Positive Changes in Political Science

Analytical Perspectives on Politics

ADVISORY EDITORS:

John Aldrich, Duke University
Bruce Bueno de Mesquita, Hoover Institution and New York University
Robert Jackman, University of California, Davis
David Rohde, Duke University

Political Science is developing rapidly and changing markedly. Keeping in touch with new ideas across the discipline is a challenge for political scientists and for their students.

To help meet this challenge, the series Analytical Perspectives on Politics presents creative and sophisticated syntheses of major areas of research in the field of political science. In each book, a high-caliber author provides a clear and discriminating description of the current state of the art and a strong-minded prescription and structure for future work in the field.

These distinctive books provide a compact review for political scientists, a helpful introduction for graduate students, and central reading for advanced undergraduate courses.

Robert W. Jackman, *Power without Force: The Political Capacity of Nation-States*

Linda L. Fowler, *Candidates, Congress, and the American Democracy*

Scott Gates and Brian D. Humes, *Games, Information, and Politics: Applying Game Theoretic Models to Political Science*

Lawrence Baum, *The Puzzle of Judicial Behavior*

Barbara Geddes, *Paradigms and Sand Castles: Theory Building and Research Design in Comparative Politics*

Rose McDermott, *Political Psychology in International Relations*

Ole R. Holsti, *Public Opinion and American Foreign Policy, Revised Edition*

Luis Fernando Medina, *A Unified Theory of Collective Action and Social Change*

John H. Aldrich, James E. Alt, and Arthur Lupia, editors, *Positive Changes in Political Science: The Legacy of Richard D. McKelvey's Most Influential Writings*

Positive Changes in Political Science

The Legacy of Richard D. McKelvey's Most Influential Writings

---

JOHN H. ALDRICH, JAMES E. ALT, AND
ARTHUR LUPIA, EDITORS

THE UNIVERSITY OF MICHIGAN PRESS

Ann Arbor

Copyright © by the University of Michigan 2007
All rights reserved
Published in the United States of America by
The University of Michigan Press
Manufactured in the United States of America
⊚ Printed on acid-free paper

2010   2009   2008   2007   4   3   2   1

No part of this publication may be reproduced,
stored in a retrieval system, or transmitted in any form
or by any means, electronic, mechanical, or otherwise,
without the written permission of the publisher.

A CIP catalog record for this book is available from the British Library.

ISBN-13: 978-0-472-09986-3 (cloth : alk. paper)
ISBN-10: 0-472-09986-8 (cloth : alk. paper)
ISBN-13: 978-0-472-06986-6 (paper : alk. paper)
ISBN-10: 0-472-06986-1 (paper : alk. paper)

In memory of William H. Riker and Jeffrey S. Banks

Contents

Acknowledgments		ix
Chapter 1.	Introduction JOHN H. ALDRICH, JAMES E. ALT, AND ARTHUR LUPIA	1
Chapter 2.	McKelvey's Democracy JOHN FEREJOHN	9
Chapter 3.	Majority Cycling and Agenda Manipulation: Richard McKelvey's Contributions and Legacy GARY W. COX AND KENNETH A. SHEPSLE	19
Chapter 4.	Intransitivities in Multidimensional Voting Models and Some Implications for Agenda Control RICHARD D. MCKELVEY	41
Chapter 5.	General Conditions for Global Intransitivities in Formal Voting Models RICHARD D. MCKELVEY	53
Chapter 6.	Statistical Tests of Theoretical Results JOHN H. ALDRICH AND KEITH T. POOLE	93
Chapter 7.	A Method of Scaling with Applications to the 1968 and 1972 Presidential Elections JOHN H. ALDRICH AND RICHARD D. MCKELVEY	103
Chapter 8.	A Statistical Model for the Analysis of Ordinal Level Dependent Variables RICHARD D. MCKELVEY AND WILLIAM ZAVOINA	143
Chapter 9.	The Competitive Solution Revisited PETER C. ORDESHOOK	165

Contents

Chapter 10. The Competitive Solution for *N*-Person Games without Transferable Utility, with an Application to Committee Games
RICHARD D. MCKELVEY, PETER C. ORDESHOOK, AND MARK D. WINER ... 187

Chapter 11. Social Choice and Elections
NORMAN SCHOFIELD ... 221

Chapter 12. Covering, Dominance, and Institution-Free Properties of Social Choice
RICHARD D. MCKELVEY ... 243

Chapter 13. Generalized Symmetry Conditions at a Core Point
RICHARD D. MCKELVEY AND NORMAN SCHOFIELD ... 281

Chapter 14. Information in Elections
DAVID AUSTEN-SMITH AND ARTHUR LUPIA ... 295

Chapter 15. Elections with Limited Information: A Fulfilled Expectations Model Using Contemporaneous Poll and Endorsement Data as Information Sources
RICHARD D. MCKELVEY AND PETER C. ORDESHOOK ... 315

Chapter 16. Centipede Game Experiments
ALAN GERBER ... 349

Chapter 17. Why the Centipede Game Is Important for Political Science
REBECCA B. MORTON ... 365

Chapter 18. An Experimental Study of the Centipede Game
RICHARD D. MCKELVEY AND THOMAS R. PALFREY ... 377

Chapter 19. McKelvey and Quantal Response Equilibrium
THOMAS R. PALFREY ... 425

Chapter 20. Quantal Response Equilibria for Normal Form Games
RICHARD D. MCKELVEY AND THOMAS R. PALFREY ... 441

Chapter 21. Computation in Finite Games: Using Gambit for Quantitative Analysis
THEODORE L. TUROCY ... 475

Chapter 22. What McKelvey Taught Us
JOHN W. PATTY AND ELIZABETH MAGGIE PENN ... 489

Index ... 493

Acknowledgments

When we first began to discuss the idea of creating this book, we made a decision that the content should be oriented as much towards looking forward as it was to looking back. This spirit is consistent with what we think Richard would have wanted as well as our collective sense of the relevance of his social scientific legacy. In the introductory chapter, we will talk about Richard as a gentleman, teacher, and scholar. Throughout the book, contributors will talk about the range of his contributions, both on the printed page and through his examples. Here, we take a moment to thank a number of people who were critical to the development of *Positive Changes*.

Many people played important roles in helping us attempt to achieve this goal. Working temporally, the first person to thank is Rebecca Morton. Rebecca organized panels on Richard's work at the first major political science conferences to be organized after his passing (the 2003 Southern and Midwest Political Science Association Meetings). The panels were very stimulating and caught the interest of several people including Jennifer Hochschild. Soon after the conference, Jennifer approached us with the idea of organizing a symposium on McKelvey's work for *Perspectives on Politics*. The three of us began to brainstorm about what such a symposium might say and how the opportunity could best be used to benefit its likely readers. We put together a list of contributors and began to contact them. We were surprised by the reaction. The support for a future-oriented retrospective on McKelvey's work was far broader and more deeply felt than we initially imagined. As we started getting feedback from other people on the contribution that such a project could make, we had a conversation with Jim Reische of the University of Michigan Press. Jim shared our energy for the project's potential and he challenged us to think about the project in greater terms. He had a crisp vision of how and where a book based on McKelvey's work could be influential (a vision sharpened even further by the contributions of Bruce Bueno de Mesquita, Bob Jackman, and Dave Rohde over lunch). Jim immediately offered to publish the project at UM Press. The book format gave us the opportunity to integrate classic McKelvey articles with new content, which by this point we saw as a key to putting past accomplishments and new contributions to the service of future generations of scholars. And so the panels became the idea for the symposium which then evolved into this book. We thank Rebecca, Jennifer, and Jim for their roles in this evolution.

Next, we contacted prospective authors. We are grateful that such an accomplished group of scholars agreed to participate. Each one was wonderful to work with. They were effective and efficient in meeting deadlines and in helping us, and each other, to refine our collective argument. A focal moment in the development of this book was a conference held at Duke University. We were allowed to fund the conference from NSF's very innovative Empirical Implications of Theoretical Modeling program. We thank Frank Scioli and Jim Granato for supporting the venture in this way, and Alexandra Cooper and Michael Tofias at Duke for organizing and running the conference so smoothly.

The conference itself was a very productive gathering. We thank the participants in the EITM Summer Seminar of that year for the very penetrating questions that they offered throughout the conference. Participants were Despina Alexiadou, Byoung-Inn Bai, Muhammet Ali Bas, Leo Blanken, Damon Centola, Daniel Corstange, Michael Crespin, Patrick Egan, Lynne Gibson-Gleiber, Matt Grossman, Nikitas Konstantinidis, Jinjie Liu, Peter Loewen, Carmela Lutmar, Monique Lyle, Linda Merola, Kevin Morrison, Kirk Randazzo, David Siroky, Mariana Sousa, Vera Troeger, Joe Ura, Stefanie Walter, and Camber Warren.

Early in 2005, William Keech gave us an opportunity to present several of the papers on a special panel at the Southern Political Science Association meetings that he organized that year in New Orleans. We received important feedback at that gathering and also appreciate the opportunity it gave many of the participants to further coordinate their contributions. We thank Bill for this opportunity.

The intellectual foundation for the book that has emerged is a series of articles by Richard McKelvey. Reprints of these articles are included among the chapters of *Positive Changes*. For assistance with these permissions we thank Zoé Ellams of Blackwell Publishing, Helen Gainford of Elsevier, Ted Gerney of Cambridge University Press, Julie Gordon of the Econometric Society, and Elaine Inverso of Taylor and Francis, Inc. Full citations to the original version of each of these chapters follow the acknowledgements.

The process connecting the electronic version of our manuscript to the book that you hold in your hands was made easier by the skills and substantial goodwill of several people. We are especially grateful to Dilyan Donchev, Ben Goodrich, and Yuki Takagi of Harvard and Adam Seth Levine and Daniel Magleby of the

University of Michigan for translating many of the chapters into LaTeX. This job was particularly important as it allowed us to present McKelvey's original work and the new articles in a common, consistent, and aesthetically pleasing manner. At the University of Michigan, Dan Corstange and Charles Taragin assisted in this process and we are grateful to them for their efforts. Elisabeth Gerber, Orit Kedar, Kenneth Kollman, and Gisela Sin also read drafts of several chapters and added helpful comments.

As you will see in the chapters that follow, Richard left a legacy of scientific ideas and practices that continues to influence our discipline. We are grateful for the opportunity to share some of these ideas with you and we are thankful that so many talented and energetic people have helped us bring the idea for a forward-looking tribute to Richard to reality.

Jim Alt, John Aldrich, and Skip Lupia
January 2006

Permissions

Grateful acknowledgment is made to the following publishers and journals for permission to reprint previously published materials.

John H. Aldrich and Richard D. McKelvey, "A Method of Scaling with Applications to the 1968 and 1972 Presidential Elections," reprinted from the *American Political Science Review*, 71, no. 1, 1977, pp. 111–130. Copyright ©1977. Reprinted with the permission of Cambridge University Press.

Richard D. McKelvey, "Intransitivities in Multidimensional Voting Models and Some Implications for Agenda Control," reprinted from the *Journal of Economic Theory*, 12, 1976, pp. 472–482. Copyright ©1976. Reprinted with the permission of Elsevier.

Richard D. McKelvey, "General Conditions for Global Intransitivities in Formal Voting Models," reprinted from *Econometrica*, 47, 1979, pp. 1085–1112. Copyright ©1979. Reprinted with the permission of The Econometric Society.

Richard D. McKelvey, "Covering, Dominance, and Institution-Free Properties of Social Choice," reprinted from the *American Journal of Political Science*, 30, no. 2, 1986, pp. 283–314. Copyright ©1986. Reprinted with the permission of Blackwell Publishing.

Richard D. McKelvey and Peter C. Ordeshook, "Elections with Limited Information: A Fulfilled Expectations Model Using Contemporaneous Poll and Endorsement Data as Information Sources," reprinted from the *Journal of Economic Theory*, 36, 1985, pp. 55–85.

Copyright ©1985. Reprinted with the permission of Elsevier.

Richard D. McKelvey, Peter C. Ordeshook, and M. Winer, "The Competitive Solution for N-Person Games without Transferable Utility, with an Application to Committee Games," reprinted from the *American Political Science Review*, 72, no. 2, 1978, pp. 599–615. Copyright ©1978. Reprinted with the permission of Cambridge University Press.

Richard D. McKelvey and Thomas R. Palfrey, "An Experimental Study of the Centipede Game," reprinted from *Econometrica*, 60, 1992, pp. 803–836. Copyright ©1992. Reprinted with the permission of The Econometric Society.

Richard D. McKelvey and Thomas R. Palfrey, "Quantal Response Equilibria for Normal Form Games," reprinted from *Games and Economic Behavior*, 10, no. 1, 1995, pp. 6–38. Copyright ©1995. Reprinted with the permission of Elsevier.

Richard D. McKelvey and Norman Schofield, "Generalized Symmetry Conditions at a Core Point," reprinted from *Econometrica*, 55, 1987, pp. 923–934. Copyright ©1987. Reprinted with the permission of The Econometric Society.

Richard D. McKelvey and William Zavoina, "A Statistical Model for the Analysis of Ordinal Level Dependent Variables," reprinted from the *Journal of Mathematical Sociology*, 4, 1975, 103–120. Copyright ©1975. Reprinted with the permission of Taylor & Francis Group, LLC, http://taylorandfrancis.com.

Each of these articles has been typeset anew to give the book a uniform appearance. To protect the integrity of the original work and to respect existing copyrights, these articles have not been altered. There are only two exceptions to this rule. The first exception is that we corrected spelling and punctuation in the few instances where corrections were appropriate. The second exception is that we edited all references to other McKelvey articles that appear in this book. All such references now include the relevant reference for this book alongside the original reference. Among the content that we have not altered is the reference section of each article. In some cases, for example, there are papers listed as forthcoming that — as of today — are 30 years old. We have preserved the original references in these cases to document the versions of the articles that were available to McKelvey at the time of his writings. Another implication of our decision to preserve the original content of these articles is that the reference sections of these chapters do not have a common format.

CHAPTER 1

Introduction

JOHN H. ALDRICH, JAMES E. ALT, AND ARTHUR LUPIA

In recent decades, political science has been the focus of an important revolution. Inventive groups of scholars have introduced powerful sets of tools that affect almost every topic the discipline studies. These tools entail increased attention to statistical inference, game theory, and laboratory experiments. Each tool allows political scientists to examine causal hypotheses and evaluate long-standing explanations with heightened degrees of logical precision and inferential validity. Today, political scientists throughout the world continue to use and develop these methods.

The increased presence of such positive analyses in political science has had a broad impact. At one end of our disciplinary continuum, it has spawned multiple generations of scholars who integrate complex logical structures into their research design. Some of these scholars use the new methods to evaluate the logical consistency of previous generations' normative or descriptive claims. In case after case, they are turning common wisdoms on their heads. At the same time, many normative and descriptive scholars are using the new methods to offer more cogent explanations of their viewpoints. A growing number of empirical researchers, moreover, now base the design of their surveys and case studies on causal propositions derived from positive analyses. The result is that political science has become a scientific discipline that is far more amenable to precise conclusions for students and scholars and to effective advice able to be offered to policymakers and institution builders, as well as to those in the academy. While important controversies remain about the most effective domain for the kinds of approaches discussed above, this positive revolution is one reason why political science is more relevant to society today than ever before.

Richard D. McKelvey was a leader among those scholars who introduced these new methods into political science. He is most famous for the theoretical work — and theorem proving in particular — that he did. But to remember him solely for those accomplishments, no matter how impressive they are, is to understate his importance to political science. One of the most remarkable things about him is his frequent and important role across the various sets of new tools for the discipline described above. Along with William Zavoina and John Aldrich, he pioneered the development of new statistical techniques for testing an important class of theoretical propositions using commonly available social science data. In the mid-1970's, he was one of the first to use game theory to clarify a core political question, How well do majority rule outcomes represent the preferences of individual voters? Later in the decade, he was among the first political scientists to use an advanced mathematical conception of incomplete information in a game theoretic setting to clarify a relationship between information and voting behavior that was present in recent empirical studies, but not in previous theory. Such work helped to launch the resurgence in interest in the role and design of political institutions that has occurred over the last quarter century. He followed this research early in the 1980's by being one of the first political scientists to design and use laboratory experiments to test critical hypotheses about how voters use information in mass elections. A decade later, he was among the first political scientists to offer a compelling alternative to Nash-based equilibrium concepts. The Quantal Response Equilibrium concept, developed with Thomas R. Palfrey, was more realistic psychologically than the more commonly used Nash-based concepts and has played a focal role in the emergence of behavioral economics — the fast-growing branch of microeconomic theory that replaces overly-simplified representations of human rationality with representations based in psychology and cognitive science.

The unifying lesson of McKelvey's work is that our discipline's ability to yield reliable and generalizable insights about political phenomena grows in proportion to our attention to the logical foundations of our arguments. His work was unprecedented in its detailed attention to such matters, and its ability to generate paradigm-changing insights. While his thesis advisor, William Riker, led the movement towards positive political analysis and deeply influenced its early practitioners, Richard McKelvey was the first to effectively and consistently deliver new insights by pairing this agenda with advanced mathematics. His methods and efforts accelerated the positive revolution's effect on political science. It also earned Richard D. McKelvey the respect of thoughtful scholars from across the social and natural sciences — many of who continue to cite his work prominently and regularly.

Such sentiments bring us to the present. The editors believe that while some scholars and students understand the impact of Richard's work, many others do not. Many are especially prone to recall only a portion of his manifold contributions. And it is surely the case that his work influences numerous leading-edge political science research agendas, often in subtle ways. But it is important to see more of the whole contribution. This is not (or not merely) to be able to appreciate the contributions of an important individual, but it is because the complete argument for the positive revolution in political science, of which he is such a central figure, can be appreciated only by the combination of deduction and inference, theory and method, in their totality. This volume reveals some of the ways in which this influence continues to improve political science and it provides a framework for building on this progress. The book shows how individual investigators and the discipline as a whole have benefited from increased attention to logic — whether it occurs through the lens of game theory, empirical work, a combination of both, or other means. It also provides many ideas for how to evolve this trend in ways that make present and future research agendas more effective.

To this end, *Positive Changes* has two kinds of chapters. Some are reprints of Richard's most influential articles. These chapters cover a range of topics. However, they are unified by several important attributes. All focus on topics that are of core importance to the study of politics. And all arguments and conclusions are built from strong and clear theoretical platforms.

However, we believe that Richard is best understood by a book that looks more to the future than to the past. Therefore, most of the book's pages are devoted to twelve compact, forward-looking articles that convey to readers the importance of Richard's methods and insights to the contemporary and future generations of research. These new chapters are written by scholars who represent multiple generations in the evolution of political science. The contributors include McKelvey's colleagues and contemporaries as well as his first and last graduate students.

While the themes of these chapters reflect the diverse areas in which McKelvey did research, they too share an important theme — a theme expressed by McKelvey when he was given an opportunity to comment on the future of political science. Shortly before his death, Richard participated in a workshop convened by the National Science Foundation on July 9–10, 2001, to discuss the problem of integrating theoretical and empirical work in political science research. The fruit of this endeavor was the development of the National Science Foundation's EITM (Empirical Implications of Theoretical Models) program. This program, like the most influential writings of Richard's career, helped scholars understand how new and evolving methods could help them engage in more effective science.

Instead of writing what we believe Richard stood for, we let him speak for himself. We have assembled from his comments and transcribed participation in the workshop his view about how political science should evolve.[1]

One of the big problems in political theory, which distinguishes it from economic theory, is the absence of any general equilibrium theory from which to start the theoretical enterprise. The lack of general equilibrium in political science has put theoretical work in political science in a kind of limbo. Economists can frequently start from well-accepted equilibrium models, and then do comparative statics by standard techniques. Political theory does not have well accepted equilibrium models to start from. So the theory must incorporate details of the situation. We agree that the underlying framework should be rational choice/game theoretic, but then to analyze a specific situation, details about the institutions must be part of the model. Thus, since the discovery of the generic non existence of equilibrium, the main trends in formal modeling have been to explicitly model the role of information, repetition and institutions in political processes. These trends have been accompanied by the increasing use of non-cooperative game theory, games of incomplete information, and explicit specification of extensive forms ...

Theorists like to prove very general results, but the institution based modeling goes in precisely the opposite direction, implying that there may be no general results. This opens up a big role for so called "applied theory." The implication is that empirical modelers, when studying a specific set of data, may not be able to find a model that they can just plug in and use. Rather, they may have to develop some of the theory themselves. This lack of ready made, plug in theories that empirical modelers can use in their work probably helps to explain some of the split between theory and empirical work. But it also opens up an opportunity for those researchers who can "speak both languages."

In terms of the body of research in political science, there is a lot of empirical research that seems purely descriptive and unmotivated by theory, but there is also a substantial body of empirical literature that is motivated by theoretical questions. Focusing on the latter literature, my impression is ... that theorists are frequently not very convinced that empirical studies have adequately tested the theoretical models that they

---

[1]These passages come from http://www.nsf.gov/sbe/ses/polisci/reports/eitmtrans (7/9/01).pdf and http://www.nsf.gov/sbe/ses/polisci/reports/eitmtrans (7/10/01).pdf.

are based on. There are a couple of reasons for this. First, the world that theorists look at is necessarily abstracted and simplified, focusing on the effects of certain variables at the exclusion of others. In the real world, it is seldom that one can find empirical situations where only the variables of theoretical interest are active. So econometric techniques, sometimes of questionable validity, must be used to introduce controls. Also, there are frequently problems measuring the variables of theoretical interest (utilities, beliefs) in natural settings. Thus it is frequently hard to get the data that is needed to test theoretical models. So empirical work encounters difficulties in implementation, because of problems with operationalization of variables and the inevitable econometric questions concerning uncontrolled confounding variables, whether the independent variables are truly exogenous, etc. This is partly because the theories are too primitive to be able to address the real world situations that empirical researchers are interested in and partly because empirical studies do not provide natural experiments.

Richard himself contributed — and for many of us, created — the "big problem," ways to address that problem and others, and define the new directions for our future. Nevertheless, in the continued and growing use of the techniques Richard advanced lie at least two very distinct possible futures for political science. One future entails one set of scholars paying greater attention to mathematics and computation at the expense of engaging in research whose social relevance is direct, while others do work that may be relevant socially, but is certainly impoverished logically. The other future — the one exemplified by Richard's work — entails scholars using these methods to clarify fundamental phenomena with unprecedented levels of logical and empirical precision. In this latter future, the chasm separating the ivory tower from advice that helps people build more effective political institutions will continue to narrow. An increasing number of observers, offering as evidence the increasing interest in quantitative and game-theoretic political science from other scientific disciplines and by governmental entities around the world, would argue that this future exists now.

Organization of the Book

The book is organized into seven sections, along with an introductory chapter and a conclusion. Each of the seven sections contains one or two of Richard McKelvey's most important articles, accompanied by one or two short articles that elaborate the contribution of his articles to subsequent developments in political science. In the chapter entitled "McKelvey's Democracy," John Ferejohn describes the importance of Richard's work to economics and social science generally.

The first section contains two core theoretical papers, "Intransitivities in Multidimensional Voting Models and Some Implications for Agenda Control" and "General Conditions for Global Intransitivities in Formal Voting Models," that were influential in reversing the naïve faith of their time that competitive party systems inevitably had centrist tendencies. They are accompanied by a chapter by Gary Cox and Kenneth A. Shepsle that relates these papers to subsequent developments in institutional analysis.

The second section contains two of Richard's papers that developed original statistical procedures. A chapter by John Aldrich and Keith Poole puts these procedures into context. An important line of argument in their chapter is that it was precisely the systematic logical formulation of the problem and consequent derivation of the new procedure that made these contributions particularly important.

The third section focuses on the Competitive Solution. In the 1970's, Richard McKelvey and Peter Ordeshook worked to develop a new solution concept for large scale voting games. While their publications on this topic are very insightful, they abandoned the enterprise before development was complete. The new article by Peter Ordeshook explains this decision. It is particularly revealing of McKelvey's scientific integrity. It also provides new clarity on the substantial benefits that will accrue to political science today if it picks up where McKelvey and Ordeshook left off.

The fourth section focuses on the characterization of election outcomes in spatial models. It focuses both on the work of Richard McKelvey and Norman Schofield. These scholars first worked on the problem of characterization independently. Each research agenda yielded results of fundamental importance. The two then joined forces to develop their ideas further. The new chapter by Schofield explains the relevance of these results, both in theory and with respect to our ability to explain differences in key characteristics of electoral outcomes (such as which voters' viewpoints are more likely to be represented in legislatures) across countries.

The fifth section focuses on the role of information and elections. In the mid and late 1980's, McKelvey and Ordeshook published models and conducted experiments that were important in several respects. Not only was their model one of the first to speak directly to the sizeable empirical literature on voting that had appeared in the late 20th century, it and their experiments also revealed that information asymmetries within the electorate need not have the damaging effects that so many other observers had presumed. In a new chapter, David Austen-Smith and Arthur Lupia describe the paper's contributions — not only to the scholarly debate of its time but to subsequent theoretical work on information and collective decision making that has followed its lead.

The sixth section focuses on experiments. The experiments in question were based on the centipede game — a game where substantial doubt existed about the applicability of its Nash-equilibrium solution. McKelvey and Thomas R. Palfrey's experiments revealed an important pattern of behavior and launched a research agenda that featured a search for a more appropriate equilibrium concept. New chapters by Alan Gerber and Rebecca Morton reflect on the impact of these experiments and their relationship to the dynamic growth in experimentation that now characterizes political science. Gerber's chapter nests a survey of centipede game research within a more general argument about the impact and relevance of laboratory experiments, while Morton's chapter reveals the relevance of centipede game controversies to fundamental questions in political science, particularly in the domain of legislative bargaining.

The seventh section describes the next step in the McKelvey-Palfrey research agenda, the development of the Quantal Response Equilibrium concept. This concept not only introduced a more realistic notion of strategic decision making to games such as centipede, it was also a harbinger of things to come — in particular, the behavioral economics movement.

The book also contains two other new chapters. One, by Theodore Turocy, motivates and explains McKelvey's gambit project. Gambit is a set of computational utilities that allows people to solve a broad class of models. It is available as freeware today and is the best available software of its kind. Turocy explains its development and provides examples of how researchers and students can use it to enhance their research. The other chapter is by McKelvey's last students, John Patty and Elizabeth Maggie Penn. Their concluding essay reflects both on Richard as a mentor and on the lasting impact of his work.

Biographical Sketch

Richard D. McKelvey was born on April 27, 1944, and died on April 22, 2002. He was the Edie and Lew Wasserman Professor of Political Science and director of the William D. Hacker Social Science Experimental Laboratory at the California Institute of Technology, having previously held faculty appointments at Rochester and Carnegie-Mellon. Near the end of his life, he was also a focal presence in the development of the National Science Foundation's EITM (Empirical Implications of Theoretical Models) program. This program, like the most influential writings of his career, helped scholars understand how new and evolving methods could help them engage in more effective science. He was elected to the American Academy of Arts and Sciences in 1992, the National Academy of Sciences in 1993, and the Econometric Society in 1994.

Richard McKelvey made wide-ranging scholarly contributions to the social sciences. He made fundamental methodological contributions to game theory, social choice theory, experimental political science, and computational economics and fundamental substantive contributions to core dynamics in the context of voting, legislating, and decision making generally. He was not afraid to innovate. He was either the first person in political science or at least one of the very first to use a mathematical version of game theory to address core problems in political theory, to use an extensive form game to address core problems in political science, to conduct laboratory experiments, to use games of incomplete information, and to write a computer program to emulate the behavior of strategic actors in political settings.

He also trained many graduate students. He was a serious and dedicated teacher. Early on, he taught semester-length statistics courses as well as a terrific econometrics course. His courses were comprehensive, thorough, and well organized. He patiently answered the dumbest questions and never made any student feel that he or she was imposing on his time. His skills included not just technical competencies in various parts of mathematics but also a remarkable intuition that combined an understanding of what was provable with what was important for understanding politics to make it worth the work of deriving results. These skills are just as apparent in his statistical work.

To quote one of the editors, who was — is — one of Richard's students, "He was dedicated. He was rigorous. He was principled. He was consistent. He was gentle. He was focused. He was constructive. And he was so dedicated to science. To political science. To doing it well. And to helping others do it more effectively."

CHAPTER 2

McKelvey's Democracy

John Ferejohn

Richard McKelvey is best known as a founder of positive political theory, a statistical methodologist, a social choice theorist, an experimental scientist, and an engineer of institutions. But, I think that he must also be considered a political theorist in the venerable tradition of Aristotle, Machiavelli, and Madison, and his ideas evaluated in that setting. Each of these writers shared with McKelvey a fundamentally empirical and pragmatic orientation to political phenomena, while at the same time deploying rigorous theoretical arguments. They had that much in common. What is more to the point however, is that each of them advanced lines of normative argument about democracy that McKelvey's various contributions put into some question.

The notion that Richard McKelvey could be considered as a traditional political theorist may be surprising to those who think of Richard as a kind of high priest of rational choice theory or a deviser of abstruse mathematics. And it may shock those who place "classical" theorists in a kind of inaccessible pantheon, or who try to erect and maintain a sharp divide between normative and positive theory. But, while each of the thinkers I mentioned aimed to give normative advice as to how to arrange institutions, each relied fundamentally on a scientific analysis of how institutions work, given his understanding of human behavior. Each was in this way a positive as well as a normative theorist.

One could object that Richard was a pure positive theorist whose work can have no normative implications because normative propositions cannot be derived from positive ones. But the separation of the normative and the positive is not nearly as simple or complete as the Humean formula seems to imply. For one thing the evaluation of an institution must depend, in part, on a descriptive characterization of its operating characteristics. And such a characterization may invoke normatively laden terms such as efficiency, equality, moderation, or justice. The first welfare theorem of neoclassical economics, for example, is a positive claim that refers to a normative entity — under certain conditions competitive equilibria are Pareto optimal. In this sense, analysis and description are prior to evaluation and necessary for it. So even if McKelvey is not seen as providing a normative case for democracy, any coherent defense of it must rely on his analysis.

But there is an important sense in which Richard is better understood as an unabashed advocate for genuine democracy. His work constitutes, I argue, a profound defense of the possibilities of genuine popular rule, of government by as well as for the people. Indeed, the case he makes is for radical or unchecked democracy and not for the tamer versions that are popularly defended nowadays.

Against Democracy

It is useful to focus on Aristotle, Machiavelli, and Madison not only because each practiced political science in a recognizably modern way but also because each was, in one way or another, profoundly skeptical about democracy or at least about the populist forms of it in which the people ruled in some direct way. Aristotle of course lived in radically democratic Athens, one of the very few extended experiments with direct democracy over a long period of time (approximately two centuries broken by a period of instability and oligarchic rule), and he concluded that decent government required checking or moderating democratic impulses either by restricting the franchise with a property qualification or by mixing aristocratic with democratic institutions. Without such tempering, democracy would be dominated by poor and unpropertied who would impose their class interest in expropriating wealth rather than seeking the public good.

Madison's reactions to what he thought were excessively democratic state constitutions were quite similar. His criticisms of the expropriative policies of the state governments and of unchecked legislatures in general as well as his pessimism about the wellsprings of human motivation are well expressed in his celebrated essays in the *Federalist*. He recognized of course that the legislature was indispensable in a republican government but saw it also as the principal source of danger to republicanism. And he thought that the only possible way to create an acceptable republican government — a government necessary to controlling the majoritarian impulses of the states — involved controlling the inherently populistic tendencies of the legislature. Most important, he insisted that the legislature be representative rather than direct and that the representatives be elected from large districts, which would tend to elect a better sort of person to office. Further he insisted on saddling the legislative body with elaborate checks such as the executive veto and perhaps (though this is a bit controversial) judicial review.

Machiavelli witnessed firsthand the populistic government of Savonarola as well as the Florentine elite's virulent rejection of it, which led to his banishment from the city. His response to these events, while in exile, was to look for lessons in the history of the Roman Republic, which he took as a kind of model for the Florentines. And, following Polybius's famous description of the Roman constitution, he attributed Rome's glory and the growth of its Mediterranean empire during the third and second centuries to a kind of equilibrium between popular and oligarchic elements. And he traced the collapse of the Republic to the erosion of that balance.

The traditional view of democracy, represented by these writers, was that it amounted to mob rule: government by poor, uneducated people, incapable of forming or acting on seriously held preferences or judgments, vulnerable to the flattery of demagogues and appeals to emotions rather than reason. Democracy was seen as essentially intemperate, turbulent, and inconsistent: a form of despotism unable to conform itself to law. And these older writers had, or thought they had, plenty of observational evidence that supported these ideas (and this view was shared by virtually everyone until well into the nineteenth century). But their evidence was drawn from the consideration of a very small and imperfectly documented set of cases. They paid special attention to Rome of course, and to a lesser extent Sparta, and in Madison's case some of the Hellenic leagues and confederacies, and a bit less to Athens, which was much less well understood before the nineteenth century. And though each of these writers was an impressive theorist, none of them had access to the analytical tools or empirical methods that Richard McKelvey did so much to develop. Nor, of course, did traditional thinkers have the advantage of seeing Richard's analyses of specific democratic institutions and how they were likely to operate in plausible human environments.

McKelvey's Democracy

Over the course of his career, McKelvey developed a much more positive picture of the possibilities of democracy — indeed of what might be called populistic or direct democracy — than any of the traditional theorists would have thought plausible. He argued, in several distinct and powerful strands of work, that ordinary democratic decision procedures such as majority rule were much better behaved than anyone had thought. Moreover, this is the case even if one takes no account whatever of institutions that may be put in place to limit majority rule. And, it is also true even where there is no possibility at all of people adjusting or moderating their preferences in order to achieve moderate compromises.

This claim may seem surprising to those who think that his celebrated "chaos" theorems must have made him a pessimist about the properties of popular rule. But, the chaos theorems are best understood as a kind of background or foil for his work on a variety of what I think are much more optimistic "possibility" theorems of democracy that showed that majoritarian voting procedures were likely to produce moderate outcomes even in "institution free" settings. Doing this required a number of deep explorations into received notions of equilibrium or, more generally, into what outcomes were likely to arise from strategic interaction.

As examples we may point to his early work with Peter Ordeshook, on the competitive solution,[1] and his papers (again, with Ordeshook) on the partial median set in two candidate competition.[2] Later work on the yolk concept[3] and on sophisticated voting[4] continued to point to moderating tendencies of majoritarian decision process. And, still later, his results (with Ordeshook) on candidate competition in a limited information environment illustrate that moderating tendencies can be produced even where voters have very little information about candidate positions in policy space.[5] These works importantly bracket the chaos theorems and must be seen as illustrating the limitations of those theorems as any kind of positive prediction as to how majoritarian bodies will actually behave. Richard believed throughout his career that actual majoritarian processes were much better behaved and more restrained than the chaos results suggested. He thought that some rough constraints could be put on how majority rule would work — the yolk concept was a rough attempt to bound the wide variety of electoral and legislative implementation of those processes. But I have no doubt that he thought that these limits were nowhere near the best that could be found.

A qualification needs to be made at this point. First, it is important to distinguish legislative from electoral implementations of democracy. Electoral democracy can be understood as a form of democratic elitism, and this is indeed how Schumpeter and Riker and other democratic elitists understood it: the electorate

---

[1] The idea was that rather than picking a single equilibrium outcome, legislative bargaining would result in a set of alternatives that are balanced with respect to each other, and is related to the Von Neumann-Morgenstern solution of a game.

[2] The idea here is that there is a relatively small set of "centrally located" outcomes that will tend to contain the platforms that vote maximizing candidates will propose.

[3] The "yolk" bounds a variety of centrally located "solutions" that can be produced either by candidate competition or, more directly, democratic legislative bargaining.

[4] If it is assumed that, in the context of "chaotic preferences," there is a monopoly agenda setter sophisticated voting will limit the outcomes that can be produced to a small and centrally located set of alternatives.

[5] Bayesian voter inferences about candidate locations from the endorsements of policy motivated groups will permit them to induce correct candidate locations and limit the range of outcomes.

chooses leaders and they do the actual governing (perhaps subject to retrospective control). However, in a direct, or legislative, implementation, the people themselves choose among alternatives without any need for intervening leaders. Since Downs' book appeared half a century ago, there has been a kind of folk intuition among positive theorists that there is a kind of equivalence between the legislative and electoral models, at least in certain circumstances. When voters have single peaked preferences for example, and when candidates can be counted on to enact their campaign promises into laws, both electoral and legislative democracy choose the same alternative. The intuition is that this equivalence, suitably qualified, extends beyond the rudimentary setting just described. And, if something like this intuition is true, it provides a way to justify direct democracy and not merely the elitist forms of it. Indeed, insofar as the elitists have an attractive case for an electoral implementation of democracy, if the folk intuition holds, that same defense holds for direct democracy too.

McKelvey's papers, of course, raise a more basic issue: even if majority decisions do exhibit a kind of moderation — in the sparse institution free, fixed preference, and limited information environments he analyzes — is that a reason to evaluate them positively? Is moderation a good thing? And if it is, what is it about moderate rule that is attractive? Aristotle had a well known view about this, thinking that moderation was a property of the good. His idea of good government was essentially a compromise of the conflicting interests of the upper and lower classes, which could be implemented either by restricting the franchise to the middle class or by constitutional balancing. But insofar as Richard subscribed to a kind of generalized utilitarian view of welfare — a view that insists that the public good is reducible to the goods enjoyed by individuals — Aristotle's path was not available to him.

Richard of course rarely took an explicit normative perspective even when evaluating explicitly normative ideas such as Pareto Optimality, or the Pareto ordering, the welfarist notions of social choice theory, or Von Neumann-Morgenstern solution ideas (some versions of which appeal to normative intuitions). Indeed he analyzed these notions with a certain impartiality, appraising their properties and holding his own endorsement in reserve. His view was, in effect, meta-ethical, in that he was more concerned with how ethical or normative principles fit together than with defending any one of them. But it seems very likely to me that he had a positive attitude toward the median voter notions developed in one-dimensional models, and sought through much of his work to see how this attractive normative idea could be realized in other settings (spatial or more general settings). And if this is right, it seems fair to say of Richard that he thought there was something positive to say about moderation itself. That is to say, if a method of collective decision making exhibited moderation, that is something in its favor.[6]

Whether or not Richard had, or whether anyone has, an acceptable normative defense of moderate government, it is important to see how Richard's theoretical findings undercut the classical criticisms of democracy. Those criticisms were based on assertions that majority rule — especially direct majority rule — was likely to be unstable and chaotic and to produce extreme policies. While we need to separate instability from extremity, several of Richard's papers cast serious doubt on both kinds of criticism. His game theoretic work (which of course was based on relatively complete institutional description) shows that the instability criticism may be unfounded. Indeed the very notion of instability needs to be theorized and not automatically associated with certain solution or equilibrium concepts, however attractive they may be in other settings. His efforts to develop other solution notions (notably in the papers developing the competitive solution and his later explorations of quantal response models) exemplify this line of thought. Moreover, the various (more general) papers on the essential moderation of majority rule suggest that extreme policies are unlikely to be selected in democratic polities.[7]

Of course most of Richard's work on these topics was theoretical and perhaps democratic critics would insist on believing "their own eyes" rather than the results of theoretical speculation. Richard thought of course it was hard to trust what your "own eyes" seemed to show. He preferred, for that reason, to engage in controlled empirical observation in a laboratory setting and, when confronting

---

[6] It is of course hard to say actually what that something is. Obviously the median can be moved around over a wide range in simple models, producing very different utility vectors, each of which would seem to lead to different overall welfare assessments. So if Richard really did subscribe to a kind of generalized utilitarian notion, he would have had to explain how to reconcile a belief that the median voter outcome was good with the fact that such an outcome could only be loosely associated with any kind of standard welfare measure.

[7] The sense in which majoritarian outcomes are "moderate" needs to be qualified. The chaos theorems are crude in the sense of being dimensionally insensitive in a certain sense. That is, under unrestrictive conditions, if the policy space has more than one dimension, there is a majority rule cycle containing virtually every alternative. These theorems make no distinction at all between the performance of majority rule in higher rather than lower dimension spaces. But, intuitively, it must be the case that the performance of majority rule is "worse" in higher dimensions and McKelvey's "moderation" results in the cited papers in fact reflect this. Consider, for example, the size of the partial median set in a two dimensional set with millions of voters with Euclidean preferences. As long as those voters are distributed more or less randomly, the partial median set will be relatively small compared, say, to the set of Pareto Optimals. But in the space of wealth distributions, with dimensionality equal to the number of voters, the set of partial medians will be as large as the Pareto set. A similar point can be made about the dispersion of outcomes in the competitive solution.

empirical evidence from the field, to be very careful in modeling how the data were likely generated. I do not want to explore this interesting topic here but to examine another postulate that underlies much of Richard's work on democracy: the rationality hypothesis.

Methodology

All this is said in the context of a simplistic theory of human nature — classical rational choice theory — that Richard employed analytically in much of his work. But it is important to see that his commitment to rationality was not ontological but methodological. A methodological commitment to rationality can be defended in several ways. One can say of the assumptions of rational choice theory that it is a "tractable" conception of human nature in the sense that a lot is known about how rational creatures would act in a range of different environments. While there is truth to this, as long as one avoids the implication that the set of well-understood environments is large in the set of real environments, it constitutes too quick a dismissal of alternative theories. That is, without careful consideration of alternative behavioral models it seems merely lazy to dismiss all of them as intractable. And Richard himself was anything but intellectually lazy.

A deeper defense of rationality could be based on the prudential guideline that it is best to design democratic institutions against the possibility that they might be populated by rational agents who would, if they were so inclined, try to take advantage of the institution for their own gain. This is the perspective articulated by James Madison and exemplified in modern work in positive political theory and in most of Richard's theoretical work. But, while this may be a good prudential strategy for analyzing how old institutions may work or for devising new ones, it is hardly defensible as a strategy for exploring how people will actually behave. And so, when Richard turns to those questions he tended, late in his career, to move away from standard rationality assumptions to explore, in a limited and controlled way, other plausible behavior assumptions. Of course, as he has developed these ideas — the papers with Palfrey on Quantal Response equilibria are excellent late examples — they have become useful and tractable tools for the analysis of institutions. In this sense, there is a dialectical aspect to McKelvey's work. One can only wonder how it would have evolved and applied to the issues of democracy which were so important to him.

What Is at Stake?

Since its birth in fifth century BCE Athens, democracy — specifically populist or majoritarian democracy — has frightened both political elites and intellectuals. The "people" which are empowered by democratic institutions have always been thought to be ignorant, fickle, easily swayed by passionate or irrational appeals, and generally not capable of making sound judgments. Popular rule amounts to rule by the poor, or at best by the lower middle class, who would be guided largely by class interests. Not a good way to run a society.

Nowadays of course, democracy is no longer feared; indeed, it seems to be at the core of President Bush's foreign policy.[8] But modern democracies are virtually all "representative" democracies where high officials are chosen in elections, where these "representatives" are not instructed, and where legislatures and executives are subject to checks both by each other and (increasingly) by courts and possibly by international institutions as well. While some democracies permit the people to have some recourse to such institutions as the popular initiative, it seems fair to say that such institutions are better seen as yet another channel for competition among elites than a route for popular government. So, modern democracy is a pale thing compared to the Athenian model, not really worth fearing much at all.

Indeed in the twentieth century the influential and elegant anti-populist arguments of Schumpeter have dominated normative democratic theory, often as a bête noir or whipping boy. Schumpeter saw modern democracy not as an attempt to implement public opinion or popular will in public policy but simply as a method of elite competition. Robert Dahl and numerous political sociologists have worried about how this process must be regulated so as to produce democratic results in some recognizable sense. These thinkers have specified "conditions" for electoral competition to produce "democratic" outcomes: frequent elections, few barriers to opposition candidates, a free press, etc. And William Riker, Richard's teacher and colleague, has developed this line of thought into a defense of liberal versus ordinary democracy. Riker's theory ended up seeing electoral competition pretty much as Schumpeter did, as a way of picking a government and (more than Schumpeter) disciplining it. And unlike Schumpeter he endorsed constitutional checks on government and judicial review too. But the basic line was similar to

---

[8]On the other hand, one doubts that the Bush administration is really committed to encouraging people to choose any kind of democracy they want. Such choices seem likely to lead to theocratic states like Iran and the administration is no fan of that regime.

Schumpeter's and, indeed, to the democratic skepticism of Aristotle, Machiavelli, and Madison.

Until quite recently it has been hard to find respectable academics who favor or even maintain scholarly neutrality about direct democracy. One could of course point to the work of Benjamin Barber and, more recently, to the revival of serious interest in Athenian politics exemplified by the studies of Josiah Ober (1991) and Mogens Hansen (1999). But, as I have shown, Richard McKelvey's work contains the basic materials for a profound theoretical defense of direct democracy whether or not Richard himself would have cared to endorse such an interpretation. If that is right, his important achievement is to offer — if anyone cares to accept it — an unromantic defense of the possibilities of popular rule. If as many believe, radical democracy is in fact deficient as an instrument of government, there is a burden on these anti-democratic thinkers to show how and why this is so. McKelvey has demonstrated that the old arguments will no longer do.

References

Morgens Hansen. 1999. *The Athenian Democracy in the Age of Demosthenes: Structure, Principles, and Ideology.* University of Oklahoma Press. Norman, Oklahoma.

Josiah Ober. 1991. *Mass and Elite in Ancient Athens: Rhetoric, Ideology, and the Power of the People.* Princeton, New Jersey. Princeton University Press.

CHAPTER 3

Majority Cycling and Agenda Manipulation: Richard McKelvey's Contributions and Legacy

GARY W. COX AND KENNETH A. SHEPSLE

Richard McKelvey's foundational work on "spatial instability" and "agenda manipulation" (McKelvey, 1979; Chapter 5 of this book) can be read in many ways. In our view, two of the enduring messages of his work concern (a) the multiplicity of outcomes that can potentially result when legislators bargain over at least two dimensions of policy at once; and (b) the importance of agenda power in determining which of the many possible outcomes will actually result.

In order to make his main points as clear as possible, McKelvey simplified many aspects of his model of legislation. Following Coase (1960), for example, he ignored the transaction costs entailed in forming legislative coalitions. Thus, in his model, any deal that makes any majority of legislators better off than the current policy is instantly and costlessly known to all concerned. Similarly, McKelvey ignored most of the institutional details of the legislative process, focusing solely on the ultimate rule regulating how many members must vote for a policy in order for it to be enacted. Later scholars have revisited and revised some of McKelvey's assumptions. His two main insights, however, have survived re-examination and, indeed, have helped spawn a large literature exploring the institutional devices by which legislatures stabilize policy and allocate agenda power.

In this essay, we consider some of the post-McKelvey literature on instability and agenda power. Most of this literature proceeds by specifying a particular set of institutional rules by which the legislature is thought to operate and then analyzing the consequences of the posited rules. McKelvey's work led naturally to this style of theorizing in several respects. First, he showed that an assembly operating under pure majority rule (with no other institutional features), and bargaining costlessly over well-understood multi-dimensional stakes, would not settle down into a single predictable pattern of legislation. Instead, almost "anything might happen." Second, he showed that adding an agenda control stage to the legislative game greatly affected the outcome, to the benefit of the agenda setter. This invited more systematic and detailed investigations of the possible and actual rules used in legislatures to structure agenda power, amendment activity, voting, and the like — an invitation that the subsequent literature has taken up.

We take up instability and agenda manipulation in the first two sections. We conclude with some thoughts about the implications of McKelvey's work for unitary actors.

Instability

We begin the discussion with a brief characterization of McKelvey's results and then examine some technical extensions these results have spawned. Needless to say, a treatise is required to treat this topic fully. Schofield (1985) and Austen-Smith and Banks (1999b, 2005) are highly recommended to the reader interested in a comprehensive technical elucidation. Following this, we trace some of the positive political theory developments stimulated by McKelvey's findings.

The Results

McKelvey's two "instability" papers (McKelvey, 1976, 1979; Chapters 4 and 5 of this book respectively) did not invent or discover "badly behaved" majority rule in spatial contexts, but they built upon this fact, and embellished it, in profound ways. Let X be a space of alternatives[1] and $W(\bullet)$ stand for the majority winset, $W(x) = \{y \in X / y \text{ preferred to } x \text{ by a majority}\}$. It had been shown by Davis, DeGroot, and Hinich (1972) in the case of Euclidean preferences that $W(x^*) = \emptyset$ for some $x \in X$, i.e., x^* is a majority Condorcet winner, if and only if x^* is a total median. This result generalized the seminal but technically more specialized result of Plott (1967).[2] Moreover, when the number of voters is odd (some qualification is required when this number is even), they show that a distribution of voter preferences possessing a total median also yields a transitive social ordering with majority rule. McKelvey reports this as Theorem 1 in his 1976 paper. This is the building block — the spatial analogue to Arrow (1963) — on which McKelvey builds, noting that "...given the severity of the restrictions needed to

---

[1] McKelvey assumes X is Euclidean in his 1976 paper (Chapter 4 in this book). In his generalization of 1979 (Chapter 5 in this book), X may be any topological space, though most of the development is in terms of a Euclidean space.

[2] Plott's condition of radial symmetry is a special instance of the total median requirement. Black's single-peakedness condition is a unidimensional instance of radial symmetry.

guarantee transitivity ... it is of considerable interest to explore the nature of the intransitivities when these symmetry conditions are not met" (McKelvey, 1976, 475). To underscore the severity of the total-median requirement, McKelvey later notes (McKelvey, 1979, 1085–86, emphasis in original. See page 54 in this volume) that "the condition is so strong that even if it *were* met, a minor perturbation of any *one* voter's preferences would cause it to be violated."[3]

The magical point, x^*, varyingly referred to in the literature as a Condorcet winner, a core point, an empty-winset point, a Plott equilibrium, or a majority-rule equilibrium, does not appear to be in the cards, generically. (See also Kramer, 1973.) This much was known, in one way or another, when McKelvey began his inquiry. His great contribution was to ask, and answer, what happens when majority rule (almost always) "fails" in this fashion.

In doing so, he provided a surprise. Much of the literature at the time was not particularly troubled by the generic non-existence of x^*. It was believed, implicitly by some and explicitly by others, that majority rule, if not perfectly well behaved, was nevertheless centripetal — that there was some small central set of points toward which majority rule was inexorably driven. Tullock (1967) typified this view, believing that the "phantom [of majority rule intransitivity] stalked the classrooms" and that general impossibility results concerning majority rule were "generally irrelevant." McKelvey suggested otherwise. For Euclidean voter preferences in his 1976 paper (Chapter 4 of this book), and for continuous preferences in his 1979 (Chapter 5) paper plus an assumption requiring modest preference diversity — see note 3), he demonstrated that there is a finite majority rule path between any two alternatives — a sequence z_0, z_1, z_K with $z_0 = x$ and $z_K = y$ — such that $z_j \in W(z_j - 1)$ for all j any $x, y \in X$ (including $x = y$). This finding undermined the sloppy optimism extant in the literature that even with majority-rule intransitivity a majority process is nevertheless centrist.

Though some of us dubbed McKelvey's theorems as "chaos" results, it is important to emphasize that his theorems are not empirical or substantive; they are logical. As Austen-Smith and Banks (1999a, 668, emphasis in original) remind us, "...the [McKelvey] theorem does not imply that observed *choices* under any strong simple rule are 'chaotic,' only that if the core is empty then (typically) *there exists a preference path* linking any two alternatives. It is a theorem on the analytical structure of a class of aggregation rules and not on the empirical behavior

---

[3]In his 1979 paper (Chapter 5 of this book) McKelvey extends his 1976 analysis (Chapter 4 of this book), which assumed Euclidean voter utilities, to any continuous voter utility function. (He additionally requires that "no two individuals' preferences coincide locally" (McKelvey, 1979, 1087. See page 53 in this volume).)

of polities using any rule within the class." McKelvey's result, that is, is not about outcomes; it is about collective preferences. It is a bit like the principle of gravity. The latter is a fact of nature and a force of nature, and as such must be factored into any analysis of physical phenomena. But it does not by itself constitute a positive description of nature, for then we would be unable to account for all those winged creatures and machines in the air. McKelvey (1979, 1106 [Chapter 5 of this book, page 81] emphasis added) put it this way: "...any attempts to construct positive descriptive theory of political processes based on majority rule (or other social choice functions satisfying the assumptions of this paper) must take account of particular institutional features of these systems, *as the social ordering by itself does not give much theoretical leverage."*

Some Technical Extensions in the Literature

These two companion results about collective preferences — the generic non-existence of core points and the all-inclusive cycling of the majority preference relation (more generally, strong simple preference aggregation rules) — stimulated a lengthy technical literature in which many facets of the McKelvey theorem have been extended. Schofield (1978), McKelvey and Schofield (1987), and Banks (1995) extend the result on generic non-existence of core points, establishing a bound on the dimensionality of the space of alternatives that guarantees the core will be generically empty. In particular, letting n denote the number of voters, q denote the number needed to make a decision, and k denote the dimensionality of the space, if $k > \frac{(n-q+1)(q-1)}{(n-q)}$, then a core point generically does not exist. A somewhat sharper bound is offered in Austen-Smith and Banks (1999b, 167), based on a result by Saari (1997): $k > 2q - n + max\left\{\frac{4q-3n-1}{2(n-q)}, 0\right\}$. In the case of the majority rule (n odd), this latter bound reduces to $k > 1$: If the number of dimensions exceeds one, then the core is generically empty. This and related work are summarized elegantly in the treatise by Austen-Smith and Banks (1999b).

Roughly contemporaneous with McKelvey's papers is the research program of Norman Schofield (see Schofield, 1985, for a summary). Schofield's major contribution for our purposes concerns the propensity toward global cycling of collective choice rules, the second of McKelvey's twin contributions (Schofield, 1978). McKelvey's theorems establish the existence of a majority path between any two alternatives when the core is empty. Schofield focuses on the "local" properties of such paths and imposes a stricter requirement, namely that such paths be continuous. Moreover, he does not restrict himself to Euclidean preferences as in McKelvey (1976; Chapter 4 of this book), requiring only continuous and differentiable utilities. He establishes a remarkable result, showing relatively mild conditions under which there is a continuous majority rule path connecting any point to any other. (Also see Schofield, 1983, and McKelvey and Schofield, 1986.)

Austen-Smith and Banks (1999a) push the cycling result in another direction. They note that the McKelvey theorem applies only to strong simple preference aggregation rules — those rules defined entirely by its winning coalitions and for which either a coalition or its complement is winning (but not both). Austen-Smith and Banks (1999a, 664) point out that "an important, but by no means exhaustive, class of simple rules are q-rules, whereby a set of individuals is decisive if and only if it includes at least q members with q strictly greater than half the population. However, the only strong q-rule is the strict majority rule (and then only when the number of individuals is odd); thus McKelvey's theorems do not apply to any super-majority rule." The McKelvey cycling result is limited in that it does not provide for situations in which blocking coalitions are possible. Austen-Smith and Banks prove that it can be extended, in weaker form, to all simple rules, including super-majority rules. In particular, they show that whenever the core is non-empty, the entire set is connected by weak majority rule. "... [A]lthough it may not be the case for non-strong simple rules that any two alternatives can be connected by a finite sequence of strict preference steps, it is the case that any two alternatives can be connected by a finite sequence of weak preference steps" (Austen-Smith and Banks, 1999a, 664).

Some Positive Political Theory Extensions

Elections. A broad class of applications of the spatial model and the McKelvey results are related to two-candidate electoral competition. Putting abstention to one side, a subject on which a light industry has sprung up (for an overview, see Feddersen, 2004), with two candidates voters vote sincerely for the candidate whose platform they most prefer. A platform is taken to be a point in a multidimensional space over which voters have preferences (usually, Euclidean or weighted Euclidean preferences are assumed). The incumbent candidate (or his heir apparent) runs on his record, while the challenger is free to choose her own platform. The candidate with a majority of votes wins and implements his or her platform. The non-existence of a core in this spatial setting means (i) that any incumbent's platform, $y \in X$, can be beaten at the next election; and (ii) the sequence of winning platforms over a series of elections is indeterminate without additional motivational or institutional detail. If candidates want to win, but also entertain policy preferences (see Calvert, 1985), then they will choose $x \in W(y)$

that generates maximal policy utility for them.[4] Kramer (1977) suggests that a challenger will pick a winning platform that *minimizes the maximum vote against it next time*. If there is a core point, she will pick it. Generically, however, from the empty-core principle, $W(y)$ is non-empty and is "star-like" (see McKelvey, 1986). Moreover, each petal in this set is convex so that well-behaved iso-vote curves imply that a minimum-maximum point as described above exists. Kramer (1977) shows that the sequence of winning platforms, so described, converges over a sequence of elections to a small centrally located set called the *minmax set*. Kramer (1978) describes both the attractive and retentive properties of this set. McKelvey (1986) proves that it is contained in the *uncovered set*, a generalization of the core (also see Miller, 1980). Thus, Tullock's conjecture about convergence of majority rule to a small central set is provided support in this setting, but not because of the irrelevance of cycling but precisely as a result of it.

Austen-Smith and Banks (2005, Chap. 7) provide an extensive survey of two-candidate spatial election models. The McKelvey theorems do not figure directly in these developments, but the empty-core condition clearly motivates this literature. The generic non-existence of a core means that equilibrium must be obtained "by other means," unless the dimensionality of the space is small. One of those is to focus on mixed-strategy equilibrium. In McKelvey (1986) it is shown that the support of these mixed strategies lies in the uncovered set. The problem is one of general existence (owing in part to the discontinuity of candidate utility functions), though Austen-Smith and Banks report progress on this front. However, it does not appear promising that two-candidate electoral equilibria can be assured without further embellishments to the model. The spatial model of the world of perfect and complete information, costless and universal participation, deterministic voting, and candidates who only want to win provides insufficient leverage to cope with the empty-core condition.

Legislatures. The earliest spatial models (Downs, 1957) were primarily models of democratic elections. The preferences to be aggregated were those of voters over platforms. The objects of choice were candidates as "carriers" of platforms. The moving part, so to speak, was candidate platform selection. These elements, however, could be relabeled — legislators for voters, motions for candidates, and motion-makers for platform-selectors — producing a model of a majority-rule

---

[4]Calvert shows in the multidimensional case in which a core exists — a symmetric distribution of voter ideal points — that the total median remains the equilibrium, despite candidate policy preferences, i.e., the model is robust to perturbations in motivational assumptions.

committee or legislature (Black, 1958). Consequently, the entire apparatus of the spatial model could be deployed in this new institutional setting. A considerable amount of research has taken this approach. Needless to say, issues of non-existent cores and global cycling carry over to this new setting, and researchers have had to grapple with these issues.

It is worth noting that investigations of core existence require universal comparison. Not only are voter (legislator) preferences complete; so, too, is the social preference. Thus x^* is an equilibrium platform (motion) if and only if x^* is socially preferred to every $y \in X - \{x^*\}$. In effect, it is assumed that no $y \in X$ can be excluded from social consideration.[5] Legislatures, however, deploy myriad rules to restrict comparisons.[6] And, while it is appropriate to be reminded that rules, themselves, are endogenous, for many purposes of analysis it is sufficient to take them as governance fixtures, at least in the short term.

Restrictions on comparisons as a means of circumventing McKelvey's empty-core condition and cyclic majority preferences were the intuition in Shepsle (1979).[7] A *structure-induced equilibrium* is a core point when comparisons are restricted. (A core point when universal comparison is permitted is a *preference-induced equilibrium*.) Although we know that the core is generically empty when comparisons are *unrestricted*, there may be circumstances in which a point cannot be beaten when only pitted against *eligible* alternatives. Institutional rules and agenda-setting roles determine comparisons. For example, the rules of the U.S. House of Representatives distinguish a class of motions governed by a *closed rule*, e.g., conference reports. Such motions may only be pitted against the status quo, x^0 — a take-it-or-leave-it vote. In these circumstances, if a motion, x, is an element of $W(x^0)$ it defeats the status quo; if not, then x^0 prevails. Suppose $x \notin W(x^0)$, but an amended version, x', is in x^0's winset. Since the rules prohibit amendments, x' is not admissible and, with only x to contend with, x^0 prevails.

To take another example, consider a motion x to change x^0 and an amendment y to this motion. A *jurisdictional germaneness rule*, common in the U.S. House, restricts x to changes in x^0 wholly contained within a pre-determined policy jurisdiction. The latter is a subset of dimensions of the policy space, X. Thus, x may not change the status quo except in the dimensions of a single jurisdiction.

---

[5]Of all the conditions of the Arrow Impossibility Theorem, that of social completeness has been the least investigated. See Fishburn (1974) for one of the few explorations.

[6]A large proportion of the pages in the 600-page *Deschler's Procedure*, the rule book governing procedure in the U.S. House of Representatives, is devoted to a determination of which motions are in order and when. See Deschler (1975).

[7]Kramer (1972) uses similar analytical tools, but for different purposes.

Likewise, the amendment, y, may only change x along these dimensions. Other examples of rules governing comparisons include the motion to adjourn — in effect to retain x^0 and permit no further motions — which is *always* in order in the House (and *never* in order in the Senate, constitutionally a continuing body). A motion containing constitutional content is also always in order.[8]

McKelvey's work also brought motivational factors into focus. This will be treated in the next section of this paper on agenda manipulation. But it is worth pointing out here that what may be voted on in a legislature is governed not only by rules on comparisons, but also by structural arrangements that generate the agenda. In the case of legislatures, a primary source of agenda content is the committee system. A committee system is a partition of the membership of the legislature into subsets given various agenda powers with respect to the dimensions assigned to their respective jurisdictions. The preferences of committee majorities will affect what motions are brought to the full legislature; indeed, they will affect whether *any* motions are brought to the full legislature. Committees, that is, possess both proposal power and veto power; they determine whether to "open the gates" in their respective jurisdictions and, if so, the content of what passes through them.

Parliaments. McKelvey's theorems launched intensive scrutiny of institutional detail, and legislatures are quintessentially highly detailed institutions. Indeed, he said as much in each of his papers which may rightfully be regarded as forerunners of what became "the new institutionalism," first in American politics and more recently in comparative politics. Of special interest is the work on parliaments. These are weighted-majority institutions in which the legislature chooses a government that, in turn, implements its policy program. Austen-Smith and Banks (1990) and Laver and Shepsle (1990, 1996) treat jurisdiction-specific *ministries* in parliaments as the analogues to committees in American-style legislatures. Ministers are endowed with the same agenda-setting powers American committees enjoy so that, given common knowledge about ministerial preferences, their policies may be anticipated. These models then ask whether a distribution of portfolios, and hence a particular jurisdiction-by-jurisdiction policy outcome, is a core point. In this setting the empty-core condition and global cycling of the majority preference relation again apply. These analysts sought institutional arrangements that

---

[8] It was this device by which Representative George Norris of Nebraska challenged and ultimately reduced the authority of Speaker Joseph Cannon in 1911, a major event in the history of the House of Representatives.

would yield an equilibrium. Laver and Shepsle specifically *restrict comparisons* by assuming that political parties are committed to particular policies ex ante and are bound to implement them if invested with ministerial authority; thus, the space of alternatives is reduced to a finite set of potential governments — namely the finite number of ways in which a fixed set of portfolios can be allocated among parties. Work by Baron (1991), Baron and Diermeier (2001), and Huber (1996) is part of a growing literature that grapples with related McKelvey problems. An extensive survey is found in Laver and Schofield (1998).

Bicameralism, Courts, and Administrative Agencies. The basic spatial legislative model, begun with a single chamber like the U.S. House in mind, has been extended to more complicated settings with multiple arenas. The underlying empty-core problem and the cycling of majority preferences are also the fulcrums for these analyses. Studies of bicameralism consider policies that are stable in the sense that no alternative exists that majorities in both chambers prefer. If, for some $x^* \in X$, it is the case that $W_H(x*) \cap W_S(x^*) = \emptyset$, where H and S are "House" and "Senate," respectively, then x^* is a *bicameral core point*. Cox and McKelvey (1984) provided an early characterization of bicameral cores that supports some of the later results in works such as Tsebelis and Money (1997), Hammond and Miller (1987), and Tsebelis (2002).

Adding courts and administrative agencies to the brew of agents, one has a multitude of players. If each has an independent and symmetric voice in determining policy, then a generalization of the set equality above may be used to characterize when core points exist (cf. Tsebelis, 2002). In non-cooperative models, there is a sequence in which House, Senate, and president bargain over a policy which is then implemented by an administrative agent or prospectively overturned by a judicial agent, judgments which, in turn, may be reversed by the legislature and president. See McCubbins, Noll, and Weingast (1987) on legislative-agency interactions, and McCubbins, Noll, and Weingast (2005) and Eskridge and Ferejohn (1992) on judicial agents. Both of these literatures are now extensive.

Can Anything Happen? Probably the most famous and widely repeated "implication" of McKelvey's theorems, more normative than positive, is wrong. Riker (1980, 1982) believed politics, not economics, is the "truly dismal science," because he inferred from the McKelvey results, among others, that democratic collective choice is chaotic and, thus, that "anything can happen." We have already cited Austen-Smith and Banks' reminder on this score, but let us cite them again:

> ... it is important to emphasize that these instability and chaos theorems are results on the consistency of the various means of aggregating individual *preferences*. As such they are not results on individual *behavior* or the aggregation of such behavior, they are facts about the formal properties of preference aggregation rules on given sets of profiles. In particular, the results do not predict that political behavior is chaotic or that "anything can happen." Instead, they demonstrate that we can *not* view or explain collective behavior as simply an exercise in selecting best alternatives according to some social preference relation. (Austen-Smith and Banks, 1999b, 184, emphasis in original)

What one may say is that the non-existence of the core and the cyclicity of the majority-rule preference relation constitute contextual features that may be exploited, but this "opportunity" will depend upon other background features. So long as the full set of alternatives is available, then absent other features or restrictions, collective preferences may give us no purchase on predicting collective outcomes. If, on the other hand, we enrich the rather Spartan model of McKelvey in various ways, we may be able to say more. With transactions costs in coalition formation, for example, in effect producing "thick" voter indifference contours, there may be a core-like equilibrium (Sloss, 1973). If, on the other hand, voters are non-myopic strategic agents, then there are limits on where a majority-rule process can be driven (Shepsle and Weingast, 1984). Finally, if institutional arrangements, a topic we address below, endow particular agents with strategic resources (proposal power, veto power, gatekeeping), then these may restrict the range of feasible results. That is, contextual features transform McKelvey's problem of aggregation into one of strategic interaction.

In personal conversation with Peter Ordeshook at a conference in memory of McKelvey, one of us was advised to read the last paragraph of each of McKelvey's intransitivity papers. There McKelvey conveys quite clearly that global cycling is not a description of majority rule, but a *condition* of it. He is one of the earliest to appreciate that these results provide a basis and a rationale for turning to other factors, especially institutional features, to understand majority rule in practice.[9] Many of the positive elaborations of the McKelvey theorems are institutional elaborations. One large class of these, to which McKelvey (1976; Chapter 4 of this book) himself devoted attention, is agenda formation and manipulation, a topic we take up next.

---

[9] In something of an about-face, McKelvey (1986; Chapter 12 of this book) seeks to sever general statements about politics from institutional detail.

Agenda Manipulation

Studies of agenda control post-McKelvey have considered many aspects and consequences of such control (cf. Cox, 2005 for a recent review). Here, we focus on the question that McKelvey himself broached most clearly, concerning how much agenda power benefits its wielder(s). In the space allotted, we can only scratch the surface and provide pointers to further sources for the interested reader.

Romer and Rosenthal's Setter Model

Romer and Rosenthal (1978) investigated a model in which an agenda setter has the exclusive right to make a single, take-it-or-leave-it proposal to another group of agents, who must then vote either to accept or reject her proposal. For example, Romer and Rosenthal's model covered the case in which a school superintendent proposes an overall budget for public schools, and the local electorate accepts or rejects it in a referendum. If the local electorate accepts the proposed budget, then that budget is implemented for the coming school year. If the local electorate rejects the proposal, however, then a pre-defined reversionary budget comes into force.

Romer and Rosenthal show that if the reversionary policy is sufficiently extreme, then the agenda setter in their model can secure her ideal policy. For example, if the consequence of rejecting the setter's proposed school budget was that the school budget would be zeroed out, forcing closure of the schools, then the local electorate would presumably accept quite a range of (positive!) budgets, rather than face the reversionary outcome. Romer and Rosenthal's finding provided surprising new insights regarding reformist proposals for sunset provisions and zero-based budgeting — reforms that render the reversionary policy extreme and thereby enable agenda setters to extract rents. Their results also resonated to some extent with McKelvey's multidimensional model, where the agenda setter was sometimes able to secure her ideal only after the reversionary policy had been strategically moved to a sufficiently extreme location. Unlike McKelvey, however, Romer and Rosenthal's original papers took the reversionary policy as an exogenous given, not something the setter (or anyone else) could manipulate. Thus, their model admitted the possibility that some reversionary policies might be so attractive to the group considering the setter's proposal that the setter could no longer secure her ideal policy. For example, if the reversionary school budget were simply "last year's budget plus an adjustment for inflation," if the median voter wants a slightly larger budget than this, and if the setter wants a much more substantial increase in funding, she can no longer attain her ideal budget. However, even in the cases where the setter's proposal has to "beat" a relatively attractive reversionary policy, as in the example just given, Romer and Rosenthal show that the setter is often able to extract the lion's share of the available "gains from trade."

Both McKelvey's and Romer and Rosenthal's models envision a single agent with the exclusive right to make proposals. The models differ in that the Romer-Rosenthal setter makes a single proposal in a unidimensional policy space, whereas the McKelvey setter makes multiple proposals in a multidimensional policy space. There are logically two other models that might be considered: a single proposal in a multidimensional policy space; and multiple proposals in a unidimensional policy space.

The first of these models yields a simple result: the setter can choose any policy in the winset of the reversionary policy. Thus, the setter can get her ideal policy in a single-proposal model only if that policy beats the reversionary policy, whereas in the multiple-proposal (McKelvey) model the setter can always get her ideal. Thus, the ability to make multiple proposals is valuable when proposals are multidimensional.

Primo (2002) has investigated the second model noted above, in which the Romer-Rosenthal stage game is repeated and, hence, the setter can make multiple proposals. In Primo's model, the consequence of rejecting the setter's initial proposal is not that an exogenous reversionary policy is implemented. Instead, rejecting the setter's initial proposal simply uses up a little bit of time and puts the ball back in the setter's court: she can then make another proposal, and keep on making new proposals until one is accepted or the number of rounds hits a predetermined level, at which point a reversionary policy is (finally) implemented. He shows that repeating the stage game neither impairs nor improves the setter's influence. Indeed, the equilibrium outcome in the repeated game remains the same as in the original one-shot game. Thus, the ability to make multiple proposals is inconsequential when proposals are unidimensional.

The Romer-Rosenthal line of models reduces the power of the agenda setter from the McKelvey baseline in two main ways: the setter can only make one proposal (that is accepted) rather than a sequence; and the setter can propose on only one dimension of policy at a time rather than on multiple dimensions at once. Despite these reductions in prerogative, however, the setter still accrues a substantial benefit.

Recent empirical works using setter models include Cameron's (2000) study of the politics of presidential vetoes, Gerber's (1996) and Feldmann's (1999) investigations of how the possibility of legislation by initiative affects the incentives of elected legislators, Dion and Huber's (1996) study of the conditions under which the House Rules Committee grants restrictive rules, Cohen and Spitzer's (1996) examination of judicial deference to agency action, and Cox and Katz's (2002) study of the reapportionment revolution. Rosenthal (1990) provides a more complete review of earlier work.

Baron and Ferejohn's Model

Baron and Ferejohn (1989) investigate a model in which the right to make proposals is not fully monopolized by a single agent. Instead, each player i has a probability π_i of being recognized at the beginning of any given stage of play. If recognized, player i proposes a division $x = (x_1, \ldots, x_n)$ of a pie, with $x_j \in [0, 1]$ denoting the share of the pie to be awarded to player j. If a majority of all players approves i's proposal, then the pie is immediately divided and consumed per that proposal (and the game ends). If no majority approves i's proposal, then the current round of bargaining ends and a new stage of the game begins (with each player i again having a probability i of being recognized to make a proposal). Players are impatient, preferring to receive and consume a given share of the pie in earlier rather than later stages. Baron and Ferejohn show that the agent initially recognized to propose a division of the pie, the analog to the agenda setter in the Romer-Rosenthal model, is able to secure a substantially larger share than other players in equilibrium.

Another way to interpret the Baron-Ferejohn model is in terms of the bonus that accrues to the formateur party in government negotiations (cf. Snyder, Ting, and Ansolabehere, 2003). The formateur party is defined as the one chosen (typically by the head of state) to take the lead in forming a government. It makes proposals regarding the allocation of ministerial positions, essentially dividing a fixed pie among its own and its prospective partners' members. In this setting, the Baron-Ferejohn model can be interpreted as arguing that formateur parties should be able to extract a bonus when forming a government.

Kalandrakis (2004) provides a more general illustration of agenda power, building on the Baron-Ferejohn approach. In particular, a near-corollary of his main result is the following: by varying a player's recognition probability from zero to one, that player's equilibrium share of the pie also varies from zero to one, regardless of the voting rule in force and regardless of players' discount factors. Eraslan (2002) also provides a broad demonstration of the value of proposal power.

The Baron-Ferejohn line of models reduces the power of the agenda setter from the McKelvey baseline, primarily by making each agent's agenda power probabilistic rather than deterministic. Despite this reduction in power, the setter still accrues a substantial benefit.

Recent works applying or empirically examining the Baron-Ferejohn model include Diermeier and Feddersen's (1998) study of how votes of confidence affect the cohesion of legislative parties, Ansolabehere et al.'s (2004) investigation of how coalition governments allocate cabinet posts among their members, and Diermeier and Merlo's (2004) study of formateur selection in European democracies. In addition, a series of experimental studies have also appeared, such as Fréchette, Kagel, and Morelli (2005) and Fréchette, Kagel, and Lehrer (2003). The works cited provide a more complete review of related work.

Cox and McCubbins' "Negative Agenda Power" Model

Building on Shepsle (1979), Cox and McCubbins (2005) consider a model in which any legislator can make proposals but these proposals may or may not be considered and voted upon by the legislature. Instead, proposals seeking access to the floor of the legislature — a necessary step if they are to be enacted — must pass muster with one or more agenda-setting agents. In their simplest model, Cox and McCubbins consider a single agent who has "negative" agenda power — i.e., the ability to *block* any proposal from reaching the floor. If the agenda setter allows a bill onto the floor, that bill is then considered under an open rule (meaning that any member may offer any germane amendment to the bill that he or she sees fit). If the agent blocks a bill from consideration, then the status quo on the policy dimension the bill proposed to change is preserved.

Cox and McCubbins point out that the agenda-setting agent is able to avoid "bad" bills — defined as those that, if allowed onto the floor for consideration, would result in policy changes contrary to the agenda setter's wishes.[10] Thus, although the setter is able neither to secure her ideal policy (as in McKelvey's model) nor to secure policies away from the floor median (as in Romer and Rosenthal's model), she can still prevent policy changes on some issue dimensions and allow them on others, a valuable ability in itself.[11] Empirical studies have emerged focusing on this sort of agenda power in various assemblies worldwide, including

---

[10] They assume that the agenda setter can anticipate the final policy outcome that will result from allowing a bill targeting dimension k to reach the floor (it will simply be the median legislator's ideal point on the kth dimension). In light of this knowledge, the agenda setter can block the "bad" bills.

[11] In another version of their model, Cox and McCubbins endow the agenda setter with the ability both to choose which bills to block and also which bills to allow onto the floor under a closed rule. In this model, the setter is able to accrue the sorts of benefits that arise in Romer and Rosenthal's take-it-or-leave-it model.

those in Argentina (Jones and Hwang, 2005), Brazil (Amorim Neto, Cox, and McCubbins, 2003), and Japan (Cox, Masuyama, and McCubbins, 2000).

Weingast's Last-Mover Model

Some legislative agents have early influence over legislation; others have late influence. For example, non-privileged committees in the U.S. House of Representatives exert most of their influence early in the legislative process; they are widely credited with the ability to delay and even kill bills referred to them by refusing to report those bills back to the House. In contrast, conference committees in the U.S. Congress exert influence late in the legislative process — that is, they are sometimes in a position to make final take-it-or-leave-it offers to the House and Senate (see Shepsle and Weingast, 1987).

In general, assemblies that allocate a lot of early negative agenda power are analogous to filtration systems: bills must pass through several filters (i.e., stages at which negative agenda power might be deployed to delay or block them) before they can reach the floor. In contrast, assemblies that allocate a lot of late positive agenda power are analogous to rapid response teams: whatever else has happened previously in the legislative process, the last-mover is given a chance to snatch victory from the jaws of defeat by making a final, take-it-or-leave-it offer. Models of this sort include Weingast (1992), analyzing the power of committees in the U.S. House; Heller (2001), analyzing the power of governments in European parliaments; and Krehbiel and Meirowitz (2002), analyzing the power of the minority party in the U.S. House. As with the other models reviewed above, agenda power — in this case, the ability to make a "last offer" — redounds to the benefit of the agent wielding it.

Summary: Varieties of Agenda Power

The models surveyed suffice to illustrate some of the varieties of agenda power that appear in legislatures worldwide. In particular, there are two distinctions that the models illustrate (for others, cf. Cox, 2005).

First, both Romer and Rosenthal (1978) and Baron and Ferejohn (1989) consider cases in which a given player has a monopoly on making legislative proposals for a given period of time. No other player can delay or prevent a vote on the agenda setter's proposal; the other players can only accept or reject (and, in some variants, amend) the setter's proposal. These are models of *positive agenda power*, in which a stipulated agent has the power to put proposals to a vote. In contrast,

Cox and McCubbins (2005) focus not on the allocation of recognition probabilities (or proposal rights), but rather on the allocation of delay or veto rights. Theirs is a model of *negative agenda power*, in which a stipulated agent has the power to prevent proposals from reaching a vote. Shepsle (1979) is a model of positive *and* negative agenda power in which jurisdiction-specific subunits (committees) may initiate change in "their" jurisdictions on the one hand, and may "keep the gates closed" on the other.

Negative agenda power helps the agent wielding it to avoid "bad" dimensions. This ability in itself can stabilize policy and ensure that all actual policy changes are to the liking of the veto agent. Positive agenda power allows the agent wielding it to push "good dimensions" — i.e., those that will result in favorable policy changes. This ability in itself ensures that all policy changes the agent wishes to make (and that will pass muster with a floor majority) actually occur.

A second distinction is between *early* and *late* agenda power. As noted above, some legislatures operate like filtration systems, by setting up several stages in which they must pass muster. Other legislatures make it easier to reach a final consideration on the floor but then also give the government (or other central actors) extraordinary rights to make "final offers."

Conclusion: Future Directions and Implications for Unitary Actors

McKelvey's original work assumed a minimal institutional structure and nil transaction costs. The ease with which alternative majorities could be formed in such a frictionless world, and the consequent instability of policies, did not jibe with empirical observations of actual legislatures, thus motivating investigation of more elaborate institutional structures and non-zero transaction costs. One branch of post-McKelvian studies has focused on institutional rules that further constrain decision-making. Under the general heading of structure-induced equilibrium (Shepsle, 1979), this branch has entered a "normal science" phase, with an increasing number of papers that explore the consequences of sundry institutional structures around the legislative world. A second branch of post-McKelvian studies is currently dominated by one particular way of modeling transaction costs (Baron and Ferejohn's time discounting approach) and has also entered a "normal science" phase, with an increasing number of papers using the Baron-Ferejohn bargaining model to achieve the twin goals of taking some account of transaction costs and helping to "close" models in which the institutional rules by themselves do not suffice to generate clear equilibrium predictions.

While there is considerable room left for more normal scientific progress along both these branches of post-McKelvian studies, we can also tentatively suggest some issues that, while not demanding a paradigm shift, suggest larger adjustments. Regarding structure-induced equilibria, a natural question that has been prominent but unresolved since the beginning concerns where institutions themselves come from and how they are stabilized. While many scholars accept, as a practical matter, that institutions have some stickiness to them, exactly how to model this in a theoretically defensible way remains less consensual. Regarding transaction costs, there are other ways to bring them into the analysis besides time discounting. For example, Sloss (1973) uses thick indifference curves and one might think also in terms of wars of attrition (e.g., Wawro and Schickler, 2004). What has not yet emerged from either of these other ways of modeling transaction costs, however, is a cumulative body of scholarship exploring empirical patterns.

As we hope to have made clear in this essay, the legacy of Richard McKelvey is reflected in the wide range of theoretical and applied work stimulated by his results on instability and agenda manipulation. Whole literatures have been launched by the two papers under review here, a sentiment that constitutes a refrain throughout this volume. While we needn't be as troubled as Riker (1980, 1982) by these characteristics of democracy, there are still theoretical puzzles that are troublesome. In political science, in all its fields, we struggle to construct a theoretical micro-foundation and the struggle is on-going. One of the most glaring signs of unfinished business in this project is our partiality toward unitary actors. Students of international relations are least apologetic and most guilty of this penchant. But students of domestic politics are guilty as well, sprinkling their analyses with references to parties, committees, chambers, bureaus, courts, and interest groups. We reify the collective and treat them as unitary. Yet, from McKelvey, we know these collectives are not unitary on the one hand, and that adding up the heterogeneous tastes comprising their memberships is problematic on the other. Even when a collective has legal standing, as do corporations and political parties in most countries, "it" is not really an it. There is much to be learned from McKelvey on (i) the conditions under which a collective may be treated as an "it," and (ii) what happens when those conditions do not prevail. These are the twin contributions of the fine papers we have considered here.

References

Amorim Neto, Octavio, Gary W. Cox, and Mathew D. McCubbins. 2003. "Agenda Power in Brazil's Câmara dos Deputados, 1989 to 1998." *World Politics* 55: 550–78.

Ansolabehere, Stephen, James Snyder, Aaron Strauss, and Michael Ting. 2004. "Voting Weights and Formateur Advantages in the Formation of Coalition Governments." Unpublished typescript. Massachusetts Institute of Technology.

Arrow, Kenneth J. 1963. *Social Choice and Individual Values*. New York: Wiley.

Austen-Smith, David and Jeffrey Banks. 1990. "Stable Governments and the Allocation of Policy Portfolios." *American Political Science Review* 84: 891–906.

Austen-Smith, David and Jeffrey Banks. 1999a. "Cycling of Simple Rules in the Spatial Model." *Social Choice and Welfare* 16: 663–672.

Austen-Smith, David and Jeffrey Banks. 1999b. *Positive Political Theory I: Collective Preference*. Ann Arbor: University of Michigan Press.

Austen-Smith, David and Jeffrey Banks. 2005. *Positive Political Theory II: Strategy and Structure*. Ann Arbor: University of Michigan Press.

Banks, Jeffrey. 1995. "Singularity Theory and the Core Existence in the Spatial Model." *Journal of Mathematical Economics* 24: 523–536.

Baron, David. 1991. "A Spatial Bargaining Theory of Government Formation in Parliamentary Democracies." *American Political Science Review* 85: 137–164.

Baron, David and Daniel Diermeier. 2001. "Elections, Governments and Parliaments in Proportional Representation Systems." *Quarterly Journal of Economics* 116: 933–967.

Baron, David and John Ferejohn. 1989. "Bargaining in Legislatures." *American Political Science Review* 83: 1181–1206.

Black, Duncan. 1958. *The Theory of Committees and Elections*. Cambridge: Cambridge University Press.

Calvert, Randall L. 1985. "Robustness of the Multidimensional Voting Model: Candidate Motivations, Uncertainty, and Convergence." *American Journal of Political Science* 29: 69–95.

Cameron, Charles. 2000. *Veto Bargaining: Presidents and the Politics of Negative Power*. Cambridge: Cambridge University Press.

Coase, Ronald. 1960. "The Problem of Social Cost." *Journal of Law and Economics* 3: 1–44.

Cohen, Linda R. and Matthew L. Spitzer. 1996. "Judicial Deference to Agency Action: A Rational Choice Theory and an Empirical Test." *Southern California Law Review* 68: 431–476.

Cox, Gary W. 2005. "The Organization of Democratic Legislatures." In Barry Weingast and Donald Wittman, eds., *The Oxford Handbook of Political Economy*. Oxford: Oxford University Press.

Cox, Gary W. and Jonathan N. Katz. 2002. *Elbridge Gerry's Salamander: The Electoral Consequences of the Reapportionment Revolution*. Cambridge: Cambridge University Press.

Cox, Gary W., Mikitaka Masuyama, and Mathew D. McCubbins. 2000. "Agenda Power in the Japanese House of Representatives." *Japanese Journal of Political Science* 1: 1–22.

Cox, Gary W. and Mathew D. McCubbins. 2005. *Setting the Agenda: Responsible Party Government in the U.S. House of Representatives*. New York: Cambridge University Press.

Cox, Gary W. and Richard D. McKelvey. 1984. "A Ham Sandwich Theorem for General Measures." *Social Choice and Welfare* 1(May): 75–83.

Davis, Otto A., Morris H. DeGroot, and Melvin J. Hinich. 1972. "Social Preference Orderings and Majority Rule." *Econometrica* 40: 147–157.

Deschler, Lewis. 1975. *Deschler's Procedure*. Washington: U.S. Government Printing Office.

Diermeier, Daniel and Timothy J. Feddersen. 1998. "Cohesion in Legislatures and the Vote of Confidence Procedure." *American Political Science Review* 92(3): 611–621.

Diermeier, Daniel and Antonio Merlo. 2004. "An Empirical Investigation of Coalitional Bargaining Procedures." *Journal of Public Economics* 88: 783–797.

Dion, Douglas and John Huber. 1996. "Procedural Choice and the House Committee on Rules." *Journal of Politics* 58: 25–53.

Downs, Anthony. 1957. *An Economic Theory of Democracy*. New York: Harpers.

Eraslan, Hülya. 2002. "Uniqueness of Stationary Equilibrium Payoffs in the Baron-Ferejohn Model." *Journal of Economic Theory* 103: 11–30.

Eskridge, William and John Ferejohn. 1992. "The Article I, Section 7 Game." *Georgetown Law Review* 80: 523–564.

Feddersen, Timothy J. 2004. "Rational Choice Theory and the Paradox of Not Voting." *Journal of Economic Perspectives* 18: 99–113.

Feldmann, Sven. 1999. "Bargaining in Legislatures with Voter Initiatives." Unpublished typescript. University of Chicago.

Fishburn, Peter C. 1974. "Impossibility Theorems without the Social Completeness Axiom." *Econometrica* 42: 695–704.

Fréchette, Guillaume, John Kagel, and Massimo Morelli. 2005. "Gamson's Law versus Non-Cooperative Bargaining Theory." *Games and Economic Behavior.* 51: 365–390.

Fréchette, Guillaume, John H. Kagel, and Steven F. Lehrer. 2003. "Bargaining in Legislatures: An Experimental Investigation of Open versus Closed Amendment Rules." *American Political Science Review* 97(2): 221–232.

Gerber, Elizabeth. 1996. "Legislative Response to the Threat of Popular Initiatives." *American Journal of Political Science* 40: 99–128.

Hammond, Thomas and Gary Miller. 1987. "Core of the Constitution." *American Political Science Review* 81: 1155–1174.

Heller, William B. 2001. "Making Policy Stick: Why the Government Gets What It Wants in Multiparty Parliaments." *American Journal of Political Science* 45(4): 780–798.

Huber, John D. 1996. *Rationalizing Parliament.* New York: Cambridge University Press.

Jones, Mark P. and Wonjae Hwang. 2005. "Party Government in Presidential Democracies: Extending Cartel Theory Beyond the U.S. Congress." *American Journal of Political Science* 49(2): 267–283.

Kalandrakis, Tasos. 2004. "Proposal Rights and Political Power." Unpublished typescript. University of Rochester.

Kramer, Gerald H. 1972. "Sophisticated Voting over Multidimensional Choice Spaces." *Journal of Mathematical Sociology* 2: 165–180.

Kramer, Gerald H. 1973. "On a Class of Equilibrium Conditions for Majority Rules." *Econometrica* 41: 285–297.

Kramer, Gerald H. 1977. "A Dynamical Model of Political Equilibrium." *Journal of Economic Theory* 16: 310–334.

Kramer, Gerald H. 1978. "Existence of Electoral Equilibrium." In Peter C. Ordeshook, ed., *Game Theory and Political Science.* New York: New York University Press.

Krehbiel, Keith and Adam Meirowitz. 2002. "Minority Rights and Majority Power: Theoretical Consequences of the Motion to Recommit." *Legislative Studies Quarterly* 27: 191–217.

Laver, Michael and Norman Schofield. 1998. *Multiparty Government*, revised edition. Ann Arbor: University of Michigan Press.

Laver, Michael and Kenneth A. Shepsle. 1990. "Coalitions and Cabinet Government." *American Political Science Review* 84: 873–890.

Laver, Michael and Kenneth A. Shepsle. 1996. *Making and Breaking Governments*. New York: Cambridge University Press.

McCubbins, Mathew, Roger Noll, and Barry Weingast. 1987. "Administrative Procedures as Instruments of Political Control." *Journal of Law, Economics and Organization* 3: 243–277.

McCubbins, Mathew, Roger Noll, and Barry Weingast. 2005. "The Positive Political Theory of Law." In A. Mitchell Polinsky and Steven Shavell, eds., *The Handbook of Law and Economics*. New York: Elsevier.

McKelvey, Richard. 1976. "Intransitivities in Multidimensional Voting Models and Some Implications for Agenda Control." *Journal of Economic Theory* 12: 472–482. Chapter 4 of this book.

McKelvey, Richard. 1979. "General Conditions for Global Intransitivities in Formal Voting Models." *Econometrica* 47: 1085–1112. Chapter 5 of this book.

McKelvey, Richard. 1986. "Covering, Dominance, and Institution-Free Properties of Social Choice." *American Journal of Political Science* 30: 283–314. Chapter 12 of this book.

McKelvey, Richard and Norman Schofield. 1986. "Structural Instability of the Core." *Journal of Mathematical Economics* 15: 179–198.

McKelvey, Richard and Norman Schofield. 1987. "Generalized Symmetry Conditions at a Core Point." *Econometrica* 55: 923–934. Chapter 13 of this book.

Miller, Nicholas R. 1980. "A New Solution Set for Tournaments and Majority Voting." *American Journal of Political Science* 24: 68–96.

Plott, Charles. 1967. "A Notion of Equilibrium and its Possibility under Majority Rule." *American Economic Review* 57: 787–806.

Primo, David. 2002. "Rethinking Political Bargaining: Policymaking with a Single Proposer." *Journal of Law, Economics and Organization* 18(2): 411–27.

Riker, William H. 1980. "Implications from the Disequilibrium of Majority Rule for the Study of Institutions." *American Political Science Review* 74: 432–446.

Riker, William H. 1982. *Liberalism Against Populism: A Confrontation between the Theory of Democracy and the Theory of Social Choice*. San Francisco: W.H. Freeman.

Romer, Thomas and Howard Rosenthal. 1978. "Political Resource Allocation, Controlled Agendas, and the Status Quo." *Public Choice* 33: 27–44.

Rosenthal, Howard. 1990. "The Setter Model." In James Enelow and Melvin Hinich, eds., *Advances in the Spatial Theory of Elections*. Cambridge: Cambridge University Press.

Saari, Donald G. 1997. "The Generic Existence of a Core for q-rules." *Economic Theory* 9: 219–260.

Schofield, Norman. 1978. "Instability of Simple Dynamic Games." *Review of Economic Studies* 45: 575–594.

Schofield, Norman. 1983. "Generic Instability of Majority Rule." *Review of Economic Studies* 50: 695–705.

Schofield, Norman. 1985. *Social Choice and Democracy*. Berlin: Springer.

Shepsle, Kenneth. 1979. "Institutional Arrangements and Equilibrium in Multidimensional Voting Models." *American Journal of Political Science* 32: 27–59.

Shepsle, Kenneth and Barry Weingast. 1984. "Uncovered Sets and Sophisticated Voting Outcomes with Implications for Agenda Institutions." *American Journal of Political Science* 25: 49–75.

Shepsle, Kenneth and Barry Weingast. 1987. "The Institutional Foundations of Committee Power." *American Political Science Review* 81: 85–105.

Sloss, Judith. 1973. "Stable Outcomes in Majority Rule Voting Games." *Public Choice* 15: 19–48.

Snyder, James, Michael Ting, and Steven Ansolabehere. 2003. "Legislative Bargaining under Weighted Voting." Unpublished typescript, MIT.

Tsebelis, George. 2002. *Veto Players*. Princeton: Princeton University Press.

Tsebelis, George and Jeannette Money. 1997. *Bicameralism*. New York: Cambridge University Press.

Tullock, Gordon. 1967. "The General Irrelevance of the General Impossibility Theorem." *Quarterly Journal of Economics* 81: 256–270.

Wawro, Gregory and Eric Schickler. 2004. "Where's the Pivot? Obstruction and Lawmaking in the Pre-cloture Senate." *American Journal of Political Science* 48: 758–774.

Weingast, Barry. 1992. "Fighting Fire with Fire: Amending Activity and Institutional Change in the Post-reform Congress." In Roger H. Davidson, ed., *The Postreform Congress*. New York: St. Martin's Press.

CHAPTER 4

Intransitivities in Multidimensional Voting Models and Some Implications for Agenda Control

RICHARD D. MCKELVEY

1. Introduction

The problem of intransitivities in social choice has been the subject of much investigation since Arrow's pioneering work in this area. In the context of social choice over multidimensional policy spaces, Plott [10] has shown the severity of the restrictions which are needed in order to generate an equilibrium policy outcome. Little attention has been paid, however, to the properties of the intransitivities when these strong equilibrium conditions are not met. One exception is Tullock [13], who has argued that Arrow's result is irrelevant in this context because the cycle set will be a fairly small area in the space. But Tullock's argument is not rigorous, and no other work has proceeded any further along this line.

In this paper, we show a rather surprising result, namely, that in the case where all voters evaluate policy in terms of a Euclidian metric, if there is no equilibrium outcome, then the intransitivities extend to the whole policy space in such a way that all points are in the same cycle set. The implications of this result are that it is theoretically possible to design voting procedures which, starting from any given point, will end up at any other point in the space of alternatives, even at Pareto dominated ones. A constructive proof is given below which does precisely this in the Euclidian case. While we only consider the case of Euclidian metrics here, there does not seem to be any reason why the results herein would not extend to more general types of utility functions.

This research was supported by NSF Grant No. SOC74-20443. A previous version of this paper was titled "Intransitivities in Spatial Voting Games." I wish to thank Richard E. Wendell and James Ward for helpful criticisms on the proof of Theorem 2.

2. Assumptions and Definitions

We assume a set $N = 1, 2, ..., n$ of *voters*, and assume that the *policy space* X is Euclidian m space, i.e., $X = R^m$. For each voter $i \in N$, we assume there is a utility function $U_i : X \to R$ which for present purposes is assumed to be a monotone decreasing function of Euclidian distance; i.e., for all $i \in N$, $\exists x_i \in R^m$ s.t.

$$U_i(x) = \Phi_i ||x - x_i||. \tag{1}$$

Here $|| \cdot ||$ represents the standard Euclidian norm, and $\Phi_i : R \to R$ is any strictly monotone decreasing function. We use the notation

$$\begin{aligned} x \succ_i y &\iff U_i(x) > U_i(y), \\ x \succeq_i y &\iff U_i(x) \geq U_i(y). \end{aligned} \tag{2}$$

Given the nature of the utility functions it follows that

$$x \succ_i y \iff ||x - x_i|| < ||y - y_i||. \tag{3}$$

We use the notation $|B|$ to represent the number of elements in a set $B \subseteq N$, and use the shorthand $|x \succeq_i y| = |\{i \in N | x \succeq_i y\}|$. Then, we can define a majority preference relation over R^m as follows. For any $x, y \in R^m$

$$x \succeq y \iff |x \succ_i y| \geq n/2. \tag{4}$$

Defining the strong majority relation in the usual way (i.e., $x \succ y \iff x \succeq y$ and $(y \succeq x)$), it follows that

$$x \succ y \iff |x \succ_i y| > n/2. \tag{5}$$

If all voters evaluate policy in terms of Euclidian distance, the conditions for equilibria can be stated in terms of the existence of a total median. We develop this formally:

For any $y \in R^m$, $c \in R$ we can define a hyperplane as follows:

$$H_{y,c} = \{x | x' \cdot y = c\}. \tag{6}$$

This partitions R^n into three sets, $H_{y,c}$, $H^+_{y,c}$, $H^-_{y,c}$, where

$$H_{y,c}^+ = \{x | x' \cdot y = c\},$$
(7) $$H_{y,c}^- = \{x | x' \cdot y < c\}.$$

Now, for any $S \subseteq R^m$, we write $|S| = |\{i | x_i \in S\}|$. Then $H_{y,c}$ is said to be a *median hyperplane* $\iff |H_{y,c}^+| \leq n/2$ and $|H_{y,c}^-| \leq n/2$. We let **M** be the set of *median hyperplanes*. It is proved in [6] that for all $y \in R^m$, there is at least one $H_{y,c} \in \mathbf{M}$, although this may not be unique.

DEFINITION 1. *A vector $x^* \in X$ is a total median iff for all $y \in R^m$, $\exists H_{y,e} \in \mathbf{M}$ such that $x_* \in H_{y,c}$. It is a strong total median if in addition, for all y, $H_{y,c} \in \mathbf{M}$ is unique.*

A total median is not necessarily unique, but a strong total median is unique. Notice that whenever there are an odd number of voters, any total median is unique, and is also strong. For even numbers of voters it is possible to have a unique total median which is not strong, as would be the case if four voters were arranged with their ideal points at the corners of a square.

DEFINITION 2. *A vector $x^* \in X$ is majority Condorcet point iff $x^* \succeq y$ for all $y \in X$.*

Davis, Degroot, and Hinich [1] prove the following theorem, which establishes necessary and sufficient conditions for the existence of a majority Condorcet point and for transitive social ordering in the Euclidian model.

THEOREM 1. *If all U_i are as in (1), then $x^* \in X$ is a Condorcet point iff it is a total median. Further, if x^* is a strong total median, the social order is transitive on X, with $x \succeq y \iff ||x - x^*|| \leq ||y - x^*||$.*

Proof. See [1, Theorems 1 and 4, and Corollary 2].

Q.E.D.

Figure 1 illustrates the necessity of the strong total median to guarantee transitivity of the social ordering. Here there is a unique total median at $x^* = \sum_{i=1}^{4} x_i/4$. but it is not a strong total median. In this example, we have $z \sim x, x \sim y$, yet $y \succ z$, violating transitivity of the social ordering.

With the exception of the above type of problem, generated by even numbers of voters, which gives rise to intransitive indifference, Theorem 1 shows that the

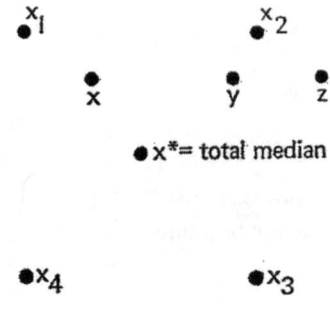

FIGURE 1

existence of Condorcet points and the existence of transitivity of the social ordering both coincide. For odd numbers of voters, the two properties completely coincide. This result is not too surprising, but given the severity of the restrictions needed to guarantee transitivity (namely, existence of a strong total median) it is of considerable interest to explore the nature of the intransitivities when these symmetry conditions are not met.

3. The Extent of Intransitivities

In this section, we show that when transitivity breaks down, it *completely* breaks down, engulfing the whole space in a single cycle set. The slightest deviation from the conditions for a Condorcet point (for example, a slight movement of *one* voter's ideal point) brings about this possibility:

THEOREM 2. *Assume $m \geq 2$, $n \geq 3$, and all voters have utility functions as in (1). If there is no total median, then for any $x, y \in X$, it is possible to find a sequence of alternatives, $\{\theta_0, \ldots, \theta_N\}$ with $\theta_0 = x, \theta_N = y$, such that $\theta_{i+1} \succ \theta_i$ for $0 \leq i \leq N - 1$.*

Proof. For each $y \in R^m$, with $||y|| = 1$, define $C_y \subseteq R$ to be the set of c satisfying $\{x | x \cdot y = c\} \in \mathbf{M}$. It is easily shown that C_y is a closed interval. So, setting $c_y = \inf C_y$, it follows that $c_y \in C_y$, and hence, we define H_y, for any y, as

(8) $$H_y = \{x | x' \cdot y = c\} \in \mathbf{M}.$$

Now it can be shown that a total median exists iff there is an $x^* \in R^m$ with

(9) $$x^* \in \bigcap_{||y||=1} \overline{H}_y^+,$$

where $\overline{H}_y^+ = H_y \cup H_y^+ = \{x | x' \cdot y = c_y\}$.

Since there is no total median, it follows that there is no common solution to the above system of inequalities. By Helley's theorem, it follows that we can find a set of $m+1$ vectors, $y_0, \ldots, y_p$, with no common solution to

(10) $$x^{*'} \cdot y_i \geq c_{yi} = c_i.$$

Out of this set, we pick a subset of vectors with no common solution (without loss of generality assume they are the first $p+1$ vectors, $y_0, \ldots, y_n$), such that for any $j, 0 \leq j \leq p$, there *is* a common solution to

(11) $$x^{*'} \cdot y_i \geq c_i \quad \text{for} \quad i \neq j, 0 \leq i \leq p.$$

For each $0 \leq j \leq p$ we set z_j to be a solution to

(12) $$z_j' \cdot y_i = c_i \quad \text{for all} \quad i \neq j, 0 \leq i \leq p,$$

and set $z = (1/(p+1)) \sum_{j=0}^{p} z_j$; we assume without loss of generality that the origin of the vector space is at z (i.e., $z = 0$, the 0 vector). Then it follows that $c_i > 0$, for all $0 \leq i \leq p$, because

(13) $$0 = z' \cdot y_i = \sum_{j=0}^{p} z_j' \cdot y_i = pc_i + z_i' \cdot y_i < (p+1)c_i.$$

Further, for any $x \in R^m$, note that

(14) $$x' \cdot y_i \leq 0 \quad \text{for some} \quad 0 \leq i \leq p.$$

Otherwise for some large $\alpha \in R$, αx is a common solution for $\alpha x' \cdot y_i \geq c_i$ for $0 \leq i \leq p$, a contradiction. Setting $H_i = H_{y_i}$ Fig. 2 illustrates a possible configuration of the y_i and H_i for the two-dimensional case.

Now, for any θ_k, we construct θ_{k+1} as follows: From (14), it follows that for some $i, \theta_k' \cdot y_i \leq 0$. Pick any such i. Then, we define θ_{k+1} as follows:

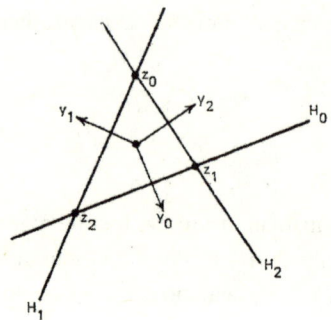

FIGURE 2

(15) $$\theta_{k+1} = \theta_k + [c_i - 2y_i \cdot \theta_k]y_i.$$

Figure 3 illustrates this for the two-dimensional case. Now,

$$\begin{aligned}
||\theta_k||^2 &= ||(y' \cdot \theta_k)y_+ (\theta_k - (y_i' \cdot \theta_k)y_i||^2 \\
&= ||(y_i' \cdot \theta_k)y_i||^2 + ||\theta_k - (y_i' \cdot \theta_k)y_i||^2 \\
&= (y_i' \cdot \theta_k)^2 + ||\theta_k - (y_i' \cdot \theta_k)y_i||^2,
\end{aligned}$$ (16)

and similarly

(17) $$||\theta_{k+1}||^2 = (y_i' \cdot \theta_{k+1})^2 + ||\theta_{k+1} - (y_i' \cdot \theta_{k+1})y_i||^2,$$

but, from (15),

$$\begin{aligned}
\theta_{k+1} - (y_i' \cdot \theta_{k+1})y_i &= \theta_k + [c_i - 2y_i' \cdot \theta_k]y_i - y_i' \cdot (\theta_k + (c_i - 2y_i' \cdot \theta_k)y_i)y_i \\
&= \theta_k + [c_i - 2y_i' \cdot \theta_k]y_i - [c_i - 2y_i' \cdot \theta_k]y_i - (y_i' \cdot \theta_k)y_i \\
&= \theta_k - (y_i' \cdot \theta_k)y_i.
\end{aligned}$$ (18)

So, substituting (18) in (17), we get

$$\begin{aligned}
||\theta_{k+1}||^2 &= (y_i' \cdot \theta_{k+1})^2 + ||\theta_k - (y_i' \cdot \theta_k)y_i||^2 \\
&= (y_i' \cdot \theta_{k+1})^2 - (y_i' \cdot \theta_k)^2 + ||\theta_k||^2 \\
&= ||\theta_k||^2 + \Delta,
\end{aligned}$$ (19)

where $\Delta = (y_i' \cdot \theta_{k+1})^2 - (y_i' \cdot \theta_k)^2$. But, now, using (15),

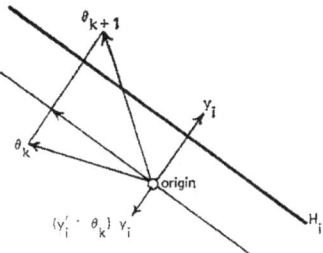

FIGURE 3

$$
\begin{aligned}
\Delta &= [y_i' \cdot (\theta_k + (c_i - 2y_i' \cdot \theta_k)y_i]^2 - (y_i' \cdot \theta_k)^2 \\
&= [y_i' \cdot \theta_k + (c_i - 2y_i' \cdot \theta_k)]^2 - (y_i' \cdot \theta_k)^2 \\
&= [c_i - y_i' \cdot \theta_k]^2 - (y_i' \cdot \theta_k)^2 \\
&= c_i^2 - 2c_i y_i' \cdot \theta_k \geq c_i^2
\end{aligned}
\tag{20}
$$

since $y_i' \cdot \theta_k \leq 0$ and $c_i > 0$. Hence,

$$||\theta_{k+1}||^2 \geq ||\theta_k||^2 + c_i^2. \tag{21}$$

It is obvious, then, by successive application of the above algorithm, we can get θ_i as far from the origin as we want.

Next we prove that $\theta_{k+1} \succ \theta_k$. To see this, note that for any $j \in N$,

$$
\begin{aligned}
\theta_{k+1} \succ_j \theta_k &\iff ||x_j - \theta_{k+1}|| < ||x_j - \theta_k|| \\
&\iff x_j \cdot (\theta_{k+1} - \theta_k) > ((\theta_{k+1} + \theta_k)'/2)(\theta_{k+1} + \theta_k) \\
&\iff x_j' \cdot y_i > ((\theta_{k+1} + \theta_k)/2)' \cdot y_i \\
&\iff x_j' \cdot y_i > c_i/2.
\end{aligned}
\tag{22}
$$

But now, since $H_i = \{x | x' \cdot y_i = c_i\} \in \mathbf{M}$ and, by assumption, $\{x | x' \cdot y_i = c_i/2\} \notin \mathbf{M}$, it follows that $|\{x | x' \cdot y_i = c_i/2\}| > n/2$ hence, $|\theta_{k+1} \succeq_j \theta_k| > n/2$ and it follows that $\theta_{k+1} \succ \theta_k$, as we wanted to show.

Thus, we have a sequence $\{\theta_1, \theta_2, \ldots\}$ such that

$$\theta_{k+1} \succ \theta_k \tag{23}$$

and such that

(24) $$\|\theta_k\| \to \infty \quad \text{as} \quad k \to \infty.$$

But now, we must show that for any x, y, we can construct a sequence satisfying (23) and (24), such that $\theta_0 = x$, and $\theta_N = y$. There is no problem with θ_0, but we must show we can get $\theta_N = y$.

To show this, we simply take $B = \{x | \|x\| < \rho\}$ to be a sphere of radius ρ satisfying $|B| > n/2$ and $y \in B$. Then, we set $B^* = \{x | \|x\| > 3\rho\}$.

It follows, for any $\theta \in B^*$, that $y \succ \theta$, since for any $x_i \in B$, $\|\theta - x_i\| > 2\rho$, and $\|y - x_i\| < 2\rho$.

Hence we pick a sequence $\{\theta_0, \ldots, \theta_{N-1}\}$ satisfying (23) and (24) with $\theta_0 = x, \theta_{N-1} \in B^*$. Then we set $\theta_N = y$, and from the above argument, $\theta_N \succ \theta_{N-1}$. But then $\{\theta_0, \ldots, \theta_N\}$ is a sequence of proposals satisfying

$$\begin{aligned} \theta_0 &= x, \\ \theta_N &= y, \end{aligned}$$

(25) $$\theta_{i+1} \succ \theta_i, \quad 0 \le i \le N-1$$

and we are done.

Q.E.D.

In Fig. 4, we illustrate the above algorithm for a simple example with five voters in two dimensions. Here we construct a cycle which arrives at a Pareto dominated point y, from a Pareto optimal point x. Note that the algorithm given is not necessarily the most efficient way of getting from x to y. In particular, as illustrated here, it is seldom necessary to actually get θ_{N-1} in B^*. Frequently one will obtain a θ_k prior to this stage which will beat y.

The theorem of the previous section shows that, at least for the Euclidian case, either the majority rule social order is completely transitive, or it is involved in a single cycle set. This result is of course dependent on the assumption of Euclidian utility functions. It seems probable, however, that the results would extend to a much larger class of utility functions. In particular it is conjectured that the same type of result would hold if each utility function were separable, i.e., of the form

$$U_i(x) = \sum_j^m U_{ij}(x^j),$$

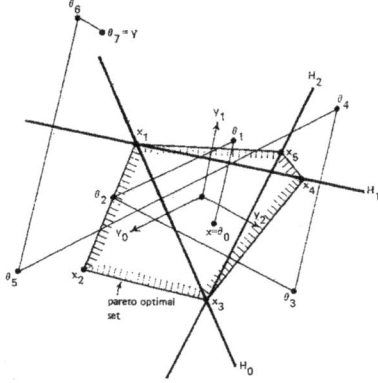

FIGURE 4

where x^j is the jth component of the vector x, and where U_{ij} is any real valued function.

In cases where majority rule is non transitive, attempts have been made in the literature to isolate subsets of alternatives which are either more stable or are in some sense normatively better than other points in the space. Some of these attempts have been based on various definitions of "top" cycle sets. Kadane [3] shows the vector of medians is always in such a set in a multidimensional model, and in a more general framework, the idea of top cycles serves as a basis for Schwartz's GOCHA set [11, 12] (called $O(a, s)$ in [11]). In the Euclidean example of this paper, the top cycle set includes the whole of R^m. If the results here extend to more general utility functions, it would suggest that such generalized equilibrium notions may not be too powerful in infinite alternative spaces.

The existence of a single cycle set implies that it is possible for majority rule to wander anywhere in the space of alternatives. The *likelihood* of this occurring probably is strongly dependent on the nature of the institutional mechanisms which generate the agenda. In the context of two-party competition, McKelvey and Ordeshook [6] prove, in the Euclidian case, that mixed strategy solutions are limited to the set of "partial medians," and recently Kramer [5] has shown that in a sequence of elections, where each candidate attempts to maximize plurality against the position of the previous winning candidate, that candidates converge towards the "minimax" set. Both the minimax set and the set of partial medians always exist, and tend to be small and centrally located subsets of the Pareto optimals. For the above institutional mechanisms then, the existence of a single

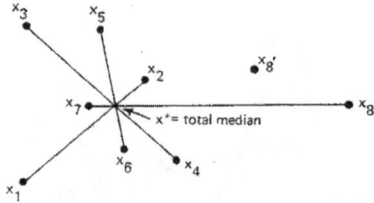

FIGURE 5

cycle set would be largely irrelevant, and the conclusions of Tullock [13] basically confirmed.

When there is the possibility of control of the agenda, either exogenously or by some member of the voting body, the existence of a single cycle set *would* be of considerable importance, as can be illustrated for the Euclidian case. From [8, 10], it follows that the existence of a Condorcet point is equivalent to a type of weak symmetry between the voters. Weak symmetry occurs when it is possible to find a point, x^*, such that voters can be divided into pairs with ideal points in opposite directions from x^*. Thus, if voters i and j are paired, we must have $(x_i - x^*) = -\alpha(x_j - x^*)$ for some $\alpha > 0$, as in Fig. 5. Any remaining voter (at most one) must be at the point x^*. This condition of weak symmetry is equivalent to the existence of a total median at x^*. With an odd number of voters it is equivalent to existence of a strong total median. Given the severity of the above conditions, the chances are very slim that such a point will exist in any particular situation. Even if a strong total median exists, it is possible for any *one* voter, by changing his preferences, to eliminate this total median. Thus, in the illustration of Fig. 5, Voter 8 could misrepresent his preferences by voting as if he had a Euclidian utility function centered at x_8' instead of at x_8. Now there is no total median, and we are in a state of flux as described in Theorem 2.

It follows from the above consideration that if any one voter, say the "Chairman," has complete control over the agenda (in the sense that he can choose, at each stage of the voting, any proposal $\theta_i \in R^n$ to be considered next) that he can construct an agenda which will arrive at any point in space, in particular at his ideal point. Even if there is a majority rule equilibrium, as in Fig. 5, the Chairman (say Voter 8) could construct an agenda which terminates at his actual ideal point (x_8) by first misrepresenting his preferences to create the intransitivities and then applying Theorem 2 to choose the appropriate agenda. This type of manipulation is possible *regardless* of the preferences of the other voters and regardless of whether the "sincere" social ordering is transitive.

The possibility outlined here for controlling the social outcome through control of the agenda depends on several assumptions which are implicit in the above scenario but which should be made more explicit. First, the Chairman must have perfect information of the other voters' preferences in order to design such an agenda. In light of the above analysis, it would obviously not be in the other voters' interests to supply such information. Second, it depends on individuals being able to make fine distinctions between alternatives without becoming indifferent. The algorithm of Theorem 2 depends on finding new alternatives which some pivotal voters just barely prefer to the previous motion. If voters cannot make such fine distinctions, this could impose some limits on the space of intransitivities such that Theorem 2 would no longer hold. Finally, the result depends on other voters voting sincerely and without collusion. If the other voters see what is occurring and know what agenda is being used they might, even without collusion, vote against their preferences at some stage (i.e., vote sophisticatedly) in order to outwit our clever Chairman. Gibbard [2] and Pattanaik [9] show that such consideration cannot be ruled out in general and Kramer [4] analyzes such behavior in a multidimensional context, proving the existence of an equilibrium to the above model if sophistication is taken into account. If collusion occurs, then one must model the above as an n-person game without sidepayments (see [6]), and for all practical purposes, the Chairman loses his power since any coalition can ensure any particular alternative in a given agenda by voting appropriately as a bloc at each stage of the agenda. Nevertheless, subject to the qualifications made above, the result of this paper, if it can be generalized, suggests that control of the agenda may be a powerful tool in a "naive" voting body.

References

[1] O. A. Davis, M. H. DeGroot, and M. M. Hinich, Social preference orderings and majority rule, *Econometrica* 40 (1972), 147–157.

[2] A. Gibbard, Manipulation of voting schemes: A general result, *Econometrica* 41 (1973), 587–601.

[3] J. B. Kadane, On division of the question, *Public Choice* 13 (Fall 1972), 47–54.

[4] G. H. Kramer, Sophisticated voting over multidimensional choice spaces, *J. Math.-Soc.* 2 (1972), 165–180.

[5] G. H. Kramer, A dynamical model of political equilibrium (sic), Cowles Foundation Discussion Paper No. 36 (June 1975).

[6] R. D. McKelvey and P. C. Ordeshook, Symmetric spatial games without majority rule equilibria, *Amer. Pol. Sci. Rev.* 70 (1976), 1172–1184.

[7] R. D. McKelvey, P. C. Ordeshook, and M. Winer, The competitive solution for n-person games without side payments, Paper presented at the meetings of the Operations Research Society of America, May 2, 1975, Chicago, IL. (Editors' Note: A later version of this conference paper became Chapter 10 of this book.)

[8] R. D. McKelvey and R. E. Wendell, Voting equilibria in multidimensional choice spaces, *Mathematics of Operations Research* 1 (1976), 144–158.

[9] P. K. Pattanaik, Strategic voting without collusion under binary and democratic group decision rules, *Rev. Econ. Studies* 42 (1976), 93–103.

[10] C. R. Plott, A notion of equilibrium and its possibility under majority rule, *Amer. Econ. Rev.* 57 (1967), 787–806.

[11] T. Schwartz, Rationality and the myth of the maximum, *Nous* 6 (1972), 97–117.

[12] T. Schwartz, Collective choice, separation of issues, and vote trading, Mimeographed, Carnegie-Mellon Univ., 1975.

[13] G. Tullock, The general irrelevance of the general impossibility theorem, *Quart. J. Econ.* 81 (1967), 256–270.

CHAPTER 5

General Conditions for Global Intransitivities in Formal Voting Models

RICHARD D. MCKELVEY

This paper proves that for majority voting over multidimensional alternative spaces, the majority rule intransitivities can generally be expected to extend to the whole alternative space in such a way that virtually all points are in the same cycle set. In other words, given almost any two points in the alternative space, it is possible to construct a majority path which starts at the first, and ends at the second. It is shown that for the intransitivities not to extend to the whole space in this manner, extremely restrictive conditions must be met on the frontier (or boundary) of the cycle set. Similar results are shown to hold for any social choice rule derived from a strong simple game. These results hold under fairly weak assumptions on individual preferences: individuals need only have continuous utility representations of their preferences such that no two individuals' preferences coincide locally. The results seem to rule out the possibility, at least in models of interest to economists, of using the transitive closure of the majority relation as a useful social choice function. They also imply that under any social choice rule meeting the conditions assumed here, it is generally possible to design agendas based on binary procedures which will arrive at virtually any point in the alternative space, even Pareto dominated points.

This research was supported, in part, by the National Science Foundation, Grant No. SOC77-08291. I am indebted to Norman Schofield for some conversations in the early stages of this research which influenced my thinking on the problem, and to Rodney Gretlein for comments on an earlier draft. In addition to the literature cited in the text, the interested reader should also see recent articles by Cohen and Matthews [4] and Schofield [21], which were written subsequent to this article, and extend some of the results of Section 4 of this paper.

1. Introduction

Since Arrow's [1] pioneering work in the area, it has been known that for most social choice mechanisms, situations can arise in which the social ordering is intransitive even though all individuals hold transitive preferences. However, Arrow's theorem only tells us that there is *some* profile of individual preferences which can yield an intransitive social ordering. It does not tell us the *likelihood* with which we can expect such a situation to arise. Nor does it tell us the seriousness, or the *extent* of the intransitivities when they do occur. This paper deals with the above questions in the context of a particular class of social choice rules, namely those based on strong simple games, where the alternatives are a subset of a multidimensional space. Particular attention is given to the special case of majority rule. For such situations it is shown that not only will intransitivities usually arise, but also, the intransitivities will generally be global, so that all points in the space are members of the same cycle set.

The question of the *likelihood* with which intransitivities arise has already received a considerable amount of attention, especially for the case of majority rule. In fact, in multidimensional models of voting, our concern here, the conditions necessary just to guarantee transitivity at the *top* of the social ordering have been shown to be so severe that one would seldom expect them to be met in practice. Plott [17] has shown if all voters have continuous, differentiable utility representations of their preferences, that a necessary condition for the existence of a core point (i.e., a point that is undefeated under the majority relation) is that a very strong symmetry condition on individual gradient vectors be met. The condition is so strong that even if it *were* met, a minor perturbation of any *one* voter's preferences would cause it to be violated. See Sloss [23], Davis, De Groot, and Hinich [5], and McKelvey and Wendell [14] for other versions of this result, and Matthews [12] and Slutsky [24] for extensions beyond simple majority rule. The generic nonexistence of a core also has been proven by Rubinstein [19] for the case when only continuity of preferences is assumed. Thus, existence of a core would seem to be a rare event. Further, transitivity at the top of the social ordering (i.e., existence of a core) does not guarantee anything about the rest of the social ordering. One is forced to conclude that the likelihood of obtaining a *completely* transitive social ordering in the case of majority rule would be *extremely* remote. Work of Kramer [10] and Schofield [20] on conditions for local transitivity reinforces this conclusion.

Although the difficulty of guaranteeing transitivity in multidimensional voting models is well known, it is not well understood how these intransitivities behave when transitivity breaks down. Thus, the question of the *extent*, or *severity* of the intransitivities is relatively unexplored. A substantial body of literature has developed recently under the implicit assumption that the intransitivities are fairly well behaved. This literature defines a derived social choice rule, called the transitive closure, which ranks two alternatives as socially indifferent if there is a cycle of which they both are members, and ranks x better than y if there is a finite path from y to x but not back. This effectively partitions the alternative space into "cycle sets," which are ordered transitively. The "top cycle set" is then of particular interest from both a normative and a descriptive point of view, the idea being that once alternatives in this set are proposed, society should not (or will not) then move to an alternative outside of the set. A review of this literature appears in Sen [22].

The usefulness of the above approach is of course dependent on the intransitivities in the social order being fairly limited in scope. Some recent research suggests that this hope may be unfounded. In a previous paper, I [Chapter 4 of this book] have shown, in a model which assumes "Euclidian" preferences (i.e., preferences based on Euclidian distance from an individual ideal point), that when transitivity breaks down at all, it breaks down completely, so that all points in the policy space, X, are in the same cycle set. By this, it is meant that for any $x_0, y_0 \in X$, it is possible to find a sequence $\theta_0, \ldots, \theta_K \in X$, with $\theta_0 = x_0$, $\theta_K = y_0$, such that θ_{i+1} is preferred to θ_i, by a majority for $1 \leq i \leq K - 1$. Thus, it is possible to find a majority rule path between any two points in the space. Recently, Cohen [3], using methods of proof quite similar to those used in this paper, has shown that the result extends to the case when preferences are "elliptical," and has also shown uniqueness of the top cycle set for general convex preferences. The assumption of Euclidian, or even elliptical preferences is clearly quite restrictive. However, Schofield [20], using a very different approach, has shown a similar result in a model requiring only that preferences be continuous and differentiable. He shows that there usually exists a continuous majority rule path between any two points in the policy space. But Schofield has only shown this result for the case when the number of policy dimensions is large in relation to the number of voters. (He requires $m \geq q + 1$, where m is the dimensionality of the policy space, and q is the number of voters in a minimal winning coalition.)

In this paper, it is shown that if the paths are not restricted to be continuous the above result extends to a very general model which places no restrictions on m. We assume only that voters have continuous utility representations of their preferences such that no two voters' preferences coincide locally. It is then shown that except under very restrictive conditions on individual preferences, global intransitivities will prevail. The conditions are such that if the alternative space, X, is any connected subset of R^2, one would usually expect them to fail, unless preferences are more or less linear over some region of X. If X is any connected subset of R^m, with $m > 2$, one would virtually always expect the conditions to fail, regardless of the nature of individual preferences. In fact, for $X \subseteq R^m$, with $m > 2$, the conditions generally fail so badly that not only is there a majority path between any two points, but that path can be chosen in such a way that it is arbitrarily close to any pre-selected curve connecting the two points.

The above describes the situation for majority rule. We also look at the general class of social choice functions generated by strong simple games. The results are more difficult to interpret here. Although they seem somewhat less pessimistic than those for majority rule, they appear to be similar in spirit to those described above: Namely, unless there is one strong player, or a fortunate distribution of preferences, we would expect global intransitivities here too.

These results imply that for social choice rules meeting the conditions required here, the transitive closure would not in general be useful as a social choice function, since it would rank all alternatives as socially indifferent. The results also imply that in most cases social choice rules of the sort studied here would be subject to manipulation by anyone in control of the agenda. A clever agenda setter, with knowledge of all voters' preferences could design an agenda to reach virtually any point in the alternative space.

The rest of the paper is organized into four sections. The following section (Section 2) begins by giving notation and definitions. We define the set $P^*(x)$ as the set of points that are "reachable" from a point x via the social relation. Section 3 then presents the main theorem, which proves that in order for $P^*(x)$ not to be the whole space, extremely restrictive conditions must be met on the "frontier" (or boundary) of $P^*(x)$. Section 4 interprets the results of Section 3 when utility functions are differentiable, and majority rule is in effect. It is proven that the main theorem then implies that for $P^*(x)$ not to be the whole space, an extremely strong symmetry condition on the gradients of individual utility functions must be met at all points on the boundary of $P^*(x)$. From this result one can see that the conditions would virtually always fail in any space of dimensionality greater than two. It also follows from this that the path can generally be chosen to follow any route desired. The final section discusses implications of these results, and gives some concluding remarks. The Appendix contains statements and proofs of a series of Lemmas used in the paper.

2. Notation and Definitions

We assume a set of *voters*, $N = \{1, 2, \ldots, n\}$, an *alternative space* X, which can be *any* topological space, although for illustrations we will assume $X \subseteq R^m$, and we let Θ denote the set of binary relations over X. For each $i \in N$, we let $\Theta_i \subseteq \Theta$ be the set of possible preference relations for voter i and we set $\bar{\Theta} = \Pi_{i \in N} \Theta_i$ to be the set of *preference profiles* over X. Elements of $\bar{\Theta}$ are written $\bar{R} = (R_1, \ldots, R_n), (\bar{R}' = (R_1', \ldots, R_n'))$, etc. For any binary relation $R \in \Theta$, we define two derived relations $P, I \in \Theta$ by $xPy \iff (xRy \text{ and } yRx)$, and $xIy \iff (xRy \text{ and } yRx)$. Thus, for any $R_i \in \Theta_i$, the associated relations are written P_i, I_i. For convenience, we will also define a relation Q by $xQy \iff yPx$, with similar definitions of Q_i, for individual voters.

A *social welfare function* is any function $f : \bar{\Theta} \to \bar{\Theta}$, which associates with each preference profile $\bar{R} \in \bar{\Theta}$, a relation $R = f(\bar{R}) = f(R_1, \ldots, R_n) \in \Theta$. In this paper, we will consider only a special class of social welfare functions, namely those which are generated from strong simple games. To formalize this, any $C \subseteq N$ is called a coalition, with $|C|$ denoting the number of members of C. For any $C \subseteq N$, and $x, y \in X$, we write $xP_c y \iff xP_i y$ for all $i \in C$. We let $\underline{W} \subseteq 2^N$ be any set of coalitions satisfying the following properties:

(2.1a)   (Monotonicity)   If $C \subseteq C'$, and $C \in \underline{W}$, then $C' \in \underline{W}$

(2.1b)   (Strong and Proper) $C \in \underline{W} \iff N - C \notin \underline{W}$.

Given any set of coalitions, $\underline{W}$, satisfying (a) and (b) above, we can define a social welfare function $R_{\underline{w}} = f_{\underline{w}}(\bar{R})$ as follows: For any $x, y \in X$,

(2.2) $$xP_{\underline{w}} y \iff xP_c y \text{ for some } C \in \underline{W}$$
$$xR_{\underline{w}} y \iff (yP_{\underline{w}} x).$$

The class of social welfare functions so generated (i.e., generated by a set of coalitions $\underline{W}$ satisfying (2.1a) and (2.1b)) will be denoted **F**. Henceforth, we will only be concerned with social welfare functions in **F**. (In general, we will drop the subscripts on $R_{\underline{w}}$ and $P_{\underline{w}}$, writing R and P for the social relations.) Note that if n is odd, majority rule is in **F**, where majority rule is defined by setting $\underline{W} = \underline{M} = \{C \subseteq N \mid |C| > n/2\}$. If n is even, then majority rule does not satisfy property 2. However, modifications of majority rule, which break ties using a chairman's preference, would be in **F**. In general, any weighted voting scheme, or representative system (which also breaks ties when all voters have strict preferences), will be in **F**.

Now, for any $y, z \in X$, we use the notation

$$(2.3) \qquad C_{y,z} = \{j \in N | y P_i z\}$$

to represent the set of voters who prefer y to z. For any $C \subseteq M$, we say voter i is *pivotal for* C if $C \notin \underline{W}$ and $C \cup \{i\} \in \underline{W}$. Then we have the following:

DEFINITION 1: Let $y, z \in X$, and $i \in N$. Then i is said to be a *dummy voter with respect to y and x* if, for any $C \subseteq N - \{i\}$ with

$$C_{y,z} - \{i\} \subseteq C \subseteq N - C_{z,y},$$

it is not the case that i is pivotal for C, i.e.,

$$C \cup \{i\} \in \underline{W} \Rightarrow C \in \underline{W}.$$

If i is not a dummy voter, he is said to be *critical between* y and z. In this case, there is a $C \subseteq N - \{i\}$ with $C_{y,z} - \{i\} \subseteq C \subseteq N - C_{z,y}$ such that $C \cup \{i\} \in \underline{W}$ and $C \notin \underline{W}$.

Thus, a voter is a dummy voter if, no matter how the indifferent votes are cast, the voter has no chance of affecting the outcome. A critical voter, on the other hand, is a voter whose vote is worth something, in the sense that there is some reassignment of preferences to the indifferent voters such that the voter in question becomes pivotal.

DEFINITION 2: Let $y, z \in X$, and $i, j \in N$; then voter i is said to be *as strong as* voter j between y and z if, for every $C \subseteq N - \{i, j\}$ with

$$C_{y,z} - \{i, j\} \subseteq C \subseteq N - C_{z,y},$$

j pivotal for $C \Rightarrow i$ pivotal for C, i.e.,

$$C \cup \{j\} \in \underline{W} \Rightarrow C \cup \{i\} \in \underline{W}.$$

Note that if $y I_i z$ and $y I_j z$, then if voter j is not a dummy voter between y and z, and voter i is as strong as voter j, then i is not a dummy voter between y and z.

Now for any $S \subseteq X$, we let S^0 denote the interior of S, $\bar{S}$ denote the closure of S, S^c denote the complement of S, and $\underline{B}(S)$ denote the boundary of S (i.e., $\underline{B}(S) = \bar{S} \cap (\overline{S^c})$). Then, we define the frontier of S, $\underline{F}(S)$, as

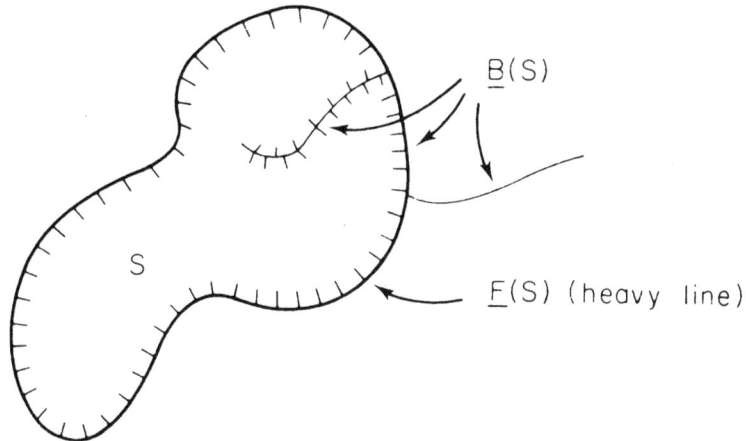

FIGURE 2.1. — Illustration of $\underline{B}(S)$ and $\underline{F}(S)$ (S includes protruding line and intruding line)

(2.4) $$\underline{F}(S) = (\overline{S^0}) \cap (\overline{(S^c)^0}).$$

All of these definitions are in the topology on X. Note that for any $S \subseteq X$; $\underline{F}(S)$ and $\underline{B}(S)$ are always closed sets, with $\underline{F}(S) \subseteq \underline{B}(S)$. The frontier of a set S, then, is simply a subset of the boundary of S, consisting of all points that are arbitrarily close to the interior of S and the interior of its complement. See Figure 2.1 for an illustration when $S \subseteq X \subseteq R^2$. In this figure S includes the line protruding from the main body of S, but does not include the line going in. The frontier of S consists only of the heavy line around S, while the boundary also includes the protruding and intruding lines.

Next, we define, for any binary relation $R \in \Theta$ and $x \in X$, a correspondence $R^j : X \to 2^X$ by

(2.5) $$\begin{aligned} R^1(x) &= R(x) = \{y \in X | yRx\} \\ R^j(x) &= \{y \in X | yRz \text{ for some}\} \in R^{j-1(x)}\} \end{aligned}$$

and

$$R^*(x) = \bigcup_{j=1}^{\infty} R'(x).$$

Thus, $R^j(x)$ is the set of points in X which can be reached in j steps, via the relation R, starting at x. $R^*(x)$ is the set of points which can be reached in some finite number of steps via the relation R (or in 1 step via the relation R^*, where R^* is the transitive closure of R). If $R = f(\bar{R})$, where $f \in \mathbf{F}$, and P and I are associated strong and equivalence relations, then $R^j(x), P^j(x)$, and $I^j(x)$ are the sets of points which can be reached in j steps via R, P, and I, respectively. Similarly, $R_j^i(x), P_j^i(x)$, and $I_j^i(x)$ are the sets of points that can be reached in j steps via the individual relations R_i, P_i, and I_i. Note that if the relation R_i is transitive, that $R_i^j(x) = R_i^j(x)$ for all j, k, so in this case $R_i(x) = R_i^*(x)$.

3. The Main Results

The main object of interest in this paper is the set $P^*(x)$. This is the set of points which are reachable, by some finite path, via the social relation, P. In other words, for any point $y \in P^*(x)$, there is an integer $K > 0$ and a sequence $\{\theta_i\}_{i=0}^K$, with $\theta_0 = x, \theta_K = y$, and $\theta_i P \theta_{i-1}$ for all $1 \leq i \leq K$. We want to determine how big $P^*(x)$ is, for arbitrary $x \in X$. In order to investigate this question, we do not investigate it directly, but rather look at properties that are satisfied on the frontier of $P^*(x)$. It will be shown that in general, very restrictive conditions must be met on $\underline{F}(P^*(x))$. For many social choice functions — in particular for majority rule — the conditions that must be satisfied on $\underline{F}(P*(x))$ are so restrictive as to imply that the frontier will be empty. But if X is connected, $\underline{F}(P^*(x)) = \emptyset$ implies (via Lemma 5 of the Appendix), that either $P^*(x) = \emptyset$ or $\overline{P^*(x)} = X$. The first possibility corresponds to the case where x is a core point (i.e., yPx for no $y \in X$), and it is known from Plott's theorem [17] that the conditions for a core point are unlikely to be met in practice. This leaves the remaining possibility, namely $\overline{P*(x)} = X$ as the situation that would be expected in general. Of course $\overline{P^*(x)} = X$ implies that virtually any point in the entire space is reachable from x.

Thus, the question of the size of $P^*(x)$ reduces to the question of the existence of its frontier. If $\underline{F}(P^*(x)) = \emptyset$, we can conclude that almost any point in X can be reached from x. The rest of this paper, then, will be devoted to studying the frontier of $P^*(x)$. This section studies the "global" properties of $\underline{F}(P^*(x))$, while Section 4 looks at the local properties of $\underline{F}(P^*(x))$.

Throughout the remainder of the paper, we assume that each individual has a continuous utility representation of his preferences, and that he has no "flat spots," or regions of indifference in his preferences. Formally, we make the following two assumptions.

ASSUMPTION 1: For each $i \in N$, there is a continuous function $u_i : X \to R$, satisfying, for all $x, y \in X, u_i(x) \geq u_i(y) \iff x R_i y$.

ASSUMPTION 2: For each $i \in N$, and all $y \in X, (I_i(y))^0 = \{x \in X | x I_i y\}^0 = \emptyset$.

It should be noted that although Assumption 2 explicitly makes restrictions only on individual preferences, it also implicitly puts some restrictions on X.

For example, X could not be a *finite* alternative set, for then it follows from Assumption 1 that regardless of the topology on X, that $I_i(y)$ is open,[1] hence $(I_i(y))^0 \neq \emptyset$. Similarly, if $X \subseteq R^m$, and R^m has the usual topology, then X can contain no isolated points, for if $y \in X$ is an isolated point, then in the relative topology on $X, y \in (I_i(y))^0$.

With the above two assumptions, a number of results about the properties of preference sets for individuals and for the social relation can be proven. These are formally stated and proven in Lemmas 2–4 of the Appendix. Using these results, we prove the following theorem which gives conditions that must be satisfied by the set $P^*(x)$.

THEOREM 1: *If each voter satisfies Assumption 1, then for any $x \in X$, and all $y \in \underline{B}(P^*(x))$,*

$$P(y) \subseteq \overline{P^*(x)} \subseteq R(y).$$

If all voters also satisfy Assumption 2, then

$$\overline{P(y)} = \overline{P^*(x)}.$$

It follows that $\underline{F}(P(y)) = \underline{F}(P^*(x))$.

PROOF: First we deal with the case when only Assumption 1 is met and prove $P(y) \subseteq \overline{P^*(x)}$. Assume the contrary. Then, we set $G = P(y) - \overline{P^*(x)}$. Since $P(y)$ is open (by Lemma 4a), it follows that G is open and non-empty, and $P(y) \cap G \neq \emptyset$. Thus, by lower semi-continuity of $P(x)$ (Lemma 4b), there is a neighborhood $N(y)$ of y such that for all $z \in N(y), P(z) \cap G \neq \emptyset$. But since $y \in B(P^*(x))$ it follows that $N(y) \cap P^*(x) \neq \emptyset$. Hence, pick $z^* \in N(y) \cap P^*(x)$. Then since $P(z^*) \cap G \neq \emptyset$, pick $w^* \in P(z^*) \cap G$. Now $z^* \in P^*(x)$ and since

---

[1] By the definition of continuity, the inverse image of every open set is open. Hence, since X is finite, we can find a small enough open neighborhood $B \subseteq R$ around $u_i(y)$ such that $u_i^{-1}(B) = I_i(y)$.

$w^* \in P(z^*)$, it follows that $w^* \in P^*(x)$. This is a contradiction since $w^* \in G$, and $G \cap P^*(x) = \emptyset$. So, we must have $P(y) \subseteq \overline{P^*(x)}$.

Now, to prove $\overline{P^*(x)} \subseteq R(y)$ it suffices to prove $P^*(x) \subseteq R(y)$, since $R(y)$ is closed (that $R(y)$ is closed follows from Lemma 3a, since $R(y) = (Q(y))^c$, and $Q(y)$ is open). We assume it is not the case that $P^*(x) \subseteq R(y)$. Then let $z \in P^*(x)$ with $z \notin R(y)$. It follows that $yPz \Rightarrow y \in P^*(x)$. But this is a contradiction since by assumption, $y \in \underline{B(P^*(x))}$, and since $P^*(x)$ is open, $y \notin P^*(x)$. Thus, $\overline{P^*(x)} \subseteq R(y)$, and we are done with the first part of the theorem.

Now, we assume all u_i satisfy Assumption 2 and prove $\overline{P(y)} = \overline{P^*(x)}$. Since $P(y) \subseteq \overline{P^*(*)}$ from the above proof, it follows that $\overline{P(y)} \subseteq \overline{P^*(x)}$. Hence we need only show that $\overline{P^*(x)} \subseteq \overline{P(y)}$. In fact it is sufficient to show $P^*(x) \subseteq \overline{P(y)}$. To show this, assume $z \in P^*(x)$ and $z \notin P(y)$. Then $z \notin \overline{P(y)} \Rightarrow z \notin P(y) \Rightarrow z \in Q(y)$ or $z \in I(y)$. But $z \in Q(y)$ is impossible, since yPz and $z \in P^*(x)$ implies $y \in P^*(x)$, a contradiction, so we must have $z \in I(y)$. But then by Lemma 3b, it follows that either $z \in \overline{P(y)}$ or $z \in \overline{Q(y)}$. By assumption, the former does not hold, so $z \in \overline{Q(y)}$. Hence, in any neighborhood of z, we can find a point $z^* \in Q(y)$. Since $P^*(x)$ is open (by Lemma 4a), and $z \in P^*(x)$, we can pick $z^* \in Q(y) \cap P^*(x)$. In other words, yPz^*, with $z^* \in P^*(x)$. It follows that $y \in P^*(X)$. However, again this is a contradiction, since by assumption that $y \in \underline{B(P^*(x))}$, it follows that $y \notin P^*(x)$. Hence $z \in \overline{P(y)}$, and $\overline{P(y)} = \overline{P^*(x)}$.

Q.E.D.

Thus, under Assumptions 1 and 2, Theorem 1 shows that it must be the case that for any point, y, on the boundary of $P^*(x)$, the set of points which can be reached in *one* step from y must *coincide* with $P^*(x)$, with the possible exception of points of closure.

This result implies restrictions on individual utility functions at frontier points of $P^*(x)$, which will be the subject of the next theorem. To obtain these implications, we first need an additional assumption.

ASSUMPTION 3 (DIVERSITY OF PREFERENCES): For all open $S \subseteq X, y \in \underline{F}(S)$, and $i, j \in N, I_i(y) \cap I_j(y)$ has no interior in the relative topology on $\underline{F}(S)$.

This assumption guarantees that no two voters have preferences whose indifference contours exactly coincide locally. To understand the assumption, consider the case when $X \subseteq R^m$. Then for an open set $S \subseteq X, \underline{F}(S)$ can be thought of as defining an arbitrary $n - 1$ dimensional manifold in X. The assumption then states that no two voters can have indifference contours which coincide on any open subset of such a manifold. Note that this does not preclude two indifference contours from crossing or being tangent at a point.

Assumption 3 would be met if all voters had "Euclidian" preferences (i.e., preferences based on Euclidean distance from some "ideal point"), as long as the ideal points of all voters were distinct. Also, as Cohen [3] proves, the assumption is met if all voters have "elliptical" preferences as long as no two voters' preferences are exactly the same over the entire space X. Finally note that Assumption 3 implies Assumption 2, so that Assumption 2 is redundant, given Assumption 3.

In the following theorem, we are concerned with a particular subset of an individual's indifference set, which we call the *"indifference frontier."* For any $i \in N$ and $y \in X$, we define the indifference frontier $\underline{IF}_i(y)$ for voter i through y by

(3.1) $$\underline{IF}_i(y) = \underline{F}(P_i(y)) \cap \underline{F}(Q_i(y)).$$

Under Assumptions 1 and 2, it follows (by Lemma 2c of the Appendix) that

(3.2) $$\underline{IF}_i(y) = \underline{F}(P_i(y)) = \underline{F}(Q_i(y)) \subseteq I_i(y).$$

Thus, the indifference frontier of voter i through y is a subset of the indifference contour of voter i through y, which coincides, under our assumptions, with the frontier of the set of points he prefers to y.

Further, for any $x \in X$, we let $Y_x = \underline{F}(P^*(x))$, and we use the notation $\hat{P}_i = P_i/Y^x$ to denote the relation P_i restricted to Y_x. $\hat{Q}_i$ is defined similarly. We then define the *indifference frontier relative to* Y_x, for voter $i \in N$, and $y \in Y_x$ by

(3.3) $$\underline{\hat{IF}}_i(y) = \underline{F}(\hat{P}_i(y)) \cap \underline{F}(\hat{Q}_i(y)),$$

where the frontiers are defined in the relative topology on Y_x. It will follow from Assumptions 1–3 together with part 1 of the following theorem that for all but one voter, say voter i, Assumptions 1 and 2 are satisfied on $\underline{F}(P^*(x))$, while voter i is indifferent between all points in $\underline{F}(P^*(x))$. Hence, as above, we can write, for all $i \in N$,

(3.4) $$\underline{\hat{IF}}_i(y) = \underline{F}(\hat{P}_i(y)) = \underline{F}(\hat{Q}_i(y)).$$

The set $\hat{IF}_i(y)$ can be thought of as voter i's indifference frontier through y relative to his preferences on $\underline{F}(P^*(x))$. Equivalently, it can be thought of as the set of points where individual i's indifference frontier crosses $\underline{F}(P^*(x))$.

With these definitions and assumptions, we can now prove the main theorem of this paper.

THEOREM 2: *Assume all voters satisfy Assumptions 1 and 2 and 3, and let $x \in X$; then:*

(i) There is some $j \in N$, such that for all $y \in \underline{F}(P^*(x)), \underline{F}(P^*(x)) \subseteq \underline{IF}_j(y) \subseteq I_j(y)$.

(ii) Let $y, z \in \underline{F}(P^*(x))$, and $z \in \hat{IF}_i(y)$ for some $i \in N - \{j\}$. Then (a) if i is not a dummy voter with respect to y and z, $\exists k \in -\{i,j\}$ with $z \in I_k(y)$; (b) if i is as strong as j with respect to y and z, $\exists k \in N - \{i,j\}$ with $z \in \hat{IF}_k(y)$.

Proof: We prove (i) first. The result is trivially true if $\underline{F}(P^*(x)) = \emptyset$, so assume $\underline{F}(P^*(x)) \neq \emptyset$. By Theorem 1, Lemma 3c, and Lemma 3d, it follows that for any $y \in \underline{F}(P^*(x))$

$$(3.5) \qquad \underline{F}(P^*(x)) = \underline{F}(P(y)) \subseteq I(y) \subseteq \bigcup_{i \in N} I_i(y).$$

We define, for any $y \in \underline{F}(P^*(x))$,

$$(3.6) \qquad V_i(y) = \underline{F}(P^*(x)) \cap I_i(y).$$

Thus,

$$(3.7) \qquad \bigcup_{i \in N} V_i(y) = \underline{F}(P^*(x)).$$

Further, since each $I_i(y)$ is closed, it follows that each $V_i(y)$ is closed in the relative topology on $\underline{F}(P^*(x))$.

We first want to show that for any $y_0 \in \underline{F}(P^*(x)), V_j(y_0) = \underline{F}(P^*(x))$ for some $j \in N$. Clearly $\underline{F}(P^*(x))$ has a relative interior, since $\underline{F}(P^*(x))$ is non-empty and open in the relative topology on $\underline{F}(P^*(x))$. So, from (3.7) and Lemma 1, it follows that some $V_i(y_0)$ must have an interior in the relative topology on $\underline{F}(P^*(x))$. We assume, without loss of generality, that $V_j(y_0)$ has a non-empty interior. We will then show that $V_j(y_0) = \underline{F}(P^*(x))$. To show this, we construct a sequence of alternatives, $y_1, \ldots, y_n \in \underline{F}(P^*(x))$, and a sequence of subsets $W_1, \ldots, W_n \subseteq \underline{F}(P^*(x))$ as follows:

$$(3.8) \qquad W_1 = v_j(y_0).$$

Then, if W_k has a non-empty interior, we construct y_k and W_{k+1} as follows:

$$(3.9) \qquad \begin{aligned} y_k &\in W_k \\ W_{k+1} &= W_k - \bigcup_{i \neq j} V_i(y_k). \end{aligned}$$

If W_k has a non-empty interior, it follows that W_{k+1} has a non-empty interior. To see this, we note first that $y_k \in W_k \subseteq W_1 = V_j(y_0)$. But by transitivity of I_j, $V_j(y_k) = V_j(y_0)$. Thus, $W_k \subseteq V_j(y_k)$ and we can rewrite W_{k+i} as

$$(3.10) \qquad \begin{aligned} W_{k+1} &= W_k - \bigcup_{i \neq j}(V_i(y_k)) \cap V_j(y_k)) \\ &= W_k - A \end{aligned}$$

where $A = \bigcup_{i \neq j} A_i$, and $A_i = V_i(y_k) \cap V(y_k)$. Clearly, each A_i is closed in the relative topology on $\underline{F}(P^*(x))$, and by Assumption 3, it follows that each A_i has no interior. Thus, A is closed, and by Lemma 1, has no interior. But now, since W_k has a non-empty interior, there is a non-empty open set $B \subseteq W_k$. Since we cannot have $B \subseteq A$, it follows that $C = B - A$ is non-empty and open and $C \subseteq W_{k+1}$. Thus W_{k+1} has a non-empty interior, as we wished to show. Hence, by induction, it follows that we can construct a sequence of alternatives $y_1, \ldots, y_n \in \underline{F}(P^*(x))$ and of sets $W_1, \ldots, W_n \subseteq \underline{F}(P^*(x))$ satisfying (3.9) for all $k \in N$.

It is easily verified that for any $r, s, k \in N$ with $k \neq j$, and $r \neq s$, the following two properties are satisfied:

$$(3.11) \qquad V_k(y_r) \cap V_k(y_s) = \emptyset$$

and

$$(3.12) \qquad \bigcup_{i \in N} V_i(y_r) = \bigcup_{i \in N} V_i(y_s) = \underline{F}(P^*(x)).$$

The second property follows directly from (3.7). To see that the first property is satisfied, assume, without loss of generality, that $r > s$. Then $y_r \in W_r \subseteq W_{s+1} = W_s - \bigcup_{i \neq j} V_i(y_s) \Rightarrow y_r \notin V_k(y_s)$. Thus, by transitivity of I_k, we get (3.11).

Now to show that $V_i(y_0) = \underline{F}(P^*(x))$, we assume this is not the case. Then $\underline{F}(P^*(x)) - V_j(y_0) \neq \emptyset$, so we pick $y^* \in \underline{F}(P^*(x)) - V_i(y_0)$. By (3.12) it follows that for each $r \in N$ there is a $k_r \in N - \{j\}$ such that

(3.13) $$y^* \in V_{k_r}(y_r).$$

But, then for some $r, s \in N$, $k_r = k_s$; i.e.,

(3.14) $$y^* \in V_{k_r}(y_r) \cap V_{k_s}(y_s).$$

But this is a contradiction to (3.11), hence $\underline{F}(P^*(x)) - V_j(y_0) = \emptyset \Rightarrow \underline{F}(P^*(x)) = V_j(y_0)$ as we wished to show.

It follows that $\underline{F}(P^*(x)) \subseteq I_i(y)$, for some $j \in N$. Now, we must show that $\underline{F}(P^*(x)) \subseteq \underline{IF}_j(y) \subseteq I_j(y)$. That $\underline{IF}_j(y) \subseteq I_j(y)$ follows directly from Lemma 2c. Now if it is not the case that $\underline{F}(P^*(x)) \subseteq \underline{IF}_j(y)$, then $\underline{F}(P^*(x)) - \underline{IF}_j(y)$ is non-empty and open in the relative topology on $\underline{F}(P^*(x))$. But by Lemma 3e $\underline{F}(P^*(x)) \subseteq \bigcup_{i \in N} \underline{F}(P_i(y)) = \bigcup_{i \in N} \underline{IF}_i(y)$. It follows that for some $i \neq j$, $\underline{IF}_i(y)$ has an interior in the relative topology on $\underline{F}(P^*(x))$. But then $(I_j(y) \cap I_i(y))$ also has an interior in the relative topology on $\underline{F}(P^*(x))$, a contradiction to Assumption 3. Thus we must have $\underline{F}(P^*(x)) \subseteq \underline{F}(P_j(y)) \subseteq I_j(y)$, and (i) is proven.

To prove (ii)(a), let $y, z \in \underline{F}(P^*(x))$, and assume $i \in N - \{j\}$ is not a dummy voter with respect to y and z, and let $z \in \underline{IF}_i(y)$. Assume the consequence of ii(a) is false. Then pick an open neighborhood $N(z)$ of z such that, for all $k \notin \{i, j\}$, either

(3.15) $$N(z) \subseteq P_k(y) \text{ or } N(z) \subseteq Q_k(y).$$

Since $z \in \underline{IF}_i(y)$, it follows that the following two sets are non-empty:

(3.16) $$\begin{aligned} A_1 &= \underline{F}(P^*(x)) \cap P_i(y) \cap N(z) \\ A_2 &= \underline{F}(P^*(x)) \cap Q_i(y) \cap N(z). \end{aligned}$$

So pick $w_1 \in A_1$ and $w_2 \in A_2$. Since $w_1, w_2 \in \underline{F}(P^*(x))$, and $\underline{F}(P^*(x)) = \underline{F}(P(y)) \subseteq I(y)$ (by Theorem 1 and Lemma 3c), it follows that $w_1 \notin P(y)$ and $w_2 \notin Q(y)$. Thus, it follows that

(3.17) $$C_{w_1,y} \notin \underline{W} \text{ and } C_{y,w_2} \notin \underline{W},$$

i.e., $C_{z,y} \cup \{i\} \notin \underline{W}$ and $C_{y,z} \cup \{i\} \notin \underline{W}$, which implies, via (2.1b),

(3.18) $$C_{z,y} \cup \{j\} \in \underline{W}.$$

But, since the game is strong, and we have

(3.19) $$\begin{aligned} C_{z,y} &= C_{z,y} - \{i\} \notin \underline{W}, \text{ and } C_{z,y} \cup \{i\} \notin \underline{W}, \\ C_{z,y} \cup \{j\} &= C_{z,y} \cup \{j\} - \{i\} \in \underline{W}, \text{ and} \\ C_{z,y} \cup \{j\} \cup \{i\} &\in \underline{W}. \end{aligned}$$

And since voters i and j are the only voters who do not hold strong preferences between y and z, it follows that voter i is a dummy voter with respect to y and z. Hence, we have a contradiction, and it follows that $z \in I_k(y)$ for some $k \notin \{i,j\}$ so ii(a) is proven.

Now to prove ii(b), let $y, z \in \underline{F}(P^*(x))$, with $z \in \hat{IF}_i(y)$ for $i \in N - \{j\}$, and assume i is as strong as j with respect to y and z. Then assume $z \notin \hat{IF}_k(y)$ for all $k \in N - \{i,j\}$. Then there is a neighborhood $N(z)$ of z such that $N(z) \cap \hat{IF}_k(y) = \emptyset$ for all $k \in N - \{i,j\}$. It follows that each of the following sets is nonempty:

(3.20) $$\begin{aligned} A_1 &= N(z) \cap Q_i(y) \cap \underline{F}(P^*(x)) - \bigcup_{k \in N-\{i,j\}} I_k(y), \\ A_2 &= N(z) \cap P_i(y) \cap \underline{F}(P^*(x)) - \bigcup_{k \in N-\{i,j\}} I_k(y). \end{aligned}$$

This follows because the sets $N(z) \cap Q_i(y) \cap \underline{F}(P^*(x))$ and $N(z) \cap P_i(y) \cap \underline{F}(P^*(x))$ are both non-empty (since $z \in \hat{IF}(y)$) and open in the relative topology on $\underline{F}(P^*(x))$. But then letting $A = A_1 \cup A_2$, it follows by construction that for all $k \in N - \{i,j\}$ that $A \subseteq P_k(y)$ or $A \subseteq Q_k(y)$. Now pick $w_1 \in A_1$, $w_2 \in A_2$; since $w_1 \in \underline{F}(P^*(x)) \subseteq \underline{F}(P(y)) \subseteq I(y)$ and $w_2 \in \underline{F}(P^*(x)) \in I(y)$, it follows that

(3.21) $$C_{w_1,y} \notin \underline{W} \text{ and } C_{w_1,y} \notin W.$$

By construction $C_{w_2,y} = C_{w_1,y} \cup \{i\}$. Further, $C_{w_1,y} \cup \{j\} = N - C_{w_2,y}$, so, since $\underline{W}$ is generated by a strong game, $C_{w_1,y} \cup \{j\} \in \underline{W}$. Setting $C = C_{w_1,y}$, we have shown

(3.22) $$C \cup \{i\} \notin \underline{W}, \text{ but } C \cup \{j\} \in \underline{W}$$

where $C_{z,y} - \{i,j\} = C_{z,y} \subseteq C \subseteq N - C_{y,z}$. In other words, it is not the case that i is as strong as j with respect to y and z, which is a contradiction. Hence, $z \in \underline{I\hat{F}}_k(y)$ for some $k \in N - \{i,j\}$.

Q.E.D.

For the case when $R = f(\bar{R})$ is generated by majority rule, condition (ii) of the above theorem can be simplified, as in this case all voters are as strong as j. We thus get the following corollary to Theorem 2 for majority rule.

COROLLARY 1: *Assume all voters satisfy Assumptions 1, 2, and 3, assume $R = f(\bar{R})$ is generated by majority rule, with n odd, and let $x \in X$; then:*
(i) *there is some $j \in N$ such that for all $y \in \underline{F}(P^*(x))$*

$$\underline{F}(P^*(x)) \subseteq \underline{IF}_i(y) \subseteq I_j(y);$$

(ii) *for all $y \in \underline{F}(P^*(x))$, and all $i \in N$,*

$$\hat{IF}_i(y) \subseteq \bigcup_{k \in N - \{i,j\}} \hat{IF}_k(y).$$

PROOF: This follows directly from Theorem 2 with the observation that if $R = f(\bar{R})$ is generated by majority rule, then for any $y, z \in X$, and $i, j \in N$, voter i is as strong as voter j. This is true because for *any* $C \subseteq N - \{i,j\}, |C \cup \{j\}| = |C \cup \{i\}|$, hence $C \cup \{j\} \in \underline{W} \iff C \cup \{i\} \in \underline{W}$.

Q.E.D.

We now interpret the above theorem and corollary. The conditions (i) and (ii) of the theorem give conditions that must be met by all points on the frontier of $P^*(x)$. Condition (i) requires that the frontier of $P^*(x)$ must be a subset of an indifference contour for some voter. In other words, there is one voter, who we label voter j, who is indifferent between all points on $\underline{F}(P^*(x))$. Condition (ii)(a) of the theorem says that for any other voter, say voter i, if his indifference curve through a point $y \in \underline{F}(P^*(x))$ crosses $\underline{F}(P^*(x))$ at z, then as long as he is not a dummy voter between y and z, there must be another voter, say voter k, whose indifference set through y also passes through z. Condition (ii)(b) is simply a modification of (ii)(a), which guarantees that if voter i is as strong as j, then voter k's indifference contour must also *cross* $\underline{F}(P^*(x))$ at z. Note that for majority rule, all voters are as strong as j, hence condition (ii) of the corollary requires that for any voter $i \in N$, if voter z's indifference frontier through y crosses through a point $z \in \underline{F}(P^*(x))$, then there must be at least one other voter whose indifference contour through y also crosses through z.

In order to illustrate the above results, we distinguish three possible cases:

CASE I: $\underline{F}(P^*(x)) = \emptyset$.

CASE II: $\underline{F}(P^*(x)) \neq \emptyset$, but $\hat{\underline{IF}}_i(y) \subseteq \{y\}$ for all $i \in N, y \in \underline{F}(P^*(x))$.

CASE III: $\underline{F}(P^*(x)) \neq \emptyset$, and $\hat{\underline{IF}}_i(y) - \{y\} \neq \emptyset$ for some $y \in \underline{F}(P^*(x)), i \in N$.

The first case is the case when the frontier of $P^*(x)$ is empty and, as we shall see, is the situation we would expect in general. In Case II, the frontier of $P^*(x)$ is not empty, but each individual indifference frontier crosses $\underline{F}(P^*(x))$ at most once. Finally, in Case III, $\underline{F}(P^*(x))$ is not empty, and at least one voter has an indifference frontier that crosses $\underline{F}(P^*(x))$ in at least two points.

Now in Case I, when $\underline{F}(P^*(x)) = \emptyset$, both conditions (i) and (ii) of the corollary (also of the theorem) are met vacuously. In Case II, condition (ii) of the corollary (theorem) is met vacuously, although condition (i) is not. An illustration of this case when $X \subseteq R^2$ and $n = 3$ is given in Figure 3.1. Here, the frontier of $P^*(x)$ must coincide with one voter's indifference frontier, and all indifference frontiers for all other voters can cross this frontier only once. Note that Case II can only occur with particular types of preferences, when dimension of the space is small. For example, if $X = R^m$, with $m \geq 2$, and $P^*(x)$ is bounded for all $i \in N, x \in X$, then Case II could not occur. Further, Case II can only occur if $m \leq 2$. Specifically, for $m \geq 3$, then $\underline{F}(P^*(x))$ would generally be an $m - 1$ dimensional manifold, and at "almost all" points $y \in \underline{F}(P^*(x))$, if $\hat{\underline{IF}}_k(y) \neq \emptyset$, then $\hat{\underline{IF}}(y)$ would have to also contain points $z \neq y$ arbitrarily close to y, which precludes Case II from occurring.

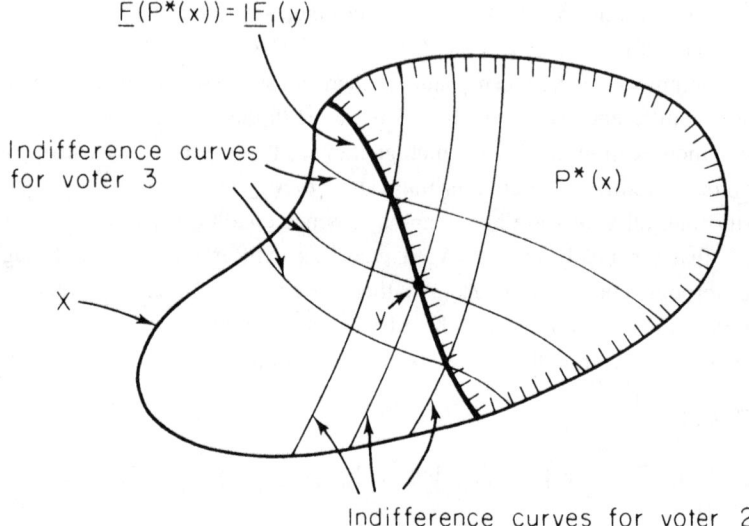

FIGURE 3.1. — Illustration of Case II

Finally, in Case III, neither conditions (i) or (ii) of the theorem and corollary are satisfied vacuously, and here the conditions imply severe restrictions on individual preferences. An illustration of this case is given in Figure 3.2. Again, the frontier of $P^*(x)$ coincides with one voter's indifference frontier, in this case that of voter 1. But now, since voter 2's indifference frontier through y also passes through the point $z \in \underline{F}(P^*(x))$, it follows, by condition (ii), that if voter 2 is not a dummy voter between y and z, there must be another voter (in this case voter 4) whose indifference frontier through y also passes through z. The same type of coincidence of indifference frontiers must occur for any other voters whose indifference frontiers cross through $\underline{F}(P^*(x))$ and who are not dummy voters.[2] Note that the figure illustrates condition (ii) for only one $y \in \underline{F}(P^*(x))$. It should be kept in mind that condition (ii) implies that similar restrictions must be satisfied for all $y \in \underline{F}(P^*(x))$. Specifically, because of continuity of preferences (Assumption 1), if $\underline{IF}_i(y)$ crosses $\underline{F}(P^*(x))$ at one point $z \neq y$, then there is a

---

[2] The theorem and corollary do not imply that the indifference frontiers must be paired in a 1-1 fashion, as drawn in the illustration (i.e., they do not prevent three voters' indifference frontiers from passing through the point z). However, for majority rule it can be shown that the above pairing is, in fact, 1-1. Further it can be shown that given any voter $i \in N - \{j\}$, $\underline{F}(P^*(x))$ can be partitioned into sets such that within each set, there is a voter $k \in N - \{j, i\}$ whose preferences on $\underline{F}(P^*(x))$ are essentially opposite to those of voter i. A future paper will report on this.

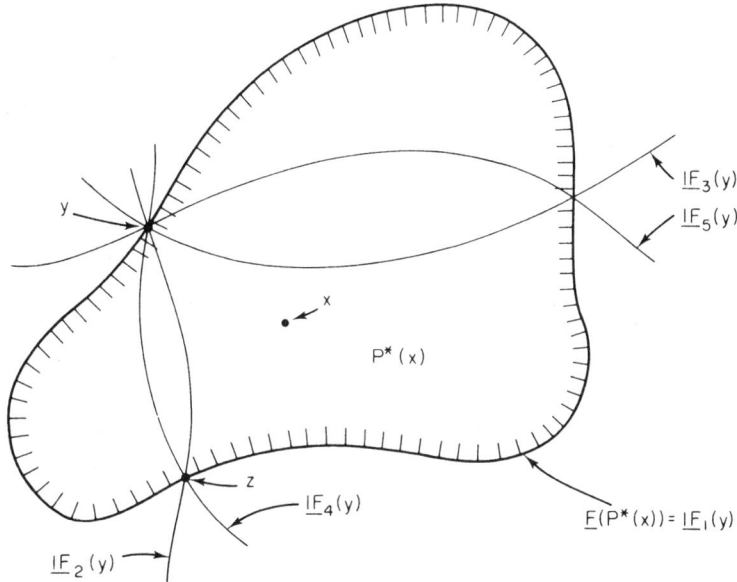

FIGURE 3.2. — Illustration of Case III

neighborhood $N(y)$ of y such that for any $\hat{y} \in N(y) \cap \underline{F}(P^*(x))$, $\underline{IF}_i(y)$ crosses $\underline{F}(P^*(x))$ at a point $\hat{z} \neq \hat{y}$. Voter k's indifference frontier must be able to be paired with another voter's indifference frontier for all such $\hat{y}$. In Case III, then, either there must be one "strong" voter with an indifference frontier that coincides with $\underline{F}(P^*(x))$, and all other voters whose indifference curves cross $\underline{F}(P^*(x))$ must be dummy voters with respect to any distinct points where they cross, or some voter must have an indifference frontier that crosses $\underline{F}(P^*(x))$ at two distinct points such that he is *not* a dummy voter between these points. The first situation, in which there is one strong voter, could arise for general social choice rules. It is obviously precluded by majority rule, and here we would *always* have the second situation. From the above discussion, we see that this implies severe restrictions on individual preferences, which one would not expect to be met in practice.

Summarizing, we have shown that for $X \subseteq R^m$, we would usually expect $\underline{F}(P^*(x)) = \emptyset$ unless there is one "strong voter," j, with an indifference contour coinciding with $\underline{F}(P^*(x))$ or unless all voters' indifference contours cross $\underline{F}(P^*(x))$ at most once. The latter case can only occur if $m \leq 2$, and preferences take a special form over X. With these exceptions, we would always expect

$\underline{F}(P^*(x)) = \emptyset$ unless extremely strong "symmetry" restrictions on individual utility functions are met at almost all points in $\underline{F}(P^*(x))$. It follows from the comments at the beginning of this section that if X is connected and x is not a core point, that $\overline{P^*(x)} = X$.

The results for general continuous utility functions, then, seem to resemble quite closely those that hold for Euclidian preferences. In general, if X is connected, and $x \in X, \overline{P(x)} = X$, and hence it is possible under the social relation to find a path which begins at x and ends arbitrarily close to any point in the space, even Pareto dominated ones.

Finally, before proceeding, it should be noted that in Theorem 2 and Corollary 1, the choice of X is arbitrary. Thus, for any $X \subseteq R^m$, if X is connected and the Assumptions 1–3 are met in the relative topology on X, then we can expect global cycles in X unless the restrictions implied under Case II or III are met. Of course, because of the severity of the conditions of Theorem 2, it is possible that the set X might be chosen in several ways, each of which would lead to global cycles. Thus, by the choice of X, there is some control over the path that will be taken from x to y. For example, we could force the path to avoid certain alternatives by eliminating them from X.

4. Local Properties of $\underline{F}(P^*(x))$

This section formalizes some of the comments of the previous section by looking at local properties of individual utility functions at points on $\underline{F}(P^*(x))$. We look only at majority rule, with n odd, in this section, and introduce the additional assumption that utility functions are everywhere differentiable. We then get a restatement of Theorem 2 in terms of individual utility gradients at points on $\underline{F}(P^*(x))$. It is shown that if $\underline{F}(P^*(x)) \neq \emptyset$, that an extremely strong symmetry condition on individual gradients must be met at all points in $\underline{F}(P^*(x))$. We call this condition the "joint symmetry" condition. The condition is a natural extension of Plott's conditions for the existence of a core point, and is such that if $X \subseteq R^m$, with $m \geq 3$, one would not, in general, expect it to be met. It is also shown that this condition is a necessary condition for transitivity of the majority relation in X. In other words, for P to be transitive on X, the joint symmetry condition must be met at all points $x \in X$. On the other hand, with arbitrary preferences on R^m, with $m \geq 3$, one would expect the condition to be violated *almost everywhere* in R^m. It follows that the existence of global intransitivities in X is almost *independent* of the choice of X. From this result it follows that not only will there generally be a majority path between any two points x and y, but the path can generally be chosen to be arbitrarily close to any pre-selected curve connecting the two points.

We make the following additional assumption.

ASSUMPTION 4: For all $i \in N$, u_i is continuously differentiable on X.

We then define the joint symmetry condition.

DEFINITION: The set $A = \{\alpha_1, \ldots, \alpha_n\} \subseteq R_m$ is said to be *jointly symmetric* with respect to j if, for all $\alpha_i \in A - \{\alpha_j\}, \exists \alpha_k \in A - \{\alpha_j, \alpha_i\}$ such that $\{\alpha_i, \alpha_j, \alpha_k\}$ are linearly dependent. The set A is *jointly symmetric* if for some $j \in N$, it is jointly symmetric with respect to j.

The condition of joint symmetry requires, then, that there be some distinguished vector $\alpha_j \in A$ such that for all the remaining vectors $\alpha_i \in A$ there is at least one additional vector in the space spanned by α_i and α_j. It should be noted that with respect to the usual product topology on $(R^m)^n$ for $m \geq 3$, the set of points where the joint symmetry condition is violated is an open, dense set in $(R^m)^n$. Hence the condition is generically violated if $m \geq 3$.

Now for any $y \in X$, we can set

(4.1) $$A(y) = \{\nabla u_1(y), \nabla u_2(y), \ldots, \nabla u_n(y)\}.$$

So $A(y)$ represents the collection of gradients at any point $y \in X$. We now prove the following extension of Theorem 2, which proves that if $P^*(x)$ has a non-empty frontier, *every* point in this frontier must satisfy the joint symmetry condition:

THEOREM 3: *Assume n odd, R is majority rule, all voters satisfy Assumptions 1, 2, 3, and 4, and $X \subseteq R^m$ is open. Then $\exists j \in N$ such that, for all $x \in X$ and $y \in \underline{F}(P^*(x))$, $A(y)$ is jointly symmetric with respect to j.*

PROOF: By Corollary 2, for some voter $j \in N$ and all $y \in \underline{F}(P^*(x))$, $\underline{F}(P^*(x)) \subseteq \underline{IF}_j(y)$. We will show that for all $y \in \underline{F}(P^*(x))$, $A(y)$ satisfies the joint symmetry condition with respect to j. We assume, for some $y \in \underline{F}(P^*(x))$, that $A(y)$ does *not* satisfy joint symmetry with respect to j, and derive a contradiction to Corollary 1.

We write $\alpha_i = \nabla u_i(y)$ for all $i \in N$, so $A(y) = \{\alpha_i | i \in N\}$. Now, since joint symmetry is violated at y, it follows that for some $i \in N$, $\{\alpha_j, \alpha_i, \alpha_k\}$ is linearly independent for all $k \in N - \{i, j\}$. Thus, in particular, $\alpha_j \neq 0$, $\alpha_i \neq 0$, and $\alpha_j \neq c\alpha_i$ for any $c \in R$. So, by Lemmas 7 and 8, there is a neighborhood, say $N(y) \subseteq X$, of y such that within this neighborhood, $I_i(y)$ coincides with $\underline{IF}_i(y)$ and $I_j(y)$ coincides with $\underline{F}(P^*(x))$. In other words

(4.2) $\quad\quad N(y) \cap I_i(y) \;=\; N(y) \cap \underline{IF}_i(y),$
$\quad\quad\quad\quad\; N(y) \cap I_j(y) \;=\; N(y) \cap \underline{IF}_j(y) = N(y) \cap \underline{F}(P^*(x)).$

Further, since u_i and u_j are continuously differentiable, $N(y)$ can be chosen so it also satisfies the condition that *for all* $u_i \in N(y)$,

(4.3) $\quad\quad\quad\quad \nabla u_i(w) \;\neq\; 0$
$\quad\quad\quad\quad\quad\; \nabla u_j(w) \;\neq\; 0$
$\quad\quad\quad\quad\quad\; \nabla u_i(w) \;\neq\; c\nabla u_j(w) \text{ for any } c \in R.$

Then, from (4.2) and Lemma 9, we have, for any $w \in N(y)$,

(4.4) $\quad\quad w \in I_i(y) \cap I_j(y) \;\Rightarrow\; w \in \underline{IF}_i(y) \cap \underline{F}(P^*(x))$
$\quad\quad\quad\quad\quad\quad\quad\quad\;\; \Rightarrow\; w \in \hat{IF}_i(y).$

Now, to derive a contradiction to Corollary 2, we must find a point $w \in \underline{F}(P^*(x))$ such that $w \in \hat{IF}_i(y)$ and $w \notin \hat{IF}_k(y)$ for any $k \in N - \{j,k\}$. In light of (4.4), and since $\hat{IF}_k(y) \subseteq I_k(y)$, it suffices to find a point $w^* \in N(y)$ such that

(4.5) $\quad\quad\quad\quad w^* \;\in\; I_i(y) \cap I_i(y)$ and
$\quad\quad\quad\quad\quad w^* \;\notin\; I_k(y) \text{ for all } k \in N - \{j,i\}.$

We pick $z \in R^m$ such that

(4.6) $\quad\quad\quad\quad\quad z \cdot \alpha_j \;=\; z \cdot \alpha_i = 0$ and
$\quad\quad\quad\quad\quad\quad z \cdot \alpha_k \;\neq\; 0$

for all $k \in N - \{j,i\}$. It is clear that we can find such a z, because for each $k \in N - \{j,i\}$, since $\{a_j, a_i, a_k\}$ is linearly independent, we can pick $z_k \in R^m$ such that $z \cdot \alpha_j = z \cdot \alpha_i = 0$, and $z \cdot \alpha_k \neq 0$. (This can be done using the Gram-Schmidt procedure, so that z_k corresponds to the third member of an orthogonal basis generated by $\{a_j, a_i, a_k\}$.) Now, we can choose $t_l \in R$ for $l \in N - \{j, i\}$ such that $z = \sum_{l \in N - \{j,i\}} t_l z_l$ satisfies (4.6).

(4.7) $\qquad D_\varepsilon = \{w | w = z + \alpha_j \beta_j + \alpha_i \beta_i, \text{ where } |\alpha_j| \leq \varepsilon, |\alpha_i| \leq \varepsilon\}.$

Now clearly D_ε is compact and convex, for all $\varepsilon > 0$. Further since the set of z satisfying $z \cdot \alpha_k \neq 0$ is an open set, it follows that we can pick ε such that for all $w \in D_\varepsilon$, $w \cdot \alpha_k \neq 0$ for all $k \in N - \{i, j\}$. Now, by Lemma 6, it follows that for all $k \in N - \{j, i\}$, we can find $t_k^* \in R^+$ such that for $t \leq t_k^*$,

(4.8) $\qquad \alpha_k \cdot z > 0 \Rightarrow y + tD_\varepsilon \subseteq P_k(y),$
$\qquad\qquad \alpha_k \cdot z < 0 \Rightarrow y + tD_\varepsilon \subseteq Q_k(y).$

Also, for $\{l, k\} = \{j, i\}$, and $|a| \leq \varepsilon$, define

(4.9) $\qquad D^*(l, a) = \{w \in D_\varepsilon | w = z + a\beta_l + a_k \beta_k \text{ for some } a_k \in R\}.$

It follows that for $l \in \{j, i\}$, $D^*(l, \varepsilon)$ and $D^*(l, -\varepsilon)$ are compact subsets of D_ε satisfying

(4.10) $\qquad w \cdot \alpha_l > 0 \quad \text{for all} \quad w \in D^*(l, \varepsilon),$
$\qquad\qquad w \cdot \alpha_l < 0 \quad \text{for all} \quad w \in D^*(l, -\varepsilon).$

Thus, by Lemma 6, it follows that we can find a $p^* \in R^+$ such that for $t \leq p^*$,

(4.11) $\qquad y + tD^*(l, \varepsilon) \subseteq P_l(y),$
$\qquad\qquad y + tD^*(l, -\varepsilon) \subseteq Q_l(y).$

Finally, since $N(y)$ is a neighborhood of y, we can pick $q^* > 0$ such that for $t \leq q^*$,

(4.12) $\qquad w \in y + tD_\varepsilon \Rightarrow w \in N(y).$

Setting

(4.13) $\qquad t^* = \min_{k \in N - \{i,j\}} (t_k^*, p^*, q^*),$

it follows that, for $t \leq t^*$, (4.8), (4.11), and (4.12) are satisfied.

We set $E = y + t^* D_\varepsilon$, $E_l^+ = y + t^* D^*(l, \varepsilon)$, and $E_l^- = y + t^* D(l, -\varepsilon)$. Now, from (4.8) it follows that for all $k \in N - \{j, i\}$, either

(4.14) $$E \subseteq P_k(y) \text{ or } E \subseteq Q_k(y).$$

Thus, since $P_k(y)$, $Q_k(y)$, and $I_k(y)$ are disjoint, it follows that

(4.15) $$E \cap I_k(y) = \emptyset$$

for all $k \in N - \{j, i\}$. However, we must prove that

(4.16) $$E \cap I_j(y) \cap I_i(y) \neq \emptyset.$$

To prove this, note first that, for $l \in \{j, i\}$, it follows from (4.11) that

(4.17) $$E_l^+ \subseteq P_l(y),$$
$$E_l^- \subseteq Q_l(y).$$

Now, setting $\varepsilon^* = t\varepsilon$, any $w \in E$ can be written in the form

(4.18) $$w = (y + t^* z) + b_j \beta_j + b_i \beta_i$$

where $|b_j| \leq \varepsilon^*$, and $|b_i| \leq \varepsilon^*$. So (4.17) can be rewritten as follows. For any $w \in E$, and $l \in \{i, j\}$,

(4.19) $$b_l = \varepsilon^* \Rightarrow u_l(w) > u_l(y),$$
$$b_l = -\varepsilon^* \Rightarrow u_l(w) < u_l(y).$$

But now, for any $w \in E$, set

(4.20) $T(w) = w + (\max[\min[u_j(y) - u_j(w), \varepsilon^* - b_j], -\varepsilon^* - b_j]) \cdot \beta_j$
$+ (\max[\min[u_i(y) - u_i(w), \varepsilon^* - b_i], -\varepsilon^* - b_i]) \cdot \beta_i.$

$T : E \to E$ is a continuous mapping on a compact convex set, and hence by the Brouwer fixed point theorem, it follows that there is a fixed point, i.e., a point $w^* \in E$ with $T(w^*) = w^*$. But from (4.19) and (4.20), it is easily shown that $T(w^*) = w^* \iff u_j(w^*) = u_j(y)$ and $u_i(w^*) = u_i(y)$. Hence, we have shown existence of a point w^* such that

(4.21) $$w^* \in E \cap I_j(y) \cap I_i(y)$$

and by (4.15), for all $k \in N - \{j, i\}$,

(4.22) $$w^* \notin I_k(y).$$

But since $E \subseteq N(y)$, w^* satisfies (4.5), and we have a contradiction. Hence, it follows that $A(y)$ must satisfy the joint symmetry condition with respect to j, as we wished to show.

Q.E.D.

Theorem 3 can be thought of as a restatement of Corollary 1 in terms of the local conditions that must be satisfied at frontier points of $P^*(x)$. As before, if $\underline{F}(P^*(x)) = \emptyset$, then the theorem is satisfied vacuously. However, if $\underline{F}(P^*(x)) \neq \emptyset$, then the joint symmetry condition must be met by the individual utility gradients at all points $y \in \underline{F}(P^*(x))$. The joint symmetry condition is a condition which, if $m \geq 3$, we would rarely, if ever, expect to be met even at just one point in X. A fortiori, we would not expect it to be met at *all* frontier points. Thus we get a further confirmation of the comments of the previous section for $m \geq 3$. Namely, if $m \geq 3$, and $X \subseteq R^m$ is connected, we can virtually always expect, under majority rule, that $\overline{P^*(x)} = X$ for any $x \in X$.

It follows further that for the majority relation to be transitive on X, we must have the joint symmetry condition met at all points in X. This is proven in the following corollary to Theorem 3. Here, for any $S \subseteq X$, and $x \in X_0$, we let $P_s^*(x) = \bigcup_{j=1}^{\infty} = P_s^j(x)$, where $P_s^1(x) = \{y \in S | yPx\}$, and $P_s^j(x) = \{y \in S | yPz \text{ for some } z \in P_s^{j-1}(x)\}$. So $P_s^*(x)$ is the set of points within S that can be reached by the majority relation.

COROLLARY 2: *If n is odd, $R = f(\bar{R})$ is majority rule, and all voters satisfy Assumptions 1, 2, 3, and 4, with X open, then a necessary condition for P to be transitive on X is that $A(y)$ be jointly symmetric for all $y \in X$. Further, for any $y \in X$, if $A(y)$ is not jointly symmetric, then there is a neighborhood $N(y)$ of y such that, for any $z \in N(y)$, $\overline{P^*_{N(y)}(z)} = N(y)$.*

PROOF: We first prove the second assertion. Assume for some $y \in X$, $A(y)$ is not jointly symmetric. Then since each u_i is continuously differentiable, it follows that we can find a neighborhood $N(y)$ of y (which we may choose to be connected) such that for any $z \in N(y)$, and any $i, j, k \in N$,

$\{\nabla u_i(y), \nabla u_j(y), \nabla u_k(y)\}$ linearly independent
$\Rightarrow \{\nabla u_i(z), \nabla u_j(z), \nabla u_k(z)\}$ linearly independent

It follows that, for all $z \in N(y)$, $A(z)$ is not jointly symmetric. But then, by Theorem 3, $\underline{F}(P^*_{N(y)}(z)) = \emptyset$ for all $z \in N(y)$. But further, we cannot have $P^*_{N(y)}(z) = \emptyset$ since then, by Plott's Theorem, the joint symmetry condition would be satisfied. Hence, since $P^*_{N(y)}(z)$ is open, and $N(y)$ is connected, it follows from Lemma 7 that we must have $\overline{P^*_{N(y)}(z)} = N(y)$. Clearly, given any $z \in N(y)$, we can construct a cycle from y to z and back again, so P is not transitive.

Q.E.D.

We now consider the implications of the previous theorem and corollary. We assume X is a connected subset of R^m, where $m \geq 3$. We define $\underline{S}(X)$ to be the set of points in X where the joint symmetry condition is satisfied, and let $\underline{V}(X) = X - \underline{S}(X)$ be the set of points in X where the joint symmetry condition is *violated*. From Assumptions 1–4 it follows that $\underline{S}(X)$ would generally be a closed set with no interior. $\underline{V}(X)$ would then be an open, dense subset of X. Now, from Theorem 1, it follows that for any $x \in X, \underline{F}(P^*(x)) \subseteq \underline{S}(X)$. But then it follows (see Lemma 5a) that unless $\underline{S}(X)$, the set of points where joint symmetry is satisfied, chops up X into at least two disjoint open sets, we must have $\underline{F}(P^*(x)) = \emptyset$. Thus, a sufficient condition for $\underline{F}(P^*(x)) = \emptyset$ is that $\underline{V}(X)$ be a connected set.

A further implication of the above arguments is that we may frequently have considerable latitude in choosing a majority path between two points. Thus, for any $X_0 \subseteq X$, we have $\underline{V}(X_0) = X_0 \cap \underline{V}(X)$, and $\underline{S}(X_0) = X_0 \cap \underline{S}(X)$. So if we wish to construct a majority path between $x, y \in X$, we can restrict the path to any subset X_0 of X such that $x \in X_0, y \in X_0$ and such that $\underline{V}(X_0)$ is connected. Thus, the path between x and y can be forced to avoid certain alternatives, as in Figure 4.1, by choosing X_0 appropriately. In fact, it follows further that if $C \subseteq X$ is any simple curve connecting x and y such that $C \cap \underline{S}(X) = \emptyset$, we can construct a "continuous" majority path between x and y, each step of which is arbitrarily close to C. To see this, note that by Corollary 2, it follows that given any $z \in C$, there is a neighborhood $N(z)$ of z, such that $N(z) \subseteq \underline{V}(X)$. Hence, there will be global intransitivities in $N(z)$. Since C is compact, it follows there is a finite subcover $N(z_1), N(z_2), \ldots, N(z_k)$ of C, with $N(z_i) \cap N(z_i + 1) \neq \emptyset$ for all i. There are global intransitivities within each $N(z_i)$, which can be pieced together to form a majority rule path from x to y. If each $N(z)$ is chosen so that

General Conditions for Global Intransitivities in Formal Voting Models

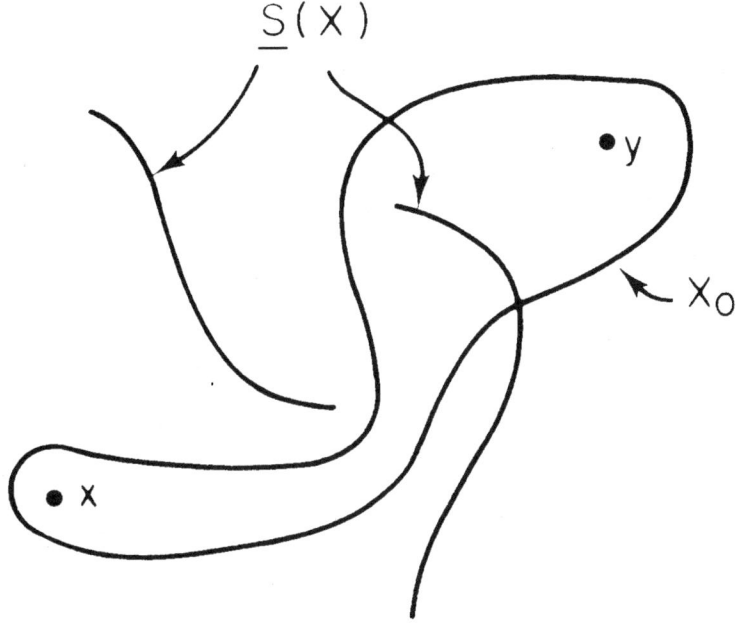

FIGURE 4.1. — Choice of X_0 to avoid certain alternatives

$N(z) \subseteq \{y | \|z - y\| < \varepsilon\}$ it follows that the resulting path can be forced arbitrarily close to C. See Figure 4.2 for an illustration.

Finally, it should be pointed out that even though we would seldom expect the joint symmetry conditions to be met, even if they are met the conditions are very fragile in the same sense that the Plott conditions for an equilibrium are fragile. Namely, when the conditions are met they are vulnerable to misrepresentations or minor perturbations of *any* one voter's preferences. Specifically, if the joint symmetry conditions *are* met at a point $y \in X$, and no two voters' gradients are linear combinations of each other, it follows that for any $k \in N$, there is a bogus representation, say $\nabla u_k^*(y)$ of $\nabla u_k(y)$, such that

$$A_k^*(y) = (A(y) - \{\nabla u_k(y)\}) \cup \{\nabla u_k^*(y)\}$$

does *not* satisfy the joint symmetry conditions. This suggests that results similar to those discussed in McKelvey [Chapter 4 of this book] may hold more generally. Namely that regardless of other voters' preferences, any one voter with complete information of other voters' preferences, control of the agenda, and the ability

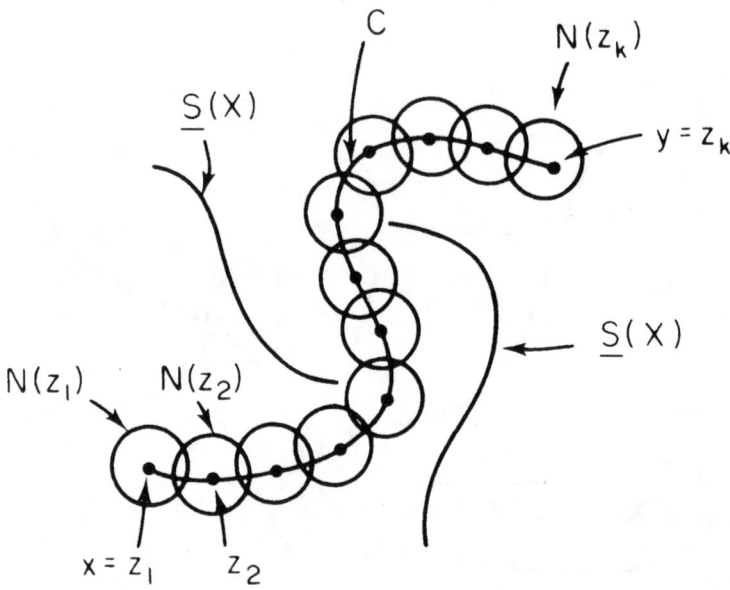

FIGURE 4.2. — Construction of majority path arbitrarily close to curve C

to cast his own vote as he chooses can *always* construct majority paths to get anywhere in the space.

In short, we have argued above that if $X \subseteq R^m$ is connected, and $m \geq 3$, the joint symmetry condition is a severe restriction which at any given point in X we would expect to fail. We would *certainly* not expect it to be satisfied on large subsets of X. Thus, in general, we would expect $\underline{V}(X)$, the set of points where joint symmetry is violated, to be a connected, dense subset of X. But then we have that $\underline{F}(P^*(x)) = \emptyset$ implying that $P^*(x) = \emptyset$ or $\overline{P^*(x)} = X$. It follows that unless x is a core point, we would generally expect to have naturally occurring majority paths between x and virtually any other point in the space. Even in the rare instances when there are not unlimited majority paths through the entire space, the conditions preventing this state of affairs are fragile enough so that any one voter, through misrepresentation of his own preferences, could give rise to this situation.

5. Conclusions

Despite the impact Arrow's impossibility theorem has had on the study of social choice, there still seems to be a tendency in much of the formal literature dealing with majority rule over multidimensional policy spaces to view majority rule as a fairly well defined notion, which will generally force the social outcome towards "median" like alternatives. Even though it is known that intransitivities will generally exist, a substantial literature has developed on the tacit assumption that these intransitivities are confined to relatively limited areas of the space.

The above results have shown that majority rule is not well defined in the above sense. Rather, the usual situation will be that majority paths exist between any two points in the space. Even in the rare situations when this is not the case, the restrictions implied on individual utility functions seem to be so severe that a minor perturbation of any one voter's preferences would be sufficient to give rise to global intransitivities.

There are several implications of the above results. First, they seem to imply that there are essentially unlimited possibilities for agenda manipulation. Any one voter, with knowledge of other voters' preferences, and the power to set the agenda could, using binary, majority rule based procedures, arrive at any outcome he wants to. See McKelvey [Chapter 4 of this book] for further elaboration on this point. Secondly, these results show the inadequacy of arriving at any useful social choice functions using the notions of top cycle set or the transitive closure of majority rule, as such methods will simply rank all alternatives as socially indifferent. Finally, the results indicate that any attempts to construct positive descriptive theory of political processes based on majority rule (or other social choice functions satisfying the assumptions of this paper) must take account of particular institutional features of these systems, as the social ordering by itself does not give much theoretical leverage. Much work has already been done in this direction, incorporating such institutional features as party competition [6, 11], sequential voting under parliamentary rules [7, 9, 15], structured and unstructured committee environments [8, Chapter 10 of this book], and agenda setters [18].

Carnegie-Mellon University
and
California Institute of Technology

Manuscript received March, 1977; final revision received October, 1978.

Appendix

Here we prove some basic properties of the preference sets for the individual relations R_i and the social relation $R = f(\bar{R})$. We first prove a general result, of which we will make frequent use.

LEMMA 1: *Let Y be any topological space, and $A \subseteq Y$. If $A \subset \bigcup_{i=1}^{n} A_i$ where each $A_i \subseteq Y$ is closed, with no interior, then A has no interior.*

PROOF: The proof is by induction on n. It is clearly true for $n = 1$. Assume, now, that the result is true for $n - 1$, but not for n. So there is an open set B with

$$\emptyset = B \subseteq A \subseteq (\bigcup_{i=1}^{n-1} A_n) \cup A_n.$$

Now if $B \subseteq A_n$, then A_n has an interior, which is a contradiction. Hence, we set

$$C = B - A_n.$$

Now $\emptyset \neq C \subseteq (\bigcup_{i=1}^{n} A_i)$, and C is open, which is a contradiction to the induction hypothesis. Hence A can have no interior.

Q.E.D.

We now prove some general properties of the individual preference sets. Note first, that for any complete binary relation R on X, that X is partitioned by $P(x)$, $Q(x)$, and $I(x)$. For the individual relations R_i, under Assumptions 1 and 2, we have the following further results.

LEMMA 2: *If Assumptions 1 and 2 are met, for $\bar{R} = (R_1, \ldots, R_n) \in \bar{\Theta}$, then for all $i \in N$, and all $x \in X$, (a) $P_i(x)$ and $Q_i(x)$ are open, and $I_i(x)$ is closed with no interior; (b) $\underline{B}(P_i(x)) \cup \underline{B}(Q_i(x)) = I_i(x)$; (c) $\underline{F}(P_i(x)) = \underline{F}(Q_i(x)) \subseteq I_i(x)$.*

PROOF: That $P_i(X)$ and $Q_i(x)$ are open follows directly from Assumption 1, because

$$P_i(x) = \{y \in X | u_i(y) > u_i(x)\} = u_i^{-1}(\{t \in R | t > u_i(x)\})$$
$$Q_i(x) = \{y \in X | u_i(x) > u_i(y)\} = u_i^{-1}(\{t \in R | t > u_i(x)\}),$$

but since u_i, is continuous, the inverse image of every open set is open, hence $P_i(x)$ and $Q_i(x)$ are both open. Next, since

$$I_i(x) = X - P_i(x) - Q_i(x),$$

it follows that $I_i(x)$ is closed. By Assumption 2, $I_i(x)$ has no interior.

Now, to prove (b), since $I_i(x)$ has no interior, it follows that any point $I_i(x)$ is an accumulation point of $P_i(x)$ or $Q_i(x)$, i.e.,

$$I_i(x) \subseteq \underline{B}(P_i(x)) \cup \underline{B}(Q_i(x))$$

But further, since $P_i(x)$ and $Q_i(x)$ are both open, with $\overline{P_i(x)} \subseteq (Q_i(x))^c$ and $\overline{Q_i(x)} \subseteq (P_i(x))^c$, it follows that $\underline{B}(P_i(x)) \subseteq I_i(x)$ and $\underline{B}(Q_i(x)) \subseteq I_i(x)$, so $\underline{B}(P_i(x)) \cup \underline{B}(Q_i(x)) \subseteq I_i(x)$. Hence,

$$I_i(x) = \underline{B}(P_i(x)) \cup \underline{B}(Q_i(x)).$$

To prove (c), we first prove that

$$\overline{P_i(x)} = \overline{[P_i(x) \cup I_i(x)]^0}$$

and

$$\overline{Q_i(x)} = \overline{[Q_i(x) \cup I_i(x)]^0}.$$

First, to prove $\overline{P_i(x)} = \overline{[P_i(x) \cup I_i(x)]^0}$, pick $y \in \overline{P_i(x)}$, and let $N(y)$ be an arbitrary neighborhood of y. Then since $P_i(x)$ is open, $P_i(x) = [P_i(x)]^0$, so $N(y) \cap P_i(x) \neq \emptyset \Rightarrow N(y) \cap P_i(x)^0 \neq \emptyset \Rightarrow N(y) \cap [P_i(x) \cup I_i(x)]^0 \neq \emptyset \Rightarrow y \in \overline{[P_i(x) \cup I_i(x)]^0}$. To show $\overline{[P_i(x) \cup I_i(x)]^0} \subseteq \overline{P_i(x)}$, pick $y \in \overline{[P_i(x) \cup I_i(x)]^0}$, and let $N(y)$ be an open neighborhood of y. Then $N(y) \cap [P_i(x) \cup I_i(x)]^0 \neq \emptyset$. So pick $z \in N(y) \cap [P_i(x) \cup I_i(x)]^0$. Since both $N(y)$ and $[P_i(x) \cup I_i(x)]^0$ are open, we can find an open neighborhood $N(z)$ of z with $N(z) \subseteq N(y)$ and $N(z) \subseteq [P_i(x) \cup I_i(x)]^0 \Rightarrow N(z) \subseteq P_i(x) \cup I_i(x)$. But then we must have $N(z) \cap P_i(x) \neq \emptyset$, otherwise $N(z) \subseteq I_i(x)$, a contradiction to Assumption 2, since $I_i(x)$ has no interior. But since $N(z) \subseteq N(y)$, it follows that $N(y) \cap P_i(x) \neq \emptyset \Rightarrow y \in \overline{P_i(x)}$, as we wished to show. Thus we have proven that $\overline{P_i(x)} = \overline{[P_i(x) \cup I_i(x)]^0}$. The proof that $\overline{Q_i(x)} = \overline{[Q_i(x) \cup I_i(x)]^0}$ is exactly equivalent.

Now to show $\underline{F}(P_i(x)) = \underline{F}(Q_i(x))$, we have, by the definition of the frontier of a set,

$$\begin{aligned}\underline{F}(P_i(x)) &= \overline{(P_i(x))^0} \cap \overline{((P_i(x))^c)^0} \\ &= \overline{P_i(x)} \cap \overline{(Q_i(x) \cup I_i(x))} \\ &= \overline{[P_i(x) \cup I_i(x)]^0} \cap \overline{Q_i(x)} \\ &= \overline{((Q_i(x))^c)^0} \cap \overline{(Q_i(x))^0} \\ &= \underline{F}(Q_i(x)).\end{aligned}$$

Finally, since $\underline{F}(P_i(x)) \subseteq \underline{B}(P_i(x))$, it follows from (b) that $\underline{F}(P_i(x)) = \underline{F}(Q_i(x)) \subseteq I_i(x)$.

Q.E.D.

The next result proves that the properties of individual preference sets given in Lemma 1 are inherited by the social relation. Also some relations between the individual and social preference sets are proven.

LEMMA 3: *If $R = f(\bar{R})$, where $f \in \mathbf{F}$, and Assumptions 1 and 2 are met, then for any $x \in X$, (a) $P(x)$ and $Q(x)$ are open, and $I(x)$ is closed with no interior; (b) $\underline{B}(P(x)) \cup \underline{B}(Q(x)) = I(x)$; (c) $\underline{F}(P(x)) = \underline{F}(Q(x)) \subseteq I(x)$; (d) $I(x) \subseteq \bigcup_{i \in N} I_i(x)$; (e) $\underline{F}(P(x)) \subseteq \bigcup_{i \in N} \underline{F}(P_i(x))$.*

PROOF: We prove (d) first. To prove (d), let $y \in I(x)$, and assume $y \notin \bigcup_{i \in N} I_i(x)$. Then let $C_1 = \{i \in N | y \in P_i(x)\}$, $C_2 = \{i \in N | y \in Q_i(x)\}$, and $C_3 = \{i \in N | y \in I-i(x)\}$. By Lemma 2a, C_1, C_2, and C_3 partition N, since any $I \in N$ must be a member of one of the three sets. Further, since $y \notin \bigcup_{n=i}^{n} I_i(x)$, it follows that $C_3 = \emptyset$. Thus $C_1 = N - C_2$. Therefore, by (2.1b), it follows that either $C_1 \in \underline{W}$ or $C_2 \in \underline{W}$. But, by construction $yP_{C_1}x$ and $xP_{C_2}y$. Hence, by (2.2), $C_1 \in \underline{W} \Rightarrow yPx$ and $C_2 \in \underline{W} \Rightarrow xPy$. So in either case, $y \notin I(x)$, a contradiction. Hence $y \in \bigcup_{i=1}^{n} I_i(x)$, and it follows that $I(x) \subseteq \bigcup_{i=1}^{n} I(x)$.

We next prove (a). To see that $P(x)$ and $Q(x)$ are open, we note that since $f \in \mathbf{F}$, we can write $P(x)$ and $Q(x)$ as follows:

$$P(x) = \bigcup_{C \in W} \bigcap_{i \in C} P_i(x)$$

and

$$Q(x) = \bigcup_{C \in W} \bigcap_{i \in C} Q_i(x).$$

Since finite unions and intersections of open sets are open, it follows that $P(x)$ and $Q(x)$ are open. Since $I(x) = X - P(x) - Q(x)$, $I(x)$ is closed. That

$I(x)$ has no interior follows directly from Lemma 1 and Lemma 3d. From Lemma 3d it follows that $I(x) \subseteq \bigcup_{i \in N} I_i(x)$, where each $I_i(x)$ is closed with no interior. Hence by Lemma 1, $I(x)$ has no interior.

The proofs of (b) and (c) follow exactly the pattern of the same proofs in Lemma 2, as the only properties that were needed in that proof were that $P_i(x)$ and $Q_i(x)$ were open, and $I_i(x)$ was closed with no interior. Since $I(x)$, $P(x)$, and $Q(x)$ satisfy these same properties, the proofs go through unchanged.

Finally, to show (e), we again argue by contradiction, and assume $y \in \underline{F}(P(x))$, with $y \notin \bigcup_{i \in N} \underline{F}(P_i(x))$. It follows that we can find an open set B, with $y \in B$ such that for all $i \in N$, either $B \cap P_i(x) = \emptyset$ or $B \cap Q_i(x) = \emptyset$. We set $C_1 = \{i \in N | B \cap P_i(x) = \emptyset\}$, and $C_2 = \{i \in N | B \cap Q_i(x) = \emptyset\}$. Then C_1 and C_2 partition N, hence by (2.1b), either $C_1 \in \underline{W}$ and $C_2 \notin \underline{W}$, or $C_1 \notin \underline{W}$ and $C_2 \in W$. In the first case, by (2.1a), it follows that for any $C \subseteq C_2$, $C \notin W$. But for any $z \in B, \{i \in N | zP_ix\} \subseteq C_2$. It follows (by (2.2)) that we cannot have zPx. In other words, $z \notin P(x)$, for any $z \in B$, or $B \cap P(x) = \emptyset \Rightarrow y \notin \underline{F}(P(x))$. Since $\underline{F}(P(x)) = \underline{F}(Q(x))$ (from Lemma 3c) it follows that $y \notin \underline{F}(P(x))$ in the second case also. Thus, we have a contradiction, and hence we must have $y \in \bigcup_{i \in N} \underline{F}(P_i(x))$. Thus $\underline{F}(P(x)) \subseteq \bigcup_{i \in N} \underline{F}(P_i(x))$, and (e) is proven.

Q.E.D.

The fourth lemma proves some properties of the higher order preference sets $P^j(x)$ and $P^*(x)$ for the social relation. We need a definition first. If $\Gamma : X \to 2^X$ is a correspondence on X, we say Γ is *lower semi-continuous* if for every $x_0 \in X$, and every open set $G \subseteq X$ with $G \cap \Gamma(x_0) \neq \emptyset$, there is a neighborhood $N(x_0)$ of x_0 such that $x \in N(x_0) \Rightarrow \Gamma(x) \cap G \neq \emptyset$. We now show that $P^j(x)$ is lower semi-continuous for all j, as is $P^*(x)$.

LEMMA 4: *If $R = f(\bar{R})$, where $f \in \mathbf{F}$, and Assumption 1 is met, then (a) for all $x \in X$ and $j \geq 1$, $P^j(x)$ and $P^*(x)$ are open sets; (b) for all $j \geq 1$, $P^j(x)$ is lower semi-continuous, as is $P^*(x)$.*

PROOF: Lemma 3a proves that $P(x) = P^1(x)$ is open. It should be noted that this proof depends only on Assumption 1. To prove that $P^j(x)$ is open, note that

$$P^j(x) = \bigcup_{y \in P^{j-1}(x)} P^1(y).$$

Since $P^j(x)$ is an infinite union of open sets, it is open. Next,

$$P^*(x) = \bigcup_{j=1}^{\infty} P^j(x).$$

So $P^*(x)$ is also an infinite union of open sets and is open, and (a) is proven.

Now, to prove (b), we first prove $P(x) = P^1(x)$ is lower semi-continuous. So let $x_0 \in X$, and let $G \subseteq X$ be open with $G \cap P^1(x_0) \neq \emptyset$. We must show there is a neighborhood $N(x_0)$ of x_0 such that $x \in N(x_0) \Rightarrow P^1(x) \cap G \neq \emptyset$. So let $y \in G \cap P^1(x_0)$, and set

$$N(x_0) = \{x \in X | y \in P^1(x)\} = Q^1(y).$$

From Lemma 2, $N(x_0)$ is open. Also $N(x_0)$ clearly contains x_0. So $N(x_0)$ is a neighborhood of x_0. Also, for all $x \in N(x_0)$, $y \in P^1(x)$. Hence $P^1(x) \cap G \neq \emptyset$, so $P^1(x)$ is lower semi-continuous.

To prove that $P^j(x)$ is lower semi-continuous, it suffices to note that P^{j-1} is the composition product of P^{j-1} and P^1. In other words, $P^j(x) = P^1 \odot P^{j-1}(x)$. Since the composition product of two lower semi-continuous correspondences is lower semi-continuous [2, Theorem 1, p. 113], it follows by a simple induction argument that $P^*(x)$ is lower semi-continuous, for all j.

Now $P^*(x) = \bigcup_{j=1}^{\infty} P^j(x)$ is the union of a family of lower semi-continuous mappings. It follows [2, Theorem 2, p. 114] that $P^*(x)$ is lower semi-continuous.

Q.E.D.

LEMMA 5: *If X is any connected topological space, and $S \subseteq X$ is open, then (a) $X - \underline{F}(S)$ connected $\Rightarrow \underline{F}(S) = \emptyset$; (b) $\underline{F}(S) = \emptyset \Rightarrow S = \emptyset$ or $\bar{S} = X$.*

PROOF: To prove (a), assume $X - \underline{F}(S)$ is connected and that $\underline{F}(S) \neq \emptyset$, say $y \in \underline{F}(S)$. Then by definition of $\underline{F}(S)$, it follows that $y \in S^0$ and $y \in (S^c)^0$. Let $A = S^0$, $B = (S^c)^0$, and $C = \underline{F}(S)$; then it is easily verified that A^0, B^0, and C partition X. Hence A^0 and B^0 partition $X - C = X - \underline{F}(S)$. Further, both A^0 and B^0 are non-empty, since $y \in A$, $y \in B$, and both A and B are the closure of open sets. But then $X - \underline{F}(S)$ is not connected, in contradiction to the assumption of the Lemma. Hence we must have $\underline{F}(S) = \emptyset$.

Now, to prove (b), by the definition of $\underline{F}(S)$, $\underline{F}(S) = \emptyset \iff$

(A.1) $$\overline{S^0} \cap \overline{(S^c)^0} = \emptyset.$$

But now if S is open, then

(A.2) $$\overline{S^0} \cap \overline{(S^c)^0} = X$$

because if $x \notin \overline{S^0}$, then there is a neighborhood $N(x)$ of x such that

$$N(x) \cap S^0 = \emptyset \Rightarrow N(x) \cap S = \emptyset \Rightarrow x \in (S^c)^0$$
$$\Rightarrow x \in \overline{(S^c)^0}.$$

But now since X is connected, it cannot be expressed as a disjoint union of two non-empty closed sets, hence (A.2) implies that $\overline{S^0} = \emptyset$ or $\overline{(S^c)^0} = \emptyset$. But since S is open, $\overline{S^0} = \emptyset \Rightarrow \bar{S} = \emptyset \Rightarrow S = \emptyset$. On the other hand $\overline{(S^c)^0} = \emptyset \Rightarrow (S^c)^0 = \emptyset$. But then for any $x \in S^c$, and every neighborhood $N(x)$ of x, $N(x) \cap (S^c)^c \neq \emptyset \Rightarrow N(x) \cap S \neq \emptyset \Rightarrow x \in \bar{S}$. Since $x \in S \Rightarrow x \in \bar{S}$, it follows that for all $x \in X$, $x \in \bar{S}$. In other words, $\bar{S} = X$. Thus we have shown that either $S = \emptyset$ or $S = X$, as we wished to show.

Q.E.D.

LEMMA 6: *Let $u_i, : X \to R$ be continuously differentiable on $X \subseteq R^m$, and let $y \in X^0$. Then if $A \subseteq R^m$ is compact, and $z \cdot \nabla u_i, (y) > 0$ for all $z \in A$ for all $\exists t^* \in R$, with $t^* > 0$, such that for all $0 < t \leq t^*$, $y + tA \subseteq P_i(y)$. Similarly if $z \cdot \nabla u_i(y) < 0$ for all $z \in A$, then $\exists t^*$ in R^+ such that for all $0 < t \leq t^*$, $y + tA \subseteq Q_i(y)$.*

PROOF: For any $z \in A$, $\exists t_z \in R$, with $t_z > 0$, such that $y + tz \in X$ and $u_i(y + tz) > u_i(y)$ for all $t \leq t_z$. (See, e.g., Zangwill [25, Theorem 2.1, p. 24] for a proof of this.) In other words, $y + tz \in P_i(y)$. But since $P_i(y)$ is open in the relative topology on X (by Lemma 2a), it follows that there is an open neighborhood, $N(z)$, of z such that $y + t(N(z)) \subseteq P_i(y)$ whenever $t < t_z$. Now, by the Axiom of Choice, for any $z \in A$, we can find an open neighborhood $N(z)$ of z, and a $t_z \in R$ with $t_z > 0$ such that $y + t(N(z)) \subseteq P_i(y)$ for $t \leq t_z$. Now $\{N(z) | z \in A\}$ is an open covering of A, hence, since A is compact, by the Heine-Borel Theorem it follows that there is a finite subcovering, say $\{N(z_1), \ldots, N(z_K)\}$. Now setting $t^* = \min_{1 < i \leq K} t_{zi}$, it follows that if $t \leq t^*$, for any $z \in A$, then $z \in N(z_i)$ for some $1 < i \leq K$. In other words, $y + t_z \subseteq P(y)$ since $t < y^* < t_{zi}$. But, then, we have just shown that $y + tA \subseteq P_i(y)$ whenever $t < t^*$, as we wished to show.

The proof of the second assertion of the theorem is exactly analogous to the above proof.

Q.E.D.

LEMMA 7: *Let $X \subseteq R^m$, $u_i : X \to R$ be continuously differentiable on X, and let $y \in X^0$ satisfy $\nabla u_i(y) \neq 0$. Then there is a neighborhood $N(y)$ of y such that $N(y) \cap I_i(y) = N(y) \cap \underline{IF}_i(y)$.*

PROOF: Since u_i is continuously differentiable, and $\nabla u_i(y) \neq 0$, we can find a neighborhood $N(y)$ of y such that $\nabla u_i(w) \neq 0$ for all $w \in N(y)$. Now let $u_i \in N(y) \cap I_i(y)$. We let $\alpha_i = \nabla u_i(w)$, and set $B = \{z \in R^m | \|z\| \leq \|\alpha_i\|/2\}$. Then we set

$$D^+ = \alpha_i + B,$$
$$D^- = -\alpha_i + B.$$

It follows that $z \cdot \alpha_i > 0$ for all $z \in D^+$, and $z \cdot \alpha_i < 0$ for all $z \in D^-$. Further D^+ and D^- are compact. Thus, by Lemma 6, $\exists t^*$ such that for $t < t^*$, $w + tD^- \subseteq P_i(w) = P_i(y)$, and $w + tD^- \subseteq Q_i(w) = Q_i(y)$. Hence, $w \in \underline{IF}(y)$, and we have shown $N(y) \cap I_i(y) \subseteq N(y) \cap \underline{IF}_i(y)$. The reverse inclusion is trivial.

Q.E.D.

LEMMA 8: *Let Assumptions 1–4 hold for all $i \in N$, let $x \in X$, and let $y \in X^0$ satisfy $y \in \underline{F}(P^*(x))$. Then if $\nabla u_i(y) \neq 0$ for all $i \in N$, there is a neighborhood, $N(y)$ of y such that for some $j \in N$,*

$$N(y) \cap \underline{F}(P^*(x)) = N(y) \cap I_j(y) = N(y) \cap \underline{IF}_j(y).$$

PROOF: By Theorem 2, for some $j \in N$, $\underline{F}(P^*(x)) \subseteq I_j(y) \subseteq \underline{IF}_j(y)$. By Lemma 7 there is an open neighborhood, $N(y)$ of y such that $N(y) \cap I_j(y) = N(y) \cap \underline{IF}_j(y)$. Further, since $\nabla u_i(y) \neq 0$, and u_j is continuously differentiable, we can pick $N(y)$ so that

$$A = N(y) \cap P_j(y) \text{ is connected and}$$
$$B = N(y) \cap Q_j(y) \text{ is connected.}$$

Further, since $y \in \underline{IF}_j(y)$, both A and B are non-empty. Now, from Theorem 2 and Lemma 7, we have

$$N(y) \cap \underline{F}(P^*(x)) \subseteq N(y) \cap I_j(y) = N(y) \cap \underline{IF}_j(y);$$

we must only show

(A.3) $$N(y) \cap \underline{IF}_j(y) \subseteq N(y) \cap \underline{F}(P^*(x)).$$

Suppose, for some $z \in N(y)$, $z \in \underline{IF}_j(y)$ and $z \notin \underline{F}(P^*(x))$. Then it follows that

(A.4) $$N(y) - \underline{F}(P^*(x)) \text{ is connected.}$$

To see this, note that if $N(y) - \underline{F}(P^*(x))$ is not connected, then we can find two disjoint open sets, say C, $D \subseteq X$ such that

$$N(y) - \underline{F}(P^*(x)) = C \cup D,$$
$$[N(y) - \underline{F}(P^*(x))] \cap C \neq \emptyset,$$

and

$$[N(y) - \underline{F}(P^*(x))] \cap D \neq \emptyset.$$

But then $z \in C$ or $z \in D$. Assume without loss of generality that $z \in C$. Then since $z \in \underline{IF}(y)$, and C is open, it follows that $C \cap A \neq \emptyset$ and $C \cap B \neq \emptyset$. Also it follows that either $D \cap A \neq \emptyset$ or $D \cap B \neq \emptyset$. Assume without loss of generality that $D \cap A \neq \emptyset$. Then

$$C \cap A \neq \emptyset,$$
$$D \cap A \neq \emptyset,$$

and

$$A \subseteq C \cup D.$$

Thus A is not connected, a contradiction. Thus we have established $N(y) - \underline{F}(P^*(x))$ is connected. But now by Lemma 5a, $N(y) - \underline{F}(P^*(x))$ connected $\Rightarrow N(y) \cap \underline{F}(P^*(x)) = \emptyset$, which contradicts the assumption that $y \in \underline{F}(P^*(x))$. Hence (A.3) is established, which proves the result.

Q.E.D.

LEMMA 9: *Let Assumptions 1–4 hold for all $i \in N$, let $x \in X$, $y \in X^0$ satisfy $y \in \underline{F}(P^*(x))$, and assume $\underline{F}(P^*(x)) \subseteq I_i(y)$. Then if $\nabla u_j(y) \neq 0$ and* *for some* $i \in N - \{j\}$, $\nabla u_i(y) \neq c\nabla u_j(y)$ *for all* $c \in R$, *there is a neighborhood* $N(y)$ *of* y *such that, for all* $w \in N(y)$,

$$w \in I_i(y) \cap I_i(y) \Rightarrow w \in \hat{IF}_i(y).$$

PROOF: We pick $N(y)$ to satisfy $\nabla u_i(w) \neq c\nabla u_j(w)$ for all $w \in N(y)$, and to simultaneously satisfy the conditions that $\nabla u_j(w) \neq 0$, $\nabla u_i(w) \neq 0$ for all $w \in N(y)$. Then by Lemmas 7 and 8 it follows that

$$N(y) \cap I_i(y) = N(y) \cap \underline{IF}_i(y)$$

and

$$N(y) \cap I_j(y) = N(y) \cap \underline{IF}_j(y) = N(y) \cap \underline{F}(P^*(x)).$$

Thus, for any $w \in N(y)$,

$$\begin{aligned} w \in I_i(y) \cap I_j(y) &\Rightarrow w \in \underline{IF}_i(y) \cap \underline{IF}_j(y) \\ &\Rightarrow w \in \underline{IF}_i(w) \cap \underline{IF}_j(w) \\ &\Rightarrow w \in \underline{IF}_i(w) \cap \underline{F}(P^*(x)). \end{aligned}$$

We need only show that in any neighborhood of w there are points in $\underline{F}(P^*(x))$ which are preferred by i to w and points to which he prefers w. Pick $z \in R^m$ such that $z \cdot \nabla u_j(w) = 0$ and $z \cdot \nabla u_i(w) > 0$. Let $N(z)$ be a closed neighborhood of z such that for all $z^* \in N(z)$, $z^* \cdot \nabla u_i(w) > 0$. Then by Lemma 6, there is a t^* such that, for $0 < t < t^*$,

$$\emptyset \neq (w + tN(z)) \cap I_j(y) \subseteq P_i(w) \cap I_j(y) = P_i(w) \cap \underline{F}(P^*(x))$$
$$\emptyset \neq (w + tN(z)) \cap I_j(y) \subseteq Q_i(w) \cap I_j(y) = Q_i(w) \cap \underline{F}(P^*(x)).$$

Q.E.D.

References

[1] Arrow, K. J.: *Social Choice and Individual Values* (2nd ed.). New Haven: Yale University Press, 1963.

[2] Berge, C.: *Topological Spaces* (translated by E. M. Patterson). New York: Macmillan, 1963.

[3] Cohen, L.: "Cyclic Sets in Multidimensional Voting Models," *Journal of Economic Theory* (forthcoming).

[4] Cohen, L., and S. Matthews: "Constrained Plott Equilibria, Directional Equilibria and Global Cycling Sets," *Review of Economic Studies* (forthcoming).

[5] Davis, O. A., M. H. Degroot, and M. J. Hinich: "Social Preference Orderings and Majority Rule," *Econometrica*, 40 (1972), 147–157.

[6] Davis, O. A., M. J. Hinich, and P. C. Ordeshook: "An Expository Development of a Mathematical Model of the Electoral Process," *American Political Science Review*, 64 (1970), 426–448.

[7] Farquharson, R.: *Theory of Voting*. New Haven: Yale University Press, 1969.

[8] Ferejohn, J., M. Fiorina, and E. Packel: "A Non Equilibrium Approach to Legislative Decision Theory," Social Science Working Paper No. 202, California Institute of Technology, 1978.

[9] Kramer, G. H.: "Sophisticated Voting Over Multidimensional Choice Spaces," *Journal of Mathematical Sociology*, 2 (1972), 165–180.

[10] Kramer, G. H.: "On a Class of Equilibrium Conditions for Majority Rule," *Econometrica*, 41 (1973), 285–297.

[11] Kramer, G. H.: "A Dynamical Model of Equilibrium," Cowles Foundation, Yale University, Discussion Paper No. 36, 1975.

[12] Matthews, S.: "The Possibility of Voting Equilibria," Mimeo, California Institute of Technology, Division of Humanities and Social Sciences, 1977.

[13] McKelvey, R. D.: "Intransitivities in Multidimensional Voting Models and Some Implications for Agenda Control," *Journal of Economic Theory*, 12 (1976), 472–482. Chapter 4 of this book.

[14] McKelvey, R. D., and R. E. Wendell: "Voting Equilibria in Multidimensional Choice Spaces," *Mathematics of Operations Research*, 1 (1976), 144–158.

[15] McKelvey, R. D., and R. G. Niemi: "A Multistage Game Representation of Sophisticated Voting for Binary Procedures," *Journal of Economic Theory*, 18 (1978), 1–22.

[16] McKelvey, R. D., P. C. Ordeshook, and M. Winer: "The Competitive Solution for N-Person Games without Side Payments," *American Political Science Review*, 72 (1978), 599–615. Chapter 10 of this book.

[17] Plott, C. R.: "A Notion of Equilibrium and Its Possibility Under Majority Rule," *American Economic Review*, 57 (1967), 787–806.

[18] Plott, C. R., and M. E. Levine: "A Model of Agenda Influence on Committee Decisions," *American Economic Review*, 68 (1978), 146–160.

[19] Rubenstein, A.: "A Note About the 'Nowhere Denseness' of Societies Having an Equilibrium Under Majority Rule," *Econometrica* (forthcoming).

[20] Schofield, N.: "Instability of Simple Dynamic Games," *Review of Economic Studies*, 40 (1978), 575–594.

[21] Schofield, N.: "Generic Instability of Voting Games," Mimeo, Department of Government, University of Texas at Austin, 1978.

[22] Sen, A. K.: "Social Choice Theory: A Re-examination," *Econometrica*, 45 (1977), 53–90.

[23] Sloss, J.: "Stable Points of Directional Preference Relations," Technical Report No. 71–7, Operations Research House, Stanford University, 1971.

[24] Slutsky, S.: "Equilibrium Under a Majority Rule," Mimeo. Paper presented at the 1978 Meetings of the Public Choice Convention, New Orleans, Louisiana.

[25] Zangwill, W. I.: *Nonlinear Programming, A Unified Approach.* Englewood Cliffs, N.J.: Prentice-Hall, 1969.

CHAPTER 6

Statistical Tests of Theoretical Results

JOHN H. ALDRICH AND KEITH T. POOLE

For the two of us these two early papers by Richard have a meaning beyond their scientific content. Richard supervised our dissertations and our memories of these two papers are forever tied to Richard the person and the University of Rochester (U of R) of the late 1960s and early 1970s.[1]

The U of R Political Science Department is justly famous for positive political theory but it also was one of the first departments to feature cutting edge statistical methods. Richard taught one of the two required semester-length statistics courses as well as his terrific econometrics course.[2] Richard was a serious and dedicated teacher. His courses were comprehensive, thorough, and well organized. He patiently answered the dumbest questions and never made any student feel that he or she was imposing on his time.

Not only is the U of R Political Science Department justly famous for positive political theory, but so, too, is Richard. Indeed, he is the most important mathematical political scientist, ever. His skills included not just technical competencies in various parts of mathematics but also a remarkable intuition that combined an understanding of what was provable with what was important for understanding politics to make it worth the effort to do the hard work (well, hard work for the authors, seemingly not very hard for Richard!!) of actually deriving results. These skills are just as apparent in his statistical work.

Arthur Goldberg, who had taught the "scope and methods" course for first-semester graduate students at the University of Rochester, liked to say that each year he taught it, he had less and less to say, condensing the course into an ever more distilled product. One of us wrote in our notebook of that class (at that point

---

[1] We were his first two Ph.D. students, and the more senior of us started graduate school when Richard was still a graduate student himself.

[2] The more senior of us also took his course on mathematics for political science in the first semester of graduate school, and it ranks as perhaps the best-taught graduate seminar taken.

taught by another faculty member, with Goldberg giving a "guest lecture") that Goldberg claimed to have reduced the course to the following two sentences:

> A scientific theory is a systematically related set of statements including some law-like generalizations that is empirically testable. Induction, in this context, is the search for suitable premises from which deduction may begin.[3]

Richard's two papers apply exactly this set of criteria to the problems he is attacking. In both cases, he sought inductively for a set of suitable premises. The most important difference between these statistical exercises and a scientific theory is that the search for suitable premises is informed at least as strongly by the need for mathematical tractability as it is by the empirical plausibility of the assumptions. These criteria are significant for both n-chotomous probit and the Aldrich-McKelvey (A-M) scaling method. The remarkable advances in computing power since the early 1970s and the resulting ability to do lots of iterations, lots of simulations, make this fact less important today, but it was of tremendous importance at the time. What is true about the empirical basis of both statistical procedures is that the premises were chosen because they were at least superior to the alternative possibilities at hand in terms of their empirical plausibility. On the other end of the process, the techniques were publishable, in Richard's opinion, because they had wonderful deductive properties and their application provided new empirical results, observations that would not have been made in the absence of the techniques.

While inductive empirics were critical in both cases, most of these two papers are about the first of Goldberg's sentences. That is, the techniques are notable above all for their being a set of systematically related statements. To the best of our knowledge, these were the first two statistical procedures developed by political scientists that were deductively rigorous. While it was quite rare, political scientists had already made occasional important contributions to statistical methods. Perhaps the most famous example was Stuart A. Rice's development of what is now known as the "Rice index" for studying roll-call votes (Rice, 1928). To develop the index, he proposed some nice properties that such a measure should have and then simply stated a formula that seemed to be consistent with those principles. Richard, by contrast, proposed a series of assumptions from which the procedure and its estimator(s) followed by deductive reasoning. Not only were these estimators the most evident fruit of the deductive process, the principles also came with additional properties. For example, because the probit model was

---

[3] Aldrich, notebook, Political Science 401, Fall, 1969.

a maximum likelihood estimator (MLE), its estimates perforce hold such desirable properties as being the best asymptotic normal estimators. While the A-M scaling procedure was derived via ordinary least squares assumptions (which bring with them fewer properties automatically), it is easy to show that they, too, are MLE, and thereby also possess desirable statistical properties.

We now turn to a discussion of the two papers.

1. *N*-Chotomous Multivariate Probit Analysis

Political science is a behavioral science. As such, its most common outcomes are the selection of one from a reasonably small set of possible (or perhaps legally permissible) set of behaviors. Most evidently, one can vote for one or another candidate or party or one can abstain, whether in large, general elections or in legislative or committee settings. Legislators can propose a bill, an amendment to the substance of the bill, an amendment to that amendment, etc. The choice of whether an idea is better accomplished by writing it into the bill in the first place, into an amendment to that bill, or at some other point in the legislative process is a choice based at least in part on the strategic setting. That is to say, the choice of behaviors is a result of a series of considerations put "on the right-hand side" of the equation (i.e., the "independent" variables). The goal of our discipline is to characterize the nature of the considerations that lead to this small set of behaviors.

The procedures we are taught in basic methods courses in graduate school, particularly estimators based on regression and related procedures, work wonderfully well when the dependent variable is an interval-level measure.[4] The regression model can easily handle independent variables that are binary, categorical, or ordinal. But it does not do well when the dependent variable is not interval because the assumptions made about the unobservable error are violated (e.g., constant error variance across observations). This is a problem, because we are usually explaining choices from a very finite list of behaviors.

The standard training, therefore, then goes on to cover procedures for estimation of dichotomous dependent variables. This is fine — wonderful even — for a great many applications, but it is obviously limited. It turned out that the

---

[4]Technically, interval scales are numerical scales in which intervals have the same interpretation throughout. For example, consider the Fahrenheit scale of temperature. The difference between 40 degrees and 50 degrees represents the same temperature difference as the difference between 70 degrees and 80 degrees. This is because each 10 degree interval has the same physical meaning. As opposed to a ratio scale, an interval scale does not have a natural zero point.

dichotomous case was, mathematically, very special, so that results could be obtained for the interval and the most extreme violation of the interval cases, but not for in-between cases.

Richard McKelvey and William Zavoina — as graduate students in their methodology courses — realized this important lacuna. To be sure, there were existing alternatives, but they were decidedly unsatisfactory for their own reasons. Certainly, there were a lot of what were then known as "nonparametric" measures of statistical association, and one could apply them to two- and three-variable cross-tabulations, but hardly for more than that. For the case of a small number of nominal categories, discriminant analysis could be used. It had the disadvantage, however, that the independent variables not only had to be interval, but they also had to be normally distributed for the resulting estimators to be justified. Enter McKelvey and Zavoina to work on the case of a dependent variable with a small number of ordinal categories coupled with independent variables that are typically found in regression analysis. They named their procedure n-chotomous multivariate probit.

Probit was originally developed by D. J. Finney in his classic book originally published in 1947 (he coined the term "probit," standing for "probability unit"). But Finney's work was strictly with a dichotomous dependent variable (and with other limitations and without full development). So, it, along with logit, was a candidate for the standard case and they are now typically covered in the first post-regression techniques in the basic sequence of methods courses. Aitchison and Silvey (1957) made a brilliant first step towards a more general model when they developed an estimator for the simple n-chotomous case with one independent variable.[5]

McKelvey and Zavoina began their work with a consideration of the nature of dependent variables in political science, much as we did here. They then developed a model designed to fit such variables. This was the probit model that Finney developed, but it was so vastly different and further developed that it was hard to recognize it. First, they reinterpreted the nature of the variable, or more accurately, added a new interpretation to those already extant. They assumed the existence of a latent interval level dependent variable (perhaps not unlike utility, although that is not required) that, if only we could only observe it, would be the

---

[5]We shouldn't be too surprised that such restrictive cases would be of interest. Probit developed in biological and agricultural applications. Finney's examples were primarily of such matters as seed germination as a function of water and sun. Experimental design made it possible to do important studies with a small number of independent variables.

perfect candidate for a regression model estimation. Instead, we only observe categories of this underlying "true" dependent variable. For example, consider the small number of categories that family income is divided into in most surveys. Obviously, much information is lost in categorizing a nearly continuous variable (indeed, that is precisely why it is done that way, to help respondents camouflage their true income, without misreporting). Still, if that is lost, the estimation question is how one might infer back from the observations to the underlying interval measure. This is the task they set for themselves.

In solving this problem, they were advantaged by being at the University of Rochester. In addition to there being a strong political science program, members of the equally strong Economics Department were also doing important work using probit.[6] But it was not just that "probit was in the air." McKelvey and Zavoina solved the problem at a very high level of generality. Their procedure was much more general than either Finney's or Aitchison and Silvey's work. In particular, they provide a totally novel and quite useful interpretation of the problem — one that students often find more intuitive, to boot. They provide new parameters to estimate, such as the cut-points between the categories. They developed, along the way, an analogue to the regression-based R^2. Their estimator, again both original and intuitive, continues to be used, independent of their statistical procedure. Finally, they derived their estimators from the use of maximum likelihood.

This process has essentially become the disciplinary standard. Nearly twenty years later, Gary King called for developing a model of the data generating process, specifying it in likelihood terms, and deriving estimators from it as a way of *Unifying Political Methodology*, as he titled it (1989). He used their paper as the rare example of what he had in mind.

Ordered probit (as the technique has come to be called), along with ordered logit and a series of related developments, has become one of the common tools of the trade throughout the social and behavioral — and even the natural — sciences. A quick web search yielded the following examples: "Provincial Credit Rating in Canada: An Ordered Probit Analysis" (Cheung, 1996); "Driver Injury Severity: An Application of Ordered Probit Models" (Kockleman and Kweon, 2002); "The Application of an Ordered Probit Model to Investigate Shippers' Perceptions of Rail Freight Services in Indonesia" (Norojono and Young, 2001); and "Modeling Migraine Severity with Autoregressive Ordered Probit Models" (Czado, Heyn, and Müller, 2005). It is easy to find many more, equally diverse, applications.

---

[6]Under Richard Rosett's tutelage, Forrest Nelson was making important advances using probit at exactly the same time. Two examples are Rosett and Nelson (1975) and Nelson and Olson (1978).

In various senses, the paper was far ahead of its time in political science. But McKelvey also wrote the program code. It turned out to be an amazing piece of coding, too. It is very robust in that it automatically caught errors that a user could easily make, and most importantly, it never "bombed." Consequently, it was perhaps the easiest of the sophisticated statistical pieces of software to use. This, done in FORTRAN, was a remarkable achievement for the early 1970s. As a result, with a clear statistical model, presented in a cogent, straightforward text, and easy-to-use software (or at least "easy-to-use" in comparison to, say, OSIRIS and other software of the day) — and a presentation in which their application made a major empirical difference — the state of the art of statistical work in this behavioral science discipline jumped forward.[7]

2. The Aldrich-McKelvey Scaling Procedure

The Aldrich-McKelvey (A-M) scaling procedure is a technique for constructing estimates of candidate locations and voter ideal points on an issue dimension using only data about voter perceptions of the candidate locations and their own position. It was originally designed to exploit the seven point issue scales that were introduced into the NES surveys beginning in 1968. A loose interpretation of the estimated candidate locations is that they are weighted averages of the voters' perceptions of the candidates' locations on the underlying true issue dimension. Because different voters may report their perceptions of this underlying true scale differently, the A-M method estimates these individual "distortion parameters" along with the positions of the candidates, under the assumption that acceptable "distortion" is that voters see candidates accurately up to a linear transformation.

It was possible to develop this estimation procedure because of advances in theory and methodology. The idea was to be able to test what was then a new, burgeoning, but essentially purely theoretical (that is, untested) literature on spatial modeling. The intuition behind the spatial model is that candidates or parties compete for votes by adopting a bundle of positions on dimensions of electoral choice. These are generally interpreted as a platform of policy positions. Voters are assumed to have preferences over these dimensions. Candidate positions thereby induce preferences for candidates among voters, because voters' preferences are assumed to be a function of distance on policy and, thus, preferences over candidates are a function of the distance separating them from the voters' most preferred policies. The spatial literature had just exploded in a number of directions. But it was McKelvey's just-completed thesis that had generalized the

---

[7]For early examples of that step forward, see Fiorina (1974) and Shepsle (1978).

spatial model of electoral competition in such a way (albeit for deeper theoretical reasons) as to make testing reasonably straightforward.[8] First, however, the spatial model continued to assume that the candidates actually had a position they were presenting to the electorate. The new survey technology of the seven point issue scales provided data to go along with the theory. It was precisely because of this conjunction that Aldrich and McKelvey sat down to begin work on this procedure, to estimate the assumed actual positions of the candidates.

One of us has argued that the Aldrich and McKelvey paper has not achieved the recognition that it deserves in political methodology (Palfrey and Poole, 1987; Poole, 1998). In part this is due to the fact that the basic measure of fit of the method (the standard error of the estimate) is biased downwards. This occurs because voters who quite literally see the world "backwards" — George W. Bush and the Republican Party to the left of John Kerry and the Democratic Party — contribute to the fit of the model. However, Palfrey and Poole (1987) show that this is an advantage, not a defect! Namely, the A-M scaling method can be used as a powerful filter. Voters who see the political universe as backward clearly have a very low level of information about politics (Palfrey and Poole, 1987).

Today, the practical problem of imposing a constraint to solve this "perceptual reversal" problem is straightforward. Had this been done, the procedure would have not been adopted only if there were practical constraints (e.g., too few candidates, parties, etc.), not the apparent theoretical one. Conversely, we would have lost what Palfrey and Poole perceive as one of the advantages of the scaling technique.

The recognition that the central result was a characteristic value problem essentially solved the problem arithmetically.[9] The initial form of the solution required an eigenvalue-eigenvector decomposition of the huge respondent by respondent matrix (n by n) rather than the more tractable candidate by candidate matrix (m by m). It was a perfectly good solution, except for the annoying practical problem that no computer in the early 1970s could extract the characteristic

---

[8]The major results of his thesis are published in McKelvey (1975). Aldrich's thesis was that straightforward test, the basic results of which can be found in Aldrich (1977).

[9]The characteristic value problem and eigenvalue-eigenvector decomposition are closely related. Let A be a symmetric n by n matrix; then $Av_i = \lambda_i v_i$, where v_i is an n-length vector known both as a characteristic vector and an eigenvector, and λ_i is known both as a characteristic value and an eigenvalue. An eigenvalue-eigenvector decomposition of A is $U\Lambda U'$, where U is an n by n matrix of the eigenvectors such that $U'U = UU' = I$, that is, the matrix product is the identity matrix, and Λ is an n by n matrix with the eigenvalues in descending order on the diagonal. In the A-M problem A is a symmetric matrix. More generally, A need not be symmetric in the context of a characteristic value problem.

equation of a 1200 by 1200 matrix. One of the other faculty at Rochester proposed seeking a brute force solution — he suggested contacting both IBM and NASA control in Houston, to see if they could solve the equation on a one-time basis. McKelvey, characteristically, found that unsatisfying. It meant that there was a theoretical solution that could not be used in practical circumstances. In a matter of days (a long time for Richard to solve a problem), he had transformed the problem into solving an m by m matrix, and therefore into finding the characteristic equation for a matrix in the range of 7 by 7 (or m by m, where m is the number of candidates or parties being scaled), that is, transforming the problem into one easily solved.

One of us has repeatedly prodded his methodological friends to read the A-M paper — especially pages 111–113 — because of its mathematical elegance. It is a beautiful tour de force. The loss function is set up as a Lagrangean multiplier problem and one of the constraints and the vector of candidate positions are an eigenvalue and an eigenvector, respectively, of an m by m matrix. Indeed, these three pages are eloquent testimony to Richard's creativity and deep mathematical abilities.

The scaling procedure had seen relatively little further development for a generation, beyond that work already cited here. Then, Gary King and colleagues (2004 [2003]) developed an extension of this procedure. As they put it, they extended the scaling procedure to "...address two long-standing survey research problems: measuring complicated concepts such as political freedom and efficacy, that researchers define best with references to examples; and what to do when respondents interpret identical questions in different ways" (2004, p. 191). One of their novel ideas was to use short vignettes to define alternatives. Aldrich and McKelvey had, in effect, allowed the candidates or parties to define the meaning of the points on a seven point issue scale. King et al. placed that under the control of the researcher, at the same time ensuring that all respondents would be presented with comparable information about the meaning of the scale.[10] They provide a non-parametric and then a parametric procedure for scaling the vignettes in the same fashion as Aldrich and McKelvey developed a procedure to scale candidates/parties and voters in an election.

3. Conclusion

We end where we began — on a personal note. Not only was Richard a brilliant scientist, he also was very perceptive when it came to the advice that he

---

[10]This is developed in detail at http://gking.harvard.edu/vign/.

gave to the two of us. One of us he told to "stay away from programming" and the other just the opposite. He correctly understood our respective talents. We are forever grateful to him and we leave it to the reader to figure out which one of us got what advice!

References

Aitchison, J. and S. D. Silvey. 1957. "The Generalization of Probit Analysis to the Case of Multiple Responses." *Biometrika* 44: 131–140.

Aldrich, John H. 1977. "Electoral Choice in 1972: A Test of Some Theorems of the Spatial Model of Electoral Competition." *Journal of Mathematical Sociology* 5: 215–237.

Cheung, Stella. 1996. "Provincial Credit Ratings in Canada: An Ordered Probit Analysis." Bank of Canada Working Paper 96-6.

Czado, Claudia, Anette Heyn, and Gernot Müller. 2005. "Modeling Migraine Severity with Autoregressive Ordered Probit Models." Unpublished paper, Technische Universität München, Boltzmannstr. 3, D-85747 Garching, Germany, March 16.

Finney, D. J. 1947. *Probit Analysis: A Statistical Analysis of the Sigmoidal Response Curve.* Cambridge, England: Cambridge University Press.

Fiorina, Morris P. 1974. *Representatives, Roll Calls, and Constituencies.* Lexington, MA: Heath.

King, Gary. 1989. *Unifying Political Methodology: The Likelihood Theory of Statistical Inference.* Cambridge, England: Cambridge University Press.

King, Gary, Christopher J. L. Murray, Joshua A. Solomon, and Ajay Tandon. 2004. "Enhancing the Validity and Cross-Cultural Comparability of Measurement in Survey Research." *American Political Science Review* 98: 191–207 (corrected version of article originally published in the November issue of the same journal, under the same authors and title).

Kockleman, Kara Maria and Young-Jun Kweon. 2002. "Driver Injury Severity: An Application of Ordered Probit Models." *Accident Analysis & Prevention* 34: 313–321.

McKelvey, Richard D. 1975. "Policy Related Voting and Electoral Equilibrium." *Econometrica* 43: 815–844.

McKelvey, Richard D. and William Zavoina. 1971. "An IBM Fortran IV Program to Perform N-Chotomous Multivariate Probit Analysis." *Behavioral Science* 16: 186–187.

Nelson, Forrest and Lawrence Olson. 1978. "Specification and Estimation of a Simultaneous-Equation Model with Limited Dependent Variables." *International Economic Review* 19: 695–709.

Norojono, O. and W. Young. 2001. "The Application of an Ordered Probit Model to Investigate Shippers' Perceptions of Rail Freight Services in Indonesia." *Road and Transportation Research*, June.
http://www.findarticles.com/p/articles/mi_qa3927/is_200106/ai_n8979652.

Palfrey, Thomas R. and Keith T. Poole. 1987. "The Relationship Between Information, Ideology, and Voting Behavior." *American Journal of Political Science* 31: 511–530.

Poole, Keith T. 1998. "Recovering a Basic Space from a Set of Issue Scales." *American Journal of Political Science* 42: 954–993.

Rice, Stuart A. 1928. *Quantitative Methods in Politics*. New York: A. A. Knopf.

Rosett, Richard N. and Forrest D. Nelson. 1975. "Estimation of the Two-Limit Probit Regression Model." *Econometrica* 43: 141–146.

Shepsle, Kenneth A. 1978. *The Giant Jigsaw Puzzle*. Chicago: University of Chicago Press.

Zavoina, William and Richard D. McKelvey. 1969. "A Statistical Model for the Analysis of Legislative Voting Behavior." Paper prepared for delivery at the 1969 APSA Meetings, New York City, New York.

CHAPTER 7

A Method of Scaling with Applications to the 1968 and 1972 Presidential Elections

JOHN H. ALDRICH AND RICHARD D. MCKELVEY

Introduction

The analysis of electoral behavior has seen a radical shift in emphasis over the last two decades. Empirically, there has been a major resurgence of interest in analysis of the relationship between issues and electoral behavior.[1] At approximately the same time, the theoretical literature has seen the development of the spatial model of party competition.[2] Based on a rational choice view of politics, this model perceives elections as a strategic contest between candidates who compete for votes by adopting positions in a multidimensional issue space. The further advancement of both the approaches has been hindered by the inability to obtain good empirically based measurements of the positions of the candidates and citizens in a common issue space.

Some recent literature along this line has attempted to estimate candidate and citizen positions by using only individual level preference data among candidates. There is a substantial body of psychological literature, culminating in the development of multidimensional proximity scaling methods[3] which, on the basis of

---

[1] See John H. Kessel, "Comment: The Issues in Issue Voting," *American Political Science Review,* 66 (June, 1972), 459–465, for an extensive bibliography of the literature.

[2] See Otto A. Davis, Melvin J. Hinich, and Peter C. Ordeshook, "An Expository Development of a Mathematical Model of the Electoral Process," *American Political Science Review,* 64 (June, 1970), 426-448, for a review of this literature.

[3] See Paul E. Green and Frank J. Carmone, *Multidimensional Scaling and Related Techniques in Marketing Analysis* (Boston: Allyn and Bacon, Inc., 1970) for a review of this literature. Applications of these methods to the 1968 and 1972 presidential elections can be found in Jerrold G. Rusk and Herbert F. Weisberg, "Perceptions of Presidential Candidates: Implications for Electoral Change," *Midwest Journal of Political Science,* 16 (August, 1972), 338–410, Herbert F. Weisberg and Jerrold G. Rusk, "Dimensions of Candidate Evaluation," *American Political Science Review,* 64 (December, 1970), 1167–1185, and Gary A. Mauser, "A Structural Approach to Predicting Patterns of Electoral

single-peakedness assumptions of individual preferences, provide means for estimating these positions. Despite the attractions of these methods, this approach has some serious drawbacks. Strong assumptions must be made about the nature of individual preferences, and only a relatively small number of all-inclusive and relatively uninterpretable dimensions can be recovered. In addition, by depending on preference rather than perceptual data, these methods end up *assuming* that voters have single-peaked preferences and vote for the candidate closest to them, rather than being able to *test* such assertions.

For the above reasons, we feel that operationalizations of tests of the spatial model have to be based on *perceptual*, as opposed to *preference* data. One method of collecting such data has been the straightforward procedure of simply asking respondents to place themselves as well as the candidates on a common issue continuum. These types of data have been collected, for example, in the 1968 and 1972 SRC election surveys in the form of "seven point scales." Here each respondent is asked to identify the positions of the major candidates and parties on a preselected set of issues. He identifies these perceptions, as well as his own "ideal point," by placing them somewhere on an equal interval scale running from 1 to 7 in which the two endpoints are identified.[4]

Unfortunately, much of the analysis of this type of data indicates that, in general, there is substantial disagreement between different individuals' perceptions of candidates, so it is not clear how to use such data to obtain representations of candidates and voters in a common space. Further, a natural interpretation of such data, and an interpretation that has been drawn by some political scientists, is that voters simply don't have the necessary information to evaluate and intelligently vote their preferences in an election, as is assumed in the spatial theories.

In this paper, we suggest an alternative interpretation of the above data, and argue that at least part of the confusion which has been attributed to the voter may be attributable purely to methodological difficulties inherent in collecting this type of perceptual data. We propose a model of the possible generation of such data which can be used to eliminate the errors attributable to these methodological difficulties. The same model serves as a scaling procedure which can be used to scale candidates and voters in a common issue space. This yields interval level data on

---

Substitution," in *Multidimensional Scaling: Theory and Applications in the Behavioral Sciences, Vol. II, Applications,* ed. Roger N. Shepard et al. (New York: Seminar Press, 1972), pp. 245–287.

[4]These particular data have been analyzed by Benjamin I. Page and Richard A. Brody, "Policy Voting and the Electoral Process: The Vietnam War Issue," *American Political Science Review,* 66 (September 1972), 979–995, and by John H. Aldrich, "Some Results about the 1968 Election Based on the Theory of the Spatial Model of Party Competition" (paper delivered at the 1973 Annual Meetings of the American Political Science Association).

TABLE 1. Some Hypothetical Voters' Scores on Seven-Point Vietnam Scale

	"Dove" 1	2	3	4	5	6	7 "Hawk"
Voter 1	H,J,N			W		S	
Voter 2	H	J		N,S		W	
Voter 3	S		H	J,N		W	

Key: H = Humphrey J = Johnson N = Nixon W = Wallace S = Self (i.e., Voter's ideal point).

candidate and voter positions which can be used to address various propositions from the spatial modeling literature.

The model we develop assumes that candidates occupy fixed positions in an issue space and that the individual perceptual data arises from this via a two-step process, the first step consisting of "true" error in perception, and the second step consisting of distortion introduced in the actual survey situation.
We then derive a least squares solution for the true parameters of this model. The solution turns out to be essentially a principal components solution for the candidate parameters together with a regression estimate of the citizen parameters. We go on to evaluate, by Monte Carlo methods, the statistical properties of these estimators, in the type of situation to which they will be applied. Finally, we use the method to analyze the candidate and citizen positions on two issues in the 1968 and 1972 presidential elections.

The Problem

Before proceeding with the formal development of the model, we shall illustrate, in greater detail, the types of methodological difficulties that can be expected to arise in the analysis of individual level perceptual data of the sort described above. In particular, we consider an example of the type of data that might arise from the "seven-point" SRC scale on Vietnam.

In the example of Table 1, we have illustrated the possible perceptions of three voters. It is evident that although these three voters differ greatly in their placement of the candidates on the Vietnam scale, they seem to agree pretty well on the underlying scale on which the candidates lie. An alternative explanation for the lack of agreement of the voters on the placement of the candidates is that the voters are simply exhibiting different reactions to the response task. Convincing arguments can be made that this may be occurring at least to some extent. Thus, even though the endpoints of the issue scales are identified, these identifiers are rather vague, and their responses are subject to interpretation. Different voters may be anchoring the scales according to their own interpretation of these endpoints. The fact that voters are also asked to locate their own ideal points on the scale can only serve to accentuate this tendency, for a voter who is himself a hawk is likely to interpret the endpoints of the Vietnam scale in order to accommodate his own ideal point, thus pushing his perceptions of the candidates farther to the left than a dove would. In addition, and associated with the ambiguity of the endpoints, is the problem that different voters may well interpret the intervals on the scale differently. Again, it is reasonable to suspect, for example, that an extreme hawk might see less difference between Nixon and Humphrey than a moderate would. Finally, the forced categorization tends to have additional undesirable effects: Not only does one lose information by forcing voters to ignore small differences, but also voters tend to place their perceptions of candidates, as well as their placement of their own ideal points, more frequently in the "prominent" categories (i.e., 1, 4, and 7) rather than in the "off" categories (i.e., 2, 3, 5, and 6). This tendency leads to curious results when one attempts to analyze data. If one uses the raw data to observe the distribution of ideal points, for example, he or she observes what one of us has likened elsewhere to a "circus tent" effect, obtaining a distribution with modes at the prominent categories. Again, this gravitation of the respondent towards the prominent categories is usually interpreted as meaning that one is asking too much of the respondent — that the voter cannot make such fine distinctions — and one then proceeds to collapse the off categories, losing further information. Here, also, an alternative explanation might be that the gravitation towards the prominent categories is due to the ambiguity of the scale. Individuals use the prominent categories as "natural anchoring" points, but each individual gives his own interpretation to the prominent points.

If the above is an accurate account of the generation of the data, then data of this type would seem to contain contaminating information, in addition to the information they carry about the true candidate positions. For it is possible that there might be complete agreement in the perceptions of the candidates, but that because of different interpretations of the scale, we might be led to believe that there was little or no agreement. In fact, one would not expect that *all* of the variation in perceptions of the candidates would be accounted for by the above type of contamination, but one would like to be able to sort out what portion of the variance is due to actual variations in perceptions and what is due to variations in response to the scale. It is this question that we try to answer in the next section. We attempt there to factor out the variations due to differential response to the response task by placing all individuals in a common space such that their perceptions are most in agreement with the common perception of the candidates.

Formal Development of the Model

We assume that the candidates occupy true positions on an issue continuum, and that the information that the citizen gives us on his perception of the candidates *is* derived from this true position in a two step process. In the first stage, we assume that there is a random disturbance in the citizen's perception of the candidate. This error in perception could arise for several reasons. For example, it may occur because the candidate is unintentionally ambiguous about his position. It may occur because voters only obtain partial information from secondary sources who distort that information in the passing. It may also arise because the voters themselves selectively perceive and distort the information they receive so that it is consistent with their prior information. Whatever the cause, we assume that the first stage, which results in the voters' perceptual space, consists in the voter observing the true space, subject to this error.

The second stage consists of the voter taking what is in his head, i.e., his perceptions, and reporting them to the interviewer. Here, we assume, since there is no common metric for placing the candidates on a scale, that the positions where the citizen reports that he sees the candidates may be an arbitrary linear transformation of his perception of the space.

More formally, we develop the following model: We assume that there are J candidates who occupy the positions $Y_1, Y_2, \ldots, Y_J$ on a one-dimensional continuum, i.e., $Y_j \in R$ for $1 \leq j \leq J$. Since this scale can only be specified up to a linear transformation, we assume that it is normalized with unit sum of squares, i.e.,

$$\sum_{j=1}^{J} Y_j = 0 \text{ and } \sum_{j=1}^{J} Y_j^2 = 1.$$

Further, we assume that there are n citizens, each of whom has a perception of each candidate. The ith citizen's perception of the jth candidate is denoted Y_{ij} and we assume that this is distributed randomly around the true candidate position, as illustrated in Figure 1, for four candidates. Thus, for the first stage, we assume that individual perceptions are generated as follows:

(1) $$Y_{ij} = Y_j + u_{ij} \text{ for } 1 \leq i \leq n, 1 \leq j \leq J,$$

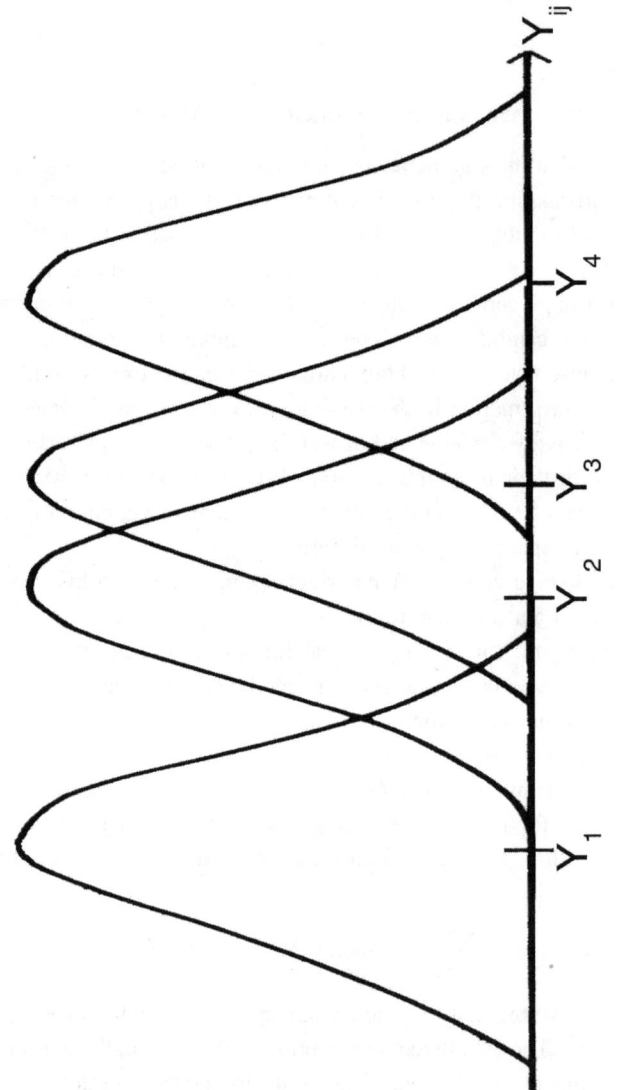

FIGURE 1. Distribution of perceptions, Y_{ij}

where u_{ij} is a random variable which satisfies the usual Gauss-Markov assumptions, i.e.,[5]

(2)
$$E(u_{ij}) = 0 \text{ for all } i, j.$$
$$E(u_{ij})^2 = \sigma^2 \text{ for all } i, j.$$
$$E(u_{ij}\, u_{kl}) = 0 \text{ for all } i, j, k, l \text{ with either } i \neq k \text{ or } j \neq l.$$

The second stage of the data generation consists in the reporting of the perceptual space. Here we assume that our observed data consists of a reported position for each candidate, for each voter, and that this consists of some linear transformation of the voter's perceptual space. I.e., we let X_{ij} represent the position where citizen i reports that he sees candidate j, and it is assumed that for each voter, there are scalars, $c_i, w_i \in R$ such that

(3)
$$c_i + w_i X_{ij} = Y_{ij} = Y_j + u_{ij}$$

for $1 \leq i \leq N$, $1 \leq j \leq J$, or equivalently,

(4)
$$X_{ij} = \frac{1}{w_i}(Y_{ij} - c_i) = \frac{1}{w_i}(Y_j - c_i) + \frac{u_{ij}}{w_i}.$$

Note that the above transformation allows us to account for different anchoring of the scale as well as for different interpretation of the intervals. It does not account for the ordinal nature of the data.

Now, the only data we actually observe is the X_{ij} matrix of reported positions, and from this, we want to recover the true parameters, Y_j, c_i, and w_i for

---

[5]The scaling model we develop here rests on Gauss-Markov type assumptions. There is good reason to question some of these assumptions, and hence attempt to extend the basic results to cover some of these potential violations. One assumption is that of "homoscedasticity" or constant error variance for each respondent and each candidate/stimulus. It may be more reasonable to expect some respondents to have greater perceptual error than others, and some stimuli to have lesser ambiguity in their positioning on issues than others. Another assumption is that of "no covariance" among an individual's perception of different candidates. It may be more realistic to assume that a respondent might identify certain candidates so that a change in perceived position of one candidate carries over to other candidates. A more general model incorporating these objections, would assume that there is a known stochastic variance/covariance matrix for each respondent:

$$E(u_i' u_i) = \begin{bmatrix} \sigma_{1i}^2 & (\sigma_{1i}\sigma_{2i}) & \cdots & (\sigma_{1i}\sigma_{Ji}) \\ & \cdot & & \\ & \cdot & & \\ & \cdot & & \\ (\sigma_{Ji}\sigma_{1i}) & (\sigma_{Ji}\sigma_{2i}) & \cdots & \sigma_{Ji}^2 \end{bmatrix}$$

While we have formulated a model of the above sort, we have not yet been able to carry through the mathematical derivations of the estimators for this case.

$1 \leq i \leq n$, $1 \leq j \leq J$. Before proceeding, we establish some matrix notation to make the calculations less burdensome. We set

$$Y = \begin{bmatrix} Y_1 \\ Y_2 \\ \cdot \\ \cdot \\ Y_J \end{bmatrix}, \quad X_i = \begin{bmatrix} 1 & X_{ij} \\ 1 & \cdot \\ \cdot & \cdot \\ \cdot & \cdot \\ 1 & X_{iJ} \end{bmatrix}, \quad \beta_i = \begin{bmatrix} c_i \\ w_i \end{bmatrix}.$$

And, using $\widehat{Y}_j$, $\widehat{c}_i$, $\widehat{w}_i$, etc., to denote our estimates of the true parameters, we set

$$\widehat{Y} = \begin{bmatrix} \widehat{Y}_1 \\ \cdot \\ \cdot \\ \cdot \\ \widehat{Y}_J \end{bmatrix}, \quad \widehat{\beta}_i = \begin{bmatrix} \widehat{c}_i \\ \widehat{w}_i \end{bmatrix}.$$

Then, the perceived candidate positions for citizen i are

$$X_i \widehat{\beta}_i = \begin{bmatrix} \widehat{c}_i + \widehat{w}_i X_{i1} \\ \cdot \\ \cdot \\ \cdot \\ \cdot \\ \widehat{c}_i + \widehat{w}_i X_{iJ} \end{bmatrix}.$$

The procedure that we will use will be to choose $\widehat{Y}$ and $\widehat{\beta}_i$, $1 \leq i \leq n$ in such a way as to get the best fit, in a least squares sense, between the estimated candidate positions and the citizen's perceptions of them. To do this, we define the vector of estimated residuals, for individual i, as

(5) $$e_i = X_i \widehat{\beta}_i - \widehat{Y}.$$

Then, the sum of the squared residuals for a particular voter is

(6) $$e_i' e_i = \left(X_i \widehat{\beta}_i - \widehat{Y} \right)' \left(X_i \widehat{\beta}_i - \widehat{Y} \right),$$

and the total sum of squared residuals is

(7) $$SS\left(\widehat{\beta}_i, \ldots, \widehat{\beta}_n \widehat{Y}\right) = \sum_{1}^{n} e_i' e_i.$$

We want to minimize (7) subject to the constraints that

(8) $$\sum_{j=1}^{J} \widehat{Y}_j = 0 \text{ and } \sum_{j=1}^{J} \widehat{Y}_j^2 = 1,$$

so if we let C be a $J \times 1$ matrix of ones, i.e.,

$$C = \begin{bmatrix} 1 \\ \cdot \\ \cdot \\ \cdot \\ \cdot \\ 1 \end{bmatrix}$$

the constraints in (8) become

$$C'\widehat{Y} = 0$$

(9)
and

$$\widehat{Y}'\widehat{Y} = 1.$$

We set the above up as a Lagrangean multiplier problem, getting

$$L\left(\widehat{\beta}_i, \widehat{Y}, \lambda_1, \lambda_2\right) = \sum_{i=1}^{n} e'_i e_i + 2\lambda_1 C'\widehat{Y}$$

$$+ \lambda_2 \left(\widehat{Y}'\widehat{Y} - 1\right) = \sum_{i=1}^{n} \left(\widehat{Y} - X_i\widehat{\beta}_i\right)'\left(\widehat{Y} - X_i\widehat{\beta}_i\right)$$

(10)
$$+ 2\lambda_1 C'\widehat{Y} + \lambda_2 \left(\widehat{Y}'\widehat{Y} - 1\right).$$

Differentiating and setting equal to 0, we get the $2n + J + 2$ equations:

(11) $$\frac{\partial L}{\partial \widehat{\beta}_i} = -2X'_i\widehat{Y} + 2X'_i X_i \widehat{\beta}_i = 0, \text{ for } 1 \leq i \leq n,$$

(12) $$\frac{\partial L}{\partial \widehat{Y}} = -2\sum_{i=1}^{n} X_i \widehat{\beta}_i + 2n\widehat{Y} + 2C'\lambda_1 + 2\lambda_2\widehat{Y} = 0,$$

(13) $$\frac{\partial L}{\partial \lambda_1} = C'\widehat{Y} = 0,$$

(14) $$\frac{\partial L}{\partial \lambda_2} = \widehat{Y}'\widehat{Y} - 1 = 0.$$

Solving (11) for $\widehat{\beta}_i$, we get

(15) $$\widehat{\beta}_i = \left(X'_i X_i\right)^{-1} X'_i \widehat{Y},$$

so that the individual transformation consists of the least-squares regression of the reported on the actual (unknown) positions of the candidates. Now, substituting in (12), gives,

(16) $$\sum_{i=1}^{n}\left[X_i\left(X_i'X_i\right)^{-1}X_i'\right]\widehat{Y} - n\widehat{Y} - C'\lambda_1 - \widehat{Y}\lambda_2 = 0.$$

Setting

(17) $$A = \sum_{i=1}^{n}\left[X_i\left(X_i'X_i\right)^{-1}X_i'\right],$$

and substituting in (16) we can reduce equations (11) through (14), getting

(18) $$(A - nI)\widehat{Y} - C'\lambda_1 - \widehat{Y}\lambda_2 = 0,$$

(19) $$C'\lambda_1 = 0,$$

(20) $$\widehat{Y}'\widehat{Y} = 1.$$

Multiplying (18) by C', we get

(21) $$C'(A - nI)\widehat{Y} - J\lambda_1 - \left(C'\widehat{Y}\right)\lambda_2 = 0.$$

But now it is straightforward, by expansions of X_i, to show that, for any $1 \leq i \leq n$

$$C'\left[X_i\left(X_i'X_i\right)^{-1}X_i'\right] = C',$$

so that

$$C'A = C'\left[\sum X_i\left(X_i'X_i\right)^{-1}X_i'\right] = nC'$$

and

(22) $$C'(A - nI) = 0.$$

And from (19), it follows that $C'\widehat{Y} = 0$, so (21) yields $J\lambda_1 = 0$, or

(23) $$\lambda_1 = 0.$$

Now (18) becomes

(24) $$(A - nI)\widehat{Y} = \lambda_2\widehat{Y}.$$

But this simply says that $\widehat{Y}$ is a characteristic vector of the matrix $(A - nI)$ which gives us our solution. To determine which characteristic vector to choose, we note that $-\lambda_2$, the negative of the characteristic root, represents the sum of the squared errors associated with the characteristic vector $\widehat{Y}$. To see this, we multiply (18) by $\widehat{Y}$, getting

$$\widehat{Y}'(A - nI)\widehat{Y} - \widehat{Y}'C\lambda_1 - \widehat{Y}'\widehat{Y}\lambda_2 = 0,$$

or, applying (19) and (20),

(25) $$\lambda_2 = \widehat{Y}'(A - nI)\widehat{Y}.$$

But, setting
$$A_i = X_i \left(X_i' X_i\right)^{-1} X_i',$$
one can easily show that $(I - A_i)$ is a symmetric, idempotent matrix, and

$$\sum_{i=1}^{n} e_i' e_i = \sum_{i=1}^{n} \left(\widehat{Y} - X_i \widehat{\beta}_i\right)' \left(\widehat{Y} - X_i \widehat{\beta}_i\right)$$

$$= \sum_{i=1}^{n} \left(\widehat{Y} - X_i \left(X_i' X_i\right)^{-1} X_i' \widehat{Y}\right)' \left(\widehat{Y} - X_i \left(X_i' X_i\right)^{-1} X_i' \widehat{Y}\right)$$

$$= \sum_{i=1}^{n} \widehat{Y}'(I - A_i)'(I - A_i)\widehat{Y}$$

$$= \sum_{i=1}^{n} \widehat{Y}'(I - A_i)\widehat{Y} = \widehat{Y}'(nI - A)\widehat{Y}$$

$$= -\widehat{Y}'(A - nI)\widehat{Y}.$$

So from (25),

(26) $$-\lambda_2 = \sum_{i=1}^{n} e_i' e_i.$$

Thus, our solution, $\widehat{Y}$, is the characteristic vector of the matrix $(A - nI)$ with the highest (negative) nonzero characteristic root. Having obtained a solution for the candidate positions, we can, of course, go back to (15), to obtain the parameters of the individual transformation by performing the least squares regression of the individual's reported positions on the estimated positions of the candidates.

With regard to the estimates of the individual perceptions, we note that $\widehat{Y}_i = X_i \widehat{\beta}_i$ is an estimate of the ith voter's perceptions of the candidate positions. Ideally, we would hope that the average perception of a candidate's position would correspond to the estimate of his position. In vector notation, we would want

$$\frac{\sum \widehat{Y}_i}{n} = \widehat{Y}.$$

In fact, this is not the case. Rather, because of a "regression towards the mean" on individuals' candidate perceptions, we get

$$\text{(27)} \qquad \frac{\sum \widehat{Y}_i}{n + \lambda_2} = \widehat{Y}.$$

To see this, we note that

$$\sum \widehat{Y}_i = \sum X_i \widehat{\beta}_i$$
$$= \sum X_i \left(X_i' X_i \right)^{-1} X_i' \widehat{Y}$$
$$= A\widehat{Y}$$
$$\text{(28)} \qquad = (n + \lambda_2) \widehat{Y},$$

from which (27) follows.

Because of this relation, in our empirical applications, we will actually present the voter's perceptions of the candidate in terms of the expanded transformation of equation (27), which differs from the least squares estimators by a factor of $\frac{n}{n+\lambda_2}$. This has the effect of normalizing the solution with respect to the mean perceptions of the candidates, and makes possible more direct comparisons with the unscaled data.

Note that from (26), it follows that the expression

$$\text{(29)} \qquad \frac{-\lambda_2}{nJ} = \frac{\sum_{i=1}^{n} e_i' e_i}{nJ}$$

represents the average squared deviations of the observed from the true candidate positions, and we can use this as an estimate of σ^2. Formally, we set

$$\text{(30)} \qquad \widehat{\sigma}^2 = \frac{-\lambda_2}{nJ}.$$

Since the estimated scale positions of the candidates are normalized to have unit sum of squares, $\widehat{\sigma}^2$ can also be used as a measure of the "goodness of fit" of the model. Actually, we will see later that $\widehat{\sigma}^2$ is generally a biased estimator of σ^2 providing a substantial underestimate of σ^2. This can be partially corrected for by computing the sum of the squared error in the expanded perceptual space described above. This results in the formula

$$\text{(31)} \qquad \widehat{\sigma}^2 = \frac{-\lambda_2}{nJ} \left(\frac{n}{n + \lambda_2} \right)^2 = -\frac{n\lambda_2}{J(n + \lambda_2)^2},$$

which is the formula we will actually use. Even with this adjustment there is substantial bias left, as we shall see. We have not yet been able to correct for this bias, however, and use σ^2 as defined above for the present, realizing that it must be interpreted cautiously.

Another point of caution regards the estimate of the individual transformations in (15). Note that no constraints are placed on $\widehat{\beta}_i$. In particular, no constraint is placed on $\widehat{w}_i$, so it is assumed that $\widehat{w}_i$ could be negative for some voters. In applications to real data, this means that voters who perceive the candidates in a "mirror image" space will be estimated as having good fits to the true model, but with negative weights. A voter who sees things backwards then contributes to a better fit to the "true" space, and this accounts for some of the underestimation of σ^2 mentioned above.

Given that the endpoints of the scales are identified in the empirical data to which we actually apply the techniques, it is not clear that one would want to treat such voters as we have above. It would be more reasonable, perhaps, to assume that the parity of the scale is given, and that any misperception of this parity is due to error in perception. In terms of the model, this would correspond to an additional set of constraints, i.e., that $\widehat{w}_i > 0$ for all voters. We have not done this for several reasons. First, the additional mathematical complexities which are introduced by this modification are substantial. Second, although the problem of negative weights is serious if one only has a small number of candidates, it should be less so as the number of candidates increases. Thus, with large numbers of candidates, the probability of obtaining a mirror-image set of observations purely by chance becomes smaller. Finally, the procedure we have developed above at least has the virtue of identifying the voters with negative weights so that one can treat them separately if need be.

All of the above analysis has dealt with scaling of the candidate positions. We have not yet discussed the treatment of individual ideal points, but this procedure is straightforward. To obtain the individual's ideal point in the common space, we merely subject it to the same transformation that his perceptions of the candidates are subjected to. Thus, if X_{i0} represents the ith individual's placement of his ideal point, then

(32) $$\widehat{Y}_{i0} = \widehat{c}_i + \widehat{w}_i X_{i0}$$

is our estimate of his ideal point in the common space.

Before proceeding, it will be worthwhile to point out some similarities between the specification of the model that we have developed in this section and the usual factor analytic model. For these purposes, we set

$$X = \begin{bmatrix} X_{11} & \cdots & X_{1J} \\ \cdot & & \\ \cdot & & \\ \cdot & & \\ X_{n1} & \cdots & X_{nJ} \end{bmatrix}, A = \begin{bmatrix} a_1 \\ \cdot \\ \cdot \\ \cdot \\ a_n \end{bmatrix},$$

$$F = \begin{bmatrix} F_1 & \cdots & F_n \end{bmatrix},$$

(33) $$D = \begin{bmatrix} d_1 & & 0 \\ & \ddots & \\ 0 & & d_n \end{bmatrix}, \text{ and } U = \begin{bmatrix} U_{11} & \cdots & U_{1J} \\ \cdot & & \\ \cdot & & \\ \cdot & & \\ U_{n1} & \cdots & U_{nJ} \end{bmatrix}.$$

Here, X generally represents the matrix of observed data, where the X_{ij} are defined above. F represents a common factor of scale positions (similar to Y above), A is a vector of individual transformations, D is a diagonal matrix of scalars, and U a matrix of errors.[6] Then the usual one-factor model can be written

(34) $$X = AF + DU$$

or

$$X_{ij} = a_i F_j + d_i u_{ij},$$

which can be compared to (4) to note the similarities. The differences are that in (34), only stretching and shrinking the original space is allowed. More important, however, the factor model generally treats F as a random variable rather than as a parameter to be estimated.[7] Hence, although one can obtain estimates of the factor scores, one does not obtain sampling distributions of these estimates. Since the candidate positions are of primary interest, we are particularly concerned about the accuracy with which they are recovered, and we would want a model that treats them as parameters rather than random variates.

In addition to the differences in the specification of the model, one should note that if the factor-analytic formulation above is used, computational problems arise in applying usual factor-analytic procedures for obtaining a solution because the usual roles of the observation and the variable are reversed. Thus a variable,

---

[6]See Harry H. Harman, *Modern Factor Analysis* (Chicago: The University of Chicago Press, 1967), for a more complete development of the factor-analytic model.

[7]See, e.g., D. N. Lawley and A. E. Maxwell, *Factor Analysis as a Statistical Method* (London: Butterworths, 1963) for a discussion of this point.

under this representation, is a respondent, while an observation is the vector of individual perceptions of a particular candidate. Because of this reversal of roles, one would end up factor analyzing a matrix of, say, four observations and 1000 variables, leading to unmanageable correlation matrices.

Despite the differences between the two formulations, it can be shown that the solution we have derived above for the candidate parameters is mathematically equivalent to extracting the first principal component of the correlation matrix XX'.

Monte Carlo Results

The last section has derived a least-squares solution for our scaling problem. In order to assess the adequacy of the solution, and its performance in a given situation, however, we should know something about the statistical properties of the estimators. Thus, unless we know the theoretical sampling distributions of the estimators, it is difficult to know how much confidence to place in the results. Since our estimators have been derived in the rather complex manner described above, analytical determination of their sampling distributions is exceptionally difficult. Although we cannot obtain mathematical derivations of these distributions, we can obtain an indication of their properties by conducting Monte Carlo type experiments.

The purpose of a Monte Carlo experiment is to generate artificial data according to a specified probabilistic model. In our case, we can specify true parameters and a stochastic term of known size and then generate data according to the model of the previous section to see how well the technique recovers these parameters. Typically, we choose, as known parameters, ones that will be as realistic as possible. To do so, we have used real data estimates to serve as parameters, and in particular, we have used those determined from the 1968 Vietnam scale data to be discussed below. Therefore, we hope to investigate the adequacy of the technique in the sort of situation we will be faced with in the real data. The true positions of the stimuli were chosen to correspond to the estimated positions of Johnson, Humphrey, Nixon, and Wallace, respectively, and the variance, σ^2, of the perceptions around the true positions was assumed to be equal to the largest variance in the estimated solution. Thus, we have $\sigma = .388$, or $\sigma^2 = .1505$. (This value of σ is actually somewhat different from the results reported below, because the Monte Carlo experiment was based on a preliminary estimation of the 1968 data.) Finally, the individual parameters, c_i and w_i, were chosen by taking a random sample of the 1968 respondents, and using their estimated values, $\hat{c}_i$ and $\hat{w}_i$, for

TABLE 2. Distribution of Candidate Estimators

	True Parameters	Candidate Parameters		Citizen Perceptions	
		Mean	Standard Deviation	Mean σ_j	Standard Deviation σ_j
Y_1	−.321	−.320	.040	.289	.021
Y_2	−.424	−.422	.035	.290	.020
Y_3	−.096	−.096	.036	.304	.013
Y_4	.841	.840	.010	.253	.021
σ	.388	.285	.013		

Average correlation of Y_j with $\widehat{Y}_j = .9977$ (over 25 samples).
Average correlation of Y_{ij} with $\widehat{Y}_j = .868$.
Correlation of Y_j with $\widehat{Y}_j = .999997$.

the Monte Carlo experiment. Using these "true parameters", we generated 25 samples with an n of 100 each, according to the model described in the previous section.

The results of the estimation of the parameters are reported in Table 2, and we are led to conclude that all the parameters describing the candidate positions are recovered exceptionally well. Figure 2 illustrates the distribution of perceptions in the assumed true model, while Figure 3 illustrates the sampling distributions of the estimated candidate positions. We see that even with a substantial amount of misperception in the original data, the technique recovers the candidate positions very well. The average correlation between the 25 estimated candidate vectors and the true candidate vector was .9977, with the average estimate of each candidate being nearly identical to the true position of the candidate. The mean estimate for each candidate is well within one standard deviation of the true position; thus if there is any bias in these estimators, it is insignificant in relation to their standard error.

The estimators for the variance in perception show a slightly different story. Here we get an overall estimate of σ of .2845, a significant underestimate of the true parameter, $\sigma = .388$. The estimates of the error in perceptions around each candidate are similar in magnitude and in their negative bias. This negative bias reveals one of the potential drawbacks of the technique, i.e., since the least-squares procedure attributes as much of the error as possible to variations in reactions to the scale, the procedure cannot recognize someone who actually perceives all candidates (say) to the left of their true positions. Such a voter is seen as perceiving

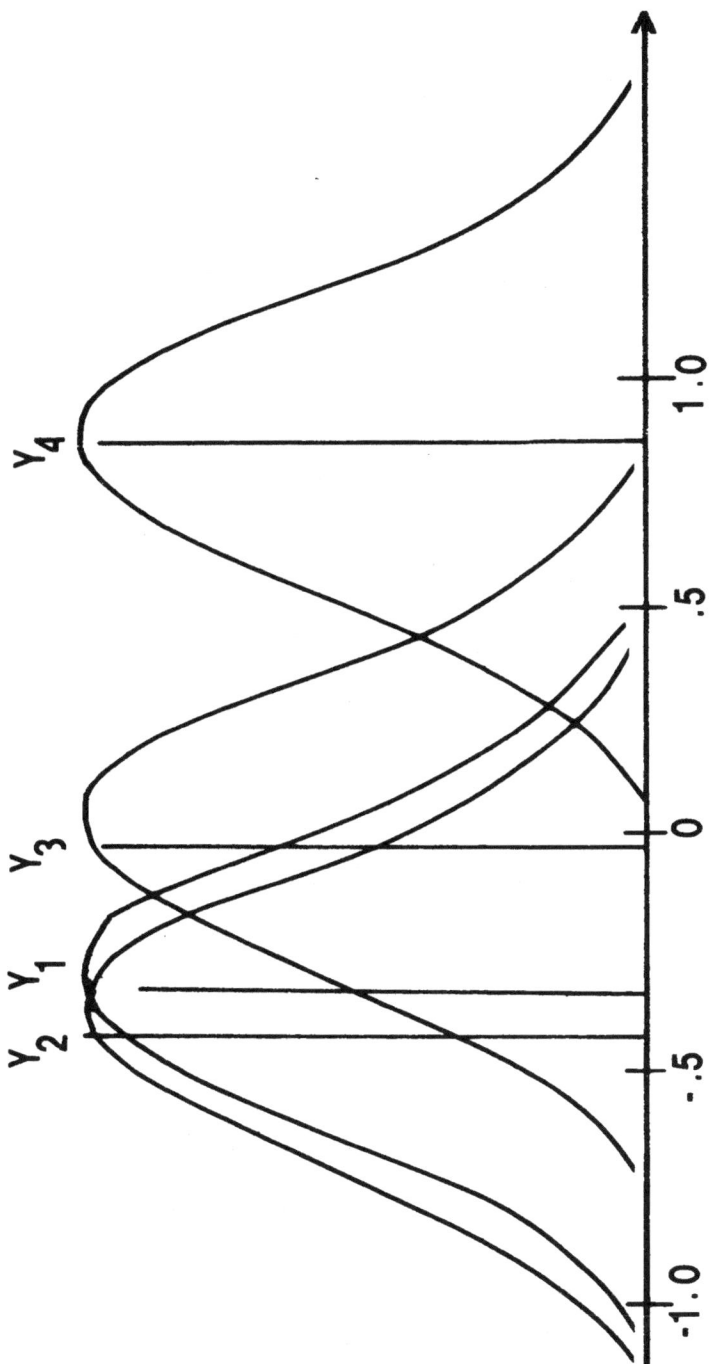

FIGURE 2. Assumed true model (distribution of perceptions)

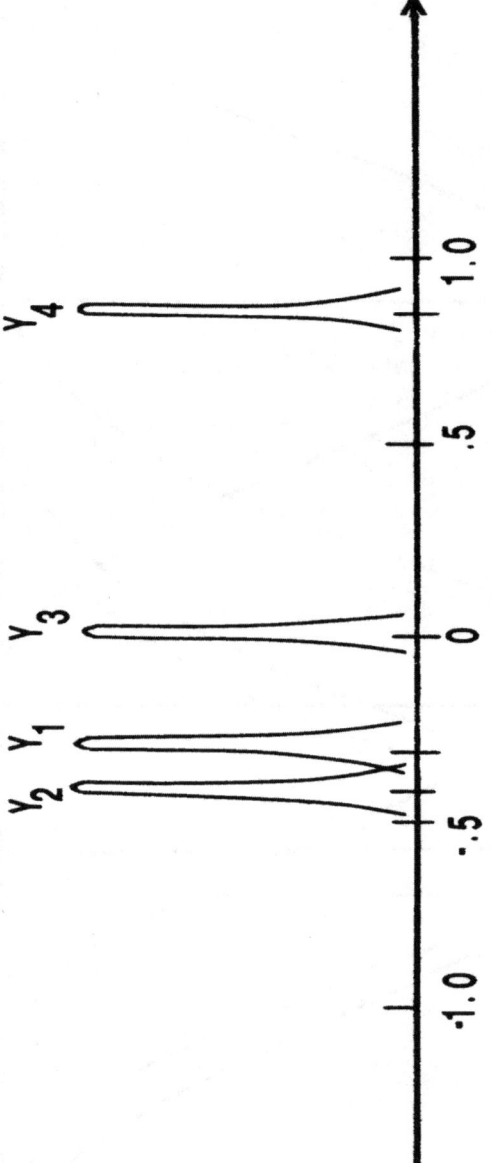

FIGURE 3. Estimated model (sampling distribution of candidate estimators)

TABLE 3. Distribution of Voter Transformation Parameters and Ideal Points

		c_i	w_i	Y_{i0}
True Distribution	Mean	−.1544	.368	−.209
	Standard Deviation	(2.242)	(.525)	1.757
Estimators	Average bias	−.0897	.0217	−.189
		(.356)	(.083)	(1.376)
	RMS bias	.1338	.0072	
	Average standard	1.080	.2511	.486
		(.865)	(.279)	(.422)

the space correctly; and consequently, we underestimate to a certain extent the variance in perceptions. Similarly, as discussed in the previous section, voters with negative weights contribute to underestimation of σ. Both of these sorts of underestimation should become less severe as the number of candidates increases.

Turning to the individual parameters, we now must view the experiment as 100 individual parameter pairs, each being estimated by 25 observations, or estimates. Rather than presenting the estimated sampling distribution of each of these 200 estimators, we present, in Table 3, some summary statistics of these sampling distributions across all 100 voters. The first set of figures gives the distribution of the true parameters, so that we have a base against which to evaluate the estimators. The next two statistics give an indication of the average bias of the estimators. First is a measure of the average (signed) bias, and the fact that these are so close to zero indicates that there is no consistent bias in one direction or the other across the 100 estimators. The second statistic is the root mean-square of the bias over all 100 estimators. This gives a better indication of the average magnitude of the bias. The third figure gives the average standard error of the 100 estimators. These indicate that the bias is generally insignificant in comparison with the standard error of the estimators. Unlike the candidate estimates, however, the standard error is fairly large. To get an idea of the amount of error that is represented in the estimators of c_i and w_i, one can compare these figures (the average standard error figures) with the standard deviations of the distributions of the true c_i and w_i. The average standard error figures are on the order of half the size of these standard deviations. This means that although these estimators may perform well on the average, in any given sample there can be a substantial amount of error in the estimation of a particular voter's transformation parameters.

It is difficult to assess the seriousness of the error in the individual estimates when they are expressed in the above form. This is because we are not really interested in the transformation parameters themselves, but are interested in them so that we can determine how accurate is the recovery of arbitrary points on the individual's perceptual scale. In particular, in our applications below, we will be interested in how well we can recover the individual's ideal point. To investigate this problem we assume that each of the 100 voters has an ideal point Y_{i0} which consists of a point in his perceptual space. Unlike his perceptions of the candidates, this is not subject to error. We then want to discover how well, for each of the 100 voters, we recover the ideal point over the course of the 25 samples. As above, we should end up with 100 estimators of 100 true parameters (in this case the Y_{i0}), each estimator based on a sample size of 25.

Just as the c_i and w_i were taken as the estimated values from an application to the 1968 Vietnam scale, the Y_{i0} were determined by setting $Y_{i0} = c_i + w_i X_{i0}$, where X_{i0} is the reported ideal point of the ith voter and c_i and w_i his estimated coefficients in the 1968 application. This computation should result in a distribution of true values much like that which we would expect to find in the actual applications. For each of the 100 voters, then, we get an estimator, $Y_{i0} = c_i + w_i X_{i0}$, for which we have 25 observations, and it is this estimator that interests us. In Table 3, we have presented information on the distributions of these estimators. We note that the average standard error of these estimators is .486, which is substantial, but comparing it to the distribution of the true ideal points, with a standard deviation of 1.757, we conclude that we can tell at least in what general area of the distribution the citizen's ideal point falls. Another way of looking at this result is to note that a 95 per cent confidence interval for an individual ideal point will be about one-half of a standard deviation either way of the estimated value. Although the amount of error may appear to be substantial, each of the individual ideal point estimates is based on a regression on four data points, and one might consider it surprising that the error is not larger than it is.

These estimates do seem to reflect a systematic bias. Points close to the mean of the true distribution are recovered with relatively greater accuracy than are those at the extremes, as reflected by the correlation of .135 between the standard error and the true value squared, and by the correlation of $-.447$ between the bias and the true value squared. Thus, there is a larger bias toward the mean and a larger standard error in the estimates of extremist ideal points, leading to a greater total mean squared error for these voters. This "regression toward the mean" suggests that a good portion of the above error in the individual estimators

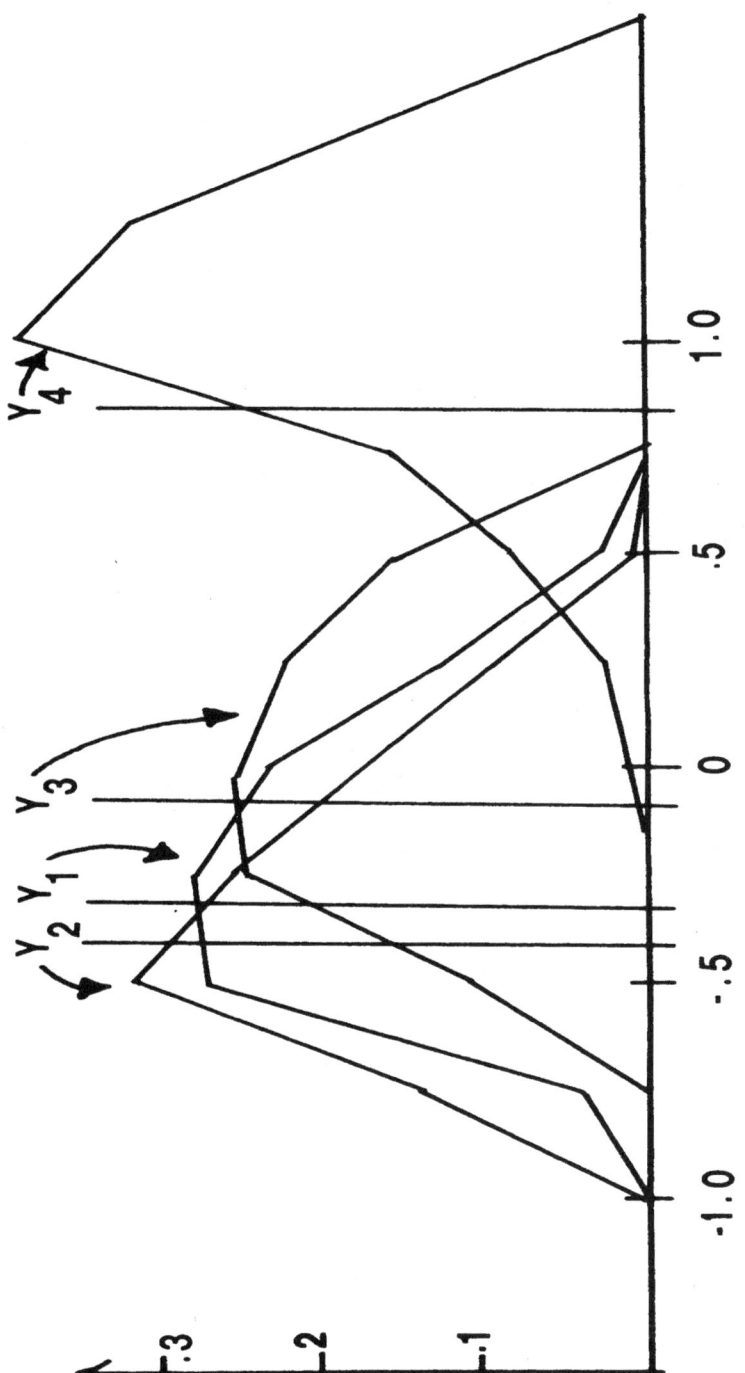

FIGURE 4. Estimated model (recovered distribution of perceptions)

may be accounted for by the extremists. From our point of view, i.e., for predicting voting behavior, we are more interested in getting good estimates of moderate ideal points than of extremists, for it is the moderate whose vote is most difficult to predict. Thus, the bias here works in our favor, giving us better estimators where we need them. As a final note, the "regression toward the mean" implies that extremists will be estimated as somewhat less extreme than they actually are. Undoubtedly this same phenomenon accounts for the skewing of the distributions of the perceptions of a candidate, as observed in Figure 4 above.

This section is rather brief, since the important findings are best presented in tabular form. This brevity does not mean that the results obtained are unimportant. On the contrary, they strongly indicate the scaling approach developed in the previous section will yield reasonably accurate estimates of the unknowns, provided that the model underlying the technique fairly describes the data being scaled. The estimators of the candidate parameters are remarkably accurate, the only deficiency being in an underestimation of the variance in individual perceptions. The recovery of the individual parameters is considerably less accurate, but there is very little bias in these estimates, and one can expect that in large samples, the method will recover these parameters well on the average. With these results in mind, we can proceed to apply the technique to some real data.

Empirical Results — Introduction

The scaling procedure we have developed provides a solution to a general scaling problem. In this section we apply this technique to some electoral data, the type of problem that catalyzed our interest in the scaling procedure in the first place. The basic data will be the two seven-point issue scales concerning urban unrest and Vietnam that were asked in the SRC's 1968 election survey and again in 1972. Following a description of the data, we will explain the candidate position estimates and the remaining variance of individual perceptions of these issues in the two very different elections. We will use the 1968 results to define a two-dimensional issue space in which we can locate both candidates and citizens. This space can be used to predict voting behavior and to demonstrate the improvement in such predictions from using the scaling results instead of the unscaled seven-point issue data. Unfortunately, the urban unrest scale was given to only a random half sample in the 1972 survey. Therefore, we are not able to relate the 1972 scaling results to the vote. Finally, we briefly report the scaling estimates for the 10 seven-point issue scales that were asked of the whole sample in 1972.

The respondents sampled in 1968 were asked to locate themselves and four "candidates," Humphrey, Nixon, Wallace, and Johnson on the two dimensions. We limit our attention to those respondents who placed all four candidates and themselves on both scales and who reported their voting behavior. Further we remove any citizen who placed all candidates on the same point on an issue, because these individual parameter estimates are undefined. For these "no-variance" people, the effect would be the same if we assigned them w_i parameter values of 0, since all candidates were seen to take the same position on that issue. These restrictions leave us with an n of 885, or about 64 per cent of the 1384 respondents asked the questions.[8] Citizens were included in the 1972 scalings if they placed themselves and all five "candidates" — McGovern, Nixon, Wallace and the two political parties — on the seven-point scale and saw at least some variance in the candidates' positions on that issue. The sample sizes are 1045 for the Vietnam scale and 519 for urban unrest. While the term "candidates" is broadly defined in these examples, it is clear that the "candidate" stimuli are all relevant to the elections and to these particular issue dimensions.

Candidate Position Estimates

The scaling estimates of the candidates' positions, the $\widehat{Y}_j$, are presented in Table 4 along with the standard deviation of the citizens' perceptions of each candidate, the $\widehat{Y}_{ij}$. Note that the mean of the distribution of $\widehat{Y}_{ij}$ is equal to $\widehat{Y}_j$. Included as well are the mean and standard deviation of the estimated distributions of citizens' ideal points (denoted by "I" in the table). The reader should keep in mind that it is not meaningful to compare candidate positions among dimensions, even for the 1968 estimates which are based on the same sample of citizens. The "unit of measurement" of each dimension has been arbitrarily set to have a mean of zero and unity sum of squares of candidate positions, reflecting our assumption that the dimensions are unique only up to a positive linear transformation. We will be able to make some cross-dimensional comparisons when we consider the individual's ideal point distributions.

The scaling results indicate that Wallace was distinctly the most conservative candidate on these two important issues in 1968. While Humphrey was the most

---

[8]The issue scales were asked on the postelection wave of the 1968 survey. Only 1384 individuals responded to this wave, down from an original N of 1557 in the initial, self-weighting, cross-sectional sample. Fifty citizens saw no differences between the candidates on Vietnam, while 14 (including 7 of the original 50) were no variance respondents on urban unrest.

TABLE 4. Scaled Estimates of Candidate Positions on Vietnam and Urban Unrest

1968	LBJ	HHH	RMN	GCW	I	
Vietnam	−.321	−.424	−.096	.841	−.238	
(std. deviation)	(.208)	(.302)	(.401)	(.403)	(1.033)	
Urban unrest	−.394	−.402	−.003	.817	−.131	
	(.239)	(.249)	(.327)	(.276)	(.645)	
1972	RMN	McG	GCW	Dem.	Rep.	I
Vietnam	.361	−.705	.376	−.355	.326	.046
	(.290)	(.338)	(.430)	(.327)	(.277)	(.694)
Urban unrest	.180	−.602	.670	−.374	.126	.243
	(.348)	(.446)	(.500)	(.363)	(.329)	(1.164)

liberal on urban unrest and dovish on Vietnam, the distance between him and the remaining two candidates is much less than that separating Wallace and Nixon.

In 1972, Wallace is once again the most right/hawkish candidate. In this election, however, Wallace and Nixon are estimated to be very similarly hawkish, while a relatively large distance remains between these two candidates on urban unrest. Balancing Wallace on the right and more, McGovern appears to be very liberal on both dimensions, relative to the positions of the other candidates. The Democratic party appears to be relatively liberal on the two issues. Nonetheless, there is a discernible gap between this party and its nominee, the party appearing more moderate. The same is not true of the competing party. The Republican party is very close to, but somewhat more liberal than, the President on both dimensions. Perhaps the most notable characteristic of these placements is the consistency of at least the ordinal properties of the four scales (we will find some examples where the ordinality is violated for the other 1972 dimensions). This ordinal consistency supports the notion that there might be a single dimension underlying the two issues in each election. The interval placements, however, are not completely consistent with this view (consider the relative placements of Nixon and Wallace in 1972).

Perceptual Variation

We will return to the consideration of the candidate point-estimations later, after we have investigated the distributions of perceptions and citizens' ideal points. The overall variance to perceptions in the scaled data, $\hat{\sigma}^2$, was defined in equation (31) of Section 3, and is reported in Table 5. These figures can be used as

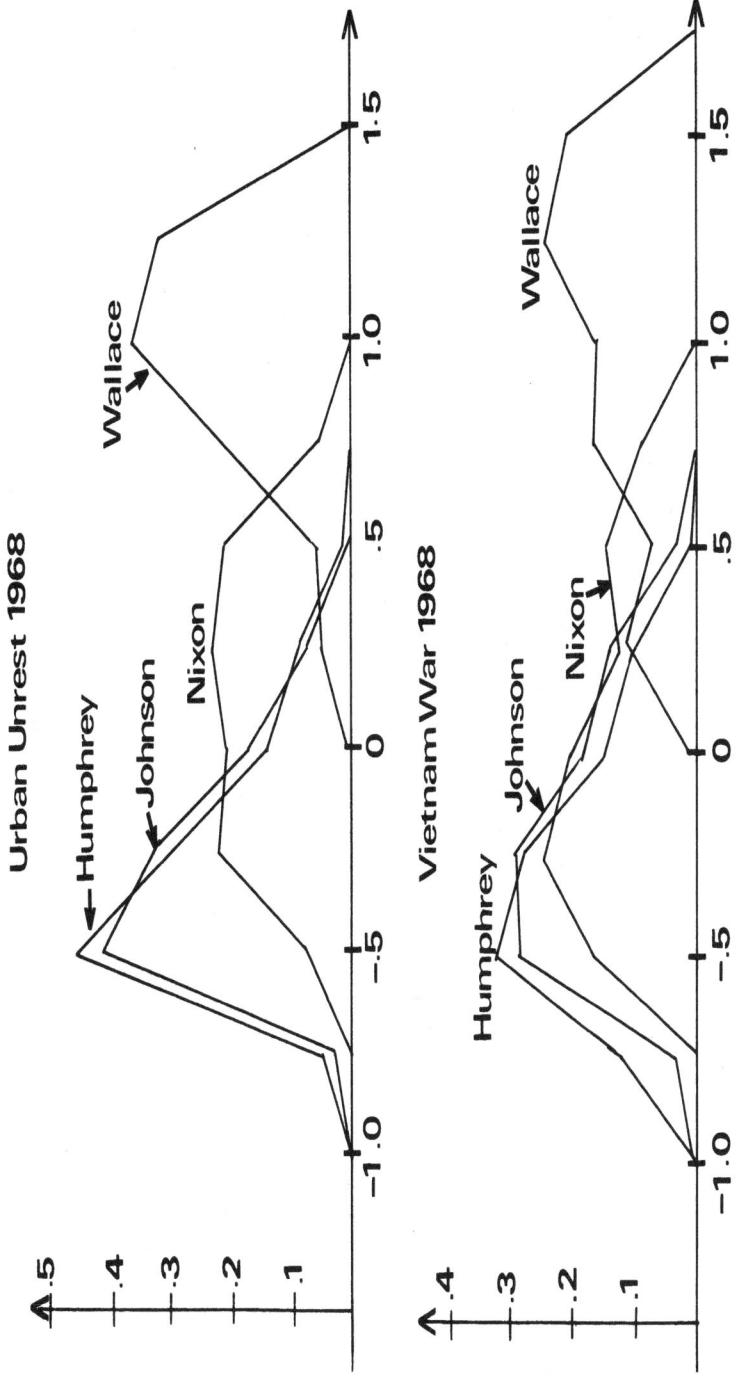

FIGURE 5. Distribution of scaled perceptions of candidates in 1968

TABLE 5. Goodness-of-Fit Measures for Scaling Solutions

	$\hat{\sigma}^2$	Average Var. 7 Point Scale Data (0,1)	Ratio of $\hat{\sigma}^2$ / Average Var.	% Negative Weights
1968				
Urban unrest	.075	.285	.264	7.5%
Vietnam	.127	1.913	.066	21.3
1972				
Urban unrest	.162	.607	.267	7.8
Vietnam	.113	.362	.313	14.5

an indication of the overall "goodness of fit" of the model and data. An alternative way of looking at the "goodness of fit" is to provide a benchmark basis of comparison to indicate the amount of reduction of the variance of the scaled over the unscaled data. To make this comparison, we normalized the seven-point scale data so that the average perceived candidate position on the seven-point scales has the same mean of zero and sum of squares of one as the scaled estimates of the candidates' positions. This restandardization of the seven-point scale data leads to an average variance to perceptions that can be compared with $\hat{\sigma}^2$ The ratio of $\hat{\sigma}^2$ to the average variance just described gives an indication of the reduction of variance of perceptions accomplished by the scaling technique. These figures, also found in Table 5, indicate substantial reductions in variance for all four dimensions. These range from about 31 per cent of the variance in the original data for the 1972 Vietnam scale to only 7 per cent for the 1968 Vietnam issue. Actually, in light of our Monte Carlo results, $\hat{\sigma}^2$ is probably an underestimate of the true stochastic component to perceptions. But even allowing for considerable bias in these estimators, it is clear that the scaling has effected a considerable reduction of the variance in perceptions. Our original suspicions seem to be confirmed: a substantial portion of the observed variance in perceptions seems to be due simply to different reactions to the interview response task, and not all variance is due to error in perceptions.

Figure 5 and Figure 6 graph the individual distributions of perceptions of each candidate, (the Y_{ij}'s), on the four dimensions.[9] The first observation that strikes one is the general similarity of these distributions to those derived from the Monte

---

[9] These graphs were drawn to scale by determining the individual frequency distributions of Y_j. The scaling dimension was divided into 16 categories, each spanning a range of .25, and the proportion of Y_j in each category determined. This is the same procedure as used in the Monte Carlo experiment.

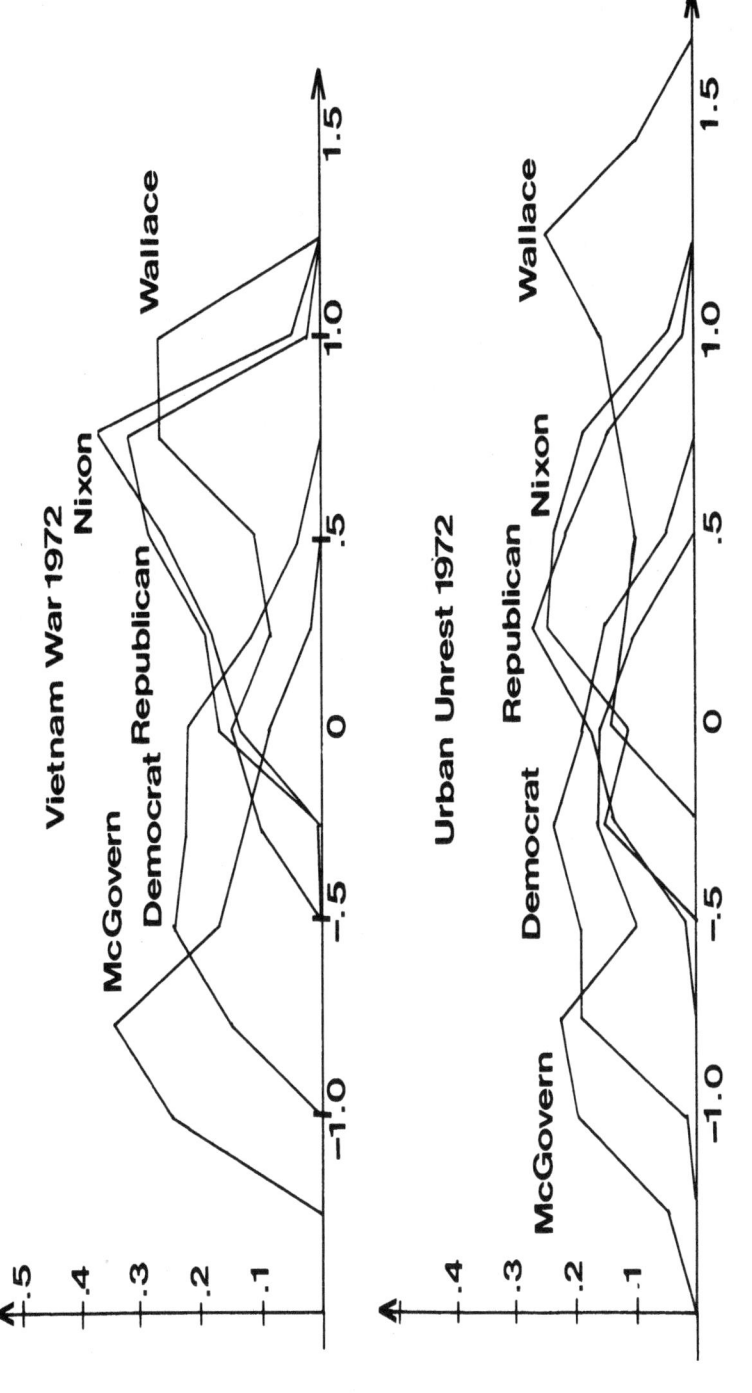

FIGURE 6. Distribution of scaled perceptions of candidates, 1972

Carlo experiment. In particular, there seems to be a similar skewing of the distribution of the more extreme candidates, indicative perhaps of a "regression toward the mean" phenomenon. Second, there seems to be a greater clarity of the perceptual distributions for the urban unrest dimension in 1968 and Vietnam in 1972. This relative clarity seems most reasonable in the contexts of the two elections. In contrast, the urban unrest dimension in 1972 in particular is rather jumbled at best. In fact, the two extreme candidates, McGovern and Wallace, have perceptual distributions with long tails toward the center of the candidate distribution and beyond, which overlap with each other and seem rather clearly not unimodal. Large portions of the sample, however, make a distinction between these two extreme candidates — a distinction that had been only slightly clearer in the 1968 version of this issue. While the perceptions of Wallace are rather distinct on Vietnam in 1968, the other three distributions are nearly identical, and even the Wallace distribution has considerable overlap with the other three. If, as Page and Brody (1972) have argued, Humphrey and Nixon (and they argue perhaps even Wallace) were purposely vague on this issue, they certainly succeeded in confusing their Vietnam policy proposals with each other's in the minds of the electorate. This finding contrasts with the relative clarity with which the Y_{ij} distributions of Nixon and McGovern are distinguished in 1972 on the Vietnam issue. The much larger overlap of the perceptual distributions of Nixon and Wallace on both issues (but especially Vietnam) in 1972 than in 1968 is noteworthy. We will shortly indicate whether this change was due to Wallace's being perceived as less conservative in 1972, or to Nixon's being viewed as more conservative. Finally, the central location and relatively large dispersal of the distributions of perceptions of Nixon in 1968 support the argument of calculated ambiguity on his part.

The entire set of candidate position estimates seems quite reasonable and helps to confirm the use of the scaling procedure for all four issues. The more refined analysis, particularly of Y_{ij}, further strengthens the argument for the "reasonableness" of the scaling estimations in our opinion. All indications, especially the distribution of perceptions, seem to point toward a greater clarity of candidate positions, and quite possibly a set of scaling estimates of higher quality, on the issues of urban unrest in 1968 and Vietnam in 1972 than on the other two dimensions. Our reading of the two elections leads us to believe that these two issues were discussed at length in the elections and that the major candidates took clear and distinguishable positions on them. This was not so obviously the case for Vietnam in 1968, when candidates were less clear in their statements, and for urban unrest in 1972, when the extent of discussion of the issue was lower and the immediacy of the riots present in 1968 was four years removed by 1972. These expectations are clearly supported by the scaling estimated distributions.

The argument of the higher quality of the scaling estimations of the issues of urban unrest in 1968 and Vietnam in 1972 receives additional support from the proportion of negative "weighting" parameters, w_i, estimated. Recall that these negative weights indicate that the citizen's perceptions can best be "fit" with the candidate position estimates by a *negative* linear transformation. In 1968, a quite small number, less than 8 per cent are estimated for the urban unrest issue (see Table 5), as is also the case for the Vietnam issue dimension in 1972. However, 14.5 per cent are estimated for urban unrest in 1972 and an unfortunately large 21.3 per cent are estimated for the 1968 Vietnam dimension. Taking the later case for example, to a fairly large extent, citizens who responded by perceiving themselves as hawks have become transformed to doves and vice versa. Perhaps the most typical case would be a hawkish respondent who claimed that Wallace is the most dovish candidate, while Humphrey or Johnson was most hawkish. Such an individual is likely to have a negative w_i and to have perceptions that correlate highly (but negatively) with the estimated candidate positions. The effect of the scaling estimations on such an individual is to treat him as if he were a dove, placing his estimated ideal point closest to Humphrey and Johnson. Thus, while it reverses his stated position, it places him closest to those candidates he claims to perceive as being closest to him.

Our interest in the individual parameter estimates, c_i and w_i, is primarily in their use in estimating the citizen's ideal point location on the set of common dimensions. The mean and variance of the distribution of ideal points for each dimension are found in Table 4. While we will be shortly putting the two 1968 distributions together to determine the distribution of citizens in the two-dimensional issue space and relating their and the candidates' positions to the citizens' voting behavior, we can also use the aggregate distributions to make some cross-dimensional comparisons. The results here can only be considered tentative, especially for the 1972 comparisons which are based on nonidentical sets of respondents. With this in mind, however, we can use the variance of ideal point distributions on each dimension to determine the relative dispersion of candidate positions on them. In particular, the estimated dimensions are unique only up to a positive linear transformation. At present, the "unit of measurement" is determined by setting the distribution of candidate positions at the "$(0, 1)$" standardization. Alternatively, we can linearly transform each dimension with respect to the distribution of ideal points so that all four have the same mean (say zero) and variance (in this case, we set all dimensions by the ideal point distribution of

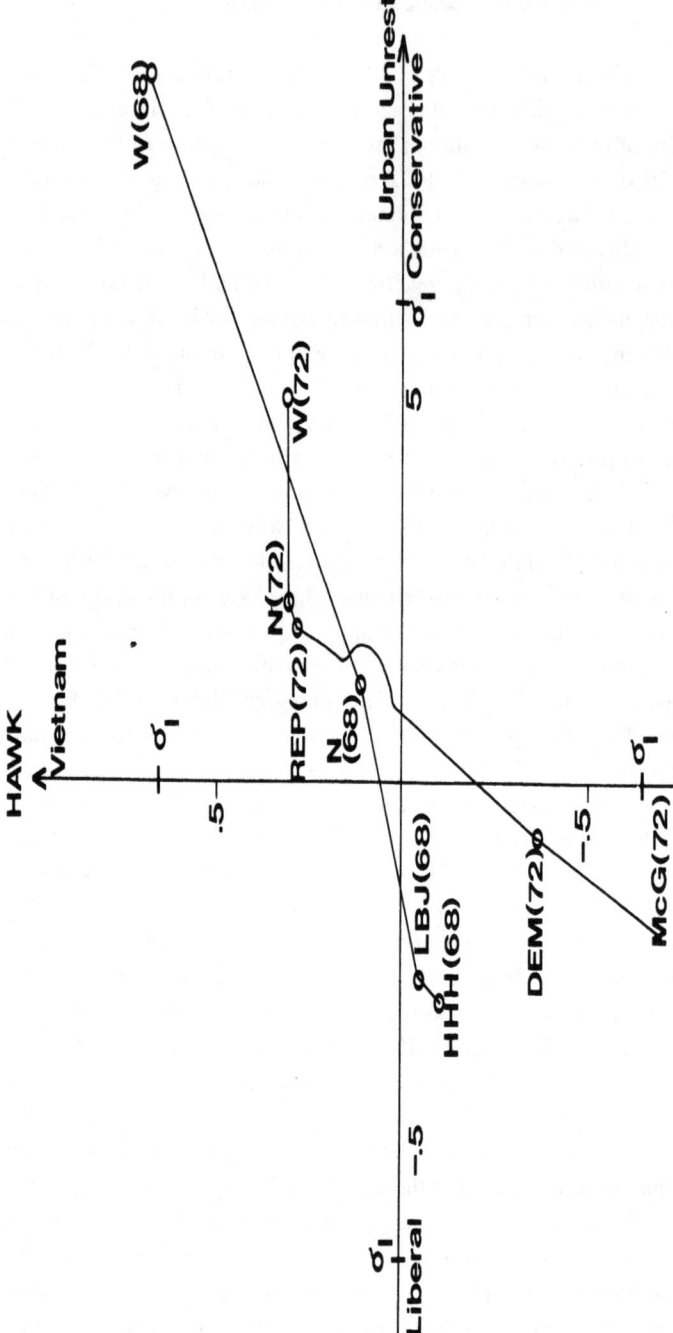

[a] σ_I indicates one (marginal) standard deviation of the ideal-point distribution from its mean of zero.

FIGURE 7. Candidate positions on urban unrest and Vietnam in 1968 and 1972 with dimensions set so that ideal point distributions have a mean of zero and variance equal to .416 (based on urban unrest 1968)

urban unrest in 1968). Therefore, all ideal point variances are set equal to .416. The new transformation of candidate position estimates would then represent the position of the candidate relative to the distribution of citizen's ideal points. Assuming that the distribution of ideal points remains constant from 1968 to 1972, we can then not only make cross-dimensional comparisons within a given year but also look at the movement of candidates between elections.

The results of the above normalization, displayed in Figure 7, tend to agree with the journalistic interpretation of the candidate positions. In 1968, Humphrey, Johnson, and Nixon were very similar and close to the average citizen on both dimensions, but especially so on Vietnam. Wallace, however, was particularly extreme on urban unrest and only somewhat less so on Vietnam. In 1972, McGovern was closer to the average citizen on urban unrest than the Democratic candidates in 1968. McGovern, however, was quite extreme on Vietnam, and the Democratic party was also more extreme than its nominees were in 1968. Nixon is estimated to have been more conservative than the average citizen in 1968, but in 1972, he is estimated to have been even more so. More dramatic movement was displayed by Wallace who appeared to have moved toward the center on both dimensions in 1972. In 1968, he was located beyond one (marginal) standard deviation of the distribution of citizens from their mean on both dimensions. By 1972, he was estimated to be well within one deviation.

Candidates appear to have been more widely dispersed on urban unrest in 1968, especially the three major party figures. By 1972, the dispersal was much greater on Vietnam. Further, while all candidates appeared to be approximately distributed along a straight line in 1968, such a "unidimensional" distribution of candidates was much less adequate in 1972.

These over-time comparisons do lend support to the scaling methodology employed. Issues that appear to us to reflect important concerns on which relatively clear positions are taken lead to better scaling estimations. Moreover, the scaling estimates conform reasonably well with a priori expectations based on (not impartially) observing the two elections.

Two-Dimensional Distribution of Ideal Points — 1968

The final stage in the analysis concerns the location of the citizen's ideal point in the common space. We have already examined the ideal-point distribution for each individual dimension. In this section, we will look at the distribution of ideal points for the two 1968 dimensions in greater detail. Beyond our concern with the extent of negative weight parameters estimated, w_i, our interest in the

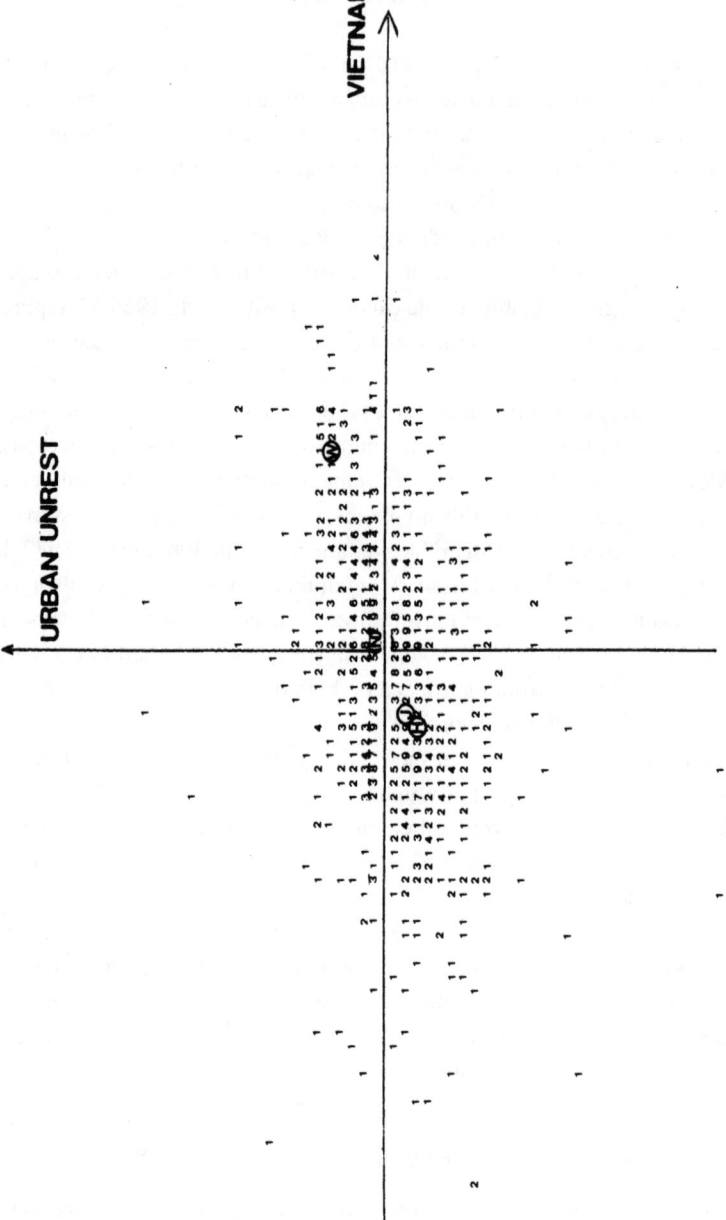

FIGURE 8. Two-dimensional ideal point distribution, 1968

individual coefficients is primarily directed at ideal-point placement, which results from solving equation (32). Figure 8 provides a scatterplot of the citizens' ideal-point locations in the common space for 1968. It is clear that most positions are estimated to be rather centrally located. Recalling the Monte Carlo results concerning the ideal-point estimates, we found that ideal points were recovered rather well over all, and that this was particularly true for less extreme estimations. Thus, this sort of distribution in the real data is likely to be somewhat more precise than a distribution with a larger number of extreme cases.

The scaling estimated distribution of ideal points differs quite extensively from the distribution obtained using the raw data. In the seven-point scale data, the individual is constrained to be located at one of the $(7 \times 7) = 49$ points of ordered pairs of positions on the two dimensions, leading to a distribution of ideal points which looks like a "circus tent." As in the scaling estimated distribution, there is some concentration of citizens towards the center, the global mode being located at the point (4,4), where one would place the large center pole of a circus tent. There were subsidiary modes, however, for each dimension at the endpoints of 1 and 7. This resulted in local modes at the four corners and at the "center edges" of such pairs of positions as (1,7) and (4,7), thus heightening the tent-like appearance of the distribution. In the transformed space, the "lumpiness" has been considerably smoothed — the distribution looking, if anything more nearly unimodal. While the distribution is not exactly unimodal or symmetric, it is greatly altered from its unscaled counterpart.

Predicting the 1968 Vote

The above estimations of the candidate positions exhibit a substantial amount of substantive reasonableness. Further, we have seen that the voter may be less confused over the candidate positions than would appear at first glance. These conclusions suggest that the assumptions of the spatial theories may constitute a reasonable model of voter behavior. The argument would be strengthened, however, if we could demonstrate that the scaling placements also lead to better predictions of electoral behavior.

To test this question, we make a simple prediction of the vote. In both the scaled and unscaled cases, the predicted vote is determined by computing the two-dimensional Euclidean distance between the voter's ideal point and the candidate position. The candidate position in the unscaled data is taken to be simply the mean perception of the sample on the seven-point scales, while we of course use the estimated position for the scaled instance. We have also computed two

TABLE 6. 1968 Vote Predictions, Comparing the Scaled and Unscaled Data

	Entire Sample				Negative Weights Removed			
	Vote		Thermometers		Vote		Thermometers	
	Unscaled	Scaled	Unscaled	Scaled	Unscaled	Scaled	Unscaled	Scaled
H-N	66%	68%	65%	69%	68%	70%	67%	72%
N-W	79	87	76	82	85	89	83	85
N-W	75	78	79	83	77	81	84	85
Both Issues Salient								
	Vote		Thermometers		Vote		Thermometers	
	Unscaled	Scaled	Unscaled	Scaled	Unscaled	Scaled	Unscaled	Scaled
H-N	67	77	69	78	72	78	74	79
N-W	86	94	81	87	93	96	86	88
N-W	78	80	83	86	81	82	88	87
Both Issues of Low Saliency								
	Vote		Thermometers		Vote		Thermometers	
	Unscaled	Scaled	Unscaled	Scaled	Unscaled	Scaled	Unscaled	Scaled
H-N	63	61	62	64	67	66	67	68
N-W	74	80	75	81	79	83	80	85
N-W	76	77	79	80	80	82	83	82

forms of the actual vote. First, we use the actually reported vote itself and examine the relationship in two way contests between pairs of candidates. In this case, we look only at those voters who actually voted for one of the pair. We use a second measure based on the SRC's 100-point-thermometer measures of candidate evaluation. Here, the "vote" is measured by assuming that the individual would vote for whichever candidate in the pair stands higher on the thermometer preference measure. Finally, it should be pointed out that this spatial prediction is a special case of the Downsian type spatial model, where it is assumed that the citizen votes, if at all, for the candidate closest to him in space.

All forms of the predictions are uniformly high, as reported in Table 6. It is noteworthy that voters seem to do remarkably well in conforming to the predictions of even this simple Downsian model, as witnessed particularly by the very high proportions of accurate predictions in those situations involving Wallace, where the citizens are generally presented two alternatives which are more easily distinguished. In this case, more than three quarters of the vote is correctly predicted.

Even with the uniformly high percentage of votes correctly predicted, the scaling based predictions consistently outperform the unsealed data. The marginal improvements run anywhere from about 2 to 8 per cent. To make sure that the improvement of the scaling results was not entirely due to the method of handling the negative weighting parameters, we reran the predictions including only those respondents who were estimated to have positive weights. These results, summarized in Table 6, indicate that the predictions continued to be improved consistently by the scaling estimations. The predictions were also improved in the unscaled data with the negative weights removed, although the scaling predictions still outperform the seven-point scale based ones. This finding illustrates the often noted tendency of people to vote their perceptions more often than they vote on the basis of the "true" positions of the candidates.

The high level of success in predicting the vote is based on a very simple model relating distance to electoral behavior. Nonetheless, some error in the prediction may result from the implicit assumption that the two issue dimensions are of equal importance. Citizens differ, of course, in the importance they attach to different issues (an argument made most forcefully by Repass).[10] Issues that the citizen believes to be of little importance to him are likely to have a smaller impact on his behavior than more salient issues. To check this possibility and any

---

[10] See David E. Repass, "Issue Salience and Party Choice," *American Political Science Review*, 65 (June, 1971), 389–400.

effect it might have on our results we applied a simple control. In particular, we looked at (a) the subset of citizens who claimed that both issues were either "very important" or "the single most important thing in the election" in the two questions following the seven-point scale responses, and (b) the subset of citizens who claimed that neither issue was very important. We then reran the same predictions for these two groups, both for the whole subsets and for the subsets with negative weights removed. These results again conform to all our expectations. The scaling-based predictions are consistently higher, and sometimes greatly so, in all but a couple of minor instances, and the saliency control improved the predictions uniformly when both issues were thought to be of importance. In fact, in the "clearest" case of predicting the actual vote between Humphrey and Wallace using the scaling estimates with high saliency control and no negative weights, 96 per cent of the vote was accurately predicted (and 94 per cent when negative parameters were included).

Scaling Estimates — 1972

We conclude this paper with a brief report of the scaling estimates for the 10 seven-point issue scales administered to the entire sample in 1972. The estimates are summarized in Table 7 and Figure 9.

The most prominent feature of the estimations is the general overall similarity of the candidates' relative positioning on most dimensions. Without exception, McGovern is clearly the most liberal candidate, followed by the estimated location of the Democratic party. As we saw earlier, McGovern is always separated from his party by a noticeable distance. Obviously, the Democrats nominated a candidate in 1972 who was not seen as a typical party member. The distance between McGovern and the Democratic party, perceptible though it may be, is always less than the sometimes very large relative distance between the Democrats and the third most liberal candidate. Thinking of the mean of the candidate distribution (i.e., 0) as the center of gravity, we see that it takes the three remaining candidates on the opposite side of the mean to balance the Democratic party and its nominee, excepting only the issue of women's rights. This contrasts with the estimates in 1968, when Wallace was estimated to be so extreme that the two Democratic candidates were not sufficient to balance him. In opposition to the distance separating McGovern and his party, the Republican party and Nixon are estimated as very similar on all ten dimensions. We cannot tell from these data whether this means that Nixon is seen as perhaps *the* typical Republican or whether it means that a "typical" party nominee, especially an incumbent president, defines much

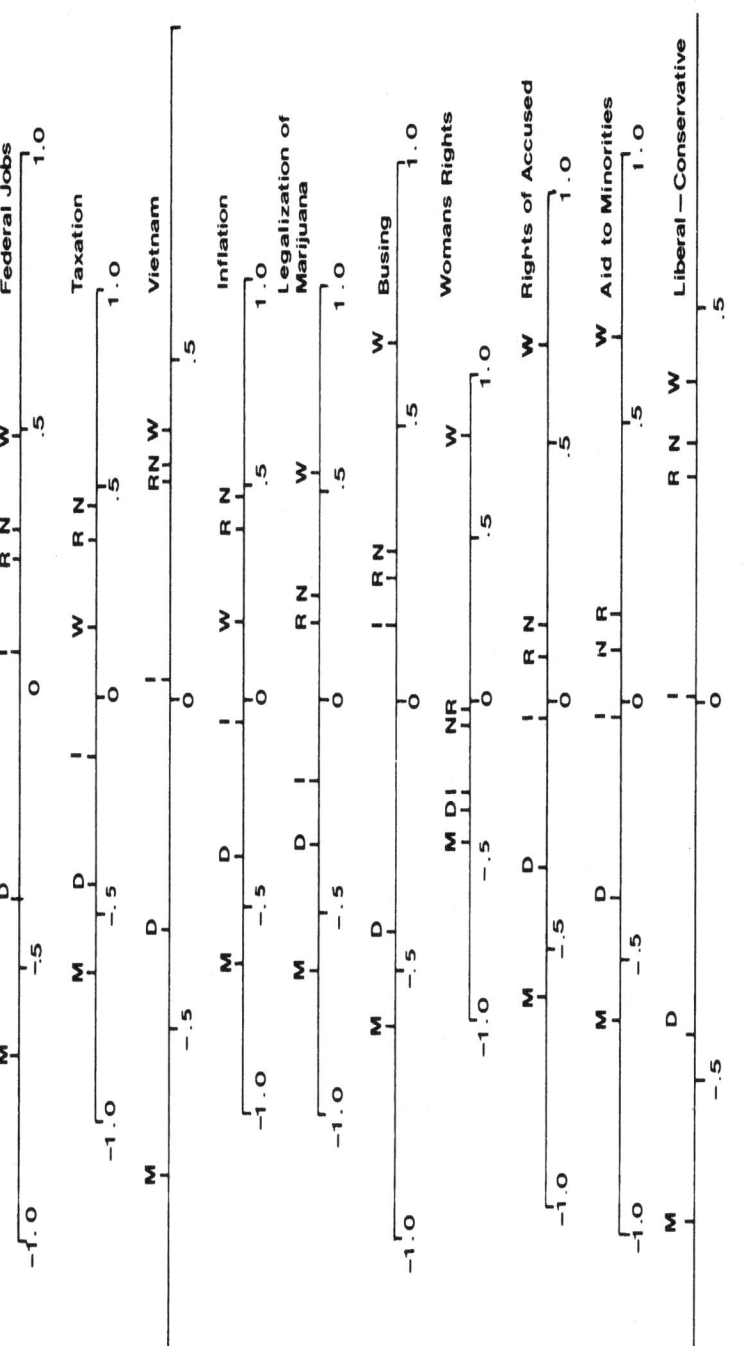

FIGURE 9. Candidate positions in 1972

of what the party stands for in the eyes of the electorate. The consistent tendency (19 out of 20 instances) to find the party closer to the mean of the distribution than its nominee may imply that parties evoke less clear cut perceptions than single individuals. This perception may be true in the eyes of each citizen, or it may be based on the obvious regional and other background differences within each party that evoke different perceptions, tending to "cancel out" extreme positionings.

The position of Wallace presents the most striking cross-dimensional differences. On most issues, Wallace is the most conservative candidate (although, as we have seen, perhaps not so obviously in 1972 as in 1968). On such issues as aid to minorities, the rights of the accused, busing, and especially women's rights, the distance separating Wallace from the two Republican stimuli is very large. The difference is much smaller on such issues as Vietnam and the general liberal/conservative continuum. Most importantly, on the two economic issues, Wallace is perceived to be only slightly on the conservative side of the mean, in a middle position dividing the Democrats from the Republicans. Again, the scaling estimated positions seem to reflect rather well the nature of the 1972 election. For example, the positioning of Wallace on the issues seems most reasonable in some detail. If he is viewed as a populist governor, his moderate economic stance could be expected.

The distribution of ideal points has been indicated in Table 7 and Figure 9. Since the distribution is only an aggregate measure, the "average citizen" not surprisingly is located rather near the center on all dimensions, dividing the two parties and nominees. Fairly consistently, then, as would be expected, the Democratic party and candidate are seen as at least somewhat liberal (this holding in 1968 as well), while the Republicans tend to be somewhat more conservative on all issues (again, the same is true in 1968). In 1972, the average citizen is consistently much closer to Nixon than McGovern. The voters tend to be, on average, slightly on the conservative side of the mean of the candidate distribution, the principal exceptions being women's rights, taxation, and the legalization of marijuana. This is not to say, of course, that the average citizen leans towards the legalization of marijuana. In fact, they are strongly conservative on the seven-point scale data. They simply see the three conservative candidates as even more conservative than themselves. These aggregate figures are, of course, only very general indicators. Our principal interest in the distribution of ideal points in this section is to rescale the unit of measurement of the dimensions, as we did previously. Recall that this would allow us to make cross-dimensional comparisons, at least to the extent of indicating the dispersal of candidates through the distribution of citizens. The relationship between the variance of ideal points and the dispersion of candidates

TABLE 7. 1972 Candidate Position Estimates

	RMN	McG	GCW	Dem.	Rep.	I
Federal jobs	.307	−.663	.474	−.401	.283	.106
	.315	.383	.438	.345	.308	.871
Taxation	.462	−.647	.166	−.402	.421	−.110
	.377	.462	.494	.424	.383	1.099
Vietnam	.361	−.705	.376	−.355	.326	.046
	.290	.338	.430	.327	.277	.694
Inflation	.457	−.628	.198	−.436	.409	−.028
	.402	.454	.515	.431	.396	1.100
Busing for integration	.240	−.587	.634	−.420	.133	.248
	.359	.406	.391	.365	.322	.857
Women's rights	−.031	−.464	.827	−.314	−.018	−.320
	.382	.437	.559	.358	.365	1.433
Rights of accused	.139	−.571	.714	−.370	.089	−.045
	.344	.414	.448	.325	.324	.927
Aid to minorities	.116	−.606	.699	−.337	.128	−.008
	.303	.361	.406	.326	.297	.876
Left / right continuum	.343	−.669	.415	−.405	.315	.006
	.261	.348	.438	.311	.272	.597

Entries are the scaled candidate or average ideal-point position on top and standard deviation underneath.

should be inverse. That is, the smaller the variance of ideal points estimated in the scaling technique, the more widely dispersed the candidates relative to the citizens. Therefore, we have taken the issue with the smallest ideal-point variance (the liberal/conservative dimension) and set all other dimensions to have the same variance, keeping the candidate positions the same on the "base" issue dimension and narrowing the distance on all others by the appropriate proportion. As Figure 9 shows, the liberal/ conservative dimension and Vietnam are quite similar in their relatively large dispersion of candidates (and especially McGovern). On the other hand, on the issue of women's rights, the candidates assume virtually identical positions. This issue has "shrunk" to less than one-half of its original size.

Conclusion

This article has attempted to apply a probabilistic model of the individual's response to questions on candidate perception to "factor out" the influences due to variations in reaction to the response task. This method then estimates the candidate positions by using the common part of individual perceptions. We have applied the method to the 1968 and 1972 election studies with reasonable success, in that the estimates correspond to a great degree with the a priori expectations, and explain voting behavior with a high degree of accuracy.

CHAPTER 8

A Statistical Model for the Analysis of Ordinal Level Dependent Variables

RICHARD D. MCKELVEY AND WILLIAM ZAVOINA

ABSTRACT. This paper develops a model, with assumptions similar to those of the linear model, for use when the observed dependent variable is ordinal. This model is an extension of the dichotomous probit model, and assumes that the ordinal nature of the observed dependent variable is due to methodological limitations in collecting the data, which force the researcher to lump together and identify various portions of an (otherwise) interval level variable. The model assumes a linear effect of each independent variable as well as a series of break points between categories for the dependent variable. Maximum likelihood estimators are found for these parameters, along with their asymptotic sampling distributions, and an analogue of R^2 (the coefficient of determination in regression analysis) is defined to measure goodness of fit. The use of the model is illustrated with an analysis of Congressional voting on the 1965 Medicare Bill.

1. Introduction

The assumptions underlying the multivariate linear model require interval level measurement of the dependent variable. Because of this, the linear model is not appropriate for many social science applications. In general, even if the dependent variable of theoretical interest is appropriately conceptualized as interval level, measurement theory in the social sciences is simply not refined enough to generate an interval level operationalization of this variable. The best that can be hoped for, in most cases, is a rather crude ordinal scale which purports to represent this true underlying variable.

The specific concern of this paper is the development of a statistical model, similar to the multivariate linear model, for utilization in situations when the observed dependent variable is of the above sort. The model investigated here is an ordinal extension of the dichotomous probit model. This model, originally developed by biometricians for the study of quantal assay (especially Finney (1947)), has also had limited application in economics and the social sciences. The probit model has been extended for polychotomous use by Aitchison and Silvey (1957) for ordinal dependent variables, and Aitchison and Bennet (1970) for categorical variables, but these extensions are only in the context of a 2 variable model, and the assumptions are somewhat different than those to be used here. A substantial literature has recently developed treating the same problem through the extension of binary logit analysis (Grizzle (1971); McFadden (1974); Theil (1969, 1970)). However, this literature generally assumes strictly categorical rather than ordinal data.

The organization of this paper is threefold. First, we illustrate the theoretical problems associated with the use of regression analysis with ordinal data, and elaborate on the types of assumptions from which an alternative model might proceed. Second, we present the maximum likelihood estimates derived from these assumptions. Finally, using some examples on legislative voting behavior, we compare the substantive conclusions drawn from regression analysis with those drawn from the ordinal probit model. Differences in substantive conclusions can be considerable.

2. The Problems of the Linear Model, and an Alternative Approach

Given a sample if n observations on a dependent variable, Y, and on K independent variables $X_1, \ldots, X_K$, the usual linear model assumes that these data satisfy

(1) $$Y = X\beta + u,$$

where

$$Y = \begin{bmatrix} Y_1 \\ \vdots \\ Y_n \end{bmatrix}, \qquad X = \begin{bmatrix} 1 & X_{11} & \ldots & X_{K1} \\ \vdots & \vdots & & \vdots \\ 1 & X_{1n} & \ldots & X_{Kn} \end{bmatrix}$$

$$\beta = \begin{bmatrix} \beta_0 \\ \vdots \\ \beta_n \end{bmatrix}, \qquad u = \begin{bmatrix} u_1 \\ \vdots \\ u_n \end{bmatrix}.$$

Here, β is a vector of unknown parameters, and u is a random disturbance term satisfying

(2)
$$E(u) = 0$$
$$E(uu') = \sigma^2 I.$$

With these assumptions, it follows that the least squares estimator

(3)
$$\hat{\beta} = (X'X)^{-1} X'Y$$

is a best linear unbiased estimator (BLUE) for β.

Although the above assumptions, (1) and (2) make no specific requirements on the level of measurement of the dependent variable, Y, it is easily seen that difficulties arise if Y is ordinal. These problems can be illustrated for the two variable model. In this case, the above assumptions amount to requiring that the data be distributed about some line, $Y = \beta_0 + \beta_1 X_1$ with an error term of zero mean and constant variance. When dealing with ordinal Y, these assumptions are generally not met. Thus, for example, in Figure 1, we have a trichotomous dependent variable, and the data indicate that there is a definite relationship between the independent and dependent variables. Yet there does not seem to be any possible linear model which could have generated the data and maintained an error term with mean zero and constant variance. The least squares line, L_1, has positive errors for small X_1 and negative errors for large X_1, so it will not do. In fact, if $E(Y|X_1)$ is nonlinear, as drawn, *no* linear model with $E(u) = 0$ would fit the data. To account for these data, one must assume either a nonlinear model or a different error structure. Actually, regardless of the *form* of the relation assumed between X_1 and Y, a different error structure seems indicated, as it will generally be the case that the error term does not have constant variance. It is clear that for these particular data, the variance of the error term is at a minimum at the extreme values of X_1, and at a maximum for moderate values.[1]

Given the above difficulties, an alternative model is clearly appropriate. In this paper, it is assumed that the above problems are due to incomplete data on the dependent variable. A distinction is made between the dependent variable of theoretical interest, Y, and the observed dependent variable, Z. We assume that the variable of theoretical interest is interval and would, if we could measure it, satisfy a linear model. Due to the inadequate measurement techniques, we only observe an ordinal version of Y, namely Z, for which the linear model is *not* satisfied.

---

[1] In the binary case, where Y is a dummy variable taking on the values 0 and 1, if $E(Y|X) = p$, then $Var(Y|X) = p(1-p)$.

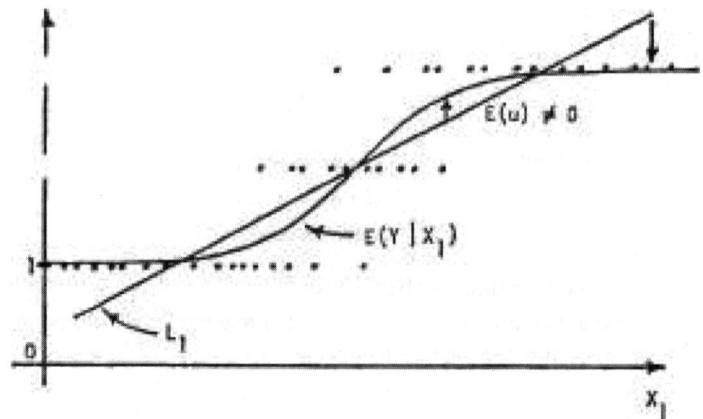

FIGURE 1

More formally, we assume, as above, that the variable of theoretical interest, Y, satisfies:

(4) $$Y = X\beta + u$$

but we make stronger assumptions on the error term, namely we assume that

(5) $$u \sim N\left(0, \sigma^2 I\right).$$

I.e., u is multivariate normal with expectation 0 and variance covariance matrix $\sigma^2 I$. Further, we assume that Z is a categorical variable with M response categories $R_1, \ldots, R_M$, which arises from the unobserved variable, Y, as follows: We assume that there are $M+1$ extended real numbers, $\mu_0, \ldots, \mu_M$ with $\mu_0 = -\infty$, $\mu_M = +\infty$ and with $\mu_0 \leq \mu_1 \leq \cdots \leq \mu_M$, such that

(6) $$Z_j \in R_i \Leftrightarrow \mu_{i-1} < Y_j \leq \mu_i$$

for $1 \leq j \leq M$.

Since Z is ordinal, it can also be represented as a series of dummy variables. In other words, we can define

$$Z_{jk} = \begin{cases} 1 & \text{if } Z_j \in R_k \\ 0 & \text{otherwise} \end{cases}$$

for $1 \leq j \leq n, 1 \leq k \leq M$.

We then write

$$Z = \begin{bmatrix} Z_{11} & \cdots & Z_{1M} \\ \vdots & & \vdots \\ Z_{n1} & \cdots & Z_{nM} \end{bmatrix}$$

Pulling together the assumptions in (4), (5), and (6), we can write directly the probability function of the observed dependent variable, Z, as follows: For any $1 \leq i \leq M$, and $1 \leq j \leq n$, we have, from (4) and (6)

(7)
$$\mu_{i-1} < Y_j < \mu_i \Leftrightarrow \mu_{i-1} < \sum_{i=0}^{K} \beta_i X_{ij} + u_j < \mu_i$$

$$\Leftrightarrow \frac{\mu_{i-1} - \sum_{i=0}^{K} \beta_i X_{ij}}{\sigma} < \frac{u_j}{\sigma} < \frac{\mu_i + \sum_{i=0}^{K} \beta_i X_{ij}}{\sigma}$$

where X_{0j} is understood to be identically one. But, since u is assumed to be multivariate normal, we can write

(8)
$$Pr[Z_{jk} = 1] = Pr[Z_j \in Rk]$$
$$= \Phi\left[\frac{\mu_k - \sum_{i=0}^{K} \beta_i X_{ij}}{\sigma}\right] - \Phi\left[\frac{\mu_{k-1} - \sum_{i=0}^{K} \beta_i X_{ij}}{\sigma}\right]$$

where $\Phi(t)$ represents the cumulative standard normal density function. I.e.,

(9)
$$\Phi(t) = \int_{-\infty}^{t} \frac{1}{\sqrt{2\pi}} e^{-x^2/2} dx.$$

Further, $Pr[A]$ is the probability of the event A.

Finally, the model of (8) is underidentified, since any linear transformation of the underlying scale Y, if applied also to the parameters $\mu_0, \ldots, \mu_M$, would lead to the same model as (8). Thus, to identify the model, we assume, without loss of generality, that $\mu_1 = 0$ and $\sigma = 1$. We get, then, the model which we will investigate:

(10)
$$Pr[Z_{jk} = 1] = \Phi\left[\mu_k - \sum_{i=0}^{K} \beta_i X_{ij}\right] - \Phi\left[\mu_{k-1} - \sum_{i=0}^{K} \beta_i X_{ij}\right].$$

Setting $Q = M + K - 1$, the problem is to find estimators for the Q parameters $\mu_2, \ldots, \mu_{M-1}$ and $\beta_0, \ldots, \beta_K$, which we proceed to do in the following section.

3. The Maximum Likelihood Estimators

Maximum likelihood methods will be used to obtain estimators of the population parameters of the model in (10). To make computations notationally easier, we set

(11) $$Y_{j,k} = \mu_k - \sum_{i=0}^{K} \beta_i X_{i,j}$$

and

$$\Phi_{j,k} = \Phi(Y_{j,k}).$$

The assumptions of (10) can then be written

(12) $$Pr[Z_{jk} = 1] = \Phi_{j,k} - \Phi_{j,k-1}$$

and the likelihood of Z, given fixed values of the parameters

(13) $$\begin{aligned} L &= L(Z|\beta_0, \ldots, \beta_K, \mu_2, \ldots, \mu_{M-1}) \\ &= \prod_{j=1}^{n} \prod_{k=1}^{M} (\Phi_{j,k} - \Phi_{j,k-1})^{Z_{j,k}}. \end{aligned}$$

So, the log likelihood function, L^*, is

(14) $$\begin{aligned} L^* &= \log L \\ &= \sum_{j=1}^{n} \sum_{k=1}^{M} Z_{j,k} \log(\Phi_{j,k} - \Phi_{j,k-1}). \end{aligned}$$

The log likelihood function, L^*, then, is a function of $(\beta_0, \ldots, \beta_K, \mu_2, \ldots, \mu_{M-1})$ and we wish to locate a maximum to L^* subject to the constraint that $\mu_1 \leq \mu_2 \leq \cdots \leq \mu_{M-1}$. This is simply a constrained maximization problem over a convex set, which we proceed to solve.

A Statistical Model for the Analysis of Ordinal Level Dependent Variables   149

Letting $N_{j,k} = \frac{1}{\sqrt{2\pi}} e^{-Y_{j,k}^2/2}$ for $1 \leq k \leq M$ and $1 \leq j \leq n$, and letting $\delta_{i,j}$ be the Kroneker delta, i.e.,

$$\delta_{i,j} = \begin{cases} 1 & \text{if } i = j \\ 0 & \text{if } i \neq j \end{cases}$$

it follows that

(15)
$$\frac{\partial}{\partial \beta_u} \Phi_{j,k} = N_{j,k} \left[\frac{\partial}{\partial \beta_M} Y_{j,k} \right] = -N_{j,k} X_{u,j} \text{ for } 0 \leq u \leq K$$
$$\frac{\partial}{\partial \mu_u} \Phi_{j,k} = N_{j,k} \left[\frac{\partial}{\partial \mu_M} Y_{j,k} \right] = -N_{j,k} \delta_{u,k} \text{ for } 2 \leq u \leq M-1$$

and

(16)
$$\frac{\partial}{\partial \beta_u} N_{j,k} = Y_{j,k} N_{j,k} X_{u,j} \text{ for } 0 \leq u \leq K$$
$$\frac{\partial}{\partial \mu_u} N_{j,k} = -Y_{j,k} N_{j,k} \delta_{u,k} \text{ for } 2 \leq u \leq M-1.$$

Equations (15) and (16) can be used to calculate the Q partial derivatives of (14) with respect to the unknown parameters, as well as the $Q \times Q$ matrix of second partials. We get, for the first partial derivatives:

(17)
$$\frac{\partial L^*}{\partial \beta_u} = \sum_{j=1}^{n} \sum_{k=1}^{M} Z_{j,k} \left[\frac{N_{j,k-1} - N_{j,k}}{\Phi_{j,k} - \Phi_{j,k-1}} \right] X_{u,j}$$

for $0 \leq u \leq K$, and

$$\frac{\partial L^*}{\partial \mu_u} = \sum_{j=1}^{n} \sum_{k=1}^{M} Z_{j,k} \left[\frac{N_{j,k} \delta_{k,u} - N_{j,k-1} \delta_{k-1,u}}{\Phi_{j,k} - \Phi_{j,k-1}} \right]$$

for $2 \leq u \leq M-1$.

Further, the second partials are:

(18)
$$\frac{\partial^2 L^*}{\partial \beta_u \beta_v} = \sum_{j=1}^{n}\sum_{k=1}^{M} Z_{j,k} \left[\frac{(\Phi_{j,k} - \Phi_{j,k-1})(N_{j,k-1}Y_{j,k-1} - N_{j,k}Y_{j,k})}{(\Phi_{j,k} - \Phi_{j,k-1})^2} \right.$$
$$\left. - \frac{(N_{j,k-1} - N_{j,k})^2}{(\Phi_{j,k} - \Phi_{j,k-1})^2} \right] X_{u,j} X_{v,j}$$

$$\frac{\partial^2 L^*}{\partial \beta_u \mu_v} = \frac{\partial^2 L^*}{\partial \mu_v \beta_u}$$
$$= \sum_{j=1}^{n}\sum_{k=1}^{M} Z_{j,k}$$
$$\left[\frac{(\Phi_{j,k} - \Phi_{j,k-1})(N_{j,k}Y_{j,k}\delta_{k,v} - N_{j,k-1}Y_{j,k-1}\delta_{k-1,v})}{(\Phi_{j,k} - \Phi_{j,k-1})^2} \right.$$
$$\left. - \frac{(N_{j,k-1} - N_{j,k})(N_{j,k}\delta_{k,v} - N_{j,k-1}\delta_{k-1,v})}{(\Phi_{j,k} - \Phi_{j,k-1})^*} \right] X_{u,j}$$

$$\frac{\partial^2 L^*}{\partial \mu_u \mu_v} = \sum_{j=1}^{n}\sum_{k=1}^{M} Z_{j,k}$$
$$\left[\frac{(\Phi_{j,k} - \Phi_{j,k-1})(N_{j,k-1}Y_{j,k-1}\delta_{u,k-1}\delta_{v,k-1} - N_{j,k}Y_{j,k-1}\delta_{u,k}\delta_{v,k})}{(\Phi_{j,k} - \Phi_{j,k-1})^2} \right.$$
$$\left. - \frac{(N_{j,k}\delta_{u,k} - N_{j,k-1}\delta_{u,k-1})(N_{j,k}\delta_{v,k} - N_{j,k-1}\delta_{v,k-1})}{(\Phi_{j,k} - \Phi_{j,k-1})^2} \right]$$

To obtain the *MLE*, then, the Q equations in (17) are set to zero and solved for the Q unknowns.[2] In order to insure that the solution is a maximum, the matrix of second partials, whose entries are given by (18), evaluated at the solution point should be negative definite. Unfortunately, the equations generated by (17) are

---

[2] If the maximum lies on the boundary of the constraint set, then Lagrangian multipliers must be introduced and these equations solved. In practice, as long as all categories of the dependent variable have observations in them, the maxima seem to naturally occur in the interior of the constraint set, so we have ignored the constraint. There do appear to be local maxima outside of the constraint set, however. So one must be careful to keep the iterative procedure from crossing into this region. We are grateful to Dr. Fritz Bedall for bringing to our attention some examples illustrating this possibility.

not linear in the unknowns, so they cannot be solved by ordinary methods for simultaneous linear equations. Rather, an iterative method of solution, the Newton-Raphson method for Q dimensions is used.[3] One of the authors has written a computer program, hereinafter referred to as NPROBIT, which uses the Newton-Raphson algorithm to iterate towards a root of the above equations.[4] Results from the use of this program are presented in the final section of this paper.

There are several difficulties with the above procedure. First, there is no guarantee of convergence of the iterative procedure. In practice, this has not been a problem, the procedure has always converged fairly rapidly, with the convergence taking between four and ten iterations, depending on the number of parameters to be estimated.

A more important problem, which is common to such nonlinear problems, is that there is no guarantee that the process converges to a global, as opposed to a relative, maximum, since there may be multiple roots to the equations generated by (17). A proof that the matrix of second partials is everywhere negative definite, or a proof that L^* is a quasi-concave function would eliminate the possibility of multiple roots. But, in the absence of such proofs, the possibility of convergence to a relative maximum cannot be excluded.

3.1. Testing Hypotheses

One of the advantages of using maximum likelihood estimates is the nice statistical properties which the *MLE* has. Under fairly general conditions the estimates are consistent and asymptotically efficient, and their asymptotic sampling distribution is known.[5] Also, hypotheses can be tested either by the use of this sampling distribution or by the use of the likelihood ratio.

If V is the $Q \times Q$ matrix of second partials of the log likelihood function evaluated at the *MLE* $\hat{\theta}$, and if V^{-1} is the inverse of this matrix, then the *MLE*, $\hat{\theta}$, has an asymptotic distribution which is multivariate normal with means equal to the true values of the parameters, and variance-covariance matrix estimated by $-V^{-1}$. Thus, in large samples $\hat{\beta}_i$ will be normal with mean β_i and standard error

---

[3] See, e.g., Draper and Smith (1966) or Hildebrand (1974) for a description of the Newton-Raphson method.

[4] Copies of this program, along with documentation and test data, can be obtained from Richard McKelvey, Political Science Department, University of Rochester, Rochester, N.Y. 14627. For a brief description of the program, see McKelvey and Zavoina (1971).

[5] See, e.g., Goldberger (1964) or Wilks (1962).

$$\text{(19)} \qquad Std(\beta_i) = \sqrt{-[V^{-1}]_{i,i}}$$

where $-V_{i,j}^{-1}$ is the i,j^{th} entry of the variance covariance matrix. For any $\beta_{i,0}$ the statistic

$$\text{(20)} \qquad z = \frac{\hat{\beta}_i - \beta_{i,0}}{\sqrt{-[V^{-1}]_{i,i}}}$$

(which is computed by NPROBIT for $\beta_{i,0} = 0$) has a standard normal distribution, and can be used to test the hypothesis $H_0 : \beta_i = \beta_{i,0}$. Similar tests apply to the μ's.

To test the significance of groups of coefficients, one can apply the likelihood ratio. If $L^*\left(\hat{\theta}\right)$ is the log of the likelihood function evaluated at the point $\hat{\theta}$, where $\hat{\theta}$ is the *MLE* $\hat{\theta} = \left(\hat{\beta}_0, \ldots, \hat{\beta}_K, \hat{\mu}_2, \ldots, \hat{\mu}_{M-1}\right)$, and if $L^*\left(\hat{\theta}'\right)$ is the log of the likelihood function evaluated at the point $\hat{\theta}'$, where $\hat{\theta}'$ is the *MLE* where r of the Q components are constrained to be fixed constants, then the likelihood ratio, λ is defined to be

$$\text{(21)} \qquad \lambda = \frac{L\left(\hat{\theta}'\right)}{L\left(\hat{\theta}\right)}.$$

For large n, it is well known that

$$\text{(22)} \qquad \lambda^* = -2\log\lambda = -2\left(L^*\left(\hat{\theta}'\right) - L^*\left(\hat{\theta}\right)\right)$$

has a χ^2 distribution with r degrees of freedom. See Wilks (1962).

To test the overall significance of the independent variables, one would let $\hat{\theta}'$ be the *MLE* when $\beta_1, \ldots, \beta_K$ are constrained to be 0. If r_k denotes the total number of observations with $Z \in R_k$, i.e., if $r_k = \sum_{j=1}^{n} Z_{j,k}$, then one would find $\hat{\theta}'$ to be the point such that

$$\text{(23)} \qquad \Phi(\mu_k - \beta_0) - \Phi(\mu_{k-1} - \beta_0) = \frac{r_k}{n}$$

for $1 \leq k \leq M$ and the probability of the sample at this point, from (13) and (15) is

$$(24) \qquad L = \prod_{k=1}^{M} \left(\frac{r_k}{n}\right)^{r_k}$$

so

$$(25) \qquad L^*\left(\hat{\theta}'\right) = \sum_{k=1}^{M} r_k \log r_k - n \log n.$$

$\hat{\theta}$ is the *MLE* when all the variables are in the equation, so $L^*\left(\hat{\theta}\right)$ is simply the log likelihood function evaluated at this point. Hence the likelihood ratio test for the overall significance of the independent variables becomes

$$(26) \qquad \lambda^* = -2\left(\sum_{k=1}^{M} r_k \log r_k - n \log n - L^*\left(\hat{\theta}\right)\right),$$

and this has a χ^2 distribution with K degrees of freedom.

3.2. Goodness of Fit

There are several statistics which can be used to measure the overall fit of the model. The most useful of these is the estimated R^2, which gives an estimate of the R^2 of the underlying regression model. This is equivalent to the R^2, or coefficient of determination, in regression analysis and has a similar interpretation, namely, it measures the portion of the original variance of the dependent variable explained by the probit analysis.

Although there is no way of knowing the variance of the dependent variable on its underlying interval scale, it can be estimated as follows: the model assumes that the dependent variable on its underlying interval scale satisfies a regression model. Moreover, the dependent variable is normalized so that the variance around the regression line, σ^2, is unity. If $\hat{\beta} = \left(\hat{\beta}_0, \ldots, \hat{\beta}_K\right)$ is the *MLE* for β, we define $\hat{Y}_0 = \sum_{i=1}^{n} \hat{\beta}_i X_{ij}$, and $e_j = \left(Y_j - \hat{Y}_j\right)$. Then, since

$$(27) \qquad \text{plim} \frac{\sum_{i=1}^{n} e_i^2}{n} = \sigma^2$$

we can get an estimate of the residual sum of squares, $\hat{S}_R^2$, to be

(28)
$$\hat{S}_R^2 = n\sigma^2 = n.$$

Next, the explained sum of squares $\hat{S}_R^2$ can be computed using ordinary procedures to be

(29)
$$S_E^2 = \sum_{i=1}^n \hat{y}_i^2 = \sum_{i=1}^n \left(\hat{Y}_i - \hat{\bar{Y}}\right)^2,$$

where $\hat{\bar{Y}} = \sum_{i=1}^n \hat{Y}_i/n$.

Thus, we can estimate the total sum of squares by summing (28) and (29) to obtain

(30)
$$\hat{S}_T^2 = S_E^2 + \hat{S}_R^2$$
$$= \sum_{i=1}^n \hat{y}_i^2 + n.$$

It follows that R^2 can be computed, in the usual manner, to be

(31)
$$\hat{R}^2 = \frac{S_E^2}{\hat{S}_T^2} = \frac{\sum_{i=1}^n \hat{y}_i^2}{[\sum_{i=1}^n \hat{y}_i^2] + n}.$$

The computer program we have written calculates $\hat{R}^2$, and as mentioned above, this statistic can be interpreted much the same as the corresponding R^2 for regression analysis. $\hat{R}^2$ represents the portion of the variance explained by the model if we could have measured the dependent variable on its underlying interval level scale. Before proceeding, however, we note some deficiencies in $\hat{R}^2$ which are not problems in the corresponding R^2 for regression.

In probit analysis, unlike in regression analysis, we cannot observe either the residuals about the regression plane or, indeed, even the deviations of the dependent variable, Y, about its mean. Thus, both the sum of squared residuals in (28) and the total sum of squares in (30) are estimates rather than actual values of these quantities. Consequently $\hat{R}^2$ is also an estimate of the true R^2, and in order to make inferences about the true R^2, we should know the distribution of $\hat{R}^2$, which we do not presently know. In addition, the partitioning of the sum of squares in (30) is not entirely valid, as this depends on using least squares estimators of the coefficients. For large samples, the probit estimates of the coefficients will approach the least squares estimates of the coefficients which we would get if we could obtain the dependent variable on its underlying interval scale (since both are consistent estimators). So the latter problem is minimized as the sample size gets large. Nevertheless, even in large samples, the $\hat{R}^2$ should be used with some caution until its sampling distribution is known.

Other summary statistics can be constructed by using the maximum likelihood predictions of the probit equation. Thus, for any combination of the independent variables, the probit equation allows us to predict the probability that the dependent variable is in each of the M categories. In particular, we have, letting $(X_{1,j}, \ldots, X_{K,j})$ be a particular observation, and letting $\hat{P}_{j,k}$ indicate the predicted probability that the dependent variable, Z_j, is in the kth category (i.e., that $Z_j \in R_k$),

$$(32) \qquad \hat{P}_{j,k} = \Phi\left[\hat{\mu}_k - \sum_{i=0}^{K} \hat{\beta}_i X_{i,j}\right] - \Phi\left[\hat{\mu}_{k-1} - \sum_{i=0}^{K} \hat{\beta}_i X_{i,j}\right]$$

Using $\hat{Z}_j$ to represent the maximum likelihood prediction of Z_j at the jth observation, we get

$$(33) \qquad \hat{Z}_j = k_j$$

where k_j is that value $1 \leq k_j \leq M$ which maximizes $P_{k_j,j}$. Both Z_j and $\hat{Z}_j$ are ordinal variables, and hence any of a number of ordinal measures of strength of association can be used to determine the strength of association between predicted and actual values of the dependent variables. NPROBIT displays both Z_j and $\hat{Z}_j$ (as well as each $\hat{P}_{k,j}$) for each observation and calculates the Spearman rank order correlation between the two.

4. Comparison of Substantive Conclusions Based on Regression Analysis and Ordinal Probit Analysis

Despite the problems discussed in Section 2, it is relatively common to see regression analyses of ordinal dependent variables. In order to illustrate some substantively interesting differences resulting from applications of the two statistical models, we have chosen to analyze the voting behavior of Congressmen in the 89th Congress on the passage of the 1965 Medicare bill.

The 1965 Medicare bill was the culmination of a twenty year campaign, which was opposed strongly by the American Medical Association, to enact some form of federal legislation to provide health insurance for the aged.[6] The bill, as reported out of the Ways and Means Committee, provided for a compulsory health

---

[6]For a more detailed discussion of the circumstances surrounding the passage of this bill, see the *Congressional Quarterly Almanac* (1965: 236 ff.).

insurance program covering hospital costs to be financed out of a payroll tax, together with an additional voluntary program covering doctor bills to be financed out of contributions of the participants and general revenues. Prior to passage of the House version of this bill, a motion by Rep. John Byrnes (R-Wis) to recommit the bill to the Ways and Means Committee was rejected. This motion would have instructed the committee to substitute a weaker version of the bill, making the entire program voluntary, and to be financed by participants. These two roll calls, first on recommittal and then passage of the Medicare bill, provide the only roll call information available on the positions of the representatives on Medicare. The bill was reported out of committee on a closed rule, allowing no amendments, and the later vote on the conference report was virtually identical to the vote on the passage of the House version. We therefore consider the voting patterns on these two roll calls as an indicator of the Congressman's position on Medicare.

The vote for recommittal (CQ34) was a move to either kill or weaken the Medicare bill, and can also be interpreted as a test vote on the bill. Thus, a vote against recommittal is a vote for Medicare. The second roll call (CQ35) on passage of the bill was straightforward, and a vote for passage was a vote for Medicare. Treating "paired for" and "paired against" as votes for and against, and abstentions as missing data, the above two roll calls Guttman scale very well with a coefficient of reproducibility of .986 and coefficient of scalability of .961. Voting patterns were thus three in number, suggesting an underlying scale of support-opposition to Medicare. Congressmen who voted for recommital and against passage were more opposed to Medicare than Congressmen who voted for recommittal and for passage, who were in turn more opposed than those who voted against recommittal and for passage.

A number of independent variables might be included in models designed to explain a legislator's position on Medicare. Party and region, of course, might be relevant. Also, since the avowed purpose of this legislation was to provide medical insurance for the aged, variables reflecting the potential usefulness or support for such programs in the Congressman's district might be relevant. Variables measuring the number of elderly people in the district and the economic problems (as measured by the rate of unemployment) of the district have therefore been included. Finally, a variable reflecting the degree of urbanization has also been included. Thus, the variables and their operationalization are as follows.[7]

---

[7]Data for the dependent variable are from the *Congressional Quarterly Almanac* (1965). Data for the independent variables are from the *Congressional District Data Book, Districts of the 88th Congress*, and from supplements indicating changes for the 89th Congress.

Variable	Measurement
Vote	Scale Score on Medicare: 0 if against (i.e., Y on CQ34, N on CQ35) 1 if weakly for (i.e., Y on CQ34, Y on CQ35) 2 if strongly for (i.e., N on CQ34, Y on CQ35)

Variable	Measurement
Party	0 if Democrat 1 if Republican
Region	0 if Non-South 1 if South
Employment	Percent civilian unemployed in district
Old	Percent over 65
Population	Population density in thousands per square mile.

We consider four different models which hypothesize that vote (or the probability of voting a particular way in the case of probit analysis) is a linear function of various combinations of the above independent variables. In Model 1, vote is a function only of the main party groupings (Party and Region). In Model 2, vote is a function also of the constituency support variables (Old and Employment), and in Models 3 and 4, we introduce the effect of urbanization (Population) into Models 1 and 2 respectively.

Table 1 represents the results of estimating the four different models, first with regression analysis and then with probit analysis. One cannot directly compare the β coefficients in the two models because they represent different things in each model. In the regression model, the β represents the amount of change in the *observed* value of the dependent variable which is brought about by a unit change in the independent variable. Since the coding of the (ordinal level) dependent variable is arbitrary, this value will depend on the particular coding which is chosen. In the probit analysis, on the other hand, β represents the amount of change in the dependent variable on its (hypothesized) *underlying* scale which is brought about by a unit change in the independent variable. (In terms of being a higher response category brought about by a unit change in the independent variable.) Because of the ordinal level assumptions of the n-chotomous probit model, this value is independent of the original coding of the dependent variable, but it is, of course, dependent on the units of the estimated underlying scale for the dependent variable. Due to the particular normalization procedure used in the n-chotomous probit analysis (i.e., setting the standard error around the hypothesized regression line to one) the units on the underlying scale may bear no relation to those of the (arbitrary) coding of the dependent variable in the corresponding regression analysis. Consequently, it follows that the β's in the two analyses are not directly comparable.

In order to overcome the above problem and to make comparisons between the two types of analysis easier, we have computed the standardized β (labelled β^* in the Table) for the probit analysis in much the same way as this is calculated for the regression analysis. Thus, for a particular coefficient β_i of the probit equation, if σ_i is the standard deviation of X_i and σ_y is the standard deviation of Y on its underlying scale, then we define

$$\beta_i^* = \beta_i \frac{\sigma_i}{\sigma_y}.$$

The standardized coefficient can be interpreted in much the same way as it is in regression analysis. It is equivalent to normalizing all variables (including the dependent variable on its underlying scale), and then performing the probit analysis on these normalized data. The resulting coefficient β^* represents the number of standard deviations of change in the (hypothetical) dependent variable brought about by a change of one standard deviation in the independent variable. When all independent variables are orthogonal, $(\beta_i^*)^2$ represents the proportion of the variance explained by variable i. The standardized coefficient thus allows us to compare the strength of different variables in the same equation. Also since it is comparable in interpretation to the corresponding standardized coefficient for the regression, it allows more meaningful comparisons between the results of the two models.

The results of Table 1 illustrate several points. The first thing to note is the general tendency, which is borne out in these tables, of the regression analysis to give lower estimates of fit (i.e., R^2) than does the probit analysis. This makes sense in light of our development above of the n-chotomous model. It is obvious, for example, that a perfect fit to the probit model would translate, under the categorization of the dependent variable, into a poor fit to the regression model. Such a possibility is illustrated in Figure 2. Even when the original fit to the probit model is not perfect, one would expect the categorization to introduce the same sort of tendency, but we would expect the differences to become more extreme the stronger the true relation, with regression always underestimating the fit. We again stress, however, that one should avoid overinterpreting the $\hat{R}^2$ of the n-chotomous probit analysis until its sampling distribution is known. Thus, although it is clear that the R^2 of the regression is generally an underestimate of the fit of a model

TABLE 1. Comparison of Regression and Probit Analysis in Four Models Explaining Congressional Voting Behavior on 1965 Medicare Bill ($N = 427$)

		Regression Analysis				Probit Analysis			
	Variables	$\hat{\beta}_i$	$\hat{\beta}^i$	t	R^2 (F)	$\hat{\beta}_i$	$\hat{\beta}^*_i$	z	$\hat{R}^2$ (λ^*)
Model 1	Party	−1.214	−.680	19.22	.50	−2.490	−.725	13.65	.62
	Region	−.792	−.433	12.24	(214.4)	−1.889	−.540	10.52	(287)
Model 2	Party	−1.161	−.651	18.29	.52	−2.460	−.691	13.2	.66
	Region	−.769	−.421	11.79	(113.4)	−1.914	−.526	10.3	(306.5)
	Old	.031	.009	.26		.050	.007	.2	
	Employment	.058	.136	3.94		.180	.213	4.2	
Model 3	Party	−1.186	−.664	18.40	.52	−2.394	−.454	12.6	.84
	Region	−.760	−.415	11.42	(145.2)	−1.706	−.316	9.0	(309.7)
	Population	.005	.070	1.97		.150	.656	3.1	
Model 4	Party	−1.142	−.640	17.67	.52	−2.397	−.382	12.3	.88
	Region	−.747	−.409	11.15	(91.5)	−1.730	−.269	8.9	(332.5)
	Old	.013	.003	.11		−.001	−.000	.0	
	Employment	.055	.131	3.75		.204	.136	4.6	
	Population	.004	.055	1.52		.192	.703	3.3	

The F statistic has an F distribution with K and $n - (K + 1)$ d.f. Here K is the number of independent variables. All the models above are significant at the .01 level.
The λ^* statistic is χ^2 with K d.f. Again, all models are significant at the .01 level.

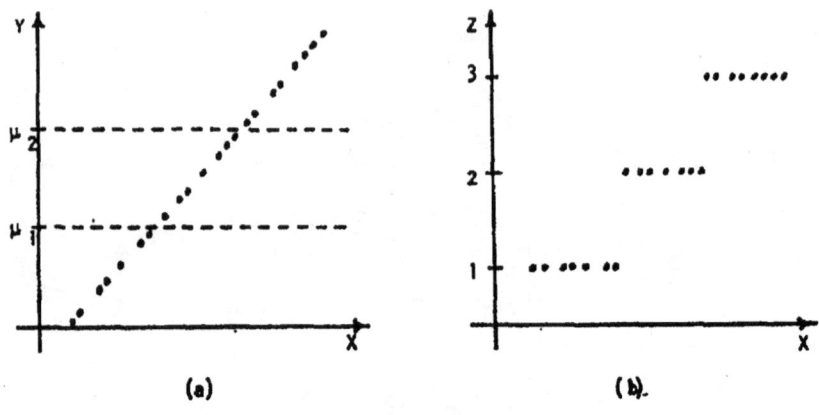

FIGURE 2

which is generated by the n-chotomous probit assumptions, it is not clear how much better $\hat{R}^2$ is. For example, it is possible that $\hat{R}^2$ may in general overestimate the true R^2 of the underlying model. More work needs to be done on the properties of $\hat{R}^2$.

The second thing to note in Table 1 is the strange behavior of the variable "Population." Thus, before the introduction of this variable (i.e., in Models 1 and 2), we can see that although there are slight differences, the basic conclusions of the probit and regression runs are similar. The relative strengths of the independent variables (as measured by the β_i^*'s) are similar, and the results of the significance tests on the coefficients are similar. However, with the introduction of the variable "Population" into the models (in Models 3 and 4), we see that now the probit and regression models differ more significantly in their conclusions. The most striking difference can be found in a comparison of the standardized coefficients (the β_i^*'s). Here, the regression analysis finds that the original party grouping variables retain their importance, and population explains a very small portion of the variance. In contrast, the n-chotomous probit analysis finds that the variable "Population" is important, explaining a larger portion of the variance than either of the original party grouping variables. Comparing the results of the significance tests, probit would retain "Population" as significant at the .05 level, while the regression analysis would not.

The characteristics of the variable "Population" which cause the different conclusions to be drawn by the two models can be illustrated by a look at the

A Statistical Model for the Analysis of Ordinal Level Dependent Variables 161

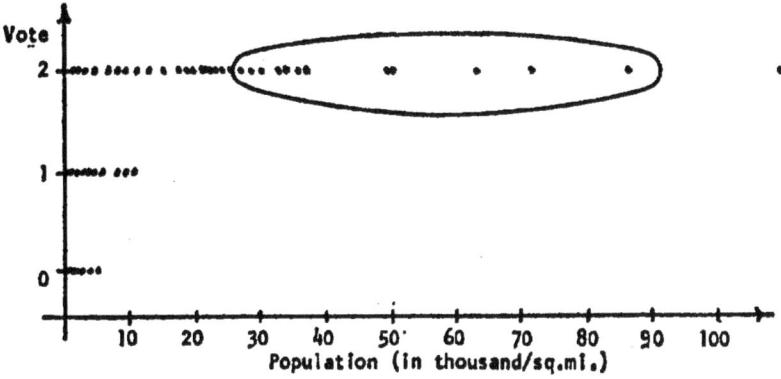

FIGURE 3

univariate relation between Population and Vote. Thus, in Figure 3, we can see that this variable has the property that *all* Congressmen from *very* densely populated areas voted for Medicare. They seem all to be very clearly for Medicare, and end up in category 2, most likely, for lack of a stronger category. But while probit analysis interprets additional data in the circled region as additional evidence for a stronger relation (as indeed it seems it should be interpreted), regression interprets such data as additional evidence for a *weaker* relation. We thus see in this example an illustration of the problems discussed from a theoretical point of view in the first two sections. In other words, the correlation between error and regressor which is introduced when using regression analysis to estimate the underlying relation causes a bias which is dependent on the distribution of the independent variable. This bias has the effect of causing the regression analysis at times to interpret data which are indicative of a strong relation as demonstrating, instead, a weak relation.

Finally, before concluding, we illustrate the use of n-chotomous probit analysis for scaling of the dependent variable and for predicting the probability of being in each response category. In Table 1, we were interested primarily in a comparison of probit to regression analysis, so we have only reported the estimated β's. In addition, of course, the n-chotomous probit analysis estimates the cutting points of the scale, or the μ_k's as they have been labeled in the formal development.

We illustrate the above for Model 1. Thus, in Table 2, we give the complete estimation of Model 1. It follows that 0 and .96 are the estimated positions of the two stimuli (i.e., CQ35 and CQ34 respectively) on the underlying scale. (Note

TABLE 2

Parameter	Represents Effect Of	MLE	Standard Error	z
β_0	Constant	2.598	.175	14.82
β_1	Party	−2.490	.182	13.65
β_2	Region	−1.899	.181	10.51
μ_1	CQ35	0.0	—	—
μ_2	CQ34	.948	.088	10.71

$L^* = -285.67.$
$\lambda^* = 286.83 \left(\chi^2 \text{ with 2 df.}\right).$

that since there are only two stimuli, the normalization procedure automatically sets one of these to 0.) It follows that respondents falling below a particular stimulus respond negatively (i.e., against Medicare) to that stimulus while respondents falling above the stimulus respond positively to it. Thus, respondents falling below $\mu_1 = 0$ fall in response category 0, and respond negatively to both stimuli. Thus, they vote for recommittal and against passage. Those respondents falling between $\mu_1 = 0$ and $\mu_2 = .96$ fall in response category 1 and respond positively to CQ35 and negatively to CQ34. Thus, they vote for recommittal and for passage. Finally, those above $\mu_2 = .96$ respond positively to both stimuli. They vote against recommittal and for passage.

Further, by substituting into the probit equation, we can find the expectation of any respondent on this underlying continuum and the estimated probability of his falling in any of the response categories. Thus, for the four main party and regional groupings, we have:

Grouping	X_1 (Party)	X_2 (Region)	$\sum \beta_i X_i$ (Expected Score)
1: Northern Democrats	0	0	2.598
2: Southern Democrats	0	1	.699
3: Northern Republicans	1	0	.108
4: Southern Republicans	1	1	−1.791

It follows that if the estimated model is the true model, one can compute the theoretical probabilities of being in each category using equation (13), i.e., by assuming that respondents are distributed around their expected score with unit variance. Thus, in Figure 4, and Table 3, we have illustrated this procedure, and have compared the predicted to the observed frequencies.

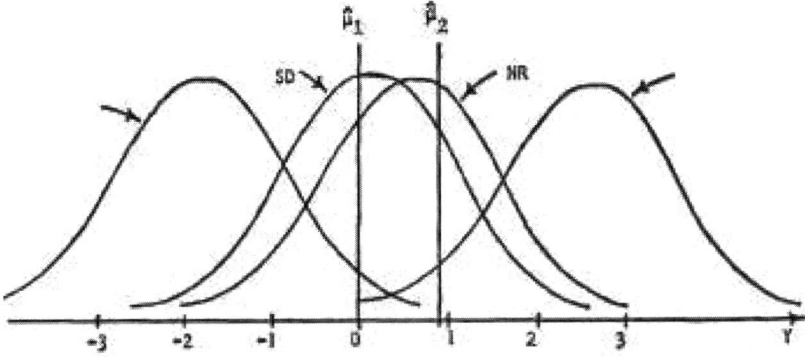

FIGURE 4

TABLE 3

Scale	Actual Frequencies				Predicted Frequencies			
Score	ND	SD	NR	SR	ND	SD	NR	SR
0	(1) .6	(35) 31.8	(57) 46.3	(16) 76.2	.5	24.3	46.1	96.4
1	(3) 1.7	(31) 28.2	(50) 40.7	(5) 23.8	4.5	35.5	34.1	3.1
2	(169) 97.7	(44) 40.0	(16) 13.0	(0) 0.0	95.1	40.2	19.8	0.3
Totals	(173) 100%	(110) 100%	(123) 100%	(21) 100%	100%	100%	100%	100%

The entries represent percentages of column totals. Figures in parentheses are the total in the cell. Columns may not add to 100 percent due to rounding error.

5. Conclusion

We have argued above that regression analysis is an inappropriate technique to apply to ordinal level dependent variables. Regression is inadequate not because of the failure to model the true relation. Rather, we assume that the true relation *is* described by a linear model, and that the failure of the regression model to describe the *observed* data is due to the inherent loss of information that is introduced when the continuous dependent variable is measured by gross techniques which lump together and identify various portions of the scale. The net effect is that if this is in fact the process by which the data have been generated, there is a correlation between error and regressor when regression is applied to the *observed* data. Consequently, a bias is introduced into the estimate of β which is dependent on the distribution of the independent variable. This bias may, in some cases, have the undesirable effect of causing regression analysis to severely underestimate the relative impact of certain variables.

References

Aitchison, J. and J. Bennet (1970) Polychotomous Quantal Response by Maximum Indicant. *Biometrica* 57, 253–262.

Aitchison, J. and S. Silvey (1957) The Generalization of Probit Analysis to the Case of Multiple Responses. *Biometrica* 44, 131–140.

Draper, N. R and H. Smith (1966) *Applied Regression Analysis*. New York: Wiley & Sons, Inc.

Finney, D. J. (1947) *Probit Analysis*. Cambridge: Cambridge University Press.

Goldberger, A. S. (1964) *Econometric Theory*. New York: Wiley & Sons, Inc.

Grizzle, J. (1971) Multivariate Logit Analysis. *Biometrica* 27, 1057–1062.

Hildebrand, F. B. (1974) *Introduction to Numerical Analysis*. 2nd edition. New York: McGraw Hill.

McFadden, D. (1974) Analysis of Qualitative Choice Behavior, in *Frontiers of Econometrics*, P. Zaremba, ed. New York: Academic Press.

McKelvey, R. and W. Zavoina. (1977) An IBM Fortran IV Program to Perform N-Chotomous Multivariate Probit Analysis. *Behavioral Science* 16, 186–187.

Theil, H. (1969) A Multinominal Extension of the Linear Logit Model. *International Economic Review* 10, 251–259.

Theil, H. (1970) On the Estimation of Relationship Involving Qualitative Variables. *American Journal of Sociology* 76, 103–154.

Wilks, S. S. (1962) *Mathematical Statistics*. New York: John Wiley and Sons.

CHAPTER 9

The Competitive Solution Revisited

PETER C. ORDESHOOK

1. Genesis

One issue dominated research in formal political theory throughout the 1970's — the search for empirically viable conditions under which some configuration of individual preferences might give rise, under majority rule, to a Condorcet winner or a Core. Although not strictly equivalent, the search for conditions under which one might exist became a search for the other (McKelvey 1986; Chapter 12 of this book). And while researchers might have hoped that some twist on Arrow's (1951) axioms would blunt the apparent implications of his proof, Black's (1958) seminal treatise, Plott's (1967) theorem, Davis and Hinich's (1966) analysis of Euclidean preferences, and Sloss's (1973) generalizations seemed to erect or reveal impenetrable obstacles. Moreover, Schwartz's (1977) demonstration that vote trading would arise in a fully informed and rational legislature only if there was no Condorcet winner seemed to confirm the view that the existence of such winners was required to predict determinate coalitional outcomes. Thus, researchers were left with the apparent conclusion that the only way to establish non-probabilistic predictions was to impose context-specific institutional constraints on choice (e.g., Shepsle 1979; Riker 1982). Indeed, McKelvey's (1976b, 1979; Chapters 4 and 5 of this book respectively) own research seemed to confirm the worst: Despite his admonitions to the contrary, the discipline labeled his result on global intransitivity a "chaos theorem" and drew from it the implication that even probabilistic predictions were problematical.

Of course, there were those who sought to circumvent these apparent obstacles by developing ideas such as the uncovered, minmax, and undominated sets so as to identify constraints on the domain of likely outcomes under alternative majoritarian procedures (Miller 1980). And even a superficial reading of McKelvey's research confirms that he never viewed his result as implying chaos. As he explicitly states with reference to the inference that only the constraints of institutional structure can provide us with the requisite predictability, "one is left with the impression that, in the absence of core alternatives, little can be said about social choice that is institution-independent ... [but] such a conclusion is not warranted" (McKelvey 1986; Chapter 12 of this book, page 244). To understand the limited interpretation he gave to his "chaos" result, one can point to the attempt to establish limits on candidate policies in multidimensional issue spaces (McKelvey and Ordeshook 1982) or his own explorations and extensions of the uncovered set (1986). However, perhaps the most critical component of this denial of the implications others drew from components of his research was our joint effort at developing a solution hypothesis for cooperative games, the Competitive Solution.

From its inception, game theory accepted the fact that cooperative games in characteristic function form possess non-empty cores — undominated imputations — under only special conditions pertaining to the additivity of coalition values. Thus, it should have come as little surprise that majority rule games had empty cores and, given the near equivalence of things, would be largely devoid of Condorcet winners except under the knife-edged conditions described by Plott (1967) and Davis and Hinich (1966). However, the implication we drew from this was not that chaos must prevail, but that one needs to look to the solution hypotheses game theorists devised to treat games generally — notably the V-set or any of the various Bargaining Sets. Focusing on the most analytically tractable class of games — "simple games," whereby coalitions are winning (because they can secure any outcome), losing (because they cannot secure anything), or blocking (because they can secure the status quo) — our initial objective was to identify these solutions when preferences had an Euclidean topology. But here we encountered a somewhat unsettling surprise with respect to an important refinement of the V-set. Briefly, to preclude degenerate V-sets (sets that satisfied the formal definition of a V solution but which nevertheless offered seemingly unreasonable predictions), game theory offered the notion of a *main simple V-set* derived from the constraint that each minimum winning coalition be uniquely paired with an outcome. This idea not only yielded reasonable predictions when utility was transferable, but it more fully established a correspondence between the V-set and Aumann and Maschler's (1964: see also Peleg 1963) Bargaining Set notions; specifically, as Wilson (1971) shows, there is a 1-to-1 correspondence between a main simple V-set and the Strong Bargaining Set (a bargaining set such that every counter to an objection is itself an element of the bargaining set). The surprise, however, was that if one makes five random dots on a sheet of paper and interprets those dots

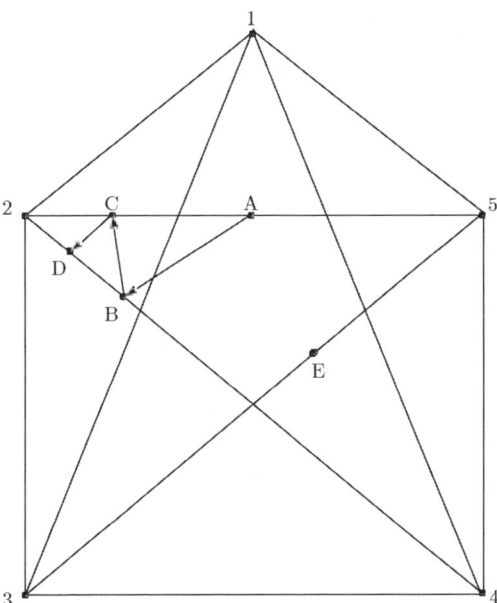

FIGURE 1. Initial bargaining with five subjects

as the ideal points of five voters or legislators with Euclidean preferences, then one is virtually guaranteed to have a counterexample to the universal existence of a main simple V-set and, thus, a counterexample to the existence of the Strong Bargaining Set.

Absent a prediction about outcomes for simple spatial bargaining games, we turned to the experimental laboratory — not with the idea of testing any hypothesis (we had none), but rather to "see what people did." Allowing our experimental subjects to bargain freely over points on a two dimensional grid, perhaps the most informative arrangement of ideal points was the one portrayed in Figure 1.

The rules of bargaining were simple: No discussion of money was allowed, a subject's monetary payoff was a function of the point finally agreed to or imposed by a majority regardless of whether the subject was a party to that agreement, and ideal points were common knowledge in addition to the fact that each subject's payoff decreased with distance from his or her ideal point. Typically, when presented with this configuration and bargaining format, subjects 1, 2, and 5 immediately presumed they were advantaged and saw a point such as A as a natural agreement. However, subjects 3 and 4, while initially resigned to an unprofitable fate, soon recognized the possibility of disrupting the $\{1, 2, 5\}$ coalition with a proposal such as B, which gives subject 2 a bit more than A. Subjects 1 and 5, seeking to shore up their initial coalition, would quickly counter with, say, C, which would lead 3 and 4 to counter now with D, and so on. However, at some point in this process of bidding for 2's loyalty (but not always before someone proposed 2's ideal point), subjects 3, 4, and 5 would realize that a point like E served their interests better than any agreement with 2. Once E entered the discussion, 2 would seek to resurrect A. But now "the game was afoot" and other coalitions and proposals would be explored in rapid and heated discussion.

A review of the transcripts of these experiments suggested that a coalition's viability depended critically on the players who pivoted between it and other seemingly viable coalitions. Hence, requiring that *all* members of some majority *strictly* prefer, say, A to B in order to say that A dominates B seemed too strong. Instead, after associating specific coalitions with A and B, it was more reasonable to allow nonpivotal players to hold weak preferences and to require only the players who pivoted between the two coalitions to hold strict preferences before saying that A "dominates" B. This, then, led us to shift our focus from outcomes (*imputations*, as is the case with the V-set and core) to the notion of a *proposal* — the pairing of an outcome with a coalition — and to the idea of a proposal's *viability* and a redefinition of *dominance* in terms of the preferences of pivotal players. Armed with these notions, we then proceeded to offer the definition of the Competitive Solution, which paralleled that of the main simple V-set at least in terms of the requirements of internal and external stability.

However, one additional and truly undesirable surprise awaited us. While we explored the possibility of the general existence of our idea, and despite the experimental evidence we had amassed in support of the Solution, two colleagues, Laing and Olmstead (1978), presented us with a simple 5-person spatial game that possessed no solution (see Figure 4, page 174).

In a fruitless attempt at overcoming the consequences of this counterexample, we attempted a variety of reformulations of the Solution, including non-cooperative conceptualizations and adjustments in our definition of "dominance," that ended with the late Rod Gretlein's (1983; see also Gretlein, McKelvey, and Ordeshook 1978) derivative notion of the Defensible Set. However, none of these reformulations appeared at the time to be satisfactory. Either the predicted set was too large or existence could not be guaranteed. Moreover, even our experimental agenda seemed to undermine our attempt at devising a universally applicable solution hypothesis. In attempting to retrace our experimental steps and see how people bargained when the Competitive Solution did not exist, we succeeded, albeit unintentionally, in devising a set of preference profiles over finite alternatives such that subjects failed to choose Competitive Solution points in the majority of cases, but reverted to those points when preference profiles were adjusted to render the Solution especially unattractive (McKelvey and Ordeshook 1983; Gretlein 1983). Specifically, for the 5 preference profiles portrayed in Table 1, the proposals $(A, \{3, 4, 5\})$, $(E, \{2, 4, 5\})$, $(F, \{2, 3, 4\})$, $(H, \{1, 3, 5\})$, and $(O, \{1, 2, 4\})$ correspond to a Competitive Solution and experimental subjects choose one of these proposals in 38 of 54 trials (70%). However, if we modify preferences only slightly by raising alternative G in profiles 1, 4, and 5 as indicated, the Solution remains unchanged but its experimental support drops to 15 out of 33 trials (45%). And if we next raise G in profiles 4 and 5 so that it becomes the ideal of these two subjects, the Competitive Solution is again unchanged and its experimental success rate, despite G's attractiveness, increases (albeit unimpressively) to 13 out of 20 experimental trials (65%).[1] Overall, then, across these 107 experiments, the Competitive Solution prevailed as the final outcome an anemic 62 percent of the time.

TABLE 1

1	2	3	4	5
N	J	B	L	B
J	O	H	E	A
F	M	A, F		
	E, F	I	D	E, H, G
I	I	K, M, D	A, O, G	K
K	K, D	J	M	D
G, O, H	G, B	G	I	M
D, M	H, C	E, C	K, B	O, C
B	L, N	L, N	F, C	L, N, J
A, C	A	O	N, J	F, I
L			H	
E				

---

[1] It is interesting to note here that the Competitive Solution's increased success rate comes almost exclusively from the fact that alternative F is now chosen in 10 of those 13 "successes" — the sole alternative in the solution that is strictly viable against G. Clearly, then, the attractiveness of alternatives within the Solution is not neutral or unaffected by alternatives outside of it, which, it would seem, is something any comprehensive or fully satisfactory theory should accommodate.

The failure of our Solution to exhibit the sort of robustness in the experimental laboratory we would otherwise demand of a viable solution hypothesis in combination with our inability to establish a variant on the Solution that guaranteed existence even when we limited our search to simple spatial games — the class of games for which it was originally designed — appeared to lead to but one conclusion: The project needed to be abandoned or set aside until some brilliant insight reignited our interest. That insight never occurred and the Competitive Solution was left "twisting in the wind." I am convinced, however, that we abandoned this enterprise prematurely. Hence, in Sections 2 and 3 I review the original formulation of the Competitive Solution and a subsequent reformulation of it in terms of non-cooperative game theory, as well as, in Section 4, Gretlein's derivative notion of the Defensible Set. I suggest a simple reinterpretation of these reformulations in Section 5 such that existence is ensured, provided it is possible to prove the existence of a mixed or pure Nash equilibrium to a particular class of games. This section also concludes with the argument that this reinterpretation not only resurrects the Competitive Solution as a viable hypothesis about coalitions in simple games, but it provides us with a handle on extending Simon's (1957) notion of satisficing as an endogenous parameter of fully rational decision making.

2. The Competitive Solution

The presentation here will be brief and without technical details. Imagine a majority rule game G among players $N = \{1, 2, ..., n\}$ over the outcome set O, which may or may not be finite. Then $p = (o, C)$ is a *proposal* if $o \in O$ and C is a winning (majority) subset of N. Next, the proposal p is *viable* against $p' = (o', C')$ iff the players in $C \cap C'$ (the intersection of C and C') do not all strictly prefer o' to o. On the other hand, p is *strictly viable* against p' if those common players strictly prefer o to o'.[2] With the notions of viable and strictly viable replacing the concepts of "undominated by" and "dominates" we can now define the Competitive Solution in a way that parallels the definition of the V-set solution. First, as the parallel to the notion of internal stability, we say that

> the set of proposals K is *balanced* if (1) for any two proposals in K, say p and p', C is not equal to C'; and (2) no proposal in K is strictly viable against any other proposal in K.

In addition to using the notion of viability in this version of internal stability, notice that we also add the requirement that no coalition can have more than one proposal in K. We do this in the spirit of thinking of coalitions as the "players"

---

[2] We can also add the requirement that the players in $C - C \cap C'$ weakly prefer o to o'.

in the game as opposed to individuals. That is, we can think of coalitions in a somewhat anthropomorphic way, with each of them attempting to offer a proposal that best serves "its interest" while maintaining itself as a viable alternative, given what other coalitions propose. There is no reason to suppose, however, that balanced sets are unique — indeed, they generally are not — and we need next to consider the possibility that new proposals can *upset* a balanced set. Specifically,

a proposal $p = (o, C)$ *upsets* K if (1) p is viable in K; and (2) for some p' in K, p is strictly viable against p'.

Next, letting M_K denote the coalitions with proposals in K, we say that

K is *competitively balanced* if it is balanced and for no C in M_K is there a proposal (o, C) that upsets K.

The notion of competitively balanced allows us to address the possibility that only specific coalitions can form. That is, if we limit the set of potential coalitions to the subset M_K we can assess whether there is a balanced set of proposals that allows for all such coalitions to make viable proposals. More generally, however, if we allow any coalition, then we say simply that

K is a *Competitive Solution* if it is balanced and there is no $p = (o, C)$ that upsets K.

We can, then, think of K as a set of proposals that are internally stable via the notion of balanced, and externally stable in the sense that no excluded proposal can "defeat" (be strictly viable against) any proposal in K while being viable against the rest.

Notice the modification here of the notion of external stability employed in the definition of V-sets. The definition of V requires that every imputation (outcome) not in V be dominated by something in V. Here, however, we require only that there be a proposal in K that is strictly viable against those proposals outside of it that might otherwise threaten K's stability. The initial logic of the traditional definition of external stability was to ensure that negotiators could "get to" V directly. This view, however, seemed entirely ad hoc to us and disconnected from any model of bargaining. The definition of external stability we employed in the definition of K, on the other hand, takes the view of coalitions attempting to enter the bargaining and that they can do so only if they "pose a threat" to the existing menu of choices (as represented by proposals in any potential solution set). Hence, the stability of that menu depends on its ability to fend off threats.

To illustrate these definitions, Figure 2 portrays a set of balanced proposals denoted $p_1 = (o_1, \{1, 2, 5\})$, $p_2 = (o_2, \{1, 2, 3\})$, $p_3 = (o_3, \{2, 3, 4\})$, $p_4 = (o_4, \{3, 4, 5\})$, and $p_5 = (o_5, \{4, 5, 1\})$. This set, however, is not balanced even if

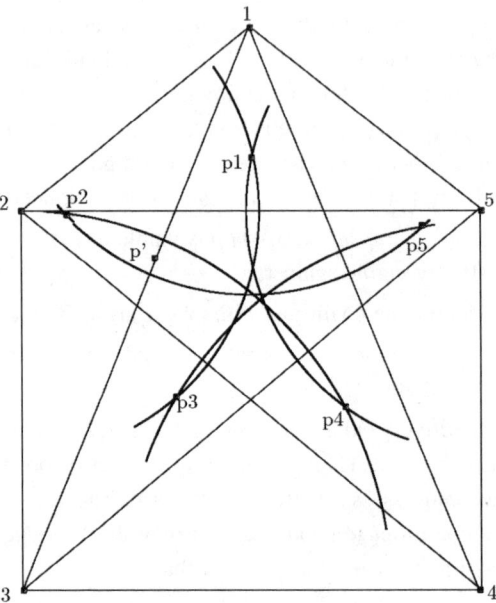

FIGURE 2. A balanced set upset by proposal p'

we limit the allowable coalitions to the set $\{\{1,2,5\},\{1,2,3\},\{2,3,4\},\{3,4,5\},\{4,5,1\}\}$. For example, the proposal $p' = (o',\{1,2,3\})$ is viable against $p_2 = (o_2,\{1,2,3\})$ — the pivots, which include 1, 2, and 3, do not all have a strict preference for the same proposal. The proposal p' is similarly viable against $p_1 = (o_1,\{1,2,5\})$ and $p_3 = (o_3,\{2,3,4\})$. However, is strictly viable against $p_4 = (o_4,\{3,4,5\})$ and $p_5 = (o_5,\{4,5,1\})$ — for example, against $p_4 = (o_4,\{3,4,5\})$, the pivot, player 3, strictly prefers o' to o_4 whereas against $p_5 = (o_5,\{4,5,1\})$, the pivot, player 1, strictly prefers o' to o_5. Thus, p' upsets $\mathbf{p} = (p_1, p_2, \ldots, p_5)$ since there is nothing in $\mathbf{p}$ that is strictly viable against p' but p' is strictly viable against elements of $\mathbf{p}$. Figure 3, in contrast, portrays the unique balanced set that comprises a Competitive Solution. Consider, for example, the proposal $p' = (o',\{1,3,4\})$. p' is clearly strictly viable against $p_3 = (o_3,\{2,3,4\})$ as well as $p_4 = (o_4,\{3,4,5\})$. However, p' is not only not viable against $p_1 = (o_1,\{1,2,5\})$, but p_1 is strictly viable against p'. Hence, p' cannot upset K.

A number of theorems can be proved about this formulation of K. Suppose we strengthen its definition somewhat to say that K is a *Strong Competitive Solution* if it is strongly balanced, where by strongly balanced we add the condition

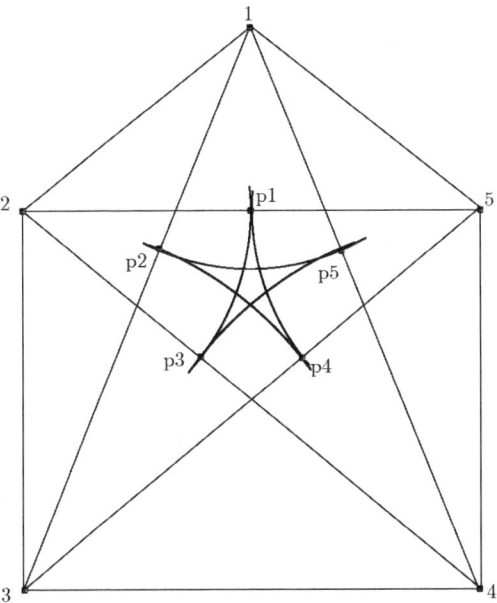

FIGURE 3. A unique balanced set that comprises a Competitive Solution

that for no $p = (o, C)$ and $p' = (o', C')$ in K is it the case that $u_i(o) \geq u_i(o')$ for all i in the intersection of C and C' with $>$ holding for at least one i in their intersection (note that the Competitive Solution portrayed in Figure 3 is strong). Then, both the Core, the game's main simple V-set, and its strong bargaining set, if any exist, correspond to a Strong Competitive Solution (McKelvey and Ordeshook 1978, p. 606). Figure 4, however, offers a devastating counterexample to any attempt at proving the universal existence of K for even simple spatial games. Although the six proposals noted there as tangencies and intersections of indifference contours form an "approximate" solution, they are not a mathematically precise one nor does one appear to exist (see Laing and Olmstead's 1978 discussion, pp. 245–250).

Good reasons can be found for rationalizing the non-existence of V-sets and bargaining sets. The V-set is itself wholly ad hoc and lacking behavioral justification. Its most important contribution to our understanding of social processes is to direct our attention to predictions that rely on the properties of sets as opposed to the individual elements of those sets taken one at a time. The various bargaining sets, in turn, although initially designed to provide a behavioral rationalization for

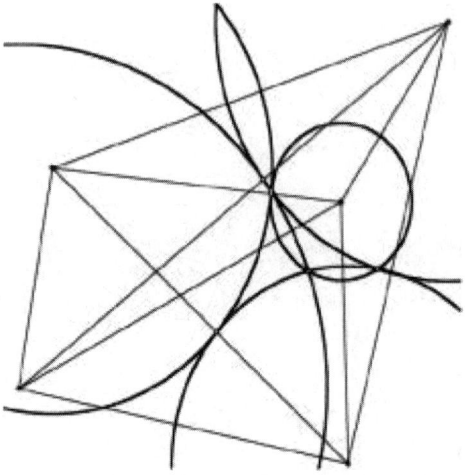

FIGURE 4. A special game without a Competitive Solution

the V-set, presume, in their rationale at least, some transferability of value. Specifically, if a player cannot defend against some objection by offering a counter that "defends" whatever payoff they are getting in the original proposal — that brings them back to the level of utility they enjoy in that proposal — then they must relinquish some value to their coalition partners. In a spatial game, however, utility is not strictly transferable as players can be awarded high (and otherwise indefensible) levels of utility merely as an externality from the actions of others. For example, any reasonable proposal by the coalition $(1, 2, 3)$ for the spatial game in Figure 1 — any proposal on the contract curve between players 1 and 3 that is not "overly close" to 1 or 3's ideal — will afford player 2 a higher level of utility than he can expect to get from any other coalition. It seems wholly unreasonable, then, to require that 2 defend that level against objections by his coalition partners. On the other hand, although it should come as no surprise that a Competitive Solution does not exist universally for majority games with finite alternatives (for a set of outcomes lacking a natural topology), that one doesn't exist for the class of games for which it was originally designed — majority spatial games — seemed a devastating fact.

3. A Non-cooperative Formulation

The seemingly evident response to counterexamples to existence is a revision of the Solution's definition. However, doing so (for instance, by "tweaking" the definitions of viable and balanced) without some guidance can lead, as it has with the Bargaining Set, to a series of wholly ad hoc definitions, none of which would necessarily hold any self-evident advantage over others. A more justifiable approach is to reconceptualize the solution in some basic way in the hope that the path to an extension that guarantees existence appears "naturally." To this end, consider a more anthropomorphic view of things whereby it is coalitions themselves who are the "players" with "strategies" that consist of the various proposals at their disposal. Specifically, let $M = \{1, 2, \ldots, C_m\}$ be a specific set of coalitions and let p_j be a proposal by C_j. Then with $\mathbf{p} = \{p_1, p_2, \ldots, p_m\}$ define $P_j = P_j(\mathbf{p})$ as a real-valued function thus:

$$(1) \qquad P_j(\mathbf{p}) = \min_{C_k \in M - \{C_j\}} \max_{i \in C_j \cap C_k} [u_i(p_j) - u_i(p_k)].$$

To illustrate this function, suppose p_j is viable against every proposal in the vector $\mathbf{p}$. Then it must be the case that for any p_k, there must be a pivot between C_j and C_k who either strictly prefers p_j to p_k or is indifferent, in which case $\max[u_i(p_j) - u_i(p_k)] \geq 0$. Hence, if p_k is viable against every proposal in p, $P_j(\mathbf{p}) \geq 0$. On the other hand, suppose there is some p_k in $\mathbf{p} = (p_1, p_2, \ldots, p_n)$ that is strictly viable against p_j. Then $\max[u_i(p_j) - u_i(p_k)] < 0$ and $P_j(\mathbf{p}) < 0$.

Notice now that expression (1), taken as a coalition's payoff, can be used to define a non-cooperative game among the coalitions in M, in which case our task is to determine when a Nash equilibrium to this game exists and when it might correspond to a Competitive Solution. To do this we say that a game is reducible at P if the elimination of coalitions with nonzero payoffs does not affect the location, with respect to the proposals of the remaining coalitions, of the Nash equilibrium to the reduced game. The critical result here now is the following:

Let $\mathbf{p}$ be a strong Nash equilibrium to the game with a payoff function as in (1). Then if $P_j(\mathbf{p}) \leq 0$ for all $1 \leq j \leq m$ and if the game is reducible at p, $K = \{p_j : P_j(\mathbf{p}) = 0\}$ is a Competitive Solution.

Clearly, if we have an equilibrium in which a coalition in M, say C_j, is afforded a negative payoff with respect to $\mathbf{p}$, then there must be some other coalition in M, say C_k, such that p_j is not viable against p_k. But suppose we can eliminate C_j without otherwise changing the nature of the equilibrium and that we can do this until all payoffs are zero for the coalitions that remain (presumably because every coalition that remains has, as is the case for the example of K in Figure 3, some other coalition with which the pivot between them is a unique player, who must thereby be indifferent between proposals). This is equivalent, then, to learning which coalitions can compete and which ones are unable to formulate viable proposals. To illustrate this result further, suppose $N = \{1, 2, 3\}$ and let M consist only of the two-person (minimal winning) coalitions. In this case expression (1) becomes

$$(2) \qquad P_j(\mathbf{p}) = \min_{C_k \in M - \{C_j\}} [u_i(p_j) - u_i(p_k)]$$

since $C_j \cap C_j$ is necessarily a single player. Hence, if u_i is continuous and concave, $P_j(\mathbf{p})$ is a concave function of p_j and continuous in $\mathbf{p}$ if preferences are spatial in the usual form. Thus, a (strong) Nash equilibrium necessarily exists (Rosen 1975). It should be evident now that this equilibrium is a Competitive Solution and corresponds to the joint pair-wise tangencies of the indifference contours of the players.

Of course, this particular non-cooperative reformulation of K is of limited value since there is no guarantee that the requisite Nash equilibrium for any specific simple game will exist (and, indeed, Laing and Olmstead's counterexample applies here as well). Nevertheless, our ability to reformulate K as an equilibrium to a non-cooperative game suggests the possibility of reformulating cooperative solutions generally using the tools of non-cooperative theory without resorting to complex and ad hoc extensive form characterizations of bargaining.[3] There is, moreover, a second implication to be drawn from this reformulation. Specifically, it reveals that the original definition of K relies, in effect, on pure as opposed to mixed strategies; and as far as I know, this is the implicit assumption of all of classical cooperative game theory to the extent that we can formulate the different components of that theory in non-cooperative terms. But allowing mixed strategies in the preceding reformulation accomplishes little since there still is the matter of requiring that a *strong* Nash equilibrium exist and that the game be reducible. The question remains as to whether there are related ideas such that neither "strong" nor "reducible" is an essential requirement for a viable solution hypothesis.

---

[3]McKelvey developed this non-cooperative conceptualization not for its own sake or any perceived need to reformulate K but rather to establish a programmable algorithm for finding K in spatial games (McKelvey 1976b [Chapter 4 of this book]; McKelvey and Wendell 1975). It was the application of this algorithm and its failure to converge that led Laing and Olmstead to their counterexample to existence.

4. Endogenous Satisficing

Consider again the Competitive Solution portrayed in Figure 3, and recall that the coalition $\{1, 2, 3\}$, like every coalition with a proposal in K, fails to be associated with an outcome in any of the Bargaining Sets since player 2 would otherwise be required to defend the level of utility he or she associates with a proposal such as B. But as we note earlier, the relatively rich reward this player gets from B is largely an "externality" of any agreement 1 and 3 might reasonably reach that is Pareto optimal for $\{1, 2, 3\}$, so absent the existence of some numeraire in the system that might allow 2 to compensate 1 and 3, it is illogical to require that 2 defend B or similar alternatives. On the other hand, notice that it is not what 2 gets from B that partially identifies K but rather what this player gets from A and C. So suppose we require only that 2 defend what the coalitions $\{1, 2, 5\}$ and $\{2, 3, 4\}$ offer, and in particular suppose we allow 2 to counter any objection to B with a proposal that brings it back only to the level of utility it associates with outcome A or C.

With this perspective we can, in fact, imagine a game that proceeds roughly as follows: Each player announces a utility level that he or she finds "satisfactory" — the implication being that each player would agree to any offer that meets his or her expectation. However, after the players make their announcements, each is free to readjust their expectation — possibly because they see that they are asking for "too much" and have inadvertently precluded the formation of a potentially profitable coalition or, given what others announce, because they are demanding too little and can demand more without injuring their chances. What we can ask here, then, is whether there is any equilibrium to this process. Of course, this abbreviated description of coalitional bargaining is imprecise, since, among other things, it leaves unspecified how players evaluate various configurations of announcements. For example, in Figure 3, if player 2 increases its expectation, then ceteris paribus alternatives A and C are no longer feasible whereas alternative B remains. Hence, if it is an alternative rationalization for K that we seek, we must ascertain the assumptions about preference and bargaining that would induce 2 to keep A and C as viable proposals.

To pursue this alternative conceptualization and questions we introduce here the notion of *levels*, $L = (l_1, l_2, \ldots, l_n)$ whereby l_i denotes the level of utility that player i is attempting to defend. Now, following the development of the Bargaining Set (see Gretlein, McKelvey, and Ordeshook 1978; and Gretlein 1983), we say that

$p = (o, C)$ is an *objection against player* i at l_i and proposal $p' = (o', C')$ if $u_i(o) < l_i$ and p is strictly viable against p'. $p = (o, C)$ is a *counterobjection by* i at l_i to $p' = (o', C')$ if $u_i(o) \geq l_i$ and p is strictly viable against p'.

The notion of levels now allows us to define the *support set* as a function of L,

$$S(L) = \{p = (o, C) : \text{for all } i \text{ in } C, u_i(o) \geq l_i\},$$

and the *support set* for player i

$$S_i(L) = S(L) \cap \{p = (o, C) : i \in C\}.$$

As a variant of (or substitute for) the Competitive Solution, the *Defensible Set* $D(L)$ consists of a set of supported proposals at level L such that each player can defend the proposals in $S(L)$ that he supports at his level against all objections and no one can defend any supported set at any higher level, given everyone else's level. More formally, as described by Gretlein (1983):

$T \subseteq S(L)$ is *defensible by* i at L if for $T_i = T \cap S_i(L)$, $\min\{u_i(o) : (o, C) \in T_i\} = l_i$ and for every $p' \in T_i$, if p is an objection against i at l_i and p', then i has a counterobjection $p'' \in T_i$.

Hence, L is defensible by i if there is some set T that is defensible by i at L. The Defensible Set, in turn, $D(L) = S(L)$, is then defined by a level L such that everyone can defend their l_i in L and no one can defend any higher level, ceteris paribus.

I am bypassing here a number of technical details in order to convey the flavor of this revised form of the Competitive Solution and to note its close relationship to the ideas that underlie the Bargaining Set. Specifically, the Defensible Set looks much like a bargaining set except that now players are not required to defend precisely the payoffs they associate from specific proposals, but rather only what we might call a satisficing level. The Defensible Set, then, corrects for an inadequacy in the original formulations of the various bargaining sets; namely, the requirement that a person defend precisely the level of utility he gets from any outcome. This assumption might be appropriate when utility is transferable and compensation can be made to other members of a coalition. But for spatial games or finite-alternative games without a transferable resource, such an assumption seems wholly out of place. At the same time, the notion of levels also renders the notion of satisficing endogenous. Players might enter a bargaining scenario with some expectation as to what they regard as an acceptable payoff, but $D(L)$ allows those expectations to change as a function of what others deem acceptable and what each person can defend.

However, in moving from the Competitive Solution to the Defensible Set, we should emphasize that K and $D(L)$ are not strictly equivalent despite the fact that they often give identical predictions (for example, for the spatial game in Figure 3, the tangent indifference contours that identify K correspond to the levels that define $D(L)$). Among other things, the definition of $D(L)$ abandons the requirement that coalitions are associated with unique proposals. But even aside from this, we note that for the finite alternative game in Table 1, K is a strict subset of $D(L)$, where $D(L)$ includes the proposal $(G, \{1, 4, 5\})$ in addition to $(A, \{3, 4, 5\})$, $(E, \{2, 4, 5\})$, $(F, \{2, 3, 4\})$, $(H, \{1, 3, 5\})$, and $(O, \{1, 2, 4\})$. Nor is it the case, of course, that any of the Bargaining Sets bears a direct relationship, in terms of predictions, to $D(L)$. For the simple game described by the preference profiles in Table 1, for instance, the M^1 Bargaining Set corresponds to the set of proposals $\{(D, \{1, 3, 4\}), (G, \{1, 2, 5\}), (G, \{1, 4, 5\}), (G, \{1, 2, 4, 5\}), (M, \{2, 3, 5\})\}$.

What is especially attractive about the Defensible Set, however, is that it lends itself in a natural way to a non-cooperative formulation. To see what we mean, first define the function

$$f_i(L) = \max\{l'_i : (l_1, l_2, \ldots, l'_i, \ldots, l_n) \text{ is defensible by } i\}.$$

Thus, f identifies the highest level of utility player i can defend, holding constant what all other players set as their levels. Next, define the payoff function[4]

(3) $$g_i(L) = l_i \text{ if } f_i(L) \geq l_i \text{ and 0 otherwise.}$$

Expression (3), then, can be used to specify an n-person non-cooperative game, G', where the strategies of the individual players are the levels they propose to defend. What remains now is to identify the properties of this game and whatever equilibria it might occasion. In this respect, Gretlein (1983, p. 28) offers the following theorem:

The following are equivalent:
  a. $P(L) > 0$ and L is a Nash equilibrium in G'
  b. L is a strong equilibrium in G'
  c. L defines a $D(L)$ solution to G.

It might seem, then, that our search for a solution is ended, but notice that this result fails to establish the existence of an equilibrium or, if it does exist, its uniqueness. Unfortunately, the prospect of uniqueness can be dispensed with easily. Consider the preference profiles portrayed in Table 2, which are a slight modification of those shown in Table 1. If these profiles correspond to a strong

---

[4]The choice of 0 as the value of this function when $f_i(L) < l_i$ is arbitrary. All we require is that g's value be less than that of the least preferred alternative outcome.

simple game, that game unremarkably (given the absence of sufficient indifference among the alternatives) fails to possess a Competitive Solution. But it has two Defensible Sets, namely (Gretlein, McKelvey, and Ordeshook 1978),

$(E, \{2,4,5\}), (A, \{3,4,5\}), (O, \{1,2,4\}), (H, \{1,3,5\}), (B, \{1,2,3,5\}),$
$(D, \{1,2,4\})$ and $(E, \{2,4,5\}), (A, \{3,4,5\}), (O, \{1,2,4\}), (H, \{1,3,5\}),$
$(F, \{1,2,3\}).$

TABLE 2

1	2	3	4	5
N	J	B	L	B
J	O	H	E	A
F	M	A	D	E
I	F	F	O	H
K	E	I	A	G
H	I	L, N	G	K
O	K, D	P	M	Q
G	G, B	Q	I	D
P, Q	H, C, P	K, M, D	P	M
D, M	L, N, Q	J	K, B	O, C
B	A	E, C	F, C	P
A, C		O	N, J, Q	L, N, J
L			H	F, I
E				

What is occurring here should not be wholly unexpected. In the first solution, the players set their levels at B, G, A, A, and H respectively whereas in the second they are O, E, F, A, and H. Thus, in the first solution, by committing to a relatively high level (A), player 3 succeeds in "trapping" players 1 and 2 into accepting B and D as the highest levels they can defend. On the other hand, if 3's level is lowered a notch to F, players 1 and 2 can raise theirs so as to exclude outcomes B and D. With alternative F now above the levels for three players, 1 and 2 can use this alternative to defend other proposals.

Insofar as the veracity of these solutions is concerned, Gretlein (1983) reports fifteen experimental runs of this game whereby outcomes A, E, F, H, and O of the "old" (but now empty) Competitive Solution are selected fourteen times and where the one exception, B, corresponds to a proposal included in the Defensible Set. Gretlein also reports twenty experimental runs of a nearly equivalent game that differs from the one corresponding to the preferences of Table 2 only insofar as the preference order for F and E for player 2 is reversed. In this instance, the second of two Defensible Set solutions expands to include the proposal $(J, \{1, 2, 3\})$. In sixteen of those experiments, outcomes A, E, F, H, or O again prevail; in one instance an outcome (I) prevails that is not associated with any proposal in K or $D(L)$, but in the remaining two cases alternative B, which $D(L)$ but not K allows, again prevails. Consider, now, the preferences portrayed in Table 1 again and recall that when G is raised in the preference profiles of players 1, 4, and 5 as indicated, the Competitive Solution's experimental success rate drops below 50 percent. In this instance, however, the Defensible Set includes $(A, \{3, 4, 5\})$, $(B, \{2, 3, 4, 5\})$, $(D, \{2, 3, 4\})$, $(E, \{2, 4, 5\})$, $(F, \{1, 2, 3\})$, $(G, \{1, 2, 4, 5\})$, $(H, \{1, 3, 5\})$, $(I, \{2, 3, 4\})$, $(J, \{1, 2, 3\})$, $(K, \{2, 3, 4\})$, $(M, \{2, 3, 4\})$, and $(O, \{1, 2, 4\})$. Thus, although $D(L)$ suffers no experimental failures, it excludes only alternatives C, L, and N. The reasons for this expansive set of predictions lie in the structure of preferences. The consequence of raising G in the profiles of players 1, 4, and 5 requires that players 2 and 3 lower their levels (from E, F to B, G and from A, F to D, J, K, M respectively) so as to offset the fact that they can no longer counter objections to proposals in which they participate. But this lowering also requires that player 4's level be lowered from A, O to B, K owing to the new proposals 2 and 3's actions admit.[5] On the other hand, if we raise G further so that it becomes 4 and 5's ideal, $D(L)$ no longer includes alternatives A, E, H, and O in addition to C, L, and N — player 1's level can now be raised to G and player 5's to A, thereby eliminating a number of potential proposals as predictions. Nevertheless, its experimental success rate is now 17 out of 20 trials.

5. Conclusions

The preceding experimental support for $D(L)$ should not distract us from the issue of existence, since if it were not for the example of a spatial game with K empty, the Defensible Set might have been an unexplored idea. Unfortunately, even the existence of $D(L)$ cannot be guaranteed. The strong simple game established by the preferences portrayed in Table 3 has neither a Competitive Solution

---

[5]This expansion of $D(L)$ suggests that a further "tweaking" of definitions (or requirements imposed for counterobjections) might be in order to develop a more refined solution. We hesitate, however, to suggest this approach since it seems more important to first develop definitions that ensure existence.

nor a Defensible Set. Nevertheless, the non-cooperative formulation provided by expression (3) in combination with what we know about some of our examples suggests an unexplored or at least an underdeveloped avenue of study. First, the existence of two solutions in pure strategies for the preferences portrayed in Table 2 means that there is a mixed strategy solution here as well in which the players randomize over levels. And then there is this fact with respect to the preferences portrayed in Table 3: If lotteries over strategies but not over outcomes are allowed, a mixed strategy solution necessarily exists since the non-cooperative game occasioned by those preferences has a finite number of players and a finite number of pure strategies or levels (Nash 1950). Moreover, even if we choose to reject the idea that equilibrium mixed strategies "solve" non-cooperative games, we can nevertheless appeal to ideas such as the support sets of those strategies to narrow the range of predicted levels, outcomes, and coalitions.

TABLE 3

1	2	3	4	5
B	D	H	E	G
H	C	I	C	I
J	A	J	B	B
D	J	C	H	E
A	I	B	J	H
F	F	A	G	D
G	E	E	A	A
C	B	G	F	C
I	H	D	D	J
E	G	F	I	F

The properties of this proposed extension of $D(L)$ are as yet unexplored (e.g., a general characterization of the support sets — the pure strategies (levels) assigned non-zero probabilities — by a solution) nor can we be certain that even a mixed strategy solution exists for spatial games since such games possess a continuum of pure strategies with discontinuous payoff functions.[6] Nevertheless, the perspectives to which we are led by the preceding non-cooperative formulation of otherwise cooperative coalition processes is more than merely promising —

---

[6]It is reasonable, nevertheless, to conjecture that the "approximate solution" identified by Laing and Olmstead (1978) in their spatial counterexample to K's existence corresponds approximately to a mixed strategy Defensible Set.

it suggests a significant reconceptualization of how, in the abstract, we ought to think about and model those processes. Briefly, bargaining and cooperation are studied formally using one of two approaches. The first (classical) approach is the one illustrated by the definitions of the V-set, Bargaining Set and Competitive Solution whereby more or less ad hoc restrictions are used to define a subset of the feasible set of imputations or proposals, possibly with some attempt at a behavioral justification. The idea here, of course, is to abandon the idea of point predictions and, by focusing on the properties of sets of outcomes rather than on the specific elements of those sets taken one at a time, to narrow the range of likely outcomes. The second approach accepts the critique of the classical approach that a set theoretic formulation fails to address the issue of how agreements are enforced (if cooperative agreements are enforceable, the argument goes, it must be the case that they are part of an equilibrium to some appropriately conceptualized non-cooperative game), and proceeds instead with an explicit model of the bargaining process in extensive form (e.g., Rubenstein 1982; Baron and Ferejohn 1987; Niou and Ordeshook 1990). Generally, however, these extensive forms are no less ad hoc than the restrictions employed by classical approaches, and are usually limited to a specific substantive context (e.g., two-person bargaining, parliamentary procedure, balance of power negotiations). The Defensible Set, in contrast, promises a simple and universally applicable conceptualization that can be applied broadly — one in which the details of the bargaining context can be subsumed in the description of outcomes. Put differently, although the bargaining context will determine how information is transmitted and how agreements are reached and enforced, and although a great deal remains to be understood as to how people learn and process information in strategic contexts (see, for example, Fudenberg and Levine 1999; Camerer 2003), the notion of levels — of people entering a cooperative decision making situation with some initial but adaptable expectation as to acceptable payoffs — seems universally applicable.

Returning to the starting point of this essay, it is evident that the search for conditions under which Condorcet winners and Cores exist, which preoccupied researchers in the 1970's, was an essential first step in uncovering the theoretical character of democratic processes. But it was precisely that — a first step. The conclusion that those processes are inherently unstable, unpredictable, or subject to the ephemeral winds of personality and rhetoric does not follow from the conclusion that the identified and typically knife-edged existence conditions are unlikely to be realized empirically. Instead, proceeding along the agenda first laid out by cooperative game theory — an agenda whereby, absent a detailed and generally impractical examination of the idiosyncrasies of a specific circumstance, predictions ought to be set theoretic — the underlying non-cooperative characterization of the Competitive Solution and the Defensible Set suggests that it is possible to hypothesize general solutions that avoid wholly ad hoc definitions of stability or definitions that rely on wholly particularistic institutional details. This, more than any implication others might draw from McKelvey's "chaos theorem," is the legacy of his research agenda, which consisted almost uniformly of the attempt to establish limits on the character of outcomes that democratic processes allow.

References

Arrow, K. J. (1951): *Social Choice and Individual Values*. Yale Univ. Press, New Haven.

Aumann, R. J., and M. Maschler (1964): "The Bargaining Set for Cooperative Games," in *Advances in Game Theory (Annals of Mathematical Studies 52)*, ed. by L. S. M. Dresher and A. Tucker. Princeton Univ. Press, Princeton.

Baron, D. P., and J. Ferejohn (1987): "Bargaining and Agenda Formation in Legislatures," *American Economic Review*, 77, 303–9.

Black, D. (1958): *The Theory of Committees and Elections*. Cambridge Univ. Press, Cambridge.

Camerer, C. F. (2003): *Behavioral Game Theory*. Princeton Univ. Press, Princeton.

Davis, O. A., and M. J. Hinich (1966): "A Mathematical Model of Policy Formation in a Democratic Society," in *Mathematical Applications in Political Science*, ed. by J. Bernd. SMU Press, Dallas.

Fudenberg, D., and D. K. Levine (1999): *The Theory of Learning in Games*. MIT Press, Cambridge.

Gretlein, R. (1983): "Ordinal Theories of Group Choice," PhD Dissertation, Carnegie Mellon University.

Gretlein, R., R. D. McKelvey, and P. C. Ordeshook (1978): "The Defensible Set," SUPA Working Paper, Carnegie Mellon University.

Laing, J. D., and S. Olmsted (1978): "An Experimental and Game-Theoretic Study of Committees," in *Game Theory and Political Science*, ed. by P. Ordeshook. NYU Press, NY.

McKelvey, R. D. (1976a): "Competitive Coalition Theory for Nonsidepayment Games: Some Further Results on the Non-cooperative Approach," mimeo, SUPA, Carnegie Mellon University.

――― (1976b): "Intransitivities in Multidimensional Voting Models and Some Implications for Agenda Control," *Journal of Economic Theory*, 12, 472–82. Also Chapter 4 of this book.

――― (1979): "General Conditions for Global Intransitivities in Formal Voting Models," *Econometrica*, 47, 1085–112. Also Chapter 5 of this book.

――― (1986): "Covering, Dominance and the Institution Free Properties of Social Choice," *American Journal of Political Science*, 30, 283–314. Also Chapter 12 of this book.

McKelvey, R. D., and P. C. Ordeshook (1976): "Symmetric Spatial Games without Majority Rule Equilibria," *American Political Science Review*, 70, 1171–84.

――― (1978): "Competitive Coalition Theory," in *Game Theory and Political Science*, ed. by P. Ordeshook. NYU Press, NY.

――― (1979): "An Experimental Test of Several Theories of Committee Decision Making under Majority Rule," in *Applied Game Theory*, ed. by S. J. Brams, A. Schotter, and G. Schwodiauer. Springer-Verlag, Wein.

――― (1980): "Vote Trading: An Experimental Study," *Public Choice*, 35, 151–84.

――― (1982): "Two-Candidate Elections without Majority Rule Equilibria: An Experimental Study," *Simulation & Games*, 13(3), 311–335.

――― (1983): "Some Experimental Results That Fail to Support the Competitive Solution," *Public Choice*, 40, 281–91.

McKelvey, R. D., P. C. Ordeshook, and M. D. Winer (1978): "The Competitive Solution for N-Person Games without Transferable Utility, with an Application to Committee Games," *American Political Science Review*, 72(2), 599–615. Also Chapter 10 of this book.

McKelvey, R. D., and R. E. Wendell (1975): "A Non-Cooperative Formulation of Competitive Coalition Theory," SUPA Working Paper, Carnegie Mellon University.

Miller, N. R. (1980): "A New Solution Set for Tournaments and Majority Voting," *Americal Journal of Political Science*, 24(1), 68–96.

Nash, J. (1950): "Equilibrium Points in n-Person Games," *Proceedings of the National Academy of Sciences*, 36, 48–9.

Niou, E. M., and P. C. Ordeshook (1990): "Stability in Anarchic International Systems," *American Political Science Review*, 84(4), 1207–34.

Peleg, B. (1963): "Bargaining Sets of Cooperative Games without Sidepayments," *Israel Journal of Mathematics*, 1, 197–200.

Plott, C. R. (1967): "A Notion of Equilibrium and Its Possibility under Majority Rule," *American Economic Review*, 57, 787–806.

Riker, W. H. (1982): *Liberalism against Populism*. Waveland Press, Prospect Heights (Ill.).

Rosen, J. B. (1975): "Existence and Uniqueness of Equilibrium Points for Concave N-Person Games," *Econometrica*, 33(3), 520–534.

Rubenstein, A. (1982): "Perfect Equilibrium in a Bargaining Model," *Econometrica*, 50(1), 97–110.

Schwartz, T. (1977): "Collective Choice, Separation of Issues and Vote Trading," *American Political Science Review*, 71(3), 999–1010.

Shepsle, K. (1979): "Institutional Arrangements and Equilibrium in Multidimensional Voting Models," *American Journal of Political Science*, 23(1), 27–59.

Simon, H. (1957): *Models of Man*. New York: Wiley.

Sloss, J. (1973): "Stable Outcomes in Majority Rule Voting Games," *Public Choice*, 15(1), 19–48.

Wilson, R. (1971): "Stable Coalition Proposals in Majority-Rule Voting," *Journal of Economic Theory*, 3, 254–271.

CHAPTER 10

The Competitive Solution for *N*-Person Games without Transferable Utility, with an Application to Committee Games

RICHARD D. MCKELVEY, PETER C. ORDESHOOK, AND
MARK D. WINER

ABSTRACT. This essay defines and experimentally tests a new solution concept for n-person cooperative games — the Competitive Solution. The need for a new solution concept derives from the fact that cooperative game theory focuses for the most part on the special case of games with transferable utility, even though, as we argue here, this assumption excludes the possibility of modelling most interesting political coalition processes. For the more general case, though, standard solution concepts are inadequate either because they are undefined or they fail to exist, and even if they do exist, they focus on predicting payoffs rather than the coalitions that are likely to form.

The Competitive Solution seeks to avoid these problems, but it is not unrelated to existent theory in that we can establish some relationships (see Theorems 1 and 2) between its payoff predictions and those of the core, the V-solution and the bargaining set. Additionally, owing to its definition and motivation, nontrivial coalition predictions are made in conjunction with its payoff predictions.

The Competitive Solution's definition is entirely general, but a special class of games — majority rule spatial games — are used for illustrations and the experimental test reported here consists of eight plays of a 5-person spatial game that does not possess a main-simple V-solution or a bargaining set. Overall, the data conform closely to the Competitive Solution's predictions.

The authors would like to thank the National Science Foundation for its support of this research. We also thank James D. Laing for his many helpful suggestions in preparing this paper and in the conduct of our experimental research, and Phillip Straffin for his perceptive comments.

Much of n-person cooperative game theory concerns the special case of games with transferable utility — games in which utility "acts like money" and can be transferred among players.[1] The transferable utility assumption, however, seriously limits the relevance of the corresponding theory, so that, as we argue later, theoretical consequences such as Riker's (1962) size principle cannot be usefully applied to the empirical analysis of, e.g., legislative coalition formation. (For an equivalent argument see De Swann, 1974, but note that the current debate over the size principle's theoretical validity assumes transferable utility. Cf., Butterworth, 1971; Shepsle, 1974; McKelvey and Smith, 1975; and Hardin, 1976.) But if we adopt a more general and appropriate model of coalition processes that does not assume transferable utility, we find that game theory is itself deficient as an analytical tool. In the transferable utility case, numerous solution concepts such as the V-set, the kernel, the nucleolis, and various bargaining sets exist to treat games with empty cores — games without undominated imputations. For games that do not assume transferable utility, on the other hand, these concepts are either undefined or, like the core, they are typically empty. Hence, for most politically important games, game theory often provides no predictions about outcomes.

Our objective is to define and to illustrate the application of a new solution concept — the *Competitive Solution* — and to report a modest experimental test of its empirical validity. This concept's definition is entirely general and thus treats games with and without transferable utility. We justify the necessity for such a concept and illustrate its application, though, by examining several examples of logrolling and spatial committee games — with particular emphasis on spatial games. In a logrolling game, the players (the members of a legislative committee) must decide by majority rule which of several bills to pass and which to fail. An analysis of the cooperative version of these games, then, reveals the consequences of vote-trading. In spatial games, the alternatives correspond to an m-dimensional subset of Euclidean space and the committee's task is to choose some point in this subset as the social choice. These games, therefore, are often used to model party parliamentary coalition processes.

We emphasize that this essay is concerned principally with developing a new solution concept and is only secondarily concerned with the analysis of specific

---

[1] In decreasing order of generality, there are three classes of games: (1) without sidepayments and without transferable utility; (2) with sidepayments but without transferable utility; and (3) with sidepayments and with transferable utility. While Aumann proves some results about (2), this case is best treated by the notation and concepts developed for (1). Hence, throughout we talk simply of the transferable — non-transferable dichotomy (cf., Aumann, 1967).

committee processes. With logrolling and spatial games, however, we can illustrate not only the necessity for abandoning the transferable utility assumption, but also the inadequacies of existing theory. *First*, this theory focuses on predicting the payoffs to players and is almost wholly silent on the question of what coalitions form. In a logrolling game, then, the specific vote trades that occur to yield a particular payoff outcome are not identified. This leads some scholars such as Michael Taylor (1972) to conclude that formal solution theory is irrelevant to the study of legislative and parliamentary coalition formation processes. *Second*, we can readily formulate spatial games for which the usual solution concepts of the Core, the V-set, and the several bargaining sets render no prediction (i.e., are empty). *Third*, concepts such as the V-set are principally mathematical abstractions without behavioral rationale. Hence, it is difficult to assess their applicability when particular rules constrain bargaining or negotiation procedures in committees.

Admittedly, there are several unresolved questions about the solution proposed here. The important theorems concerning existence and uniqueness await proof or counterexamples. Also, as the current debate over the theoretical validity of the size principle illustrates, this principle as well as the several ad hoc hypotheses designed to model coalition processes (e.g., only connected or compact coalitions form) should be linked to the Competitive Solution. The particular examples considered in this essay suggest that these hypotheses are consistent with the Competitive Solution; but, again, the relevant theorems await proof. Nevertheless, the Competitive Solution seems the most promising candidate for usefully applying game theory. First, it predicts coalitions as well as payoffs and links coalitions to specific payoffs. Second, it solves those spatial games that serve as counterexamples to the existence of V-sets, etc. Moreover, the Competitive Solution necessarily exists and is equivalent to the Core or a main-simple V-solution if either of these exist (see Theorems 1 and 2). Hence, it is a natural extension of these classical solution concepts. Third, like bargaining set theory, it is motivated principally by a specific conceptualization of the bargaining process.

Section 1 briefly reviews the differences between games with and without transferable utility and illustrates the necessity for a nontransferable utility formulation of committee processes. This section also develops the spatial conceptualization of a simple majority game and illustrates the shortcomings of standard solution theory. Section 2 defines the Competitive Solution for cooperative games in general, and, via two theorems, reports on this solution's relationship to the core, to the main-simple V-set and to bargaining set theory. Section 3 applies this concept to some simple spatial games, while Section 4 describes the results of eight 5-person experiments that test the solution's empirical validity.

1. Transferable Utility, Committee Games, and Solution Theory

We begin with some preliminary notation:
$N = \{1, 2, \ldots, n\}$: the set of *players*,
$C \subseteq N$: a *coalition*,
$|C|$: *the number of players in coalition C*.
$u = \{u_1, \ldots, u_n\} \in R^n$, an ordered utility payoff vector, where u_i denotes the utility of player i.
$H \subseteq R^n$: the set of possible *payoff vectors or outcomes*.

The theory of n-person games is formulated now in terms of a *characteristic function*, $v(C)$, which specifies the payoffs that the members of C can jointly secure for themselves, regardless of the actions of other players. The most familiar version of the characteristic function equates $v(C)$ with some real number, r_C, with the implication that r_C is a quantity of utility that the members of C can secure and divide among themselves. This is referred to as the transferable utility case. More generally, though, we can abandon the transferable utility assumption by letting $v(C)$ be a set of payoff vectors, i.e., $v(C) \subseteq R^n$.[2]

To see why this reformulation of $v(C)$ is essential, consider *simple games*, which are important because they model committee processes that entail formal voting procedures. A game is *simple* if it is "superadditive" and if a coalition can guarantee its members any payoff vector in H (plus all lesser payoffs), or nothing, in that it cannot guarantee its members more than they can obtain individually. Thus, for all coalitions C, either $H \subseteq v(C)$, in which case C is *winning*, or $v(C) \cap H^{int} = \Phi$ in which case C is *losing*. A simple game is superadditive if any superset of a winning coalition is also winning. Further, a simple game is *strong* (decisive) if for every coalition $C \subseteq N$, exactly one of $C, N-C$ is winning (i.e., there are no blocking coalitions), and it is *symmetric* if $v(C)$ depends only on the size of C (e.g., all players possess equal weight in the voting). We let W

---

[2]The conditions imposed on $v(C)$ vary in the literature. But, the three most common are: (i) for all $C \subseteq N$, $v(C)$ is closed and convex; (ii) for any $C \subseteq N$, if $u_i \leq w_i$ for all $i \in C$ and if $w \in v(C)$, then $u \in v(C)$; (iii) for any $C_1, C_2 \subseteq N$ with $C_1 \cap C_2 = \Phi$, $v(C_1) \cap v(C_2) \subseteq (C_1 \cup C_2)$. These conditions are imposed typically to establish particular results or to render analysis tractable. We state them here, then, only as a matter of convention. One assumption, however, warrants discussion. In particular, by letting $v(C) \subseteq R^n$, such that no constraints are placed on u_j, $j \notin C$, $v(C)$ is a "cylinder." Some treatments assume that $v(C) \subseteq R^{|C|}$. We emphasize that adopting one assumption over the other is made simply on the basis of notational convenience. Hence, while we let $v(C) \subseteq R^n$, when graphing $v(C)$ in Figures 1a and 1b, we graph only the $|C|$-projection.

denote the set of winning coalitions, and then define the set of *minimal winning coalitions*,

$$W^* = \{C \in W | C - \{i\} \notin W \quad \text{for all } i \in C\}.$$

If we intend, now, to model a committee that uses majority rule to choose one outcome from the set A, and if the number of players, $n = |N|$, is odd so that there are no blocking coalitions, the set of winning coalitions is

$$W = \left\{C \subseteq N | |C| > \frac{n}{2}\right\}.$$

Letting each player's utility be a function over A, we can associate the utility vector $u(\theta) = (u_1(\theta), u_2(\theta), \cdots, u_n(\theta))$ with each θ in A, and express the set of all possible payoff vectors as (ignoring lotteries) $H = \{u | u = u(\theta), \theta \in A\}$. Since winning coalitions secure any alternative, if C is winning,

$$v(C) = \{u | \text{ for some } \theta \in A, u_i \leq u_i(\theta) \text{ for all } i \in C \supseteq H\}$$

while the value of a losing coalition is simply the intersection of the values of its members. (Thus, for each $i \in N$,

$$v(\{i\}) = \left\{u | u_i \leq \min_{w \in H} w_i\right\}$$

and

$$v(C) = \bigcap_{i \in C} v(\{i\})$$

if C is losing.)

To illustrate, suppose a 3-member legislature is confronted with three bills and that it must decide by majority vote which bills to pass and which to fail. Hence, $A = \{\theta = (\theta_1, \theta_2, \theta_3) | \theta_i = 0 \text{ or } 1 \text{ for } i = 1, 2, 3\}$, so that, excluding lotteries, the committee must choose one of $2^3 = 8$ possible outcomes, including the passage of no bills or the passage of all bills. Table 1 portrays some possible utility payoffs for each legislator over the eight outcomes.

Since player 1 is not a majority, he cannot be certain that his least preferred outcome — bills 2 and 3 passing — does not prevail. Hence, $v(1) = \{u | u_1 \leq -2\}$. Similarly, for legislator 2, $v(2) = \{u | u_2 \leq -4\}$. Together, however, players 1 and 2 can secure any outcome, and Figure 1a graphs the joint payoffs that these two players can attain as a winning coalition. Assuming that

TABLE 1. 3-Person, 3-Bill Logrolling Example

Legislator	Bills Passed by the Committee							
	None	1	2	3	1 and 2	1 and 3	2 and 3	All
1	0	5	−1	−1	4	4	−2	3
2	0	−2	5	−2	3	−4	3	1
3	0	−3	−3	6	−6	3	3	0

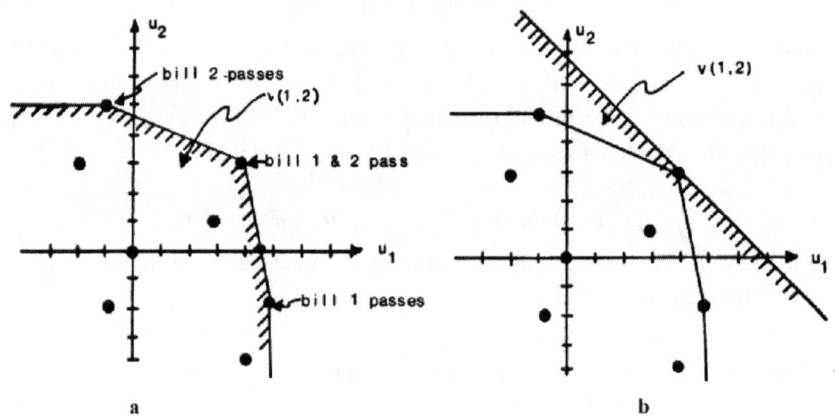

FIGURE 1

players 1 and 2 also consider all possible lotteries, the shaded region in Figure 1a describes $v(1,2)$.

Figure 1a, then, illustrates a characteristic function defined simply as some collection of utility vectors. For the more familiar transferable utility case, on the other hand, $v(C)$ is summarized by a single number thus:

$$v(C) = \left\{ u \mid \sum_{i \in C} u_i \leq r_C \right\},$$

which is to say that C can secure any distribution of utility among its members provided that the sum over its members (given suitable normalizations) does not exceed r_C. (In the traditional development of games with side payments and transferable utility, $v(C)$ is treated as a real valued function rather than a set valued function; and in this case we have $v(C) = r_C$.) In the example, however, no single number adequately summarizes $v(1,2)$. To suppose that such a number exists necessitates assuming, for instance, that the payoffs in Table 1 are dollars and that each legislator's utility is linear in money, so that the members of a coalition could, after agreeing to a particular outcome, transfer utility by transferring money from one player to another.[3] For example, legislators 1 and 2 could pass bills 1 and 2, secure a total dollar payoff of 7 and then transfer dollars between themselves to secure any utility payoff in the shaded region of Figure 1b — any payoff distribution between 1 and 2 such that $u_1 + u_2 < 7$. To model this logrolling example with transferable utility, then, necessarily limits the interpretation or scope of the analysis. If the legislators' payoffs correspond to votes won or lost in their respective constituencies, then in addition to trading votes on bills, we must also assume that their constituents' votes (and hence utility) can be transferred as well. Or, equivalently, we must assume that legislators can compensate one another in dollars for lost votes. While we might be interested in studying the consequences of such legislatures, it is inappropriate to so limit ourselves theoretically.

If we abandon the transferable utility formulation of $v(C)$ and hypothesize (for simplicity) that players do not consider lotteries, then, for simple games at least, a far more analytically convenient representation of $v(C)$ can be used. Specifically, instead of assuming that $v(C)$ is in the utility space, R^n, we can assume that $v(C) \subseteq A$, where A is the set of feasible outcomes. If $v(C)$ is the outcomes in A that C can secure then,

$v(C) = A$ if C is winning

$v(C) = \Phi$ if C is losing.

The utility function u_i, in turn, defines a preference relation for player i over A thus: for any $\theta, \theta' \in A$,

---

[3]To understand the assumptions implicit in the transferable utility formulation of $v(C)$, suppose player i is a consumer and let $x^i = (x_1^i, x_2^i, \cdots, x_m^i)$ denote the amount of each of m commodities that he consumes or possesses. Suppose further that at least one commodity, say the mth, is separable, i.e., that we can write

$$u_i(x_1^i, \cdots, x_m^i) = u_i^0(x_1^i, \cdots, x_{m-1}^i) + u_i'(x_m^i)$$

which is to say that player i's utility for commodity m is independent of his utility for the first $m-1$ commodities and vice versa. Third, suppose that u_i' is linear in x_m^i. If these assumptions hold for all players and if the mth commodity is freely transferable between and among all players, then we can assume transferable utility. Specifically, if C is winning, it can pick the distribution of the m commodities that maximizes the sum of the utilities of the members of C, and trade commodity m from there. Since utility is separable and linear in x_m, transferring m is equivalent to transferring utility. Hence, we set r_C equal to this maximum attainable sum. We emphasize that the non-transferable utility representation of $v(C)$ does not preclude the possibility that the players can exchange resources, and in fact admits transferable utility as a special case.

$$\theta \left\{\begin{array}{c}\succsim_i \\ \succ_i \\ \sim_i\end{array}\right\} \theta' \text{ if and only if } u_i(\theta) \left\{\begin{array}{c}\geq_i \\ >_i \\ =_i\end{array}\right\} u_i(\theta')$$

Thus, in the logrolling example, if C is a majority coalition, $v(C)$ is simply the set of all possible dispositions of all bills while Table 1 summarizes the preferences over these outcomes.

To develop this further and to illustrate the inadequacies of existent solution theory, suppose, as many analyses of parliamentary processes assume (e.g., tests of the size principle), that conflict occurs over issues or ideology as when party leaders attempt to form governments by manipulating their policy commitments. In particular, let us adopt the spatial structure used in the several extensions of the "Downsian" model of election competition (cf., Ordeshook, 1976). That is, we suppose that the set of alternatives, A, confronting a committee is *any* subset of m-dimensional space (in the previous example, A is a discrete subset of R^m), that the dimensions correspond to the criteria players use to evaluate alternative outcomes (so that an outcome can be characterized by its position on each dimension), and that each player possesses a utility function, u_i, over this space. The particular form assumed for u_i is that all players evaluate alternatives in terms of a Euclidean metric: For all $i \in N$ and $\theta \in A$, there is a point $x_i \in R^m$ such that

$$(1) \qquad u_i(\theta) = f\left(\|\theta - x_i\|\right),$$

where $f : R \to R$ is a monotone-decreasing function. The point x_i represents player i's ideal point in A — the issue positions he most prefers — while the utility player i associates with other alternatives in A decreases the further one moves from x_i. Thus, for two dimensions (two issues), a player's indifference contours are concentric circles about x_i, where circles of smaller radius correspond to higher utility levels.

Figure 2 illustrates a 3-player 2-issue representation of a spatial game, and it also illustrates the necessity for abandoning the transferable utility assumption. Specifically, suppose that the coalition $\{1, 2, 3\}$ considers only policies on the line connecting x_1 and x_2 and that u_1 and u_2 are linear along this line so that $u_1 + u_2$ equals a constant. However, $u_1 + u_2 + u_3$ is not a constant since player 3 prefers x_2 to x_1. Thus, $v(1, 2, 3)$ cannot be summarized by a single number. The problem with transferable utility becomes even more apparent for larger games so that to impose this condition we must, as with the logrolling example, assume that the

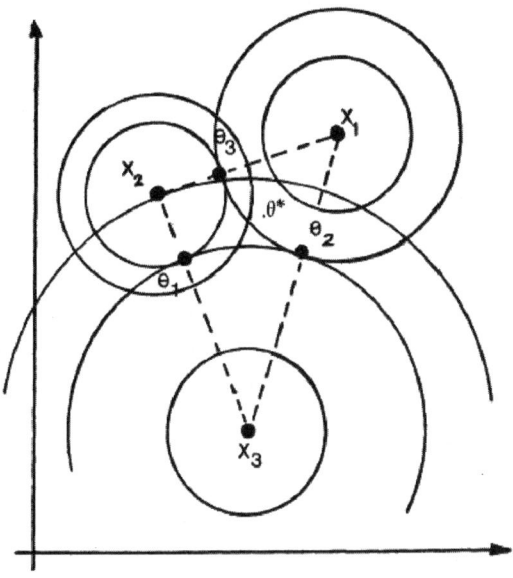

FIGURE 2

game entails some unspecified, divisible and unrestrictedly transferable commodity over which each player possesses a linear utility function and that each player's utility for this commodity is independent of policy. Schofield (1976) usefully assumes that the allocation of ministerships approximates these conditions, but by thus constraining $v(C)$ the essence of the original problem — policy conflict — is lost in favor of the distribution of some commodity. For example, Riker's size principle, the theoretical justifications of which assume transferable utility, must be interpreted as irrelevant to a broad range of parliamentary coalition processes or, minimally, in need of proof in the more general non-transferable context.

Game theory can be usefully applied only if we let $v(C)$ be a collection of utility n-tuples or, in the case of simple games without lotteries, if we let $v(C)$ be A if C is winning and the empty set if C is losing. A spatial map, such as the one portrayed in Figure 2, is used then to summarize individual preferences over A. Simple spatial games, though, also illustrate the problems one encounters when applying existent solution theory.

Turning to this theory, we consider first the core, ℓ. Briefly ℓ is defined as all payoff n-tuples in H that are undominated. In the present context, ℓ corresponds to all outcomes in A that cannot be defeated in a majority vote by some other outcome in A (i.e., $\ell = \{\theta \in A |$ for no $\theta' \in A$ and $C \in W$ is $\theta' \succ_i \theta$ for all $i \in C\}$). It is well known that if a committee is concerned with a single issue (if preferences are single-peaked), then ℓ is non-empty and corresponds to the median preference. For more than one issue, however, the existence of a non-empty core is not as readily assured. For both the 3-person and 5-person examples in Figures 2 and 3, ℓ is empty. This follows from Plott's (1967) necessary and sufficient conditions for majority rule equilibrium and Sloss's (1973) extension of them. Specifically, if at most one player's ideal policy is at a point presumed to be in ℓ, then that point is in the core *if and only if* we can pair all remaining voters so that the contract curve of each pair includes it. For the case of circular indifference contours, the contract curve is the line connecting the two players' ideal points. Hence, the existence of a non-empty core requires a form of symmetry in the distribution of ideal points that is not satisfied in Figures 2 and 3 and that is sufficiently restrictive to lead to the conclusion that, in general ℓ is empty for majority rule spatial games.

Spatial counterexamples to the existence of ℓ are well known, and the lack of existence provides the motivation for considering other game theoretic solution notions, such as the V-set and bargaining sets. Unfortunately, as we show subsequently, these solutions also cannot be guaranteed to exist generally, and when they do exist, they possess other problems.

In the present context, $V \subseteq A$ is a V-set or Von Neumann-Morgenstern solution if it is (1) *internally stable* — if no element of V dominates (defeats under majority rule) another element of V— and (2) *externally stable* — if for every element not in V, there is at least one in V that dominates it. The problem with most games, however, is that they possess too many V-sets and, hence, to restrict predictions in simple games, the ad hoc concept of a main-simple V-set is introduced. Briefly, a V-set is *main-simple* if and only if for each minimal winning coalition, C, there is an element of V, say θ, such that θ is weakly preferred by each member of C to any other element of V.[4]

For the game in Figure 2, note first that $\{\theta_1, \theta_2, \theta_3\}$ is internally stable. For example, player 1 prefers θ_2 to θ_1, player 2 prefers θ_1 to θ_2, and player 3 is indifferent. Hence, θ_1 and θ_2 do not dominate each other under majority rule. It is easily shown that $\{\theta_1, \theta_2, \theta_3\}$ is externally stable as well, since every point in the space (except θ_1, θ_2, and θ_3) is outside at least two of the three tangent circles and, hence, is dominated by the point corresponding to the intersection of these

---

[4]That is, if $C \in W^*$ and if V is main-simple, then there exists a $\theta \in V$ such that $\theta \succeq_i \theta'$ for all $\theta' \in V$. This definition is taken from an equivalence theorem (Theorem 2) by Robert Wilson (1971).

two circles. Thus, $\{\theta_1, \theta_2, \theta_3\}$ is a V-set. And, further, it is a main-simple V-set since the minimal winning coalition $\{1, 2\}$ weakly prefers θ_3 to θ_1 and θ_2, $\{1, 3\}$ weakly prefers θ_2 to θ_1 and θ_3, and $\{2, 3\}$ weakly prefers θ_1 to θ_2 and θ_3.

Because the predictions of main-simple V-sets are intuitively satisfying, most experimental tests of V focus on them (cf., Riker, 1967; Riker and Zavoina, 1970; Kahn and Rapoport, 1972; Horowitz and Rapoport, 1974). Their definition, however, contains no behavioral justification for supposing that players adopt outcomes in them. As such, V-sets and main-simple V-sets are mathematical inventions without a behavioral rationale. For this reason, Aumann and Maschler (1964) define several variants of the bargaining set — a solution theory with predictions that often correspond closely to the main-simple V-set, but which nevertheless is motivated by some behavioral considerations.

The intuitive idea behind bargaining set theory is that for a particular payoff vector and coalition structure to be "stable," the members of every coalition must be able to "defend" their payoff agaist the possible objections of their partners. In a sense, the players must possess counter-threats to all conceivable threats against them. Rather than present any formal definitions, though, we note simply that the points θ_1, θ_2, and θ_3, in conjunction with the respective coalition structures $(\{2, 3\}, \{1\})$, $(\{1, 3\}, \{2\})$, and $(\{1, 2\}, \{3\})$ are in all of the several variants of the bargaining set. The simple game portrayed in Figure 3, however, is more interesting, since this game does not possess a bargaining set in the traditional sense and since from this it follows that it does not possess a main-simple V-set either.

To begin, consider the point θ and the payoff configuration

$$(\theta; \{1, 2, 3\}, \{4, 5\})$$

(i.e., the minimal winning coalition $\{1, 2, 3\}$ proposes to exclude players 4 and 5 and to pass θ). Suppose, however, that player 3 feels that the coalition should adopt a policy closer to his ideal preference and consequently he *objects* against player 2 with the configuration (see Figure 3):

$$(\theta^*; \{1, 2, 3\}, \{1, 2\}).$$

In accordance with the definitions of bargaining set theory, this is a legitimate objection since θ^* is Pareto optimal for $\{3, 4, 5\}$, $\{3, 4, 5\}$ is winning, and

$$\theta^* \succ_3 \theta,$$
$$\theta^* \succcurlyeq_4 \theta,$$
$$\theta_5^* \succcurlyeq_5 \theta.$$

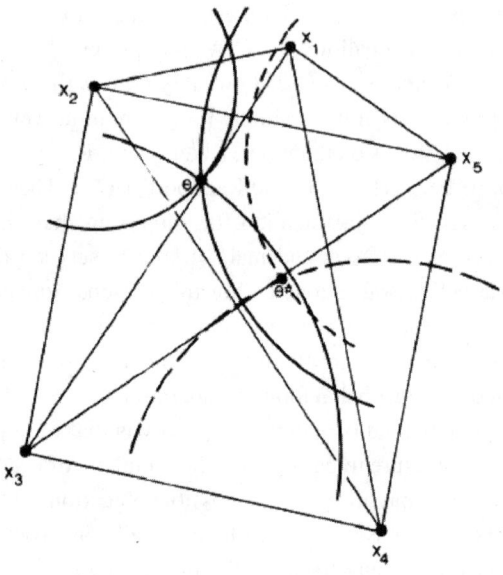

FIGURE 3

For player 2 to defend what he is getting from θ, i.e., for $(\theta; \{1,2,3\}, \{4,5\})$ to be a candidate for an element of a bargaining set, player 2 must find a counterobjection — a third payoff configuration such that 3 is excluded from the winning coalition, player 2 does at least as well as he does at θ, and 2's new coalition partners do at least as well at θ^* as at θ. To see that player 2 does not possess such a counterobjection, note that since he is prohibited from using player 3 — the objector — in a counter, and since (from the construction of Figure 3) he cannot find a point that gives him at least $u_2(\theta)$ while simultaneously giving player 4 at least $u_4(\theta^*)$, player 2's only possible counter is with the coalition $\{1,2,5\}$. But, as Figure 3 shows, he cannot lure player 5 away from θ^* and recover $u_2(\theta)$. Hence, there exists an objection that cannot be countered, so $(\theta; \{1,2,3\}, \{4,5\})$ is not in any bargaining set.

While the choice of θ in this example is not entirely arbitrary (it is a point in the solution we propose later) it can be shown that for every point and for every such coalition, there exist objections that cannot be countered. Thus, by the usual definition of existence (i.e., for every coalition structure, there exists a payoff configuration in the bargaining set), the various bargaining sets are empty. Further, from the correspondence Wilson proves between the main-simple V-set and the strong bargaining set and from his result that a main-simple V-set is an "admissible" set of proposals by each of the minimal winning coalitions, we conclude that *the main-simple V-set is empty as well.*

Is this example a special case? We cannot answer this question definitively since Peleg's (1963) existence results are not relevant here. But, a succession of counterexamples using spatial games (including three-dimensional configurations of ideal points) suggest that, like the core, existence of other solution concepts is assured only under special conditions. An examination of the game in Figure 3 reveals why the principles underlying bargaining set theory are inappropriate for spatial games. Since a coalition cannot freely transfer utility, a coalition's proposal exhibits a particular type of externality. It cannot withhold the benefits of the policy it chooses from anyone, including players that are admitted to the coalition simply to render it winning. Player 2, for example, cannot defend the payoff he associates with θ, but he cannot also be excluded from this payoff; players 1 and 3 necessarily give player 2 more than he is worth — in violation of the bargaining set notion that every player defend his payoff from all possible objections. Since these externalities are inescapable, bargaining set theory yields no stable payoff configuration for $\{1, 2, 3\}$.

There is, however, an alternative interpretation of this example and of bargaining set theory suggested by Laing and Morrison (1974) that yields an interesting contrast between this theory and the solution concept we propose. Suppose coalition structures that do not possess stable payoff configurations are interpreted as structures that bargaining set theory predicts will not form. For the game in Figure 3 it is possible to show that, with respect to the minimal winning coalitions, the bargaining set makes the following predictions,

Coalitions that will not form (i.e., have no stable payoff configurations)	**Coalitions that can form (i.e., have stable payoff configurations)**
$\{1, 2, 3\}$	$\{1, 3, 4\}$
$\{2, 3, 4\}$	$\{2, 4, 5\}$
$\{3, 4, 5\}$	$\{1, 3, 5\}$
$\{4, 5, 1\}$	$\{1, 2, 4\}$
$\{5, 1, 2\}$	$\{2, 3, 5\}$

That is, the only minimal winning coalitions with stable payoff configurations are those that geometrically "split the opposition." These configurations, moreover, correspond to proposals in the interior pentagon of Figure 3. It is important to keep these predictions in mind when we turn to the Competitive Solution, and to the experimental results.

2. The Competitive Solution

Turning to n-person games in general (as opposed to only simple or spatial games) the solution concept proposed here hypothesizes that potential coalitions must bid for their members in a competitive environment via the proposals they offer. Given that several coalitions are attempting to form simultaneously, each coalition must, if possible, bid efficiently by appropriately rewarding its "critical" members. Thus, if any one player or set of players is pivotal between two coalitions and if each coalition is to have a chance of forming, the pivotal players should be indifferent between the offers of both coalitions lest their preferences insure that one of the two cannot form. This can result in certain coalitions being unable to compete, and thus, we must identify not only the competitive offers of coalitions, but also, the coalitions that can make them.

To formalize this imprecise and anthropomorphic perspective, we define:

Proposal: A *proposal* of $C \subseteq N$ is an ordered pair $(u : C)$ such that $u \in v(C)$ and $u \in v(N)$.

Viable: For any two proposals $(u_1; C_1)$ and $(u_2; C_2)$, $(u_1; C_1)$ is *viable* against $(u_2; C_2)$ if it is not the case that $u_1 <_i u_2$ for all $i \in C_1 \cap C_2$.[5]

For any two coalitions C_1, $C_2 \subseteq N$, the set $C_1 \cap C_2$ is referred to as the *pivotal players between C_1 and C_2*. The proposal $(u_1; C_1)$ is viable against $(u_2; C_2)$, then, if the pivotal players do not strictly prefer the proposal of the coalition into which they pivot. Now let $\mathcal{K}$ be any set of proposals. A proposal $(u; C)$ is viable in $\mathcal{K}$ if it is viable against all proposals in $\mathcal{K}$. Then,[6]

Balanced: $\mathcal{K}$ *is balanced* if

(i) For any distinct $(u; C)$ and $(u'; C') \in \mathcal{K}$, $C \neq C'$.
(ii) Every $(u; C) \in \mathcal{K}$ is viable in $\mathcal{K}$.

---

[5]In an earlier version of this paper we also required for viability that
$u_1 \geq_i u_2$ for all $i \in C_1 - (C_1 \cap C_2)$.

i.e., that the non-pivotal players weakly prefer their coalition's proposal. For simple games this condition is redundant. For non-simple games, though, this modification in the definition of viability may be necessary to insure the existence of a Competitive Solution.

[6]The word "balanced" is unrelated to and should not be confused with the notions of "balanced collection" and "balanced game" that are used to establish sufficient conditions for non-empty cores. See, for example, Herbert E. Scarf (1967).

Condition i requires that each coalition represented in $\mathcal{K}$ can have exactly one proposal. Condition ii requires all proposals in $\mathcal{K}$ to be viable against each other.

There may exist many distinct balanced sets of proposals. We focus, then, on the class of proposals in which the coalitions represented in $\mathcal{K}$ make offers that are as attractive as possible to their respective critical members. To define this precisely, we say that

Upset: A proposal $(u; C)$ upsets $\mathcal{K}$ if
  (i) $(u; C)$ is viable in $\mathcal{K}$.
  (ii) For some $(u'; C') \in \mathcal{K}$ $u >_i u'$ for all $i \in C \cap C'$.

Then, letting $M_\mathcal{K}$ be the set of coalitions represented in $\mathcal{K}$, i.e., $M_\mathcal{K} = \{C \subseteq N |$ for some $(u'; C') \in \mathcal{K}, C' = C'\}$, we define

Competitively Balanced: $\mathcal{K}$ is *competitively balanced* if it is balanced and if for no $C \in M_\mathcal{K}$ is there a proposal $(u; C)$ that upsets $\mathcal{K}$.

Clearly, competitively balanced sets are particular to an assumed coalition structure: with a different initial assumption about the coalitions that make proposals, we might arrive at a different competitively balanced set. The dependence of $\mathcal{K}$ on $M_\mathcal{K}$ can be viewed as an advantage since it permits us to model situations in which there are legal or sociological restrictions on alignments. Nevertheless, a completely general solution should admit the possibility that any coalition can enter the bidding, and to this end we say that

$\mathcal{K}$ *is a Competitive Solution if* $\mathcal{K}$ *is balanced and if there is no proposal* $(u; C)$ *that upsets* $\mathcal{K}$.

As a possible further refinement of this definition, we note that the notion of "balanced" used to formulate this definition permits pivotal groups of players to weakly prefer one proposal over another. Later, we illustrate this possibility and show how it raises problems for the hypothesis of minimal winning coalitions. But, at least for the examples we examine, a stronger definition of "balanced" and, hence, of $\mathcal{K}$, excludes coalitions greater than minimal winning size.

Strongly Balanced: $\mathcal{K}$ is strongly balanced if it is balanced and, if for no $(u_1; C_1), (u_2; C_2) \in \mathcal{K}$, is it the case that

$$u_1 \geq_i u_2$$

for all $i \in C_1 \cap C_2$, with $>_i$ holding for at least one $i \in C_1 \cap C_2$.

For a stronger version of $\mathcal{K}$, then, we have,

$\mathcal{K}$ *is a Strong Competitive Solution if it is a Competitive Solution that is strongly balanced.*

Before illustrating these definitions, we observe that there is a close correspondence between $\mathcal{K}$ and the solution concepts of the Core, the V-set, and the bargaining set. This, of course, is desirable since the imputations identified by main-simple V-sets, for example, often are intuitively plausible. Further, there already exists some experimental support for these predictions as well as the predictions of the Core and the bargaining set. Theorems 1 and 2, then, formally establish a relationship between $\mathcal{K}$ and the Core, ℓ, and the V-set (for proofs, see McKelvey and Ordeshook, 1978).

THEOREM 1. *If $u \in \ell$, then $\mathcal{K} = \{(u; N)\}$ is a Strong Competitive Solution.*

THEOREM 2. *If V is a main-simple V-set for a strong simple game, then there is a Strong Competitive Solution $\mathcal{K}$ such that $(u; C) \in \mathcal{K} \Longrightarrow C \in W^*$, $u \in V$.*

With respect to the bargaining set, Wilson shows that for all simple games, the "strong" bargaining set is equivalent to the main-simple V-solution. It follows from Theorem 2, then, that the strong bargaining set is a Strong Competitive Solution.

The links Theorems 1 and 2 establish between $\mathcal{K}$ and ℓ and between $\mathcal{K}$ and V are important. A great deal is already known about ℓ and V mathematically. More importantly, though, if the definition of $\mathcal{K}$ is behaviorally meaningful, these links suggest that $\mathcal{K}$ can provide a behavioral motivation for solution concepts that presently are little more than mathematical inventions.

To illustrate this, as well as the several earlier definitions, consider again the logrolling example from Table 1 and the following proposals:

Majority Decision	Proposal	
pass only bills 1 and 2	$(4, 3, -6; \{1, 2\})$	
pass only bills 1 and 2	$(4, -4, 3; \{1, 3\})$	$\equiv \mathcal{K}$
pass only bills 1 and 2	$(-2, 3, 3; \{2, 3\})$	

Note that the coalitions offering proposals here are winning and, hence, these are legitimate proposals (i.e., $u \in v(C)$). Second, note that these proposals are viable against each other and thus are (strongly) balanced; for example, player 1 pivots between the proposals of $\{1, 2\}$ and $\{1, 3\}$ and holds no strict preference either way. Further, referring to Table 1, no minimal winning coalition can offer an alternative proposal that makes all of its members strictly better off — these proposals cannot be upset by $\{1, 2\}$, $\{1, 3\}$ or $\{2, 3\}$. Hence, $\mathcal{K}$ is competitively balanced. Finally, to check whether $\mathcal{K}$ is a competitive solution, suppose that the coalition of the whole, $\{1, 2, 3\}$ attempts to enter the bidding with a proposal of its own. But, this is impossible since for any proposal by $\{1, 2, 3\}$, the pivotal players will correspond to a minimal winning coalition and we know already that there does not exist another possibility that makes all members of any such coalition strictly better off. That is, condition ii in the definition of upset cannot be satisfied by any proposal for $\{1, 2, 3\}$.

Consider, on the other hand, the following proposals:

$$\left\{ \begin{array}{l} (4, 3, -6; \{1, 2, 3\}) \\ (4, -4, 3; \{1, 3\}) \\ (-2, 3, 3; \{2, 3\}) \end{array} \right\} \equiv \mathcal{K}'$$

$\mathcal{K}'$ is identical here to $\mathcal{K}$ except that $\{1, 2, 3\}$ proposes the payoffs $(4, 3, -6)$ rather than $\{1, 2\}$. Following the earlier argument, it follows that $\mathcal{K}'$ is a competitive solution as well. It is not, however, a strong solution. For example, the pivots between $\{1, 2, 3\}$ and $\{1, 3\}$ — players 1 and 3 — weakly prefer $(4, -4, 3)$ to $(4, 3, -6)$. In this instance, then, the strong but not the weak version of $\mathcal{K}$ predicts that only minimal winning coalitions form.

It is possible to show now that the payoffs in these three proposals also constitute a main-simple V-set. However, the advantage of $\mathcal{K}$ is that, by linking payoffs to specific coalitions, $\mathcal{K}$, but not V, tells us the vote trades that correspond to particular payoff outcomes. For example, the proposal $(4, 3, -6; \{1, 2\})$ implies that player 1 trades his vote on bill 2 for player 2's vote on bill 1. Similarly, $(-2, 3, 3; \{2, 3\})$ implies that player 2 trades his vote on bill 3 for player 3's vote on bill 2.

The preceding theorems and example should not be interpreted to mean that there is correspondence between $\mathcal{K}$ and V-sets for all games. To illustrate, consider the five-person, five-bill logrolling game described in Table 2. We assume as before that utility is separable across bills so that, for example, legislator 2's utility from passing bills 2, 3, and 4 is -4 (i.e., $0 + 1 - 2 - 3 + 0$). Excluding lotteries, the following outcomes correspond to the unique Competitive Solution to this majority game.

TABLE 2. 5-Person, 5-Bill Logrolling Example

	Utility from Individual Bills if Passed					
Legislator	None	1	2	3	4	5
1	0	1	−2	−3	1	2
2	0	2	1	−2	−3	1
3	0	1	2	1	−2	−3
4	0	−3	1	2	1	−2
5	0	−2	−3	1	2	1

Coalition	Majority Decision
$\{1,2,3\}$	pass bill 1, defeat remainder
$\{2,3,4\}$	pass bill 2, defeat remainder
$\{3,4,5\}$	pass bill 3, defeat remainder
$\{1,4,5\}$	pass bill 4, defeat remainder
$\{1,2,5\}$	pass bill 5, defeat remainder

$\mathcal{K}$, then, does predict vote trading since, if everyone voted sincerely, all bills pass, yielding the payoff vector $(-1, -1, -1, -1, -1)$. More interestingly, though, note that the payoffs corresponding to outcomes in $\mathcal{K}$ do not constitute a V-set: the condition of internal stability is not satisfied. For example, the payoff vector $(1, 2, 1, -3, -2)$, which corresponds to $\{1,2,3\}$'s proposal, dominates $(-2, 1, 2, 1, -3)$, which corresponds to $\{2,3,4\}$'s proposal. In fact, excluding lotteries, this game does not possess a main simple V-set.

3. Spatial Games

The preceding example is a prelude to the application of $\mathcal{K}$ to spatial games. Recalling that $u_i(\theta) = f(\|\theta - x_i\|)$, the following definitions are useful for analyzing such games. Letting

$$\bar{V}_C = \{\theta | \theta \in A \text{ and for no other } \theta' \in A \text{ is it the case that } \theta' \succ_i \theta \text{ for all } i \in C\}$$

then, a coalition $C \in W$ is *external* if there is some other coalition $C' \in W$ with $C \cup C' = N, C \cap C' = \{i\}$ for some $i \in N$ and $\bar{V}_C \cap \bar{V}_{C'} = \{x_i\}$. Any winning coalition that is not external is *internal*.

In Figure 3, for example, the coalitions not possessing stable payoff configurations — predicted not to form by bargaining set theory — are external while those with stable configurations are internal. This is particularly interesting in light of the following conjecture, which assists us in finding solutions:

Conjecture: In any spatial game there exists a competitive solution, $\mathcal{K}$, such that if $(\theta; C) \in \mathcal{K}$, then C is an external coalition.

We can prove this conjecture for $n \leq 5$ person games and are unable to find a counterexample in any larger game for which $\mathcal{K}$ has been computed. Despite the fact that we are unable to prove this conjecture more generally, it is especially interesting because of two properties of external coalitions in majority rule games: (1) if C is external, then it is minimal winning, and (2) if C is external, then it is *connected*, where by connected we mean that for no $i \in N$, $i \notin C$, is it the case that x_i is in the interior of $\bar{V}_C$. Hence, the close correspondence between $\mathcal{K}$ and at least two hypotheses about legislative and parliamentary coalitions suggests the possibility of deducing these hypotheses directly from a formal solution concept.

Finding a solution based on the external coalitions, moreover, is rendered easier oftentimes by the following property: If $C \in M_\mathcal{K}$, and $i \in C$, i is *critical* if $C \cap C' = \{i\}$, for some $C' \in M_\mathcal{K}$. Then,

Property 1: If a set of proposals $\mathcal{K}$ is balanced and if for all $(\theta; C) \in \mathcal{K}, \theta \in \bar{V}_{C^*}$, where $C^* \subseteq C$ is the set of critical members in C, then $\mathcal{K}$ is competitively balanced.

We illustrate the application of this result by proceeding directly to some examples of spatial games.

Example 1, Three Players. Consider the three-person spatial game portrayed in Figure 2, and recall that $\{\theta_1, \theta_2, \theta_3\}$ corresponds there to a main-simple V-set and to a bargaining set. Turning to the Competitive Solution, the set of minimal winning coalitions is $W^* = \{\{1,2\},\{1,3\},\{2,3\}\}$, which is also the set of external winning coalitions. Hence, we let $M = W^*$ and seek a set of balanced proposals, based on M satisfying Property 1. We have then, the following coalitions, individual pivots and proposals.

External Coalitions	Individual Pivots	Policy Proposal
$\{2,3\}$	$2,3$	$\theta_1 \in \bar{V}_{23}$
$\{1,3\}$	$1,3$	$\theta_2 \in \bar{V}_{13}$
$\{1,2\}$	$1,2$	$\theta_3 \in \bar{V}_{12}$

Letting $\mathcal{K} = \{(\theta_1; \{2,3\}), (\theta_1; \{1,3\}), (\theta_3; \{1,2\})\}$, where θ_i is the proposal of the coalition that excludes player i, $\mathcal{K}$ is balanced only if

$$u_1(\theta_2) = u_1(\theta_3)$$
$$u_2(\theta_1) = u_2(\theta_3)$$
$$u_3(\theta_1) = u_3(\theta_2)$$

otherwise player 1 is not indifferent between the two proposals, θ_2 and θ_3, for which he is a pivot, and so on. The solution to these three expressions is, of course, the joint pairing of tangencies portrayed in Figure 2.[7] Further, since θ_1 is obviously in $\bar{V}_{23}$, and so on, the conditions of Property 1 are satisfied. To check then whether $\mathcal{K}$ is a Competitive Solution, we need only consider the possibility that the coalition of the whole can upset $\mathcal{K}$ by entering the bidding. First it follows that any proposal of N, say θ, cannot correspond to θ_1, θ_2 or θ_3. For if it does, it will not upset $\mathcal{K}$. But if $\{1,2,3\}$ proposes some other policy, say θ^*, θ^* is not viable against θ_1 since the pivots between $\{2,3\}$ and $\{1,2,3\}$ both prefer θ_1. Thus, $\mathcal{K}$ is a Competitive Solution.

It is easily seen, moreover, that $\mathcal{K}$, as defined above, constitutes a Strong Competitive Solution. We note, however, that,

$$\{(\theta_1; \{2,3\}), (\theta_2; \{1,3\}), (\theta_3; \{1,2,3\})\}$$

which admits a greater than minimal winning coalition, is a Competitive Solution as well, but it is not a strong solution. Specifically, the pivots 2 and 3 between $\{2,3\}$ and $\{1,2,3\}$ weakly prefer θ_1 to θ_3 (i.e., player 2 is indifferent between θ_1 and θ_3, but player 3 strictly prefers θ_1 to θ_3). Thus, as in the previous logrolling examples, a *Strong Competitive Solution eliminates coalitions that are greater than minimal winning.*

Example 2, Four Players. A four-person spatial game with Euclidean utility is interesting here only if the dimensionality of the policy space exceeds 2 or if the players are not equally weighted. Otherwise, the game possesses a Core. Consider, then, a four-person weighted voting game in which $W^* = \{\{1,2\}, \{1,3\}, \{1,4\}, \{2,3,4\}\}$, which could model a cabinet formation game, where the voting weights, w_i, of the players (parties) are: $w_1 = 40$, $w_2 = w_3 = w_4 = 20$. Suppose now that the set of external coalitions is $\{1,2\}, \{1,4\}$,

---

[7]The exact location of the solution points is given by
$$\theta_i = \frac{r_j}{r_j + r_k} x_i + \frac{r_j}{r_j + r_k} x_j \quad \text{for } i,j,k \in \{1,2,3\}$$
where for $1 \leq i \leq 3$,
$$r_i = \frac{\|x_i - x_j\| - \|x_j - x_k\| + \|x_i - x_k\|}{2}$$

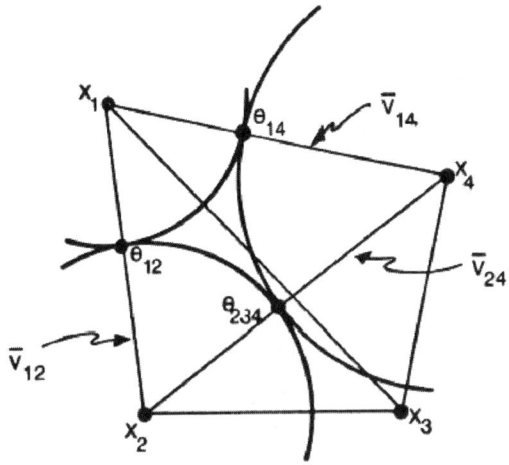

FIGURE 4

$\{2, 3, 4\}$, as portrayed in Figure 4. (Note that $\{1, 3\}$ is not external since it "divides the opposition.") We proceed, then, by setting M equal to this set and by solving for points that satisfy Property 1.

External Coalitions	Individual Pivots	Policy Proposal of Coalition
$\{1, 2\}$	1, 2	$\theta_{12} \in \bar{V}_{12}$
$\{1, 4\}$	1, 4	$\theta_{14} \in \bar{V}_{14}$
$\{2, 3, 4\}$	2, 4	$\theta_{234} \in \bar{V}_{24}$

Figure 4 portrays the appropriate competitively balanced set.

A quick check reveals that these three proposals are *strongly* competitively balanced. To see that they constitute a strong *Competitive Solution* we need to check whether $\{1, 3\}$ and the greater than minimal winning coalitions can upset $\mathcal{K}$ by entering the bidding. For brevity, we consider only $\{1, 3\}$ here. First, if $\{1, 3\}$'s proposal is to be viable, it must provide player 1 with at least as much utility as does θ_{12} and θ_{14}, since player 1 is pivotal between $\{1, 3\}$ and $\{1, 2\}$ and between $\{1, 3\}$ and $\{1, 4\}$. Similarly, $\{1, 3\}$'s proposal must give player 3 at least as much as he gets from θ_{234}. But, as is evident from Figure 4, both conditions cannot be satisfied simultaneously. Hence, $\{1, 3\}$ cannot compete. Since a similar argument holds for the greater than minimal winning coalitions,

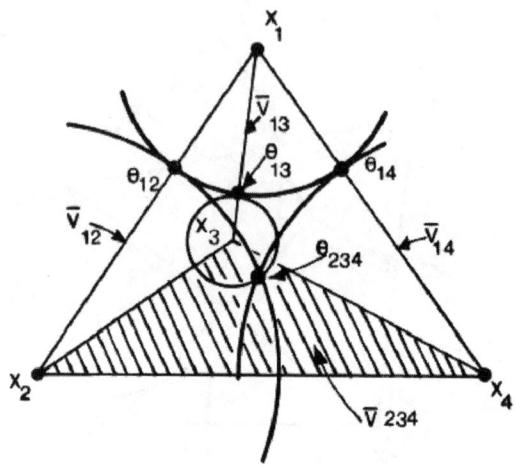

FIGURE 5

$\mathcal{K} = \{(\theta_{12}; \{1,2\}), (\theta_{14}; \{1,4\}), (\theta_{234}; \{2,3,4\})\}$ constitutes a Strong Competitive Solution.

It is interesting to observe in this example that $\mathcal{K}$ also constitutes a V-set (but, not main-simple). However, unlike V-set theory, $\mathcal{K}$ also predicts that only minimal winning coalitions form and that the minimal winning coalition $\{1,3\}$ does not form. $\mathcal{K}$, then, provides a stronger and more readily tested prediction.

To ascertain the influence of spatial location, though, consider the four-person configuration in Figure 5, which differs from the configuration in Figure 4 only in that $\{1,3\}$ is now external. Hence, we set $M = W^*$, and

External Coalitions	Individual Pivots	Policy Proposal of Coalition
$\{1,2\}$	1, 2	$\theta_{12} \in \bar{V}_{12}$
$\{1,3\}$	1, 3	$\theta_{13} \in \bar{V}_{13}$
$\{1,4\}$	1, 4	$\theta_{14} \in \bar{V}_{14}$
$\{2,3,4\}$	2, 3, 4	$\theta_{234} \in \bar{V}_{24}$

Figure 5 portrays the corresponding (strong) competitively balanced set, which is (without proof) a Strong Competitive Solution. Clearly, then, $\mathcal{K}$ is sensitive to spatial location since, now, $\{1,3\}$ has a viable proposal.

Example 3, Five-Person Games. The variety of types of spatial games becomes quite rich for five-player games, and it is here that the correspondence between $\mathcal{K}$ and the V-set disappears. To ease exposition we consider only simple games in R^2 without weighted voting. Nevertheless, the location and number of the external coalitions can vary considerably, depending on the configuration of ideal points. Specifically, let $G \subseteq R^m$ be the convex hull of the players' ideal points, and let G^{int} be the interior of this set. There are, then, three classes of ideal point configurations:

a)   no player's ideal point is in G^{int}
b)   exactly one player's ideal point is in G^{int}
c)   exactly two player's ideal points are in G^{int}

We illustrate here only cases (a) and (b).

(a) No $x_i \in G^{int}$: A typical configuration of type (a), which reproduces Figure 3, is portrayed in Figure 6. Since here $\{\{1,2,3\}, \{2,3,4\}, \{3,4,5\}, \{4,5,1\}, \{5,1,2\}\}$ is the set of external coalitions, we let M equal this set and, let $\mathcal{K}$ be the set of proposals on the joint tangencies of the pivotal players, as illustrated in Figure 6.[8]

External Coalitions	Individual Pivots	Group Pivots	Policy Proposal of Coalition
$C_1 = \{5,1,2\}$	5, 2	$\{5,1\}, \{1,2\}$	$\theta_1 \in \bar{V}_{52}$
$C_2 = \{1,2,3\}$	1, 3	$\{1,2\}, \{2,3\}$	$\theta_2 \in \bar{V}_{13}$
$C_3 = \{2,3,4\}$	2, 4	$\{2,3\}, \{3,4\}$	$\theta_3 \in \bar{V}_{24}$
$C_4 = \{3,4,5\}$	3, 5	$\{3,4\}, \{4,5\}$	$\theta_4 \in \bar{V}_{35}$
$C_5 = \{4,5,1\}$	4, 1	$\{4,5\}, \{5,1\}$	$\theta_5 \in \bar{V}_{41}$

We emphasize that this method of solving for the Competitive Solution is valid only if the pivotal groups do not hold preferences among the proposals of the coalitions for which they are pivotal. A quick glance at Figure 6 reveals that

---

[8]The exact location of the solution points is as follows: If $j, k, l, m, n \in N$, with $k = j+l$ (mod 5), $l = k+1$ (mod 5), etc., then

$$\theta_j = \frac{1}{2}[s_{km} - s_{mj} + s_{jl} - s_{ln} - s_{nr}]$$

$$r_n = \frac{1}{2}[s_{nk} - s_{kn} + s_{mj} - s_{jl} - s_{ln}]$$

and $s_{pq} = \|x_p - x_q\|$ for any $p, q \subseteq N$. Cf. McKelvey and Ordeshook (1978) for a description of an algorithm for locating $\mathcal{K}$ for general configurations of ideal points and also for more general types of preferences.

this condition holds. For example, $\{1,2\}$ pivots between θ_1 and θ_2; but while player 1 prefers θ_1 to θ_2, player 2 prefers θ_2 to θ_1. This argument reveals also, of course, that $\mathcal{K} = \{(\theta_i, C_i) | 1 \leq i \leq 5\}$ is a *Strong* Competitive Solution. It is not, however, a V-set; while $\mathcal{K}$ is externally stable it is not internally stable. Specifically, θ_5 dominates θ_1 via the coalition $\{3, 4, 5\}$, θ_2 dominates θ_5 via $\{2, 3, 4\}$, and so on. This game does possess V-sets, but, while we may be missing something, those we can identify are discriminatory and consist of arc segments that together justify every point in the interior pentagon of Figure 6.[9] None possess the simple intuitive geometric plausability of $\mathcal{K}$. More importantly, though, $\mathcal{K}$ predicts exactly those coalitions that bargaining set theory can be interpreted to predict will not form, while none of the coalitions predicted by bargaining set theory are predicted by $\mathcal{K}$. The experimental use of this example, then, should provide a critical test of these alternative solution theories.

(b) *Exactly one* $x_i \in G^{int}$: Thus far in the spatial examples, all Competitive Solutions are also strong solutions. Consider, however, the configuration in Figure 7. The set of external coalitions here is $\{\{1, 5, 4\}, \{1, 5, 2\}, \{2, 5, 3\}, \{4, 5, 3\}, \{2, 3, 4\}, \{1, 3, 4\}\}$, and these are the coalitions for which we first attempt to find a competitively balanced set of proposals.

---

[9] An illustrative discriminatory V-solution is portrayed in the figure below:

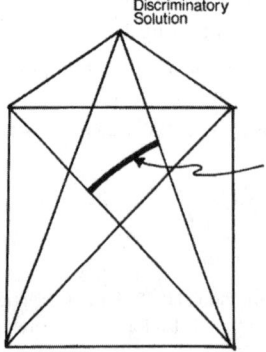

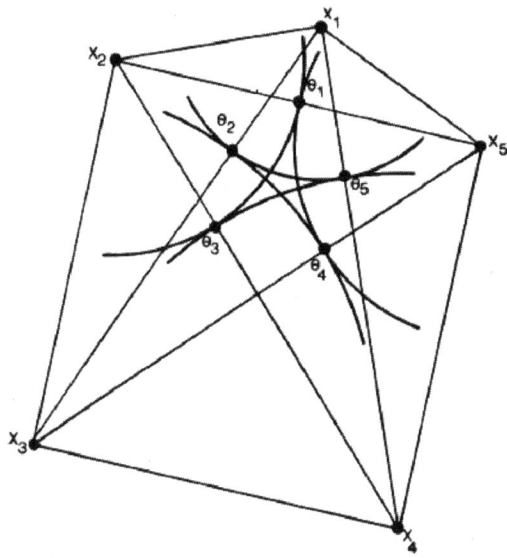

FIGURE 6

External Coalitions	Individual Pivots	Group Pivots	Policy Proposal of Coalition
$C_1 = \{1,5,4\}$	4, 5	all	$\theta_1 \in \bar{V}_{45}$
$C_2 = \{1,5,2\}$	1, 5, 2	$\{1,5\}, \{1,2\}$	$\theta_2 \in \bar{V}_{152}$
$C_3 = \{2,5,3\}$	3, 5	all	$\theta_3 \in \bar{V}_{35}$
$C_4 = \{4,5,3\}$	5	all	θ_4
$C_5 = \{2,3,4\}$	2, 4	$\{2,3\}, \{3,4\}$	$\theta_5 \in \bar{V}_{23}$
$C_6 = \{1,3,4\}$	1, 3	$\{3,4\}, \{1,4\}$	$\theta_6 \in \bar{V}_{13}$

In this example, however, we cannot use Property 1. To see this, note that $\theta_4 \in \bar{V}_5$ implies $\theta_4 = x_5$. And, since player 5 is the sole individual pivot between the coalitions $\{4,5,3\}$ and $\{1,5,2\}$, 5 must be indifferent between θ_2 and θ_4, i.e., $\theta_2 = x_5$. But, now the proposals θ_5 and θ_6 are preferred by $\{3,4\}$ to the proposal of $\{4,5,3\}$ and, since $\{3,4\}$ pivots between $\{4,5,3\}$ and $\{2,3,4\}$, the conditions for $\mathcal{K} = \{(\theta_i, C_i) | 1 \leq i \leq 6\}$ being balanced are violated. Despite the fact that we cannot use Property 1, we can nevertheless find a balanced set of proposals. We do not solve for them here analytically, but the five proposals portrayed in

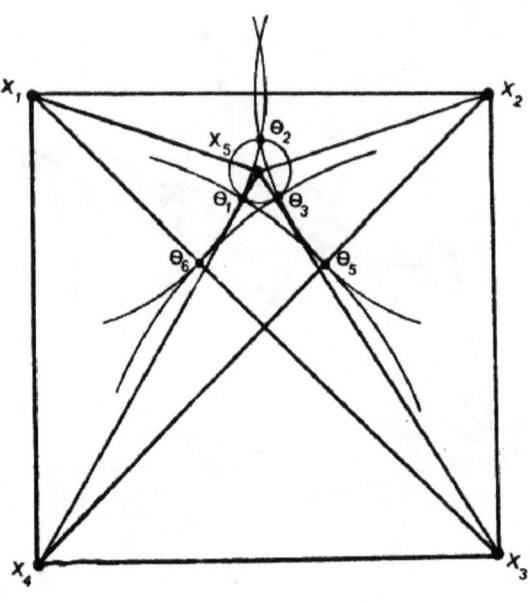

FIGURE 7

Figure 7 constitute a Competitive Solution. Note that the proposal θ_4 is excluded since the coalition $\{3, 4, 5\}$ has no viable proposal.

As before, the five proposals of coalitions in $\mathcal{K}$ which are portrayed in Figure 7 do not constitute a V-solution: while they are externally stable, they are not internally stable. Specifically, θ_3 and θ_1 dominate θ_2 via the coalition $\{3, 4, 5\}$. Unlike our previous examples, however, $\mathcal{K}$ is not a *Strong* Competitive Solution: the pivots $\{1, 4\}$ weakly prefer θ_6 to θ_1. In fact this particular configuration does not appear to possess a strong solution.

4. Experimental Results

This section reports a preliminary test of the Competitive Solution's empirical validity. The correspondence established in Section 2 between $\mathcal{K}$ and the Core, the V-set, and bargaining set theory suggests that much experimental research which tests these concepts is also a test of the Competitive Solution. We cannot review this literature here except to say that its conclusions are encouraging but fragmentary. But also, almost without exception, this experimental research assumes that utility is linear in money and that money (and thus utility) is freely transferable. The experiments we report here use money to induce preferences, but we do not permit money to be transferred among players. Hence, the context of these experiments is a game without transferable utility.

The game we use is the simple five-person spatial game portrayed in Figure 6, which is particularly interesting because, first, it does not possess a main-simple V-set. Second, the discriminatory V-sets justify outcomes in the interior pentagon of Figure 6, while the Strong Competitive Solution predicts five distinct points on this pentagon's hull. Third, $\mathcal{K}$ is not internally stable and thus any apparent empirical support for the Competitive Solution here would seriously question the behavioral imperative of the internal stability property of V-sets. Finally, $\mathcal{K}$ predicts that only five of the ten minimal winning coalitions possess proposals and these five are exactly those that do not correspond to stable payoff configurations under bargaining set theory.

Briefly, eight games were played using 33 students from the MS program of C-MU's Graduate School of Industrial Administration. All participants had played a three-person spatial game previously to familiarize them with the game's concepts and rules, but no two subjects played together more than once. Further, no subject received any formal training in game theory nor were any of them, at any time, instructed about the Competitive Solution.

The format of these experiments is detailed elsewhere and so we note only briefly here that the players' task is to reach a majority agreement on some point on a grid corresponding to the game in Figure 6.[10] To induce preferences, each player is given a grid that portrays several of his indifference contours and each contour is assigned a dollar value that decreases as the distance from x_i increases. No player knows another's payoff (but they do know each other's preferences, including each other's ideal preferences). To retain the non-transferable utility context of the experiment, players are prohibited from any discussion of schemes to divide their winnings or, in fact, from any mention of money whatsoever during the experiment. Bargaining is allowed to proceed freely, and the experiment is terminated when members of a majority coalition agree to jointly sign a form indicating the final agreement. Each player (including those not in the majority coalition) is then paid in accordance with his payoff schedule and the agreement point.

---

[10]In the context of testing the core as a solution concept, the structure of these experiments and the instructions read to subject (with obvious appropriate modifications) are given in J. Berl, R. McKelvey, P. C. Ordeshook, and M. Winer, 1976. We would like to note, in addition, that the procedures used here closely parallel those of Morris Fiorina and Charles Plott (1978).

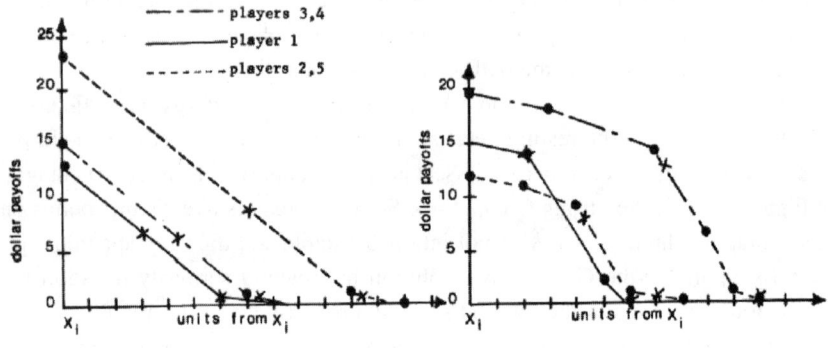

FIGURE 8

The players' payoff schedules take either of two forms — linear or nonlinear (see Figure 8). We did not, however, mix forms in a game. While this procedure might permit players to infer the schedules of others from their own, the players were told that there is no symmetry to payoff schedules and that they cannot infer the schedules of others from their own. Ideal point payoffs range between $12 and $23 while zero is a player's minimum payoff. The approximate total payoff in each game is $25.

Assuming the validity of these procedures, we know that this game does not possess a main-simple V-set or a bargaining set for the external coalitions, whereas Figure 6 displays its Strong Competitive Solution. Figure 9 contrasts this solution with the actual outcomes of the experiments while Table 3 summarizes the relevant data.

Even a casual glance at these results reveals a remarkable correspondence between outcomes and the Competitive Solution's predictions. First, in only one game (No. 5) is there a "significant" deviation from the Solution. Second, all outcomes lie in the Pareto optimals of the winning coalitions that proposed them. Finally, *all five external minimal winning coalitions predicted by K formed at least once and only these coalitions formed.* Stated differently, *no coalition formed that corresponds to a stable payoff configuration under bargaining set theory.*

Figure 9 reveals another interesting pattern in the outcomes. Noting that the various discriminatory V-sets predict outcomes in the interior pentagon, note also that no outcome in these experiments lies in this pentagon. *To the extent, then, that the data support the Competitive Solution, they also weaken the argument for V-sets as appropriate definitions of a solution.* Instead, all deviations occasioned

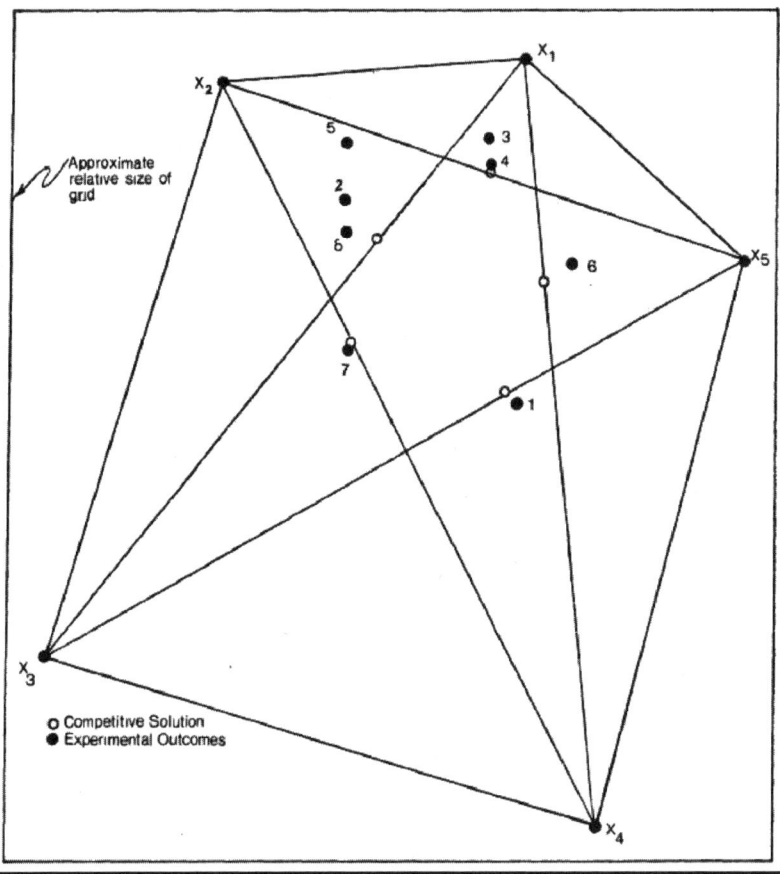

FIGURE 9

by, for example, the coalition $\{1,2,3\}$ favor player 2, those occasioned by the coalition $\{5,1,2\}$ favor player 1, and so on. That is, in every game the two players furthest apart (the critical members of the coalition) appear to be "buying" the third off. Thus, it seems as if the third player has some bargaining power in the coalition, which, of course, is untrue according to the theory since this player does not pivot into another coalition with a proposal in $\mathcal{K}$ (i.e., the player is not critical). Given the properties of the players' indifference contours, however, we note that small deviations towards 2's ideal away from player 1 and 3's contract curve decrease 1 and 3's payoff by only pennies, whereas the benefit to 2 can be

TABLE 3. Summary of Experiments

Game and Type	Payoffs — Predicted/Actual					Coalition
	1	2	3	4	5	
1. Linear	1.25 / 1.00	.75 / .75	5.00 / 5.00	9.00 / 9.00	5.00 / 5.00	{3, 4, 5}
2. Non-linear	6.00 / 6.00	9.25 / 10.00	6.00 / 6.00	.50 / 0	1.50 / 1.50	{1, 2, 3}
3. Non-linear	13.75 / 14.25	5.00 / 5.00	0 / 0	0 / .50	5.00 / 5.00	{1, 2, 5}
4. Linear	8.50 / 8.50	5.00 / 5.00	1.00 / 1.00	1.00 / 1.00	5.00 / 5.00	{1, 2, 5}
5. Linear	5.00 / 6.00	8.25 / 10.00	5.00 / 3.25	2.00 / 1.00	1.50 / 1.50	{1, 2, 3}
6. Non-linear	6.00 / 7.50	.50 / .50	.50 / 0	6.00 / 4.00	9.25 / 9.75	{1, 4, 5}
7. Non-linear	.50 / 0	5.00 / 5.00	13.00 / 13.00	6.00 / 6.00	.50 / .25	{2, 3, 4}
8. Non-linear	6.00 / 5.00	9.25 / 9.75	6.00 / 7.00	.50 / 0	.50 / .50	{1, 2, 3}

considerable (on the order of fifty cents to a dollar). Only three players in winning coalitions received less than predicted whereas six received more, thereby adding weight to the argument that the third non-critical player is being "bought" at near-zero cost to his partners.

Finally, we note that in no game was the coalition of the whole seriously considered, and the issue of equity or fairness arose explicitly in the bargaining only once (the idea of an equitable proposal was quickly rejected and never mentioned again). Most subjects recognized the instability of the situation and a few noted after the game that their objective was to form a winning and acceptable coalition as quickly as possible (despite the fact that several games ran for nearly an hour). Hence, in some cases a form of satisficing appears to have affected calculations and strategies. Again, though, several players commented on the necessity for revising their assessment of "acceptable payoffs" as the game progressed.

Clearly, much additional analysis and experimentation are required. The subjects in these experiments are not known for their lack of competitiveness and, doubtless, this improves our results. Further, alternative configurations of preferences and utility functions should be considered. In particular, a configuration with an internal ideal point should provide a more critical test of $\mathcal{K}$ since a Strong

Solution does not exist there and since the meaning of internal and external coalitions is less obvious.

5. Conclusions

The Competitive Solution's motivation is most compatible with the unrestricted bargaining process of our experiments. It seems less well suited to processes that use formal voting procedures or to procedures that admit secret negotiations. $\mathcal{K}$, nevertheless possesses several important advantages over classical concepts. First, in many examples, the proposals by coalitions in $\mathcal{K}$ reduce to the main-simple V-set and thereby provide a behavioral rationale for hypothesizing outcomes in V. Second, neither the Core nor the V-set identify the coalitions that form to support payoff vectors in them, while bargaining set theory in general takes the coalition structure as a given and identifies the proposals it can support. $\mathcal{K}$, on the other hand, isolates the coalitions that can compete successfully for members as well as the proposals they offer. And, in one instance where bargaining set theory can be interpreted as making coalition predictions, the experimental evidence conclusively supports $\mathcal{K}$ as opposed to that theory's predictions.

Third, in all spatial examples, the (strong) Competitive Solution corresponds to proposals made only by minimal winning and connected coalitions (i.e., no excluded player lies within the convex hull of a coalition with a proposal in $\mathcal{K}$). And, while we may have missed some possibilities, we are unable to find solutions in these examples that entail coalitions that are other than minimal winning and connected. Hence, these are good reasons for conjecturing that the minimal winning and connected coalitions hypotheses can be deduced from the properties of $\mathcal{K}$.

Finally, the Competitive Solution treats those examples that classical concepts fail to solve. Since these examples correspond to the implicit or explicit conceptualizations others use to model legislative or parliamentary coalition processes, the implication is that $\mathcal{K}$ is the more useful concept.

References

Aumann, Robert J. (1967). "A Survey of Cooperative Games Without Side Payments." In M. Shubik (ed.), *Essays in Mathematical Economics in Honor of Oskar Morgenstern*. Princeton: Princeton University Press.

Aumann, Robert J., and M. Maschler (1964). "The Bargaining Set for Cooperative Games." In M. Dresher, L. S. Shapley and A. W. Tucker (eds.), *Advances in Game Theory*. Annals of Mathematical Studies, No. 52, Princeton: Princeton University Press.

Berl, J., R. McKelvey, P. C. Ordeshook, and M. Winer (1976). "An Experimental Test of the Core in a Simple N-Person Cooperative Non Sidepayment Game." *Journal of Conflict Resolution* 20:453–79.

Butterworth, Robert (1971). "Research Note on the Size of Winning Coalitions." *American Political Science Review* 65:741–48.

deSwaan, Abraham (1973). *Coalition Theories and Cabinet Formation.* San Francisco: Jossey Bass.

Downs, Anthony (1957). *An Economic Theory of Democracy.* New York: Harper and Row.

Fiorina, Morris, and Charles Plott (1978). "Committee Decisions Under Majority Rule: An Experimental Study," *American Political Science Review* 72:575–98.

Frohlich, Norman (1975). "The Instability of Minimum Winning Coalitions." *American Political Science Review* 69:943–46.

Horowitz, Abraham D., and Amnon Rapoport (1974). "Test of the Kernel and Two Bargaining Set Models in Four- and Five-person Games." In Anatol Raport (ed.), *Game Theory as a Theory of Conflict Resolution.* Boston: Reidel Publishing Company.

Kahn, J. P., and Amnon Rapoport (1972). "Test of the Bargaining Set and Kernel Model in Three-Person Games." Report No. 112, Thurston Psychometric Laboratory, University of North Carolina, pp. 161–92.

Laing, J. D., and Richard J. Morrison (1974). "Sequential Games of Status." *Behavioral Science* 19:177–96.

McKelvey, R. D., and R. Smith (1975). "Internal Stability and the Size Principle." Mimeographed, Carnegie-Mellon University.

McKelvey, R. D., and P. C. Ordeshook (1976). "Symmetric Spatial Games Without Majority Rule Equilibria." *American Political Science Review* 70:1172–84.

——— (1978). "Competitive Coalition Theory." In P. C. Ordeshook (ed.), *Game Theory and Political Science.* New York: New York University Press.

Ordeshook, P. C. (1976). "Spatial Models of Election Competition: A Survey and Critique." In Budge and Crewe (eds.), *Party Identification and Beyond.* New York: Wiley.

Peleg, B. (1963). "Bargaining Sets of Cooperative Games Without Sidepayments." *Israel Journal of Mathematics* 1:197–200.

Plott, Charles R. (1967). "A Notion of Equilibrium and Its Possibility Under Majority Rule." *American Economic Review* 57:787–806.

Riker, William H. (1967). "Bargaining in a Three-Person Game." *American Political Science Review* 61:642–56.

Riker, W. H., and W. J. Zavoina (1970). "Rational Behavior in Politics: Evidence from a Three-Person Game." *American Political Science Review* 64:48–60.

Riker, W. H. (1962). *The Theory of Political Coalitions*. New Haven: Yale University Press.

Scarf, Herbert E. (1967). "On the Core of an N-Person Game." *Econometrica* 35, 1:50–69.

Schofield, Norman (1976). "The Kernel and Payoffs in European Government Coalitions." *Public Choice* 26:29–49.

Shepsle, Kenneth (1974). "On the Size of Winning Coalitions." *American Political Science Review* 68:505–18. (Comment and Rejoinder, 519–24.)

Sloss, Judith (1973). "Stable Outcomes in Majority Voting Games." *Public Choice* 15:19–48.

Taylor, Michael (1972). "On the Theory of Government Coalition Formation." *British Journal of Political Science* 2:361–73.

Wilson, Robert (1971). "Stable Coalition Proposals in Majority-Rule Voting." *Journal of Economic Theory* 3:254–71.

CHAPTER 11

Social Choice and Elections

NORMAN SCHOFIELD

1. Social Choice Theory

The electoral models based on the early work of Hotelling (1929) and Downs (1957) essentially suppose that the motivation of parties is to win a majority of the votes or seats. A very considerable literature developed in the period up to 1973 (ably summarized by Riker and Ordeshook, 1973), focusing on two party competition and the existence of convergent equilibrium at the electoral median. McKelvey's thesis (1972) and his first technical paper (McKelvey, 1975) made a significant contribution to this literature. A feature of this literature was that symmetry in the electoral distribution was the sufficient condition for existence. Plott's (1967) previous analysis indicated that symmetry was also a necessary condition. Indeed, Gerry Kramer's (1972, 1973) papers suggested that equilibria might generally not even exist. The papers by McKelvey (1976 (Chapter 4 of this book)) and Schofield (1977), though independently arriving at somewhat similar conclusions on the existence of voting cycles, used entirely different formal methods.[1] McKelvey supposed that the electoral distribution was not symmetric, so that the electoral equilibrium, or core, was empty, and then showed that disconnected preference cycles could wander throughout the preference space. Schofield (1977) first generalized Kramer's result by showing that there was a local electoral condition sufficient to generate voting cycles near the point, and then demonstrated

---

This chapter is based on research supported by NSF Grant SES 024173.

[1]McKelvey (1976 (Chapter 4 of this book)) was submitted to the *Journal of Economic Theory* in May 1975, and my own paper on a similar topic (Schofield, 1977) was also submitted to the same journal that April. We both met at the APSA meeting in San Francisco in August 1975 and were surprised to learn of each other's results, based as they were on completely different mathematical tools. McKelvey (1979, Chapter 5 of this book) and Schofield (1978) were also written independently and were submitted in March 1977 and January 1976 respectively.

that this condition could be expected to hold somewhere, whenever two dimensions were involved. Extensions of these two papers (Schofield, 1978; McKelvey, 1979 (Chapter 5 of this book)) showed that very stringent symmetry conditions on voter preferences were necessary to avoid the kind of generic instability that became known as chaos. Essentially, these results suggested that, with majority rule, chaos in some form could be expected in two dimensions (when the size of the society was odd) or in three dimensions, when the size was even (Schofield, 1983). While these may be seen as the end of the Hotelling-Downs research program, they also, in a sense, concluded a long line of formal explorations of voting models to determine what exactly the implications were.[2]

It seemed likely that democratic polities were neither in the state of rigid equilibrium posited by the Hotelling-Downs theory, nor in a state of permanent chaos, and much work has concentrated on showing how institutional arrangements could lead to some kind of equilibrium. In this chapter I shall argue that a useful model of elections is essentially stochastic, and based on the judgments made by voters of the candidates' competence or ability. These judgments, or candidate valences, provide a natural framework within which to consider what Madison, in *Federalist 10*, called a "fit choice." It can readily be shown that "local equilibria" occur in such models, but they involve "heterogeneous" locations for the candidates or parties. The framework is thus compatible with the observation, made particularly with respect to European multiparty polities, that there may be many small "radical" parties positioned far from the electoral center. The theory indicates that these parties are small because their valence is low, and their positions on the electoral periphery are chosen to maximize their electoral support. Thus proportional electoral systems will tend to generate small radical parties, whose policy preferences may make government formation difficult. Under plurality rule, third parties will typically have lower valence, will be forced to take up radical positions, and may face extinction. Thus there is a "feedback effect" that may be the underlying mechanism that can be used to explain the Riker-Duverger thesis (Duverger, 1954; Riker, 1953) about the relationship between the plurality electoral mechanism and the stability of the two party system.

---

[2]The two papers by McKelvey and Schofield (1986, 1987 (Chapter 13 of this book)) were the fruit of a happy collaboration between us made possible by my tenure of the Fairchild distinguished fellowship at Caltech. These papers were the culmination of about ten years work aimed at an understanding of the formal properties of party competition. It extended the analyses from two party competition to multiparty competition and generalized the earlier results of Cohen and Matthews, 1980; Riker, 1982; Schofield, 1980, 1985, 1986. Later work in this vein can be found in Banks, 1995; Saari, 1997; Austen-Smith and Banks, 1999.

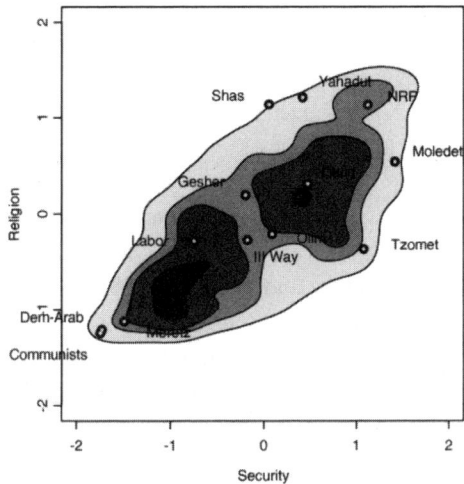

FIGURE 1. Party positions and electoral distribution (at the 95%, 75%, 50% and 10% levels) in the Knesset at the election of 1996.

2. Multiparty Democracy and Proportional Electoral Methods

Perhaps the most important application of the McKelvey-Schofield (1987, Chapter 13 of this book) symmetry conditions for existence of a core is not to majority rule elections, but to existence of an equilibrium in coalition bargaining, where a small number of parties have policy preferences, and differing political weights. As an illustration, consider the situation in the Israel Knesset after the election of 1996.

Figure 1 shows the estimated positions of thirteen parties in the Knesset in 1996 in a two-dimensional policy space. The background to this figure is the estimated electoral distribution of voter ideal points, obtained from factor analysis of survey data (Arian and Shamir, 1999). The party positions were estimated from the party manifestos, using the same factor model derived from the electoral survey (Schofield and Sened, 2005a,b). Suppose that these party positions are indeed the preferred positions of the various party leaders, and that these leaders have "Euclidean" preferences, derived from monotonically decreasing utility from the preferred positions. There are three obvious post-election winning coalitions: {Likud, Shas, Third Way, NRP} with 62 seats, {Likud, Labor} with 64 seats, and {Labor, Meretz, Third Way, Shas} with 66 seats. A coalition of {Labor,

Meretz, Shas} with the support of the small Arab parties is improbable because of the unwillingness of the Arab parties to join in coalition. Let us designate the set of winning coalitions after this election by the symbol D_0. Given Euclidean preferences of the party leaders, each winning coalition can be associated with a compromise set, defined as the convex hull of the preferred positions of the leaders of the parties belonging to the coalition. However these compromise sets do not intersect. In terms of the spatial model there is no "core point."[3] This can be shown formally by verifying that the McKelvey-Schofield symmetry conditions are nowhere satisfied (McKelvey and Schofield 1987, Chapter 13 of this book). The results of McKelvey and Schofield, mentioned above, suggest that in the absence of a core point, there can be cycling among possible coalition outcomes. However, while there was indeed a degree of coalition instability after 1996, it is more in accord with the actual events to postulate that the outcome of political bargaining would be a lottery across a number of different coalition governments and policy positions within the convex hull of all the preferred positions of party leaders. Various theories of post-election bargaining have been constructed, some based on cooperative game theory,[4] social choice theory,[5] or Bayesian non-cooperative game theory.[6] These theories all postulate that the lottery will depend on the party positions and on the coalition structure D_0 but not on the particular seat shares of the parties. Note that, although Labor was the largest party in 1996, it was unable to form a government. In fact, Netanyahu (of Likud) won a separate prime-ministerial election against Peres (of Labor) and formed a coalition government with Shas. The point to note about this election is that it was the position of Shas in Figure 1 that made it pivotal between the two possible coalitions led either by Likud or Labor.

The election of 1992 brought about a very different coalition structure, D_1, say. For the 1992 seat distribution, the Likud-led coalition, including Shas, controlled only 59 seats. The estimated positions of party leader positions for 1992 imply that the convex compromise sets of all winning coalitions intersect in the position of the Labor party leader. Because the McKelvey-Schofield symmetry conditions are satisfied at the Labor position, this party is at the policy core. As suggested by bargaining theory (Laver and Schofield, 1990; Schofield, 1993,

---

[3] Austen-Smith and Banks, 1999; Schofield, 1986; Schofield, Grofman and Feld, 1988; Laver and Schofield, 1990.

[4] McKelvey, Ordeshook and Winer 1978, Chapter 10 of this book; Ordeshook and McKelvey, 1978.

[5] Schofield, 1999; Banks, Duggan and Le Breton, 2002.

[6] Banks and Duggan, 2000.

1995; Banks and Duggan, 2000), the Labor party, under Rabin, was able to form a minority government and implement its declared policy position (Sened, 1996; Nachmias and Sened, 1997). Thus, under the coalition structure, D_1, at the vector of party positions holding in 1992, the outcome of coalition negotiation was, in fact, an essentially unique policy outcome, namely the position z_{labor}, of the Labor party.

Under D_1, Shas could expect a minority government under Peres, from which it would gain no government perquisites. If the electoral outcome were D_0, then coalition governments under either Peres or Netanyahu would both be possible. Indeed the separate prime ministerial election race was closely run, and in expectation, both of these coalitions would be equally likely. Both governments would require a majority in the Knesset for which Shas would be crucial. Obviously, coalition possibilities for Shas under D_0 were much more attractive than under D_1, so an optimal strategy for Shas would be to position itself in order to maximize π_0, conditional on the positions of the other parties. The same conclusion obviously holds for Likud. One way for Likud to maximize π_0 is to position itself so as to maximize its expected vote share vis-à-vis Labor. Conversely, the coalition structure D_1 is much more attractive for Labor, and a proxy for this is for Labor to attempt to maximize its vote share. Notice that the two situations that occurred in 1992 and 1996 were qualitatively very different. After 1996, a sequence of minimal winning or surplus coalitions formed (Riker, 1962; Laver and Schofield, 1990), whereas in 1992 a non-winning minority coalition of Labor, with the support of Meretz, was able to govern.

While the various post-election bargaining theories give some insights into multiparty negotiations, they start from the given positions and strengths of the parties. To model pre-election party positioning it is necessary to construct a theory of elections that provides a plausible "non-Downsian" account of the divergent configuration of party positions illustrated in Figure 1. This is the motivation for the next section.

3. A Stochastic Model of Elections

Partly as a result of the theoretical difficulties over the non-existence of equilibria in the two party electoral model, and also because of the need to develop empirical models of voter perception and choice that involve a "stochastic" element (Aldrich and McKelvey 1977, Chapter 7 of this book), attention has focused on "probabilistic" vote models. A formal basis for such models is provided by the notion of "quantal response equilibria" (McKelvey and Palfrey, 1992 (Chapter 18 of this book), 1996, 1998). In such models, behavior of each voter is modeled by a vector of choice probabilities (Hinich, 1977; Enelow and Hinich, 1984; Coughlin, 1992; Lin, Enelow and Dorussen, 1999; Banks and Duggan, 2005). A standard result in this class of models is that all parties converge to the electoral origin when the parties are motivated to maximize vote share (McKelvey and Patty, 2006).

However, this convergence result need not hold if there is an asymmetry in the electoral perception of the "quality" or "valence" of party leaders (Stokes, 1992). The early empirical model of Poole and Rosenthal (1984) on US presidential elections included these valence terms and noted that there was no evidence of candidate convergence. Formal models of elections incorporating valence have been developed recently (Ansolabehere and Snyder, 2000; Groseclose, 2001; Aragones and Palfrey, 2004, 2005), but results to date have been obtained only for the two party case. This section will present a "classification theorem" for the formal probabilistic model of voter choice, in a policy space of dimension w, with an arbitrary number of parties, in which party leaders exhibit differing valences. A "convergence coefficient," incorporating all the parameters of the model, will be defined. It is shown that there are necessary and sufficient conditions for the existence of a pure strategy vote maximizing equilibrium at the mean of the voter distribution. When the necessary condition fails, then parties, in equilibrium, will adopt divergent positions. In general, parties whose leaders have the lowest valence will take up positions furthest from the electoral mean.

The empirical studies of voter behavior for Israel in 1992–1996, discussed in the previous section, can then be used to show that the necessary condition for party convergence fails in these elections. The equilibrium positions as obtained from the formal result, under vote maximization, are, in general, comparable with, but not identical to, the estimated positions. It is suggested that the observed discrepancy can be accounted for by a more refined model that involves strategic calculations by parties with respect to post-election coalition possibilities.

The electoral model to be presented is an extension of the multiparty stochastic model of Lin, Enelow and Dorussen (1999), constructed by acknowledging the empirical asymmetries in terms of valence. The basis for this extension is the extensive empirical evidence that valence is a significant component of the judgments made by voters of party leaders.[7] There are a number of possible choices for

---

[7] The earliest paper was Schofield, Sened and Nixon (1998), which was presented at a conference at Northwestern University in June 1995. I am indebted to my colleagues Andrew Martin, Gary Miller, David Nixon, Kevin Quinn, Robert Parks, Itai Sened, and Andrew Whitford, whose collaboration on empirical and computation modeling was crucial in tracking down the electoral theorem. These results have appeared in Schofield, Martin, Quinn and Whitford, 1998; Quinn, Martin and Whitford, 1999;

the appropriate game form for multiparty competition. The simplest one, which is used here, is that the utility function for party j is proportional to its vote share, V_j. With this assumption, we can examine the conditions on the parameters of the stochastic model which are necessary for the existence of a pure strategy Nash equilibrium (PNE).

The key idea underlying the formal model is that party leaders attempt to estimate the electoral effects of party declarations, or manifestos, and choose their own positions as best responses to other party declarations, in order to maximize their own vote share. The stochastic model essentially assumes that party leaders cannot predict vote response precisely, but can compute the expected vote share function. In the model with "exogenous" valence, the stochastic element is associated with the weight given by each voter, i, to the average perceived quality or valence of the party leader.

DEFINITION 1. **The Stochastic Vote Model.**

The data of the spatial model is a distribution, $\{x_i \in X\}_{i \in N}$, of voter ideal points for the members of the electorate, N, of size n. As usual we assume that X is a compact convex subset of Euclidean space, $\Re^w$, with w finite. Each of the parties, or agents, in the set $P = \{1, \ldots, j, \ldots, p\}$ chooses a policy, $z_j \in X$, to declare. Let $\mathbf{z} = (z_1, \ldots, z_p) \in X^p$ be a typical vector of agent policy positions. Given $\mathbf{z}$, each voter, i, is described by a vector $\mathbf{u}_i(x_i, \mathbf{z}) = (u_{i1}(x_i, z_1), \ldots, u_{ip}(x_i, z_p))$, where

(1) $$u_{ij}(x_i, z_j) = \lambda_j - \beta \|x_i - z_j\|^2 + \varepsilon_j = u_{ij}^*(x_i, z_j) + \varepsilon_j$$

Here $u_{ij}^*(x_i, z_j)$ is the observable component of utility. The term λ_j is the "exogenous" valence of agent j, β is a positive constant, and $\|\cdot\|$ is the usual Euclidean norm on X. The terms $\{\varepsilon_j\}$ are the stochastic errors, whose multivariate cumulative distribution function will be denoted by Ψ.

There are a number of possible distribution functions that can be used. The most common assumption in empirical analyses is that Ψ is the "extreme value Type I distribution" (sometimes called log Weibull). Empirical estimation based on this assumption is known as multinomial logit (MNL). The formal "quantal response model" introduced by McKelvey and Palfrey (1995) essentially supposes that individuals make logistic errors in estimating optimal responses, where these errors are distributed by the extreme value distribution. The electoral theorem

---

Schofield and Parks, 2003; Schofield and Sened, 2005a,b, 2006; Schofield, 2004, 2005a,b, 2006a,b, 2007; Miller and Schofield, 2003; Schofield, Miller and Martin, 2003. Richard McKelvey, Jeffrey Banks, and John Duggan gave me very helpful comments on my earlier work on the vote model.

presented here is based on this assumption. An alternative assumption is that the errors are independently and identically distributed by the normal distribution (iind), with zero expectation, each with stochastic variance σ^2 (Lin, Enelow and Dorussen, 1999). An even more general assumption is that the stochastic error vector $\varepsilon = (\varepsilon_1, \ldots, \varepsilon_p)$ is multivariate normal with general variance/covariance matrix Ω. Empirical estimation based on this assumption is known as multinomial probit (MNP).[8]

We assume that the valence vector

$$\Gamma = (\lambda_1, \lambda_2, \ldots, \lambda_p) \text{ satisfies } \lambda_p \geq \lambda_{p-1} \geq \cdots \geq \lambda_2 \geq \lambda_1.$$

Because of the stochastic assumption, the behavior of voter i is modeled by a probability function ρ_i. The probability that a voter i chooses party j at the vector **z** is

$$\text{(2)} \quad \rho_{ij}(\mathbf{z}) = \Pr\left[[u_{ij}(x_i, z_j) > u_{il}(x_i, z_l)], \text{ for all } l \neq j\right]$$
$$\text{(3)} \quad = \Pr\left[\varepsilon_l - \varepsilon_j < u_{ij}^*(x_i, z_j) - u_{il}^*(x_i, z_l), \text{ for all } l \neq j\right]$$

Here Pr stands for the probability operator generated by the distribution assumption on ε. The expected vote share of agent j is

$$\text{(4)} \quad V_j(\mathbf{z}) = \frac{1}{n} \sum_{i \in N} \rho_{ij}(\mathbf{z})$$

I shall use the notation $V : X^p \longrightarrow \Re^p$ and call V the *party profile function*. In the vote model it is assumed that each agent j chooses z_j to maximize V_j, conditional on $\mathbf{z}_{-j} = (z_1, \ldots, z_{j-1}, z_{j+1}, \ldots, z_p)$.

Because of the differentiability of the cumulative distribution function, the individual probability functions $\{\rho_{ij}\}$ are differentiable in the strategies $\{z_j\}$. Thus, the vote share functions will also be differentiable. Let $x^* = (1/n)\sum_i x_i$. Then the mean voter theorem for the stochastic model asserts that the "joint mean vector" $\mathbf{z}_0^* = (x^*, \ldots, x^*)$ is a "pure strategy Nash equilibrium." Lin, Enelow and Dorussen (1999) used differentiability of the expected vote share functions, in the situation with zero valence, as well as "concavity" of the vote share functions, to assert this theorem. They argued that a sufficient condition for the validity of the theorem was that *error variance* was "sufficiently large." Because concavity cannot in general be assured, we shall utilize a weaker equilibrium concept, that of *Local Strict Nash Equilibrium* (LSNE). A strategy vector $\mathbf{z}^*$ is an LSNE if, for

---

[8]See Dow and Endersby (2004) and Quinn, Martin and Whitford (1999) for discussion of the various empirical models. Results based on the normal distribution can be obtained, but are quite difficult to demonstrate (see Schofield, 2004, 2005a,b).

each j, z_j^* is a critical point of the vote function $V_j(z_1^*, \ldots, z_{j-1}^*, -, z_{j+1}^*, \ldots, z_p^*)$ and the eigenvalues of the Hessian of this function (with respect to z_j) are negative. More formally, a strategy vector $\mathbf{z}_j(z_1^*, \ldots, z_{j-1}^*, z_j^*, z_{j+1}^*, \ldots, z_p^*) \in X^p$ is a *local strict pure strategy Nash equilibrium* (LSNE) for the profile function $V : X^p \longrightarrow \Re^p$ iff, for each agent $j \in P$, there exists a neighborhood X_j of z_j^* in X such that z_j^* is the strictly best response in the neighborhood X_j by j to $z_{-j}^* = (z_1^*, \ldots, z_{j-1}^*, z_{j+1}^*, \ldots, z_p^*)$. That is:

$$V_j(z_1^*, \ldots, z_{j-1}^*, z_j^*, z_{j+1}^*, \ldots, z_p^*) > V_j(z_1^*, \ldots, z_j, \ldots, z_p^*) \text{ for all } z_j \in X_j - \{z_j^*\}$$

Say the strategy z_j^* is a *local strict best response* to z_{-j}^*.

We can also define local weak best response, global strict best response, and global weak best response to z_{-j}^* by weakening the inequality sign and by requiring that the response is best not just in a neighborhood, but in X itself. This allows us to define the notions of *local weak pure strategy Nash equilibrium* (LNE), *global weak pure strategy Nash equilibrium* (PNE), and *global strict pure strategy Nash equilibrium* (PSNE).

Obviously if $\mathbf{z}^*$ is an LSNE or a PNE then it must be an LNE, while if it is a PSNE then it must be an LSNE. We use the notion of LSNE to avoid problems with the degenerate situation when there is a zero eigenvalue to the Hessian. The weaker requirement of LNE allows us to obtain a necessary condition for $\mathbf{z}_0^* = (x^*, \ldots, x^*)$ to be an LNE and thus a PNE, without having to invoke concavity. The result below also gives a sufficient condition for the joint mean vector $\mathbf{z}_0^*$ to be an LSNE. A corollary of the theorem shows, in situations where the valences differ, that the necessary condition is likely to fail. In dimension w, the theorem can be used to show that, for $\mathbf{z}_0^*$ to be an LSNE, the necessary condition is that a "convergence coefficient," defined in terms of the parameters of the model, must be strictly bounded above by w. Similarly, for $\mathbf{z}_0^*$ to be an LNE, then the convergence coefficient must be weakly bounded above by w. The main point of the result is that when this condition *fails*, then the joint mean vector $\mathbf{z}_0^*$ *cannot* be an LNE and therefore *cannot* be a PNE. Of course, even if the sufficient condition is satisfied, and $\mathbf{z}_0^* = (x^*, \ldots, x^*)$ is an LSNE, it need not be a PNE.

To state the theorem, we first transform coordinates so that in the new coordinates, $x^* = 0$. We shall refer to $\mathbf{z}_0^* = (0, \ldots, 0)$ as the *joint origin* in this new coordinate system. Whether the joint origin is an equilibrium depends on the distribution of voter ideal points. These are encoded in the voter covariance matrix. We first define this, and then show that the vote share Hessians depend on the covariance matrix.

DEFINITION 2. **The Electoral Covariance Matrix, $\frac{1}{n}\nabla$.**

To characterize the variation in voter preferences, we represent in a simple form the covariation matrix (or data matrix), ∇, given by the distribution of voter ideal points. Let X have dimension w and be endowed with a system of coordinate axes $(1,\ldots,r,s,\ldots,w)$. For each coordinate axis let $\xi_r = (x_{1r}, x_{2r}, \ldots, x_{nr})$ be the n-vector of the rth coordinates of the set of n voter ideal points. We use (ξ_r, ξ_s) to denote scalar product.

The symmetric $w \times w$ voter covariation matrix ∇ is then defined to be the matrix $\nabla = [(\xi_r, \xi_s)]$, while the covariance matrix is defined to be $\frac{1}{n}\nabla$.

We write $v_r^2 = \frac{1}{n}(\xi_r, \xi_r)$ for the electoral variance on the rth axis and

$$v^2 = \sum_{r=1}^{w} v_r^2 = \frac{1}{n}\sum_{r=1}^{w}(\xi_r, \xi_s) = trace\left(\frac{1}{n}\nabla\right)$$

for the total electoral variance. The electoral covariance between the rth and s^{th} axes is $(v_r, v_s) = \frac{1}{n}(\xi_r, \xi_s)$.

DEFINITION 3. **The Extreme Value Distribution, Ψ.**

(i) The cumulative distribution Ψ and probability density function φ have the closed forms

$$\Psi(h) = \exp\left[-\exp\left[-h\right]\right],$$
$$\varphi(h) = \exp\left[-h\right]\exp\left[-\exp\left[-h\right]\right]$$

with variance $\frac{1}{6}\pi^2$.

(ii) With this distribution it follows from Definition 1 that, for each voter i and party j, the probability $\rho_{ij}(\mathbf{z})$ is given by the logistic quantal response expression

(5) $$\rho_{ij}(\mathbf{z}) = \frac{\exp\left[u_{ij}^*(x_i, z_j)\right]}{\sum_{k=1}^{p}\exp\left[u_{ik}^*(x_i, z_k)\right]}$$

Note that (ii) implies that the model satisfies the independence of irrelevant alternative property (IIA): for each individual i and each pair j, k, the ratio $\frac{\rho_{ij}(\mathbf{z})}{\rho_{ik}(\mathbf{z})}$ is independent of a third party l (see Train, 2003, p. 79).

While this distribution assumption facilitates estimation, the IIA property may be violated. It is possible to obtain results for the case of covariant errors, so that IIA is not imposed (Schofield, 2005a).

The formal model just presented and based on Ψ is denoted $M(\Gamma, \beta; \Psi, \nabla)$, though we shall usually suppress the reference to ∇.

It can then easily be shown that, at the vector $\mathbf{z}_0 = (0, \ldots, 0)$, the probability $\rho_{ij}(\mathbf{z}_0)$ that i votes for party j is the same for every individual, and is given by

(6) $$\rho_j = \left[1 + \sum_{k \neq j} \exp[\lambda_k - \lambda_j]\right]^{-1}$$

Then the Hessian of the vote share function of the lowest valence party, 1, at $\mathbf{z}_0$ is given by the symmetric matrix

$$C_1 = \left[2[1 - 2\rho_1](\frac{\beta}{n}\nabla) - I\right]$$

where I is the $w \times w$ identity matrix. Since it is trivial to show that the first order conditions, $\frac{dV_j}{dz_j} = 0$ are satisfied at $\mathbf{z}_0$, it follows that the necessary condition for existence of an LSNE at $\mathbf{z}_0$ is that C_1 has negative eigenvalues. Moreover, if C_1 has negative eigenvalues at $\mathbf{z}_0$, then so will the Hessians for $j = 2, \ldots, p$. Thus we obtain necessary and sufficient conditions in terms of C_1. Because this condition is determined by the determinant and trace of C_1, it can be re-expressed in terms of a convergence coefficient

(7) $$c(\Gamma, \beta; \Psi, \nabla) = 2[1 - 2\rho_1]\beta v^2$$

Then, in dimension w, the *sufficient and the necessary* conditions for existence of an LNE at $\mathbf{z}_0$ are respectively that

(8) $$c(\Gamma, \beta; \Psi, \nabla) < 1 \text{ and } c(\Gamma, \beta; \Psi, \nabla) \leq w$$

Obviously if all valences are identical then $\rho_1 = \frac{1}{p}$, as expected. The effect of increasing λ_j, for $j \neq 1$, or of decreasing λ_1 is clearly to decrease ρ_1, and therefore to increase $c(\Gamma, \beta; \Psi, \nabla)$, thus rendering existence of an LNE less likely. Ceteris paribus, an LNE at the joint origin is "less likely" the greater are the parameters β, $\lambda_p - \lambda_1$, and v^2. The proof of this result is given in Schofield (2006a).

Even when the sufficient condition is satisfied, so the joint origin is an LSNE, the concavity condition (equivalent to the negative semi definiteness of all Hessians *everywhere*) is so strong that there is no good reason to expect it to hold. The empirical analyses of Israel, which we shall present below, show that the necessary condition fails. In this polity, a vote maximizing PNE, even if it exists, will generally not occur at the origin. In these analyses, the policy space is two-dimensional, and in this case it is possible to demonstrate that the eigenvalues a_1, a_2 of the Hessian of the lowest valence party, 1, are given by the expressions

$$a_{1,2} = [1 - 2\rho_1]\beta\{[v_1^2 + v_2^2] \pm [[v_1^2 - v_2^2]^2 + 4(v_1, v_2)^2]^{\frac{1}{2}}\} - 1$$

Note that the case $\lambda_p = \lambda_1$ was studied by Lin, Enelow and Dorussen (1999), under the assumption that the errors were independently and identically normally distributed. A similar result to the above can be obtained for this formal model based on multivariate normal errors (Schofield, 2004). The only difference is that with the normal distribution, the convergence coefficient has the error variance σ^2 in the denominator, and has the average of the valence difference in the numerator. It follows that if all valences are identical, then the average valence difference is zero, and thus the electoral origin is assured of being an LSNE. However, this does not guarantee that it is a PSE. However, if the error variance is sufficiently great (in comparison to the spatial coefficient, β, and the electoral variance, v^2) then all Hessians will be negative definite everywhere. This implies that the joint origin will indeed be a PSE.

In the next section we use this result to determine whether convergence can be expected in the complex multiparty situation in the Israel Knesset.

4. Empirical Analysis for Israel: The Election of 1996

To provide an explanation for the non-convergent positions of the parties at the time of the 1996 election, an MNL estimation of the election based on the Arian–Shamir survey was carried out.[9] The MNL model with valence was found to be statistically superior to both an MNL model and a multinomial probit (MNP) model without valence. The two dimensions of policy deal with attitudes to the PLO (the horizontal axis) and religion (the vertical axis). The policy space was derived from voter surveys (obtained by Arian and Shamir, 1999) and the party positions from analysis of party manifestos. Using the formal analysis, we can readily show that one of the eigenvalues of the lowest valence party, the NRP, is positive. Indeed it is obvious that there is a principal component of the electoral distribution, and this axis is the eigenspace of the positive eigenvalue. It follows that low valence parties should then position themselves on this eigenspace.

In 1996, the lowest valence party was the NRP with valence -4.52, while the valences for the major parties, Labor and Likud, were 4.15 and 3.14 respectively. The spatial coefficient was $\beta = 1.12$, so for the extreme value model $M(\Psi)$ we compute $\rho_{NRP} \cong 0$. Since $v_1^2 = 1.0$, $v_2^2 = 0.732$, and $(v_1, v_2) = 0.591$, we can compute $c(\Gamma, \beta; \Psi, \nabla) = 3.88$, which clearly exceeds the necessary bound of 2. The matrix C_{NRP} is readily computed.[10]

---

[9] Details are given in Schofield and Sened (2005b) and Schofield, Sened and Nixon (1998).

[10] $C_{NRP} = 2(1.120) \begin{pmatrix} 1.0 & 0.591 \\ 0.591 & .732 \end{pmatrix} - I = \begin{pmatrix} 1.24 & 1.32 \\ 1.32 & 0.64 \end{pmatrix}.$

Using the expression for the eigenvalues presented above, we find that the eigenvalues are 2.28 and -0.40, giving a saddlepoint. The major eigenvector for the NRP is (1.0,0.8), and along this axis the NRP vote share function increases as the party moves away from the origin. The minor, perpendicular axis is given by the vector $(1, -1.25)$ and on this axis the NRP vote share decreases. Simulation of the model showed that, as predicted by the formal model, all vote maximizing positions lay on the principal axis through the origin and the point (1.0,0.8). Five different LSNE were located. However, in all the equilibria, the two high valence parties, Labor and Likud, were located at precisely the same positions. The only difference between the various equilibria was that the positions of the low valence parties were perturbations of each other.

The simulated vote maximizing party positions in all three elections indicated that there was no deviation by parties off the principal axis or eigenspace associated with the positive eigenvalue. Thus the simulation was compatible with the predictions of the formal model based on the extreme value distribution. All parties were able to increase vote shares by moving away from the origin, along the principal axis. In particular, the simulation confirms the logic of the above analysis. Low valence parties, such as the NRP and Shas, in order to maximize vote shares must move far from the electoral center. Their optimal positions will lie either in the "northeast" quadrant or the "southwest" quadrant. The vote maximizing model, without any additional information, cannot determine which way the low valence parties should move from the origin.

In contrast to these low valence parties, because the valence differences between Labor and Likud were relatively low in all three elections, their equilibrium positions would be relatively close to, but not identical to, the electoral mean. The simulation figures for all three elections are also compatible with this theoretical inference. Intuitively it is clear that once the low valence parties vacate the origin, then high valence parties like Likud and Labor will position themselves almost symmetrically about the origin, and along the major axis. It should be noted that the positions of Labor and Likud, particularly, closely match their positions in the simulated vote maximizing equilibria.

Clearly, the configuration of equilibrium party positions will fluctuate as the valences of the large parties change in response to exogenous shocks. The logic of the model remains valid however, since the low valence parties will be obliged to adopt relatively "radical" positions in order to maximize their vote shares.

The relationship between the empirical work and the formal model, together with the possibility of strategic reasoning of this kind, suggests the following hypothesis.

Hypothesis. The close correspondence between the simulated LSNE based on the empirical analysis and the estimated actual political configuration suggests that the true utility function for each party j has the form $U_j(\mathbf{z}) = V_j(\mathbf{z}) + \delta_j(\mathbf{z})$, where $\delta_j(\mathbf{z})$ may depend on the beliefs of party leaders about the post-election coalition possibilities, as well as the effect of activist support for the party.

This hypothesis leads to the further conjecture, for the set of feasible strategy profiles in the Israel polity, that $\delta_j(\mathbf{z})$ is "small" relative to $V_j(\mathbf{z})$. A formal model to this effect could indicate that the LSNE for $\{U_j\}$ would be close to the LSNE for $\{V_j\}$.

The discussion of coalition bargaining offered in the first section of this chapter suggests that the primary motivation of high valence parties can be assumed to be to maximize the probability of bringing about the more favorable coalition structure, and a proxy for this can be taken to be expected vote share. Low valence parties like Shas or NRP may have more complex motivations, involving positioning themselves to be able to bargain effectively over coalition formation. Thus, to construct a formal model of political behavior it would appear necessary to combine elements of social choice, as discussed in the first section, together with a theory of electoral competition.

The construction of a formal model involving both electoral and coalitional concerns would have appealed to Richard McKelvey. Such a theory requires integrating social choice theory, multinomial logit electoral models based on quantal response, and factor analysis, together with computation and simulation of the equilibria (McKelvey and McLennan, 1996).

5. Conclusion

In an attempt to model this complex political game, this chapter has introduced the idea of a *local Nash equilibrium* (Schofield and Sened, 2002, 2006). This general concept can incorporate the quantal response idea for modeling electoral response, as developed by McKelvey and Palfrey (1992, Chapter 18 of this book) and McKelvey and Patty (2006) as well as the spatial notions of equilibrium studied in the earlier analyses of McKelvey (1976 (Chapter 4 of this book), 1979 (Chapter 5 of this book)) and Schofield (1977, 1978). The underlying premise of this concept is that party principals will not consider "global" changes in party policies, but will instead propose small changes in the party leadership in response to changes in beliefs about electoral response and the likely consequences of policy negotiations. It is also evident that the electoral model depends on the notion of "valence." Valence can be regarded as that element of a voter's choice which is

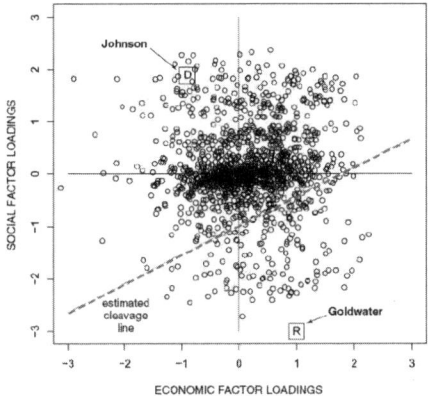

FIGURE 2. The two-dimensional factor space, with voter positions and Johnson's and Goldwater's respective policy positions in 1964

determined by judgment rather than preference. This accords well with the arguments of James Madison in *Federalist 10* of 1787 and of Condorcet in his treatise of 1785 on social choice theory (Schofield, 2005c, 2006c), and can be interpreted as a justification for the democratic process. Pursuing this line of development suggests a new and very interesting way of thinking about politics in terms of "belief games." Indeed, it is natural to speculate that political processes, regarded as belief games, are in some kind of dynamic equilibrium (Miller and Schofield, 2003) between the opposed convergent and centripetal tendencies implicit in the models that we have discussed here. As a second example, Figure 2 shows the underlying distribution of the sample voter positions and the estimated positions of Goldwater and Johnson in the 1964 presidential election. The cleavage line in the figure separates those voters more likely to vote for Johnson than for Goldwater. The fact that this line does not pass through the origin indicates that Johnson's estimated valence exceeded that of Goldwater. Goldwater's position hints at the socially conservative positions taken by future Republican presidential candidates. Miller and Schofield (2003) and Schofield (2007) have used these ideas to give an account of the realignment of the principal electoral dimensions in terms of the "clockwise rotation" of this electoral cleavage line.

References

Aldrich, John and Richard D. McKelvey. 1977. "A Method of Scaling with an Application to the 1968 and 1972 Presidential Elections." *American Political Science Review* 71:111–130.

Ansolabehere, Steven and James Snyder. 2000. "Valence Politics and Equilibrium in Spatial Election Models." *Public Choice* 103:327–336.

Aragones, Enriqueta and Thomas Palfrey. 2002. "Mixed Equilibrium in a Downsian Model with a Favored Candidate." *Journal of Economic Theory* 103:131–161.

Aragones, Enriqueta and Thomas Palfrey. 2004. "The Effect of Candidate Quality on Electoral Equilibrium: An Experimental Study." *American Political Science Review* 98:77–90.

Aragones, Enriqueta and Thomas Palfrey. 2005. "Spatial Competition between two Candidates of Different Quality: The Effects of Candidate Ideology and Private Information," in *Social Choice and Strategic Decisions: Essays in Honor of Jeffrey S. Banks*, David Austen-Smith and John Duggan (eds.). Heidelberg: Springer.

Arian, Asher and Michael Shamir. 1999. *The Election in Israel: 1996*. Albany: SUNY Press.

Austen-Smith, David and Jeff Banks. 1999. *Positive Political Theory I: Collective Preferences*. Ann Arbor: University of Michigan Press.

Austen-Smith, David and Jeff Banks. 2005. *Positive Political Theory II: Strategy and Structure*. Ann Arbor: University of Michigan Press.

Banks, Jeff. 1995. "Singularity Theory and Core Existence in the Spatial Model." *Journal of Mathematical Economics* 24:523–536.

Banks, Jeff and John Duggan. 2000. "A Bargaining Model of Collective Choice." *American Political Science Review* 103:73–88.

Banks, Jeff and John Duggan. 2005. "The Theory of Probabilistic Voting in the Spatial Model of Elections," in *Social Choice and Strategic Decisions: Essays in Honor of Jeffrey S. Banks*, David Austen-Smith and John Duggan (eds.). Heidelberg: Springer.

Banks, Jeff, John Duggan and Michel LeBreton. 2002. "Bounds for Mixed Strategy Equilibria and the Spatial Model of Elections." *Journal of Economic Theory* 103:88–105.

Banks, Jeff, John Duggan and Michel LeBreton. 2006. "Social Choice and Electoral Competition in the General Spatial Model." *Journal of Economic Theory* 126:194–234.

Cohen, Linda and Matthews Steven. 1980. "Constrained Plott Equilibria, Directional Equilibria and Global Cycling Sets." *Review of Economic Studies* 47:975–986.

Coughlin, Peter. 1992. *Probabilistic Voting Theory*. Cambridge: Cambridge University Press.

Dow, John. 2001. "A Comparative Spatial Analysis of Majoritarian and Proportional Elections." *Electoral Studies* 20:109–125.

Dow, John and Jay Endersby. 2004. "Multinomial Logit and Multinomial Probit: A Comparison of Choice Models for Voting Research." *Electoral Studies* 23:107–122.

Downs, Anthony. 1957. *An Economic Theory of Democracy*. New York: Harper and Row.

Duverger, Maurice. 1954. *Political Parties*. New York: Wiley.

Enelow, James and Melvin Hinich. 1984. *The Spatial Theory of Voting: An Introduction*. Cambridge: Cambridge University Press.

Groseclose, Timothy. 2001. "A Model of Candidate Location when One Candidate Has a Valence Advantage." *American Political Science Review* 45:862–886.

Hinich, Melvin. 1977. "Equilibrium in Spatial Voting: The Median Voter Result Is an Artifact." *Journal of Economic Theory* 16:208–219.

Hotelling, Harold. 1929. "Stability in Competition." *Economic Journal* 39:41–57.

Kramer, Gerald. 1972. "Sophisticated Voting over Multidimensional Choice Spaces." *Journal of Mathematical Sociology* 2:165–180.

Kramer, Gerald. 1973. "On a Class of Equilibrium Conditions for Majority Rule." *Econometrica* 41:285–297.

Laver, Michael and Norman Schofield. 1990, 1998. *Multiparty Government: The Politics of Coalition in Europe*. Oxford: Oxford University Press. Reprinted, Ann Arbor: University of Michigan Press.

Lin, Tse-min, James Enelow and Han Dorussen. 1999. "Equilibrium in Multicandidate Probabilistic Spatial Voting." *Public Choice* 98:59–82.

McKelvey, Richard D. 1972. Some Extensions and Modifications of the Spatial Models of Party Competition. PhD Dissertation, University of Rochester.

McKelvey, Richard D. 1975. "Policy Related Voting and Electoral Equilibrium." *Econometrica* 43:815–844.

McKelvey, Richard D. 1976. "Intransitivities in Multidimensional Voting Models and Some Applications for Agenda Control." *Journal of Economic Theory* 12:472–482. Chapter 4 of this book.

McKelvey, Richard D. 1979. "General Conditions for Global Intransitivities in Formal Voting Models." *Econometrica* 47:1085–1112. Chapter 5 of this book.

McKelvey, Richard D. 1986. "Covering, Dominance, and Institution Free Properties of Social Choice." *American Journal of Political Science* 30:283–314. Chapter 12 of this book.

McKelvey, Richard D. and Andrew McLennan. 1996. "Computation of Equilibria in Finite Games," in *The Handbook of Computational Economics*, H. Amman, D. Kendrick and J. Rust (eds.). Amsterdam: Elsevier.

McKelvey, Richard D., Peter Ordeshook and Mark Winer. 1978. "The Competitive Solution for N-Person Games without Transferable Utility, with an Application to Committee Games." *American Political Science Review* 72:599–615. Chapter 10 of this book.

McKelvey, Richard D. and Thomas Palfrey. 1992. "An Experimental Study of the Centipede Game." *Econometrica* 60:803–836. Chapter 18 of this book.

McKelvey, Richard D. and Thomas Palfrey. 1995. "Quantal Response Equilibria for Normal Form Games." *Games and Economic Behavior* 10:6–38. Chapter 20 of this book.

McKelvey, Richard D. and Thomas Palfrey. 1996. "A Statistical Theory of Equilibrium in Games." *Japanese Economic Review* 47:186–209.

McKelvey, Richard D. and Thomas Palfrey. 1998. "Quantal Response Equilibria for Extensive Form Games." *Experimental Economics* 1:9–41.

McKelvey, Richard D. and John Patty. 2006. "A Theory of Voting in Large Elections." *Games and Economic Behavior* 57:155–180.

McKelvey, Richard D. and Norman Schofield. 1986. "Structural Instability of the Core." *Journal of Mathematical Economics* 15:179–198.

McKelvey, Richard D. and Norman Schofield. 1987. "Generalized Symmetry Conditions at a Core Point." *Econometrica* 55:923–934. Chapter 13 of this book.

Miller, Gary and Norman Schofield. 2003. "Activists and Partisan Realignment in the US." *American Political Science Review* 97:245–260.

Nachmias, David and Itai Sened. 1997. "The Bias of Pluralism," in *The Election of 1996 in Israel*, A. Arian and M. Shamir (eds.). Albany: SUNY Press.

Ordeshook, Peter C. and Richard D. McKelvey. 1978. "Competitive Coalition Theory," in *Game Theory and Political Science*, Peter C. Ordeshook (ed.). New York: New York University Press.

Plott, Charles. 1967. "A Notion of Equilibrium and Its Possibility under Majority Rule." *American Economic Review* 57:787–806.

Poole, K. and H. Rosenthal. 1984. "US Presidential Elections 1968–1980: A Spatial Analysis." *American Journal of Political Science* 43:283–312.

Quinn, Kevin and Andrew Martin. 2002. "An Integrated Computational Model of Multiparty Electoral Competition." *Statistical Science* 17:405–419.

Quinn, Kevin, Andrew Martin and Andrew Whitford. 1999. "Voter Choice in Multiparty Democracies." *American Journal of Political Science* 43:1231–1247.

Riker, William H. 1953. *Democracy in the United States*. New York: Macmillan.

Riker, William H. 1962. *The Theory of Political Coalitions*. New Haven: Yale University Press.

Riker, William H. 1982. *Liberalism Against Populism*. San Francisco: Freeman.

Riker, William H. and Peter Ordeshook. 1973. *An Introduction to Positive Political Theory*. Englewood Cliffs: Prentice Hall.

Saari, Donald. 1997. "Generic Existence of a Core for q-Rules." *Economic Theory* 9:219–260.

Schofield, Norman. 1977. "Transitivity of Preferences on a Smooth Manifold." *Journal of Economic Theory* 14:149–172.

Schofield, Norman. 1978. "Instability of Simple Dynamic Games." *Review of Economic Studies* 45:575–594.

Schofield, Norman. 1980. "Generic Properties of Simple Bergson-Samuelson Welfare Functions." *Journal of Mathematical Economics* 7:175–192.

Schofield, Norman. 1983. "Generic Instability of Majority Rule." *Review of Economic Studies* 50:695–705.

Schofield, Norman. 1985. *Social Choice and Democracy*. Heidelberg: Springer.

Schofield, Norman. 1986. "Existence of a 'Structurally Stable' Equilibrium for a Non-Collegial Voting Rule." *Public Choice* 51:267–284.

Schofield, Norman. 1993. "Political Competition in Multiparty Coalition Governments." *European Journal of Political Research* 23:1–33.

Schofield, Norman. 1994. "Coalition Politics: A Formal Model and Empirical Analysis." *Journal of Theoretical Politics* 7:245–281.

Schofield, Norman. 1999. "The Heart and the Uncovered Set." *Journal of Economics Supp.* 8:79–113.

Schofield, Norman. 2003. "Valence Competition and the Spatial Stochastic Model." *Journal of Theoretical Politics* 15:371–383.

Schofield, Norman. 2004. "Equilibrium in the Spatial Valence Model of Politics." *Journal of Theoretical Politics* 16:447–481.

Schofield, Norman. 2005a. "A Valence Model of Political Competition in Britain: 1992–1997." *Electoral Studies* 24:347–370.

Schofield, Norman. 2005b. "Local Political Equilibria," in *Social Choice and Strategic Decisions*, David Austen-Smith and John Duggan (eds.). Heidelberg: Springer.

Schofield, Norman. 2005c. "The Intellectual Contribution of Condorcet to the Founding of the US Republic." *Social Choice and Welfare* 25:303–318.

Schofield, Norman. 2006a. "The Mean Voter Theorem: Necessary and Sufficient Conditions for Convergent Equilibrium." Forthcoming in *Review of Economic Studies*.

Schofield, Norman. 2006b. "Equilibria in the Spatial Stochastic Model of Voting with Party Activists." *Review of Economic Design* 10:183–203.

Schofield, Norman. 2006c. *Architects of Political Change: Constitutional Quandaries and Social Choice*. Cambridge: Cambridge University Press.

Schofield, Norman. 2007. "Political Equilibrium with Electoral Uncertainty." *Social Choice and Welfare* 28:461–490.

Schofield, Norman, B. Grofman and S. Feld. 1988. "The Core and the Stability of Group Choice in Spatial Voting Games." *American Political Science Review* 82:195–211.

Schofield, Norman, Andrew Martin, Kevin Quinn and Andrew Whitford. 1998. "Multiparty Electoral Competition in the Netherlands and Germany: A Model Based on Multinomial Probit." *Public Choice* 97:257–293.

Schofield, Norman, Gary Miller and Andrew Martin. 2003. "Critical Elections and Political Realignments in the US: 1860–2000." *Political Studies* 51:217–240.

Schofield, Norman and Robert Parks. 2003. "Nash Equilibrium in a Spatial Model of Coalition Formation." *Mathematical Social Science* 39:133–174.

Schofield, Norman, Itai Sened and David Nixon. 1998. "Nash Equilibrium in Multiparty Competition with Stochastic Voters." *Annals of Operations Research* 84:3–27.

Schofield, Norman and Itai Sened. 2002. "Local Nash Equilibrium in Multiparty Politics." *Annals of Operations Research* 109:193–211.

Schofield, Norman and Itai Sened. 2005a. "Modeling the Interaction of Parties, Activists and Voters: Why Is the Political Center So Empty?" *European Journal of Political Research* 44:355–390.

Schofield, Norman and Itai Sened. 2005b. "Multiparty Competition in Israel 1988–1996." *British Journal of Political Science* 35:635–663.

Schofield, Norman and Itai Sened. 2006. *Multiparty Democracy: Parties, Elections and Legislative Politics*. Cambridge: Cambridge University Press, in press.

Sened, Itai. 1995. "Equilibria in Weighted Voting Games with Side-payments in Two-dimensional Spaces." *Journal of Theoretical Politics* 7:283–300.

Sened, Itai. 1996. "A Model of Coalition Formation: Theory and Evidence." *Journal of Politics* 58:350–372.

Stokes, Donald. 1992. "Valence Politics," in *Electoral Politics*, D. Kavanagh (ed.). Oxford: Clarendon Press.

Train, Kenneth. 2003. *Discrete Choice Methods for Simulation*. Cambridge: Cambridge University Press.

CHAPTER 12

Covering, Dominance, and Institution-Free Properties of Social Choice

RICHARD D. MCKELVEY

ABSTRACT. This paper shows that different institutional structures for aggregation of preferences under majority rule may generate social choices that are quite similar, so that the actual social choice may be rather insensitive to the choice of institutional rules.

Specifically, in a multidimensional setting, where all voters have strictly quasi-concave preferences, it is shown that the "uncovered set" contains the outcomes that would arise from equilibrium behavior under three different institutional settings. The three institutional settings are two-candidate competition in a large electorate, cooperative behavior in small committees, and sophisticated voting behavior in a legislative environment where the agenda is determined endogenously.

Because of its apparent institution-free properties, the uncovered set may provide a useful generalization of the core when a core does not exist. A general existence theorem for the uncovered set is proven, and for the Downsian case, bounds for the uncovered set are computed. These bounds show that the uncovered set is centered around a generalized median set whose size is a measure of the degree of symmetry of the voter ideal points.

1. Introduction

Recent results in social choice theory for multidimensional choice spaces have shown not only the genericity of nonexistence of core alternatives (Plott, [1967]; Rubinstein, [1979]; Schofield, [1983]), but also the genericity of global

---

This research was supported in part by NSF grants No. SES-82-08 184 and SES-84-09654 to the California Institute of Technology. I benefitted from discussion with Nicholas Miller, Ken Shepsle, and Barry Weingast. Section 5 of this paper began as joint work with Ken Shepsle and Barry Weingast. They have kindly permitted me to present it here.

cycle sets (McKelvey, [1976, Chapter 4 of this book], [1979, Chapter 5 of this book]; Schofield, [1978], [1983]). The conclusions drawn from these results have led to renewed interest in the role of rules and institutions in determining social outcomes (e.g., Shepsle and Weingast, [1981]; and Ordeshook and Shepsle, [1982]). The result has been a growing body of literature which explicitly models the institutional structure, and then looks for game theoretic equilibria conditional on the strategies that are implied by that structure (e.g., Shepsle, [1979]; Kramer, [1972], [1977]; McKelvey, Ordeshook, and Winer, [1978, Chapter 10 of this book]; and Ferejohn, Fiorina, and Packel, [1980], [1984]). While these directions are a healthy development in the field, one is left with the impression that, in the absence of core alternatives, little can be said about social choice that is institution-independent. We argue here that such a conclusion is not warranted.

While it may be necessary to model explicitly the institutional structure to obtain exact solutions, there appears to be enough commonality among the outcomes selected under different institutional arrangements so that nontrivial bounds on social choice, which hold under several different institutions, can be determined. Miller (1980) in a very insightful paper, argued that, for finite alternative spaces, the "uncovered set" performs just such a function. The covering relation, as defined by Miller, provides a method for transitively ordering alternatives for social choice. Miller argues that the resulting set of "uncovered" alternatives serves as a general solution set for majority voting games. Specifically, he shows that under a variety of institutional settings, game theoretic behavior by participants leads to outcomes in the uncovered set.

The covering relation is akin to the notion of dominance between strategies in two-person games. As such it has also been studied by other authors in slightly different versions. McKelvey and Ordeshook (1976) define an "admissibility relation" which is quite similar to the covering relation, and show the connection between the admissible set and outcomes resulting from two-candidate competition. Fishburn (1977) defines and investigates the normative properties of a set based on a dominance-like relation. Richelson (1980) shows the connection between Fishburn's set and the uncovered set, and introduces a choice set based on a more natural definition of dominance. More recently, Shepsle and Weingast (1984) have applied and extended Miller's results to show how the covering relation can be used to get bounds on agenda-reachable outcomes in multidimensional choice spaces.

This paper studies the dominance and covering relations in a setting that is of more immediate interest to economists and political theorists. Namely, we assume multidimensional choice spaces with quasi-concave preferences. This is more general than Miller's setup in terms of the assumptions on the alternative set and the social order, because we allow for infinite alternative sets, social indifference between alternatives, and more general social choice functions than majority rule. But it is less general than Miller in the assumptions on preferences, because restrictions are placed on the allowable preference profiles. These are the standard continuity and convexity assumptions used by economists, however.

The results here are similar in spirit to those of Miller, and reaffirm the importance of the uncovered and undominated sets. Specifically, it is shown that the uncovered and undominated sets *exist* in this more general setting, that the undominated set is contained in the uncovered set, and that the uncovered set contains, as subsets, the solutions that arise as game theoretic equilibria in several different institutional settings. Namely, the uncovered set contains as a subset *any* von Neumann-Morgenstern solution. It contains the support set of any mixed strategy equilibrium to the related two-candidate competition game. Finally, it contains the outcomes that result from sophisticated voting when agendas are determined endogenously.

It thus appears that the uncovered set may be an important generalization of the core when core points do not exist. Namely, it allows us to give restrictions on what outcomes might arise as the result of game-theoretic or "incentive-compatible" behavior of individuals, under a number of different institutional mechanisms. It is thus of interest to determine the properties and relative size of the uncovered set.

A final section of the paper obtains bounds on the uncovered set for the case of "Downsian," or "Euclidian-based" preferences. These results confirm a conjecture of Miller's — that the uncovered set is a centrally-located set that collapses to the core when a core exists, and that grows smaller when the configuration of preferences grows closer to having a core.

The remainder of the paper introduces assumptions on voter preferences and derives some basic properties of the social preference relation; defines the covering and dominance relations, giving properties of both; gives the basic existence theorems for the uncovered and undominated sets; shows the relation between the three different institutional mechanisms and the uncovered set; and derives bounds on the uncovered set under the assumption of "Downsian" preferences.

2. Assumptions: Voters and the Social Preference Order

We assume there is a finite set, N, of voters, a convex set $X \subseteq \mathbb{R}^m$ of alternatives, and for each $i \in N$, a weak order, $R_i \subseteq X \times X$ representing i's *preferences.* So each R_i is reflexive, complete, and transitive. We let P_i and I_i denote the asymmetric and symmetric parts of R_i, respectively.

We assume X is endowed with the standard metric topology, and for any set $A \subseteq X$, we use the notation $\beta(A)$, $\overline{A}$, A^c, and A° for the boundary, closure, complement, and interior of A, respectively. For any binary relation $Q \subseteq X \times X$, we use the notation

$$xQy \iff (x,y) \in Q, \text{ and } Q(x) = \{y \in X | yQx\}.$$

Thus, Q can be viewed as a correspondence: $Q : X \twoheadrightarrow X$. Also, we write $Q^1 = Q$, and for any integer $k > 1$, $Q^k = Q^{k-1} \circ Q$. We write Q^{-k} for the relation satisfying $xQ^{-k}y \iff yQ^k x$. So $xQ^k y$ iff there is a k step path, via Q, from y to x, and $xQ^{-k}y$ iff there is a k step path, via Q^{-1} from y to x.

We now introduce the assumptions we make on individual preferences. Throughout, we always make the following assumption (A0):

ASSUMPTION A0. *Continuous Preferences*: For all $i \in N$, and all $x \in X$, $R_i(x)$ and $R_i^{-1}(x)$ are closed.

This assumption guarantees that each voter's preferences can be represented by a continuous utility function. In addition to assumption A0, we will make the following assumptions when they are needed:

ASSUMPTION A1. *Strict Quasi-Concave Preferences*: For all $i \in N$, and for all $x, y \in X$ with $y \in R_i(x)$, if $z = ty + (1-t)x$, with $0 < t < 1$, then $z \in P_i(x)$.

ASSUMPTION A2. *Compact Preferences*: For all $i \in N$ and $x, y \in X$, $R_i(x)$ is compact.

Assumption A1 requires that for all voters, the set of points that are preferred or indifferent to any alternative, x, is always a convex set. Further, there can be no "thick" indifference curves. Assumption A2 requires that the set of points at least as good as x must be a compact set. Typical economic preferences on $\mathbb{R}_+^m$ (where more is better) generally satisfy assumption A1, but not A2, whereas the usual preferences assumed in political science, where there is an implicit budget constraint, and individuals can be satiated, would satisfy both assumptions A1 and A2. In particular the quadratic-based preferences of Davis and Hinich (1968) satisfy both assumptions A1 and A2.

We now define the social preference order based on a set $\mathbf{W} \subseteq 2^N$ of coalitions in N. We call $\mathbf{W}$ the set of winning coalitions. Throughout, we always assume:

ASSUMPTION B0. **W** *Is Monotonic*: $C \in \mathbf{W}$ and $C \subseteq C' \implies C' \in \mathbf{W}$ and **W** *Is Proper*: $C \in \mathbf{W} \implies C^c \notin \mathbf{W}$.

So every superset of a winning coalition is winning, and a coalition and its complement cannot both be winning. Another condition, which will be used when needed, is:

ASSUMPTION B1. **W** *Is Strong*: $C \notin \mathbf{W} \implies C^c \notin \mathbf{W}$.

We define $\mathbf{B} = \{C \subseteq N | C^C \notin \mathbf{W}\}$ to be the set of *blocking* coalitions (clearly $\mathbf{W} \subseteq \mathbf{B}$), and $\mathbf{L} = 2^N - \mathbf{B}$ to be the *losing* coalitions. (Here 2^N represents the set of all subsets of N.) Note if **W** satisfies assumption B1, then $\mathbf{B} = \mathbf{W}$, and **L** and **W** partition 2^N. For any coalition $C \subseteq N$, we use the notation:

(2.1) $\qquad xP_c y \iff xP_i y$ for $\forall i \in C$

$\qquad\qquad xR_c y \iff xR_i y$ for $\forall i \in C$

for the coalition preference relations, and

(2.2) $\qquad xPy \iff xP_C y$ for some $C \in \mathbf{W}$

$\qquad\qquad xRy \iff xR_C y$ for some $C \in \mathbf{B}$

for the social preference relation. Note that P and R are related in that P is the asymmetric part of R, but P_C is not necessarily the asymmetric part of R_C. Also, for $C \subseteq N$, and $x \in X$, $R_C(x)$ is the closure of $P_C(x)$ if the assumption A1 on preferences is met (see lemma 1 of appendix A).

Assumption B0 requires only that the set of winning coalitions be monotonic and proper, and it allows for the existence of nontrivial (i.e., nonwinning) blocking coalitions. Committee systems, bicameral systems, weighted voting, and α-majority rule are all examples of systems whose winning coalitions satisfy assumption B0. Assumption B1 requires that there cannot be nontrivial blocking coalitions. So every coalition must be either winning or losing. Systems satisfying assumption B1 must always have rules for "breaking ties." Majority rule with n odd, or majority rule with n even and a tiebreaking chairman are examples (but not the only examples) of systems satisfying assumption B1.

Throughout this paper, we will *always* assume both A0 and B0 are true. Hence, these assumptions will not be explicitly stated in the assumptions of any of the theorems. The other assumptions will sometimes be required, and they will be identified when they are needed.

In appendix A, we prove a number of properties of the social order, P. The most important of these are listed here:

FIGURE 1. Illustration of $P(x)$ for three voters. Note $P(x)$ is starlike about x. For any $y \in P(x)$, $z' \in P(x)$ and $z'' \in P^{-1}(x)$.

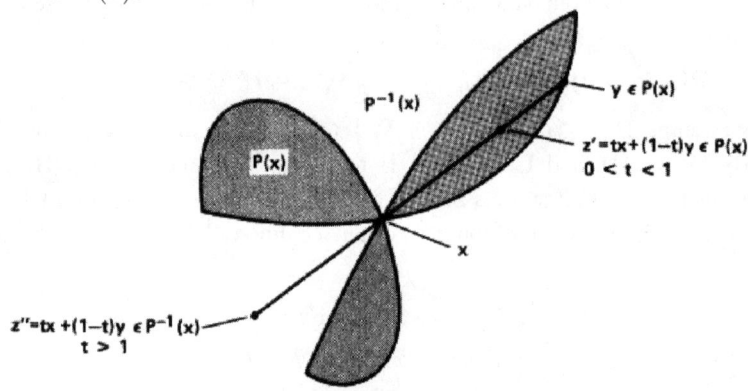

(1) Lemma 4: Under assumption A1, for all $k = \pm 1, \pm 2, \ldots$, both P^k and R^k are lower hemicontinuous.
(2) Lemma 5, 6: Under assumption A1, for all $x \in X$,
   a: $P(x)$ is starlike about x, and for all $y \in P^{-1}(x)$ and $z = ty + (1 - t)x$, with $t < 0$, $z \in P^{-1}(x)$.
   b: Consequently, if $P(x) \neq \varnothing$, for every neighborhood, $N(x)$ of x, $N(x) \cap P(x) \neq \varnothing$ and $N(x) \cap P^{-1}(x) \neq 0$.
(3) Lemma 7: Under assumptions A1 and B1, for all $x \in X$, if $P(x) \neq \varnothing$ then $I(x) = \beta(P(x)) = \beta(P^{-1}(x))$. So $R(x) = \overline{P(x)}$.

The first property establishes continuity properties of the social order. Lower hemicontinuity ensures that points in $P^k(x)$ (or $R^k(x)$) cannot suddenly disappear with arbitrarily small changes in x. The second property is illustrated in Figure 1. The first part says that if $y \in P(x)$ and $z = ty + (1 - t)x$, then if z is on the line segment connecting x and y (i.e., $0 < t < 1$), then $z \in P(x)$, whereas if z is on the ray emanating from x in the opposite direction from y (i.e., $t < 0$), then $z \in P^{-1}(x)$. From this result, part b follows immediately. Namely, whenever $P(x)$ is empty, then any neighborhood of x must contain points both of $P(x)$ and of $P^{-1}(x)$. The last property shows that when the social order is generated by a strong game, then $R(x)$ is the closure of $P(x)$.

3. The Dominance and Covering Relations

We define two binary relations, which we call the dominance and covering relations. They are both variations of the *weak dominance* relation, $\mathcal{D} \in X \times X$, which is defined as follows. For any $x, y \in X$,

(3.1) $\qquad x\mathcal{D}y \iff P(x) \subseteq P(y) \text{ and } R(x) \subseteq R(y).$

The *dominance relation*, $D \in X \times X$, is just the asymmetric part of $\mathcal{D}$. So, for any $x, y \in X$,

(3.2) $\qquad xDy = x\mathcal{D}y \;\&\; \sim y\mathcal{D}x \iff P(x) \subseteq P(y) \text{ and } R(x) \subseteq R(y),$

with one inclusion strict.

The second relation we define is a slight variation of the dominance relation, and we call it the covering relation. The definition we give is somewhat different than that of Miller (1983). The *covering relation*, denoted $C \subseteq X \times X$ is defined by the following, for all $x, y \in X$,

(3.3) $\qquad xCy \iff x\mathcal{D}y \;\&\; xPy.$

In appendix A, we prove the following propositions, which give properties of the dominance and covering relations.

PROPOSITION 3.1. Both D and C are symmetric, irreflexive, transitive and acyclic. Further $C \subseteq D$.

PROPOSITION 3.2. Under assumption A1, $\mathcal{D}(x)$ is closed for all x.

Under assumptions A1 and B1, the definitions of dominance and covering simplify considerably, so that we need only verify one inclusion:

PROPOSITION 3.3. Under assumptions A1 and B1, we have, for all $x, y \in X$

$$x\mathcal{D}y \iff P(x) \subseteq P(y) \iff R(x) \subseteq R(y),$$
$$xDy \iff P(x) \subseteq P(y) \iff R(x) \subseteq R(y),$$
$$xCy \iff \{x\} \cup P(x) \subseteq P(y) \iff \{x\} \cup P(x) \subset P(y).$$

The next result is a version of Miller's "two step" principle, which, under assumptions A1 and B1, also holds in the spatial framework developed here. Namely, x weakly dominates y if and only if it is not possible to reach y, in two steps, from x.

PROPOSITION 3.4. For any $y, x \in X, x \in P^{-2}(y) \implies \sim x\mathcal{D}y$. Under assumptions A1 and B1, $x \in P^{-2}(y) \iff \sim x\mathcal{D}y$. Equivalently, $y \notin P^2(x) \iff x\mathcal{D}y$.

4. The Undominated and Uncovered Sets

The undominated and uncovered sets are defined to be the maximal elements of the dominance and covering relations, respectively. More formally, for any binary relation, $Q \subseteq X \times X$ and set $A \subseteq X$, the *maximal* elements of the relation Q in A are defined:

$$\mathbf{M}(Q, A) = \{x \in A | \forall y \in A, xQy \text{ or } \sim yQx\}.$$

If Q is asymmetric (as are the covering and dominance relations), then we can write:

$$\mathbf{M}(Q, A) = \{x \in A | \forall y \in A, \sim yQx\}.$$

Then we define the *undominated set of X in A*, written $\mathbf{UD}(X|A)$, and the *uncovered set of X in A*, written $\mathbf{UC}(X|A)$ by:

$$\mathbf{UD}(X|A) = \mathbf{M}(D, A),$$

and

$$\mathbf{UC}(X|A) = \mathbf{M}(C, A).$$

We write $\mathbf{UD}(X)$ for $\mathbf{UD}(X|X)$ and $\mathbf{UC}(X)$ for $\mathbf{UC}(X|X)$, and refer to $\mathbf{UD}(X)$ and $\mathbf{UC}(X)$ as the *undominated* and *uncovered* sets of X, respectively. Since $C \subseteq D$, it follows easily that $\mathbf{UD}(X) \subseteq \mathbf{UC}(X)$.

Our first theorem establishes *existence* of the uncovered set and the undominated set. With quasi-concave preferences (assumption A1), to guarantee existence, it is sufficient to assume either that the alternative set is compact or that individual preferences are compact (i.e., individuals always have compact "preferred to" sets).

THEOREM 1. Under assumption A1, for any compact $A \subseteq X$, $\mathbf{UD}(X|A) \neq \varnothing$ and $\mathbf{UC}(X|A) \neq \varnothing$. If assumption A2 is also satisfied, then for any $X \subseteq \mathbb{R}^m$, $\mathbf{UD}(X) \neq \varnothing$ and $\mathbf{UC}(X) \neq \varnothing$.

PROOF. For any $A \subseteq X$, it follows easily that $\mathbf{M}(D, A) \subseteq \mathbf{M}(C, A)$. This follows directly by proposition 3.1, since $C \subseteq D$. But now, it suffices to prove the theorem for $\mathbf{M}(D, A)$ and $\mathbf{M}(D, X)$, since the corresponding results for $\mathbf{M}(C, A)$ and $\mathbf{M}(C, X)$ follow from the above inclusion.

Let $A \subseteq X$ be compact, and let $E \subseteq A$ be a chain under the partial ordering induced by $\mathcal{D}$. We will show that any such chain has an upper bound in A. Set $F = \bigcap_{x \in E} [\mathcal{D}(x) \cap A]$. If $F \neq \varnothing$, then pick $x^* \in F$. So $x^* \mathcal{D} x$ for all $x \in E$. Hence x^* is an upper bound for E. If $F = \varnothing$, then $\{\mathcal{D}(x)^c | x \in E\}$ is an open cover of A, since by proposition 3.2, each $D(x)$ is closed. But then there is a finite subset $G \subseteq E$ such that $\{\mathcal{D}(x)^c | x \in G\}$ is an open cover of A. By transitivity of $\mathcal{D}$ and the fact G is a chain, there is an $x^* \in G$ with $x^* \mathcal{D} x$ for all $x \in G$. Also by transitivity of $\mathcal{D}$, $\mathcal{D}(x^*) \subseteq \mathcal{D}(x)$ for all $x \in G$. But then $A \subseteq \mathcal{D}(x^*)^c$, so $\mathcal{D}(x^*) \cap A = \emptyset$, and a fortiori, $\mathcal{D}(x^*) \cap E = \emptyset$. I.e., we have $x^* \in E$ with xDx^* for no $x \in E$. But since E is a chain, we must have $x^* Dx$ for all $x \in E$. But then x^* is an upper bound for E. Thus, we have shown every chain $E \subseteq A$ has an upper bound in A; hence, by Zorn's lemma, there is a maximal element in A, i.e., $\mathbf{M}(D, A) \neq \emptyset$. But $\mathbf{M}(D, A) = \mathbf{M}(\mathcal{D}, A)$, since D is the asymmetric part of $\mathcal{D}$. Hence $\mathbf{M}(D, A) \neq \emptyset$.

Now if assumption A2 is satisfied, and X is any (not necessarily compact) subset of $\mathbb{R}^m$ then let $E \subseteq X$ be a chain. Pick arbitrary $x_0 \in E$, and set $E^+ = \{y \in E | y D x_0\}$, $E^- = \{y \in E | x_0 D y\}$. Now E^+ is a chain contained in $\mathcal{D}(x_0)$, which, by assumption A2, is compact. By the proof of theorem 1, E has an upper bound, say x^*, but x^* is also an upper bound for E, by transitivity. Hence every chain $E \subseteq X$ has an upper bound. Applying Zorn's lemma again, $\mathbf{M}(\mathcal{D}, X) = \mathbf{M}(D, X) \neq \emptyset$. Q.E.D.

The two-step principle can be extended to get upper and lower bounds on the uncovered set in terms of the set of points that are reachable in two steps from all other alternatives. When both assumptions A1 and B1 are met, then with the exception of points of closure, the uncovered set (and undominated set) is characterized as the set of points which are reachable in two steps, via P, from every other point in X. In this case, it follows that $\overline{\mathbf{UD}(X)} = \overline{\mathbf{UC}(X)}$, so the two sets are identical except for points of closure.

PROPOSITION 4.1. In general, $\bigcap_{y \in X} P^2(y) \subseteq \mathbf{UD}(X) \subseteq \mathbf{UC}(X) \subseteq \bigcap_{y \in X} R^2(y)$. If assumptions A1 and B1 are satisfied, and $P(z) \neq \emptyset$ for all $z \in X$, then $\bigcap_{y \in X} P^2(y) \subseteq \mathbf{UD}(X) \subseteq \mathbf{UC}(X) \subseteq \overline{\bigcap_{y \in X} P^2(y)}$.

When assumptions A1 and B 1 are met, proposition 4.1 gives a potential "brute force" method for computing $\overline{\mathbf{UC}(X)}$ up to any desired degree of accuracy. One could simply check whether $x \in P^2(y)$ for all y on some fine-enough grid in X.

The next two results give properties of the uncovered set and undominated set that are useful later in dealing with endogenous agendas:

PROPOSITION 4.2. Under assumptions A1 and B1, for all $A \subseteq X$ with either $X = A$ or A compact, and for all $x \in A$, if $x \notin \mathbf{UD}(X|A)$ then $\exists y \in \mathbf{UD}(X|A)$ with yDx. Similar results hold for $\mathbf{UC}(X|A)$.

PROPOSITION 4.3. For any collection $\{x^j\} \subseteq X$ with $\bigcap_j P(x^j) \neq \varnothing$, we have $\bigcap_j P(x^j) \cap \mathbf{UD}(X) \neq \varnothing$, and $\bigcap_j P(x^j) \cap \mathbf{UC}(X) \neq \varnothing$.

Note that, for all $x \in \bigcap_j P(x^j)$, either $x \in \mathbf{UD}(X)$ or there is a $y \in \bigcap_j P(x^j) \cap \mathbf{UD}(X)$ with yDx. (Similarly for $\mathbf{UC}(X)$.)

5. Small Committees

Small committee behavior is usually modeled as a cooperative game, in characteristic function form. This provides a good model of the social outcomes that would occur in small groups operating with unstructured rules of procedure. In this section, we define a simple characteristic function form game, without sidepayments, whose winning coalitions are $\mathbf{W}$. We then show that every von Neumann-Morgenstern solution to this game is included in the uncovered set.

Before proceeding, we warn the reader of some terminological ambiguity which leads to considerable confusion. The word "dominance" is used in game theory with two different meanings. In one usage, it refers to the relation between two strategies in a noncooperative game. Here, one strategy dominates another if it is better no matter what strategy the opponents adopt. We will see, in the next section, that this usage of the word coincides with our relation D, which we have thus called the dominance relation. The second usage of "dominance" is in *cooperative* games, where it refers to a relation between two strategies adopted by perhaps different coalitions. Here, one strategy (or alternative) "dominates" another if there is some coalition which both prefers and can unilaterally ensure the first over the second. This second usage of the word "dominance" is the usage which is meant in this section of the paper. Since we will have occasion to use "dominance" in both of its meanings in this paper, when there is the possibility of confusion, we will use the terms Φ-dominance and v-dominance to refer to the noncooperative and cooperative usages of the term. Here Φ refers to the payoff function of the corresponding noncooperative game, and v to the characteristic function of the corresponding cooperative game.

We define the characteristic function, $v: 2^N \to 2^X$ for a simple game without sidepayments by:

$$v(C) = X \text{ if } C \in \mathbf{W},$$
$$v(C) = \varnothing \text{ if } C \notin \mathbf{W}.$$

For any $x, y \in X$ and $C \subseteq N$, we say x v-*dominates* y *via* C, written $x \rightarrowtail Cy$, iff $xP_C y$ and $x \in v(C)$. We say x v-*dominates* y, written $x \rightarrowtail y$ iff $x \rightarrowtail Cy$ for some $C \subseteq N$. It is trivial to verify that, for the simple characteristic function defined above, $x \rightarrowtail Cy$ iff $xP_C y$ and $x \rightarrowtail y$ iff xPy.

A *von Neumann-Morgenstern* solution is defined to be any set $K \subseteq X$ satisfying:
(a) *Internal Stability*. $\forall x, y \in K, \sim (x \rightarrowtail y)$.
(b) *External Stability*. $\forall x \notin K, \exists y \in K$ such that $y \rightarrowtail x$.

THEOREM 2. *Let assumptions A1 and B1 be met, and let K be a von Neumann-Morgenstern solution. Then $K \subseteq \mathbf{UC}(X)$.*

PROOF. We first show that for any $x \in K$, $z \notin K$, that $\sim zDx$. To prove this, by external stability it follows that $\exists y \in K$ with yPz. By openness of $P(z)$, it follows there is a neighborhood $N(y)$ of y such that $y'Pz$ for any $y' \in N(y)$. By internal stability, xIy. By lemma 8, $P(x) \neq \varnothing$. By lemma 7, we can find $y' \in N(y)$ with $y' \in P^{-1}(x)$. But then $y' \in P^{-1}(x)$ and $zP^{-1}(y')$, so $z \in P^{-2}(x)$. By proposition 3.4, $\sim zDx$.

To show that $K \subseteq \mathbf{M}(C, X)$, note that from the first paragraph, whenever $x \in K$, $z \notin K$, we have $\sim zDx$. But since $zCx \Longrightarrow zDx$, it follows that $\sim zCx$. But also, if $x \in K$, and $z \in K$, then by internal stability, $\sim zPx$ so $\sim zCx$. Thus for all $x \in K$, $z \in X$, $\sim zCx$. Hence $x \in \mathbf{M}(C, X)$, so $K \subseteq \mathbf{M}(C, X)$. Q.E.D.

Typically, a von Neumann-Morgenstern solution is not unique. In addition to finite solutions (where it is possible to view each alternative in K as the proposal of some winning coalition), there may be an infinite number of "discriminatory" solutions. The discriminatory solutions each contain an infinite number of alternatives, and in some games (for example, majority rule "divide the dollar" games) their union covers the whole set of Pareto Optimals. It is worth emphasizing that theorem 2 holds for *any* von Neumann-Morgenstern solution. Hence it follows that the union of all von Neumann-Morgenstern solutions (i.e., the set of all points which could result from some von Neumann-Morgenstern solution) is also in the uncovered set.

6. Two-Candidate Competition

The covering relation also turns out to have a close connection with models of two-candidate competition. We can model two-candidate competition as a two-person, zero-sum game, with the candidates as players, who compete for the votes of the electorate through the policy positions they adopt. Thus, candidate strategies consist of an announcement of a policy position that they will adopt if elected, and then voters are assumed to vote for the candidate whose policy position they prefer. Formally, we define a two-player, symmetric zero-sum game as follows: the strategy spaces for both players will be $S_1 = S_2 = X$. The payoff function, $\Phi : S_1 \times S_2 \to R$ for player 1 is defined by, for $\mathbf{s} = (s_1, s_2) \in S_1 \times S_2$

(6.1) $$\Phi(\mathbf{s}) = \begin{cases} 1 & \text{if} & s_1 P s_2 \\ -1 & \text{if} & s_2 P s_1 \\ 0 & \text{otherwise.} \end{cases}$$

Since the game is zero sum, the payoff to player 2 is just $-\Phi(\mathbf{s})$.

It is easily shown that the game modeled in equation 6.1 has a pure strategy equilibrium if and only if there is a majority rule core point (i.e., iff $\mathbf{M}(P, X) \neq \emptyset$). Hence, it follows from Plott's Theorem (1967) that, generally, there will not exist pure strategy equilibria to the game. Even though there are no pure strategy equilibria, we can still make some statements about the policy outcomes that might occur. There are two ways of doing this: one is to look for mixed strategy equilibria, and the other is to use Farquharson's concept (1969) of "sophisticated" strategies.

Before proceeding, we recall the definition of domination of two strategies for a noncooperative game, and show that it corresponds to the dominance relation, D, defined earlier. Given two strategies, $s_1, t_1 \in S_1$ for player 1, we say that s_1 Φ-dominates t_1 if, for all choices of strategy $s_2 \in S_2$ by player 2,

(6.2) $$\Phi(s_1, s_2) \geq \Phi(t_1, s_2),$$

with strict equality for some $s_2 \in S_2$. But, from equation 3.2,

(6.3a) $\quad s_1 D t_1 \iff P(s_1) \subseteq P(t_1)$ and $R(s_1) \subseteq R(t_1)$,

and

(6.3b) $\quad P(s_1) \subset P(t_1)$ or $R(s_1) \subset R(t_1)$.

However, 6.3a holds iff

$$(\forall s_2 \in X)(s_2 P s_1 \implies s_2 P t_1) \text{ and } (s_2 R s_1 \implies s_2 R t_1)$$
$$\iff (\forall s_2 \in X)(\Phi(s_1, s_2) = -1 \implies \Phi(t_1, s_1) = -1) \text{ and }$$
$$(\Phi(s_1, s_2) \leq 0 \implies (t_1, s_2) \leq 0)$$
(6.4) $$\iff (\forall s_2 \in X)(\Phi(s_1, s_2) > \Phi(t_1, s_2)).$$

Similarly 6.3b holds iff

(6.5) $$(\exists s_2 \in X)(\Phi(s_1, s_2) > \Phi(t_1, s_2)).$$

Together, equations 6.4 and 6.5 yield equation 6.2. Thus, $s_1 D t_1$ if and only if s_1 Φ-dominates t_1 in the two-person noncooperative game of equation 6.1.

Farquharson's analysis of sophisticated behavior is based on the idea that players will eliminate from consideration any strategies that are Φ-dominated. The remaining strategies are called admissible (or primarily admissible). Once the dominated strategies have been eliminated, a reduced game results, and strategies that were previously not dominated can now be dominated. Players can now eliminate strategies from the reduced game. The remaining strategies are called secondarily admissible, and the resulting game is called the second reduction. Proceeding in this fashion, one arrives eventually at ultimately admissible, or sophisticated strategies, which are those that survive all successive reductions. It is reasonable to think that when there is no pure strategy equilibrium, candidates should confine themselves to ultimately admissible strategies (or at least to admissible strategies). The following theorem shows that any sophisticated strategy as well as the support of any mixed strategy equilibrium must be inside the uncovered set.

THEOREM 3. (a) All admissible strategies (and hence all ultimately admissible strategies) for the game in equation 6.1 are included in $\mathbf{UC}(X)$.

(b) If $\lambda : X \to \mathbb{R}^m$ is a mixed strategy equilibrium for the game in equation 6.1, then the support for λ, $\text{supp}(\lambda)$ must satisfy $\text{supp}(\lambda) \subseteq \mathbf{UC}(X)$.

PROOF. (a) The relation D corresponds to Φ-dominance in the game in equation 6.1. Thus the primarily admissible strategies are included in $\mathbf{UD}(X)$, which are in turn included in $\mathbf{UC}(X)$.

(b) A mixed strategy equilibrium can not put positive measure on the set of dominated strategies. Q.E.D.

On the question of existence of mixed strategy equilibria see Kramer (1978) who shows that for games similar to that in equation 6.1, mixed strategy equilibria will exist.

In the context of "Downsian," or "Euclidian-based preferences," McKelvey and Ordeshook (1976) studied properties of a set very similar to the uncovered set (called the admissible set in their paper), and showed that it contains the mixed-strategy solutions and is a subset of the convex hull of the "partial medians." Unfortunately, this set is frequently not very restrictive. On the other hand, under similar assumptions on preferences, the uncovered set can frequently be quite restrictive, as the final section of this paper shows. Hence, theorem 3 can be used to calculate nontrivial bounds on the support set of the mixed-strategy solution to the candidate-competition game.

7. Sophistication and Endogenous Agendas

The third institutional setting we consider is a legislature operating under a set of parliamentary rules, where the motions on the agenda are generated endogenously. We consider only amendment-type procedures, where voters vote in a sophisticated fashion. Some preliminary definitions are in order.

We first define versions of the dominance and covering relations which apply to a subset of $A \subseteq X$. They are defined in the natural way. Thus, for any $x, y \in X$,

(7.1) $\quad x\mathcal{D}_A y \iff [P(x) \cap A \subseteq P(y) \cap A]$ and $[R(x) \cap A \subseteq R(y) \cap A]$

and D_A is defined to be the asymmetric part of $\mathcal{D}_A$. I.e.,

(7.2) $\quad\quad\quad\quad x\mathcal{D}_A Y \iff x\mathcal{D}_A y$ and $\sim y\mathcal{D}_A x.$

Also, we define

(7.3) $\quad\quad\quad\quad xC_A y \iff x\mathcal{D}_A y$ and $xPy.$

For any $A, B \subseteq X$, the *undominated set of A in B*, written $\mathbf{UD}(A|B)$, is $\mathbf{M}(D_A, B)$, and the *uncovered set of A in B*, written $\mathbf{UC}(A|B)$, is $\mathbf{M}(C_A, B)$. Again we use the notation $\mathbf{UD}(A) = \mathbf{UD}(A|A)$ and $\mathbf{UC}(A) = \mathbf{UC}(A|A)$.

The following properties are easily verified. For any $A, B \subseteq X$, and $x, y \in X$:

(a): if $A \subseteq B$, then $x\mathcal{D}_B y \implies x\mathcal{D}_A y$; i.e., $A \subseteq B \implies \mathcal{D}_B \subseteq \mathcal{D}_A$,
(b): if $B \subseteq A$, and $x, y \in B$, then $xC_A y \implies x\mathcal{D}_A y$; i.e., $C_A \cap B \subseteq D_A \cap B$,
(c): if $B \subseteq A$, $\mathbf{UD}(A|B) \subseteq \mathbf{UC}(A|B)$.

FIGURE 2. Illustration of the agenda $(x_1, x_2, \ldots, x_t)$ with sophisticated equivalent $(x_1^*, x_2^*, \ldots, x_t^*)$

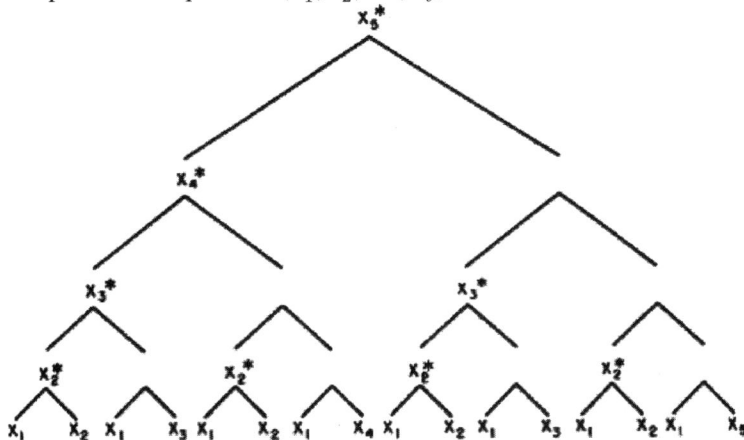

Now an *agenda based on the amendment process* is simply a t-tuple $(x_1, \ldots, x_t)$ together with a voting tree, as illustrated in Figure 2. x_1 is called the *status quo*, x_2 the *motion*, x_3 the *amendment*, x_4 the *amendment to the amendment*, etc.

Given an agenda based on the amendment process, $(x_1, x_2, \ldots, x_t)$, we define its *sophisticated equivalent*, $(x_1^*, x_2^*, \ldots, x_t^*)$ as follows:

(7.4a) $\qquad x_1^* = x_1,$

(7.4b) $\qquad$ for $1 < i \leq t, x_i^* = \left\{ \begin{array}{ll} x_i & \text{if } x_i P x_j^* \text{ for } \forall j < i \\ x_{i-1}^* & \text{otherwise.} \end{array} \right\}$

The ith element, x_i^*, of the sophisticated equivalent is called the *sophisticated equivalent of node i* and represents the outcome that would occur for the agenda $(x_1, \ldots, x_i)$ if no further amendments are introduced, and all voters vote sophisticatedly.

As discussed in the previous section, Farquharson's (1969) notion of sophisticated behavior amounts to successive elimination of dominated strategies. However, in this case, the underlying game is an n-person, noncooperative game, where individual strategy spaces are possible instructions as to how to vote at each node in the voting tree, and where the payoff function is the payoff that the voter gets from the final node reached, given an n-tuple of voter strategies. We will not write out the payoff function of this game formally, but results of McKelvey and Niemi (1978) and Gretlein (1983) show that sophisticated voting in this game is equivalent to the type of behavior described by equation 7.4, i.e., all voters vote at early nodes on the basis of what they realize will happen at successive nodes.

We now consider a fixed agenda $\mathbf{x} = (x_1, \ldots, x_t)$ and set $A = \{x_1, x_2, \ldots, x_t\}$. Then the following proposition extends a theorem of Miller (1980) to deal with a social ordering, P, which may or may not be antisymmetric (a "tournament" in Miller's terminology) over A:

PROPOSITION 7.1. (*Miller*): In general, $x_t^* \in \mathbf{UC}(A)$. If P is antisymmetric on A, $x_t^* \in \mathbf{UD}(A)$.

While proposition 7.1 shows that $x_t^* \in \mathbf{UC}(A)$, in general there may be an even more restrictive subset of $\mathbf{UC}(A)$ that contains x_t^*. See Banks (1985) for a characterization of the set of alternatives achievable by sophisticated agendas.

Proposition 7.1 relates to a fixed agenda $(x_1, \ldots, x_t)$, where the alternatives, x_i, on the agenda are given exogenously. Further, the proposition only shows that the outcome resulting from sophisticated behavior is in the uncovered set of $A = \{x_1, x_2, \ldots, x_t\}$, where the covering relation, C_A, is defined with respect to the set A rather than with respect to X. It does not follow that x_t^* must be in the uncovered set of the whole space. Even if $A \cap \mathbf{UC}(X) \neq \emptyset$, we might have $\mathbf{UC}(A) \cap \mathbf{UC}(X) = \emptyset$. For example, if $A = \{x_1, x_2\}$, where $x_2 P x_1$, and $x_1 \in \mathbf{UC}(X)$ but $x_2 \notin \mathbf{UC}(X)$, then $\mathbf{UC}(A) = \{x_2\}$.

Even though proposition 7.1 does not establish that x_t^* must be in the uncovered set of X, it does prove a powerful result that becomes useful in analyzing what might occur if there is any *endogeneity* to the process of agenda formation. Namely, the proposition shows that, for any $x \in X$, no alternative $y \in X$, for which xCy, can be the sophisticated outcome of an agenda that contains the two. If $A = \{x_1, x_2, \ldots, x_t\}$ is such an agenda, then $xCy \implies xC_Ay \implies y \notin \mathbf{UC}(A)$. So by the proposition, $y \neq x_t^*$. It follows that an individual can *unilaterally* quash any alternative in $C^{-1}(x)$ by introducing x on the agenda anywhere in the amendment process. Furthermore, the introduction of x on the agenda will have the desired effect (namely the elimination of $C^{-1}(x)$) regardless of whether the individual knows the other proposals on the agenda and regardless of whether other players are allowed to propose amendments subsequent to the introduction of x.

To formalize these ideas, we first define $\mathbf{A}$ to be the set of all possible agendas. I.e.,

(7.5) $\qquad \mathbf{A} = \{\mathbf{x} | \mathbf{x} = (x_1, x_2, \ldots, x_t) \in X^t \text{ for some } t\}$

and for any $x \in \mathbf{A}$, we let $x^* \in X$ be the sophisticated outcome of the agenda x. I.e., if $\mathbf{x} = (x_1, \ldots, x_t)$, then $x^* = x_t^*$. Also, for any $\mathbf{x} = (x_1, \ldots, x_t) \in \mathbf{A}$, we write $A(\mathbf{x}) = \{x_1, \ldots, x_t\}$ for the set of proposals on the agenda $\mathbf{x}$; and for any $z \in X$, we write $\mathbf{A}(z) = \{\mathbf{x} \in \mathbf{A} | z \in A(\mathbf{x})\}$ for the set of agendas containing z.

We can now define an n-person game as follows: let the set of players be $N = \{1, 2, \ldots, n\}$, for each $i \in N$; let $u_i : X \to \mathbb{R}$ be a continuous utility representation of R_i, and define the strategy space for player i to be $S_1 = X$. Given choices $\mathbf{s} = (s_1, \ldots, s_n) \in \mathbf{S} = \prod_i S_i$, we define the payoff function $\Phi_i : \mathbf{S} \to \mathbb{R}$ by the equation:

(7.6) $$\Phi_i(\mathbf{s}) = \inf_{\mathbf{x} \in \mathbf{A}(s_t)} u_i(x^*),$$

where "inf" is the infimum, or greatest lower bound of the $u_i(x^*)$. Thus, this game models the type of outcomes that might occur if alternatives on the agenda emerge endogenously and are then voted on in the following two-step procedure: First, there is a period of agenda formation during which any individual has access to the floor and can introduce motions. During this stage, motions are made in an environment of incomplete information about how the amendments might be ordered for voting or what additional motions might arise. Once all motions have been made, they are placed on the agenda and voting occurs in a specific order, according to the amendment process. During this stage, all voters are assumed to know the entire agenda and to vote sophisticatedly.

For any two strategy n-tuples, $\mathbf{s}$ and $\mathbf{t}$, we say that $\mathbf{s}$ and $\mathbf{t}$ are *payoff equivalent* if $\Phi_i(\mathbf{s}) = \Phi_i(\mathbf{t})$ for all i. We obtain the following result:

THEOREM 4. *If X is compact, and assumptions A1 and B1 are met, the game defined by equation 7.6 has a pure strategy equilibrium. Further, for any equilibrium, $\mathbf{s}$, there is a payoff equivalent strategy n-tuple, $\mathbf{t} = (t_1, \ldots, t_n) \in \mathbf{S}$ such that for any permutation $\varphi : N \to N$, and resulting agenda $(t_{\varphi(i)}, \ldots, t_{\varphi(n)})$, $t^*_{\varphi(n)} \in \mathbf{M}(C, X)$.*

PROOF. We first show that there is an equilibrium, $\mathbf{s}$. We let $W(s_i) = \{y \in X | y = x^* \text{ for some } \mathbf{x} \in \mathbf{A}(s_i)\}$. So

(7.7) $$\Phi_{(\mathbf{s})} = \inf_{y \in W(s_i)} u_i(y).$$

We first note that, for any $x \in X$, $W(x) = X - C^{-1}(x)$. Miller's theorem gives us that $W(x) \subseteq X - C^{-1}(x)$ and to see $X - C^{-1}(x) \subseteq W(x)$, note for any $y \in X - C^{-1}(x)$, we have $\sim (xCy) \implies (xDy \text{ and } xPy) \implies \sim (xDy)$ or yRx. But if yRx, then the agenda (y, x) has sophisticated outcome y, and if

$\sim (xDy)$, then by proposition 3.4, $x \in P^{-2}(y) \implies \exists z \in X$ with yPz and zPx. But then the agenda (z, y, x) has y as its sophisticated outcome. So we have proven $W(x) = X - C^{-1}(x)$. But now, from proposition 3.4, it follows easily that $X - C^{-1}(x) = P^2(x) \cup R(x)$. Hence, we have that

(7.8) $$W(x) = P^2(x) \cup R(x).$$

Next, from lemma 7, it follows that $\overline{P(z)} = R(z)$ whenever $P(z) \neq \emptyset$, and that $\overline{P^2(x)} = R^2(x)$ whenever $P(x) \neq \emptyset$. Hence $\overline{W(x)} = R^2(x)$ when $P(x) \neq \emptyset$. By lemma 4, $R(x)$, and hence $R^2(x)$ is a lower hemicontinuous correspondence. But now,

(7.9) $$\Phi_i(\mathbf{s}) = \inf_{y \in W(s_t)} u_i(y) = \inf_{y \in \overline{W(s_t)}} u_i(y) = \inf_{y \in R^2(s_t)} u_i(y).$$

But since $R^2(s_i)$ is lower hemicontinuous and u_i is continuous, Φ_i is upper semicontinuous on X. Hence, since X is compact, Φ_i attains a maximum. Hence an equilibrium exists to equation 7.9. It also follows that if $\mathbf{s} = (s_1, \ldots, s_n)$ is an equilibrium, then either $s_i \in \mathbf{M}(C, X)$ for all i, or there exists a "payoff equivalent equilibrium" in which all strategies are undominated: i.e., there are strategies $\mathbf{t} = (t_1, \ldots, t_n)$ with $t_i \in \mathbf{M}(C, X)$ such that $\mathbf{t}$ is in equilibrium and $\Phi_i(\mathbf{t}) = \Phi_i(\mathbf{s})$ for all i. To see this, note that if for some $i \in N$, $s_i \notin \mathbf{M}(C, X)$, then by proposition 4.2, $\exists t_i \in \mathbf{M}(C, X)$ with $t_i C s_i$. In this fashion, pick $\mathbf{t}$ with $t_i \in \mathbf{M}(C, X)$ for all $i \in N$. But by transitivity of C,

$$t_i C s_i \implies C^{-1}(s_i) \subseteq C^{-1}(t_i) \implies X - C^{-1}(t_i) \subseteq X - C^{-1}(s_i)$$
$$\implies W(t_i) \subseteq W(s_i) = \Phi_i(\mathbf{t}) \geq \Phi_i(\mathbf{s}).$$

But since $\mathbf{s}$ is an equilibrium, it must be that $\Phi_i(\mathbf{t}) = \Phi_i(\mathbf{s})$. So $\mathbf{t}$ is an equivalent equilibrium. We can proceed in this fashion to eventually obtain an equilibrium, $\mathbf{t}$, with all t_i in $\mathbf{M}(C, X)$. But now, the result that $t_{\Phi(n)} \in \mathbf{M}(C, X)$ follows from the fact that all t_i are in $\mathbf{M}(C, X)$. Q.E.D.

The game defined by equation 7.8 represents only *one* possible way of modeling endogenous formation of agendas, and the theorem then shows that all equilibria are payoff equivalent to equilibria in which all players restrict themselves to the uncovered set. Alternative methods of modeling the endogeneity of the proposals on the agenda would be indicated if legislators had more complete information during the motion-making stage. We do not investigate those models here, but the same sort of considerations that drive motions into the uncovered set in the above model might also be expected to do so in other models. Proposition 4.3 shows that it is impossible to construct any agenda, $\mathbf{x} = (x_1, \ldots, x_t)$, that will eliminate all uncovered points; i.e., for any such agenda, there always exists a proposal $x_{t+1} \in \mathbf{M}(C, X)$ which, when added into the existing agenda, will be the sophisticated outcome. And Miller's theorem together with proposition 4.2 shows the attractiveness of uncovered points in eliminating covered points. Based on these two statements, we would conjecture that any model of endogenous agenda formation that allows all legislators the right to introduce motions will result in outcomes inside the uncovered set.

8. Size of the Uncovered Set

Given the results of the previous sections, it would be of interest to characterize the uncovered set as a function of the particular preference profile. Miller (1980) conjectures that the uncovered set will generally be a small, centrally-located set. We have not been able to obtain results for general preference profiles satisfying assumptions A1 or A2. However, for the special case of Euclidian-based preferences, we have been able to calculate bounds on the uncovered set. These results show that the uncovered set is indeed a "centrally-located" set that collapses to the core when a core exists, and that is small if the preference configuration is "close" to having a core.

We assume in this section that $X = \mathbb{R}^m$, and that preferences are of the following form:

ASSUMPTION A3. *Euclidian-Based Preferences*: For all $i \in N$, $\exists x^i \in X$ such that for all $x, y \in X$

$$xRy \iff \|x - x^i\| \leq \|y - x^i\|.$$

These are the usual "Downsian" preferences, and x^i is called voter i's *ideal point*. Additionally, we assume that the social preference order is generated by majority rule. Here we write $n = |N|$.

ASSUMPTION B2. *Majority Rule*: The number n is odd and

$$\mathbf{W} = \left\{ C \subseteq N \,\big|\, |C| \geq \frac{n+1}{2} \right\}.$$

Clearly preferences satisfying assumption A3 satisfy A0–A2, and if assumption B2 is satisfied, then B0 and B1 are satisfied. Hence, all of the results of the previous sections apply here.

Now, for any $\alpha \in \mathbb{R}^m$ and $c \in \mathbb{R}$ write:

(8.1) $$H(\alpha, c) = \{x \in \mathbb{R}^m \,|\, x \cdot \alpha = c\}.$$

So $H(\alpha, c)$ is an $m - 1$ dimensional hyperplane in $\mathbb{R}^m$. The hyperplane $H(\alpha, c)$ is a *median hyperplane* if:

(8.2) $\quad |\{i \in N | x^i \cdot \alpha < c\}| \leq \dfrac{n}{2}$ and $|\{i \in N | x^i \cdot \alpha > c\}| \geq \dfrac{n}{2}$.

We let **H** denote the set of all median hyperplanes.

Next, for any $y \in X$ and $t \in \mathbb{R}^+$, let $\mathcal{B}(y, t)$ be the closed ball with center at y and radius t. So

(8.3) $\qquad\qquad \mathcal{B}(y, t) = \{x \in X | \, \|y - x\| \leq t\}$.

We let **B** denote the set of all such balls which have nonempty intersections with each $H \in \mathbf{H}$. I.e.,

(8.4) $\quad \mathbf{B} = \{\mathcal{B}(y, t) | y \in X, t \in \mathbb{R}^+, \text{ and for } \forall H \in \mathbf{H}, H \cap \mathcal{B}(y, t) \neq \varnothing\}$.

It is easily shown that under the assumptions made, there is a unique element, say $\mathcal{B}(\overline{y}, \overline{t})$ of **B** satisfying, for $\forall \mathcal{B}(y, t) \in \mathbf{B}$, $\overline{t} \leq t$. The element $\mathcal{B}(\overline{y}, \overline{t})$ of **B** is called the *Generalized Median Set* (or alternatively, the *Yolk*). It is the ball of minimum radius, which intersects every median hyperplane. The point $\overline{y}$ is referred to as the *generalized median point*. See Figure 3 for an illustration of this construction.

The generalized median set can be computed as a solution to a linear programming problem. Let $H_1, H_2, \ldots, H_k$ be the set of all median hyperplanes that contain at least two ideal points on the hyperplane. Assume α_i and c_i are the parameters describing H_i. Without loss of generality we can assume that $\|\alpha_i\| = 1$ for all i. So $H_i = \{x \in \mathbb{R}^m | x \cdot \alpha_i = c\}$. Since the distance from any $y \in \mathbb{R}^m$ to H_i is given by $|y \cdot \alpha_i - c_i|$, it follows that $\overline{y}$ and $\overline{t}$ are the solution to the following linear program: minimize t such that, for $\forall 1 \leq i \leq K$,

$t \geq y \cdot \alpha_i - c_i$,
$t \geq c_i - y \cdot \alpha_i$.

Next, given $x^*, y^* \in X$, and $t^* \in \mathbb{R}$, define $\mathcal{C}^m(x^*, y^*, t^*)$ to be the region bounded by the *m-dimensional cardioid* which has *cusp* at x^*, *center* at y^*, *eccentricity* of t^*, and *radius* of $r^* = \|x^* - y^*\|$ (see Figure 4). This is defined formally in appendix B.

The following results are proven in appendix B. See Figure 5 for an illustration.

PROPOSITION 8.1. *Under assumptions A3 and B2, for all $x \in X$:*

$$\mathcal{C}^m(x, \overline{y}, -2\overline{t}) \subseteq P(x) \subseteq R(x) \subseteq \mathcal{C}^m(x, \overline{y}, 2\overline{t}).$$

FIGURE 3. The construction of $B(\bar{y}, \bar{t})$ for a preference configuration of seven voters in two dimensions

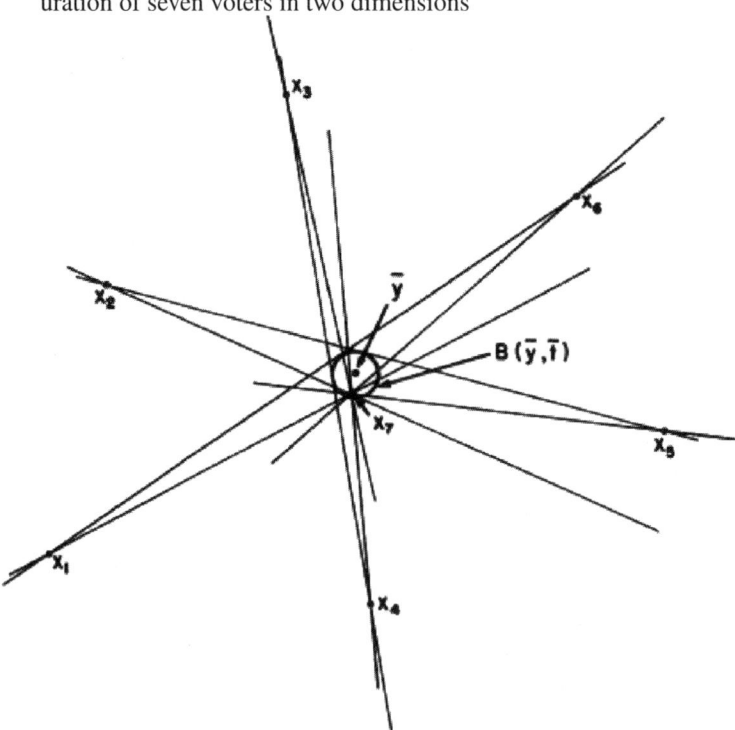

Further, proposition 8.2 follows directly from the definition of the sets $\mathcal{C}^m(x, y, t)$:

PROPOSITION 8.2. Under assumptions A3 and B2, for all $x \in X$, if $t = \|x - \bar{y}\|$, then
$$\mathcal{C}^m(x, \bar{y}, 2\bar{t}) \subseteq \mathcal{B}(\bar{y}, t + 2\bar{t}),$$
$$\mathcal{B}(\bar{y}, t - 2\bar{t}) \subseteq \mathcal{C}^m(x, \bar{y}, -2\bar{t}).$$

Putting together these results, we get the following proposition:

FIGURE 4. The cardioid $C^2(x^*, y^*, t^*) : r^* = \|x^* - y^*\|$

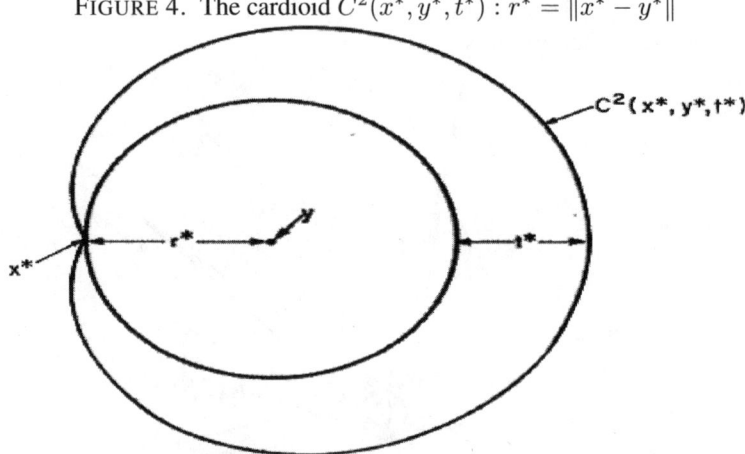

FIGURE 5. Example of $P(x)$ and $R(x)$ for a two-dimensional case

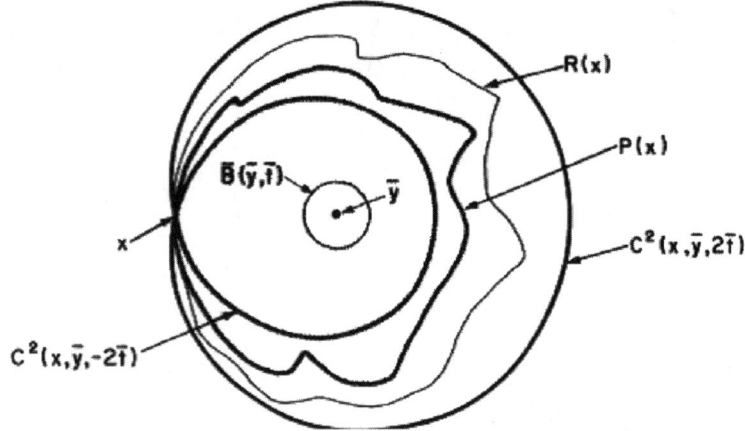

PROPOSITION 8.3. Under assumptions A3 and B2, then for all $x \in X$, if $t = \|x - \bar{y}\|$, we have:
$$\mathcal{B}\left(\bar{y}, t - 4\bar{t}\right) \subseteq D(x),$$
and
$$X - D^{-1}(x) \subseteq \mathcal{B}\left(\bar{y}, t + 4\bar{t}\right).$$

The proposition gives bounds on the set of points that cover and are covered by a point $x \in X$. While the proposition is not our primary concern, it does have some implications worth noting. Shepsle and Weingast (1984) prove that the set of reachable points under "forward" agendas, (i.e., agendas of the form $(x_i, x_2, \ldots, x_k, x)$, where first x_k is voted against x, then the winner against x_{k-1}, etc.) is exactly $X - D^{-1}(x)$. It follows that with a sophisticated agenda, one can never reach from a point x, an alternative y for which $\|y - \overline{y}\| > \|x - \overline{y}\| + 4\overline{t}$. So "forward"-building sophisticated agendas are constrained in how far they can wander from the generalized median point, $\overline{y}$.

THEOREM 5. Under the assumptions of proposition 8.3,

$$\mathbf{UC}(X) \subseteq \mathcal{B}\left(\overline{y}, 4\overline{t}\right).$$

PROOF. For any $x \in \mathcal{B}\left(\overline{y}, 4\overline{t}\right)$, by proposition 8.3, $\overline{y} \in D(x)$ and $\overline{y} \in P(x)$, hence $x \notin \mathbf{UC}(X)$. Q.E.D.

Proposition 8.3 and theorem 5 are illustrated in Figures 6 and 7. The crucial parameter here is $\overline{t}$. As is described in Ferejohn, McKelvey, and Packel (1984), the size of $\overline{t}$ can be thought of as a measure of the symmetry of the distribution of ideal points. In the case when a total multidimensional median point exists, then $\overline{t}$ will be zero, since all median planes go through that point. In the more general cases, $\overline{t}$ is the radius of a smallest sphere needed to intersect all medians. So if there is just a small deviation from the case when a total median exists, $\overline{t}$ would be small. For larger deviations it would be larger. The smaller $\overline{t}$ is, the less latitude there is in terms of the size of the uncovered set, and the size of the set of reachable points.

As far as the location of the uncovered set, we see from the theorem, together with the observations that have been made on the size of the generalized median set, that at least for the "Downsian" case, the conjecture of Miller is correct. Namely, the uncovered set is a centrally-located set. It collapses to the core, or majority-rule equilibrium when one exists, and will be small when the configuration of ideal points is perturbed slightly from a core configuration. It is centered around a generalized median set whose size is a measure of the degree of nonsymmetry of the ideal points.

9. Conclusion

We have shown that three different institutional processes all lead to points inside the uncovered set. Also, in the case of Euclidian-based preferences, we

FIGURE 6. Illustration of proposition 8.3 for a two-dimensional example

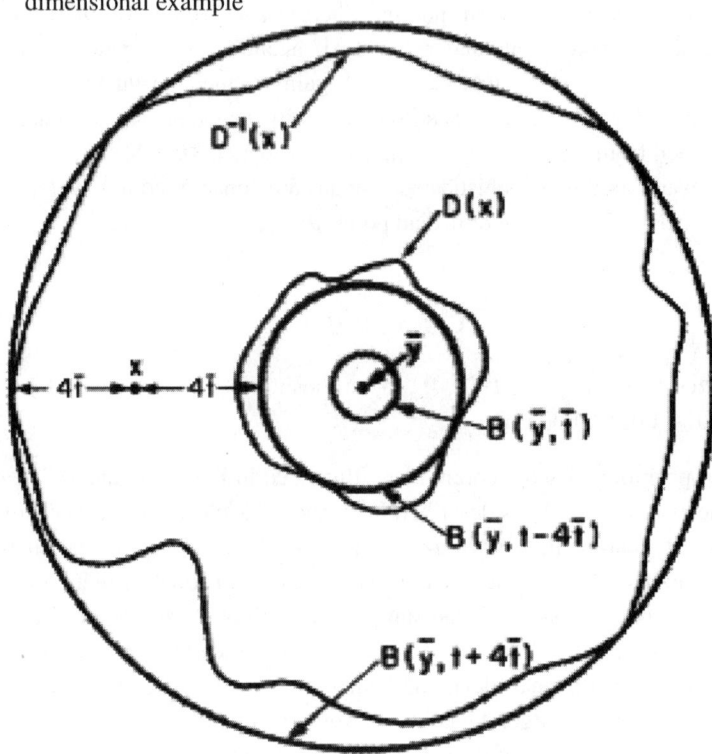

have shown that the uncovered set is bounded by a sphere centered about a generalized median set. This set, in turn, is shown to be a centrally-located set that is equal to the core, or to the total median when one exists, and that is small when preferences are "close" to having a core.

Other results have also identified the generalized median set to be of particular importance. Ferejohn, McKelvey, and Packel (1984) show that a Markov process, where new proposals are generated randomly to beat the previous status quo, has a limiting distribution which is centered about this set.

Although the uncovered set encompasses the equilibria for several different institutions, it should be emphasized that the uncovered set is *not* a catch-all. In particular, Kramer and McKelvey (1984) show that the "minmax set" is not included in the uncovered set. Further, any process that can pick Pareto-dominated

FIGURE 7. Limits for the uncovered set given in Figure 2 $\left(\mathbf{UC}\left(X\right) \subseteq \mathbf{B}\left(\overline{y}, 4\overline{t}\right)\right)$

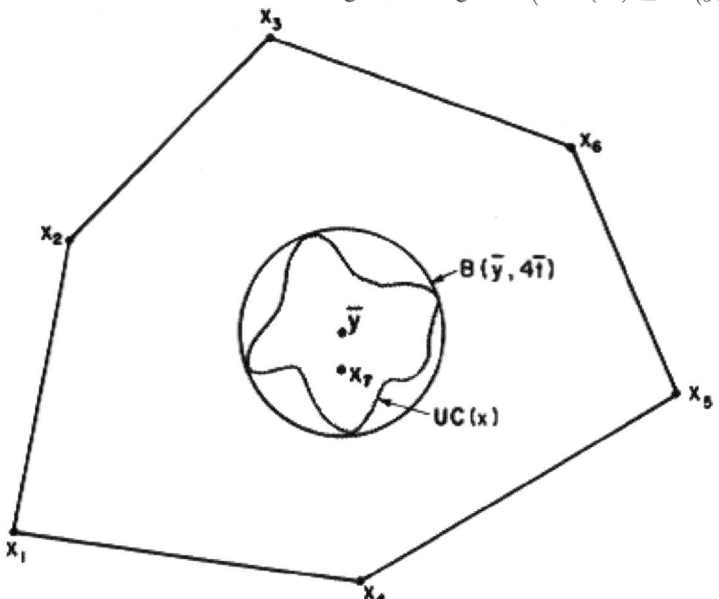

points — such as the "sophisticated voting equilibrium" of Kramer (1972), or the "institution-induced equilibrium" of Shepsle (1979), can clearly lead to points outside the uncovered set. Even the Markov process of Ferejohn, McKelvey, and Packel (1984), described above, can select points outside the uncovered set. While the limiting distribution for the Markov process is centered about the generalized median set, it can put some probability beyond the distance $(4\overline{t})$ that bounds the uncovered set. A subject for future research will be to try and identify the characteristics of institutions whose equilibria lie in the uncovered set.

Appendix A

In this appendix, we prove the results labeled as "propositions" in the body of the paper. We first round up a herd of lemmas, which characterize various properties of the social order, P, and which are used in the proofs of the main results, Throughout this appendix, since assumptions A0 and B0 are always true, they will not be explicitly stated as assumptions in the results.

LEMMA 1. Under assumption A1, for any $x \in X$ and $C \subseteq N$, if $P_C(x) \neq \emptyset$, then $R_C(x) = \overline{P_C(x)}$.

PROOF. We first show that

(A.1) $$\bigcap_{i \in C} \overline{P_i(x)} = \overline{P_C(x)}.$$

We can use the properties of closure of intersections of sets to obtain $\overline{P_C(x)} = \bigcap_{i \in C} \overline{P_i(x)} = \overline{P_i(x)}$. To show the reverse inclusion, let $y \in \bigcap_{i \in C} \overline{P_i(x)}$. Then $y \in R_i(x)$ for all $i \in C$. But now let $L = \{z = ty + (1-t)x | 0 < t < 1\}$. Then, by assumption A1, $L \subseteq P_i(x)$ for all $i \in C$, and $N(y) \cap L \neq \emptyset$ for all neighborhoods $N(y)$ of y. Hence, $N(y) \cap P_i(x) \neq \emptyset$, so $y \in P_C(x)$. Using assumption A1, we now get

$$R_C(x) = \bigcap_{i \in C} R_i(x) = \bigcap_{i \in C} \overline{P_i(x)} = \overline{P_C(x)}.$$

This completes the proof of lemma 1. Q.E.D.

LEMMA 2. For all $i \in N$, P_i is an open correspondence.

PROOF. Let $u_i : X \to \mathbb{R}$ be a continuous utility representation of P_i, and let $(x_0, y_0) \in P_i$; i.e., $x_0 P y_0$, or $u_i(x_0) > u_i(y_0)$. Set $\varepsilon = u_i(x_0) - u_i(y_0)$, and find neighborhoods $N(x_0)$ and $N(y_0)$ of x_0 and y_0 respectively such that $x \in N(x_0) \Longrightarrow u_i(x) > u_i(x_0) - \frac{\varepsilon}{2}$ and $y \in N(y_0) \Longrightarrow U(y) < U(y_0) + \frac{\varepsilon}{2}$. Then, for $x \in N(x_0)$ and $y \in N(y_0)$,

$$u_i(x) > u_i(x_0) - \frac{\varepsilon}{2} = u_i(y_0) + \frac{\varepsilon}{2} > u_i(y).$$

So $N(x_0) \times N(y_0)$ is an open neighborhood of (x_0, y_0) contained in P_i. Hence P_i is open. Q.E.D.

LEMMA 3. For all $k = \pm 1, \pm 2, \ldots$, P^k is an open correspondence.

PROOF. For $k = 1$, we have $P^1 = P = \bigcup_{c \in \mathbf{W}} \bigcap_{i \in C} P_i$, so since, by lemma 2, each P_i is open, so is P. Now assume P^k is open, and we show that P^{k+1} is. If $(x_0, y_0) \in P^{k+1}$, then there exists $z \in X$, such that $x_0 P z$ and $z P^k y_0$. By openness of P^k and P^1, there are neighborhoods $N(x_0)$ and $N(y_0)$ of x_0 and y_0 such that $x \in N(x_0) = x P z$ and $y \in N(y_0) = z P^k y$.

But then $N(x_0) \times N(y_0) \subseteq P^{k+1}$, so P^{k+1} is open. Finally, for $k < 0$, the result follows from the observation that $(x, y) \in P^k \iff (y, x) \in P^{-k}$. Q.E.D.

LEMMA 4. Under assumption A1, for all $k = \pm 1, \pm 2, \ldots$, both P^k and R^k are lower hemicontinuous correspondences.

PROOF. Lower hemicontinuity of P follows directly from lemma 3, since $P = P^1$ is an open correspondence. Then by induction, lower hemicontinuity of P^k follows because $P^k = P \circ P^{k-1}$ is the composition of two lower hemicontinuous correspondences. Note that lower hemicontinuity of P^k does not depend on assumption A1.

To show that R is lower hemicontinuous, apply lemma 1 to get, for $P(x) \neq \emptyset$, $R(x) = \bigcup_{C \in \mathbf{B}} R_C(x) = \bigcup_{C \in \mathbf{B}} \overline{P_C(x)} = \overline{\bigcup_{C \in \mathbf{B}} P_C(x)}$. For $P(x) = \emptyset$, $R(x) = \{x\}$. Since $x \in R(x)$ for $P(x) \neq \emptyset$, we can write $R(x) = \{x\} \cup \overline{\bigcup_{C \in \mathbf{B}} P_C(x)}$. But $\bigcup_{C \in \mathbf{B}} P_C(x)$ is open, hence it is lower hemicontinuous. Then, by proposition 11.19(b) of Border, $\overline{\bigcup_{C \in \mathbf{B}} P_C(x)}$ is lower hemicontinuous. Also $\{x\}$ is lower hemicontinuous. Then since the union of two lower hemicontinuous correspondences is lower hemicontinuous, this proves R is lower hemicontinuous. The result for R^k follows as above for P^k. Q.E.D.

LEMMA 5. Under assumption A1, for all $x \in X$, $P(x)$ is starlike about x. Further, for all $y \in P(x)$, if $z = ty + (1-t)x$, with $t < 0$, then $z \in P^{-1}(x)$.

PROOF. To show that $P(x)$ is starlike about x, we must show that for all $y \in X$, if $y \in P(x)$, then $z = ty + (1-t)x \in P(x)$ whenever $0 < t < 1$. But by strict quasi concavity, for all $i \in N$, if $y \in P_i(x)$, then $z \in P_i(x)$. So, for any $C \subseteq N$, $yP_Cx \Longrightarrow zP_Cx$. To show the second assertion, pick $x \in X$, $y \in P_i(x)$ and $z = ty + (1-t)x$ for $t < 0$. Then $x = rz + (1-r)y$, where $r = 1/(1-t)$. So $0 < r < 1$, and x is a convex combination of z and y. Now for all $i \in N$, we have $yP_ix \Longrightarrow xP_iz$. To see this, suppose not; i.e., suppose yP_ix and zR_ix. By completeness of R_i, either yR_iz or zR_iy. But by strict quasi concavity, $yR_iz \Longrightarrow xP_iz$, and $zR_iy \Longrightarrow xP_iy$. Either of these yields a contradiction, so we must have $yP_ix \Longrightarrow xP_iz$, but then for any $C \subseteq N$, $yP_Cx \Longrightarrow xP_Cz$, hence $yPx \Longrightarrow xPz \Longrightarrow z \in P^{-1}(x)$. Q.E.D.

LEMMA 6. Under assumption A1, for all $x \in X$, if $P(x) \neq \emptyset$, then for every neighborhood, $N(x)$ of x, $N(x) \cap P(x) \neq \emptyset$ and $N(x) \cap P^{-1}(x) \neq \emptyset$.

PROOF. The result follows immediately from lemma 5. Q.E.D.

LEMMA 7. Under assumptions A1 and B1, then for all $x \in X$, if $P(x) \neq \emptyset$, $I(x) = \beta(P(x)) = \beta(P^{-1}(x))$. So $R(x) = \overline{P(x)}$.

PROOF. First, it is clear that $\beta(P(x)) \subseteq I(x)$ and $\beta(P^{-1}(x)) \subseteq I(x)$. To see this, assume $y \in \beta(P(x))$. Then any neighborhood of y must intersect $P(x)$ and $X - P(x) = R^{-1}(x)$. But then $y \notin P(x)$ because $P(x)$ is open, and $y \notin P^{-1}(x)$ because $P^{-1}(x)$ is open and $P^{-1}(x) \cap P(x) = \emptyset$. But $P(x)$, $P^{-1}(x)$, and $I(x)$ partition X, so we must have $y \in I(x)$. A similar argument shows $\beta(P^{-1}(x)) \subseteq I(x)$.

Now, to show $I(x) \subseteq \beta(P(x))$ and $I(x) \subseteq \beta(P^{-1}(x))$, pick $y \in I(x)$. If $y = x$, then the result follows from lemma 6. If $y \neq x$, then pick $z = ty + (1-t)x$ where $0 < t < 1$, and $w = sy + (1-s)x$, where $s > 1$. By strict quasi concavity, we have, for all $i \in N$,

(A.2)
$$yR_ix \implies zP_ix$$
$$xR_iy \implies xP_iw$$

But then n odd and xIy means $\{i \in N | xP_iy\} \notin \mathbf{W}$ and $\{i \in N | yP_ix\} \notin \mathbf{W}$ or, equivalently $\{i \in N | yP_ix\} \in \mathbf{B}$ and $\{i \in N | xP_iy\} \in \mathbf{B}$. By the assumption that $\mathbf{W}$ is strong and proper, it follows $\mathbf{B} = \mathbf{W}$, so we can replace $\mathbf{B}$ by $\mathbf{W}$ in the above expressions, but then, from equation (A.2), it follows that

$$\{i \in N | yR_ix\} \subseteq \{i \in N | zP_ix\}$$

and

$$\{i \in N | xR_iy\} \subseteq \{i \in N | xP_iw\}$$

Hence, by assumption B0 on $\mathbf{W}$, $\{i \in N | zP_ix\} \in \mathbf{W}$ and $\{i \in N | xP_iy\} \in \mathbf{W}$. So $z \in P(x)$ and $w \in P^{-1}(x)$. Since t and s are arbitrary, z and w can be chosen to be in any neighborhood $N(y)$ of y. Hence $y \in \beta(P(x))$ and $y \in \beta(P^{-1}(x))$. This completes proof of the first statement of the lemma. The fact that $R(x) = \overline{P(x)}$ now follows immediately from the fact that $I(x) = \beta(P(x))$. Q.E.D.

LEMMA 8. Under assumptions A1 and B1, if $x, y \in X$ with $x \neq y$, and $z = ty + (1-t)x$ with $0 < t < 1$, then $y \in R(x) \implies z \in P(x)$. Further, $R(x)$ satisfies the same properties as $P(x)$ in lemmas 5 and 6.

PROOF. Let x, y, z be as described in the lemma, and $y \in R(x)$. Then $\sim xPy$ means $\{i \in N | xP_iy\} \notin \mathbf{W}$ or, taking the complement and using the fact $\mathbf{W}$ is strong and proper, $\{i \in N | yR_ix\} \in \mathbf{B} = \mathbf{W}$. But then, by strict quasi-concavity, $yR_ix \implies zP_ix$ for all i, so

$$\{i \in N | yR_ix\} \subseteq \{i \in N | zP_ix\},$$

so, by property (a) of **W**, $\{i \in N | zP_i x\} \in \mathbf{W}$. Hence zPx. The remainder of the lemma follows by similar arguments to those of lemmas 5 and 6. Q.E.D.

LEMMA 9. *Under assumptions A1 and B1, for all $x, y \in X$ with $x \neq y$, $P(x) \cap P(y) \neq \varnothing$ whenever $P(x)$ and $P(y)$ are nonempty.*

PROOF. Assume, for some $x, y \in X$ that

(A.3) $$P(x) \cap P(y) = \varnothing.$$

Then, we must have xIy. Otherwise, if for example xPy, then by openness of $P(y)$, there is a neighborhood $N(x)$ of x such that $N(x) \subseteq P(y)$, and since $P(x) \cap P(y) = \varnothing$, we must have $N(x) \cap P(x) = \varnothing$. But this contradicts lemma 6. A similar argument shows we cannot have yPx. So we must have xIy. But then pick $z = 1/2x + 1/2y$. By lemma 8 it follows that zPx and zPy is a contradiction to assumption A3. So we must have $P(x) \cap P(y) \neq \varnothing$. Q.E.D.

PROOF OF PROPOSITION 3.1. We first show that D satisfies the properties stated.

If $x = y$, then $P(x) = P(y)$ and $R(x) = R(y)$, so $\sim xDy$. Hence D is irreflexive.

If $x \neq y$, and xDy, then either $P(x) \subseteq P(y)$ or $R(x) \subseteq R(y)$. In either case $\sim yDx$. So D is asymmetric.

If xDy and yDz then $P(x) \subseteq P(y)$ and $P(y) \subseteq P(z)$, so $P(x) \subseteq P(z)$. Also $R(x) \subseteq R(y)$ and $R(y) \subseteq R(z)$. So $R(x) \subseteq R(z)$. Also at least one of these inclusions is strict since for the inclusions $P(x) \subseteq P(y)$ and $R(x) \subseteq R(y)$, at least one is strict. So xDz.

Acyclicity follows directly from the fact that D is asymmetric and transitive. So D satisfies the stated properties. We now show that C does also.

If $x = y$, then $\sim xPy \implies \sim xCy$. So C is irreflexive.

If $x \neq y$, then $xCy \implies xPy \implies \sim yPx \implies \sim yCx$. Hence C is asymmetric.

If xCy and yCz, then xDy and yDz and xPy and yPz. By an argument similar to that given above, it follows $\mathcal{D}$ is transitive, so xDz. But since yDz, it follows that $P(y) \subseteq P(z)$. Thus $xPy \implies x \in P(y) \implies x \in P(z) \implies xPz$. Thus xDz and xPz; i.e., xCz. So C is transitive.

As above, acyclicity of C follows from transitivity and asymmetry.

Finally, for any $x, y \in X$, $xCy \implies x\mathcal{D}y$ and $xPy \implies x \in P(y)$ and $P(x) \subseteq P(y)$. But $x \notin P(x)$, so $P(x) \subsetneq P(y)$. Hence xDy. Thus $C \subseteq D$. Q.E.D.

PROOF OF PROPOSITION 3.2. Let $\{y\}_{i=1}^{\infty}$ be a sequence with $y_i \to y^* \in X$, and with $y_i \in \mathcal{D}(x)$ for all i. Thus for all i, $P(y_i) \subseteq P(x)$ and $R(y_i) \subseteq R(x)$. Assume $y^* \notin \mathcal{D}(x)$. Then either $P(y^*) \not\subseteq P(x)$ or $R(y^*) \not\subseteq R(x)$. If $P(y^*) \not\subseteq P(x)$, then set $G = X - \overline{P(x)}$. Since $P(x)$ is open, G is open, and $G \cap P(y^*) \neq \emptyset$. Hence, by lower hemicontinuity of P, lemma 4, there is a neighborhood $N(y^*)$ of y such that $P(y) \cap G \neq \emptyset$ for all $y \in N(y^*)$. In particular, since $y_i \to y^*$, $P(y) \cap G \neq \emptyset$ for some y. But this contradicts $P(y_i) \subseteq P(x)$, so we must have $P(y^*) \subseteq P(x)$.

Now assume $R(y^*) \not\subseteq R(x)$. Now set $G = X - R(x)$. Again G is open and $R(y^*) \cap G \neq \emptyset$. Again, we can apply lower hemicontinuity of R to get a neighborhood $N(y^*)$ of y for which $R(y) \cap G \neq \emptyset$ for $y \in N(y^*)$, but then $R(y) \cap G \neq \emptyset$ for some i, which contradicts $R(y_i) \subseteq R(x)$. Q.E.D.

PROOF OF PROPOSITION 3.3. $x\mathcal{D}y = P(x) \subseteq P(y)$ and $x\mathcal{D}y \implies R(x) \subseteq R(y)$ follows directly from the definition of $\mathcal{D}$, so we need only show the reverse implications. We show $P(x) \subseteq P(y) \iff R(x) \subseteq R(y)$. Then clearly either one of these inclusions implies $x\mathcal{D}y$. By lemma 7, $P(x) = [R(x)]°$ for all x, hence $R(x) \subseteq R(y) \implies [R(x)]° \subseteq [R(y)]° \implies P(x) \subseteq P(y)$. Now assume $P(x) \subseteq P(y)$. If $P(x) \neq \emptyset$, then lemma 7 implies $R(x) = \overline{P(x)} \subseteq \overline{P(y)} = R(y)$. If $P(x) = \emptyset$, then lemma 8 implies $R(x) = \{x\}$. But $P(x) = \emptyset \implies y \notin P(x) \implies x \in R(y)$ so $R(x) \subseteq R(y)$. This proves the first line of implication. The second and third lines follow directly using the definitions of D and C in terms of $\mathcal{D}$. Q.E.D.

PROOF OF PROPOSITION 3.4. For any $x, z \in X$

$$z \in P^{-2}(x) \iff \exists y \in X \text{ such that } xPy \text{ and } yPz$$
$$\iff \exists y \in X \text{ such that } y \notin R(x) \text{ and } y \in P(z)$$
$$\iff P(z) \not\subseteq R(x)$$
$$\implies P(z) \not\subseteq P(x)$$
$$\implies\, \sim z\mathcal{D}x.$$

Now if assumptions A1 and B1 are met, then by lemma 7 and proposition 3.3, the last two implications become $\iff$. Q.E.D.

PROOF OF PROPOSITION 4.1. To show $\bigcap_{y \in X} P^2(y) \subseteq \mathbf{UD}(X)$, pick $x \in \bigcap_{y \in X} P^2(y)$ (the proof is trivial if this set is empty). Then, for all $y \in X$, $y \in P^{-2}(x)$. By proposition 3.4, $\sim y\mathcal{D}x$. Thus $x \in \mathbf{UD}(X)$.

Covering, Dominance, and Institution-Free Properties of Social Choice 273

The fact that $\mathbf{UD}(X) \subseteq \mathbf{UC}(X)$ follows directly from $C \subseteq D$.

To show $\mathbf{UC}(X) \subseteq \bigcap_{y \in X} R^2(y)$, let $x \in \mathbf{UC}(X)$. Then, for all $y \in X$, $\sim yCx$: i.e., $\sim (P(y) \subseteq P(x))$ or $\sim (R(y) \subseteq R(x))$ or $\sim yPx$. But $\sim yPx \Longrightarrow xRy \Longrightarrow x \in R^2(y)$. Next, $\sim (R(y) \subseteq R(x)) \Longrightarrow \exists z \in X$ with zRy and $\sim zRx$; i.e., zRy and xPz, so $x \in R^2(y)$.

Finally, $\sim (P(y) \subseteq P(x)) \Longrightarrow \exists z \in X$ with zPy and $\sim zPx$; i.e., zPy and xRz. So $x \in R^2(y)$.

To show the second assertion, we need only show that under assumptions A1 and B1, $\bigcap_{y \in X} R^2(y) \subseteq \bigcap_{y \in X} \overline{P^2(y)}$. First we show that $R^2(y) \subseteq \overline{P^2(y)}$ for any $y \in X$. Let $z \in R^2(y)$. Then there exists $w \in X$ with wRy and zRw. But now, by lemma 7, $R(w) = \overline{P(w)}$, so for any neighborhood $N(z)$ of z, $N(z) \cap P(w) \neq \varnothing$. By lower hemicontinuity of P (lemma 4), there is a neighborhood, $N(w)$ of w such that, for all $w' \in N(w)$, $N(z) \cap P(w') \neq \varnothing$. Now, since $R(y) = \overline{P(y)}$, we can pick $w' \in N(w)$ with $w'Py$. Then picking $z' \in P(w') \cap N(z)$, we have $z' \in P^2(y)$, so $z \in \overline{P^2(y)}$. But now, we have $\bigcap_{y \in X} R^2(y) \subseteq \bigcap_{y \in X} \overline{P^2(y)} = \overline{\bigcap_{y \in X} P^2(y)}$.

To show the last equality, note that $z \in \bigcap_{y \in X} \overline{P^2(y)} \iff$ for all $y \in N$, and every neighborhood, $N(z)$ of z, $N(z) \cap P^2(y) = \varnothing \iff$ for every neighborhood, $N(z)$ of z, $N(z) \cap \left[\bigcap_{y \in X} P^2(y)\right] \neq \varnothing \iff z \in \overline{\bigcap_{y \in X} P^2(y)}$. Q.E.D.

PROOF OF PROPOSITION 4.2. $x \notin \mathbf{M}(D, A) \Longrightarrow$ there exists $z \in A$ with zDx. But then $\{x, z\}$ is a chain, which, by the Kuratowski lemma, is part of a maximal chain, say $E \subseteq A$. But by the proof of theorem 1, E has an upper bound, say y; i.e., yDw or $y = w$ for all $w \in E$. It follows that $y \in E$ but by transitivity of D, we must have $D(y) = \varnothing$. Otherwise E is not maximal.

PROOF OF PROPOSITION 4.3. Suppose $\bigcap_j P(x^j) \cap \mathbf{M}(D, X) = \varnothing$, and pick $x \in \bigcap_j P(x^j)$. Then since $x \notin M(D, X)$, by proposition 4.2, there exists $y \in \mathbf{M}(D, X)$ with yDx; i.e., $P(y) \subseteq P(x)$ and $R(y) \subseteq R(x)$ (one strict). But since $x \in \bigcap_j P(x^j)$, we have $x^j Px$ for all j, or $\{x^j\} \subseteq P^{-1}(x) \subseteq P^{-1}(y)$. So

yPx^j for all j. But then $y \in \bigcap_j P(x^j) \cap \mathbf{M}(D, X)$, a contradiction. The proof of the second inequality is similar. Q.E.D.

PROOF OF PROPOSITION 7.1. Assume there is some $x_i \in A$ with $x_i C_A x_t^*$; i.e., $x_i P x_t^*$ and $x_i \mathcal{D}_A x_t^*$. By the definition of the sophisticated equivalent, it follows that $x_t^* = x_k^* = x_k$ for some $x_k \in A$. There are two cases:

CASE 1. $i < k$. Here, from the definition of the sophisticated equivalent, since $x_k = x_k^*$, we have $x_k P x_j^*$ for all $j < k$. But since $x_i \mathcal{D}_A x_k$, it follows that for $j < i$, $x_i P x_j^*$. Otherwise $x_j^* \in R(x_i) \Longrightarrow x_j^* \in R(x_k) \Longrightarrow \sim x_k^* P x_j^*$, a contradiction. But then, by the definition of the sophisticated equivalent, $x_i^* = x_i$. But $x_k^* = x_k$ and $i < k \Longrightarrow x_k P x_i^* \Longrightarrow x_k P x_i$, a contradiction.

CASE 2. $i > k$. Now, since $x_k = x_k^*$, $x_k P x_j^*$ for all $j < k$. By $x_i \mathcal{D}_A x_k$, it follows that $x_i P x_j^*$ for all $j < k$. But for $k \le j \le i$, $x_j^* = x_k$, since $x_n^* = x_k$. But then $x_i P x_k$ for $k \le j < i$. Hence $x_i P x_j^*$ for all $j < i$, which means, by the definition of the sophisticated equivalent, that $x_i^* = x$. But this is a contradiction to $x_n^* = x_k$, since this would imply $x = x_k$ also.

So, in both cases, we get a contradiction, implying that for any $x_k \in A$, we cannot have $x_k P x_t^*$ and $x_k \mathcal{D}_A x_t^*$. It follows that $\sim x_k C_A x_t^*$, so $x^* \in \mathbf{M}(C_A, A)$. This proves the first assertion; the second follows immediately from the observation that if P is antisymmetric, then $x\mathcal{D}_A x_t \Longrightarrow xPx_t$, hence by the first part of the theorem, $xPx_t \Longrightarrow \sim x\mathcal{D}x_t \Longrightarrow \sim x\mathcal{D}_A x_t$, a contradiction. So for all $x \in A$, $\sim x\mathcal{D}_A x_t$, i.e., $x_t \in \mathbf{M}(D_A, A)$. Q.E.D.

Appendix B

This appendix provides formal definitions of the sets $\mathcal{C}^m(x, y, t)$ as well as a proof of the propositions of section 8. Further details can be found in Ferejohn, McKelvey, and Packel (1984).

Let $\theta(x) = (\theta_1(x), \theta_2(x), \ldots, \theta_{m-1}(x), \rho(x))$ denote the m-dimensional, spherical coordinates of the vector $x \in R^m$. Thus

(B1) $$\rho(x) = \|x\|$$

and, for $1 \le i \le m - 1$,

(B2) $$\theta_i(x) = \sin^{-1} \left\{ \frac{x_i}{\rho(x) \prod_{J < i} \cos \theta_J(x)} \right\}.$$

Here, the θ_J range between $-\pi/2$ and $\pi/2$, except for θ_{m-1}, which ranges between $-\pi/2$ and $3\pi/2$. Now for any $x^*, y^* \in R^m$, and $t^* \in R$, we set $r^* = \|x^* - y^*\|$, and let Q be an $m \times m$, orthonormal-rotation matrix such that

(B3) $$Q(y^* - x^*) = (t, 0, \ldots, 0).$$

Write $Q(x - x^*) = (z_1, \ldots, z_m) = z$. Then define $\zeta_{x^*y^*}(x) = \theta(Q(y^* - x^*)) = \theta(z)$. So $\zeta_{x^*y^*}(x)$ are m-dimensional spherical coordinates of x which are centered at x^* and have one axis coincident with the vector $y^* - x^*$. Now, where $-\pi/2 \le \alpha \le \pi/2$, set

(B4) $$\alpha = \sin^{-1} \frac{-t^*}{r^*}.$$

So that the above is also well-defined for the case when $|t^*| \ge r^*$, we use the convention that, for $r \in \mathbb{R}$, $|r| \ge 1$, $\sin^{-1} r = \pi/2 \sin(r)$. Then,

(B5) for $m > 2$, we set $\beta = \dfrac{\pi}{2}$,

for $m = 2$, we set $\beta = \pi - \alpha$.

Then define, for $t^* \in \mathbb{R}$,

(B6) $$\mathcal{C}^m(x^*, y^*, t^*) = \{x \in X | 0 \le \rho(z) \le 2r^* \sin\theta_t(z) + t^* \text{ and}$$
$$a \le \theta_1(z) \le \beta \text{ (where } z = Q(x - x^*))\}.$$

Thus, $\mathcal{C}^m(x^*, y^*, t^*)$ is the m-dimensional cardioid with cusp at x, center at y, eccentricity of t, and radius of r^*. Note that if $t^* = 0$, then $\mathcal{C}^m(x^*, y^*, t^*)$ becomes a sphere, with center at y and radius r^*. If $t^* < 0$, then the resulting cardioid is contained in this sphere, otherwise it contains the sphere. Also note that if $t^* < -r^*$, then $\mathcal{C}^m(x^*, y^*, t^*) = \emptyset$.

PROPOSITION 8.1. Let assumptions A3 and B2 be met. Let $\bar{y} \in X$ and $\bar{r} \in \mathbb{R}^+$ be chosen so that for every median hyperplane $H(\alpha, c)$, with $\alpha \in \mathbb{R}^m$, $c \in \mathbb{R}$, that $H(\alpha, c) \cap \mathcal{B}(\bar{y}, \bar{r}) \ne \emptyset$. Then

$$\mathcal{C}^m(x, \bar{y}, -2\bar{r}) \subseteq P(x) \subseteq R(x) \subseteq \mathcal{C}^m(x, \bar{y}, 2\bar{r}).$$

PROOF. We write B_0 for $\mathcal{B}(\bar{y}, \bar{r})$, and $\mathbf{M}$ for the set of all median hyperplanes. Pick $x \in \mathbb{R}^m$, and set $r = \|x - \bar{y}\|$. We choose coordinates so that B_0 is centered at $(r, 0, \ldots, 0)$, (which translates to $(\pi/2, 0, \ldots 0, r)$ in spherical coordinates), and so that x is at the origin. Now θ_1 (actually $\pi/2 - \theta_1$) measures the angle an arbitrary point y, with spherical coordinates $(\theta_1, \ldots, \theta_{m-1}, \rho)$ makes with the axis between the origin and the center of B_0. We consider the points on the ray from the origin through y, and characterize those points on the ray which are in $P(x)$ and $R(x)$. We assume y is of unit length, so $\rho(y) = \|y\| = 1$. A point on the ray is of the form λy, with $\lambda > 0$, and has spherical coordinates which are the same as those of y, except $\rho(\lambda y) = \lambda$.

First note that the set of median hyperplanes in the direction y is a closed set; i.e., $\{c \in \mathbb{R} | H(y, c) \in \mathbf{M}\}$ is closed. So we let c_L and C_H be the infimum and supremum of $\{c \in \mathbb{R} | H(y, c) \in \mathbf{M}\}$, and set $H_L = H(y, c_L)$ and $H_H = H(y, c_H)$. Of course if n is odd, $H_L = H_H$. By virtue of assumption A3, we get, for $\lambda > 0$,

(B7)
$$\lambda y \in P(x) \iff y < 2c_L,$$
$$\lambda y \in P(x) \iff y \leq 2c_H$$

But, by assumption of the lemma, $\{c_L, c_H\} \subseteq \{c \in \mathbb{R} | H(y, c) \cap B_0 \neq \varnothing\}$. Letting b_L and b_H be the infimum and supremum of this latter set, we get

(B8)
$$b_L \leq c_L \leq c_H \leq b_H.$$

Consequently

(B9)
$$\lambda < 2b_L \implies \lambda < 2c_L \implies \lambda y \in P(x),$$
and
$$\lambda y \in R(x) \implies \lambda \leq 2c_H \implies \lambda \leq 2b_H.$$

But, by construction, b_L and b_H are obtained simply by projecting the center, $\bar{y}$, of $\mathcal{B}$ on y, and then adding or subtracting the radius, $\bar{r}$ of $\mathcal{B}$. I.e.,

(B10)
$$b_L = r \sin \theta_1 - \bar{r},$$
$$b_H = r \sin \theta_1 + \bar{r}.$$

So, since $\lambda = \rho(\lambda y) = \lambda \rho(y)$, we have for any $w = \lambda y, \lambda > 0$

(B11)
$$\rho(w) < 2r \sin \theta_1(w) - 2\bar{r} \implies w \in P(x),$$
$$w \in R(x) \implies \rho(w) \leq 2r \sin \theta_1(w) + 2\bar{r}.$$

Now, applying definition B6, we get for any $w = \lambda y, \lambda > 0$:

(B12)
$$w \in \mathcal{C}^m(x, \bar{y}, -2\bar{r}) \implies w \in P(x),$$
$$w \in R(x) \implies w \in \mathcal{C}^m(x, \bar{y}, 2\bar{r})$$

Since y is an arbitrary unit length vector, the result of the lemma follows directly. Q.E.D.

Figure 8 illustrates the construction of lemma 8.1 for the two-dimensional case.

FIGURE 8. Illustration of construction for lemma 1

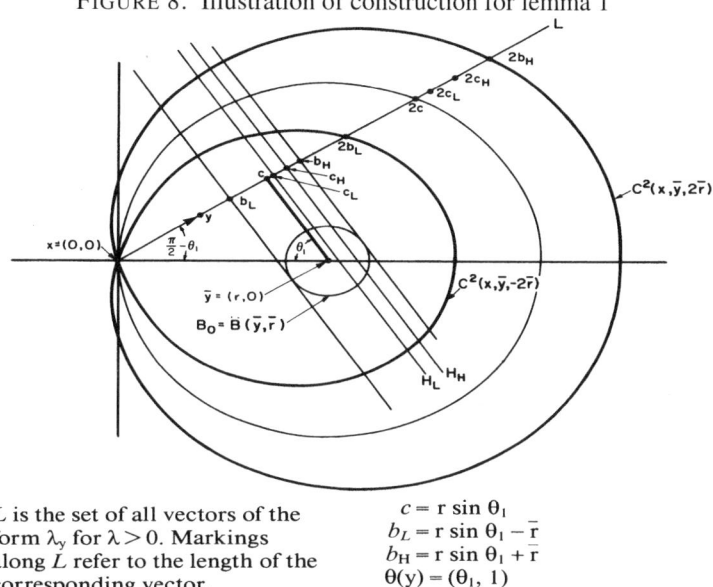

L is the set of all vectors of the form λy for $\lambda > 0$. Markings along L refer to the length of the corresponding vector.

$c = r \sin \theta_1$
$b_L = r \sin \theta_1 - \bar{r}$
$b_H = r \sin \theta_1 + \bar{r}$
$\theta(y) = (\theta_1, 1)$
$\theta(\bar{y}) = (\pi/2, r)$

PROOF OF PROPOSITION 8.3. Let $y \in \mathcal{B}(\bar{y}, t - 4\bar{t})$. So $\|y - \bar{y}\| \leq \|x - \bar{y}\| - 4\bar{t}$. Then from lemmas 8.1 and 8.2,

$$P(y) \subseteq \mathcal{C}^m(y, \bar{y}, 2\bar{t}) \subseteq \mathcal{B}(\bar{y}, \|y - \bar{y}\| + 2\bar{t}) \subseteq B(\bar{y}, \|x - \bar{y}\| - 2\bar{t}) \subseteq \mathcal{C}^m(\bar{x}, \bar{y}, -2\bar{t}) \subseteq P(x).$$

So $P(y) \subseteq P(x)$, and a similar chain shows $R(y) \subseteq R(x)$. Also $y \in P(x)$ and $y \notin P(y)$, so the inclusion $P(y) \subseteq P(x)$ is strict, hence $y \in D(x)$, as we wished to show. The second assertion follows in exactly analogous argument. Q.E.D.

References

Banks, J. S. 1985. Sophisticated voting outcomes and the covering relation. *Social Choice and Welfare*, 1:295–306.

Davis, O. A., and M. J. Hinich. 1968. On the power and importance of the mean preference in a mathematical model of democratic choice. *Public Choice*, 5:59–72.

Farquharson, R. 1969. *Theory of Voting*. New Haven: Yale University Press.

Ferejohn, J. A., M. P. Fiorina, and E. W. Packel. 1980. Nonequilibrium solutions for legislative systems. *Behavioral Science*, 25:140–48.

Ferejohn, J. A., R. D. McKelvey, and E. W. Packel. 1984. Limiting distributions for continuous state Markov models. *Social Choice and Welfare*, 1:45–67.

Fishburn, P. C. 1977. Condorcet social choice functions. *SIAM Journal of Applied Mathematics*, 33:469–89.

Gretlein, R. J. 1983. Dominance elimination procedures on finite alternative games. *International Journal of Game Theory*, 12:107–13.

Kramer, G. H. 1977. A dynamical model of political equilibrium. *Journal of Economic Theory*, 16:310–34.

Kramer, G. H. 1978. Existence of electoral equilibrium. In P. C. Ordeshook, ed., *Game Theory and Political Science*. New York: New York University Press, 375–91.

Kramer, G. H. 1972. Sophisticated voting over multidimensional choice spaces. *Journal of Mathematical Sociology*, 2:165–80.

Kramer, G. H., and R. D. McKelvey. 1984. The relation between the generalized median and the minimax sets: A correction. *Social Choice and Welfare*, 1:243–44.

McKelvey, R. D. 1976. Intransitivities in multidimensional voting models and some implications for agenda control. *Journal of Economic Theory*, 12:472–82. Also Chapter 4 of this book.

McKelvey, R. D. 1979. General conditions for global intransitivities in formal voting models. *Econometrica*, 47:1085–112. Also Chapter 5 of this book.

McKelvey, R. D., and P. C. Ordeshook. 1976. Symmetric spatial games without majority rule equilibrium. *American Political Science Review*, 70:1171–84.

McKelvey, R. D., P. C. Ordeshook, and M. Winer. 1978. The competitive solution for N-person games without transferable utility, with an application to committee games. *American Political Science Review*, 72:599–615. Also Chapter 10 of this book.

McKelvey, R. D., and R. G. Niemi. 1978. A multistage game representation of sophisticated voting for binary procedures. *Journal of Economic Theory*, 18:1–22.

Miller, N. R. 1980. A new solution set for tournaments and majority voting. *American Journal of Political Science*, 24:68–96.

Miller, N. R. 1983. The covering relationship in tournaments: Two corrections. *American Journal of Political Science*, 27:382–85. (See also Errata in volume 28, p. 434.)

Ordeshook, P. C., and K. A. Shepsle, eds. 1982. *Political Equilibrium*. Boston: Kluwer-Nijhoff.

Plott, C. R. 1967. A notion of equilibrium and its possibility under majority rule. *American Economic Review*, 57:787–806.

Richelson, J. T. 1980. Social choice solution sets. Analytical Assessments Corporation, Marina Del Rey. mimeo.

Riker, W. H. 1980. Implications from the disequilibrium of majority rule for the study of institutions. *American Political Science Review*, 74:432–46.

Rubinstein, A. 1979. A note about the "nowhere denseness" of societies having an equilibrium under majority rule. *Econometrica*, 47:511–14.

Schofield, N. 1978. Instability of simple dynamic games. *Review of Economic Studies*, 45:575–94.

Schofield, N. 1983. Generic instability of majority rule. *Review of Economic Studies*, 50:695–705.

Shepsle, K. A. 1979. Institutional arrangements and equilibrium in multidimensional voting models. *American Journal of Political Science*, 23:27–59.

Shepsle, K., and B. Weingast. 1981. Structure induced equilibrium and legislative choice. *Public Choice*, 37:503–19.

Shepsle, K., and B. Weingast. 1984. Uncovered sets and sophisticated voting outcomes with implications for agenda institutions. *American Journal of Political Science*, 28:49–74.

CHAPTER 13

Generalized Symmetry Conditions at a Core Point

RICHARD D. MCKELVEY AND NORMAN SCHOFIELD

> ABSTRACT. Previous analyses have shown that if a point is to be a core of a majority rule voting game in Euclidean space, when preferences are smooth, then the utility gradients at the point must satisfy certain restrictive symmetry conditions. In this paper, these results are generalized to the case of an arbitrary voting rule, and necessary and sufficient conditions, expressed in terms of the utility gradients of "pivotal" coalitions, are obtained.

1. Introduction

It is now well known that if the set of alternatives can be represented as a subset of Euclidean space, and individual preferences are smooth, then the individual utility gradients at a point in the majority core must satisfy strong symmetry conditions (Plott (1967)). The necessity that these symmetry conditions be satisfied can be used to prove the generic nonexistence of core points in certain situations (McKelvey and Schofield (1986)). The same symmetry conditions can be used to show that if the majority rule core is empty, then it will generally be the case that voting trajectories can be constructed throughout the space.

This paper generalizes the Plott symmetry conditions to deal with arbitrary voting rules, obtaining restrictions on the gradients at a point which are necessary and sufficient for that point to be in the core. The generalized gradient restrictions that we identify show the central role of what we term the "pivotal" coalitions in determining when core points exist. Specifically, we define a coalition, M, to

---

The contribution of the first author is supported, in part, by NSF Grant SES-84-09654 to the California Institute of Technology, and that of the second author is based on work supported by NSF Grant SES-84-18295 to the School of Social Sciences, University of California at Irvine. We are grateful to David Austen-Smith, Charles Plott, and Jeff Strand for a number of helpful observations.

be *pivotal* in a subset L of the voters, if it is the case that whenever we partition $L - M$ into two subsets, at least one of these subsets, together with the members of M, constitutes a decisive coalition. Our symmetry conditions specify that for x to be a core point, the utility gradients of the members of any subset, L, of voters must satisfy the following condition: For every pivotal coalition M in L, the set of utility gradients which lie in the subspace spanned by those in M, must positively span 0 (the zero vector). Taking L to be the set of nonsatiated voters, it is easily shown that the Plott symmetry conditions for the existence of a majority core point are implied by this condition. The pivotal gradient condition can also be applied to get necessary conditions for a point to be in the constrained core, and hence for a point to be outside the cycle set of an arbitrary voting rule.

2. Definition and Notation

We let $W \subseteq \mathbf{R}^w$ represent the set of *alternatives*. Let $N = \{1, 2, ..., n\}$ be a finite set indexing *voters*. Let U denote the set of smooth, real valued functions on W, and let $u = (u_1, ..., u_n) \in U^n$, with u_i representing the *utility function* for voter i. Throughout this paper, we consider only a fixed $u \in U^n$, and call such a $u \in U^n$ a *smooth profile*.

For any binary relation $Q \subseteq W \times W$, we use the standard notation $xQy \iff (x, y) \in Q$. We write P_i for the binary relation on W defined by $xP_iy \iff u_i(x) > u_i(y)$, and for any $C \subseteq N$, write $P_C = \bigcap_{i \in C} P_i$.

We are given a set $\mathbf{D}$ of subsets $C \subseteq N$, called the set of *decisive coalitions*, which is assumed to satisfy: (a) $C \in \mathbf{D}$ and $C \subseteq C' \implies C' \in \mathbf{D}$ ($\mathbf{D}$ is monotonic); (b) $C \in \mathbf{D} \implies N - C \notin \mathbf{D}$ ($\mathbf{D}$ is proper). We can then define the *social order* $P \subseteq W \times W$ by

$$xPy \iff xP_Cy \quad \text{for some} \quad C \in \mathbf{D}.$$

For any binary relation, $Q \subseteq W \times W$, and $x \in W$, define $Q(x) = \{y \in X : yQx\}$, and write $Q^1(x) = Q(x)$. For any integer $j \geq 1$, define $Q^j(x) = \{y \in W : yQz \text{ for some } z \in Q^{j-1}(x)\}$. Then define $Q^*(x) = \bigcup_{j=1}^{\infty} Q^j(x)$. Also, for any $V \subseteq W$, and $Q \subseteq W \times W$, define $Q|_V = Q \cap (V \times V)$ to be the binary relation Q, restricted to V. We can then define the *core*, or *global optima set* to be the set of socially unbeaten alternatives in V:

$$GO(V, \mathbf{D}) = \{x \in V : (P|_V)(x) = \varnothing\},$$

and the *local optima set* on V by

$$LO(V, \mathbf{D}) = \{x \in V : x \in GO(V', \mathbf{D}) \text{ for some neighborhood} \\ V' \text{ of } x \text{ in } V\}.$$

We define the *global cycle set* to be the set of points which are elements of a cycle in V, under the social order:

$$GC(V, \mathbf{D}) = \{x \in V : x \in (P|_V)^*(x)\},$$

and the *local cycle set* by

$$LC(V, \mathbf{D}) = \{x \in V : x \in GC(V', \mathbf{D}) \text{ for all neighborhoods} \\ V' \text{ of } x \text{ in } V\}.$$

When there is no fear of ambiguity we write $GO(V)$, $LO(V)$, etc. for these sets. We will also write $GO = GO(W)$, $LO = LO(W)$, etc. and call these the global or local optima sets with respect to $\mathbf{D}$. Clearly,

$$GO \subseteq LO \quad \text{and} \quad LC \subseteq GC.$$

3. Constraints on Gradients at a Core Point

In this section, we define the critical optima set, $IO(W, \mathbf{D})$, give its relation to the global and local optima sets, and characterize this set in terms of conditions on the utility gradients of members of decisive coalitions.

For any $x \in W$, and $i \in N$, let $p_i(x) = \nabla u_i(x) \in \mathbf{R}^w$ represent voter i's utility gradient at the point x. For $C \subseteq N$, let

$$p_C(x) = \left\{ y \in \mathbf{R}^w : y = \sum_{i \in C} \alpha_i p_i(x),\ \alpha_i \geq 0\ \forall\ i \in C \text{ and } \exists i \in C \text{ s.t. } \alpha_i \neq 0 \right\}$$

be the semi-positive cone generated by $\{p_i(x) : i \in C\}$, and let

$$sp_C(x) = \left\{ y \in \mathbf{R}^w : y = \sum_{i \in C} \alpha_i p_i(x) \text{ with } \alpha_i \in \mathbf{R} \right\}$$

be the subspace spanned by $\{p_i(x) : i \in C\}$.[1]

We use the notation Int W to refer to the interior of W in the standard topology on $\mathbf{R}^w$, and write $\partial W = W \backslash \text{Int } W$ for the boundary of W. We also make the assumption that $W \subseteq$ clos Int W where clos means the closure in the topology on $\mathbf{R}^w$. This eliminates the possibility that W includes isolated points. Define the

---

[1] We use the convention that $sp_\varnothing(x) = \{0\}$, and $p_\varnothing(x) = \varnothing$.

preference cone of coalition $C \subseteq N$ at x by
$$H_C^+(x) = \{y \in W : p_i(x) \cdot (y - x) > 0 \; \forall i \in C\}.$$

Define the *critical* (or infinitesimal) *optima set* on $V \subseteq W$ with respect to **D** by
$$IO(V, \mathbf{D}) = \{x \in V : V \cap H_C^+(x) = \emptyset \; \forall C \in \mathbf{D}\}.$$

The critical optima set for **D** may be thought of as the analogue, for a social order, of the set of critical points of a smooth function. It is the set of points which, on the basis of "first derivative" information, are candidates for global optima. Thus the critical optima set contains the global optima set, but may also contain other points. We shall obtain necessary and sufficient conditions on the utility gradients at x for x to belong to $IO(W, \mathbf{D})$. Consequently these conditions will be necessary for a point to belong to the core. Under some conditions the critical and global optima sets coincide, and in this case, our conditions are necessary and sufficient for a point to belong to the core.

Say the smooth profile $(u_1, ..., u_n)$ is *strictly pseudo-concave* iff $\forall i \in N$, and for any $x, y \in W$ it is the case that $u_i(y) \geq u_i(x)$ implies that $p_i(x)(y - x) > 0$. More generally, say the preference profile is *semi-convex* iff $\forall i \in N$, and for any $x \in W$
$$\{y \in W : y P_i x\} \subseteq H_{\{i\}}^+(x).$$

It is easy to show that if the profile is strictly pseudo-concave then it is semi-convex in the above sense, and then $GO(W, \mathbf{D}) = IO(W, \mathbf{D})$.

LEMMA 1: *(i) $GO(W) \subset LO(W) \subset IO(W, \mathbf{D})$. Moreover if preferences are semiconvex, then these sets are identical. (ii) If $x \in$ Int W then a necessary and sufficient condition for $x \in IO(W, \mathbf{D})$ is that $0 \in \bigcap_{c \in \mathbf{D}} p_C(x)$.*

Proof: (i) Using Taylor's Theorem, we can prove that if $H_C^+(x) \neq \emptyset$, for some $C \in \mathbf{D}$, then in any neighborhood V of x, $\exists y \in V$ such that $y P_C x$ (e.g., see Schofield (1984a), Lemma 4.19). Thus $x \notin IO(W, \mathbf{D})$ implies $x \notin LO(W)$ and hence $x \notin GO(W)$. When preferences are semi-convex, then for any $C \subseteq N$,
$$\{y \in W : y P_C x\} \subseteq H_C^+(x).$$
Thus,
$$x \notin GO(W) \implies H_C^+(x) \neq \emptyset \text{ for some } C \in \mathbf{D}$$
$$\implies x \notin IO(W, \mathbf{D}).$$

(ii) From a standard argument (see, e.g., Schofield (1978 and 1983)) if $x \in$ Int W then for any $C \subseteq N$,
$$H_C^+(x) = \emptyset \quad \text{iff} \quad 0 \in p_C(x).$$

Q.E.D.

Thus a necessary condition for $x \in \text{Int } W \cap GO(W)$ is that $0 \in p_C(x) \ \forall C \in \mathbf{D}$. We now show that this latter condition is equivalent to a condition on *pivotal* rather than decisive coalitions.

4. Symmetry Conditions for a Core

In this section we define the notion of "pivotal" coalitions and use this notion to develop symmetry conditions, similar to the Plott (1967) symmetry condition for majority rule, which characterize $IO(W, \mathbf{D})$ for a fixed smooth profile, u.

DEFINITION 1: Given any family $\mathbf{D}$ of subsets of N and any $L \subseteq N$, we define the set of *pivotal coalitions for* $\mathbf{D}$ *in* L, written $\mathbf{E}_L(\mathbf{D})$, as the set of all coalitions $M \subset L$ such that for every binary partition $\{C, D\}$ of $L - M$, either $M \cup C \in \mathbf{D}$ *or* $M \cup D \in \mathbf{D}$. We write $\mathbf{E}_L$ for $\mathbf{E}_L(\mathbf{D})$ when there is no danger of confusion.

It is easy to see that, since $\mathbf{D}$ is monotonic, so is $\mathbf{E}_L$; i.e., any superset of a pivotal coalition is also pivotal.

DEFINITION 2: Let $x \in W$. We say x satisfies the *pivotal gradient restrictions* (PGR) with respect to $\mathbf{D}$ iff, for every $L \subseteq N$ and every $M \in E_L(\mathbf{D})$, $0 \in p_{M^*}(x)$, where $M^* = \{i \in L : p_i(x) \in sp_M(x)\}$.

We offer a loose interpretation of the above definition: Say that the pivotal coalition, $M \in E_L$ is "blocked" if $0 \in p_{M^*}(x)$. If M is blocked, then there are some members of L, whose gradients lie in the same subspace as those of M, but *not* in the same half space. See Figure 1. Thus, the members of M^* cannot agree on any common direction to move. The PGR condition, then, simply specifies that every pivotal coalition, in every subset L of N, must be blocked in the above sense.

THEOREM 1: *If $x \in$ Int W then a necessary and sufficient condition for $x \in IO(W, \mathbf{D})$ is that x satisfies PGR with respect to $\mathbf{D}$.*

Proof: (i) Let $L \subseteq N$ and suppose, for some $M \in \mathbf{E}_L$, that $0 \notin p_{M^*}(x)$. Suppose that $\dim[sp_M(x)] = w$. Then $M^* = L$. But since $M \in \mathbf{E}_L$, then L contains some decisive coalition, C say. But then $0 \notin p_{M^*}(x)$ implies $0 \notin p_C(x)$, a contradiction. Suppose that $\dim[sp_M(x)] < w$. Then $\exists \beta \in \mathbf{R}^\omega$ with $\beta \cdot p_i(x) = 0$ for all $i \in M^*$, and $\beta \cdot p_i(x) \neq 0$ for all $i \in L - M^*$. Let

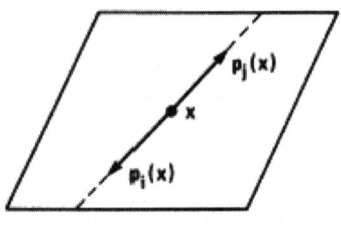

(a) $\{i,j\}$ blocked internally

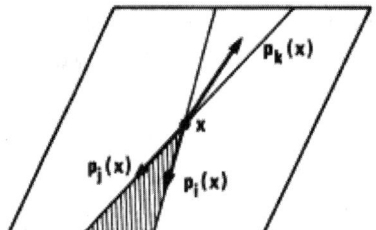 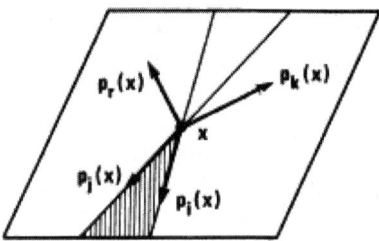

(b) $\{i,j\}$ blocked by other players

FIGURE 1. Examples of ways in which $\{i,j\}$ can be locked

$A = \{i \in L : \beta \cdot p_i(x) > 0\}$ and $B = \{i \in L : \beta \cdot p_i(x) < 0\}$. But since $M \in \mathbf{E}_L$, and $M^* \supseteq M$, we have $M^* \in \mathbf{E}_L$. Hence $M^* \cup A \in \mathbf{D}$ or $M^* \cup B \in \mathbf{D}$. Without loss of generality, assume $M^* \cup A \in \mathbf{D}$. Now if $0 \notin p_{M^*}(x)$, then by the separating hyperplane theorem, $\exists \alpha \in sp_{M^*}(x) = sp_M(x)$ with $\alpha \cdot p_i(x) > 0$ for all $i \in M^*$. Now pick $\delta \in \mathbf{R}^+$ with $(\beta + \delta\alpha) \cdot p_i(x) > 0$ for all $i \in A$ and set $\gamma = \beta + \delta\alpha$. Then $\gamma \cdot p_i(x) > 0$ for all $i \in M^* \cup A$. But then $0 \notin p_C(x)$ where $C = M^* \cup A \in \mathbf{D}$. By Lemma 1, $x \notin IO(\text{Int } W, \mathbf{D})$. Hence PGR is a necessary condition.[2]

(ii) To prove sufficiency, note that for any $M \in \mathbf{D}$ if we set $L = M$ then $M \in \mathbf{E}_L$ and $M^* = M$. Hence PGR $\Longrightarrow$ that $0 \in p_M(x) \forall M \in \mathbf{D}$.

---

[2]The reader may wish to verify that, with the convention described in footnote 1, the proof of the theorem is valid in the case $M = \emptyset$.

Q.E.D.

COROLLARY 1: *PGR is a necessary condition for an interior point of W to belong to GO(W). Moreover, with semi-convex preferences the condition is also sufficient.*

Proof: This follows directly from Theorem 1 together with Lemma 1.

Q.E.D.

5. Applications to General Rules

We now show how the PGR conditions can be applied to particular social choice functions, and how for majority rule, the conditions imply the Plott symmetry conditions.

Note that the PGR conditions specify symmetry conditions that must hold for *every* $L \subseteq N$. However, if $p_i(x) = 0$ for some $i \in L$, then the PGR symmetry conditions are trivially satisfied for that L. Hence the most useful gradient restrictions are obtained by setting $L \subseteq \{i \in N : p_i(x) \neq 0\}$. In particular, a *necessary* condition for x to be a core point is that the PGR symmetry conditions be met for the set $L = \{i \in N : p_i(x) \neq 0\}$.

As an example, consider a q-*rule*, whose decisive coalitions are given by $\mathbf{D} = \{C \subseteq N : |C| \geq q\}$. The q-rule contains majority rule (with n odd or even) as a special case. Supra-majority rules of this kind have been studied by a number of writers (e.g., Ferejohn and Grether (1974), Greenberg (1979), Peleg (1978), Sloss (1973), Matthews (1980), Slutsky (1979)). To obtain the core symmetry conditions for such a rule, assume that $q < n$ and define $e(n, q) = 2q - n - 1$. Then it is easy to verify (McKelvey and Schofield (1986)) that

(a) if $|L| = n$, then $E_L = \{M \subseteq N : |M| \geq e(n, q)\}$;
(b) if $|L| = n - 1$, then $E_L = \{M \subseteq L : |M| \geq e(n, q) + 1\}$.

Now, setting $L = \{i \in N : p_i(x) \neq 0\}$, we obtain necessary conditions for a point x to be a core point of a q-rule when no more than one person is satiated at x: Either no one is satiated at x, and all coalitions of size $e(n, q)$ are blocked, or one person is satiated at x, and all coalitions of size $e(n, q) + 1$ (among the remaining individuals) are blocked. (Compare to Slutsky (1979).)

We now show how the Plott (1967) symmetry conditions for the existence of a majority rule core obtain as a special case of Theorem 1. Specifically, the Plott conditions deal with the case of majority rule when n is odd and when no two voters have common satiation points. The conditions specify the following:

CONDITION 1. (PO): $p_j(x) = 0$ for some $j \in N$, and for all $i \in N - \{j\}, \exists k \in N - \{i,j\}$ with $p_j(x) = -\alpha_k p_k(x)$ for some $\alpha_k > 0$.

However, majority rule is a q-rule, with $q = (n+1)/2$, and $e(n,q) = 0$, when n is odd. Setting $L = \{i \in N : p_i(x) \neq 0\}$ and using the characterization of the pivotal sets given above, it is easily verified that the pivotal gradient restrictions imply condition PO:

(a) If $|L| = n$, then $\mathbf{E}_L = \{M : |M| \geq 0\}$, so $\varnothing \in \mathbf{E}_L$. Since $sp_\varnothing(x) = \{0\}$ we see that $\varnothing^* = \varnothing$. But $p_\varnothing(x) = \varnothing$ contradicting the pivotal gradient restriction that $0 \in p_\varnothing(x)$. Hence $x \notin IO(W, \mathbf{D})$.

(b) If $|L| = n-1$, then $L = N - \{j\}$ for some $j \in N$ (i.e., $p_j(x) = 0$), and $\mathbf{E}_L = \{C \subseteq N - \{j\} : |C| \geq 1\}$. Hence, for all $i \in N - \{j\}, \{i\} \in \mathbf{E}_L$. Hence $0 \in p_{i^*}(x)$, which implies that $\exists k \in N - \{i,j\}$ with $p_i(x) = -\alpha_k p_k(x)$ for some $\alpha_k > 0$.

This gives Plott's theorem as an immediate corollary of Theorem 1.

COROLLARY 2: *Let P be majority rule, with n odd, and assume $x \in W$ satisfies $|\{i \in N : p_i(x) = 0\}| \leq 1$. Then $x \in GO \cap Int\ W$ implies that condition PO is met.*

To show how Theorem 1 may be used in the general case, we let $n = 5$ and consider a social choice rule with the following decisive coalitions (we only list the minimal decisive sets): $\mathbf{D} = \{\{1,2,5\}, \{1,3,5\}, \{2,3,4\}, \{2,3,5\}, \{4,5\}\}$. Then the pivotal sets for $|L| \geq 4$ can be described as follows (we only list the minimal pivotal sets). Let $L_i = N - \{i\}$, and write $\mathbf{E}_L = \mathbf{E}_i$:

L	Pivotal Sets
N	$\mathbf{E}_N = \{\{1\}, \{2\}, \{3\}, \{4\}, \{5\}\}$
L_1	$\mathbf{E}_1 = \{\{2\}, \{3\}, \{4\}, \{5\}\}$
L_2	$\mathbf{E}_2 = \{\{1,3\}, \{4\}, \{5\}\}$
L_3	$\mathbf{E}_3 = \{\{1,2\}, \{4\}, \{5\}\}$
L_4	$\mathbf{E}_4 = \{\{1,2\}, \{1,3\}, \{5\}\}$
L_5	$\mathbf{E}_5 = \{\{2,4\}, \{3,4\}, \{2,3\}\}$.

Thus, as above, setting $L = \{i \in N : p_i(x) \neq 0\}$, we obtain necessary conditions for x to be a core point if no more than one individual is satiated at x: Either no individual is satiated, and all coalitions in $\mathbf{E}_N$ are blocked, or individual i is satiated and all coalitions in $\mathbf{E}_i$ are blocked. Figure 2 illustrates how a core can occur at individual 5's ideal point in two dimensions, and Figure 3 illustrates how a core can occur at 5's ideal point in three dimensions. In these figures, we assume,

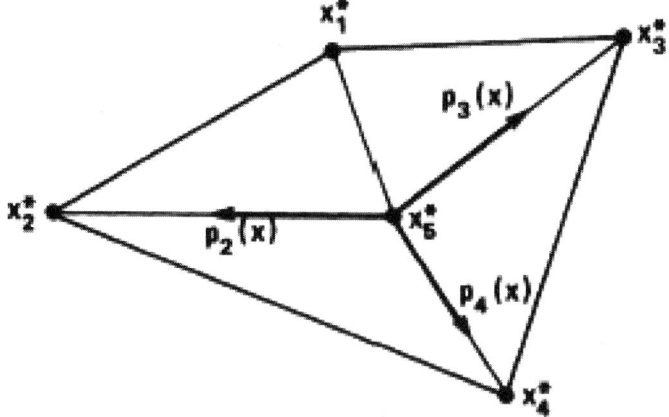

FIGURE 2. Example of core for D in two dimensions, at ideal point of individual 5

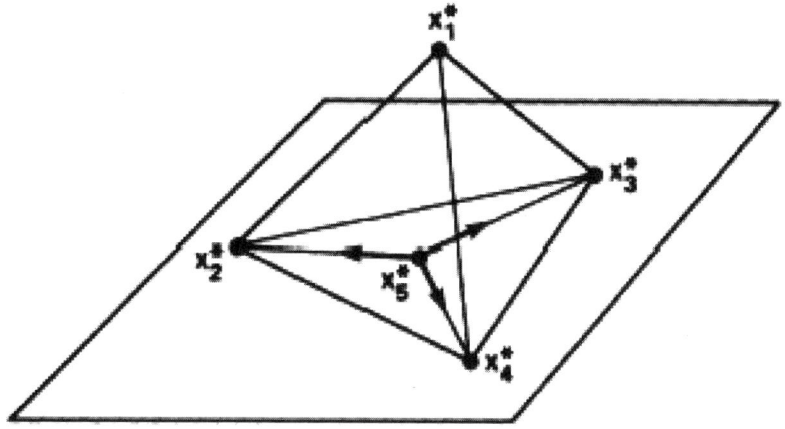

FIGURE 3. Example of core for D in three dimensions, at ideal point of individual 5. The ideal points x_2^*, x_3^*, x_4^*, and x_5^*, are all in the subspace represented by the plane drawn. The ideal point x_1^*, may be off the plane.

for ease of illustration, that each player has a "Type I" or Euclidean preference of the type $u_i(x) = -1/2 \, \|x - x_i^*\|^2$ where $\| \; \|$ is the standard Euclidean norm, and x_i^* is the ideal point of player i, where $p_i(x_i^*) = 0$.

In Figure 3, if x_5^* is the core, then this point must belong to the set A, defined to be the convex hull of $\{x_2^*, x_3^*, x_4^*\}$. Transversality arguments (McKelvey and Schofield (1986), and Smale (1973)) show that for an open dense set of profiles, the objects $\{x_5^*\}$ and A are respectively zero- and two-dimensional and do not intersect in $\mathbf{R}^3$. Thus the core in Figure 3 is "structurally unstable"; i.e., arbitrarily small perturbation will destroy the conditions for a core. On the other hand, in the two-dimensional case of Figure 2, the pivotal gradient restrictions are robust under small perturbations and so the core is "structurally stable." Arguments of this sort can be used to establish the maximum dimension which will yield existence of structurally stable cores for arbitrary social choice functions. See McKelvey and Schofield (1986) and Schofield (1986) for further discussion.

The results of Section 4 and these examples above are valid when the set of alternatives is unconstrained. Political institutions frequently impose feasibility constraints on social choice, and in the following section we show how these can be incorporated in more general pivotal gradient restrictions.

6. Applications: Constrained Cores and Cycle Sets

We can use Theorem 1 to characterize points in a constrained core. We fix $x \in W$. Then for any $v \in \mathbf{R}^W$, define the v restriction on W by

$$W_v = \{y \in W : y \cdot v \geq x \cdot v).$$

Say that x is a v *constrained core*, whenever $x \in GO(W_v)$; i.e., x is a core in the constrained set W_v.

Another way of thinking of a constrained core is to introduce another voter, say voter "$n+1$," who has utility gradient $p_{n+1}(x) = v$, and who must be included in any winning coalition. Using this motivation, we define a new set $N_v = N \cup \{n+1\}$ of voters, and the corresponding set $\mathbf{D}_v$ of decisive coalitions by

$$\mathbf{D}_v = \{C \subseteq N_v : n+1 \in C \text{ and } C \backslash \{n+1\} \in \mathbf{D}\}.$$

Given $\mathbf{D}_v$, and any $L \in N_v$, then as before $E_L(\mathbf{D}_v)$ is the set of pivotal coalitions for $\mathbf{D}_v$ in L. An easy argument shows that $IO(W_v, \mathbf{D}) = IO(W, \mathbf{D}_v)$. Then Theorem 1 immediately gives the following corollary.

COROLLARY 3: *If $x \in Int\ W$ then $x \in IO(W_v, \mathbf{D})$ iff x satisfies PGR with respect to $\mathbf{D}_v$.*

Applying Lemma 1 yields the following corollary.

COROLLARY 4: *If $x \in \text{Int } W$ then a necessary condition for x to be a v-constrained core is that x satisfies PGR with respect to $\mathbf{D}_v$. If preferences are semi-convex, then the condition is sufficient.*

To illustrate, consider the case of majority rule with n odd. As we have noted, $\varnothing \in \mathbf{E}_N(\mathbf{D})$, so $\{n+1\} \in \mathbf{E}_{N_v}(\mathbf{D}_v)$. Hence, it follows from the pivotal gradient restrictions that there exists $k \in N$ with $p_k(x) = -\lambda v$ for some $\lambda \in \mathbf{R}$ with $\lambda > 0$. Now let $L = N_v \backslash \{k\}$. Then it follows that any set of the form $M = \{j, n+1\}$ is pivotal if $j \notin \{k, n+1\}$. It follows again, from the pivotal gradient conditions, that $0 \in p_{M^*}(x)$, where $M^* = \{i \in L : p_i(x) \in sp_M(x)\}$. In particular, it follows that $\exists i \in N \backslash \{j, k\}$ with $p_i(x) \in sp_M(x)$. But, if all gradients are nonzero, this is exactly the "joint symmetry" condition given by McKelvey (1979).

The symmetry properties for a majority rule constrained core which can be deduced from Corollary 4 are identical to those mentioned by Plott (1967). The corollary also shows how to obtain necessary symmetry properties at a constrained core for an arbitrary social order. Note also that Corollary 3 can be easily extended to the case where there exists a family of constraints at the point.

The notion of a constrained core is also helpful in characterizing the cycle set $LC(W)$. Define the *critical cycle set* (Schofield (1978)) written $IC(W)$ by $x \in IC(W)$ iff (i) $0 \notin p_C(x)$ for at least one $C \in \mathbf{D}$, and (ii) $\phi = \bigcap_{C \in \mathbf{D}(x)} p_C(x)$ where $\mathbf{D}(x) = \{C \in \mathbf{D} : O \notin p_C(x)\}$.

The critical cycle set bears the same relation to the local and global cycle sets as the critical optima bear to the local and global core points. It is the set of points which, on the basis of "first derivative information," are candidates for the cycle sets. Earlier results have shown that $IC(W)$ is open in W and

$$IC(W) \subseteq LC(W) \subseteq \text{clos } IC(W)$$

where clos $IC(W)$ is the closure of $IC(W)$ in W (Schofield (1978, 1984b)).

THEOREM 2: $x \in (\text{Int } W) \backslash IC(W)$ *iff there exists a vector $v_x \in \mathbf{R}^w \backslash \{0\}$ such that x satisfies PGR with respect to $\mathbf{D}_{v_x}$.*

Proof: If $x \in (\text{Int } W) \backslash IC(W)$, then either (i) or (ii) in the definition of $IC(W)$ must fail. If (i) fails, then $0 \in \bigcap_{C \in \mathbf{D}(x)} p_C(x)$, implying $x \in IO(W, \mathbf{D})$. Moreover, for any $v \in \mathbf{R}^w \backslash \{0\}$, $IO(W, \mathbf{D}) \subseteq IO(W_v, \mathbf{D})$. By Corollary 1, x must satisfy PGR with respect to $\mathbf{D}_v$. If (ii) fails, then there exists $v_x \in \mathbf{R}^w \backslash \{0\}$ such that, for all $B \in \mathbf{D}$ either $0 \in p_B(x)$ or $-v_x \in p_B(x)$. Define $p_{n+1}(x) = v_x$. Now for any $B \subseteq N$, $B \in \mathbf{D} \iff B' = B \cup \{n+1\} \in \mathbf{D}_{v_x}$. Hence $0 \in p_B(x)$

or $-v_x \in p_B(x), \forall B \in \mathbf{D} \iff 0 \in p_{B'}(x) \forall B' \in D_{v_x} \iff x$ satisfies PRG with respect to D_{v_x}, by Theorem 1.

Q.E.D.

COROLLARY 5: *If $LC(W)$ is empty then at every point in the interior of W, there exists a vector $v_x \in R^w$ such that x satisfies PGR with respect to D_{v_x}.*

Proof: By previous results $LC(W)$ is empty iff $IC(W)$ is empty which implies that Int $W \cap IC(W)$ is empty. The result follows by Theorem 2.

Q.E.D.

Early results by Cohen and Matthews (1980), McKelvey (1979 (Chapter 5 of this book)), and Schofield (1983) only considered the cycle set for majority rule. Theorem 2, together with Corollary 5 and the comments following Corollary 4, gives symmetry conditions which are necessary if a point is to lie outside the cycle set not just for majority rule but for an arbitrary social order.

Notice that Plott (1967, p. 793) in his analysis of majority rule observed that a constraint could be represented by an "invisible" veto player. For an arbitrary social order the new player $(n + 1)$ introduced in the proof of Corollary 3 and Theorem 2 has precisely the same function. This means effectively that $LC = \emptyset$ if and only if it is the case that, at each point x, there exists an "invisible" veto player i_x who in fact "represents" the social order.

Our work is related to that of Slutsky (1979) and Matthews (1980, 1982), who derive symmetry conditions for cores of alpha-majority rule and anonymous simple games, respectively. (Matthews also obtains conditions for constrained cores.) Their symmetry conditions give inequalities on the number of voters with gradients in opposing cones, in contrast to those here, which give classes of coalitions whose gradients must be "blocked." In addition to being applicable to arbitrary voting rules, our conditions have proven more useful than previous symmetry conditions in extending generic existence results for cores and cycle sets to more general voting rules (McKelvey and Schofield (1986)).

Finally, we note that the analysis of the previous sections can be extended to the case where W is a smooth manifold of dimension $(\dim(W))$ equal to w.

References

Cohen, L., and S. A. Matthews (1980): "Constrained Plott Equilibria, Directional Equilibria and Global Cycling Sets," *Review of Economic Studies*, 47, 975–986.

Ferejohn, J. A., and D. M. Grether (1974): "On a Class of Rational Social Decision Procedures," *Journal of Economic Theory*, 8, 471–482.

Greenberg, J. (1979): "Consistent Majority Rules over Compact Sets of Alternatives," *Econometrica*, 47, 285–297.

Matthews, S. A. (1980): "Pairwise Symmetry Conditions for Voting Equilibria," *International Journal of Game Theory*, 9, 141-156.

——— (1982): "Local Simple Games in Public Choice Mechanisms," *International Economic Review*, 23, 623–645.

McKelvey, R. D. (1979): "General Conditions for Global Intransitivities in Formal Voting Models," *Econometrica*, 47, 1085–1112. Also Chapter 5 of this book.

McKelvey, R. D., and N. Schofield (1986): "Structural Instability of the Core," *Journal of Mathematical Economics*, 15, 179–198.

Peleg, B. (1978): "Consistent Voting Systems," *Econometrica*, 46, 153–161.

Plott, C. R. (1967): "A Notion of Equilibrium and its Possibility under Majority Rule," *American Economic Review*, 57, 787–806.

Schofield, N. (1978): "Instability of Simple Dynamic Games," *Review of Economic Studies*, 45, 575–594.

——— (1980): "Generic Properties of Simple Bergson-Samuelson Welfare Functions," *Journal of Mathematical Economics*, 7, 175-192.

——— (1983): "Generic Instability of Majority Rule," *Review of Economic Studies*, 50, 695–705.

——— (1984a): *Mathematical Methods in Economics*. New York: New York University Press.

——— (1984b): "Existence of Equilibrium on a Manifold," *Mathematics of Operations Research*, 9, 545–557.

——— (1986): "Existence of a 'Structurally Stable' Equilibrium for a Non-Collegial Voting Rule," *Public Choice*, 51, 267–284.

Sloss, J. (1973): "Stable Outcomes in Majority Voting Games," *Public Choice*, 15, 19–48.

Slutsky, S. (1979): "Equilibrium under α-Majority Voting," *Econometrica*, 47, 1113-1125.

Smale, S. (1973): "Global Analysis and Economics I: Pareto Optimum and a Generalization of Morse Theory," in *Dynamical Systems*, ed. by M. Peixoto. New York: Academic Press.

CHAPTER 14

Information in Elections

DAVID AUSTEN-SMITH AND ARTHUR LUPIA

1. Introduction

In the scientific study of elections, there is a growing emphasis on the role of information. Of particular importance are the conditions under which certain kinds of informational asymmetries affect voter strategies, candidate strategies, and electoral outcomes. For claims about such effects to apply generally, interactions between voters and candidates must share an underlying logic. To the extent that political information is sought and produced by goal-oriented actors, this logic will include attention to the role of incentives. We can, for example, expect that actors who can influence others through the selective provision of information may have an incentive to exercise their influence in the service of only their own interests. At the same time, if those who are subject to such influence recognize these incentives, then they are likely to have an incentive to be selective about who and what to believe.

Game theory provides a means for understanding the logic of information transmission and reception in circumstances where at least some actors have an incentive to be at least partially strategic in their conveyance or acceptance of information. In such circumstances, game theory can clarify how clearly stated premises about voter, candidate, and contextual attributes relate to clearly stated conclusions about communicative and behavioral outcomes. It can help us understand the conditions under which certain kinds of information, such as polls and endorsements, affect voter and candidate strategies. Such understanding, in turn, can clarify the credibility and applicability of many election related claims, including those made elsewhere in the scientific literature.

One of the first attempts to employ game theory to this end is McKelvey and Ordeshook's 1985 paper, "Elections with Limited Information: A Fulfilled

Expectations Model Using Contemporaneous Poll and Endorsement Data as Information Sources" (Chapter 15 of this book). In the next section, we sketch the context and substance of this paper. Subsequent sections address some developments in the theory of electoral competition under uncertainty, paying particular attention to the extent to which electoral competition promotes information aggregation across individuals (section 3) and to the conditions under which commonly available kinds of political endorsements affect voter beliefs and behavior (section 4). A final section points to some open issues for future research.

2. Some Context and the Paper

When McKelvey and Ordeshook began working on their paper, there was precious little interaction between formal modelers and other political scientists who were interested in information and elections. On the empirical side, there existed a large literature documenting a considerable lack of information among voters (for instance, Berelson, Lazarsfeld, and McPhee, 1954; Almond and Verba, 1963; Converse, 1975). Conclusions from these studies tended to reflect variations on a theme. Relative to the sorts of elections one might expect under full information and universal participation, an uninformed electorate was presumed to induce low-powered incentives for voter turnout, to create inefficiencies in legislative decision-making, and to attenuate electoral control of political agents. Moreover, an asymmetrically informed electorate was characterized as promoting unequal turnout among more and less informed voters, as well as partisan bias and manipulability of policy choice. At the same time, there was a much smaller (formal) theoretical literature in political science that began to address related issues. For example, Downs (1957) suggested problems involved with the "rationally ignorant voter," while Stokes (1963) criticized the standard spatial model of the day for its informational assumptions. Later, the depth of theoretical inquiry increased. Early probabilistic voting models were being developed to reflect candidate uncertainties and, at about the same time as the McKelvey and Ordeshook paper, Ledyard (1984) developed a rational expectations model of turnout with incomplete information about voting costs.[1] Nevertheless, the conventional wisdom at the time (and still, for many audiences) was that, without a uniformly well-informed electorate, elections are poor instruments for democratic policy selection. McKelvey and Ordeshook's particular contribution in their paper was to suggest that such a pessimistic conclusion is premature.

---

[1] See also Palfrey and Rosenthal (1985).

McKelvey and Ordeshook 1985 (McK&O = Chapter 15 of this book) was one of the very first papers in positive political theory to apply the concept of a rational expectations equilibrium from the economic theory of large markets to study a spatial model of electoral competition. The key feature of rational expectations equilibria is that although players in a game make decisions without full information about their consequences, in equilibrium everyone's expectations must prove correct; thus equilibrium actions must induce beliefs in observers that confirm their prior expectations. McK&O was also one of the first election-oriented formal theory articles to speak directly to the empirical literature referenced above. Indeed, they describe their paper "as an attempt to bring the informational assumptions of [formal] models more in line with what we know empirically" (1985:56. See Chapter 15 in this book, page 316).

In the McK&O model, two symmetric candidates compete by choosing policies in a one-dimensional policy space under plurality rule. Although candidates know that all voters have symmetric, single-peaked preferences over the policy space, they do not know and no individual voter knows the true distribution of these preferences. In addition to the candidates, there are two non-strategic interest groups with opposing and extreme policy preferences. Each group's sole role in the model is to endorse a candidate. Since all voters are assumed to know the endorsers' preferences, the endorsements reveal to all players the relative positions of the candidates' platforms (i.e., whose platform is to the left of the other's). The endorsements, however, do not reveal the candidates' exact platforms. This matters because not all voters observe the policy platforms directly. Instead, the electorate is partitioned into two subgroups, a set of *informed voters* who directly observe the candidates' platforms and a set of *uninformed voters* who do not observe the platforms. Instead, uninformed voters observe the endorsements and the results of a poll. Intuitively, we can think of the poll as reporting the distribution of votes that would occur if everyone voted as they say they would in answer to the question, "If the election were held today, for whom would you vote, given the endorsements?" In any equilibrium of voter strategies that is conditional on the candidates' platforms, the poll data must, in expectation, reflect the realized distribution of votes. Finally, McK&O assume that indifferent voters abstain and that every uninformed voter believes dogmatically that he or she is the only uninformed voter.

The equilibrium concept, a *rational expectations political equilibrium* (REPE), is a list of payoff-maximizing mutual best response strategies, one for each agent in the polity, such that the expected equilibrium distribution of votes justifies each agent's beliefs when choosing his or her strategy. Today, a theorist might use a more commonly-known and more widely evaluated equilibrium concept, such as perfect Bayesian equilibrium (PBE) or a variant of the self-confirming equilibrium (SCE), to solve this kind of model. At the time McK&O were working on their problem, however, concepts such as SCE did not exist and concepts such as PBE were neither as well known nor as widely accepted as they are today. So it was quite reasonable (and enterprising) for them to develop their own concept — a concept that adapted elements of the rational expectations logic, itself quite popular in economics at the time, into the empirical context of mass elections with two candidates.

McK&O establish three main results regarding such equilibria. The first result is that, given any pair of candidate platforms, almost all voters vote as if fully informed about these platforms. This outcome occurs because voters use the polls and endorsements to infer how to vote. Those voting for the rightist candidate e, for example, reason from the poll data that "if *that* many voters are voting for candidate e, he can't be *too* liberal" (1985:63. See Chapter 15 in this book, page 323). The second result exploits this logic to prove that, in any REPE, candidates converge on a common platform and there is a continuum of such equilibria. In any such equilibrium, the poll data splits the population in half and, consequently, no uninformed individual receives any information that suggests that a change of vote would be advisable, in which case neither candidate has any incentive to change his or her platform. A potential problem with this finding is that these sets of consistent beliefs can in principle arise at a great many policy positions. Mitigating such an inference is McK&O's third main result, which shows that there exists a unique "informationally stable" REPE and it is such that both candidates converge on the true median of the distribution of all voters' ideal points. Here, an REPE is said to be "informationally stable" if it is robust with respect to candidates making small decision errors with respect to voter beliefs. Intuitively, any deviation from the equilibrium induced by such errors is self-correcting.

As a heuristic for thinking about how REPE might be realized in the model, McK&O suggest a dynamic process under which the candidates first adopt platforms, the groups make their endorsements, and there follows an arbitrarily long sequence of polls asking the question, "For whom would you vote?" Voters are presumed to update their beliefs between polls and report honestly at each step. Once the polls converge (if they do) to a stable distribution, the candidates adjust their platforms and the procedure repeats until no candidate wishes to change his or her platform. Fixing the candidate platforms arbitrarily with the associated endorsements and focusing exclusively on the poll sequence, McK&O provide two ancillary results. First, they demonstrate that "*regardless* of the initial starting behavior of the uninformed voters, this process converges to the full information voter equilibrium" (1985:73, below, p. 334). In other words, as long as some informed voters are in the population, the entire electorate eventually casts the same votes they would have cast if all were informed. Second, they show that the speed of convergence to the fully informed outcome depends on the extent to which pivotal voters are informed. In other words, if voters whose ideal points are close to the midpoint between the two candidates' platforms also tend to be informed, then the polls reveal more to uninformed voters. If, by contrast, such "pivotal voters" are uninformed, then the poll provides a less precise signal of how uninformed voters whose ideal points are near the midpoint should vote. These dynamics are worth emphasizing: the uninformed voters have no candidate-specific information beyond the endorsement and the poll, and the endorsement merely reveals which candidate is to the left of the other. So even in relatively extreme informational conditions, every person in the electorate eventually behaves as if fully informed.

Taking these results together, it follows that if we restrict attention to the stable REPE, none of the main inferences from the descriptive literature regarding electoral inefficiencies obtain! In the stable REPE, highly uninformed voters vote as if fully informed and highly uninformed candidates converge on the platform predicted when all agents are fully informed and everyone participates. Moreover, McK&O provide qualitative support for their thesis with experimental data.[2]

From a contemporary theoretical perspective, not everything about McK&O's model is compelling. The assumption that each uninformed voter assumes he or she is the *only* uninformed voter and thus treats poll data as reflecting the true distribution of realized ideal points is worrisome, especially so when McK&O offer the dynamic mechanism described above through which REPE might be achieved. Along the sequence, the polls can change quite dramatically, reflecting bandwagon voting behavior, and it is these changes that drive the convergence of beliefs. But an uninformed voter's observations in such sequences can be inconsistent with the rational expectations idea that he believes himself to be uniquely uninformed (i.e., a single vote should not lead to any observable change in the poll data over the sequence.) A second, and more subtle, analytical concern is with the assumptions that indifferent voters necessarily abstain and that voters vote sincerely. Abstention is admissible but voting is costless and there is uncertainty. Thus an instrumentally rational uninformed voter should condition his or her vote

---

[2]Ledyard (1984) proved a similar result using a rational expectations approach. However, his model rests on quite different informational assumptions. In particular, Ledyard assumed costly voting with the distribution of voter preferences and the candidates' platforms being common knowledge. The only source of uncertainty in his setup concerned the realized distribution of voting costs.

(or abstention) decision on the event that he or she is pivotal. Whether or not such behavior is consistent with the McK&O assumptions is unclear. Moreover, the introduction of costly voting makes the stability result less convincing; for instance, frictions due to voting costs might render multiple equilibria stable. And finally, McK&O presume the candidates are committed to implement the policy platform on which they are elected even though not everyone knows exactly what the platform might be. (But having said this, it should be noted that neither candidate has a policy preference so there is little reason for either to do otherwise.)

The McK&O paper explicitly addressed two issues and raised a variety of other interesting questions. The two explicitly considered topics concern the ability of the electoral process to aggregate privately held and asymmetric information within a large electorate, and the candidates' strategic choice of electoral platforms under uncertainty with a rational electorate. Less directly, McK&O also address questions regarding policy bias, information acquisition, the impact of endorsements on information aggregation, and the effect of candidate advertising. Their work and that of their contemporaries mark an important turning point in the effort to understand the role of information in political decision making. We now turn to some of the subsequent insights that this work helped to promote.

3. Developments in Understanding Electoral Competition under Uncertainty

In this section, we consider the progress made on the questions addressed in McK&O (1985), focusing especially on the ability of electoral competition to aggregate information and on strategic candidate behavior in the presence of informational limitations. As observed earlier, these questions have been the subject of discussion and speculation for a long time. With the exception of studies on various properties and implications of the Condorcet Jury Theorem, formal analysis of these issues is relatively recent.[3]

The first significant attempt following McK&O to address information aggregation questions in electoral competition is due to Ledyard (1989). Ledyard focuses on the consequences of asymmetrically informed candidates, rather than voters, and assumes that candidates acquire private information about the distribution of voter preferences by commissioning polls. In this setting, his findings are more sanguine than those of McK&O. Specifically, the zero-sum character of

---

[3]The Condorcet Jury Theorem is concerned with the problem of a committee choosing one of two given alternatives when individuals have common full information preferences but differ with respect to their beliefs about which alternative is most in their interests. Young (1988) provides an excellent account of the Jury Theorem. See also Ladha (1992) and Austen-Smith and Banks (1996).

two-candidate elections with plurality rule, coupled with the strategic advantage to a candidate of keeping any private information private, greatly mutes any candidate's incentive to collect information or to reveal what they have learned through their choice of electoral platform. Similar results were discovered independently by Harrington (1992). Banks (1990a) attacked this problem in a different way. Taking the classical Downsian model, Banks assumes that a candidate knows her *type* and that all voters do not. In his model, a candidate's type refers to the policy that she would implement if elected. Moreover, voters are fully rational and, in equilibrium, draw inferences about a candidate's type using her choice of electoral platform. In a (suitably refined) sequential equilibrium, Banks shows that as it becomes more costly for a candidate to misrepresent her true policy intentions during a campaign, the closer do candidate platforms and the final policy outcome converge to the full information median voter outcome in equilibrium. On the other hand, when such costs are not so severe, there is no assurance that the full information equivalent electoral outcome is realized, although all voters' beliefs in equilibrium satisfy a rational expectations property.

Unlike McK&O, in which there are both fully and only partially informed voters, neither the Ledyard nor the Banks model admits asymmetric information across the electorate. These models focus instead on candidate platform selection. In a paper on information aggregation and turnout in large elections, Feddersen and Pesendorfer (1996) reverse this focus, allowing for greater informational asymmetries across voters than McK&O but fixing candidate platforms exogenously. Their model assumes there are two given and distinct candidate platforms, A, B, and two possible states of the world, a, b. There is a finite number of voters, where the actual number is unknown to any individual. Each individual in the realized electorate is either a "partisan" for one or the other of the candidates, or an "independent." Partisans prefer a given candidate whatever the true state of the world whereas independents prefer candidate A in state a and prefer candidate B in state b. Initially, all members of the electorate know only their type (partisan for A, partisan for B, or independent) and have a common belief about both the size of the electorate and the likely true state of the world. Before voting, assumed costless as in McK&O, each voter privately observes a signal about the true state. With some probability, this signal reveals the true state to the voter. With the complementary probability, the signal conveys no new information to the voter. Everyone is assumed to understand the process by which information is distributed. Although voting is costless, Feddersen and Pesendorfer make no assumptions about individual voting behavior beyond those implicit in the presumption that voters are instrumentally rational and Bayesian.

Feddersen and Pesendorfer demonstrate two remarkable results. First, in any perfect Bayesian equilibrium in undominated strategies, there is positive but not full participation: in particular, costless voting does not imply all individuals with a strict preference (conditional on beliefs) necessarily vote, or that all indifferent individuals (conditional on beliefs) necessarily abstain. And second, despite such voting behavior and informational limitations, the probability that the electoral outcome is exactly the outcome arising when the electorate is fully informed and participation is 100% converges to one as the size of the electorate increases to infinity. In other words, Feddersen and Pesendorfer confirm the full information equivalent voting results reflected in McK&O's analysis. Moreover, they do this without any endorsements; poll data; or, in contrast to McK&O, ad hoc assumptions about voters' beliefs and, when indifferent, their voting behavior. The "trick" here is to observe that rational voters who do not use dominated strategies condition their decision on the event of being pivotal in the election and, in turn, this event implies a great deal about the distribution of information in the electorate at large.[4] In particular, as the size of the electorate grows to infinity, the *proportion* of the population voting informatively on the basis of the counterfactual event of being pivotal becomes vanishingly small, but the absolute *number* of such voters is growing arbitrarily large. Feddersen and Pesendorfer prove that the latter tendency dominates the former, thus establishing full information equivalence.

In two subsequent contributions, Feddersen and Pesendorfer (1997, 1999) extend their analysis to the spatial model in which voters have single-peaked preferences and there is considerably more heterogeneity in both preferences and information than assumed in their first paper. These papers establish that the full information equivalent voting results for large electorates obtain for any supermajority rule shy of unanimity and, furthermore, that they are robust to variations in informational quality and to extreme correlations between partisan bias and informational asymmetries. On the other hand, it turns out that apparently "technical" assumptions on the coarseness of the signal space governing individuals' information (i.e., the extent to which available information about the true state of the world is vague/coarse or specific/fine) can be substantively consequential, and this is a topic that warrants deeper investigation.

Subsequently, other scholars have built on Feddersen and Pesendorfer by examining the information aggregation properties of majoritarian elections in richer

---

[4]To the best of our knowledge, the first recognition of the implications of conditioning behavior on being pivotal in the presence of incomplete information is due to Ordeshook and Palfrey (1988), who study committee voting over amendment agendas with incomplete information.

settings. Razin (2003), for example, explores a spatial model in which the winning candidate may change his or her policy platform after the election (that is, the post-election legislative policy and the policy promoted during the campaign might differ). In the model, voters do not abstain, are uncertain about the true state of the world, and have symmetric single-peaked preferences over a one-dimensional issue space. However, the Left (respectively, Right) candidate must choose from a moderate or a relatively extreme position to the left (respectively, to the right) of the median voter. In this model, Razin shows that uncertain voters weigh a signaling motive (to influence the candidates) against a pivot motive (to influence the post-election policy choice). When these incentives operate in opposing directions, it is possible for electoral outcomes to be different than would be the case if all voters were completely informed. Further limitations on the full information equivalence results have been established by Kim (2004) and Gul and Pesendorfer (2006). That such limitations arise in richer models should not be surprising; what is surprising is that, as McK&O clearly saw, there exist non-pathological settings for which the full information equivalence results obtain at all.

Despite the Ledyard (1989) and Banks (1990a) papers discussed above, far less progress has been made regarding how voter uncertainty affects candidates' strategies. Although there now exists a sizeable literature on probabilistic voting models in which candidates are uncertain about everything that affects voter decisions or about the true distribution of voter preferences itself, voters in this literature are not making decisions under incomplete information about which candidate is most in their interest.[5] Prominent examples here include Coughlin and Nitzan (1981) and Banks and Duggan (2004), who show that, when candidates are unsure about the realized distribution of non-policy (but decision-relevant) attributes within the electorate, candidates' equilibrium platforms maximize expected utility aggregated across the electorate.[6] Unfortunately, when there is a unique policy that maximizes aggregate utility, these models also predict zero expected turnout when voting is costly. Unlike in Ledyard (1989), Banks (1990a), and Razin (2003), therefore, the candidates' decision calculus in these models need not internalize strategic responses by voters who might learn about other decision-relevant parameters from the candidates' choices. An exception here is Gul and Pesendorfer (2006), who consider a spatial competition model that is

---

[5]Coughlin (1992) provides an excellent survey and synthesis of the probabilistic voting literature to that date. See also Calvert (1986).

[6]Ledyard (1984) establishes a similar result without probabilistic voting in a model in which the only source of uncertainty is the distribution of voting costs.

similar to Razin's, allowing for voter ignorance about candidate platforms and the distribution of other voters' preferences. As with Razin, they find conditions under which the electoral outcome is different than would have occurred if all voters were completely informed. In particular, the median voter's ideal point may not be an equilibrium policy outcome. Moreover, these failures are more acute when candidates care more about winning than about policy.

In addition to the two central concerns in McK&O (1985), information aggregation and strategic candidate policy choice, the paper raised several related issues about whether an electorate containing uninformed voters can produce the same electoral outcome as when all voters have complete information. Subsequent work has addressed this issue in different ways. For instance, Harrington (1993) considers the signaling role of candidate platform choice when candidates know more than voters about the policy consequences of their platform choices. Harrington proves that competition constrains, but does not eliminate, politicians' abilities to use their knowledge advantages to manipulate electorates for self-serving purposes. In particular, as signaling costs rise, electoral outcomes converge to those that would be realized under complete information.[7] Martinelli (2003), in turn, extends the standard Downsian framework to voter uncertainty about candidate platforms. He assumes that voting is costless but that individual information acquisition is costly. He proves that even though most voters do not become informed as the electorate grows, full information and full participation equivalence results remain for large elections. And while McK&O observed bandwagon-like behavior between successive polling results in the dynamic version of their model, Fey (2001) and Callander (2003) use dynamic, sequential voting models with fully rational and incompletely informed individuals to develop richer equilibrium theories of bandwagon voting. Callander, in particular, identifies conditions under which an equilibrium bandwagon can lead to the full information equivalent outcome in large elections.

McK&O also raise questions about how to conceptualize voter reasoning in an election model. Much of their attempt to advance the debate is contained within the structure of the model (in particular, the inclusion of polls and endorsements) and in the development of the REPE concept. While the perfect Bayesian equilibrium concept used by much of the post-McK&O literature on electoral competition under incomplete information also implies a rational expectations property

---

[7] See also Piketty (2000), who, like Razin (2003), considers the signaling role of voting on candidate behavior in elections with incomplete information.

on agents' beliefs, tracking differences between these concepts reveals subsequent trends in how theorists model voter reasoning.

Save for the assumption that uninformed voters believe themselves to be uniquely uninformed, voters in McK&O are rational to the extent that they make appropriate inferences about how best to vote. They do not, however, condition their voting decision on being pivotal. Moreover, to insure that individuals do vote when they have a strict preference, despite each individual being an infinitesimally small proportion of the electorate in the limit, McK&O assume voters receive an arbitrarily small consumption benefit from voting for their most preferred candidate. In effect, voters recognize that they have negligible weight in the election and seek to choose rationally on this basis (there is no cost to voting). Perhaps the closest model to McK&O in this respect is due to Myerson and Weber (1993), who consider large electorates with multiple candidates and strategic, rather than substantive, uncertainty among voters under a variety of vote counting rules. The focal uncertainty for voters in Myerson and Weber regards the decisions of other voters rather than the policy positions of the candidates. M&W's analysis hinges on a rational expectations equilibrium in voter behavior consistent with the motivation underlying McK&O. Individuals do not explicitly condition on the event of being pivotal, but use polls as in McK&O, adjusting beliefs so that, in equilibrium, all voters are choosing best decisions relative to their beliefs, and the expected and the realized aggregate vote distributions are mutually consistent. In other words, both McK&O and Myerson and Weber build models of voter behavior in large electorates that mirror the price-taking models of individual choice behavior in large economic markets. More recently, Myerson (1998, 2000 2002) has introduced a theory of large Poisson games to allow for very rich informational environments, including uncertainty about the electorate's size, policy preference uncertainties, voting cost uncertainties, and so forth. The theory of large Poisson games is an innovation on par with McK&O's and Ledyard's (1984) introduction of rational expectations ideas to the theory of elections with imperfect and incomplete information.

4. Developments in Understanding Endorsement Credibility

The role of the endorsers in McK&O is essentially technical: they are nonstrategic and their endorsements insure that all voters know the relative spatial locations of the two candidates. Without this knowledge, prima facie absurd equilibria could arise in which, say, all uninformed voters who would surely prefer the leftmost candidate surely vote for the rightmost candidate, and conversely. But as suggested by Grossman and Helpmann (1999) among others, endorsers have substantive interests in the outcome of the election and cannot be expected to reveal all of their private information regardless of the circumstance. Endorsements are instances of strategic information transmission from possibly self-interested agents. This fact raises important questions about the credibility and influence of those offering endorsements and has led theorists to examine the role of endorsements when endorsers are more strategic than those of McK&O.

The focal theoretical insight on what an endorser will do in this situation comes from Crawford and Sobel (1982).[8] Their model features a sender and a receiver. The receiver's job is to make a choice, and we can think of this player as somewhat analogous to a voter in McK&O. Before the receiver chooses, a sender sends a message to the receiver about the consequences of her choice. In the electoral context, the message can be interpreted as an endorsement, although the quality of this endorsement is endogenously determined rather than fixed as presumed in McK&O. Unlike the receiver, the sender knows the consequences of the receiver's actions.

Crawford and Sobel (1982:1431) find that "equilibrium signaling is more informative when agents' preferences are more similar." The intuition underlying the results is as follows: if outcomes that are good for the receiver also benefit the sender, then the sender has an incentive to reveal what he knows and the receiver should follow the endorsement (see also Calvert 1986; Farrell and Gibbons 1989). By contrast, if what is good for a sender is bad for a receiver, and vice versa, then the receiver rationally places little weight on the sender's endorsement and the sender similarly has little incentive to offer any useful information. This result calls into question the extent to which McK&O's results are robust to cases where the endorsement comes from a goal-oriented actor rather than the truth-telling endorsement device of the initial model. It leads us to ask about what and how much a receiver must know about a sender to treat the endorsement as credible. Several lines of research in political science address this question and the literature is large and growing (see Banks 1990b for a relatively early survey). Here, we focus on two of many game-theoretic efforts to show how variations in player and institutional attributes affect whether or not endorsements are credible, thus promoting more informed choices.

Austen-Smith (1994) extends Crawford and Sobel's model to a case where the sender is not automatically endowed with superior knowledge about what choice

---

[8]In an unpublished working paper, Green and Stokey (1980) independently established related results in a very different model.

is good for the receiver. Instead, prior to playing the Crawford-Sobel game, the sender can purchase such information. Only the sender knows the price of becoming informed. If he chooses to become informed, he can demonstrate as much to the receiver, but he has no way to document his lack of information when he is uninformed. The paper's main result is that such uncertainty about the sender's knowledge actually expands the set of circumstances in which the receiver can use the endorsement to make the same choice she would have made if fully informed. The intuition underlying this counterintuitive result is that receiver uncertainty about the sender's knowledge and the sender's cost of becoming informed can induce the receiver to be uncertain as to whether certain messages are being sent by an informed or uninformed sender. Such uncertainty, in turn, can induce the receiver to treat seriously some messages that would otherwise be dismissed as wholly unreliable. This paper thus demonstrates how the credibility of endorsements depends on receiver knowledge of speaker attributes as well as contextual variables such as the cost of being informed.

Lupia and McCubbins (1998) expand on Crawford and Sobel's template in a different way. Like McKelvey and Ordeshook, they base their inferences on models and experiments. In each endeavor, the sender's expertise (i.e., whether he knows more than the voter), the sender's interests (i.e., whether he prefers the same outcomes as the receiver), and the receiver's knowledge of these and other factors are parameterized and independently determined. Varying these factors one at a time or in multiples, Lupia and McCubbins demonstrate conditions under which the endorsement is credible. A preliminary result (shown theoretically and in experiments) is that the receiver's *perceptions* of key sender attributes trump the sender's actual attributes in determining whether the receiver will base her choice on the endorsement. Later, they further introduce institutional forces such as observable costly effort (a cost for making any statement, following Spence 1974 and Lupia 1992) and threats of verification. They clarify how such forces affect what senders say and what receivers believe. Their main result shows that even if voters are relatively ignorant about an endorser's knowledge and interests, there exist institutional settings under which endorsements remain effective in promoting relatively informed voter decisions.

Collectively, such work clarifies the conditions under which the endorsements of strategic agents can nevertheless induce voters to vote as they would under full information. This theoretical work is increasingly complemented by empirical work that yields comparable results, particularly in developed countries (see, e.g., Lupia 1994; Bowler and Donovan 1998; Sekhon 2005). That such conditions exist in a general set of circumstances, and appear in real elections, is a testament to the applicability of McKelvey and Ordeshook's original claim. So while endorsements are not a universal remedy for voter ignorance, theorists and empirical scholars in political science have made considerable progress in clarifying the conditions under which they are sufficient for "informed voting."

5. What Has Been Learned and What Is to Be Done?

As suggested by the preceding brief survey of the literature, since McK&O's seminal contribution a good deal has been learned about information aggregation in large two-candidate elections with fixed candidate platforms, the relative values of which are uncertain to voters. We have also learned about the signaling role of policy choice and about voting equilibria in elections with strategic uncertainty and we have engaged in deeper inquiries about strategic endorsements, communication in campaigns, costly information acquisition, and the dynamics of sequential voting (bandwagons). On the other hand, there has been no major advance on McK&O in regard to strategic platform choice (or strategic obfuscation thereof) in the spatial model (although Gul and Pesendorfer 2006 is promising), and we are unaware of any general model of information dynamics in elections with more than two candidates (although Kedar 2005 provides a platform focusing on important aspects of electoral institutions from which such a theory can be built). Similarly, there is still no generally intuitive and analytically tractable model of strategic voting in large elections (although Myerson's theory of Poisson games is an attempt at such).

The gaps in our understanding of the role of information in large elections, and in the tools available for improving that understanding, suggest the main open research problems on the topic. Rather than offer personal (and doubtless idiosyncratic) lists of problems here, we want to highlight three that we think both pressing and promising topics for study.

The first problem concerns integrating a general strategic theory of candidate behavior with a similar theory of voter choice under incomplete information. One benefit of pursuing such a theory will be a better understanding of how electoral institutions influence policy outcomes. This benefit will arise because candidates have an incentive to think about voter responses when selecting policy platforms and while legislative policy outcomes rarely correspond exactly to winning candidates' platforms they are nevertheless affected by the policy goals that candidates for office espouse. In this regard, it is worth noting that relatively few elections around the world involve only two candidates. However, the properties of information aggregation in multicandidate elections, even with fixed (uncertain) candidate platforms, are as yet quite opaque to social science. Since a general theory of strategic candidate behavior includes a theory of the number of candidates who run for office, clarifying the information aggregation properties of multicandidate elections can provide a wide range of interesting inferences.

The second problem is closely related and involves how best to model incomplete information among voters. There are many ways in which voters' lack of information might be modeled. In any given model, it is not always transparent exactly which particular informational assumptions are generating the focal conclusion. McK&O, for example, assume that voters know the location of their ideal point relative to the population at large and, as discussed in some detail above, that each voter believes that all others are fully informed and rational. These are relatively restrictive assumptions. It is reasonable to ask whether McK&O's formal conclusions are robust, for instance, to settings in which voters have mistaken or varying beliefs about each other. Analogous questions can be asked about many other election theories.

In formal models, such questions have long been difficult to explore. A common practice is to assume that even incompletely informed players share with all other players (whether informed or not) correct and common prior beliefs about the true state of the world or about the type of a focal player. Indeed, the equilibrium concepts used to solve most existing models of incomplete information presume that all players share such beliefs — at least along the equilibrium path. In many political contexts, however, we know that players can have wildly different beliefs about important phenomena. Liberals and conservatives, for example, hold different beliefs about the social ramifications of topics such as gay marriage, abortion, and religious education. Similarly, before, during, and after the O. J. Simpson murder trial, blacks and whites in the United States had very different beliefs about Mr. Simpson's guilt. In some situations, it is possible that people are so polarized in their background assumptions that any presumption of complete and common priors is prima facie implausible.

One approach that game theorists are now exploring with increasing frequency is to study games where players do not assume that all other players are utility-maximizing (McKelvey and Palfrey 1992, 1995) or where players have distinct prior beliefs (see, e.g., Piketty 1995). An important and emerging line of theorizing goes further, relaxing the assumption that players' prior beliefs are complete. In the self-confirming equilibrium concept, for example, players need not have well defined beliefs about all aspects of the game, such as other players' types or preferences (see, e.g., Dekel, Fudenberg, and Levine 2003). Instead, theoretical inferences are drawn from steady state relationships between players' (possibly very incomplete) conjectures about cause-and-effect in the game and their (possibly very uninformative) observations.[9]

A complementary approach to modeling individual uncertainty is through a political analogue of behavioral economics, where theorists pay more attention to cognitive and psychological phenomena than is admitted by the canonical rational choice model. In this framework, empirical findings from brain-and-mind oriented fields are used both as premises to game-theoretic models and as phenomena to be explained, at least in part, as a result of strategic adaptation. The explicit integration of psychological phenomena into formal models is relatively new. The practice of integrating such phenomena into studies of political science, by contrast, is more established. Political psychology has been a growing and recognized subfield for at least two decades now, making substantial contributions to our understanding of individual behavior, especially in elections and collective decision-making (see Kuklinski 2002 for a recent overview of the literature). There may be new gains from trade available in new interactions between formal theorists and scholars who are knowledgeable about psychology.

The final problem of concern is with the role of the media in electoral politics. McK&O exploited the endorsements of interest groups as an information source for voters. Newspapers and television networks, although more-or-less committed to reporting facts about politics, tend to have clearly articulated positions (loosely, preferences) of their own regarding desirable political outcomes. It is unlikely that such preferences are irrelevant to decisions on what and how they report. Indeed, newspapers routinely endorse candidates for many different electoral offices and, in this respect at least, behave as the interest groups in McK&O's model. Formal work on how the media affect information aggregation and electoral outcomes is just beginning to emerge. While game-theoretic approaches are not yet widely accepted among the large contingent of empirically oriented scholars who write about media and politics (similar to the reaction of many voting and election scholars to formal model of elections in the McK&O era), they are beginning to provide effective counterarguments and replicable logic that can be used to evaluate the many speculative claims that exist on the topic (see, e.g., Hamilton 2004).[10]

---

[9]Lupia, Zharinova, and Levine (2007) suggest applications of this approach in political contexts.
[10]See for example Bovitz, Druckman, and Lupia (2002), Baron (2004), Shleifer and Mullainathan (2002), Stromberg (2004), and Chan and Suen (2004, 2006), each of whom address important but

References

Almond, G. and S. Verba. 1963. *The Civic Culture*. Princeton: Princeton University Press.

Austen-Smith, D. 1994. Strategic transmission of costly information. *Econometrica* 62: 955–963.

Austen-Smith, D. and J. S. Banks. 1996. Information aggregation, rationality and the Condorcet Jury Theorem. *American Political Science Review* 90: 34–45.

Banks, J. S. 1990a. A model of electoral competition with incomplete information. *Journal of Economic Theory* 50: 309–325.

Banks, J. S. 1990b. *Signaling Games in Political Science*. Chur: Harwood Academic Press.

Banks, J. S. and J. Duggan. 2004. Probabilistic voting in the spatial model of elections: The theory of office-motivated candidates (with John Duggan). In Austen-Smith, D. and J. Duggan (eds.), *Social Choice and Strategic Decisions: Essays in Honor of Jeffrey S. Banks*. Berlin: Springer.

Baron, D. P. 2004. Persistent media bias. Research paper 1845R, Stanford Graduate School of Business.

Berelson, B., P. Lazarsfeld and W. McPhee. 1954. *Voting*. Chicago: University of Chicago Press.

Bovitz, G. L., J. N. Druckman and A. Lupia. 2002. When can a news organization lead public opinion? Ideology versus market forces in decisions to make news. *Public Choice* 113: 127–155.

Bowler, S. and T. Donovan. 1998. *Demanding Choices: Opinion, Voting and Direct Democracy*. Ann Arbor: University of Michigan Press.

Callander, S. 2003. Bandwagons and momentum in sequential voting. Working paper, Northwestern University.

Calvert, R. 1986. *Models of Imperfect Information in Politics*. Chur: Harwood Academic Publishers.

Chan, J. and W. Suen. 2004. Media as watchdogs: The role of the news media in electoral competition. Working paper, The Johns Hopkins University.

Chan, J. and W. Suen. 2006. A spatial theory of news consumption and electoral competition. Working paper, Shanghai University of Finance and Economics.

---

complementary aspects of the manner in which the industrial organization of the media as a whole, or the internal organization of media-producing firms, affects the distribution of information and voter knowledge in elections.

Converse, P. 1975. Public opinion and voting behavior. In Greenstein, F. and N. Polsby (eds.), *Handbook of Political Science*. Reading, MA: Addison-Wesley.

Coughlin, P. J. 1992. *Probabilistic Voting Theory*. Cambridge: Cambridge University Press.

Coughlin, P. J. and S. Nitzan. 1981. Electoral outcomes with probabilistic voting and Nash social welfare maxima. *Journal of Public Economics* 15: 113–122.

Crawford, V. and J. Sobel. 1982. Strategic information transmission. *Econometrica* 50: 1431–1451

Dekel, E., D. Fudenberg and D. K. Levine. 2003. Learning to play Bayesian games. *Games and Economic Behavior* 46: 282–303.

Downs, A. 1957. *An Economic Theory of Democracy*. New York: Harper.

Farrell, J. and R. Gibbons. 1989. Cheap talk with two audiences. *American Economic Review* 79: 1214–1223.

Feddersen, T. J. and W. Pesendorfer. 1996. The swing voter's curse. *American Economic Review* 86: 408–424.

Feddersen, T. J. and W. Pesendorfer. 1997. Voting behavior and information aggregation in elections with private information. *Econometrica* 65: 1029–1058.

Feddersen, T. J. and W. Pesendorfer. 1999. Abstentions in elections with asymmetric information and diverse preferences. *American Political Science Review* 93: 381–398.

Fey, M. 2001. Informational cascades and sequential voting. Working paper, University of Rochester.

Green, J. R. and N. L. Stokey. 1980. A two-person game of information transmission. CMS-EMS Working paper #418, Northwestern University.

Grossman, G. and E. Helpmann. 1999. Competing for endorsements. *American Economic Review* 89: 501–524.

Gul, F. and W. Pesendorfer. 2006. Partisan politics and aggregation failure with ignorant voters. Working paper, Princeton University.

Hamilton, J. 2004. *All the News That's Fit to Sell: How the Market Transforms Information into News*. Princeton: Princeton University Press.

Harrington, J. 1992. The revelation of information through the electoral process: An exploratory analysis. *Economics and Politics* 4: 255–275.

Harrington, J. 1993. Economic policy, economic performance and elections. *American Economic Review* 83: 27–42.

Kedar, O. 2005. When moderate voters prefer extreme parties: Policy balancing in parliamentary elections. *American Political Science Review* 99: 185–200.

Kim, J. 2004. Private values and the swing-voter's curse. Working paper, University of Rochester.

Kuklinski, J. H. 2002. *Thinking about Political Psychology.* New York: Cambridge University Press.

Ladha, K. 1992. The Condorcet jury theorem, free speech and correlated votes. *American Journal of Political Science* 36: 617–634.

Ledyard, J. 1984. The pure theory of large two-candidate elections. *Public Choice* 44: 7–43.

Ledyard, J. 1989. Information aggregation in two-candidate elections. In Ordeshook, P. C. (ed.), *Models of Strategic Choice in Politics.* Ann Arbor: University of Michigan Press.

Lupia, A. 1992. Busy voters, agenda control and the power of information. *American Political Science Review* 86: 390–403.

Lupia, A. 1994. Shortcuts versus encyclopedias: Information and voting behavior in California insurance reform elections. *American Political Science Review* 88: 63–76.

Lupia, A. and M. D. McCubbins. 1998. *The Democratic Dilemma: Can Citizens Learn What They Need to Know?* New York: Cambridge University Press.

Lupia, A., N. Zharinova and A. S. Levine. 2007. Should political scientists use the self-confirming equilibrium concept: Explaining the choices of cognitively limited actors. Working paper posted at http://mpra.ub.uni-muenchen.de/1618/ .

Martinelli, C. 2003. Would rational voters acquire costly information? Working paper, University of Rochester.

McKelvey, R. D. and P. C. Ordeshook. 1985. Elections with limited information: A fulfilled expectations model using contemporaneous poll and endorsement data as information sources. *Journal of Economic Theory* 36: 55–85. Chapter 15 of this book.

McKelvey, R. D. and T. R. Palfrey. 1992. An experimental study of the centipede game. *Econometrica* 60: 803–836. Chapter 18 of this book.

McKelvey, R. D. and T. R. Palfrey. 1995. Quantal response equilibria for normal form games. *Games and Economic Behavior* 10: 6–38. Chapter 20 of this book.

Myerson, R. B. 1998. Population uncertainty and Poisson games. *International Journal of Game Theory* 27: 375–392.

Myerson, R. B. 2000. Large Poisson games. *Journal of Economic Theory* 94: 7–45.

Myerson, R. B. 2002. Comparison of scoring rules in Poisson voting games. *Journal of Economic Theory* 103: 217–251.

Myerson, R. B. and R. Weber. 1993. A theory of voting equilibria. *American Political Science Review* 87: 102–114.

Ordeshook, P. C. and T. Palfrey. 1988. Agendas, strategic voting, and signaling with incomplete information. *American Journal of Political Science* 32: 441–466.

Palfrey, T. R. and H. Rosenthal. 1985. Voter participation and strategic uncertainty. *American Political Science Review* 79: 62–78.

Piketty, T. 1995. Social mobility and redistributive politics. *Quarterly Journal of Economics* 100: 551–584.

Piketty, T. 2000. Voting as communicating. *Review of Economic Studies* 67: 169–191.

Razin, R. 2003. Signaling and election motives in a voting model with common values and responsive candidates. *Econometrica* 71: 1083–1120.

Sekhon, J. S. 2005. The varying role of voter information across democratic societies. Working paper, Harvard University.

Shleifer, A. and S. Mullainathan. 2002. Media bias. MIT Department of Economics Working paper 02-33.

Spence, A. M. 1974. *Market Signaling*. Cambridge, MA: Harvard University Press.

Stokes, D. E. 1963. Spatial models of party competition. *American Political Science Review* 57: 368–377.

Stromberg, D. 2004. Mass media competition, political competition and public policy. *Review of Economic Studies* 71: 265–284.

Young, H. P. 1988. Condorcet's theory of voting. *American Political Science Review* 82: 1231–1244.

CHAPTER 15

Elections with Limited Information: A Fulfilled Expectations Model Using Contemporaneous Poll and Endorsement Data as Information Sources

RICHARD D. MCKELVEY AND PETER C. ORDESHOOK

ABSTRACT. A one-dimensional model of two candidate elections under asymmetric information is theoretically developed and experimentally tested. Candidates do not know voter utility functions, and most voters are uninformed about candidate policy positions. A fulfilled expectations equilibrium is defined, using poll and endorsement data as information sources. It is proved that with any positive fraction of informed voters, any equilibrium extracts all available information: all participants — voters and candidates alike — act as if they were fully informed. For fixed candidate strategies, a dynamic is given for convergence to voter equilibrium, and this process is shown to imply a "bandwagon effect."

1. Introduction

In the last 30 years or so, considerable effort has been expended at attempting to develop a formal theory of political systems and processes based on the economic paradigm of rational choice. Labeled variously positive political theory, public choice, or social choice, this effort encompasses a broad area of study, including spatial election models, coalition processes. voting rules, and agenda manipulation. (See Riker and Ordeshook [23] for a review of the early work in this area and Shepsle [24], Kramer [10], McKelvey, Ordeshook, and Winer [13, Chapter 10 of this book] for a sampling of the recent directions of this literature.) Generally, however, the models and theories that form the component parts of this effort are subject to a common and compelling criticism — they assume that political actors such as voters, candidates, legislators, etc., possess a level of knowledge of other voters' preferences, candidate positions and the like that empirical investigation does not support. Thus, in these models, it is supposed typically that candidates adopt well-defined positions on all issues and that voters know these positions and the issues (at least up to some well-defined probability measure) — despite the well-documented empirical fact that voters oftentimes do not even know the names of the candidates, much less the policies they espouse (cf. Berelson, Lazarsfeld, and McPhee [2], Almond and Verba [1], Converse [3], and for an up-to-date review of this literature, Kinder and Sears [9]). The effort of this paper can be thought of as an attempt to bring the informational assumptions of such models more in line with what we know empirically.

This paper is one in a series of papers in which we study election processes under limited and decentralized information conditions. (See also McKelvey and Ordeshook [15, 16, 17].) Specifically, in this and other papers, we develop models of policy formation in two candidate elections where most voters have little or no information about the policies or platforms adopted by the candidates, and where candidates have little or no information about the voter preference functions.

The key to understanding and modeling systems in which participants have limited access to information seems to us to be related to the ideas that have recently been applied succesfully to similar situations in economics. When voters do not possess the perfect information assumed in earlier models, and when it is costly to obtain this information relative to the presumed expected benefits, we assume that voters take cues from other sources, endogenous in the system, that are easily observable and which they believe may convey useful information. Such sources may be other voters, interest groups, historical behavior of the candidates, or poll results. Regardless of the source, we assume voters will condition their choices on such "low cost" data. Candidates, too, may condition their actions on such data. Thus, there are variables, endogenous in the system, which carry information to the uninformed participants. When actors condition their behavior on the information from these endogenous sources, this, in itself will change the observed values of some of the endogenous variables. The system is in equilibrium only if all participants are acting optimally given available information, and further if the information generated when participants act in such a fashion does not change — i.e., it is stable and consistent with this optimization behavior of all participants.

Several questions of considerable theoretical interest can be addressed by models of this sort. The most important and interesting of these questions is the extent to which the equilibria of systems with limited information correspond to the equilibria of systems with full information. That is, do the policy outcomes correspond to the outcomes that would prevail were all participants to have full information? As we show, in this and other papers, such a correspondence can frequently be established.

The model developed in this paper assumes the information source for uninformed voters is poll data and interest group endorsements. Our model is a model of a *single* election, so no historical information is available. There are two classes of participants: voters and candidates. However, the voters are further partitioned into informed and uninformed voters. All voters have single peaked preferences over a one-dimensional issue space, X. Strategies available to candidates are to adopt positions in the policy space, and strategies available to voters are to vote for one candidate or the other. The candidates do not know voter utility functions, and the uninformed voters do not know the candidates' positions. The only source of information for the uninformed agents is "interest group endorsement" information and the results of a "Gallup poll" of all voters. In addition, uninformed voters know where their ideal point is in the distribution of total ideal points, i.e., they know how liberal or conservative they are with respect to the remaining population.

In this model one might expect that the informed voters, by virtue of their better information, would have a disproportionate impact on the final outcome. On the contrary, the informed voters, by acting on their superior information, end up revealing it (through the poll and endorsement data) to others, so that in equilibrium, we obtain the result described above: The equilibrium extracts all choice relevant information so that all voters vote as if they had full information. The policies adopted by the candidate in equilibrium reflect the preferences of the uninformed as well as the informed voters.

Our approach in this and companion papers parallels the development of rational expectations models in economics (cf. Muth [18], Lucas [12], Radner [21, 22], and Grossman [5, 7] for development and references to some of this extensive literature). In that literature, the actors are buyers and sellers, and the information that is of concern is the future state of the world — a state that affects the future market value of the commodity being traded. The question addressed by the rational expectations literature is what will happen to the market price of a commodity when only a few specialized participants, called *insiders*, have information regarding the future state of the world. In those models, agents are able to condition their choices, and derive information from endogenous variables such as the price or historical market data. The principal result to emerge is called the efficient markets hypothesis, which asserts that the market will behave as if everyone had information, since the relevant information about the state of the world is itself conveyed to the other participants through the price.

This paper shows how the rational expectations view can be applied to models of political processes. The correspondence between the models we develop and the rational expectations models in economics is that in our models interest groups or informed voters perform the same function as the insiders in the rational expectation market models: their choices provide signals to the other participants (voters and candidates alike) that convey information about the relevant properties of the election system. Namely, they convey some sketchy, but useful, information about the relative positions of the candidates. Further, an election or poll outcome serves the same role as the price in the market models. Just as the price elicits demand information in market models, so the election outcome conveys information to the candidates about the preferences of the voters. In the model developed here, the true distribution of voter preferences is, to the candidates, the unknown state of the world, so the price conveys information about the true state of the world. Only when no participant wants to change his behavior given the information that is being revealed by the behavior of the interest groups and the outcome of the election can the system be in equilibrium. This is the type of equilibrium we search for in these models.

The organization of the paper is as follows: Section 2 develops the basic model and defines the equilibrium notion used here. Section 3 presents the main results, which prove the existence of and derive properties of equilibria to our model. Section 4 specifies a dynamic "tâtonnement" process, corresponding to a series of successive polls, which converges to a voter equilibrium for any fixed candidate positions. Finally, in addition to the theoretical work, we design and run some experiments intended to test certain implications of the model. Section 5 reports on these experimental results.

2. The Formal Development

We are given a measure space $\Omega = (\Omega, \mathbf{F}, \mu)$ of *voters*, a set $K = \{1, 2\}$ of *candidates*, and a closed convex set $X \subseteq R$ of *alternatives*. Voters in Ω are partitioned into two classes, I and U, which are referred to as *informed* and *uninformed* voters, respectively. There is a function $y^* : \Omega \longrightarrow \mathbb{R}$ which assigns to each voter, $\alpha \in \Omega$, a characteristic, $y^*(\alpha)$, referred to as voter α's *ideal* point. We write $y^*_\alpha = y^*(\alpha)$. All voters then have *utility functions* $u_\alpha : X \longrightarrow \mathbb{R}$ which are assumed to be of the form

(2.1) $$u_\alpha(x) = u(x, y^*_\alpha) = -|x - y^*_\alpha|$$

for all $x \in X$.

We now define a game, with players consisting of the voters and candidates. The strategy sets are

(2.2) $$\text{Voter } \alpha : B_\alpha = K_0 = K \cup \{0\}$$
$$\text{Candidate } k : S_k = X.$$

We let **B** denote the set of measurable functions from Ω into K_0. Elements of **B** are denoted b, with $b_\alpha = b(\alpha) \in B_\alpha$, representing the choice of strategy by $\alpha \in \Omega$. Similarly, let **S** denote the set of functions from K to X. Elements of **S** are denoted s, with $s_k = s(k) \in S_k$ representing the choice of strategy by candidate k. We call b_α voter α's *ballot*, with $b_\alpha = k$ representing a vote for candidate k if $k \in K$, and an abstention if $k = 0$. We call s_k candidate k's *policy position*. For any $b \in \mathbf{B}$, $\alpha \in \Omega$, and $b'_\alpha \in B_\alpha$, we use the notation b/b'_α to denote the ballot which results when we replace b_α by b'_α in b. Similarly, for $s \in \mathbf{S}$, $s_k \in S_k$, the notation s_k/s'_k denotes the strategy pair resulting when we replace s_k by s'_k in s. For any $k \in K$, we use the notation $\bar{k}$ for k's *opponent*. I.e., $\bar{k} \in K - \{k\}$.

A choice of strategies $(s, b) \in \mathbf{S} \times \mathbf{B}$ by all players yields a *vote*, in any measurable $C \subseteq \Omega$ defined by

(2.3) $$v_k^C(b) = \mu(\{\alpha \in C | b_\alpha = k\})$$

for each $k \in K_0$. Thus for $k \in K$, $v_k^C(b)$ represents the vote in C for candidate k, and for $k = 0$, it represents the total abstentions in C. We write $v_k(b) = v_k^\Omega(b)$ for the *total vote* for k, and $v_k^{-\alpha}(b) = v_k^{\Omega - \{\alpha\}}(b)$ for the vote of all voters except α.

The election *outcome* is then

(2.4) $$\begin{aligned} j(b) &= k && \text{if } v_k(b) > v_{\bar{k}}(b) \text{ and } k \in K \\ &= 0 && \text{otherwise.} \end{aligned}$$

I.e., the candidate with the greatest number of votes wins unless there is a tie. (If there is a tie — i.e., $k(b) = 0$, we assume below that a coin is flipped.)

We pick $\delta \in \mathbb{R}$ with $\delta \geq 0$. The payoff functions, $M_\alpha : \mathbf{S} \times \mathbf{B} \longrightarrow \mathbb{R}$ and $M_k : \mathbf{S} \times \mathbf{B} \longrightarrow \mathbb{R}$, to voters and candidates, are now defined by

(2.5) $$M_\alpha(s,b) = u_\alpha(s_{j(b)}) + \delta u_\alpha(s_{b_\alpha})$$

and

(2.6) $$\begin{aligned} M_k(s,b) &= 1 && \text{if } j(b) = k \\ &= -1 && \text{if } j(b) = \bar{k} \\ &= 0 && \text{otherwise,} \end{aligned}$$

for all $\alpha \in \Omega$, $k \in K$, and $(s,b) \in \mathbf{S} \times \mathbf{B}$. We use the convention that $u_\alpha(s_0) = \frac{1}{2}u_\alpha(s_1) + \frac{1}{2}u_\alpha(s_2)$. So the payoff to the voter consists of the utility he receives for the policy position of the winning candidate plus some small increment of utility of the candidate he votes for. The candidates care only about winning. The reason for the second term in (2.5) is to deal with the nonatomic case, where $\mu(\{\alpha\}) = 0$. In order to insure that, in equilibrium, such voters have positive incentives to vote for their preferred candidate, the second term must be added. For the finite voter case, it is immaterial if we set $\delta = 0$ or $\delta > 0$.

In addition to the above, rather standard, development, we introduce some structure to allow us to model the imperfect information. Specifically, each player has beliefs over certain parameters of the above model which he does not observe. We define $\mathbf{Y}^0 = \{y | y : \Omega \longrightarrow \mathbb{R}$ such that y is $\mathbf{F}$ measurable$\}$ to be a set of possible assignments of ideal points to voters, and let $\mathbf{Y} \subseteq \mathbf{Y}^0$ be a set of feasible assignments. For any measurable set $C \subseteq \Omega$, $x \in \mathbb{R}$, and $y \in \mathbf{Y}$, we use the notation

(2.7) $$F_C(x|y) = \mu(\{\alpha \in C | y_\alpha \leq x\})$$
$$G_C(x|y) = \mu(\{\alpha \in C | y_\alpha \geq x\})$$
$$H_C(x|y) = \mu(\{\alpha \in C | y_\alpha = x\}).$$

Thus, $F_C(x|y)$ is the cumulative density function of y in C, while $G_C(x|y)$ is the "reverse" cumulative density function. We write $F_C(x|y^*) = F_C(x)$ and $F_\Omega(x|y) = F(x|y)$ so $F(x) = F_\Omega(x|y^*)$ is the cumulative density function of the true ideal points y_α^*. Also, we write $F^{-\alpha}(x)$ for $F_{\Omega - \{\alpha\}}(x)$. Similar notation is used for G and H.

We now define the *belief spaces* for voters and candidates by

(2.8) $$\text{Voter } \alpha : \Lambda_\alpha = \tilde{\mathbf{S}}$$
$$\text{Candidate } k : \Gamma_k = \tilde{\mathbf{Y}}.$$

Here, $\tilde{\mathbf{S}}$ denotes the set of probability measures over the Borel sets of $\mathbf{S}$, and $\tilde{\mathbf{Y}}$ denotes the set of probability measures over some σ algebra of $\mathbf{Y}$. (We assume sets of the form $\{y \in \mathbf{Y} | F_C(x|y) \geq t\}$ and $\{y \in \mathbf{Y} | G_C(x|y) \geq t\}$ are $\mathbf{Y}$ measurable for all $x, t \in \mathbb{R}$, $C \in \mathbf{F}$.) Thus, voters have beliefs about candidate policy positions, while candidates have beliefs about voter ideal points. A belief is simply a probability measure over the relevant space.

We let Λ be the set of functions from Ω into $\tilde{\mathbf{S}}$, and Γ denote the set of functions from K into $\tilde{\mathbf{Y}}$. Elements of Λ are denoted λ, with $\lambda_\alpha = \lambda(\alpha) \in \Lambda_\alpha$

Elections with Limited Information

denoting the belief of $\alpha \in \Omega$. Elements of Γ are denoted γ, with $\gamma_k = \gamma(k) \in \Gamma_k$ denoting the belief by $k \in K$. We will routinely use shorthand notation of the form $\lambda_\alpha(s_k < s_{\bar{k}})$ to represent $\lambda_\alpha(\{s \in \mathbf{S} | s_k < s_{\bar{k}}\})$, $\gamma_k(F(x|y) < t)$ to represent $\gamma_k(\{y \in \mathbf{Y} | F(x|y) \le t)\})$, etc.

For any $s \in \mathbf{S}$, we define the *endorsement*

(2.9) $\quad\quad\quad e(s) = k \quad\quad$ if $s_k < s_{\bar{k}}$ for $k \in K$,
$\quad\quad\quad\quad\quad = 0 \quad\quad$ otherwise,

and the *anti-endorsement*,

(2.10) $\quad\quad\quad \bar{e}(s) = \bar{k} \quad\quad$ if $s_k < s_{\bar{k}}$ for $k \in K$,
$\quad\quad\quad\quad\quad = 0 \quad\quad$ otherwise.

So the endorsed candidate is the candidate whose policy position is to the left, while the anti-endorsement represents the candidate to the right. Also, we let $q = (\frac{1}{2}, \frac{1}{2})$, so for any $s \in \mathbf{S}$, the *candidate midpoint* between s_1 and s_2 is $q \cdot s = (s_1 + s_2)/2$.

For any $s \in \mathbf{S}$, and $y \in \mathbf{Y}$, we define the *predicted ballot* $\hat{b}(s, y) \in \mathbf{B}$ by

(2.11) $\quad\quad\quad \hat{b}_\alpha(s, y) = k \quad\quad$ if $u(s_k, y_\alpha) > u(s_{\bar{k}}, y_\alpha)$ for $k \in K$,
$\quad\quad\quad\quad\quad\quad = 0 \quad\quad$ otherwise.

With this notation, we can now define the equilibrium conditions used here.

DEFINITION 2.1. Let $s^* \in \mathbf{S}$. A *voter equilibrium*, conditional on s^*, is a profile $(b^*, \lambda^*) \in \mathbf{B} \times \mathbf{\Lambda}$ satisfying

(a) $\forall \alpha \in \Omega, \forall b \in \mathbf{B}, b_\alpha^* \in \arg\max_{b_\alpha' \in B_\alpha} E_{\lambda_\alpha^*}[M_\alpha(s^*, b/b_\alpha')]$
(b) $\forall \alpha \in I, \lambda_\alpha^*(\{s^*\}) = 1$
(c) $\forall \alpha \in U$, if $e \in K$, then
  (i) $\lambda_\alpha^*(s_e < s_{\bar{e}}) = 1$
  (ii) $v_e^{-\alpha}(b^*) > F^{-\alpha}(y_\alpha^*) \Rightarrow \lambda_\alpha^*(q \cdot s > y_\alpha^*) = 1$
  (iii) $v_{\bar{e}}^{-\alpha}(b^*) > G^{-\alpha}(y_\alpha^*) \Rightarrow \lambda_\alpha^*(q \cdot s < y_\alpha^*) = 1$,

where $e = e(s^*)$, and $\bar{e} = \bar{e}(s^*)$.

DEFINITION 2.2. A *full equilibrium* is a candidate profile $(s^*, \lambda^*) \in \mathbf{S} \times \mathbf{\Gamma}$, together with a voter profile $(b^*, \lambda^*) \in \mathbf{B} \times \mathbf{\Lambda}$, such that (b^*, λ^*) is a voter equilibrium, conditional on s^*, and (s^*, γ^*) satisfies $\forall k \in K$,

(a) $s_k^* \in \arg\max_{s_k \in S_k} E_{\gamma_k^*}[M_k(s^*/s_k, \hat{b}(s^*/s_k, y))]$
(b) If $e \in K, \gamma_k^*(F(q \cdot s^*|y) \ge v_e^*) = 1$, and $\gamma_k^*(G(q \cdot s^*|y) \ge v_{\bar{e}}^*) = 1$

where $v_e^* = v_e(s^*)$ and $v_{\bar{e}}^* = v_{\bar{e}}(s^*)$.

Thus, in full equilibrium, each player chooses a strategy which maximizes his payoffs subject to his beliefs (i.e., voters satisfy Definition 2.1(a), candidates satisfy Definition 2.2(a)). Further, the beliefs of each player must be consistent with the data he observes (i.e., informed voters satisfy Definition 2.1(b), uninformed voters satisfy Definition 2.1(c), and candidates satisfy Definition 2.2(b)).

For players to be able to behave according to the above equilibrium definitions, some implicit assumptions are made about what contemporaneous information each player observes, and about what each player knows about the structure of the model. Before discussing the equilibrium conditions, we specify these information assumptions.

The contemporaneous data each player observes is:

$$I : s^*$$
$$U : e(s^*), v_k(s^*)$$
$$K : s^*, v_k(s^*).$$

Thus, informed voters observe the actual candidate positions. The uninformed voters, on the other hand, only observe the contemporaneous endorsement and vote (or poll) totals. The candidates observe candidate positions and contemporaneous poll data.

Also, all players are assumed to have some knowledge of the basic structure of the model: Specifically, they know that all voters have utility functions of the form (2.1), although they do not know other voters' ideal points. Further, each voter α is assumed to know the relative position of his own ideal point in the issue space: Thus, voter α knows $F(y_\alpha^*)$ and $G(y_\alpha^*)$ — the number of voters to his left and right. Note that we do *not* require that he know $F(x)$ or $G(x)$ for $x \neq y_\alpha^*$. Finally, when there is no reason to conclude otherwise, each player assumes that all other players are fully informed and rational. As we will see, in equilibrium, this assumption is justified.

We now discuss each of the conditions in the equilibrium definitions, in turn.

Voter Strategies: Definition 2.1(a)

This condition requires each voter to pick a strategy which maximizes his expected payoff subject to his beliefs — *regardless* of the behavior of other voters. Thus, he must pick a dominant strategy to the game whose payoff is $E_{\lambda_\alpha^*}[M_\alpha(s, b)]$. Fortunately, since the choice is discrete, and the payoff $M_\alpha(s, b)$ is "positively responsive," a strategy of choosing b_α to maximize $E_{\lambda_\alpha^*}[u_\alpha(s, b)]$ achieves this, as is shown in the next section.

Informed Voter Beliefs: Definition 2.1(b)

Informed voters each observe the true candidate positions s^*. Their beliefs about the candidate positions must be consistent with this information. Hence, their beliefs must be degenerate point masses centered on s^*.

Uninformed Voter Beliefs: Definition 2.1(c)

Uninformed voters observe the endorsement $e(s^*)$ and the vote $v_k(b^*)$ for each $k \in K_0$.

Condition (i) insures that voter α's belief is consistent with the endorsement. I.e., he assigns zero probability to situations where the endorsed candidate is to the right of the other candidate.

Conditions (ii) and (iii) bring the voter's beliefs in agreement with the observed vote outcome. Voter α knows that, excluding his own vote, all votes for the endorsed candidate must come from voters with ideal points at or to the left of the candidate midpoint, $q \cdot s^* = (s_1^* + s_2^*)/2$, wherever that might be. This follows from his assumption that all voters who are voting are informed and rational. Hence condition (ii) requires that if he observes the vote for the endorsed candidate to be greater than the number of voters he knows to have ideal points at or to his left, then he must infer that the candidate midpoint is to his right. Similarly, condition (iii) requires that if more voters are voting for the unendorsed candidate than voter α knows to be at or to his right, then he must infer that the candidate midpoint is to his left.

Conditions (ii) and (iii) are the key conditions driving the results in the subsequent sections. These conditions formalize the notion of how it is possible for uninformed voters to gather useful information from contemporaneous poll data. A very loose idea of the type of inference being required of the uninformed voter in condition (ii) can be captured in the statement "Well if *that* many voters are voting for candidate e, he can't be *too* liberal."

Figure 1 illustrates the situation for the case when Ω is infinite and F is invertible. In this case we have $\mu(\{\alpha\}) = 0$ for all α, so $v_e^{-\alpha} = v_e$, $F^{-\alpha} = F$, etc. Also $G(x) = \mu(\Omega) - F(s)$ for all x. Here, voters in group A (with $y_\alpha^* < F^{-1}(v_e)$) must infer that the candidate midpoint is to the right of their ideal point. Voters in group B (with $u_\alpha^* > G^{-1}(v_{\bar{e}})$ or $y_\alpha^* > F^{-1}(v_e + v_0)$) must infer that the candidate midpoint is to the left of their ideal points. The remaining voters, those in group C, can make no inference.

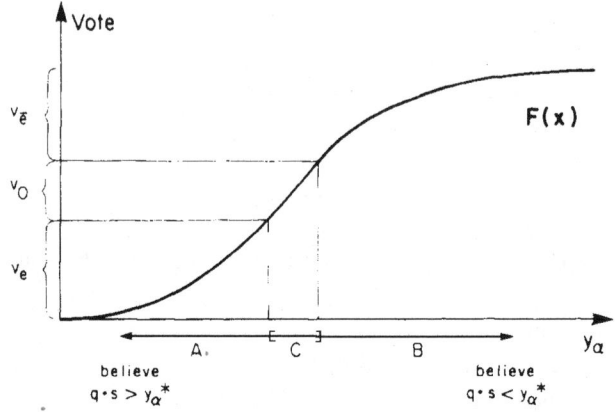

FIGURE 1. Illustration of voter inferences

Candidate Strategies: Definition 2.2(a)

This condition requires that each candidate chooses a policy position to maximize his expected payoff, based on his belief of the voter ideal points.

Note that each candidate knows the position of the other candidate, but does not know the true voter ideal points y_α^*; hence his belief γ_k^* over $\mathbf{Y}$. Further, each candidate, in choosing his optimal strategy, assumes that all voters are informed and rational. I.e., given ideal points $y \in \mathbf{Y}$ for each voter, and candidate positions $s \in \mathbf{S}$, the candidate assumes that voters vote according to $\hat{b}(s, y)$. The results in Section 3 show that if the voters are in equilibrium, then they satisfy this condition.

Candidate Beliefs: Definition 2.2(b)

These conditions require that candidate beliefs about voter characteristics be consistent with the observed vote. The candidates observe s^* as well as $v_k(s^*)$. Hence they know the candidate midpoint $q \cdot s^* = (s_1^* + s_2^*)/2$. Since all voters who are voting are assumed to be voting rationally, it must be that all voters voting for $e(s^*)$ have ideal points at or to the left of $q \cdot s^*$, while all those voting for $\bar{e}(s^*)$ must have ideal points at or to the right of $q \cdot s^*$. Hence for any $y \in \mathbf{Y}$ in the support set of γ_k^*, it must be that $F(q \cdot s^*|y) \geq v_e^*$ and $G(q \cdot s^*|y) \geq v_{\bar{e}}^*$.

In concluding this section, we relate our equilibrium definition to other types of equilibria for games with incomplete information. Our equilibrium is similar to

Harsanyi's Bayesian equilibrium (see Harsanyi [8]) in that each player has beliefs about the unknown characteristics of other players. However, we differ significantly from the Bayesian equilibrium framework in that we allow for revision of beliefs based on observed strategy choices of other players. The beliefs are *part of the equilibrium* in our setup, unlike in Bayesian equilibria, where they are data. In this respect our equilibrium resembles more closely the "rational expectations" or "fulfilled expectations" equilibria. Like these equilibria (see, e.g., Kreps [11] or Grossman [7]), our players optimize subject to beliefs, and then beliefs cannot be countermanded by observed data. However, our equilibrium also differs somewhat from these equilibria. In a fulfilled expectations equilibrium, there is exogenous uncertainty, and the function relating states of the world to observed data (prices) is determined as part of the equilibrium. In our equilibrium, at least part of the uncertainty — namely the candidate strategies — is endogenously determined, and since uninformed voters assume that all other voters are informed, the correspondence relating states of the world (i.e., candidate positions and voter ideal points) to observed data (i.e., endorsement and vote totals) is known. In the context of voting models, we believe these assumptions make more sense than the assumption that uninformed voters must learn the voting correspondence.

3. Results

This section states and proves some properties of equilibria to the above model. Lemmas 1 and 2 deal with voter equilibria, while Theorems 1 and 2 deal with full equilibria.

LEMMA 1. *Assume Ω is finite, with $|\Omega| = n$, and with $\mu(C) = |C|$ for all $C \subseteq Q$. Let $s^* \in \mathbf{S}$ satisfy $s_1^* \neq s_2^*$. Then if $(b^*, \lambda^*) \in \mathbf{B} \times \mathbf{\Lambda}$ is a voter equilibrium conditional on s^*, it must satisfy*

(a) *For all $\alpha \in I$,*

$$y_\alpha^* < q \cdot s^* \Rightarrow b_\alpha^* = e(s^*)$$
$$y_\alpha^* > q \cdot s^* \Rightarrow b_\alpha^* = \bar{e}(s^*)$$

(b) $\exists x_L, x_R \in X$, *satisfying*

$$F_I(x_R) \leq F_I(q \cdot s^*) + T - 1$$
$$G_I(x_L) \leq G_I(q \cdot s^*) + T - 1,$$

where $T = \max_{x \in X} H(x)$, such that for all $\alpha \in U$,
$$y_\alpha^* < x_L \Rightarrow b_\alpha^* = e(s^*)$$
$$y_\alpha^* > x_R \Rightarrow b_\alpha^* = \bar{e}(s^*).$$

Proof. From Definition 2.1(a) and (2.5), it follows that, $\forall \alpha \in \Omega$,

(3.1) $$b_\alpha^* \in \arg\max_{b_\alpha \in B_\alpha} E_{\lambda_\alpha^*}[u_\alpha(s_{j(b)}) + \delta u_\alpha(s_{b_\alpha})].$$

But, from the definition of $j(b)$, it follows that by voting for candidate k, voter α can never cause candidate k to do worse than he would if α voted for k or abstained. Further, by finiteness of Ω, for some b, voter α is pivotal. Hence, regardless of whether $\delta > 0$ or $\delta = 0$, (3.1) can be rewritten as, $\forall \alpha \in \Omega$,

(3.2) $$b_\alpha^* \in \arg\max_{b_\alpha \in B_\alpha} E_{\lambda_\alpha^*}[u_\alpha(s_{b_\alpha})].$$

For $\alpha \in I$, from Definition 2.1(b), $\lambda_\alpha(\{s^*\}) = 1$, so, for $\alpha \in I$,

(3.3) $$b_\alpha^* \in \arg\max_{b_\alpha \in B_\alpha}[u_\alpha(s_{b_\alpha}^*)] = \arg\min_{k \in K}[|s_k^* - y_\alpha^*|].$$

But $y_\alpha^* < q \cdot s^* \Rightarrow |s_e^* - y_\alpha^*| < |s_{\bar{e}}^* - y_\alpha^*|$, where $e = e(s^*)$ and $\bar{e} = \bar{e}(s^*)$. So

(3.4) $$y_\alpha^* < q \cdot s^* \Rightarrow b_\alpha^* = e(s^*).$$

Similarly,

(3.5) $$y_\alpha^* > q \cdot s^* \Rightarrow b_\alpha^* = \bar{e}(s^*),$$

which proves (a). For part (b), we first show, for all $\alpha \in U$, that

(3.6) $$F(y_\alpha^*) \le v_e^* \Rightarrow b_\alpha^* = e$$
$$F(y_\alpha^*) \le v_{\bar{e}}^* \Rightarrow b_\alpha^* = \bar{e},$$

where $v_e^* = v_e(b^*)$ and $v_{\bar{e}}^* = v_{\bar{e}}(b^*)$. To see this, suppose $F(y_\alpha^*) \le v_e^*$ and $b_\alpha^* \ne e$. Then $F^{-\alpha}(y_\alpha^*) = F(y_\alpha^*) - 1$ and $v_e^{-\alpha}(b^*) = v_e^*$. So for all $\alpha \in U$, using (ii) of Definition 2.1(c),

(3.7) $$F(y_\alpha^*) \le v_e^* \Rightarrow F^{-\alpha}(y_\alpha^*) < v_e^{-\alpha}(b^*)$$
$$\Rightarrow \lambda_\alpha^*(q \cdot s > y_\alpha^*) = 1.$$

But now, for a set of s of λ_α^* measure 1, we have $q \cdot s > y_\alpha^*$ and (from (i) of Definition 2.1(c)), $s_e < s_{\bar{e}}$. For such s, $u_\alpha(s_e) > u_\alpha(s_{\bar{e}})$ so $\{e\} = \arg\max_{b_\alpha \in B_\alpha}$

$[u_\alpha(s_{b_\alpha})]$. Hence

(3.8) $$\{e\} = \arg\max_{b_\alpha \in B_\alpha} E_{\lambda_\alpha^*}[u_\alpha(s_{b_\alpha})].$$

So, from (3.2), it follows that $b_\alpha^* = e$, a contradiction. It follows that $F(y_\alpha^*) \leq v_e^* \Rightarrow b_\alpha^* = e$. The second inequality of (3.6) follows in analogous fashion. Now, we set

(3.9) $$x_L = \sup\{x \in X | F(x) \leq v_e^*\}$$
$$x_R = \inf\{x \in X | F(x) \leq v_{\bar{e}}^*\}$$

then, using (3.6), for all $\alpha \in U$,

(3.10) $$y_\alpha^* < x_L \Rightarrow F(y_\alpha^*) \leq v_{\bar{e}}^* \Rightarrow b_\alpha = e$$
$$y_\alpha^* > x_R \Rightarrow G(y_\alpha^*) \leq v_{\bar{e}}^* \Rightarrow b_\alpha = \bar{e}$$

So x_L and x_R satisfy the last inequalities in part (b) of the lemma. We must only show the first inequalities in (b). Using (3.10) together with (a) of the lemma, we get

(3.11) $$v_0^* + v_e^* \leq F_I(q \cdot s^*) + F_U(x_R)$$
$$v_0^* + v_{\bar{e}}^* \leq G_I(q \cdot s^*) + G_U(x_L)$$

where $v_0^* = v_0(b^*)$. (For example, the contrapositive of the second equation in (a) and the second equation in (3.10) yield the first equation of (3.11).) Adding and subtracting $F_I(x_R)$ to the first equation of (3.11), using $F_I(x_R) + F_U(x_R) = F(x_R)$, and rearranging, we get

(3.12) $$v_0^* + v_e^* - F(x_R) \leq F_I(q \cdot s^*) - F_I(x_R).$$

But, from the definition of x_R, and since G is a lower semi-continuous, monotone decreasing step function, we have $G(x_R) > v_{\bar{e}}^*$. So $G(x_R) \geq v_{\bar{e}}^* + 1$. Hence, $n - F(x_R) + H(x_R) \geq n - v_e^* - v_0^* + 1$, which implies

(3.13) $$v_0^* + v_e^* - F(x_R) \geq 1 - H(x_R) \geq 1 - T.$$

Now (3.12) together with (3.13) yields $1 - T < F_I(q \cdot s^*) - F_I(x_R)$ or

(3.14) $$F_I(x_R) \leq F_I(q \cdot s^*) + T - 1.$$

A similar argument yields

(3.15) $$G_I(x_L) \leq G_I(q \cdot s^*) + T - 1$$

which completes the proof of the lemma.

Q.E.D.

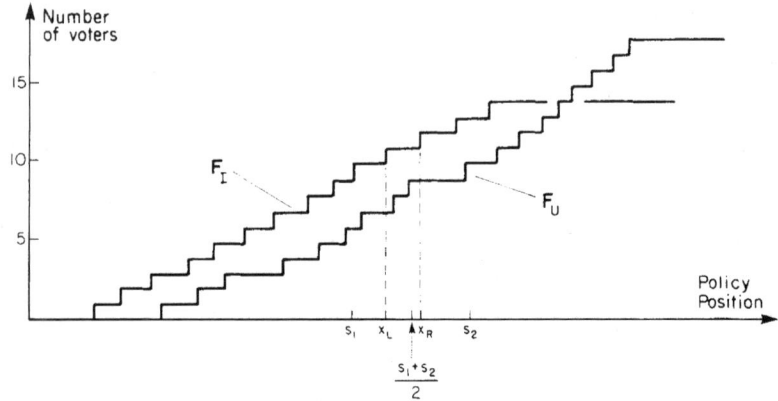

FIGURE 2. Illustration of Lemma 1, where $T = 1$. All voters with $y_\alpha \leq x_L$ vote for candidate 1. Those with $y_\alpha \geq x_R$ vote for candidate 2.

The above lemma establishes that in equilibrium, all voters (informed and uninformed voters alike) with the exception of a few uninformed voters with ideal points in the neighborhood of the candidate midpoint vote as if they had correct information about candidate positions. In the special case when $T = \sup_{x \in X} H(x) = 1$, we get that the equations in (b) of the lemma become

(3.16) $$F_I(x_L) \geq F_I(q \cdot s^*)$$
$$G_I(x_G) \geq G_I(q \cdot s^*).$$

Figure 2 illustrates the interpretation of this result.

Clearly, as the number of informed voters around $q \cdot s^*$ becomes denser and denser, the uninformed voters' voting will also become more and more informed.

It is of considerable interest to determine the limiting behavior of the model as the number of voters becomes large. To do this, we consider the infinite voter model. Here, we can formalize the above notion of the denseness of the informed voters through the invertibility of the cumulative density function of ideal points. We get the following analogue of Lemma 1.

LEMMA 2. *Assume Ω is infinite, $\mu(I) > 0$, F_I and F are invertible, and $\delta > 0$. Let $s^* \in \mathbf{S}$ satisfy $s_1^* \neq s_2^*$, and let $(b^*, \lambda^*) \in \mathbf{B} \times \Lambda$ be a voter equilibrium conditional on s^*. Then it must satisfy, for all $\alpha \in \Omega$,*

$$y_\alpha^* < q \cdot s^* \Rightarrow b_\alpha^* = e(s^*)$$
$$y_\alpha^* > q \cdot s^* \Rightarrow b_\alpha^* = \bar{e}(s^*).$$

Or, equivalently, for all $\alpha \in \Omega$, all $k \in K$,
$$u_\alpha(s_k^*) > u_\alpha(s_{\bar{k}}^*) \Rightarrow b_\alpha^* = k.$$

Proof. Invertibility of F implies $H_I(x) = H_U(x) = 0$ for all $x \in X$, which further implies that $\mu(\{a\}) = 0$ for all $\alpha \in \Omega$. Thus for all $\alpha \in \Omega$ and $b_\alpha' \in B_\alpha$, we have $j(b/b_\alpha') = j(b)$. So, using (2.5), and the fact $\delta > 0$, for all $b \in \mathbf{B}$, we have

(3.17)
$$\arg \max_{b_\alpha' \in B_\alpha} E_{\lambda_\alpha^*}[M_\alpha(s^*, b/b_\alpha')]$$
$$= \arg \max_{b_\alpha' \in B_\alpha} E_{\lambda_\alpha^*}[u_\alpha(s_{j(b)}) + \delta u_\alpha(s_{b_\alpha'})]$$
$$= \arg \max_{b_\alpha' \in B_\alpha} E_{\lambda_\alpha^*}[u_\alpha(s_{b_\alpha'})].$$

Hence, Definition 2.1(a) reads, for all $\alpha \in \Omega$,

(3.18)
$$b_\alpha^* \in \arg \max_{b_\alpha \in B_\alpha} E_{\lambda_\alpha^*}[u_\alpha(s_{b_\alpha})].$$

Using the same argument as in Lemma 1, it follows that if $\alpha \in I$, the result of Lemma 2 holds. Hence we need only show that it holds for $\alpha \in U$.

Since $\mu(\{a\}) = 0$ for all $\alpha \in \Omega$, we have $F^{-\alpha}(x) = F(x)$ and $v_k^{-\alpha}(b) = v_k(b)$ for all $x \in \mathbb{R}$, $k \in K$, $b \in \mathbf{B}$. Hence (ii) and (iii) of Definition 2.1(c) read, for all $\alpha \in U$,

(3.19)
$$v_e^* > F(y_\alpha^*) \Rightarrow \lambda_\alpha^*(q \cdot s > y_\alpha^*) = 1$$
$$v_{\bar{e}}^* > G(y_\alpha^*) \Rightarrow \lambda_\alpha^*(q \cdot s < y_\alpha^*) = 1,$$

where $v_e^* = v_e(s^*)$ and $v_{\bar{e}}^* = v_{\bar{e}}(s^*)$. But then, together with (i) of Definition 2.1(c), it follows that if $v_e^* > F(y_\alpha^*)$, there is a set of $s \in \mathbf{S}$, of λ_α^* measure 1, for which $q \cdot s > y_\alpha^*$ and for which $s_e < s_{\bar{e}}$. For any such s, it follows that $|s_e - y_\alpha^*| < |s_{\bar{e}} - y_\alpha^*| \Rightarrow u_\alpha(s_e) > u_\alpha(s_{\bar{e}})$, so $\{e\} = \arg\max_{k \in K_0} u_\alpha(s_k)$. It follows from (3.18) that $b_\alpha^* = e$. Using a similar argument when $v_{\bar{e}}^* > G(y_\alpha^*)$, we get that Eqs. (3.19) imply, for all $\alpha \in U$,

(3.20)
$$v_e^* > F(y_\alpha^*) \Rightarrow b_\alpha = e$$
$$v_{\bar{e}}^* > G(y_\alpha^*) \Rightarrow b_\alpha = \bar{e}.$$

Now, define $x_L = F^{-1}(v_e^*)$ and $x_R = G^{-1}(v_{\bar{e}}^*)$. Then $x_L \leq x_R$, since $x_L = F^{-1}(v_e^*) < F^{-1}(\mu(\Omega) - v_{\bar{e}}^*) = G^{-1}(v_{\bar{e}}^*) = x_R$. And, by monotonicity of F and G,

(3.21)
$$y_\alpha^* < x_L \Rightarrow F(y_\alpha^*) < F(x_L) = v_e^* \Rightarrow b_\alpha = e$$
$$y_\alpha^* > x_R \Rightarrow G(y_\alpha^*) < F(x_R) = v_{\bar{e}}^* \Rightarrow b_\alpha = \bar{e}.$$

Putting this together with the informed voters (for whom the result of the lemma holds), and using the fact that for all $x \in \mathbb{R}$, $H_I(x) = H_U(x) = 0$, we get

(3.22)
$$v_e^* \geq F_I(q \cdot s^*) + F_U(x_L)$$
$$v_{\bar{e}}^* \geq G_I(q \cdot s^*) + G_U(x_R).$$

Adding and subtracting $F_I(x_L)$ and $G_I(x_R)$, respectively, to each of these equations, as in the proof of Lemma 1, we get, in the first equation, $F_I(q \cdot s^*) - F_I(x_L) < v_e^* - F(x_L) = 0$ or

(3.23) $$F_I(x_L) \geq F_I(q \cdot s^*).$$

And the second yields

(3.24) $$G_I(x_R) \geq G_I(q \cdot s^*).$$

From the monotonicity and invertibility of F_I and G_I, it follows that $x_R \leq q \cdot s^* \leq x_L$. But we have already shown $x_L \leq x_R$. So $x_L = x_R = q \cdot s^*$. Together with (3.21), this yields the desired result.

Q.E.D.

Thus, the above lemmata show that equilibrium behavior by all voters implies that the aggregate voting behavior of the voters extracts all the relevant information about the candidate positions. As we see, for any choice of strategies by the candidates, in equilibrium, *all voters vote as if they had perfect information*, regardless of whether they are informed or uninformed. It should be noted that in equilibrium the uninformed voters still do not know, or even have any common probability distribution of, the positions of the candidates. However, they each have enough probabilistic information about the location of the midpoint between s_1 and s_2 to allow them to make correct voting decisions. So the equilibrium extracts correct voting decisions without disseminating fully the information on candidate positions.

We next investigate the characteristics of full equilibria to the game. Here, for simplicity, we look only at the infinite voter case, where F_I and F are invertible.

In addition to requiring the true cdf's to be invertible, we also require the cdf's of the candidate beliefs to be invertible. This we do by setting $\mathbf{Y} = \mathbf{Y}' = \{y \in \mathbf{Y}^0 | F(x|y) \text{ is invertible}\}$. Similar theorems can be proven for finite Ω, but they are messier, because of the nonuniqueness of admissible strategies for uninformed voters with ideal points near the candidate midpoint. We do not present results for finite voters here, since (via Lemma I), in the limiting case, as n gets large, they become equivalent to the infinite voter results presented here.

THEOREM 1. *There exists a full equilibrium to the game defined by (2.5)–(2.6). Further, if $\mu(I) > 0$, F_I and F are invertible, $\mathbf{Y} = \mathbf{Y}'$, and $\delta > 0$, any equilibrium $((s^*, \gamma^*), (b^*, \lambda^*)) \in \mathbf{S} \times \mathbf{\Gamma} \times \mathbf{B} \times \mathbf{\Lambda}$ must satisfy $s_1^* = s_2^*$.*

Proof. To show existence, we set $s_1^* = s_2^* = F^{-1}(t)$, where $t = \mu(\Omega)/2$. Let $\lambda_\alpha^*\{s^*\} = 1$ for all $\alpha \in \Omega$ and $\gamma_k^*(\{y^*\}) = 1$ for all $k \in K$. It is easily verified that this is a full equilibrium for any choice of b^*. (In particular, we could choose $b_\alpha^* = 0$ for all α.)

Now assume $((s^*, \gamma^*), (b^*, \lambda^*))$ is a full equilibrium, and $s_1^* \neq s_2^*$. Pick $k \in K$ with $s_k^* < s_{\bar{k}}^*$. I.e., $e = e(s^*) = k$ and $\bar{e} = \bar{e}(s^*) = \bar{k}$. Then by Lemma 2, we have

(3.25)
$$y_\alpha^* < q \cdot s^* \Rightarrow b_\alpha^* = k$$
$$y_\alpha^* > q \cdot s^* \Rightarrow b_\alpha^* = \bar{k}.$$

So, since $H(x) = 0$ for all x, we have $v_0^* = 0$, $v_k^* = F(q \cdot s^*)$, and $v_{\bar{k}}^* = G(q \cdot s^*)$. Hence $v_k^* + v_{\bar{k}}^* = \mu(\Omega)$. So, writing $t = \mu(\Omega)/2$, either $v_k^* \leq t$ or $v_{\bar{k}}^* \leq t$. Assume, w.l.o.g., that $v_k^* \leq t$.

Now, for arbitrary $s \in \mathbf{S}$, $y \in \mathbf{Y}$,

(3.26)
$$\begin{aligned} M_k(s, \hat{b}(s,y)) &= 1 && \text{if } v_k(\hat{b}(s,y)) > v_{\bar{k}}(\hat{b}(s,y)), \\ &= -1 && \text{if } v_k(\hat{b}(s,y)) < v_{\bar{k}}(\hat{b}(s,y)), \\ &= 0 && \text{otherwise.} \end{aligned}$$

But, using the definitions of $\hat{b}$ and v_k, and manipulating the above expressions, we can rewrite

(3.27)
$$\begin{aligned} M_k(s, \hat{b}(s,y)) &= 1 && \text{if } |s_k - m(y)| < |s_{\bar{k}} - m(y)|, \\ &= -1 && \text{if } |s_k - m(y)| > |s_{\bar{k}} - m(y)|, \\ &= 0 && \text{otherwise,} \end{aligned}$$

where $m(y) \in \mathbb{R}$ is chosen to satisfy $F(m(y)|y) = t$. I.e., $m(y)$ is the median of the y_α. (Since $F(x|y)$ is invertible, it exists and is unique.) It follows that

$$(3.28) \quad \begin{aligned} E_{\gamma_k^*}[M_k(s,\hat{b}(s,y))] &= \gamma_k^*(|s_k - m(y)| < |s_{\bar{k}} - m(y)|) \\ &\quad -\gamma_k^*|s_k - m(y)| > |s_{\bar{k}} - m(y)|. \end{aligned}$$

Now, we define m_k^* to be a median of the $m(y)$s with respect to γ_k^*. I.e. $\gamma_k^*(m(y) \leq m_k^*) \geq \frac{1}{2}$ and $\gamma_k^*(m(y) \geq m_k^*) \geq \frac{1}{2}$. Then, for $s_k = m_k^*$, we have $E_{\gamma_k^*}[M_k(s^*/s_k, \hat{b}(s^*/s_k, y))] \geq \frac{1}{2} - \frac{1}{2} = 0$. So it follows from Definition 2.2(a) that we must have

$$(3.29) \quad E_{\gamma_k^*}[M_k(s^*, \hat{b}(s^*, y))] \geq 0.$$

But invertibility of $F(\cdot|y)$ implies that $H(q \cdot s^*|y) = 0$ for all y. Using this together with $v_0^* = 0$, Definition 2.2(b) becomes $\gamma_k^*(F(q \cdot s^*|y) = v_k^*) = 1$. Since $v_k^* \leq t$, and $F(\cdot|y)$ is monotonic for all y, we must have $\gamma_k^*(m(y) \geq q \cdot s^*) = 1$. Now if $\gamma_k^*(m(y) \geq q \cdot s^*) > 0$, we have from (3.28), $E_{\gamma_k^*}[M_k(s^*, \hat{b}(s^*, y))] < 0$, a contradiction to (3.29). Hence $\gamma_k^*(m(y) \geq q \cdot s^*) = 1$. But then, for $s_k = q \cdot s^*$, we have from (3.28) that $E_{\gamma_k^*}[M(s^*/s_k, \hat{b}(s^*/s_k, y))] = 1$, while $E_{\gamma_k^*}[M_k(s^*, \hat{b}(s^*, y))] = 0$. But this is a contradiction to Definition 2.2(a). Hence, $s_1 \neq s_2$ leads to a contradiction so we must have $s_1 = s_2$, which proves the theorem.

Q.E.D.

Unfortunately it happens that the full equilibria of the game (2.5)–(2.6) cannot be narrowed down any further than the set of candidate strategies defined by Theorem 1. In fact, it happens that if voters are in equilibrium, then all candidate profiles, (s^*, y^*), where $s_1^* = s_2^*$ and $\gamma_1^*(F(q \cdot s^*|y) = t) = \gamma_2^*(F(q \cdot s^*|y) = t) = 1$ yield full equilibria under the definition we have given. However, it seems apparent that if $s_1^* = s_2^* \neq x^*$, where x^* is the median of the true distribution of voter ideal points, then the equilibrium is somewhat unstable. Under our definition, this is formally an equilibrium by virtue of the fact that both candidates maintain the same incorrect beliefs about the median. Since they both agree on their incorrect beliefs, they both adopt the same position as their strategy. There is no endorsement, and voters vote randomly between them, yielding an outcome which is consistent with the candidates' incorrect beliefs. However, this equilibrium is unstable in the sense that if either candidate makes a slight error in choice strategy, then the beliefs of both candidates will be subjected to reality testing, and will be found to be inconsistent with the observed voting behavior. These considerations lead us to define a somewhat stronger notion of equilibrium. This stronger version requires that beliefs must be consistent not only with the information that is generated when candidates adopt their equilibrium strategies, but also with the information that is generated when they make small errors.

DEFINITION 3.1. Let $((s^*, \gamma^*), (b^*, \lambda^*)) \in \mathbf{S} \times \mathbf{\Gamma} \times \mathbf{B} \times \mathbf{\Lambda}$ be a full equilibrium to the game (2.5)–(2.6). Then it is said to be an *informationally stable equilibrium* iff there is a neighborhood $N(s^*)$ of s^*, such that whenever $s' \in N(s^*)$, and (b', λ') is a voter equilibrium conditional on s', then for each $k \in K$, if $e(s') \in K$,

$$\gamma_k^*(F(q \cdot s'|y) \geq v_e') = 1$$

and

$$\gamma_k^*(F(q \cdot s'|y) \geq v_{\bar{e}}') = 1,$$

where $e = e(s')$, $e = \bar{e}(s')$, and $v_e' = v_e(s')$, $v_{\bar{e}}' = v_{\bar{e}}(s')$.

THEOREM 2. *There exists an informationally stable equilibrium to the game defined by (2.5)–(2.6). Further, if $\mu(I) > 0$, F_I and F are invertible, $\mathbf{Y} = \mathbf{Y}'$, and $\delta > 0$, any equilibrium $((s^*, \gamma^*), (b^*, \lambda^*)) \in \mathbf{S} \times \mathbf{\Gamma} \times \mathbf{B} \times \mathbf{\Lambda}$ must satisfy $s_1^* = s_2^* = F^{-1}(t)$, where $t = \mu(\Omega)/2$.*

Proof. Existence follows from the same example as in Theorem 1. Assume the second part of the theorem is false. From Theorem 1, we must have $s_1^* = s_2^*$. Assume w.l.o.g., that $s_1^* = s_2^* < F^{-1}(t)$. Pick $N(s^*)$ as in Definition 3.1, and pick $s' \in N(s^*)$ such that $s_1' < s_2'$ and such that $q \cdot s' = q \cdot s^*$. From Lemma 2, it follows that $v_1' = F(q \cdot s') = F(q \cdot s^*) < t$, $v_2' = G(q \cdot s') = G(q \cdot s^*) > t$, and $v_0' = 0$. From Definition 3.1 the invertibility of $F(\cdot|y)$ and $v_0' = 0$, it follows that $\gamma_1^*(F(q \cdot s'|y) \geq v_1') = 1$. So $\gamma_1^*(m(y) > q \cdot s^*) = 1$, where $m(y)$ is defined, as in Theorem 1, to be the median of the y_α. But now, by an argument similar to that in the previous theorem, this leads to a contradiction to (3.29). Hence, we must have $s_1^* = s_2^* = F^{-1}(t)$.

Q.E.D.

In summary, we have shown that the only informationally stable equilibria involve both candidates converging to the true median of the *entire electorate*. If the candidates have converged exactly to the equilibrium, then, of course, there is no useful endorsement or poll information generated for the voters. They must vote arbitrarily and the outcome is also arbitrary. If either of the candidates deviates at all from the equilibrium strategy, then the endorsement and poll information *will* be useful, and, in light of Lemma 1, the equilibrium behavior of the voters will extract all information. The outcome will be the same as the full information outcome, and all voters — informed and uninformed — will end up voting correctly.

4. Additional Results: Dynamics, Speed of Convergence, Bandwagons, and Manipulability

The previous section proves the existence of an equilibrium which extracts all relevant information. However, there is no guarantee that this equilibrium will ever be located. Here we concentrate on voter equilibria, when Ω is infinite, and we present a dynamic process by which such equilibria might be attained. The process corresponds to a series of successive polls. Candidate positions are fixed, and at each stage, all voters act rationally on the basis of information generated by the previous poll. We show that *regardless* of the initial starting behavior of the uninformed voters, this process converges to the full information voter equilibrium. The convergence properties of this process resemble in some respects a "bandwagon effect." I.e., the vote share for one candidate increases monotonically, at the expense of the other candidate. Further, we obtain some results bearing on the speed of convergence. While any positive density of informed voters at the candidate midpoint guarantees eventual convergence, the speed of this convergence depends on the ratio of the density of informed and uninformed voters at that point. Finally, although we do not prove this formally, it appears that the above process, as well as the equilibrium associated with it is nonmanipulable. I.e., given our restrictions on preferences, no voter can gain by adopting strategies different from those prescribed in the above dynamic. Similarly, and more obviously, in equilibrium no one can gain by misrepresenting his preferences.

DEFINITION 4.1. Fix $s^* \in \mathbf{S}$ and $(b^0, \lambda^0) \in \mathbf{B} \times \mathbf{\Lambda}$. We then define, inductively on t, a sequence of profiles $(b', \lambda') \in \mathbf{B} \times \mathbf{\Lambda}$ satisfying:

(a) $\forall \alpha \in \Omega, b_\alpha^t \in \arg\max_{b_\alpha \in B_\alpha} E_{\lambda_\alpha^{t-1}}[u_\alpha(s_{b_\alpha})]$
(b) $\forall \alpha \in I, \lambda_\alpha^t(\{s^*\}) = 1$
(c) $\forall \alpha \in U,$
  (i) $\lambda_\alpha^t(s_e < s_{\bar{e}}) = 1$
  (ii) $v_e^{t-1} > F(y_\alpha^*) \Rightarrow \lambda_\alpha^t(q \cdot s > y_\alpha^*) = 1$
  (iii) $v_{\bar{e}}^{t-1} > G(y_\alpha^*) \Rightarrow \lambda_\alpha^t(q \cdot s < y_\alpha^*) = 1,$

where $e = e(s^*)$, and $\bar{e} = \bar{e}(s^*)$, $v_e^{t-1} = v_e(b^{t-1})$, $v_{\bar{e}}^{t-1} = v_{\bar{e}}(b^{t-1})$.

Thus, each profile satisfies the conditions required in Definition 2.1 for a voter equilibrium with respect to the data generated from the previous profile. I.e., b^t is the best ballot conditional on the beliefs λ^{t-1}, and λ^t are beliefs consistent with the data generated by the ballot b^{t-1}. For the case of Ω infinite, with F invertible, the conditions in Definition 2.1 become those given above.

Using an argument similar to that in Lemma 2, it is easily shown that if F is invertible, the ballots b^t in the above process satisfy:

(4.1) $$\text{for } \alpha \in I, b_\alpha^t = e \quad \text{if } y_\alpha^* < x^*$$
$$= \bar{e} \quad \text{if } y_\alpha^* > x^*;$$

(4.2) $$\text{for } \alpha \in U, b_\alpha^t = e \quad \text{if } y_\alpha^* < x^{t-1}$$
$$= \bar{e} \quad \text{if } y_\alpha^* > x^{t-1},$$

where

(4.3) $$x^* = q \cdot s^* = \frac{s_1 + s_2}{2}$$

and, for $0 \leq t$,

(4.4) $$x^t = F^{-1}(v_e^t).$$

It follows that the only voters voting incorrectly for $t \geq 1$ are the uninformed voters with ideal points in the interval between x^t and x^*. The measure of these voters is precisely $|v_e^t - v_e^*|$, where $v_e^* = F(q \cdot s^*) = F(x^*)$. We can now prove

THEOREM 3. *If Ω is infinite, with $\mu(I) > 0$, with F, F_I, and F_U invertible, and $\delta > 0$, then the process defined by Definition (4.1) converges to a voter equilibrium in the sense that $v_e^t \to v_e^*$, $v_{\bar{e}}^t \to v_{\bar{e}}^*$, and $x^t \to x^*$. The asymptotic speed of convergence of v_e^t to v_e^* is $f_U(x^*)/f(x^*)$, where f_U and f are the pdf's of F_U and F, respectively.*

Proof. Since F is monotone increasing and invertible, it is continuous, so all three convergence results follow if we prove $v_e^t \to v_e^*$. We have from (4.1) and (4.2)

(4.5) $$v_e^t = F_I(x^*) + F_U(x^{t-1})$$
$$= F_I(x^*) - F_I(x^{t-1}) + F_I(x^{t-1}) + F_U(x^{t-1})$$
$$= [F_I(x^*) - F_I(x^{t-1})] + F(x^{t-1}).$$

But since $v_e^{t-1} = F(x^{t-1})$,

(4.6) $$v_e^* - v_e^t = F_I(x^*) - F_I(x^{t-1}).$$

In a similar fashion, adding and subtracting $F_U(x^*)$ to Eq. (4.5), we get

(4.7) $$v_e^* - v_e^{t-1} = F_U(x^*) - F_U(x^{t-1}).$$

Adding (4.6) and (4.7), we get the identity

(4.8) $$v_e^* - v_e^{t-1} = F(x^*) - F(x^{t-1}).$$

Further, by monotonicity of F, F_I, and F_U, it follows that $\left(v_e^* - v_e^{t-1}\right)$ has the same sign as $x^* - x^{t-1}$, which has the same sign as the righthand side of Eqs. (4.6)–(4.8). But then, it follows that we can write v_e^t as the following convex combination of v_e^{t-1} and v_e^*

(4.9) $$v_e^t = r_1 v_e^{t-1} + r_2 v_e^*,$$

where

(4.10) $$r_1 = \frac{F_U(x^{t-1}) - F_U(x^*)}{v_e^{t-1} - v_e^*} \quad \text{and} \quad r_2 = \frac{F_I(x^{t-1}) - F_I(x^*)}{v_e^{t-1} - v_e^*}.$$

It is easily verified that $1 > r_i > 0$ for $v_e^{t-1} \neq v_e^*$ and $r_1 + r_2 = 1$. Thus, it follows that the sequence $\{v_e^t\}_{t=0}^{\infty}$ is either a monotone increasing or monotone decreasing sequence, converging to v_e^*.

To address the speed of convergence, we note that if $\rho_t = |v_e^t + v_e^*|$, then, for large t

(4.11) $$\frac{\rho_t}{\rho_{t-1}} = \frac{F_U(x^*) - F_U(x^{t-1})}{F(x^*) - F(x^{t-1})}$$
$$= \frac{F_U(x^*) - F_U(x^{t-1})}{x^* - x^{t-1}} \bigg/ \frac{F(x^*) - F(x^{t-1})}{x^* - x^{t-1}} \approx \frac{f_U(x^*)}{f(x^*)}$$

Q.E.D.

To illustrate the above dynamic model, we give an example. Figure 3 portrays the cumulative distribution of ideal points for the uninformed, informed, and all voters (denoted F_U, F_I, and F, respectively). The corresponding density functions for the uninformed, informed, and all voters are illustrated in the lower half of the figure and are denoted f_U, f_I, and f. Now suppose that candidates 1 and 2 adopt $s^* = (s_1^*, s_2^*)$, as shown in Fig. 3. An initial poll of voters might reveal a random response by uninformed voters (hence they split 50–50 between candidates 1 and 2) while the informed voters vote correctly, and split 30–70, yielding an overall straw vote of 0.40 for candidate 1, 0.60 for candidate 2. We have assumed that uninformed voters know where they are on the issue relative to the entire electorate, and that each uninformed voter assumes he is the only uninformed voter. Hence, voters can infer where the midpoint between the candidates is and hence how they ought to vote. Specifically, using the poll data together with the endorsement information that candidate 1 is to the left of candidate 2, uninformed voters can infer that the candidate midpoint is at $x^0 = F^{-1}(v_1^0)$. So everyone to the left of the point x^0 ought to vote for candidate 1 and everyone to the right ought to vote for candidate 2. That is, in accordance with (4.2) and (4.4), uninformed voters who are below the 40th percentile on the overall distribution vote for candidate 1, the remaining vote for candidate 2. This produces a second poll result of 51% for candidate 1, 49% for candidate 2. Repeating this for a third poll yields a 57.5%–42.5% division. Continuing in this fashion, the polls converge to a voter equilibrium, in which the vote is the correct vote of 63% for candidate 1, 37% for candidate 2. As was shown formally in Section 3, in equilibrium, *all voters vote as if they had perfect information.*

Finally, we say a few words about manipulability of the above dynamic process. Although we do not formally prove it here, it should be evident that given his state of information at time t, it will never be to any voter's advantage to vote differently than it is assumed he votes in the above dynamic process. The reason for this is because of the "multiplier effect" which drives the above process. Namely, uninformed voters cue off of the total vote, and the larger the vote for a given candidate, the greater is the number of uninformed voters who will infer it is in their interest to vote for that candidate (since all uninformed voters to the left of $x^{t-1} = F^{-1}(v_e^{t-1})$ vote for e and those to the right vote for $\bar{e}$). Thus, given his state of information at time t, in order to encourage other voters to vote for the candidate he believes he prefers, a voter should always vote his truthful preferences, as we assume he does.

5. Test of the Model

This section describes two experiments that are designed to test the model developed above. We wish to test both the hypothesis that uninformed voters use poll information to inform their vote and the hypothesis that candidates converge to positions that reflect the preferences of the uninformed as well as of the informed voters. Thus, it is necessary to design an experiment that allows candidates to adjust their policy positions, but at the same time keeps candidate positions stationary enough to allow voters to collect useful information on candidate positions through the poll results.

The experiments we conducted each had between forty and fifty subjects. The subjects consisted of students at California Institute of Technology (Experiment 1) and Carnegie Mellon University (Experiment 2). In each experiment, two of

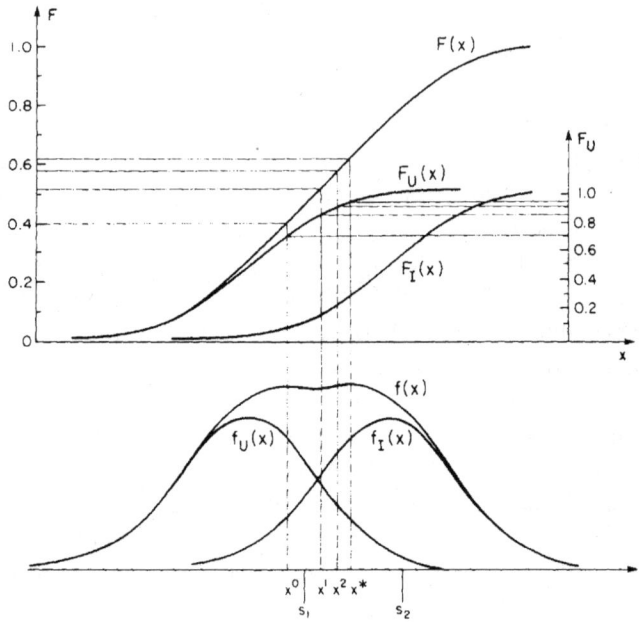

FIGURE 3. Example of successive polls

the subjects played the part of candidates, labeled candidate A and B for these experiments, while the rest of the subjects were voters. Each experiment consists of a sequence of periods, or elections. (See Fig. 4 for a schematic diagram of the sequence of events.) In each period, the two candidates first adopt policy positions in a one-dimensional policy space. Candidate positions are fixed for the duration of the period, after which the candidates are able to adopt new positions.

Once the candidates have selected positions, a sequence of two polls is taken, followed by a final election. Each poll is like a Gallup poll, in that voters are asked how they would vote if the election were held now. There are two classes of

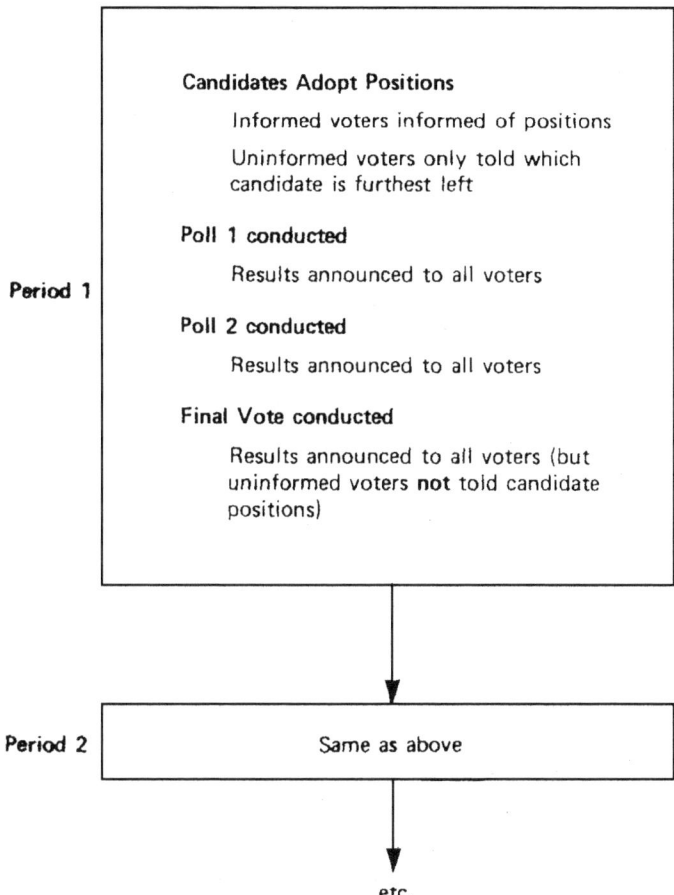

FIGURE 4. Sequence of events for experiments 1 and 2. Note: All polls and votes are by secret ballot.

voters: informed and uninformed, who are selectively provided with information about the candidate positions. The informed voters are told the positions of both candidates at the beginning of each period. The uninformed voters, on the other hand, are never told the position of the candidates. The uninformed voters are only told which candidate position is furthest to the left. All voters, however, are informed of the poll results, and hence, if they wish, can attempt to infer candidate positions on the basis of these results.

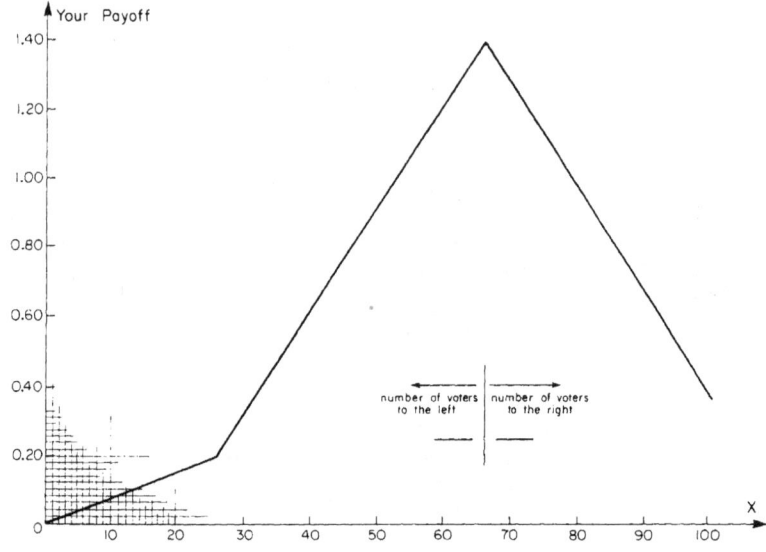

FIGURE 5. Sample payoff function

Voters are paid for their participation in each period on the basis of the position of the winning candidate and their individual payoff functions. A sample payoff function for a typical voter is given in Fig. 5. The payoff function determines the amount the voter will be paid if the winning candidate adopts a given position. For example, in this sample, if the winning candidate adopted the position 70, the voter would earn $1.28 in that period. All voters have single peaked payoff functions, but the location of the individual ideal points differs for different voters. Although voters do not know the distribution of voter ideal points, they do know where their own ideal point is in relation to those of the rest of the electorate. As seen in the sample of Fig. 5, each voter is informed about how many voters have ideal points to the left and to the right of his.

Although the experiment consists of a number of periods, voter preferences remain fixed across periods, as does the partition of informed and uninformed voters. Voters know only their own ideal points, not those of any other voters, and candidates do not have any information about voter ideal points. Further, the uninformed voters never learn anything about the policy position adopted by either candidate in a given period until the termination of the entire experiment. Thus, there is no possibility for uninformed voters to make inferences about candidate

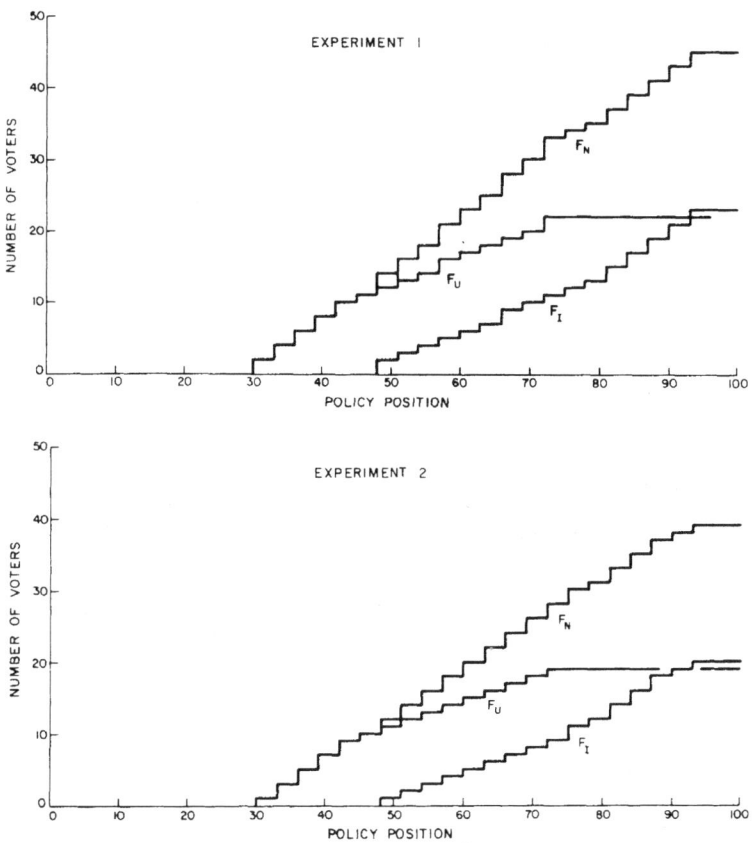

FIGURE 6. Cumulative distributions of voter ideal points, experiments 1 and 2

positions from the historical record of candidate positions in previous periods. A complete listing of the instructions can be found in McKelvey and Ordeshook [14]. They are similar to those used in two-dimensional experiments published elsewhere (McKelvey and Ordeshook [15]).

The distribution of ideal points of the informed and uninformed voters for our two experiments is given in Fig. 6. Notice that in each experiment there are approximately equal numbers of informed and uninformed voters, with the distribution of the uninformed voters being stochastically dominated by that of the informed voters. The median informed voter is at 75, the median uninformed voter is at 45–48, and the overall median is at 60.

Our model makes predictions about the candidate behavior as well as about voter choice. First, with regard to voters, we would expect, in each period, the poll results to converge to the perfect information poll result. In the first poll, the informed voters should vote correctly, with the uninformed being indifferent or voting arbitrarily. In the second poll and in the final vote, uninformed voters should sort themselves into the appropriate category, by using information available from the previous polls. If no voters err, then as proven in the previous section, this process should converge to the situation where uninformed voters vote as if they had complete information.

Table 1 summarizes the results of the final vote in each experiment, showing the number of voters making errors.

TABLE 1. Summary of Errors in Final Vote

	Expt 1	Expt 2	All
Informed voters			
Correct choice	160 (99.4)	149 (94.9)	309 (97.2)
Error	1 (0.6)	8 (5.1)	9 (2.8)
Total	161	157	318
Uninformed voters			
Correct choice	121 (75.2)	131 (83.4)	252 (79.2)
Error	40 (24.8)	26 (16.6)	66 (20.8)
Total	161	157	318

Note: Errors based on assumption of full information.

An "error" is simply a difference from the behavior the subject would exhibit if he had full information. We see that the informed voters virtually always vote correctly. In Experiment 1 there is only one error in the entire experiment (for the final votes), while for Experiment 2, there are 8 errors, or an average of one per period. Of all the votes cast by the informed voters in the final period, over 97% are cast correctly. The error rate for the uninformed voters is substantially higher than that for the informed voters, but still, across both experiments, approximately 80% of the votes cast by the uninformed voters are cast correctly.

TABLE 2. Summary of Individual Error Levels

	Expt 1	Expt 2	All
Second poll			
Correct choice	88 (71.5)	88 (68.8)	176 (70.1)
Abstain	14 (11.4)	29 (22.7)	43 (17.1)
Error	21 (17.1)	11 (8.6)	32 (12.8)
Total	123	128	251
Final poll			
Correct choice	119 (83.2)	118 (86.8)	237 (84.9)
Error	24 (16.8)	18 (13.2)	42 (15.1)
Total	143	136	279

Note: Errors based on failure of Eq. (2.18).

It is important to note that the above computation of the error rate is actually an overestimate of the *individual level* errors. Since uninformed voters can only make inferences about candidate positions on the basis of poll data, it follows that errors made by one voter can affect the decisions made by other voters. Under the above computation, a voter may be making a completely rational vote based on the information he observes, but if this information is itself incorrect, he will not necessarily vote as if he had complete information. We wish, therefore, to determine the proportion of voters who make correct voting decisions *based on the information available* to them. We assume, then, that uninformed voters use the decision rule in Eq. (3.6) modified for a dynamic setting — as described in Section 4. Thus, we assume that for $\alpha \in U$, $t = 2, 3$

(5.1)
$$y_\alpha^* \leq F^{-1}(v_e^{t-1}) \Rightarrow b_\alpha^t = e$$
$$y_\alpha^* \geq G^{-1}(v_{\bar{e}}^{t-1}) \Rightarrow b_\alpha^t = \bar{e},$$

where $v_k^t = v_k(b^t)$ is the vote for candidate k in poll t. We look only at those voters who have a unique choice given the information available to them. Table 2 compiles this data for the second poll and final vote in all periods of Experiments 1 and 2. We see that the error rate for uninformed voters averages around 15% across both experiments for both the final vote and the second poll. Finally, a

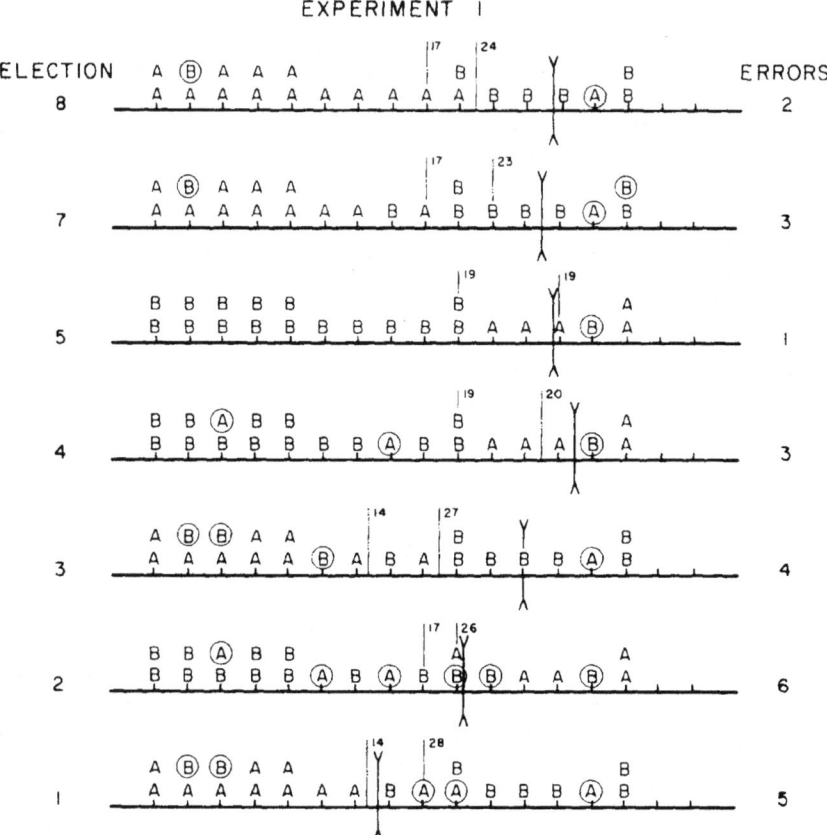

FIGURE 7. Individual votes of uninformed voters (final vote). Key: The vote of each voter is listed above his ideal point. Circled votes denote errors. For each experiment, an inverted arrow depicts the true candidate midpoint. The two vertical lines represent $F^{-1}(v_e^2)$ and $G^{-1}(v_{\bar{e}}^2)$. The numbers next to these lines are v_e^2 and $v_{\bar{e}}^2$: the votes for the left and right candidate in round 2.

glance at Fig. 7 illustrates that most of the errors which do occur can be attributed to two or three voters in each experiment.

Our second hypothesis concerns candidate behavior. Figure 8 shows the sequence of candidate positions in each experiment. We see that in both experiments, the candidates converge quickly to a point between 63 and 65. The point

EXPERIMENT 2

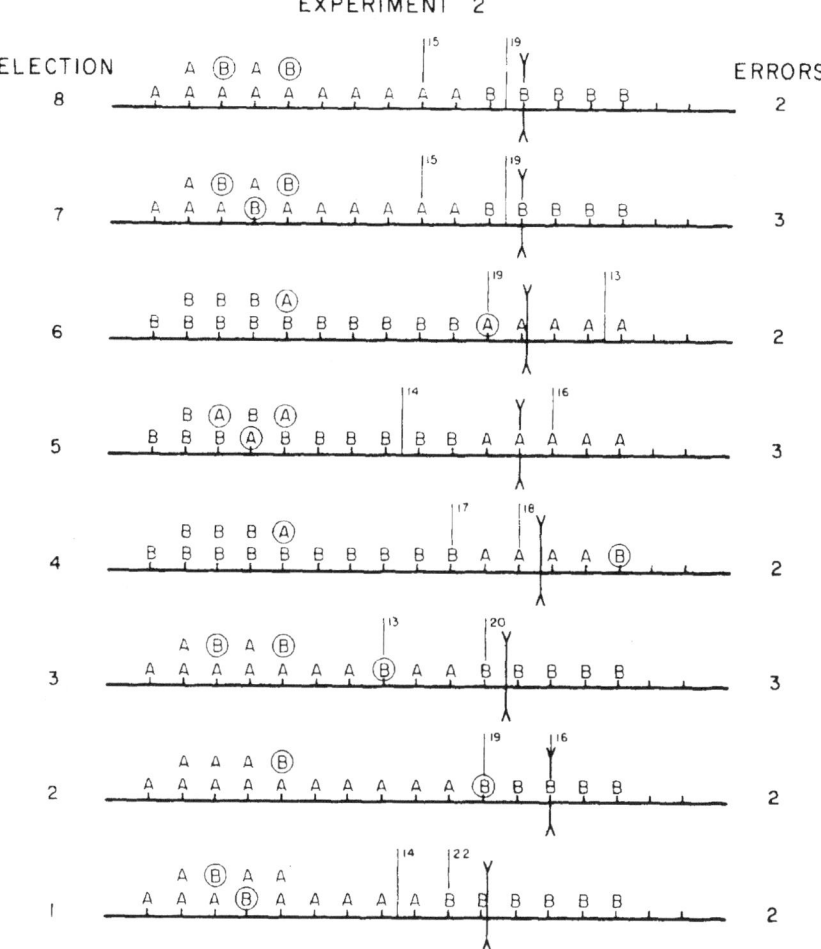

FIGURE 7. *Continued*

to which they converge lies between the median of the informed voters and that of the total electorate, but they are closer to the total median. This is consistent with what we should anticipate given the individual voting behavior of the uninformed voters. The fact that some proportion (about $\frac{1}{3}$) of the uninformed voters are not utilizing the poll information causes the effective equilibrium for the candidates to slide up by several voters from the total median.

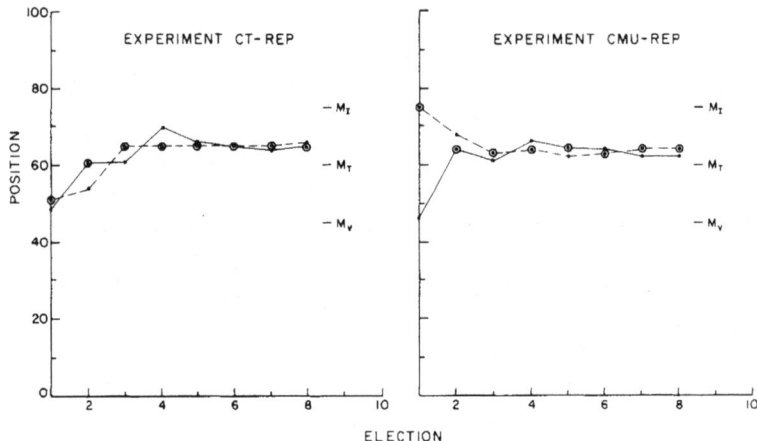

FIGURE 8. Candidate behavior positions in experiments 1 and 2. Key: —— candidate A; - - - - candidate B; circle — winning candidate.

Overall, this experiment provides qualified support for the model. We do not have full support for either hypothesis. Rather about $\frac{2}{3}$ of the uninformed voters appear to end up voting as if they had perfect information, and the position to which the candidates converge is correspondingly to a point about $\frac{2}{3}$ of the distance from the informed median to the total median.

References

[1] G. Almond and S. Verba, *The Civic Culture*, Princeton Univ. Press, Princeton, N.J., 1963.

[2] B. R. Berelson, P. F. Lazarsfeld, and W. N. McPhee, *Voting*, Univ. of Chicago Press, Chicago, 1954.

[3] P. E. Converse, Public opinion and voting behavior, in *Handbook of Political Science* (F. Greenstein and N. Polsby, Eds.), Addison-Wesley, Reading, Mass., 1975.

[4] O. A. Davis and M. J. Hinich, On the power and importance of the mean preference in a mathematical model of democratic choice, *Public Choice* (1968), 59–72.

[5] S. Grossman, Further results on the informational efficiency of competitive stock markets, *J. Econ. Theory* 18 (1978), 81–101.

[6] S. Grossman and J. E. Stiglitz, On the impossibility of informationally efficient markets, *Amer. Econ. Rev.* 70 (1980), 393–408.

[7] S. J. Grossman, An introduction to the theory of rational expectations under asymmetric information, *Rev. Econ. Stud.* 48 (1981), 541–559.

[8] J. C. Harsanyi, Games with incomplete information played by "Bayesian" players, 1–111, *Manage. Sci.* 14 (1968), 159–182, 320–334, 486–502.

[9] D. R. Kinder and D. O. Sears, Political psychology, in *The Handbook of Political Psychology* (G. Lindzey and E. Aronson, Eds.), 1985.

[10] G. H. Kramer, A dynamical model of political equilibrium, *J. Econ. Theory* 16 (1977), 310–334.

[11] D. M. Kreps, A note on fulfilled expectations equilibria, *J. Econ. Theory* 14 (1977), 32–43.

[12] R. E. Lucas, Expectations and the neutrality of money, *J. Econ. Theory* 4 (1972), 103–104.

[13] R. D. McKelvey, P. C. Ordeshook, and M. Winer, The competitive solution for N-person games without transferable utility, with an application to committee games, *Amer. Polit. Sci. Rev.* (June 1978), 599–615. Chapter 10 of this book.

[14] R. D. McKelvey and P. C. Ordeshook, "Elections with Limited Information: A Fulfilled Expectations Model Using Contemporaneous Poll and Endorsement Data as Information Sources," Social Science Working Paper No. 434, California Institute of Technology, 1983.

[15] R. D. McKelvey and P. C. Ordeshook, Rational expectations in elections: Some experimental results based on a multidimensional model, *Public Choice* 44 (1984), 61–102.

[16] R. D. McKelvey and P. C. Ordeshook, Sequential elections with limited information, *Amer. J. Polit. Sci.* (1985), in press.

[17] R. D. McKelvey and P. C. Ordeshook, "Elections with Limited Information: A Multidimensional Model," Social Science Working Paper No. 529, California Institute of Technology, 1984.

[18] J. F. Muth, Rational expectations and the theory of price movements, *Econometrica* 29 (1961), 315–335.

[19] C. R. Plott, "A Comparative Analysis of Direct Democracy, Two Candidate Elections, and Three Candidate Elections in an Experimental Environment," Social Science Working Paper No. 457, California Institute of Technology, 1982.

[20] C. R. Plott and S. Sunder, Efficiency of experimental security markets with insider information. An application of rational expectations models, *J. Polit. Econ.* 90 (1982), 663–698.

[21] R. Radner, Existence of equilibrium in plans, prices, and price expectations in a sequence of markets, *Econometrica* 40 (1972), 289–303.

[22] R. Radner, Rational expectations equilibrium: Generic existence and the information revealed by price? *Econometrica* 47 (1979), 655–678.

[23] W. H. Riker and P. C. Ordeshook, *An Introduction to Positive Political Theory*, Prentice-Hall, Englewood Cliffs, N.J., 1973.

[24] K. A. Shepsle, Institutional arrangements and equilibrium in multidimensional voting models, *Amer. J. Polit. Sci.*, February (1979).

CHAPTER 16

Centipede Game Experiments

ALAN GERBER

There has been explosive growth in the use of laboratory experimentation in political science and economics. McKelvey and Palfrey (1992 (Chapter 18 of this book)) illustrates the attraction of this style of research. Laboratory experiments can be designed to address specific theoretical issues and are relatively easy to perform. By producing evidence of where theories succeed and fail, experiments accelerate and direct the development of alternative models. McKelvey and Palfrey's quantal response equilibrium (QRE) model, an important theoretical innovation, was encouraged in part by a desire to provide a more accurate and theoretically satisfying account of the data produced by the centipede game experiment (McKelvey and Palfrey 1998, 11). Here, I focus more narrowly on experimental investigations of the centipede game.

I begin with a brief introduction to McKelvey and Palfrey's "centipede game" paper.[1] After describing the centipede game and McKelvey and Palfrey's main findings, I discuss some of the subsequent experimental research examining play in variations of the game. My own experimental research involves field experiments and this background shapes my views regarding laboratory experiments. I will briefly comment on how field experiments can complement laboratory-based experimentation. My essay on implications of the centipede game complements that of the following chapter, in which Rebecca Morton links the centipede game to broader substantive themes in political science.

1. Centipede Game

The centipede game is a complete information, finite period alternate-move game. A 4 move version of the centipede game adapted from Aumann (1992)

---

[1] Why is this game named after an insect? When the game has 100 moves, the extensive form resembles (in an abstract rendering) a centipede (Binmore 1987).

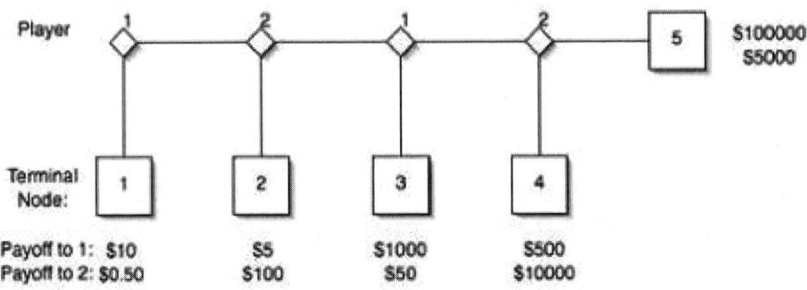

FIGURE 1

and Rapoport, Parco, and Stein (2002) is shown here as Figure 1. There are two players, Player 1 and Player 2. Player 1 is initially presented with the option of taking the larger share of a sum of money ($10.50), $10 going to Player 1 and 50 cents for Player 2. Player 1 can accept this division ("Take") or reject it ("Pass"). If Player 1 rejects the division the total amount available for division increases by 10×, to $105, and the option to Take or Pass goes to Player 2. Player 2 is now offered the larger share, $100. If Player 2 accepts this division, the game ends, while if Player 2 passes the game continues, with the option going back to Player 1, the sum of money available for division again increased by 10× (to $1050), and Player 1 offered the larger share.[2] Figure 1 illustrates the centipede game's basic tension. If Player 1 selects Pass and Player 2 responds with Take, Player 1's payoff is lower than she would have received by selecting Take rather than Pass. The prospect of this loss pushes Player 1 to select Take right away. However, if Player 2 responds to Player 1's selection of Pass by Passing, then Player 1 now faces the Take/Pass decision again, this time with a payoff to selecting Take that is 100 times larger than at the previous opportunity. The prospect of this larger payoff encourages Player 1 to Pass rather than Take.

---

[2] A common but not universal feature of centipede games is that if Player 1 selects Pass and then Player 2 selects Pass, if Player 1's next move is Take, the payoffs are Pareto superior to those received if the game had ended 2 moves earlier. Both players are better off if they somehow manage to play in a cooperative fashion. In some experimental studies the sum of payoffs is held constant over the game, but the payoff shares are varied. In one recent study (Huck and Jehiel [HJ] 2004) the sum of the payoffs increases, but the lower payoff does not, and therefore payoffs later in the game are not Pareto superior to the payoffs received if the game ends at the first move.

The standard game theoretic solution to the centipede game can be found using backward induction.[3] In all Nash equilibria the game ends at the first move, with Player 1 selecting Take. This prediction follows from the basic behavioral assumptions employed in public choice, namely "that man is an egoistic, rational, utility maximizer" (Mueller 1989, 2), along with the assumption that the game — and the fact that the players will act according to the standard behavioral postulates — is common knowledge. If the Nash equilibrium prediction fails empirically, then one of these assumptions has failed. The experiments discussed here typically give great care to making the game common knowledge through public explanation of the game or use of a written description supplied to all subjects. The common knowledge assumption will fail if a subject believes that there is deception about the game or thinks that other subjects suspect deception.[4] Even if this difficulty can be avoided, the Nash equilibrium prediction is not robust to minor relaxation of the standard behavioral assumptions.

Due to its vulnerability to departures from the standard behavioral model, it is (and was) widely believed that the Nash equilibrium is not a convincing prediction of how people would play the game. Given the payoffs in Figure 1, if Player 1 believes there is even a 1% chance that Player 2 selects Pass, it pays for Player 1 to Pass at the first choice node. There are many reasons why Player 2 might choose Pass rather than Take. Suppose that players are not perfectly "rational" and occasionally select inferior options by mistake. Then Player 1 might Pass in hope that Player 2 will, perhaps in error, move Pass. What if some players are altruistic or wish to appear so to others? The total payoffs increase each period and so altruism encourages cooperative play. For the game depicted in Figure 1, only a slight deviation from egoism is needed to produce cooperation. At the final choice node if Player 2 chooses Pass rather than Take, the loss to Player 2 ($5000) is much less than the gain enjoyed by Player 1 ($99,500). Lastly, the Nash equilibrium prediction of Take at the first move rests on a fairly complicated chain of reasoning about how players will act at later moves (this is especially true in longer versions of the game). Though it is assumed that subjects will perform the required calculation, these impose a cognitive burden on subjects. A desire to avoid this effort may encourage non-rational play or use of simple rules. For example, Player 1 might elect not to reason backward from the end of the game, but rather observe that the potential prize from playing Pass is so great compared

---

[3]There is an extensive theoretical literature that analyzes the centipede game, focusing on what the backward induction solution requires of the players. See Rapoport (2001) for an accessible discussion.

[4]In comments on this paper, Skip Lupia also noted that the equilibrium prediction may not hold if the game can effectively be altered by players communicating and pledging side payments.

to the loss from foregoing Take that it is worth it to gamble on Pass and then see what happens. When playing the game repeatedly, the subject might develop rules of play based on what worked in previous games.

2. McKelvey and Palfrey (1992; Chapter 18 of this book)

Prior to McKelvey and Palfrey, there was extensive theoretical discussion of play in the centipede game but no systematic empirical evidence showing how people actually played. McKelvey and Palfrey(MP) (1992) perform the first experimental study. They examine how students from Cal Tech and Pasadena Community College play 3 versions of the game (a 4 move version where the game ends after either a player selects Take or each player chooses Pass twice, a 6 move version where the game ends after Take or each player chooses Pass 3 times, a "high" payoff version where the payoffs for the 4 move version are quadrupled) in sessions consisting of 10 games. The experimental design incorporated features to eliminate the potential for cooperative or supergame behavior. Subjects registered their choices through computer terminals and did not communicate with one another except through their strategy choices. Further, subjects were paired up according to a rotation scheme that prevented players from ever being matched to a player more than once or even being matched to someone who had played someone a player had played previously.

There are two main empirical findings. First, the outcome does not follow the Nash equilibrium prediction. Subjects very rarely select Take at the first choice node (only 7% of the time in the 4 move version of the game, 1% of the time in the 6 move version, 15% of the time in the high stakes game). Second, with experience, there is some convergence of play toward the Nash equilibrium prediction. In both the 4 move and the 6 move versions of the game, behavior later in the 10 game sessions is closer to the Nash equilibrium outcome than play early in the sessions. Convergence suggests that in situations where people have a chance to learn, the Nash equilibrium prediction may be more accurate.[5]

MP (1992) offer two explanations for the observed deviations from the Nash equilibrium prediction. First, some percentage of players are by nature "altruistic"

---

[5]MP (1992) also emphasize that the finding that the conditional probability of selecting Take increases at each choice node. This is consistent with both the incomplete information model employed in MP (1992) and the quantal response equilibrium model used in later work (e.g., MP 1998; Fey, McKelvey, and Palfrey [FMP] 1996). MP (1992) also report some unusual play. In the 4 move game subjects Pass 25% of the time they reach the final choice node; in the 6 move game they Pass 15% of the time. In MP (1992), as in Figure 1, Passing in the final period is a strictly dominated strategy. A small percentage of players in MP (1992) choose Pass at every opportunity.

types, defined by MP (1992) as players who care about the combined payoffs, and will therefore select Pass at every opportunity. Further, when there are altruistic types, it is rational for non-altruists to select Pass early in the game, since they have an incentive to mimic the altruists to build a reputation for altruism (e.g., Kreps and Wilson 1982). A second explanation for observing Pass is that players make errors. These include errors in play (selecting the wrong strategy by chance) or errors in beliefs (incorrectly estimating the chances your opposite player is an altruist). Strategic responses to anticipated errors in play can produce additional use of Pass. If players make fewer errors as they gain experience, play will move closer to the Nash equilibrium outcome over the course of a session as subjects learn.

MP (1992) derive the sequential equilibrium and estimate a structural model that includes altruistic types, errors, and learning. They find that slightly over 5% of the players are "altruists," players make a sizable number of errors, and the error rate declines with experience.

3. Subsequent Experimental Literature

Following MP's seminal work, there have been half a dozen experimental analyses of the centipede game. These papers are each briefly described here and some of the main findings are summarized at the end of the section. The experimental literature explores how variations in the experimental design affect outcomes of the game, assesses the effects of experience, and analyzes alternative learning models. Several questions receive significant attention. Are there conditions where the backward induction solution works better? Does play converge toward the Nash equilibrium outcome, or if the session is long enough, perhaps even arrive at the Nash equilibrium? Is there a better model to explain how subjects are making their decisions?

Altruism was cited by MP (1992) as a reason why the Nash equilibrium prediction failed. To exclude the influence of altruistic preferences, FMP (1996) design a version of the centipede game where payoff shares change but the sum of the payoffs stays constant. In the constant sum game any gain by one player is offset by the other player's loss and so there is no justification for a player to deviate from the Nash equilibrium on grounds of altruism.[6] As expected, FMP (1996) find that the Nash equilibrium outcome occurs much more often in the constant sum

---

[6]Take in period 1 is the equilibrium outcome of the game. A further feature of the Nash equilibrium outcome in FMP (1996) is that payoffs for both players are equal when the game ends at the first move, an outcome that is attractive because it is most "fair."

than in the increasing sum version of the centipede game studied by MP (1992). However, the game still ends on the first move less than half the time. As players get experience playing the constant sum game the outcome clearly moves in the direction of the Nash equilibrium over the course of the 10 game sessions.[7]

An additional aspect of FMP (1996) merits a slight digression. In their initial analysis of the centipede game, MP (1992) modeled subjects making errors but these were random noise. When MP turn to analyze the data from their new experiment, they had in the intervening years developed the quantal response equilibrium model (QRE). In the QRE (MP 1995 (Chapter 20 of this book), 1998), described in detail by Morton (Chapter 17 of this book), the subject's error rate for a given strategic choice is a function of the difference in the expected payoffs from alternative choices; the more costly the error, the less often the error is made.[8] FMP (1996) consider several simple alternative models to explain the experimental results (such as a model where subjects select Take with some probability p that changes as the subject gets more experience) and find that the data is best explained by an extension of the newly developed QRE model. In related work, MP (1998) reanalyze the data from the original centipede experiment to see how well it fits a version of the QRE model that excludes altruistic types. They find that while the fit is not as good as that obtained in the original analysis, the QRE model excluding altruistic players explains the data reasonably well with fewer free parameters.[9]

People often make decisions in groups and perhaps the Nash equilibrium prediction works better for group decision making. It has been suggested groups make fewer mistakes and are also less altruistic than individuals acting alone. Given the explanations in MP (1992), if this is true then competing groups will produce outcomes closer to the Nash equilibrium prediction. Bornstein, Kugler, and Ziegelmeyer [BKZ] (2004) find that in an increasing payoff centipede game

---

[7]It is unclear from the data presented whether the movement toward the Nash equilibrium had stabilized or not by the end of the sessions.

[8]Details of how to calculate the QRE are found in FMP (1996) and MP (1998).

[9]The evidence for excluding altruistic types is ambiguous, however, since fit improves noticeably when altruistic types are added to the QRE model (MP 1998, Tables 7 and 8). Without altruistic players the QRE model substantially underestimates the amount of Pass in the first period. More generally, other laboratory experiments show substantial evidence of altruism (e.g., Andreoni and Miller 2002). For a review of the experimental conditions favoring altruistic play, see Frolich and Oppenheimer (2000).

when groups play other groups the games do tend to end earlier than when individuals play individuals.[10] In their constant sum game, where altruism is not relevant, groups still select Take earlier than individuals, but the difference between the group and individual outcomes is smaller than in the increasing sum version. For both individuals and groups, the game ends much more quickly in the constant sum version of the game than the increasing sum version, which is consistent with the pattern found earlier in MP (1992) and FMP (1996).[11]

The payoffs used in the centipede game experiments are fairly small. Perhaps the failure of Nash equilibrium is due to the low stakes, which makes "nice behavior" or errors relatively inexpensive. The centipede game typically has only two players who alternate moves, a design that might facilitate cooperation. Parco, Rapoport, and Stein [PRS] (2002) and Rapoport, Stein, Parco, and Nicholas [RSPN] (2003) explore these issues in a study of a centipede game where three players alternate moves. They compare the outcomes from a series of 60 game sessions of a low stakes and very high stakes version of the game (in the high payoff game, payoffs rise over the course of the game to $2560 versus $25.60 in the low stakes version).

The results from the low stakes version of the 3 player game are very similar to MP (1992 (Chapter 18 of this book)). The game almost never ends at the first move. Further, there is no evidence of convergence to the Nash equilibrium during the session. In contrast, using high stakes has a large effect on subjects' choices. The game ended at the first move nearly 40% of the time, and one of the three players selected Take at their first chance over 80% of the time. There is also substantial evidence of convergence. By the last games of the 60 game sessions the Nash equilibrium was the outcome about 75% of the time and the game almost never went beyond the first round of player moves. These results suggest that, especially when there is opportunity to learn, the predictions that follow from assuming egoism and optimization are more accurate when the stakes are high. RSPN (2003) also examine how subjects change their moves in response to their experience in the previous game. They note that the probability a subject selects Pass in the first move is strongly increasing in the length of their previous game. This finding is consistent with a learning model where subjects adapt their choices to perform well against the choices they observe.

---

[10]The hypothesis that groups are less altruistic is bolstered by evidence obtained from recordings of group deliberations, which supports the intriguing claim from previous studies that if one person in a group suggests acting selfishly the others will go along.

[11]Subjects played only once and so the study provides no evidence regarding convergence.

Two recent experimental studies also use the centipede game to study learning models. Nagel and Tang [NT] (1998) study a normal form representation of the centipede game.[12] They examine play in 100 game sessions, which is perhaps long enough to see full convergence to the Nash equilibrium if it occurs. NT (1998) find that the game ends at the first move less than 1% of the time. Despite the long sessions, there is no movement toward the Nash equilibrium prediction. Further, they disaggregate the data from MP (1992) and upon re-examination suggest that there was in fact very little movement toward the Nash equilibrium within each MP (1992) 10 game session (see Table 3, MP 1992; Figure 3, NT 1998). While the average game length in MP (1992) was, in fact, lower in the last 5 games than in the first 5 games, the mean game length was stable after the 6th game in each session.

One difference between the experimental design used in NT (1998) and MP (1992) is that while in NT (1998) players were randomly and anonymously matched (NT 1998, 360), the pool of players was relatively small. Subjects in NT (1998) meet more than once and meet players whom they might have influenced indirectly through a subject they were paired with in a previous game. This presents an explanation for why the Nash equilibrium is not played in NT (1998), since there is a theoretical possibility of cooperation or other strategic dependencies across games within a session. However, even very near the end of the 100 game sessions, where these strategic issues dissipate, there appears to be no movement toward the Nash equilibrium in 4 of the 5 sessions, and only slight movement in the remaining session.

NT compare Nash equilibrium and the quantal response equilibrium model to learning models that, unlike standard game theory models, do not assume mutually consistent strategies. In these learning models subjects may tally up the track record of payoffs produced by their choices in prior play and play successful moves more, or reflect on how previous opponents played and then select strategies that would have worked well in these previous cases.[13] NT (1998) find the best fit for a model of re-enforcement learning in which players choose strategies according to the payoffs produced by the strategy in previous rounds.

Huck and Jehiel [HJ] (2004) examine the effect of providing subjects varying amounts of information about how the entire pool of subjects plays at individual

---

[12]In the normal form representation a strategy specifies the choice node where the player moves Take. While the extensive form reveals the strategy of the player that ends the game, the normal form permits NT to learn the strategy of both players. This is helpful, since they are interested in how players alter their strategies in response to their experiences.

[13]See RSPN (2003, 253) for a discussion and useful typology of these models.

choice nodes and at collections of choice nodes. For example, in one variation, players at choice node t are told the percentage of the time all other subjects have moved Take at choice node $t + 1$. In all the games they examine the payoffs are slightly unusual: the "losing" player's payoff stays the same, but the winner's payoff doubles after each Pass. In contrast to games where the payoffs later in the game tree are Pareto superior, this payoff structure reduces the incentive for players to select Pass and may be expected to lead to less "cooperative" play.

For the experiments where players have only their own private information (the familiar case) the results confirm earlier findings. The Nash equilibrium is almost never played. There was convergence toward the Nash equilibrium as in FMP (1996), which similar to HJ (2004) had a payoff structure that provided no Pareto superior payoffs later in the game. However, HJ (2004) run 50 game sessions, which are longer sessions than those in FMP (1996), and find that movement toward "Take" first period stabilizes well short of the Nash equilibrium.[14] In contrast, when subjects are provided information about how the population of subjects has played the next move, there is steady convergence toward the Nash equilibrium.

Recent papers focus much greater attention than MP (1992) on how the individual subject's strategy changes during sessions (RSPN 2003; NT 1998; HJ 2004). The NT study illustrates two benefits from this focus: the analysis can help explain the failure of convergence and can identify weaknesses in previous theory.

NT (1998) note features of their data, as well as the data reported by MP (1992), that are consistent with "learning direction theory," which posits that if players elect to adjust their play, they do so by assessing whether there was a better way to play versus the previous opponent and then moving in the direction of the improvement. Consistent with this model, NT find that when a player "wins" the

---

[14]Players were randomly matched, but as in NT (1998), there was a possibility of facing the same subject or a subject influenced by one's earlier play in later sessions. It appears that play does not converge to the Nash equilibrium because many of the subjects do not change their strategy in response to experience (they are labeled "non-adaptive") and select Pass each time. Those subjects that do change their play adapt to experience and information. HJ find that they respond to how often other players have selected Pass. The large number of subjects playing Pass evidently stabilizes outcomes away from the Nash equilibrium. HJ also report other interesting findings. When there is no public information, subjects appear to use a decision rule based on the play of their own opponents during the past 5 iterations of the game. In contrast, when a public statistic is available they use all the information from their own experience. The tables (e.g., Table 9) appear to show an unexpected finding that subjects place greater weight on their own experience at each decision node than on the public information that summarizes all previous decisions made at the node, despite the fact that there are more observations, and presumably more information, contained in the public statistic.

game by Taking first, they are more likely to alter their strategy and Take later in the next game they play (perhaps because if they had waited longer their payoff would have been larger); when the player "loses," the player is more likely to move Take earlier next game. NT also find that as the session continues players are less likely to switch their strategies. These two findings suggest why there is no convergence to Nash equilibrium in their experiment. Players tend to settle into a strategy and stay with it, which produces stable outcomes; when strategies do change it is not always in the direction of the Nash equilibrium, since players who "win" tend to Pass more the following period.

Examining the details of how individual choices change over the course of a session suggests patterns of strategic adaptation not part of the MP (1992) model. NT show that whether the subject was the first to move Take in the previous game has a very strong effect on how the subject plays the next game. This pattern of change does not appear to be consistent with the equilibrium in the theoretical model used by MP (1992). Setting aside any error reduction from experience, in MP (1992) subjects change their moves from one game to the next because they are playing mixed strategies. The distribution of subsequent moves by the subject should be independent of the realization of the random move by the subject's opponent, and therefore independent of whether a given strategy by the player resulted in Taking first or not. NT show that, in fact, the choice of move is clearly affected by the opponent's choice in the prior game (the same pattern holds in HJ and RSPN).

To summarize, the experimental studies are typically different on many dimensions (the subjects, the stakes, the length of the game, the number of players, groups versus individuals, the number of games per session, constant versus increasing payoffs, algorithm for how players are paired) and so it is difficult to isolate the effect of variation in particular features. A few things clearly emerge.

First, the failure of the Nash equilibrium prediction occurs across many variations in the experimental design.[15] In no case is the backward induction solution played initially more than half the time. The experiments most similar to MP (1992) found the Nash equilibrium outcome as rarely as they did (HJ, NT). There is some evidence that higher stakes encourage players to choose Take earlier (MP

---

[15] Backward induction fails to predict laboratory results in other contexts. In a finite period repeated prisoner's dilemma with complete information the standard game theoretic prediction is that both parties defect in the first period. Laboratory experiments show that there is very often significant cooperation (Ledyard 1995). The subgame perfect Nash equilibrium frequently fails in alternate offer bargaining games (Roth 1995).

1992; RSPN 2003).[16] The Nash prediction does much better in the constant payoff case than in experiments where there are gains to cooperation. However, even when the sum of the payoffs stays constant, more than half the time the game goes beyond the first period (BKZ, FMP).[17]

Second, there is only weak evidence that more experience leads to convergence to Nash equilibrium in the typical low stakes, increasing payoff game, even when sessions are many games long. The reported trend toward convergence during the 10 game session in MP (1992) hinted that, if the sessions had been longer, Nash equilibrium might have turned out to be a reasonable prediction. Subsequent work in similar games (low stakes, increasing payoffs) suggests otherwise (RSPN, NT, HJ) and in retrospect the evidence for convergence in the MP (1992) data is not strong to begin with (NT, 362). There is evidence of some limited convergence in low stakes, non-increasing-sum versions of the game (FMP, HJ) and much greater convergence when subjects are given more information about how other subjects have played at forthcoming moves (HJ). The most substantial convergence occurs in the 3 player high stakes version of the game (RSNP). Since there is no convergence in the low stakes version of the 3 player game, the high stakes appears to be driving this result.

Third, recent work (RSPN, NT, HJ) shows that learning models can help explain how subjects change strategies in response to experience during a session. These models can explain features of the data not explained by the models advocated by MP (1992) and FMP (1996), and perform well in formal comparisons of how alternative models fit the experimental data. It is common for papers to report a "horse race" between new and old models, and new models win this contest. I have elected not to emphasize the results of these horse races or other tests of model fit. First, the old model is known ex-ante, while the new models are, to varying degrees, constructed in light of the data. Second, the tests involve particular specification of the previous models that may not capture their full merit.

---

[16] In contrast to PRS (2002), increasing the stakes does not necessarily produce strong movement toward the backward induction solution in other contexts. For example, Roth reports the findings presented in the Hoffman, McCabe, and Smith (1993) ultimatum game (Roth 1995, 303). An experimental study of the ultimatum game using large payoffs found equilibrium demands still tended to be close to equal division.

[17] In the QRE model, changing payoffs will also change the error rates, without the requirement that players are "cooperative." How the QRE plays out in the particular experiments considered here is not clear to me. In increasing sum games, the higher payoffs later in the game will encourage Pass for any given level of player errors; this effect will be countered by a reduction in the error rate if there is an increase in the difference in expected payoff from Pass versus Take in the later portions of the game.

For instance, RSNP evaluate a static version of QRE, when this model could be adapted to permit error reduction with experience.

4. Some Remarks on Lab and Field Experiments

Experiments are commonly evaluated by examining their internal and external validity (Campbell and Stanley 1966). Threats to internal validity are factors that undermine the ability of the researcher to correctly measure the experimental effect. These include problems like non-blinded assessments and inadequate randomization. Threats to external validity are factors that limit the applicability of the experimental findings to new contexts.

Proponents of laboratory experiments suggest that in the future "experiments will provide the test-bed in which new organizations will be tested before implementation" (Ledyard 1985, 173). In the face of these ambitions stands a familiar challenge to laboratory experiments: given the artificiality of the laboratory setting, can the results be generalized to the "real world"? Concerns about specific design features of the laboratory experiment, such as the payoffs levels or the use of student subjects, can be addressed in follow-up experiments that vary these conditions. But showing that results are robust to experimental variation along theoretically meaningless dimensions is not the same as establishing that there is no common factor across laboratory experiments that might make the findings irrelevant to more typical decision environments.[18]

Field experiments can help us learn about how laboratory results travel to other contexts (Harrison and List 2004). Field experiments, where treatments are applied unobtrusively to subjects in natural settings, are an increasingly common research strategy for obtaining accurate measurement of causal effects. Applications of this work in political science include the investigation of alternative types of partisan and non-partisan Get-Out-The-Vote stimuli (Gerber and Green 2000; Gerber, Green, and Green 2003); examples from economics include measuring

---

[18]Skeptics can raise a number of familiar reasons for concern: People have heuristics to assist them in real life and it is not clear what analogies people draw on when facing the abstract decisions considered in the lab. The lab version of a situation misses important elements of the real world decision environment. For example, if laboratory results stem from errors in calculation, in external environments if gains are sufficiently great there might be organizations or experts that assist in decision making and/or players might seek out assistance. Participating in a laboratory experiment may be more like playing a game than making a decision. There are social norms associated with game playing, such as how you are allowed to treat an opponent and how you should treat a potential teammate, that differ from the norms in other contexts. There is the strong possibility of expectancy effects if subjects are attuned to investigators' presumed values and/or demand effects. Subjects may attempt to impress with "skilled" play or "ethical" play. I am unaware of evidence regarding whether blinding, if it is used, is believed by the subjects.

the flow of information through social networks and detecting labor market discrimination (Bertrand and Mullainathan 2003).[19]

I am unaware of any work in political science that attempts to corroborate the ordering or calibrate laboratory effects by comparing laboratory results to those produced by field experiments. An example of such work from psychology is a recent study of Prospect Theory by Salovey and Williams-Piehota (2004). They examined the relative effectiveness of a series of negative- and positive-framed health messages. One set of studies compared the effectiveness of messages about sunblock in the lab and the field. They found that, when the messages were delivered on a public beach and effectiveness measured by whether the subject actually obtained sunblock, the prediction (derived from Prospect Theory) that the positive framed message would be most effective was confirmed. However, things were different in the lab; they report that "in the sterile setting of the laboratory, some of our framing effects on sunscreen have failed to produce any framing effects, most likely because participants could not muster much concern about skin cancer prevention in this environment" (Salovey and Williams-Piehota 2004).

In economics there have also been efforts to see how well findings from the lab fare in the field. These include using more "realistic subjects," such as the use of experienced bidders rather than students in analyzing auctions, or more realistic experimental environments. An example of work in this spirit is List (2001), which investigates how well the findings of a laboratory experiment hold up when tested in a more natural setting. In a laboratory experiment using students Cummings and Taylor (1999) found that an upward bias in contingent valuations (a method of hypothetical valuation of a non-market commodity commonly used in assigning a value to environmental protection) was eliminated when the subjects were provided a discussion of the problem of upward bias prior to being surveyed about their valuations. List performed a series of actual auctions of a baseball cards at card shows and found that the "cheap talk" script eliminated bias for inexperienced consumers but not for dealers (and the valuations in the hypothetical auctions were about twice those in the real auction for both groups of subjects).

In principle, it should be possible to discover how the results from one context, such as a laboratory setup, translate into another context, the "real world."

---

[19] Assumptions are always required to apply the findings of research from one context to another, whether that evidence comes from the field or the lab. In this sense, all research has an "external validity" problem. However, it seems natural to apply research findings from field experiments to other "similar" real world settings, though a complete analysis would need to spell out (and investigate) exactly what variables affect the size of the treatment effects and account for the levels of these variables when making predictions.

Building up a body of empirical work that demonstrates how laboratory experiments predict behavior in natural environments across a range of applications will overcome residual skeptics and bring the compelling advantages of laboratory experiments into sharper relief.

5. Conclusion

Prior to the MP (1992) study of the centipede game, it was suspected that the Nash equilibrium prediction of Take first period was not a good prediction of how people would play the game. MP's experimental work confirmed this and subsequent research investigated the robustness of this result and how it is modified under a variety of alternative conditions. Since the assumptions supporting prediction of the Nash equilibrium include fundamental assumptions about behavior, such as the role of self interest and rationality, the experimental literature analyzing the centipede game has implications for these basic issues.

Perhaps the most important thing about the centipede game experiment, however, is that it played a role in advancing the analysis of strategic interaction. Documenting the details of the empirical failure of Nash equilibrium and constructing explanations for the observed deviations are part of the process by which theories are improved. In their discussion of the results, MP (1992) foreshadow subsequent theoretical developments. Rather than model errors as noise as they do in MP (1992), MP suggest that it "might be reasonable to assume instead that individuals make more errors ... when they are indifferent between alternatives ... than when they have preferences over alternatives. ... In other words, the error rate may be a function of the utility differences between the choices" (MP 1992, 826. See Chapter 18 in this book, page 408). They proceed to observe that such a model might be able to reconcile the differences seen in the error rates in the 4 and 6 move games, and in turn lead to a better fit and explanation of the trends in the 6 move game. This modeling suggestion is developed in their subsequent work on the quantal response equilibrium (MP 1995 (Chapter 20 of this book), 1998), which is now a standard analytical tool, applied to a wide variety of problems in economics and political science (Signorino 1999; Goeree, Holt, and Palfrey 2005). This attractive interplay of theory and data is a textbook example of the process of scientific discovery, and shows how MP's paper possesses those elements that have been described in another context as "the best of experimental economics. It tests the clear prediction of a general theory, on a difficult test case. And the results allow alternative hypotheses to be developed" Roth (1995, 10).

References

Andreoni, James, and John H. Miller (2002):"Giving According to GARP: An Experimental Study of Rationality and Altruism," *Econometrica*, 70, 737–753.

Aumann, R. J. (1992): "Irrationality in Game Theory," in *Economic Analysis of Markets and Games*, ed. by D. G. P. Dasgupta, and E. Maskin. MIT Press, Cambridge.

——— (1995): "Backward Induction and Common Knowledge of Rationality," *Games and Economic Behavior*, 8, 6–19.

Bertrand, M., and S. Mullainathan (2003): "Are Emily and Greg More Employable than Lakisha and Jamal? A Field Experiment on Labor Market Discrimination," NBER Working Paper No. 9873.

Binmore, K. (1987): "Modeling Rational Players I," *Economics and Philosophy*, 3, 179–214.

Bornstein, G., T. Kugler, and A. Ziegelmeyer (2004): "Individual and Group Decisions in the Centipede Game: Are Groups More "Rational" Players?" unpublished manuscript.

Campbell, D. T., and J. C. Stanley (1966): *Experimental and Quasi Experimental Designs for Research*. Rand McNally, Chicago.

Cummings, R. G., and L. O. Taylor (1999): "Unbiased Value Estimates for Environmental Goods: A Cheap Talk Design for Contingent Valuation Method," *American Economic Review*, 89(3), 649–665.

Fey, M., R. D. McKelvey, and T. Palfrey (1996): "An Experimental Study of Constant Sum Centipede Games," *International Journal of Game Theory*, 25, 269–287.

Frohlich, Norman, and Joe A. Oppenheimer (2000): "How People Reason about Ethics," in *Elements of Political Reason: Cognition, Choice and the Bounds of Rationality*, ed. by Arthur Lupia, Matthew McCubbins, and Sam Popkin. Cambridge University Press.

Gerber, A. S., and D. P. Green (2000): "The Effects of Canvassing, Direct Mail, and Telephone Contact on Voter Turnout: A Field Experiment," *American Political Science Review*, 80, 540–550.

Gerber, A. S., D. P. Green, and M. Green (2003): "Partisan Mail and Voter Turnout: Results from Randomized Field Experiments," *Electoral Studies*, 22(4), 563–579.

Goeree, Jacob, Charles A. Holt, and Thomas R. Palfrey (2005): "Regular Quantal Response Equilibrium," *Experimental Economics*, 8, 347–367.

Harrison, Glenn W. and John A. List (2004): "Field Experiments," University of Central Florida Economics Working Paper No. 03-12, July 2004.

Huck, S., and P. Jehiel (2004): "Public Statistics and Private Experience: Varying Feedback Information in a Take-or-Pass Game," unpublished manuscript. University College, London.

Kreps, D. M., and R. Wilson (1982): "Reputation and Imperfect Information," *Journal of Economic Theory*, 27, 245–252.

Ledyard, J. (1995): "Public Goods: A Survey of Experimental Research," in *Handbook of Experimental Economics*, ed. by J. Kagel, and A. Roth.

List, J. A. (2001): "Do Explicit Warnings Eliminate the Hypothetical Bias in Elicitation Procedures? Evidence from Field Auctions for Sportscards," *American Economic Review*, 91(5), 1498–1507.

McKelvey, R. D., and T. Palfrey (1992): "An Experimental Study of the Centipede Game," *Econometrica*, 60(4), 803–836. Chapter 18 of this book.

——— (1995): "Quantal Response Equilibria for Normal Form Games," *Games and Economic Behavior*, 10(1), 6–38. Chapter 20 of this book.

——— (1998): "Quantal Response Equilibria for Extensive Form Games," *Experimental Economics*, 1(1), 9–41.

Mueller, D. C. (1989): *Public Choice II*. Cambridge University Press.

Nagel, R., and F. Tang (1998): "Experimental Results on the Centipede Game in Normal Form: An Investigation on Learning," *Journal of Mathematical Psychology*, 42, 356–384.

Parco, J., A. Rapoport, and W. Stein (2002): "Effects of Financial Incentives on the Breakdown of Mutual Trust," *Psychological Science*, 13, 292–297.

Rapoport, A. (2001): "Centipede Games," unpublished manuscript.

Rapoport, A. S., J. W. E. Parco, and T. Nicholas (2003): "Equilibrium Play and Adaptive Learning in the Three-Person Centipede Game," *Games and Economic Behavior*, 43, 239–265.

Roth, A. (1995): "Bargaining Experiments," in *Handbook of Experimental Economics*, ed. by J. Kagel, and A. Roth. Princeton University Press.

Salovey, P., and P. Williams-Piehota (2004): "Field Experiments in Social Psychology: Message Framing and the Promotion of Health Protective Behaviors," *American Behavior Scientist*, 47(5), 488–505.

Signorino, C. S. (1999): "Strategic Interaction and the Statistical Analysis of International Conflict," *American Political Science Review*, 93(2), 279–297.

CHAPTER 17

Why the Centipede Game Is Important for Political Science

REBECCA B. MORTON

The centipede game is odd. It is hard to imagine a real world situation, particularly one in the world of politics, where two individuals would play such a stylized game. Furthermore, what are we to make of the results from the laboratory experiments — where undergraduates at Caltech were given monetary payoffs represented by such a game? What do these actions by highly intelligent subjects in an artificial environment in an unreal game have to tell us about politics? For example, suppose the research goal was to gain a better understanding of how legislatures operate. Wouldn't it be better to work with a much more realistic theory and to do empirical research using data from naturally occurring legislatures? Or, if we wanted to do experiments, maybe we could try to do something in the field — somehow manipulating the choices before legislators and seeing how that manipulation affects their actions.

Using this sort of reasoning, many political scientists dismiss the centipede game experiments of McKelvey and Palfrey. My goal in this short essay is to challenge that reasoning. I will do so by putting the experiments in the context of a general research program — by looking at the research that preceded those experiments and the research that has followed. The goal of the research program was indeed the study of how legislatures operate. In particular, the researchers desired to build a positive theory of coalition formation that would explain how voting led to outcomes in legislatures and other political bodies which used majority rule. Such a theory would be logically consistent, have realistic assumptions, and make empirical predictions that were supported. I take it as a given that such a program is deeply important for political science.

Figure 1 summarizes how I put the centipede game experiments into the context of that research program. The figure presents a small slice of the program and highlights just five papers — McKelvey and Ordeshook (1983), Baron and Ferejohn (1989a), McKelvey (1991), McKelvey and Palfrey (1992 (Chapter 18 of this book)), and Fréchette, Kagel, and Morelli (2005). However, I contend that examining how the centipede game experiments fit into this slice shows how fundamental these experiments are to the research program and the importance of McKelvey's experimental contributions to that program and the value of laboratory experiments like his in general to political science.

1. Understanding Legislative Behavior through Cooperative Game Theory

Deciding when this program began is arbitrary, but the seminal theoretical work that started much of the research I discuss was William Riker's *The Theory of Political Coalitions*, published in 1962. The approach taken by Riker was to model coalition formation as a cooperative game and use solution concepts to derive predictions about the payoffs in the coalitions. But in the late 1970s the solution proposed by Riker as well as other similar ones could not "be usefully applied to the empirical analysis of, e.g., legislative coalition formation" as Riker's students, McKelvey, Ordeshook, and Winer, hereafter MOW (1978, p. 599 (Chapter 10 of this book, page 188)), pointed out, because they assumed transferable utility — that side payments could be made. Moreover, the existing theories only predicted payoffs, not which coalitions would form, and the solution concepts did not have behavioral foundations — they were as MOW wrote (p. 600 in original, Chapter 10 in this book, page 189) "principally mathematical abstractions without behavioral rationale." As a consequence, MOW advocated a new idea, the competitive solution, which they put forward as a way of understanding coalition formation in legislatures without assuming the unreal idea of transferable utility. Furthermore, the competitive solution provided predictions about coalitions and payoffs and it had a behavioral foundation of coalition formation as a bargaining process (the competitive solution is discussed in more detail in the contribution to this volume by Peter Ordeshook in Chapter 9 of this book)).

2. Using Experiments to Test Theory

Although MOW's motives were to propose a more realistic, behavioral theory of legislative coalition formation that would be more useful for empirical analysis of real legislatures, they turned to laboratory experiments to test that theory. Why? Why not go directly to legislatures? The advantage of going to the lab was that the researchers could use financial incentives to induce preferences for the subjects and thus more accurately test whether their proposed solution did predict

FIGURE 1. Putting the centipede game experiments in context

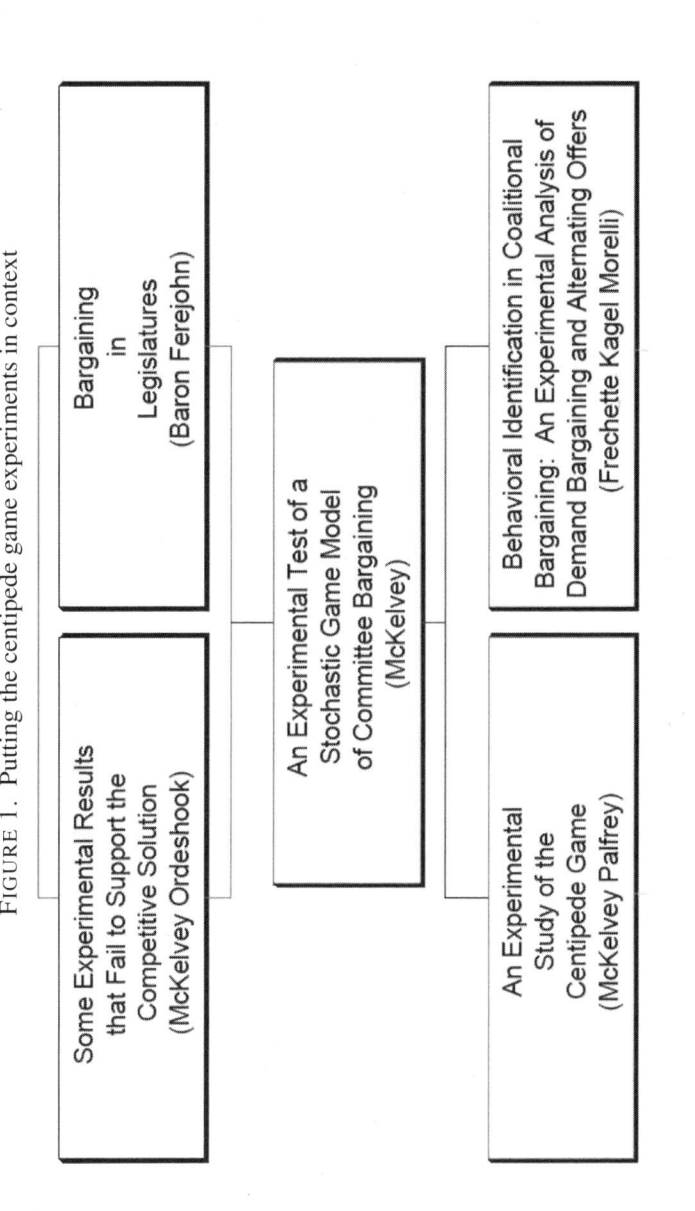

accurately. If they had gone to a real legislature they would have had to estimate those preferences. This was before the important work of Poole and Rosenthal and others, which now provides us with a way of computing such estimates. However, even if MOW had had such data available, those estimates would still have had error. Moreover, the researchers would not have been able to vary those preferences to see if under different preference profiles, number of actors, and number of alternatives the solution concept worked — they would not have the control they had and used in the laboratory. Thus, the lab provided MOW with a strong test of their theory.

The experiments on the competitive solution were experiments that Alvin Roth (1995) labels as "speaking to theorists." And they did. Although at first the results showed support for the competitive solution, the experiments also showed problems with the solution as discussed in McKelvey and Ordeshook (1983) and McKelvey (1991). Importantly, the experiments showed that the solution concept, because it was ordinal in nature, often did not explain the behavior of subjects. Specifically, the solution concept could not explain the fact that subjects chose alternatives with different probabilities and that subjects were influenced by differences in cardinal utilities in preference profiles that were ordinally equivalent. There were important disconnects between what the theory predicted and the behavior in the lab.

It is important to remember that the goal of the experimentalists was not to design a world that was like real world legislatures. The goal was to design a world that looked like the theory and then see if indeed real individuals, placed in that world, behaved as predicted. But that makes the experiments seem like a trivial demonstration. The experiments were much more than that. In the experiments, the researchers were able to vary things — preference profiles, the number of alternatives, the number of actors — that they would not have been able to do using naturally occurring data from legislatures or field experiments. If there is some variation in these factors in naturally occurring legislatures it is possible to use statistical inference to posit how changes in these factors affect behavior. But generally there is little variation in these factors — Congress has not changed the number of members in over 50 years — or the variation is not random, forcing us to rely heavily on inference over observation. Field experiments that vary legislative preferences, number of alternatives, and number of legislators seem highly improbable.

As Gerber's essay (Chapter 16 of this book) points out many are skeptical of the results from laboratory experiments because they are seen as poor substitutes for empirical knowledge gained from examining naturally occurring legislatures.

If that were the purpose, then these skeptics are justified in dismissing the laboratory experiments. But those who dismiss experiments for this reason show a fundamental lack of understanding of what can be learned from experiments that it is not possible to learn directly from the field. Laboratory experiments provide something unique — a chance to see if the theory works under variations and control that simply is not possible or highly difficult to observe in the field. There is no perfect substitute for the laboratory data, just as there is no perfect substitute for the data derived from naturally occurring legislatures or from field experiments when they are possible. Hence, it is silly to debate whether data from the lab is superior or inferior to data from the field, either naturally occurring or manipulated. Such analyses should be seen as complements, each telling us something different and unique, since each provides us with a different piece of information not available otherwise, which together can provide us with a fuller understanding of the usefulness of the theory.

The experiments on the competitive solution and other similar cooperative game theoretic solutions showed that when preference profiles were varied, behavior changed in a systematic fashion according to cardinal payoffs that was unpredicted by the theory. In this sense, as Roth (1995) discusses, the experiments brought to light new facts that were unknown before they were conducted. The experimentalists found that varying something that was not theoretically meaningful was empirically meaningful and thus discovered something new about behavior — something that showed that the theory was inadequate.

3. Noncooperative Legislative Bargaining Theory, Experiments, and Subgame Perfection

It is my belief that without those lab experiments, the limitations of cooperative game theory as an approach to studying legislatures would have not been manifested for some time. As a consequence of the experiments, researchers like McKelvey (1991) began to turn to noncooperative game theoretic models of coalition formations to understand legislatures. Noncooperative game theory could provide some explanations for the relationships between cardinal payoffs and voting choices made by the subjects and provide explicit microfoundations for observed behavior that could be empirically tested. McKelvey (1991) used a model like Baron and Ferejohn (1989a), hereafter BF. In the BF model legislative bargaining is modeled as an infinitely repeated game where one individual makes an offer, the remaining individuals vote whether or not to accept the offer, and the game ends when an offer is accepted. Individuals are assumed to prefer bargains made earlier rather than later, the proposer is selected randomly each period, and a majority vote is needed for a proposal to be passed.

The predictions of the finite version of BF model rely heavily on the solution concept of subgame perfection. That is, suppose that there are three political parties, A, B, and C, choosing how to allocate a fixed number of ministerial portfolios. Assume that party A has 40 percent of the votes in the legislature, B has 35 percent, and C has 25 percent. Party A is chosen to make a proposal on how to divide the portfolios. Suppose that it is the last period of bargaining and if a proposal is not accepted the portfolios will be divided by vote shares. Thus party B should vote for a proposal that offers them more than 35 percent of the portfolios and party C should vote for a proposal that offers them more than 25 percent. Because A only needs a majority and C is cheaper, then A should propose that C gets slightly more than 25 percent of the portfolios, while A gets the remaining amount and B receives nothing. If we fold back the game to earlier proposal periods we find that whichever party is selected as the initial proposer should calculate for each party a reversion level using subgame perfection and propose an allocation that gives the party with the lowest reversion level just enough portfolios so that the party benefits over the reversion while keeping the majority of the portfolios to itself.

As Diermeier and Morton (2005) note the BF model is one of the most widely used formal frameworks in the study of legislative politics. Variants of the model have been used in the study of legislative voting rules (Baron and Ferejohn 1989a), committee power (Baron and Ferejohn 1989b), pork-barrel programs (Baron 1991a), government formation (Baron 1989, 1991b; Baron and Ferejohn 1989a), multi-party elections (Austen-Smith and Banks 1988; Baron 1991b), and inter-chamber bargaining (Diermeier and Myerson 1994; Ansolabehere, Snyder, and Ting 2003).

Because the BF model does make precise predictions about voting choices and coalition formation that can be related to actual payoffs, it has been subject to evaluation using both experimental and naturally occurring data (I am unaware of field experiments). McKelvey (1991) was the first to conduct laboratory experiments on BF (I discuss the evaluations of BF using field data below). McKelvey found that proposers offered too much. He speculated that the proposers were reluctant to give as small shares to coalition partners as predicted out of fear of retaliation should their proposal not be accepted. He suspected that the results showed a problem with assuming that individuals would follow subgame perfection.

4. How Centipede Game Experiments Inform Legislative Bargaining

The predictions of the centipede game, described in the accompanying chapters by McKelvey and Palfrey (Chapter 18) and Gerber (Chapter 16), like the BF model, heavily depend on subgame perfection. Like the BF model, at each stage the game potentially ends. Like the BF model the players are predicted to look down the tree and using backwards induction make a choice in the first play of the game that effectively ends the game. Yet, unlike the BF model, the centipede game is not seen as representative of legislative bargaining. For one thing, it is a much simpler two-person game. Players do not have to choose proposals but the options before them are exogenous. Furthermore, calculating what a player expects to receive if later branches of the tree are reached is straightforward rather than dependent on the probability that a player is selected to make a proposal and so on. Finally, the benefits to a player for violating subgame perfection are sizeable and increase the more willing the player is to do so.

Yet, the centipede game, because it is simpler and more straightforward, provides a more conclusive test of the assumption that players choose subgame perfect strategies than a test of the BF model. That is, the only reason why behavior may not be as predicted is if subjects do violate subgame perfection. The centipede game also allows for a careful investigation of what subjects anticipate about other subjects' behavior. In the centipede game, the first mover might pass if he or she is fairly confident that the second mover will pass and thus the first mover will be able to get a higher payoff for sure. But the first mover is assuming that the second mover may violate subgame perfection. In McKelvey's experiments on the BF model, he suspected that the tendency to give larger shares to coalition partners was because individuals were afraid that other subjects would violate subgame perfection and reject payoffs that they should accept. But the BF model had too many moving parts to be able to conclude that the subjects' choices were made for those reasons. In particular McKelvey could not observe rejections of equilibrium payoffs if payoffs were above equilibrium in anticipation of rejection. The centipede game, in contrast, allowed for the measurement of both non-equilibrium behavior and how anticipation of such behavior affected the choices of other players. By conducting experiments on the centipede game it was possible to learn something about behavior in other games, such as the BF model, which are more realistic, that an experiment on the BF model itself could not reveal. As discussed in Gerber, the centipede game experiments did show violations of subgame perfection and the anticipation of violations, thus suggesting that McKelvey's suspicion that the failure of the BF model to predict well in the laboratory experiments was related to a tendency to violate subgame perfection.

5. Behavioral Game Theory, Experiments, and Legislative Bargaining

As discussed in the contributions by Gerber (Chapter 16) and Palfrey (Chapter 19), the results from the centipede game experiments led McKelvey and Palfrey to derive a new equilibrium concept, quantal response equilibrium, that would allow for subjects to violate subgame perfection. This concept was one of the first in a new approach to game theory, behavioral game theory, an approach that incorporates the fact that individuals may not always choose rationally in games. This concept has been applied to more specific questions in political science using naturally occurring data such as in the work of Signorino (1998) analyzing strategic interaction in international conflict. Hence, even if the centipede game experiments did not tell us something useful about legislative bargaining, they indirectly have informed our understanding of international conflict.

Although the centipede game experiments took the basics of the BF model and focused on those aspects that may be causing the results McKelvey (1991) found — fairer distributions within coalitions than predicted — other research on legislative bargaining took the alternative approach of testing the BF model directly on naturally occurring data (see Warwick and Druckman 2001; Ansolabehere et al. 2003). This analysis is also concerned with determining whether bargaining leads to unequal distributions of payoffs in coalitions as predicted by BF. However, the research contrasts the predictions of the BF model with an alternative model of bargaining called demand bargaining similar to that formulated in Morelli (1999). In the demand model actors make sequential demands until every member has made a demand or someone forms a majority by demanding the residual payoff that is implicitly left by one short of a majority of other coalition members. If no majority coalition forms after all players have made a demand, a new first demander is randomly selected, all previous demands are void, and the game continues. Demand bargaining provides different predictions from the BF model in that the allocations of portfolios will be proportional to bargaining power and that proposers will not receive an undue share. Yet the results using naturally occurring data have been inconclusive — Warwick and Druckman (2001) find support for a proportional relationship and demand bargaining in legislatures while Ansolabehere et al. (2003) find evidence of proposal power, supporting the BF model.

What to make of the contrasting empirical results? The problem with the results is that it is difficult to determine the nature of the underlying bargaining process within the legislature simply by looking at what can be observed, proposal and bargaining power and portfolio allocations. Theoretically the two different models provide different predictions about the relationship between the observables. But the results from McKelvey (1991) and the centipede game experiments suggest that even when the underlying model is BF, the behavior of the individuals will lead to more equitable proposals, resembling demand bargaining. Thus, it might be the case that the predictions of the two models when behavioral violations of subgame perfection occur will not be dissimilar enough for the naturally occurring data to distinguish between them.

In an innovative study, Fréchette, Kagel, and Morelli (2005), hereafter FKM, investigate this hypothesis. First they tested to see if the methods used by Warwick and Druckman and Ansolabehere et al. could distinguish between the two models if subjects behaved as the standard theory would predict (that is, without behavioral errors as discussed above). They generated simulated data and analyzed that data in the same way that the researchers using field data had. They found that the approaches using field data, if subjects make decisions as predicted by the standard game theoretic approach, could distinguish between the two theories. Thus, in theory the methods used by the field researchers should work to determine how legislatures bargain.

But FKM also conducted experiments on both the BF and demand bargaining models — thus generating actual choices by real subjects. As with the simulated data they treated the data as if it they could only measure the same observables that a researcher with field data can measure. FKM found that the empirical approaches used by Warwick and Druckman and Ansolabehere et al. could not distinguish between the two models using the data from the subjects in the experiments. Specifically, the regression analysis used on the field data, when used on the experimental data, cannot identify the underlying data generating processes and the regression results are similar to those found on the field data independent of whether the underlying data is generated with subjects participating in a BF game or a demand bargaining game. FKM (p. 6, italics in the original) contend that

> there is a *behavioral identification* problem with the regression approach advocated for the field data, in that even though the specifications used are well identified with respect to theoretical behavior, the parameters of interest are not identified with

respect to how agents actually behave. As such there is no clear mapping from the estimated parameters to the rules of the game that the investigator is trying to infer given how people actually play these games. To fully address this behavioral identification problem, one would need to observe actual institutional differences and/or come up with other ways to distinguish between the two models given the available field data.

The analysis of FKM shows that laboratory experiments provide researchers who work with field data unique opportunities. That is, the choices made by the subjects are better than simulated choices in that they incorporate differences between how individuals actually choose in games like BF or demand bargaining.

6. Concluding Remarks

The centipede game experiments when viewed in isolation may seem to be mainly of interest to theorists. But when put in context, we can see that the experiments were a direct consequence of a research program designed to understand legislative bargaining — a research program highly directed to building an empirically relevant theory. Experimental research on cooperative game theoretic models led to a more realistic noncooperative approach. Field data analysis is unlikely to have revealed the problems that the experimental research revealed. However, the assumptions about individual behavior in the noncooperative approach appeared to be violated in further experiments, leading to a more careful study of those assumptions in the centipede game experiments and a new equilibrium concept that allows for more realistic behavior. The violations found in the centipede game experiments and McKelvey's BF experiments also imply, as FKM demonstrate, that tests of theories using field data must recognize that the predictions of the theory may not be distinguishable when violations are a possibility. Laboratory experiments not only can lead to more realistic theories but can also be a testbed for methodologists who wish to evaluate formal theories on field data.

References

Ansolabehere, Stephen, James Snyder, and Michael Ting. 2003. "Bargaining in Bicameral Legislatures: When and Why Does Malapportionment Matter?" *American Political Science Review* 97:471–81.

Austen-Smith, David and Jeffrey S. Banks. 1988. "Elections, Coalitions, and Legislative Outcomes." *American Political Science Review* 82:405–22.

Baron, David P. 1989. "A Noncooperative Theory of Legislative Coalitions." *American Journal of Political Science* 33:1048–84.

Baron, David P. 1991a. "Majoritarian Incentives, Pork Barrel Programs, and Procedural Control." *American Journal of Political Science* 35:57–90.

Baron, David P. 1991b. "A Spatial Theory of Government Formation in Parliamentary Systems." *American Political Science Review* 85:137–65.

Baron, David P. and John A. Ferejohn. 1989a. "Bargaining in Legislatures." *American Political Science Review* 89:1181–1206.

Baron, David P. and John A. Ferejohn. 1989b. "The Power to Propose." In *Models of Strategic Choice in Politics*, ed. by Peter C. Ordeshook. Ann Arbor: University of Michigan Press, pp. 343–66.

Diermeier, Daniel and Rebecca Morton. 2005. "Proportionality versus Perfectness: Experiments in Majoritarian Bargaining." In *Social Choice and Strategic Behavior: Essays in Honor of Jeffrey Banks*, ed. by David Austen-Smith and John Duggan, Berlin et al.: Springer, pp. 201–227.

Diermeier, Daniel and Roger B. Myerson. 1994. "Bargaining, Veto Power, and Legislative Committees." CMSEMS working paper no. 1089. Northwestern University.

Fréchette, Guillaume, John Kagel, and Massimo Morelli. 2005. "Behavioral Identification in Coalitional Bargaining: An Experimental Analysis of Demand Bargaining and Alternating Offers." Working paper. New York University Department of Economics.

McKelvey, R. D. 1991. "An Experimental Test of a Stochastic Game Model of Committee Bargaining." In *Contemporary Laboratory Research in Political Economy*, ed. by Thomas R. Palfrey. Ann Arbor: University of Michigan Press.

McKelvey, Richard D. and Peter C. Ordeshook. 1983. "Some Experimental Results That Fail to Support the Competitive Solution." *Public Choice* 40:281–91.

McKelvey, Richard D., Peter C. Ordeshook, and Mark D. Winer. 1978. "The Competitive Solution for N-Person Games without Transferable Utility, with an Application to Committee Games." *American Political Science Review* 72(2):599–615. Chapter 10 of this book.

McKelvey, Richard D. and Thomas R. Palfrey. 1992. "An Experimental Study of the Centipede Game." *Econometrica* 60:803–36. Chapter 18 of this book.

Morelli, M. (1999): "Demand Competition and Policy Compromise in Legislative Bargaining." *American Political Science Review* 93:809–20.

Riker, William H. 1962. *The Theory of Political Coalitions*. New Haven: Yale University Press.

Roth, Alvin E. 1995. "Bargaining Experiments." In *The Handbook of Experimental Economics*, ed. by John Kagel and Alvin Roth. Princeton: Princeton University Press, pp. 253–348.

Signorino, Curt. 1998. "Strategic Interaction and the Statistical Analysis of International Conflict." *American Political Science Review* 93(2):279–98.

Warwick, Paul V. and James N. Druckman. 2001. "Portfolio Salience and the Proportionality of Payoffs in Coalition Governments." *British Journal of Political Science* 31:627–49.

CHAPTER 18

An Experimental Study of the Centipede Game

RICHARD D. MCKELVEY AND THOMAS R. PALFREY

ABSTRACT. We report on an experiment in which individuals play a version of the centipede game. In this game, two players alternately get a chance to take the larger portion of a continually escalating pile of money. As soon as one person takes, the game ends with that player getting the larger portion of the pile, and the other player getting the smaller portion. If one views the experiment as a complete information game, all standard game theoretic equilibrium concepts predict the first mover should take the large pile on the first round. The experimental results show that this does not occur. An alternative explanation for the data can be given if we reconsider the game as a game of incomplete information in which there is some uncertainty over the payoff functions of the players. In particular, if the subjects believe there is some small likelihood that the opponent is an altruist, then in the equilibrium of this incomplete information game, players adopt mixed strategies in the early rounds of the experiment, with the probability of taking increasing as the pile gets larger. We investigate how well a version of this model explains the data observed in the centipede experiments.

1. Overview of the Experiment and the Results

This paper reports the results of several experimental games for which the predictions of Nash equilibrium are widely acknowledged to be intuitively unsatisfactory.[1] We explain the deviations from the standard predictions using an approach that combines recent developments in game theory with a parametric specification of the errors individuals might make. We construct a structural econometric model

---

[1]Support for this research was provided in part by NSF Grants #IST-8513679 and #SES-878650 to the California Institute of Technology. We thank Mahmoud El-Gamal for valuable discussions concerning the econometric estimation, and we thank Richard Boylan, Mark Fey, Arthur Lupia, and David Schmidt for able research assistance. We thank the JPL-Caltech joint computing project for granting us time on the CRAY X-MP at the Jet Propulsion Laboratory. We also are grateful for comments and suggestions from many seminar participants, from an editor, and from two very thorough referees.

and estimate the extent to which the behavior is explainable by game-theoretic considerations.

In the games we investigate, the use of backward induction and/or the elimination of dominated strategies leads to a unique Nash prediction, but there are clear benefits to the players if, for some reason, some players fail to behave in this fashion. Thus, we have intentionally chosen an environment in which we expect Nash equilibrium to perform at its worst. The best known example of a game in this class is the finitely repeated prisoners' dilemma. We focus on an even simpler and, we believe more compelling, example of such a game, the closely related alternating-move game that has come to be known as the "centipede game" (see Binmore (1987)).

The centipede game is a finite move extensive form two person game in which each player alternately gets a turn to either terminate the game with a favorable payoff to itself, or continue the game, resulting in social gains for the pair. As far as we are aware, the centipede game was first introduced by Rosenthal (1982), and has subsequently been studied by Binmore (1987), Kreps (1990), and Reny (1988). The original versions of the game consisted of a sequence of a hundred moves (hence the name "centipede") with linearly increasing payoffs. A concise version of the centipede game with exponentially increasing payoffs, called the "Share or Quit" game, is studied by Megiddo (1986), and a slightly modified version of this game is analyzed by Aumann (1988). It is this exponential version that we study here.

In Aumann's version of the centipede game, two piles of money are on the table. One pile is larger than the other. There are two players, each of whom alternately gets a turn in which it can choose either to take the larger of the two piles of money or to pass. When one player takes, the game ends, with the player whose turn it is getting the large pile and the other player getting the small pile. On the other hand, whenever a player passes, both piles are multiplied by some fixed amount, and the play proceeds to the next player. There are a finite number of moves to the game, and the number is known in advance to both players. In Aumann's version of the game, the pot starts at $10.50, which is divided into a large pile of $10.00 and a small pile of $.50. Each time a player passes, both piles are multiplied by $10. The game proceeds a total of six moves, i.e., three moves for each player.

It is easy to show that any Nash equilibrium to the centipede game involves the first player taking the large pile on the first move — in spite of the fact that in an eight move version of the game, both players could be multi-millionaires if they were to pass every round. Since all Nash equilibria make the same outcome prediction, clearly any of the usual refinements of Nash equilibrium also make the same prediction. We thus have a situation where there is an unambiguous prediction made by game theory.

Despite the unambiguous prediction, game theorists have not seemed too comfortable with the above analysis of the game, wondering whether it really reflects the way in which anyone would play such a game (Binmore (1987), Aumann (1988)). Yet, there has been no previous experimental study of this game.[2]

In the simple versions of the centipede game we study, the experimental outcomes are quite different from the Nash predictions. To give an idea how badly the Nash equilibrium (or iterated elimination of dominated strategies) predicts outcomes, we find only 37 of 662 games end with the first player taking the large pile on the first move, while 23 of the games end with both players passing at every move. The rest of the outcomes are scattered in between.

One class of explanations for how such apparently irrational behavior could arise is based on reputation effects and incomplete information.[3] This is the approach we adopt. The idea is that players believe there is some possibility that their opponent has payoffs different from the ones we tried to induce in the laboratory. In our game, if a player places sufficient weight in its utility function on the payoff to the opponent, the rational strategy is to always pass. Such a player is labeled an *altruist*.[4] If it is believed that there is some likelihood that each player may be an altruist, then it can pay a selfish player to try to mimic the behavior of an altruist in an attempt to develop a reputation for passing. These incentives to mimic are very powerful, in the sense that a very small belief that altruists are in the subject pool can generate a lot of mimicking, even with a very short horizon.

The structure of the centipede game we run is sufficiently simple that we can solve for the equilibrium of a parameterized version of this reputational model. Using standard maximum likelihood techniques we can then fit this model. Using this assumption of only a single kind of deviation from the "selfish" payoffs normally assumed in induced-value theory[5] we are able to fit the data well, and obtain an estimate of the proportion of altruistic players on the order of 5 percent of the subject pool. In addition to estimating the proportion of altruists in the subject

---

[2]There is related experimental work on the prisoner's dilemma game by Selten and Stoecker (1986) and on an ultimatum bargaining game with an increasing cake by Güth et al. (1991).

[3]See Kreps and Wilson (1982a), Kreps et al. (1982), Fudenberg and Maskin (1986), and Kreps (1990, pp. 536–543).

[4]We called them "irrationals" in an earlier version of the paper. The equilibrium implications of this kind of incomplete information and altruism have been explored in a different kind of experimental game by Palfrey and Rosenthal (1988). See also Cooper et al. (1990).

[5]See Smith (1976).

pool, we also estimate the beliefs of the players about this proportion. We find that subjects' beliefs are, on average, equal to the estimated "true" proportion of altruists, thus providing evidence in favor of a version of rational expectations. We also estimate a decision error rate to be on the order of 5%–10% for inexperienced subjects and roughly two-thirds that for experienced subjects, indicating two things: (i) a significant amount of learning is taking place, and (ii) even with inexperienced subjects, only a small fraction of their behavior is unaccounted for by a simple game-theoretic equilibrium model in which beliefs are accurate.

Our experiment can be compared to that of Camerer and Weigelt (1988) (see also Neral and Ochs (1989) and Jung et al. (1989)). In our experiment, we find that many features of the data can be explained if we assume that there is a belief that a certain percentage of the subjects in the population are altruists. This is equivalent to asserting that subjects did not believe that the utility functions we attempted to induce are the same as the utility functions that all subjects really use for making their decisions. I.e., subjects have their own personal beliefs about parameters of the experimental design that are at odds with those of the experimental design. This is similar to the point in Camerer and Weigelt, that one way to account for some features of behavior in their experiments was to introduce "homemade priors"— i.e., beliefs that there were more subjects who always act cooperatively (similar to our altruists) than were actually induced to be so in their experimental design. (They used a rule-of-thumb procedure to obtain a homemade prior point estimate of 17%.) Our analysis differs from Camerer and Weigelt partly in that we integrate it into a structural econometric model, which we then estimate using classical techniques. This enables us to estimate the number of subjects that actually behave in such a fashion, and to address the question as to whether the beliefs of subjects are on average correct.

Our experiment can also be compared to the literature on repeated prisoner's dilemmas. This literature (see e.g., Selten and Stoecker (1986) for a review) finds that experienced subjects exhibit a pattern of "tacit cooperation" until shortly before the end of the game, when they start to adopt noncooperative behavior. Such behavior would be predicted by incomplete information models like that of Kreps et al. (1982). However, Selten and Stoecker also find that inexperienced subjects do not immediately adopt this pattern of play, but that it takes them some time to "learn to cooperate." Selten and Stoecker develop a learning theory model that is not based on optimizing behavior to account for such a learning phase. One could alternatively develop a model similar to the one used here, where in addition to incomplete information about the payoffs of others, all subjects have some chance of making errors, which decreases over time. If some other subjects might be

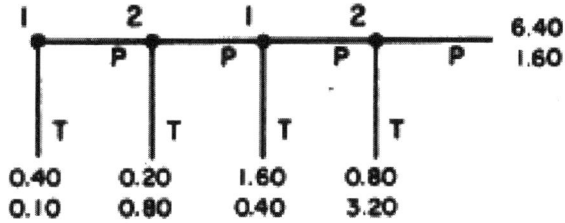

FIGURE 1. The four move centipede game

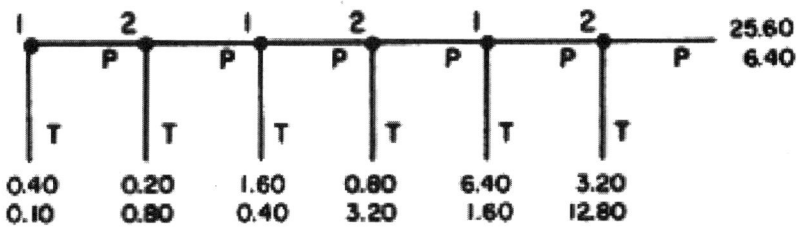

FIGURE 2. The six move centipede game

making errors, then it could be in the interest of all subjects to take some time to learn to cooperate, since they can masquerade as slow learners. Thus, a natural analog of the model used here might offer an alternative explanation for the data in Selten and Stoecker.

2. Experimental Design

Our budget is too constrained to use the payoffs proposed by Aumann. So we run a rather more modest version of the centipede game. In our laboratory games, we start with a total pot of $.50 divided into a large pile of $.40 and a small pile of $.10. Each time a player chooses to pass, both piles are multiplied by two. We consider both a two round (four move) and a three round (six move) version of the game. This leads to the extensive forms illustrated in Figures 1 and 2. In addition, we consider a version of the four move game in which all payoffs are quadrupled. This "high payoff" condition therefore produced a payoff structure equivalent to the last four moves of the six move game.

In each experimental session we used a total of twenty subjects, none of whom had previously played a centipede game. The subjects were divided into

TABLE I. Experimental Design

Session #	Subject Pool	# Subjects	Games / Subjects	Total # Games	# Moves	High Payoffs
1	PCC	20	10	100	4	No
2	PCC	18	9	81	4	No
3	CIT	20	10	100	4	No
4	CIT	20	10	100	4	Yes
5	CIT	20	10	100	6	No
6	PCC	18	9	81	6	No
7	PCC	20	10	100	6	No

two groups at the beginning of the session, which we called the Red and the Blue groups. In each game, the Red player was the first mover, and the Blue player was the second mover. Each subject then participated in ten games, one with each of the subjects in the other group.[6] The sessions were all conducted through computer terminals at the Caltech Laboratory for Experimental Economics and Political Science. Subjects did not communicate with other subjects except through the strategy choices they made. Before each game, each subject was matched with another subject, of the opposite color, with whom they had not been previously matched, and then the subjects who were matched with each other played the game in either Figure 1 or Figure 2 depending on the session.

All details described above were made common knowledge to the players, at least as much as is possible in a laboratory setting. In other words, the instructions were read to the subjects with everyone in the same room (see Appendix B for the exact instructions read to the subjects). Thus it was common knowledge that no subject was ever matched with any other subject more than once. In fact we used a rotating matching scheme which insures that no player i ever plays against a player who has previously played someone who has played someone that i has already played. (Further, for any positive integer n, the sentence which replaces the phrase "who has previously played someone who has played someone" in the previous sentence with n copies of the same phrase is also true.) In principle, this matching scheme should eliminate potential supergame or cooperative behavior, yet at the same time allow us to obtain multiple observations on each individual's behavior.

---

[6] Only one of the three versions of the game was played in a given session. In sessions 2 and 6, not all subjects showed up, so there were only 18 subjects, with 9 in each group, and consequently each subject played only 9 games.

We conducted a total of seven sessions (see Table I). Our subjects were students from Pasadena Community College (PCC) and from the California Institute of Technology (CIT). No subject was used in more than one session. Sessions 1–3 involved the regular four move version of the game, session 4 involved the high payoff four move game, and sessions 5–7 involved the six move version of the game. This gives us a total of 58 subjects and 281 plays of the four move game, and 58 subjects with 281 plays of the six move game, and 20 subjects with 100 plays of the high payoff game. Subjects were paid in cash the cumulative amount that they earned in the session plus a fixed amount for showing up ($3.00 for CIT students and $5.00 for PCC students).[7]

3. Descriptive Summary of Data

The complete data from the experiment is given in Appendix C. In Table II, we present some simple descriptive statistics summarizing the behavior of the subjects in our experiment. Table IIA gives the frequencies of each of the terminal outcomes. Thus f_i is the proportion of games ending at the ith terminal node. Table IIB gives the implied probabilities, p_i of taking at the ith decision node of the game. In other words, p_i is the proportion of games among those that reached decision node i, in which the subject who moves at node i chose TAKE. Thus, in a game with n decision nodes, $p_i = f_i / \sum_{j=1}^{n+1} f_j$.

All standard game theoretic solutions (Nash equilibrium, iterated elimination of dominated strategies, maximin, rationalizability, etc.) would predict $f_i = 1$ if $i = 1$, $f_i = 0$ otherwise. The requirement of rationality that subjects not adopt dominated strategies would predict that $f_{n+1} = 0$ and $p_n = 1$. As is evident from Table II, we can reject out of hand either of these hypotheses of rationality. In only 7% of the four move games, 1% of the six move games, and 15% of the high payoff games does the first mover choose TAKE on the first round. So the subjects clearly do not iteratively eliminate dominated strategies. Further, when a game reaches the last move, Table IIB shows that the player with the last move adopts the dominated strategy of choosing PASS roughly 25% of the time in the four move games, 15% in the six move games, and 31% in the high payoff games.[8]

The most obvious and consistent pattern in the data is that in all of the sessions, the probability of TAKE increases as we get closer to the last move (see

---

[7]The stakes in these games were large by usual standards. Students earned from a low of $7.00 to a high of $75.00, in sessions that averaged less than 1 hour — average earnings were $20.50 ($13.40 in the four move, $30.77 in the six move, and $41.50 in the high payoff four move version).

[8]For sessions 1–3, 7 of the 14 cases in this category are attributable to 2 of the 29 subjects. In the high payoff condition, 4 of the 5 events are attributable to 1 subject.

TABLE II. A. Proportion of Observations at Each Terminal Node

		Session	N	f_1	f_2	f_3	f_4	f_5	f_6	f_7
Four Move	1	(PCC)	100	.06	.26	.44	.20	.04		
	2	(PCC)	81	.10	.38	.40	.11	.01		
	3	(CIT)	100	.06	.43	.28	.14	.09		
	Total	1–3	281	.071	.356	.370	.153	.049		
High Payoff	4	(High-CIT)	100	.150	.370	.320	.110	.050		
Six Move	5	(CIT)	100	.02	.09	.39	.28	.20	.01	.01
	6	(PCC)	81	.00	.02	.04	.46	.35	.11	.02
	7	(PCC)	100	.00	.07	.14	.43	.23	.12	.01
	Total	5–7	281	.007	.064	.199	.384	.253	.078	.014

TABLE II. B. Implied Take Probabilities for the Centipede Game

		Session	p_1	p_2	p_3	p_4	p_5	p_6
Four Move	1	(PCC)	.06 (100)	.28 (94)	.65 (68)	.83 (24)		
	2	(PCC)	.10 (81)	.42 (73)	.76 (42)	.90 (10)		
	3	(CIT)	.06 (100)	.46 (94)	.55 (51)	.61 (23)		
	Total	1–3	.071 (281)	.38 (261)	.65 (161)	.75 (57)		
High Payoff Six Move	4	(CIT)	.15 (100)	.44 (85)	.67 (48)	.69 (16)		
	5	(CIT)	.02 (100)	.09 (98)	.44 (89)	.56 (50)	.91 (22)	.50 (2)
	6	(PCC)	.00 (81)	.02 (81)	.04 (79)	.49 (76)	.72 (39)	.82 (11)
	7	(PCC)	.00 (100)	.07 (100)	.15 (93)	.54 (79)	.64 (36)	.92 (13)
	Total	5–7	.01 (281)	.06 (279)	.21 (261)	.53 (205)	.73 (97)	.85 (26)

The number in parentheses is the number of observations in the game at that node.

TABLE III. A. Cumulative Outcome Frequencies ($F_j = \sum_{i=1}^{j} f_i$)

Treatment	Game	N	F_1	F_2	F_3	F_4	F_5	F_6	F_7
Four	1–5	145	.062	.365	.724	.924	1.00		
Move	6–10	136	.081	.493	.875	.978	1.00		
Six	1–5	145	.000	.055	.227	.558	.889	.979	1.00
Move	6–10	136	.015	.089	.317	.758	.927	.993	1.00

Table IIB). The only exception to this pattern is in session 5 (CIT) in the last two moves, where the probabilities drop from .91 to .50. But the figure at the last move (.50) is based on only two observations. Thus any model to explain the data should capture this basic feature. In addition to this dominant feature, there are some less obvious patterns of the data, which we now discuss.

Table III indicates that there are some differences between the earlier and later plays of the game in a given treatment which are supportive of the proposition that as subjects gain more experience with the game, their behavior appears "more rational." Recall that with the matching scheme we use, there is no game-theoretic reason to expect players to play any differently in earlier games than in later games. Table IIIA shows the cumulative probabilities, $F_j = \sum_{i=1}^{j} f_i$, of stopping by the jth node. We see that the cumulative distribution in the first five games stochastically dominates the distribution in the last five games both in the four and six move experiments. This indicates that the games end earlier in later matches. Table IIIB shows that in both the four and six move sessions, in later games subjects chose TAKE with higher probability at all stages of the game (with the exception of node 5 of the six move games). Further, the number of subjects that adopt the dominated strategy of passing on the last move drops from 14 of 56, or 25%, to 4 of 27, or 15%.

A third pattern emerges in comparing the four move games to the six move games (in Table IIB). We see that at every move, there is a higher probability of taking in the four move game than in the corresponding move of the six move game (.07 vs .01 in the first move; .38 vs .06 in the second move, etc.). The same relation holds between the high payoff games and the six move games. However, if we compare the four move games to the *last* four moves of the six move games, there is more taking in the six move games (.75 vs .85 in the last move; .65 vs .73 in the next to last move, etc.). This same relationship holds between the high payoff games and the six move games even though the payoffs in the high payoff games are identical to the payoffs in the last four moves of the six move games.

TABLE III. B. Implied Take Probabilities Comparison of Early versus Late Plays in the Low Payoff Centipede Game

Treatment	Game	p_1	p_2	p_3	p_4	p_5	p_6
Four Move	1–5	.06 (145)	.32 (136)	.57 (92)	.75 (40)		
	6–10	.08 (136)	.49 (125)	.75 (69)	.82 (17)		
Six Move	1–5	.00 (145)	.06 (145)	.18 (137)	.43 (112)	.75 (64)	.81 (16)
	6–10	.01 (136)	.07 (134)	.25 (124)	.65 (93)	.70 (33)	.90 (10)

There is at least one other interesting pattern in the data. Specifically, if we look at individual level data, there are several subjects who PASS at every opportunity they have.[9] We call such subjects *altruists*, because an obvious way to rationalize their behavior is to assume that they have a utility function that is monotonically increasing in the *sum* of the red and blue payoffs, rather than a selfish utility function that only depends on that player's own payoff. Overall, there were a total of 9 players who chose PASS at every opportunity. Roughly half (5) of these were red players and half (5) were in four move games. At the other extreme (i.e., the Nash equilibrium prediction), only 1 out of all 138 subjects chose TAKE at every opportunity. This indicates the strong possibility that players who will always choose PASS do exist in our subject pool, and also suggests that a theory which successfully accounts for the data will almost certainly have to admit the existence of at least a small fraction of such subjects.

Finally, there are interesting *non-patterns* in the data. Specifically, unlike the ten cases cited above, the preponderance of the subject behavior is inconsistent with the use of a single pure strategy throughout all games they played. For example, subject #8 in session #1 (a red player) chooses TAKE at the first chance in the second game it participates in, then PASS at both opportunities in the next game, PASS at both opportunities in the fourth game, TAKE at the first chance in the fifth game, and PASS at the first chance in the sixth game. Fairly common irregularities of this sort, which appear rather haphazard from a casual glance, would seem to require some degree of randomness to explain. While some of this behavior may indicate evidence of the use of mixed strategies, some such behavior

---

[9] Some of these subjects had as many as 24 opportunities to TAKE in the 10 games they played. See Appendix C.

is impossible to rationalize, even by resorting to the possibility of altruistic individuals or Bayesian updating across games. For example, subject #6 in session #1 (a blue player), chooses PASS at the last node of the first game, but takes at the first opportunity a few games later. Rationalization of this subject's behavior as altruistic in the first game is contradicted by the subject's behavior in the later game. Rational play cannot account for some sequences of plays we observe in the data, even with a model that admits the possibility of altruistic players.

4. The Model

In what follows, we construct a structural econometric model based on the theory of games of incomplete information that is simultaneously consistent with the experimental design and the underlying theory. Standard maximum likelihood techniques can then be applied to estimate the underlying structural parameters.

The model we construct consists of an incomplete information game together with a specification of two sources of errors — errors in actions and errors in beliefs. The model is constructed to account for both the time-series nature of our data and for the dependence across observations, features of the data set that derive from a design in which every subject plays a sequence of games against different opponents. The model is able to account for the broad descriptive findings summarized in the previous section. By parameterizing the structure of the errors, we can also address issues of whether there is learning going on over time, whether there is heterogeneity in beliefs, and whether individuals' beliefs are on average correct.

We first describe the basic model, and then describe the two sources of errors.

4.1. The Basic Model

If, as appears to be the case, there are a substantial number of altruists in our subject pool, it seems reasonable to assume that the possible existence of such individuals is commonly known by all subjects. Our basic model is thus a game of two sided incomplete information where each individual can be one of two types (selfish or altruistic), and there is incomplete information about whether one's opponent is selfish or altruistic.

In our model, a *selfish* individual is defined as an individual who derives utility only from its own payoff, and acts to maximize this utility. In analogy to our definition of a selfish individual, a natural definition of an altruist would be as an individual who derives utility not only from its own payoff, but also from the payoff of the other player. For our purposes, to avoid having to make parametric assumptions about the form of the utility functions, it is more convenient to define an altruist in terms of the strategy choice rather than in terms of the utility function. Thus, we define an *altruist* as an individual who always chooses PASS. However, it is important to note that we could obtain an equivalent model by making parametric assumptions on the form of the utility functions. For example, if we were to assume that the utility to player i is a convex combination of its own payoff and that of its opponent, then any individual who places a weight of at least $\frac{2}{9}$ on the payoff of the opponent has a dominant strategy to choose PASS in every round of the experiment. Thus, defining altruists to be individuals who satisfy this condition would lead to equivalent behavior for the altruists.

The extensive form of the basic model for the case when the probability of a selfish individual equals q is shown in Figure 8 in Appendix A. Hence, the probability of an altruist is $1 - q$. This is a standard game of incomplete information. There is an initial move by nature in which the types of both players are drawn. If a player is altruistic, then the player has a trivial strategy choice (namely, it can PASS). If a player is selfish, then it can choose either PASS or TAKE.

4.1.1. Equilibrium of the Basic Model. The formal analysis of the equilibrium appears in Appendix A, but it is instructive to provide a brief overview of the equilibrium strategies, and to summarize how equilibrium strategies vary over the family of games indexed by q. We analytically derive in Appendix A the solution to the n-move game, for arbitrary values of q (the common knowledge belief that a randomly selected player is selfish) ranging from 0 to 1.

For any given q, a strategy for the first player in a six move game is a vector, (p_1, p_3, p_5), where p_i specifies the probability that Red chooses TAKE on move i conditional on Red being a selfish player. Similarly, a strategy for Blue is a vector (p_2, p_4, p_6) giving the probability that Blue chooses TAKE on the corresponding move conditional that Blue is selfish. Thus a strategy pair is a vector $p = (p_1, p_2, \ldots, p_6)$, where the odd components are moves by Red and the even components are moves by Blue. Similar notation is used for the four move game.

In Appendix A, we prove that for generic q there is a unique sequential equilibrium to the game, and we solve for this equilibrium as a function of q. Let us write $p(q)$ for the solution as a function of q. It is easy to verify the following properties of $p(q)$, which are true in both the four move and six move games.

Property 1: For any q, Blue chooses TAKE with probability 1 on its last move.

Property 2: If $1 - q > \frac{1}{7}$, both Red and Blue always choose PASS, except on the last move, when Blue chooses TAKE.

Property 3: If $1 - q \in \left(0, \frac{1}{7}\right)$, the equilibrium involves mixed strategies.
Property 4: If $q = 1$, then both Red and Blue always choose TAKE.

From the solution, we can compute the implied probabilities of choosing TAKE at each move, accounting for the altruists as well as the selfish players. We can also compute the probability $s(q) = (s_1(q), \ldots, s_7(q))$ of observing each of the possible outcomes, T, PT, PPT, PPPT, PPPPT, PPPPPT, PPPPPP. Thus, $s_1(q) = qp_1(q), s_2(q) = q^2(1 - p_1(q))p_2(q) + q(1 - q)p_2(q)$, etc. Figures 3 and 4 graph the probabilities of the outcomes as a function of the level of altruism, $1 - q$.

It is evident from the properties of the solution and from the outcome probabilities in Figures 3 and 4 that the equilibrium predictions are extremely sensitive to the beliefs that players have about the proportion of altruists in the population. The intuition of why this is so is well-summarized in the literature on signalling and reputation building (for example, Kreps and Wilson (1982a), Kreps et al. (1982)) and is exposited very nicely for a one-sided incomplete information version of the centipede game more recently in Kreps (1990). The guiding principle is easy to understand, even if one cannot follow the technical details of the Appendix. Because of the uncertainty in the game when it is not common knowledge that everyone is self-interested, it will generally be worthwhile for a selfish player to mimic altruistic behavior. This is not very different from the fact that in poker it may be a good idea to bluff some of the time in order to confuse your opponent about whether or not you have a good hand. In our games, for *any* amount of uncertainty of this sort, equilibrium will involve some degree of imitation. The form of the imitation in our setting is obvious: selfish players sometimes pass, to mimic an altruist. By imitating an altruist one might lure an opponent into passing at the next move, thereby raising one's final payoff in the game. The amount of imitation in equilibrium depends directly on the beliefs about the likelihood $(1 - q)$ of a randomly selected player being an altruist. The more likely players believe there are altruists in the population, the more imitation there is. In fact, if these beliefs are sufficiently high (at least $\frac{1}{7}$, in our versions of the centipede game), then selfish players will always imitate altruists, thereby completely reversing the predictions of game theory when it is common knowledge that there are no altruists. Between 0 and 1, the theory predicts the use of mixed strategies by selfish players.

4.1.2. Limitations of the Basic Model. The primary observation to make from the solution to the basic model is that this model can account for the main feature of the data noted in the previous section — namely that probabilities of taking

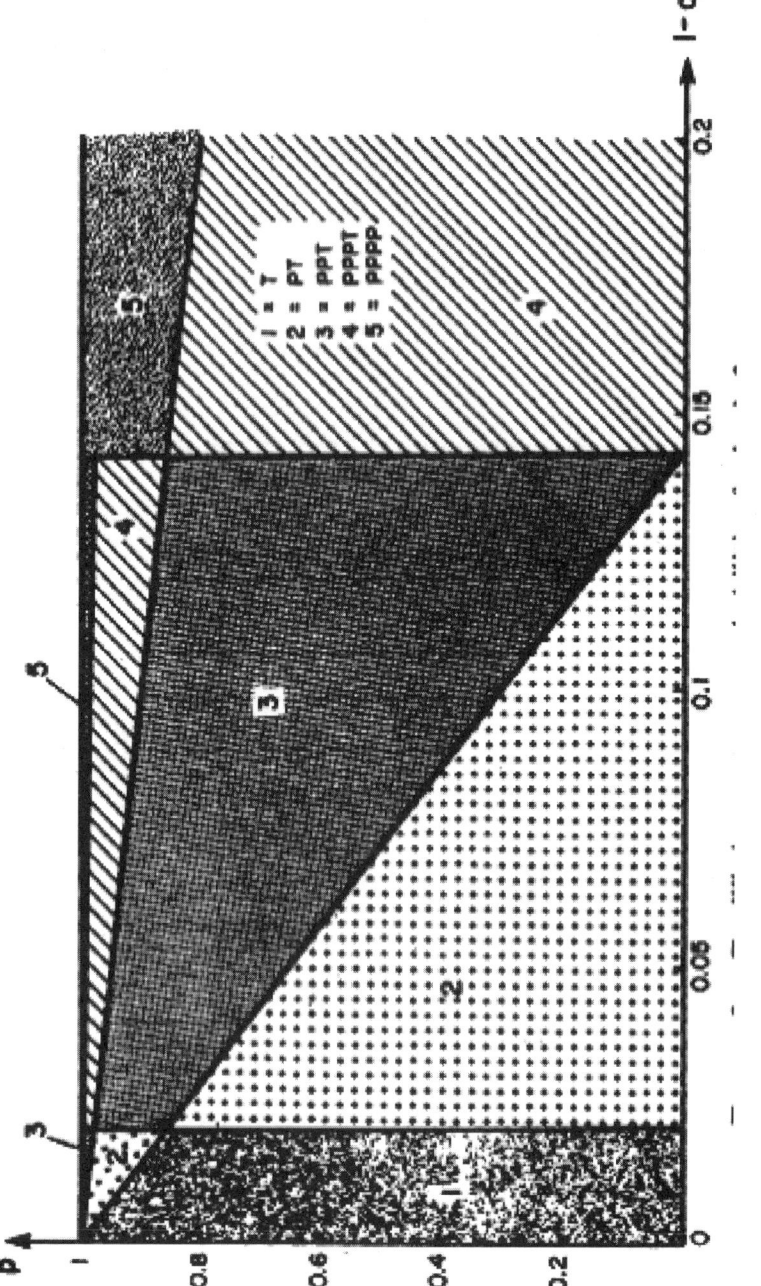

FIGURE 3. Equilibrium outcome probabilities for basic four move game

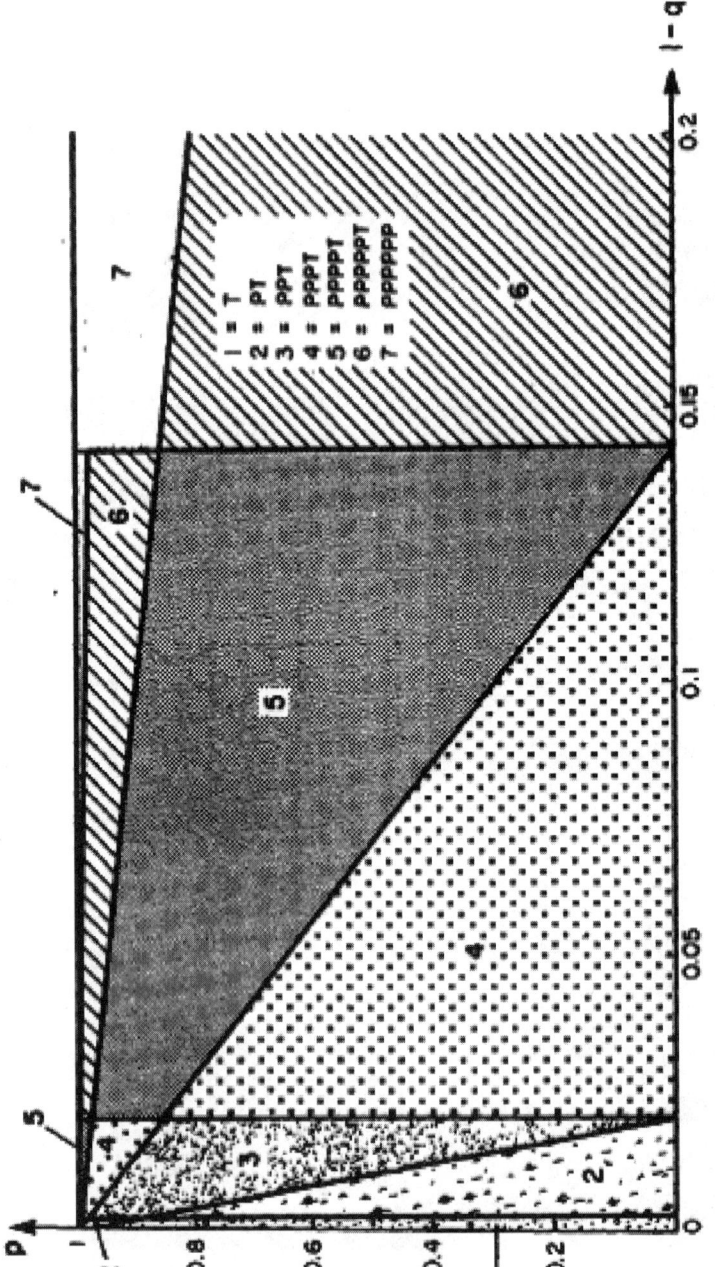

FIGURE 4. Equilibrium outcome probabilities for basic six move game

increase as the game progresses. For any level of altruism above $1/7^2$ in the four move game, and for any value above $1/7^3$ in the six move game, the solution satisfies the property that $p_i \geq p_j$, whenever $i > j$.

Despite the fact that the basic model accounts for the main pattern in the data, it is just as obvious that the basic model cannot account for the remaining features of the data. It is apparent from Figures 3 and 4 that for any value of q, there is at least one outcome with a 0 or close to 0 probability of occurrence. So the model will fit poorly data in which all of the possible outcomes occur. Nor can it account for any consistent patterns of learning in the data, for substantial variations across individuals, or for some of the irregularities described earlier. To account for these features of the data, we introduce two additional elements to the model — the possibility of errors in actions, and the possibility of errors in beliefs.

4.2. Errors in Actions — Noisy Play

One explanation of the apparently bizarre irregularities that we noted in the previous section is that players may "experiment" with different strategies in order to see what happens. This may reflect the fact that, early on, a subject may not have settled down on any particular approach about how to play the game. Alternatively, subjects may simply "goof," either by pressing the wrong key, or by accidentally confusing which color player they are, or by failing to notice that is the last round, or some other random event. Lacking a good theory for how and why this experimentation or goofing takes place, a natural way to model it is simply as noise. So we refer to it as *noisy play*.

We model noisy play in the following way. In game t, at node s, if p^* is the equilibrium probability of TAKE that the player at that node attempts to implement, we assume that the player actually chooses TAKE with probability $(1 - \varepsilon_t)p^*$, and makes a random move (i.e., TAKE or PASS with probability .5) with probability ε_t. Therefore, we can view $\varepsilon_t/2$ as the probability that a player experiments, or, alternatively, goofs in the tth game played. We call ε_t the error rate in game t. We assume that both types (selfish and altruistic) of players make errors at this rate, independently at all nodes of game t, and that this is common knowledge among the players.

4.2.1. Learning.
If the reasons for noisy play are along the lines just suggested, then it is natural to believe that the incidence of such noisy play will decline with experience. For one thing, as experience accumulates, the informational value of experimenting with alternative strategies declines, as subjects gather information

about how other subjects are likely to behave. Perhaps more to the point, the informational value will decline over the course of the 10 games a subject plays simply because, as the horizon becomes nearer, there are fewer and fewer games where the information accumulated by experimentation can be capitalized on. For different, but perhaps more obvious reasons, the likelihood that a subject will goof is likely to decline with experience. Such a decline is indicated in a wide range of experimental data in economics and psychology, spanning many different kinds of tasks and environments. We call this decline *learning*.

We assume a particular parametric form for the error rate as a function of t. Specifically, we assume that individuals follow an exponential learning curve. The initial error rate is denoted by ε and the learning parameter is δ. Therefore,

$$\varepsilon_t = \varepsilon e^{-\delta(t-1)}.$$

Notice that, while according to this specification the error rate may be different for different t, it is assumed to be the same for all individuals, and the same at all nodes of the game. More complicated specifications are possible, such as estimating different ε's for altruistic and selfish players, but we suspect that such parameter proliferation would be unlikely to shed much more light on the data. When solving for the equilibrium of the game, we assume that players are aware that they make errors and learn, and are aware that other players make errors and learn too.[10] Formally, when solving for the Bayesian equilibrium TAKE probabilities, we assume that ε and δ are common knowledge.

4.2.2. Equilibrium with Errors in Actions. For $\varepsilon > 0$, we do not have an analytical solution for the equilibrium. The solutions were numerically calculated using GAMBIT, a computer algorithm for calculating equilibrium strategies to incomplete information games, developed by McKelvey (1990 — also see Chapter 21 of this book). For comparison, the equilibrium outcome probabilities as a function of q, for $\varepsilon_t = .2$, are illustrated graphically in Figures 5 and 6.

4.3. Errors in Beliefs — Heterogeneous Beliefs

In addition to assuming that individuals can make errors in their strategies, we also assume that there can be errors in their beliefs. Thus, we assume that there is a *true probability* Q that individuals are selfish (yielding probability $1 - Q$ of altruists),

---

[10] An alternative specification would have it common knowledge that subjects believe others make errors, but believe they do not commit these "errors" themselves. Such a model is analytically more tractable and leads to similar conclusions, but seems less appealing on theoretical grounds.

but that each individual has a *belief*, q_1, of the likelihood of selfish players, which may be different from the true Q.[11] In particular, individuals' beliefs can differ from each other, giving rise to heterogeneous beliefs.

For individual i, denote by q_i the belief individual i holds that a randomly selected opponent is selfish. (We assume that each individual maintains its belief throughout all 10 games that it plays.) Because this converts the complete information centipede game into a Bayesian game, it is necessary to make some kind of assumption about the beliefs a player has about its opponent's beliefs, etc. etc. If there were no heterogeneity in beliefs, so that $q_i = q$ for all i, then one possibility is that a player's beliefs are correct — that is, q is common knowledge, and $q = Q$. We call this *rational expectations*. One can then solve for the Bayesian equilibrium of the game played in a session (which is unique), as a function of ε, δ, t, and q. An analytical solution is derived in Appendix A for the case of $\varepsilon = 0$.

To allow for heterogeneity, we make a parametric assumption that the beliefs of the individuals are independently drawn from a Beta distribution with parameters (α, β), where the mean of the distribution, q, is simply equal to $\alpha/(\alpha + \beta)$. There are several ways to specify higher order beliefs. One possibility is to assume it is common knowledge among the players that beliefs are independently drawn from a Beta distribution with parameters (α, β) and that the pair (α, β) is also common knowledge among the players. This version of higher order beliefs leads to serious computational problems when numerically solving for the equilibrium strategies. Instead, we use a simpler[12] version of the higher order beliefs, which might be called an *egocentric model*. Each player plays the game as if it were common knowledge that the opponent had the same belief. In other words, while we, the econometricians, assume there is heterogeneity in beliefs, we solve the game in which the players do have heterogeneous beliefs, but believe that everyone's beliefs are alike. This enables us to use the same basic techniques in solving for the Bayesian equilibrium strategies for players with different beliefs as one would use if there were homogeneous beliefs. We can then investigate a weaker form of rational expectations: is the average belief $(\alpha/(\alpha, \beta))$ equal to the true proportion (Q) of selfish players?

---

[11] This is related to the idea proposed independently by Camerer and Weigelt (1988) and Palfrey and Rosenthal (1988), where they posit that subjects' beliefs about the distribution of types may differ from the induced-value distribution of types announced in the instructions.

[12] While it is simpler, it is no less arbitrary. It is a version of beliefs that does not assume "common priors" (Aumann (1987)), but is consistent with the standard formulation of games of incomplete information (Harsanyi (1967–68)).

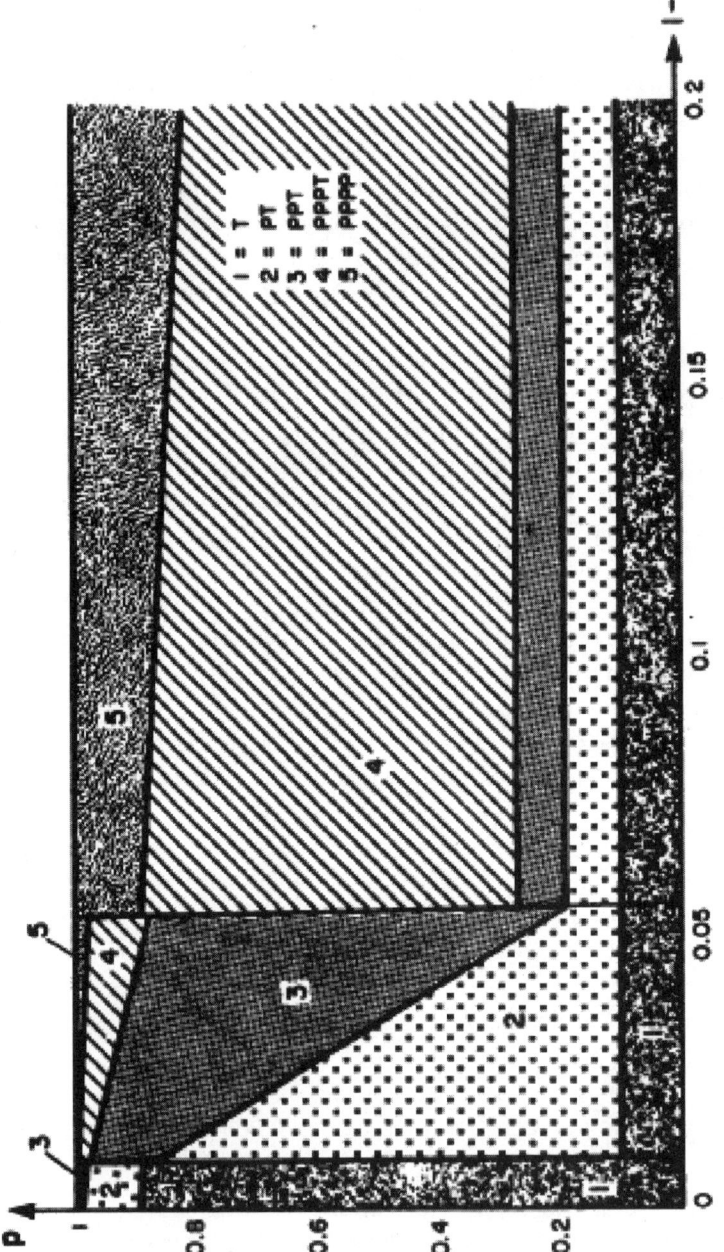

FIGURE 5. Equilibrium outcome probabilities for four move game ($\varepsilon_t = .2$)

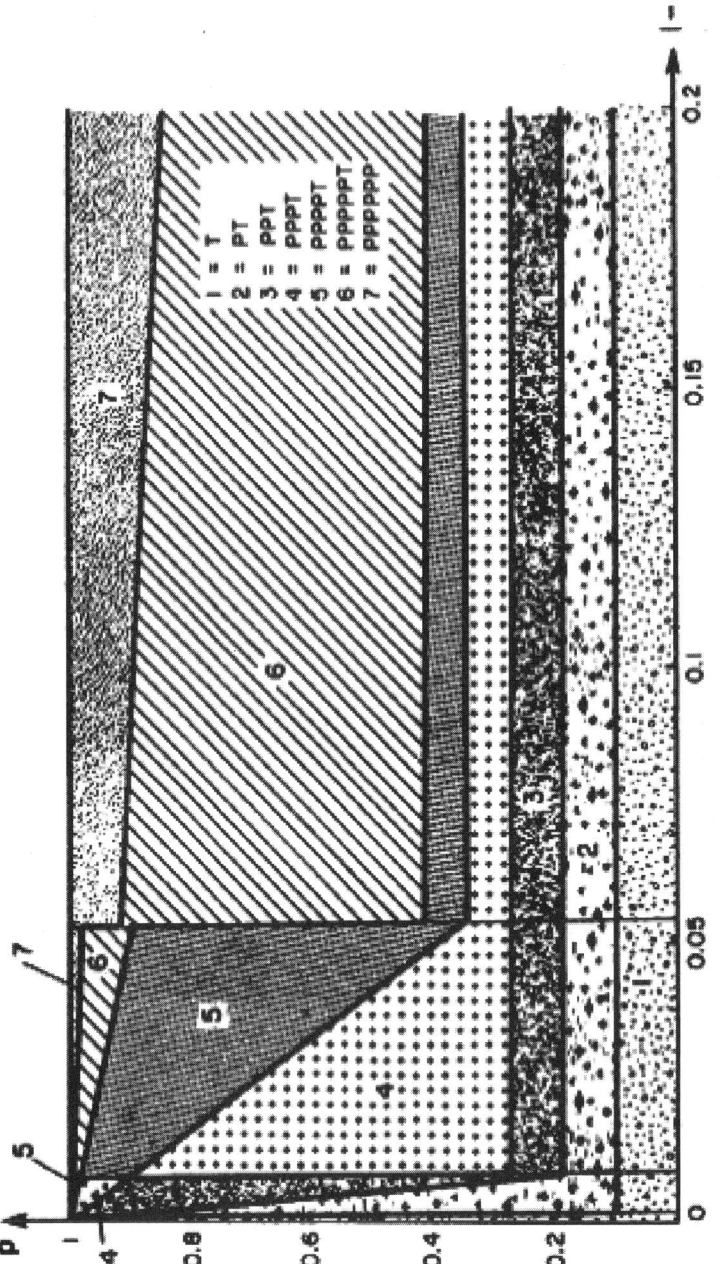

FIGURE 6. Equilibrium outcome probabilities for six move game ($\varepsilon_t = .2$)

Given the assumptions made regarding the form of the heterogeneity in beliefs, the introduction of errors in beliefs does not change the computation of the equilibrium for a given individual. It only changes the aggregate behavior we will expect to see over a group of individuals. For example, at an error rate of $\varepsilon_t = .2$, and parameters α, β for the Beta distribution, we will expect to see aggregate behavior in period t of the six move games which is the average of the behavior generated by the solutions in Figure 6, when we integrate out q with respect to the Beta distribution $B(\alpha, \beta)$.

5. Maximum Likelihood Estimation

5.1. Derivation of the Likelihood Function

Consider the version of the game where a player draws belief q. For every t, and for every ε_t, and for each of that player's decision nodes, v, the equilibrium solution derived in the previous section yields a probability that the decision at that node will be TAKE, conditional on the player at that decision node being selfish, and conditional on that player *not* making an error. Denote that probability $p_s(\varepsilon_t, q, v)$. Therefore, the probability that a selfish type of that player would TAKE at v is equal to $P_s(\varepsilon_t, q, v) = (\varepsilon_t/2) + (1 - \varepsilon_t) p_s(\varepsilon_t, q, v)$, and the probability that an altruistic type of this player would take is $P_a(\varepsilon_t, q, v) = \varepsilon_t/2$. For each individual, we observe a collection of decisions that are made at all nodes reached in all games played by that player. Let N_t denote the set of decision nodes visited by player i in the tth game played by i, and let D_{ti} denote the corresponding set of decisions made by i at each of those nodes. Then, for any given $(\varepsilon, \delta, q, v)$ with $v \in N_{ti}$, we can compute $P_s(\varepsilon_t, q, v)$ from above, by setting $\varepsilon_t = \varepsilon e^{-\delta(t-1)}$. From this we compute $\pi_{ti}(D_{ti}; \varepsilon, \delta, q)$, the probability that a selfish i would have made decisions D_{ti}, in game t, with beliefs q, and noise/learning parameters (ε, δ), and it equals the product of $P_s(\varepsilon, q, v)$ over all v reached in game t. Letting D_i denote the set of all decisions by player i, we define $\pi_i^s(D_i; \varepsilon, \delta, q)$ to be the product of the $\pi_{ti}(D_{ti}; \varepsilon, \delta, q)$ taken over all t. One can similarly derive $\pi_i^a(D_i; \varepsilon, \delta, q)$, the probability that an altruistic i would have made that same collection of decisions. Therefore, if Q is the true population parameter for the fraction of selfish players, then the likelihood of observing D_i without conditioning on i's type is given by:

$$\pi_i(D_i; Q, \varepsilon, \delta, q) = Q\pi_i^s(D_i; \varepsilon, \delta, q) + (1-Q)\pi_i^a(D_i; \varepsilon, \delta, q).$$

Finally, if q is drawn from the Beta distribution with parameters (α, β), and density $B(q; \alpha, \beta)$, then the likelihood of observing D_i without conditioning on

q is given by:

$$s_i(D_i; Q, \varepsilon, \delta, \alpha, \beta) = \int_0^1 \pi_i(D_i; Q, \varepsilon, \delta, q) B(q; \alpha, \beta) \, dq.$$

Therefore, the log of the likelihood function for a sample of observations, $D = (D_1, \ldots, D_i)$, is just

$$L(D; Q, \varepsilon, \delta, \alpha, \beta) = \sum_{i=1}^{I} \log[s_i(D_i; Q, \varepsilon, \delta, \alpha, \beta)].$$

For any sample of observations, D, we then find the set of parameter values that maximize L. This was done by a global grid search using the Cray X-MP at the Jet Propulsion Laboratory.

5.2. Treatments and Hypotheses

We are interested in testing four hypotheses about the parameters of the theoretical model.

(1) Errors in action: Is ε significantly different from 0?

(2) Heterogeneity (errors in beliefs): Is the variance of the estimated distribution of priors significantly different from 0?[13]

(3) Rational Expectations: Is the estimated value of Q equal to the mean of the estimated distribution of priors, $\alpha/(\alpha + \beta)$?

(4) Learning: Is the estimated value of δ positive and significantly different from 0?

The first two hypotheses address the question of whether the two components of error in our model (namely errors in action and errors in belief) are significantly different from 0. The second two hypotheses address issues of what properties the errors have, if they exist.

In our experimental design, there were three treatment variables:

(1) The length of the game (either four move or six move).

(2) The size of the two piles at the beginning of the game (either high payoff, ($1.60, $.40), or low payoff, ($.40, $.10)).

(3) The subject pool (either Caltech undergraduates (CIT) or Pasadena City College students (PCC)).

We also test whether any of these treatment variables were significant.

---

[13] While homogeneity of beliefs is not strictly nested in the Beta distribution model (since the Beta family does not include degenerate distributions), the homogeneous model can be approximated by the Beta distribution model by constraining $(\alpha + \beta)$ to be greater than or equal to some large number.

TABLE IV. Results from Maximum Likelihood Estimation[a]

	Treatment	$\hat{\alpha}$	$\hat{\beta}$	$\hat{\mu}$	$\hat{Q}$	$\hat{\varepsilon}$	$\hat{\delta}$	$-\ln L$
	Unconstrained	42	2.75	.939	.956	.18	.045	327.35
Four	$\mu = Q$	44	2.75	.941	.941	.18	.045	327.41
Move	$\delta = 0$	68	2.50	.965	.950	.21	.000	345.08
	$\sigma = 0$	—	—	.972	.850	.23	.020	371.04
	Unconstrained	40	2.00	.952	.904	.06	.030	352.07
Six	$\mu = Q$	38	2.00	.950	.950	.06	.030	352.76
Move	$\delta = 0$	34	1.75	.951	.908	.05	.000	371.01
	$\sigma = 0$	—	—	.976	.850	.22	.030	442.96
	Unconstrained	42	2.75	.939	.974	.14	.030	464.14
PCC	$\mu = Q$	40	2.75	.936	.936	.11	.040	464.57
	$\sigma = 0$	—	—	.952	.882	.18	.050	508.60
	Unconstrained	42	1.25	.971	.880	.22	.040	340.27
CIT	$\mu = Q$	28	1.00	.966	.966	.22	.040	342.57
	$\sigma = 0$	—	—	.994	.994	.27	.010	424.83
	High payoff	64	2.25	.966	.900	.22	.050	107.11
	All four move	48	2.25	.955	.938	.22	.050	435.73
	All low	28	1.75	.941	.938	.14	.050	702.80
	All sessions	40	2.00	.952	.930	.18	.050	813.38

[a] Rows marked $\mu = Q$ report parameter estimates under the rational expectations restriction that $\hat{\alpha}/(\hat{\alpha} + \hat{\beta}) = \hat{Q}$. Rows marked $\delta = 0$ are parameter estimates under the hypothesis of no learning. Rows marked $\sigma = 0$ are parameter estimates under the assumption of no heterogeneity.

5.3. Estimation Results

Table IV reports the results from the estimations. Before reporting any statistical tests, we summarize several key features of the parameter estimates.

First, the mean of the distribution of beliefs about the proportion of altruists in the population in all the estimations was in the neighborhood of 5%. Figure 7 graphs the density function of the estimated Beta distribution for the pooled sample of all experimental treatments for the four and six move experiments, respectively. Second, if one looks at the rational expectations estimates (which constrain $\hat{\mu} = \hat{\alpha}/(\hat{\alpha} + \hat{\beta})$ to equal $\hat{Q}$), the constrained estimate of the Beta distribution is nearly identical to the unconstrained estimate of the Beta distribution.

Furthermore, the rational expectations estimates of μ are nearly identical across all treatments. Therefore, if we are unable to reject rational expectations,

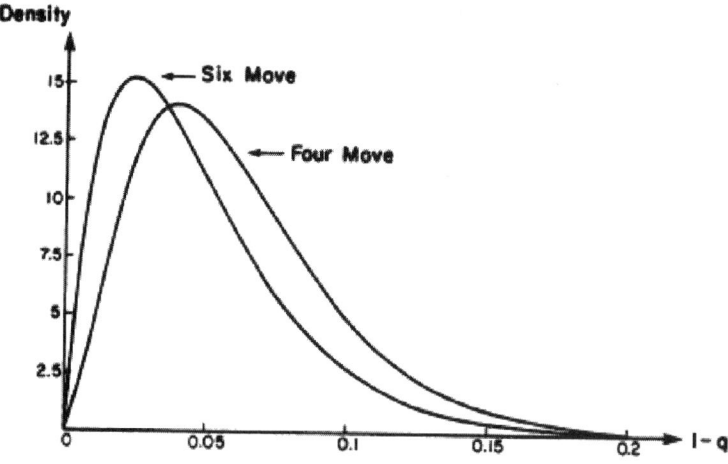

FIGURE 7. Estimated distribution of beliefs for four and six move games

then it would seem that these beliefs, as well as the true distribution of altruists are to a large extent independent of the treatments. The greatest difference across the treatments is in the estimates of the amount of noisy play. While the estimates of δ are quite stable across treatments, the estimates of ε are not. This is most apparent in the comparison of the four move and the six move estimates of ε. We discuss this below after reporting statistical tests. Finally, observe that in the $\sigma = 0$ estimates (no heterogeneity of beliefs), the estimate of μ is consistently much larger than the estimate of Q, and the recovered error rates are higher.

It might seem paradoxical that we estimate a level of altruism on the order of 5%, while the proportion of subjects who choose pass on the last move is on the order of 25% for the four move experiments and 15% for the six move experiments. One reason for the low estimate of the level of altruism is that in the theoretical model, part of this behavior is attributed to errors in action. But less obviously, it should be noted that because our equilibrium is a mixed strategy, there is a sample selection bias in the set of subjects who get to the last move: altruists are more likely to make it to this stage, since they pass on earlier moves whereas selfish subjects mix. Thus, even with no errors, we would expect to see a higher proportion of passing on the last move than the proportion of altruists in the subject pool.

5.4. Statistical Tests

Table V reports likelihood ratio χ^2 tests for comparisons of the various treatments, and for testing the theoretical hypotheses of rational expectations, learning, and heterogeneity.

Our first hypothesis — that $\varepsilon = 0$ — can be dispensed with immediately. In both the four and six move experiments, setting $\varepsilon = 0$ yields a likelihood of zero. So this hypothesis can be rejected at any level of significance, and is not included in Table V.

To test for heterogeneity, we estimate a model in which a single belief parameter, q, is estimated instead of estimating the two parameter model, α and β (see Table IV, rows marked $\sigma = 0$). As noted earlier, homogeneity is approximately nested in our heterogeneity model. Therefore, we treat the homogeneous model as if it is nested in the heterogeneous model, and report a standard χ^2 test based on likelihood ratios. All statistical tests were highly significant (see Table V). Note that by setting Q and all q_i to one, then one obtains a pure random model where individuals PASS with probability $\varepsilon/2$. Hence for any probability of passing less than or equal to $\frac{1}{2}$, the pure random model is a special case of the homogeneous model. Thus the above findings mean we also reject the pure random model ($\varepsilon = 1$).

In the test for learning, the null hypothesis that $\delta = 0$ is clearly rejected for all treatments, at essentially any level of significance. We conclude that learning effects are clearly identified in the data. Subjects are experimenting less and/or making fewer errors as they gain experience. The magnitude of the parameter estimates of δ indicates that subjects make roughly two-thirds as many errors in the tenth game, compared to the first game.

The test for rational expectations is unrejectable in most cases. The one exception is for the CIT subject pool, where the difference is significant at the 5% level, but not the 1% level.

The payoff level treatment variable is not significant. This is reassuring, as it indicates that the results are relatively robust.

The other treatment effects, CIT/PCC and four move/six move, are both significant. One source of the statistical difference between the PCC and CIT estimates apparently derives from the fact that two-thirds of the CIT data were for four move games, while only half of the PCC data were for four move games. Consequently, we break down the statistical comparison between PCC and CIT into the four and six move game treatments (see Table VI). The subject pool effect

TABLE V. Likelihood Ratio Tests

	Hypothesis	Treatment	d.f.	$-2\log$ likelihood ratio
Theoretical Hypotheses	Heterogeneity ($\sigma = 0$)	4-move	1	87.38*
	Rational expectations ($\mu = Q$)	4-move	1	0.12
		6-move	1	1.38
	Learning ($\delta = 0$)	4-move	1	35.46*
		6-move	1	37.88*
Treatment effects	4-move vs. 6-move		5	51.16*
	4-high vs 4-low (payoff treatment)		5	2.54
	PCC vs. CIT	All	5	17.94*
		4-move	5	9.63
		6-move	5	8.42

* Significant at 1% level.

TABLE VI. Estimates Broken down into Four Move and Six Move Treatments

	$\hat{\alpha}$	$\hat{\beta}$	$\hat{\mu}$	$\hat{Q}$	$\hat{\varepsilon}$	$\hat{\delta}$	$-\ln L$
PCC 4	74.0	3.75	.95	.996	.210	.04	216.47
CIT 4	36.0	1.50	.96	.866	.220	.05	214.35
PCC 6	40.0	2.50	.94	.906	.060	.04	231.28
CIT 6	80.0	2.25	.97	.902	.060	.03	116.58

TABLE VII. Chi Squared Tests for Differences in ε and δ across Treatments (under Assumption that $\mu = Q$)

Parameter	Treatment	d.f.	$-2\log L$ ratio
ε	4-move vs. 6-move	1	39.28[a]
	CIT vs. PCC	1	3.90
δ	4-move vs. 6-move	1	5.76
	CIT vs. PCC	1	.02

[a] Significant at $p = .01$ level.

is not significant in the six move treatment and is barely significant at the 10% level in the four move treatment (see Table V).

In order to pin down the source of the treatment effects we performed several tests. The first one was to test for differences in learning effects across treatments. This test is done by simultaneously reestimating the parameters for each of the different treatments, subject to the constraint that δ is the same for each treatment, and then conducting a likelihood ratio test. Second, we tested for differences in the noise parameter, ε. The χ^2 tests are reported in Table VII. The results reflect the estimates in Tables IV and V. The only significant (1% level) difference is the estimated initial error rate in the four move versus six move games. The CIT/PCC difference is significant at the 5% level, but this is due to reasons given in the previous paragraph. The difference between δ in the six move game and four move game is significant at the 5% level.

5.5. Fit

In order to get a rough measure of how well our model fits the data, we use the unconstrained parameter estimates from Table IV to obtain predicted aggregate outcomes. Table VIII displays the predicted frequencies of each of the five possible outcomes of the four move game, and compares these frequencies to the observed frequencies. This comparison is done for each of the ten periods, $t, t = 1, \ldots, 10$, and for the time-aggregated data. Table IX displays similar numbers for the six move games. The last column of the table displays a χ^2 for each period, comparing the predicted to the actual values.[14]

It is evident from Tables VIII and IX that the fit to the four move games is better than that of the six move games. For the four move games, in only one of the periods (period 7), are the predicted and actual frequencies significantly different at the .05 level. In the six move games, there are six periods in which there are differences significant at the .05 level, and four of these differences are significant at the .01 level. The predicted frequencies for the four move games also pick up reasonably well the trends in the data between periods. Thus $\widehat{f_2}$ and $\widehat{f_3}$ increase over time, while $\widehat{f_4}$ decreases, all in accordance with the actual data. In the six move data, on the other hand, the predicted frequencies show very small trends in comparison with those in the actual data. The tables can also be used to help identify where the model seems to be doing badly. In the four move games, the model overestimates f_1 and f_4 and underestimates f_2 and f_3. In the six move games, the model underestimates f_3.

The differences in fit between the four and six move games can be accounted for by the limitations of the model we fit. As noted earlier, the main difference between the estimates for the four and six move games is in the estimate of ε. In the four move games, we find a high value of $\varepsilon = .18$, while in the six move game we find a lower value of $\varepsilon = .06$. The reason for the differences in the estimates of ε between the four and six move games is fairly clear. In order to obtain a high value of the likelihood function in the six move games, the model is forced to estimate a low error rate, simply because there are almost no observations at the first terminal node.[15]

The difference in the estimates of ε also accounts for the failure of the model to explain the trends in the six move data. The way that our model explains time trends is through the learning parameter, δ, which represents the rate at which the error rate, ε_t, declines over time. As ε_t declines, the model implies that the game will end sooner, by predicting more frequent outcomes at the earlier terminal nodes. In the four move game, the initial error rate is $\varepsilon = .18$. With this high initial error rate, a decay of $\delta = .045$ is able to lead to substantial changes in predicted behavior. However, in the six move games, we estimate a significantly

---

[14]The χ^2 statistic is not reported for the time-aggregated data, since the assumption of independence is violated.

[15]In fact, there were *no* such observations in the first 9 periods and only 2 in the last period.

TABLE VIII. Comparison of Predicted (First) vs. Actual (Second) Frequencies, Four Move (Cells 4 and 5 Combined for Computation of χ_2^2)

Period	n	ε	Predicted					Actual					χ^2
			$\hat{f}_1$	$\hat{f}_2$	$\hat{f}_3$	$\hat{f}_4$	$\hat{f}_5$	f_1	f_2	f_3	f_4	f_5	
1	58	.18	.106	.269	.291	.291	.042	.000	.276	.379	.241	.103	7.72
2	58	.17	.101	.292	.298	.271	.037	.103	.276	.345	.241	.034	0.69
3	58	.16	.097	.314	.316	.241	.032	.034	.310	.379	.172	.103	3.11
4	58	.16	.096	.314	.316	.241	.032	.103	.276	.379	.172	.069	1.24
5	58	.15	.100	.329	.320	.223	.028	.069	.379	.310	.172	.069	1.04
6	58	.14	.095	.349	.335	.197	.024	.103	.310	.414	.172	.000	2.00
7	58	.14	.095	.349	.335	.197	.024	.069	.414	.448	.069	.000	9.39*
8	58	.13	.090	.369	.338	.181	.021	.069	.414	.345	.138	.034	0.87
9	58	.13	.090	.369	.338	.182	.021	.103	.483	.310	.069	.034	5.10
10	40	.12	.095	.380	.348	.159	.017	.050	.450	.400	.050	.050	2.99
Total	562	—	.097	.333	.324	.218	.028	.071	.356	.370	.153	.050	

* Significant at the .05 level.

TABLE IX. Comparison of Predicted (First) vs. Actual (Second) Frequencies, Six Move (Cells 1 and 2 and 6 and 7 Combined for Computation of χ_2^2)

			Predicted							Actual							
Period	n	ε	$\widehat{f}_1$	$\widehat{f}_2$	$\widehat{f}_3$	$\widehat{f}_4$	$\widehat{f}_5$	$\widehat{f}_6$	$\widehat{f}_7$	f_1	f_2	f_3	f_4	f_5	f_6	f_7	χ^2
1	58	.06	.035	.077	.096	.435	.275	.072	.010	.000	.103	.103	.310	.345	.103	.034	5.33
2	58	.06	.035	.077	.096	.435	.275	.072	.010	.000	.069	.172	.276	.379	.103	.000	10.41*
3	58	.06	.035	.076	.096	.435	.275	.072	.010	.000	.069	.103	.345	.345	.069	.069	5.32
4	58	.05	.030	.076	.113	.432	.273	.068	.009	.000	.034	.241	.414	.207	.103	.000	12.72*
5	58	.05	.030	.076	.113	.432	.273	.068	.009	.000	.000	.241	.310	.379	.069	.000	18.99**
6	58	.05	.030	.076	.113	.432	.273	.068	.009	.000	.069	.172	.552	.138	.069	.000	8.39
7	58	.05	.030	.076	.113	.432	.273	.068	.009	.000	.069	.276	.448	.132	.034	.000	17.98**
8	58	.05	.030	.076	.113	.432	.273	.068	.009	.000	.069	.276	.345	.241	.034	.034	15.68**
9	58	.05	.030	.076	.113	.432	.273	.068	.009	.000	.069	.172	.483	.207	.069	.000	3.86
10	40	.05	.030	.076	.113	.432	.273	.068	.009	.001	.100	.250	.350	.050	.150	.000	20.66**
Total	562		.031	.076	.108	.433	.274	.069	.009	.007	.064	.199	.384	.253	.078	.014	

* Significant at the .05 level. ** Significant at .01 level.

lower $\varepsilon = .06$. With this lower initial error rate, a similar rate of learning will lead to less dramatic changes in behavior.

Our model of errors assumes that in any given game, the error rate is a constant. In other words the likelihood of making an error is the same at each node regardless of whether the equilibrium recommends a pure or mixed strategy at that node. It might be reasonable to assume instead that individuals make more errors when they are indifferent between alternatives (i.e., when the equilibrium recommends a mixed strategy) than when they have preferences over alternatives (i.e., when the equilibrium recommends a pure strategy). In other words, the error rate may be a function of the utility differences between the choices. Such a model might be able to explain the behavior of the six move games with error rates on the same order of magnitude as those of the four move games. This in turn might lead to a better fit, and a better explanation of the trends in the six move games. We have not investigated such a model here because of computational difficulties.

One final point regards the comparisons between the take probabilities in the four move games and the six move games. As noted in Section 3, the aggregate data from the four move games exhibit higher take probabilities than the six move games at each of the decision nodes 1, 2, 3, and 4. But in contrast to this, when one compares the take probabilities of the last four moves of the six move game with the four move game (where the terminal payoffs are exactly comparable), this relationship is reversed; the six move data exhibit the higher take probabilities. Both of these features of the data are picked up in the estimates from our model. From Tables VIII and IX, the predicted take probabilities for the four move and six move games are $\widehat{p}_4 = (.097, .368, .568, .886)$, and $\widehat{p}_6 = (.031, .078, .120, .552, .778, .885)$, respectively.

6. Conclusions

We conclude that an incomplete information game that assumes the existence of a small proportion of altruists in the population can account for many of the salient features of our data. We estimate a level of altruism on the order of 5%. In the version of the model we estimate, we allow for errors in actions and errors in beliefs. Both sources of errors are found to be significant. Regarding errors in action, we find that there are significant levels of learning in the data, in the sense that subjects learn to make fewer errors over time. Subjects make roughly two thirds as many mistakes at the end of a session as they make in early play. Regarding errors in beliefs, we reject homogeneity of beliefs. However, we find that rational expectations, or on-average correct beliefs, cannot be rejected.

While we observe some subject pool differences, they are small in magnitude and barely significant. The payoff treatment had no significant effect. The only significant difference between the parameter estimates of the four and the six move games was that the estimated initial error rate was lower in the six move game. A model in which the error rate is a function of the expected utility difference between the available action choices might well account for the observed behavior in both the four and the six move games with similar estimates of the error rate. This might be a promising direction for future research.

Division of the Humanities and Social Sciences, California Institute of Technology, Pasadena, CA 91125, USA. Manuscript received May, 1990; final revision received February, 1992.

Appendix A

In this appendix, we prove that there is a unique sequential equilibrium to the n move centipede game with two sided incomplete information over the level of altruism (see Figure 8).

There are n nodes, numbered $i = 1, 2, \ldots, n$. Player 1 moves at the odd nodes, and Player 2 moves at the even nodes. We use the terminology "player i" to refer to the player who moves at node i. Let the payoff if player i takes at node i be (a_i, b_i) where a_i is payoff to player i and b_i is payoff to player $i-1$ (or $i+1$). Also, if $i = n+1$, then (a_i, b_i) refers to the payoff if player n passes at the last node. Define

$$\eta_i = \frac{a_i - b_{i+1}}{a_{i+2} - b_{i+1}}.$$

We assume that $a_{i+2} > a_i > b_{i+1}$, and that η_i is the same for all i. We write $\eta = \eta_i$. (A similar solution can be derived when the η_i are different.)

Now a strategy for the game can be characterized by a pair of vectors $p = (p_1, \ldots, p_n)$ and $r = (r_1, \ldots, r_n)$, where for any node i, p_i is the probability that a selfish type takes at that node, and r_i is the conditional probability, as assessed by player i at node i, of the other player being selfish. Let q be the initial probability of selfishness. So $r_1 = q$.

LEMMA 1. If $p \in \mathbb{R}^n$ and $r \in \mathbb{R}^n$ are a sequential equilibrium, then:
(a) for all i, $p_i = 0 \Longrightarrow p_j = 0$ for $j \leq i$;
(b) $p_n = 1$. Also, $p_i = 1 \Longrightarrow i = n$ or $i = n-1$.

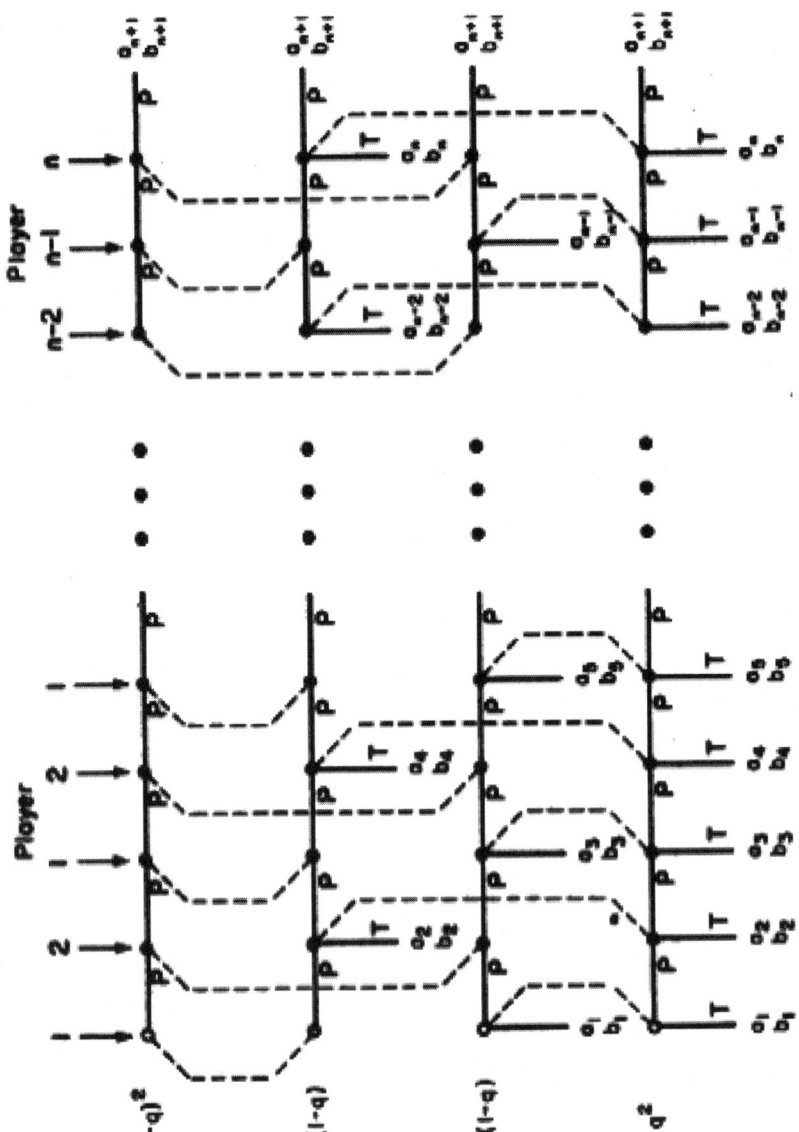

FIGURE 8. Centipede game with incomplete information (dashed lines indicate information sets and open circles are starting nodes, with probabilities indicated)

PROOF. (a) Assume $p_i = 0$. Clearly $p_{i-1} = 0$, because at node $i - 1$, the value to player $i - 1$ of passing is at least a_{i+1}, which is by assumption greater than a_{i-1}, the payoff from taking.

(b) By dominance, $p_n = 1$. Suppose $p_i = 1$ for $i < n - 1$. Then by Bayes rule $r_{i+1} = 0$, so $p_{i+1} = 0$ is the best response by player $i + 1$, since i's type has been revealed. But $p_{i+1} = 0 \implies p_i = 0$ by part (a), which is a contradiction. Q.E.D.

Define $\underline{k}$ to be the first node at which $0 < p_i$ and $\overline{k}$ to be the first node for which $p_i = 1$. Clearly $\underline{k} < \overline{k}$. Then $\underline{k}$ and $\overline{k}$ partition the nodes into at most three sets, which we refer to as the *passing stage* ($i < \underline{k}$), the *mixing stage* ($\underline{k} < i < \overline{k}$), and the *taking stage* ($\overline{k} < i$). From Lemma 1 it follows that there are no pure strategies in the mixing stage. From Lemma 1(b), it follows that the taking stage is at least one and at most two moves.

LEMMA 2. In any sequential equilibrium (p, r), for $1 \leq i \leq n - 1$,
(a) $0 < p_i < 1 \implies r_i p_{i+1} = 1 - \eta$;
(b) $r_i p_{i+1} < 1 - \eta \implies p_i = 0$;
(c) $r_i p_{i+1} > 1 - \eta \implies p_i = 1$.

PROOF. (a) Assume $0 < p_i < 1$. Let v_i, be the value to player i at node i given equilibrium play from node i on. Write $v_{n+1} = a_{n+1}$. Now if $i = n - 1$, then $v_{i+2} = v_{n+1} = a_{n+1} = a_{i+2}$. If $i < n - 1$, then by Lemma 1, $0 < p_i \implies 0 < p_{i+2}$, which implies $v_{i+2} = a_{i+2}$. Now in both cases $0 < p_i$ implies $v_i = a_i = r_i p_{i+1} + (1 - r_i p_{i+1}) a_{i+2}$. Solving for $r_i p_{i+1}$, we get

$$r_i p_{i+1} = \frac{a_{i+2} - a_i}{a_{i+2} - b_{i+1}} = 1 - \eta.$$

(b) If $r_i p_{i+1} < 1 - \eta$, then at node i, $v_i \geq r_i p_{i+1} b_{i+1} + (1 - r_i p_{i+1}) a_{i+2} = a_{i+2} - r_i p_{i+1} (a_{i+2} - b_{i+1}) > a_{i+2} - (a_{i+2} - a_i) = a_i$. So $v_i > a_i \implies p_i = 0$.

(c) If $r_i p_{i+1} > 1 - \eta$, then $p_{i+1} > 0 \implies p_{i+2} > 0$ (by Lemma 1). Hence, $v_{i+2} = a_{i+2}$. By similar argument to (b), $v_i < a_i \implies p_i = 1$. Q.E.D.

LEMMA 3. For generic q, for any sequential equilibrium there are an even number of nodes in the mixing stage. I.e., $\overline{k} = \underline{k} + 2K$ for some integer $0 < K < n/2$. For any $k < K$,
(a) $r_{\underline{k}+2k} = 1 - (1 - q)/\eta^k$;
(b) $r_{\overline{k}-1-2k} = 1 - \eta^{k+1}$.

PROOF. We first show (a) and (b), and then show $\overline{k} = \underline{k} + 2K$.

(a) For any node i, Bayes rule implies

$$(1) \quad r_{i+2} = \frac{(1-p_{i+1})r_i}{(1-p_{i+1})r_i + (1-r_i)} = \frac{r_i - p_{i+1}r_i}{1 - p_{i+1}r_i}.$$

By assumption $r_1 = q$. And since in the passing stage $p_i = 0$, it follows that $r_{\underline{k}} = q$. Now if both i and $i+2$ are in the mixing stage, it follows from Lemma 1 that $i+1$ is also, implying $0 < p_{i+1} < 1$. So by Lemma 3, $r_i p_{i+1} = 1 - \eta$. Hence, (1) becomes

$$(2) \quad r_{i+2} = \frac{r_i - (1-\eta)}{1-(1-\eta)} = 1 - \frac{(1-r_i)}{\eta}.$$

By induction, it follows that as long as $k < \frac{1}{2}\left(\overline{k} - \underline{k}\right)$, then $\underline{k} + 2k < \overline{k}$ is in the mixing stage. So

$$r_{\underline{k}+2k} = 1 - \frac{1-r_{\underline{k}}}{\eta^k} = 1 - \frac{1-q}{\eta^k}.$$

(b) As above, as long as both i and $i-2$ are in the mixing stage, we get

$$r_i = 1 - \frac{(1-r_{i-2})}{\eta}.$$

Solving for r_{i-2}, we get

$$r_{i-2} = 1 - \eta(1-r_i).$$

Now from Lemma 2, it follows, since $p_{\overline{k}} = 1$,

$$r_{\overline{k}-1} = \frac{1-\eta}{p_{\overline{k}}} = 1 - \eta.$$

Hence, by induction, as long as $k < \frac{1}{2}\left(\overline{k}-\underline{k}\right)$, we have

$$r_{\overline{k}-1-2k} = 1 - \eta^k\left(1 - r_{\overline{k}-1}\right) = 1 - \eta^{k+1}.$$

Finally, to show that there are an even number of nodes in the mixing stage, assume, to the contrary that there are an odd number. Then we can write $\overline{k} = \underline{k} + 2k + 1$ for some $k \geq 0$. Thus $\underline{k} = \overline{k} - 1 - 2k$. So by part (b) we have $r_{\underline{k}} = 1 - \eta^{k+1}$. But by (a) we have $r_{\underline{k}} = 1 - (1-q) = q$, implying that $q = 1 - \eta^{k+1}$. For generic q, this is a contradiction, implying that $\overline{k} = \underline{k} + 2K$ for some $K \geq 0$. If $k \geq n/2$, then $\overline{k} \geq \underline{k} + n > n$, which contradicts Lemma 1(b). Hence $\overline{k} = \underline{k} + 2K$ for some $0 \leq K < n/2$. Q.E.D.

THEOREM 4. *For generic q, there is a unique sequential equilibrium (p,r) which is characterized as follows: Let I be the smallest integer greater than or equal to $n/2$. If $1 - q < \eta^f$, set $K = I - 1$, $\underline{k} = 1$, and $\overline{k} = 2I - 1$. If $1 - q > \eta^I$,* let K be the largest integer with $1 - q < \eta^K$, $\overline{k} = n$, and $\underline{k} = \overline{k} - 2K$. The solution then satisfies:

(a) if $i < \underline{k}$, then $r_{i+1} = q$ and $p_i = 0$;
(b) if $i \geq \overline{k}$, then $r_{i+1} = 0$ and $p_i = 1$;
(c) if $\underline{k} \leq i < \overline{k}$: (i) if $i = \underline{k}$, then $r_{i+1} = 1 - \eta^K$, and $p_i = (q + \eta^K - 1)/q\eta^K$; (ii) if $i = \underline{k} + 2k$, with $i \leq k < K$, then $r_{i+1} = 1 - \eta^{K-k}$, and $p_i = (1 - \eta)/(1 - \eta^{K+1-k})$; (iii) if $i = \underline{k} + 2k + 1$, with $0 \leq k \leq K$, then $r_{i+1} = 1 - (1-q)/\eta^{k+1}$, and $p_i = \eta^k(1-\eta)/(\eta^k - (1-q))$.

PROOF. The formulae for r_i and p_i in parts (a), (b), and (c) follow by application of the previous lemmas together with Bayes rule. In particular in (a), $p_i = 0$ follows from the definition of $\underline{k}$, and $r_{i+1} = q$ follows from $p_i = 0$ for $j < i$ together with Bayes rule. In (b), $p_i = 1$ follows from the definition of $\overline{k}$, and $r_{i+1} = 0$ then follows by Bayes rule. In (c), all the formulae for r_{i+1} follow from Lemma 3. In (c) part (i), we set $\underline{k} = i + 1$ in (1) and solve for $p_{\underline{k}}$ to get

$$p_{\underline{k}} = \frac{r_{\underline{k}-1} - r_{\underline{k}+1}}{r_{\underline{k}-1} - r_{\underline{k}-1} r_{\underline{k}+1}}.$$

But $r_{\underline{k}-1} = q$ and $r_{\underline{k}+1} = 1 - \eta^K$. So

$$p_{\underline{k}} = \frac{q - 1 + \eta^K}{q\eta^K}.$$

In parts (ii) and (iii) of (c), we apply Lemma 2a to get that $p_i = (1 - \eta)/(r_{i-1})$. Substituting in for the values of r_{i-1} gives the required formulae.

Thus, it only remains to prove the assertions about $\overline{k}$ and $\underline{k}$. We first prove two preliminary inequalities. First, note, $\underline{k} > 1$ implies, by Lemma 2,

$$p_{\underline{k}-1} = 0 \implies r_{\underline{k}-1} p_{\underline{k}} \leq 1 - \eta$$
$$\implies q\left(\frac{q + \eta^K - 1}{q\eta^K}\right) \leq 1 - \eta$$
$$\implies q + \eta^K - 1 \leq \eta^K - \eta^{K+1}$$
$$\implies 1 - q \geq \eta^{K+1}.$$

Hence,

(3) $\qquad 1 - q < \eta^{K+1} \implies \underline{k} = n.$

Second, note $\bar{k} = n - 1$ implies, by Lemma 2,

$$p_{\bar{k}-1} = 1 \implies r_{\bar{k}-1} p_{\bar{k}} \geq 1 - \eta$$
$$\implies \frac{q + \eta^K - 1}{\eta^K} \geq 1 - \eta$$
$$\implies 1 - q \leq \eta^{K+1}.$$

Hence,

(4) $$1 - q > \eta^{K+1} \implies \bar{k} = n.$$

Let

$$I = \left\lceil \frac{n}{2} \right\rceil.$$

There are two cases.

Case I: $1 - q < \eta^I$. From Lemma 3, we have

$$K < \frac{n}{2} \implies K \leq \left\lceil \frac{n}{2} \right\rceil - 1 \implies I \geq K + 1.$$

Thus we have $1 - q < \eta^I \leq \eta^{K+1}$. But from (3), this implies $\underline{k} = 1$. Now since $\bar{k} \geq n - 1$, it follows that $K = I - 1$, and $\bar{k} = \underline{k} + 2K = 2I - 1$.

Case II: $1 - q > \eta^I$. Now $p_{\underline{k}} > 0 \implies (q + \eta^K - 1)/q\eta^K > 0 \implies 1 - q < \eta^K$. Suppose $1 - q < \eta^{K+1}$. Then, from (1), we have $\underline{k} = 1$, and by the same argument as Case I, $K = I - 1 \implies 1 - q < \eta^{K+1} = \eta^I$, a contradiction. Hence we must have

$$\eta^{K+1} < 1 - q < \eta^K.$$

So K is the largest integer with $1 - q < \eta^K$. But now, from (4), it follows that $\bar{k} = n$. Q.E.D.

In the centipede games described in the text, the piles grow at an exponential rate: There are real numbers $c > d > 1$ with $a_i = cb_i$ and $a_{i+1} = da_i$ for all i. So $\eta = (c - d)/(cd^2 - d)$. In our experiments $c = 4$, and $d = 2$, so $\eta = \frac{1}{7}$. The figures in the text correspond to the solution for the two and three round games ($n = 4$ and $n = 6$) for these parameters.

It is interesting to note that since the solution depends only on η, the above solution also applies if there are linearly increasing payoffs of the form $a_{i+1} = a_i + c$, and $b_{i+1} = b_i + c$ (with $c > 0$), as long as $a_i > b_{i+1} = b_i + c$. Hence picking a_i, b_i, and c so that

$$\frac{a_1 - b_2}{a_3 - b_2} = \frac{a_1 - b_1 - c}{a_i - b_i + c} = \frac{1}{7}$$

(e.g., $a_i = 60$, $b_i = 20$, $c = 30$) one can obtain a game with linearly increasing payoffs whose solution is exactly the same as the solution of the game with exponentially increasing payoffs treated in this paper.

Appendix B

Experiment Instructions

This is an experiment in group decision making, and you will be paid for your participation in cash, at the end of the experiment. Different subjects may earn different amounts. What you earn depends partly on your decisions, partly on the decisions of others, and partly on chance.

The entire experiment will take place through computer terminals, and all interaction between you will take place through the computers. It is important that you not talk or in any way try to communicate with other subjects during the experiments. If you disobey the rules, we will have to ask you to leave the experiment.

We will start with a brief instruction period. During the instruction period, you will be given a complete description of the experiment and will be shown how to use the computers. You must take a quiz after the instruction period. So it is important that you listen carefully. If you have any questions during the instruction period, raise your hand and your question will be answered so everyone can hear. If any difficulties arise after the experiment has begun, raise your hand, and an experimenter will come and assist you.

The subjects will be divided into two groups, containing 10 subjects each. The groups will be labeled the RED group and the BLUE group. To determine which color you are, will you each please select an envelope as the experimenter passes by you.

[EXPERIMENTER PASS OUT ENVELOPES]

If you chose BLUE, you will be BLUE for the entire experiment. If you chose RED, you will be RED for the entire experiment. Please remember your color, because the instructions are slightly different for the BLUE and the RED subjects.

In this experiment, you will be playing the following game, for real money.

First, you are matched with an opponent of the opposite color. There are two piles of money: a Large Pile and a Small Pile. At the beginning of the game the Large Pile has 40 cents and the Small Pile has 10 cents.

RED has the first move and can either "Pass" or "Take." If RED chooses "Take," RED gets the Large Pile of 40 cents, BLUE gets the Small Pile of 10 cents, and the game is over. If RED chooses "Pass," both piles double and it is BLUE's turn.

The Large Pile now contains 80 cents and the Small Pile 20 cents. BLUE can take or pass. If BLUE takes, BLUE ends up with the Large Pile of 80 cents and RED ends up with the Small Pile of 20 cents and the game is over. If BLUE passes, both piles double and it is RED's turn again.

This continues for a total of six turns, or three turns for each player. On each move, if a player takes, he or she gets the Large Pile, his or her opponent gets the Small Pile, and the game is over. If the player passes, both piles double again and it is the other player's turn.

The last move of the game is move six, and is BLUE's move (if the game even gets this far). The Large Pile now contains $12.80 and the Small Pile contains $3.20. If BLUE takes, BLUE gets the Large Pile of $12.80 and RED gets the Small Pile of $3.20. If BLUE passes, then the piles double again. RED then gets the Large Pile, containing $25.60, and BLUE gets the Small Pile, containing $6.40. This is summarized in the following table.

| Move # | | | | | | Large Pile | Small Pile | RED's Payoff | BLUE's Payoff |
1	2	3	4	5	6				
T						.40	.10	.40	.10
P	T					.80	.20	.20	.80
P	P	T				1.60	.40	1.60	.40
P	P	P	T			3.20	.80	.80	3.20
P	P	P	P	T		6.40	1.60	6.40	1.60
P	P	P	P	P	T	12.80	3.20	3.20	12.80
P	P	P	P	P	P	25.60	6.40	25.60	6.40

[EXPERIMENTER HAND OUT PAYOFF TABLE]

Go over table to explain what is in each column and row.

The experiment consists of 10 games. In each game, you are matched with a different player of the opposite color from yours. Thus, if you are a BLUE player, in each game, you will be matched with a RED player. If you are a RED player, in each game you are matched with a BLUE player. Since there are ten subjects of each color, this means that you will be matched with each of the subjects of the other color exactly once. So if your label is RED, you will be matched with each of the BLUE subjects exactly once. If you are BLUE, you will be matched with each of the RED subjects exactly once.

An Experimental Study of the Centipede Game

We will now begin the computer instruction session. Will all the BLUE subjects please move to the terminals on the left side of the room, and all the RED subjects move to the terminals on the right side of the room.

[SUBJECTS MOVE TO CORRECT TERMINALS]

During the instruction session, we will teach you how to use the computer by going through a few practice games. During the instruction session, *do not hit any keys until you are told to do so*, and when you are told to enter information, *type exactly what you are told to type*. You are not paid for these practice games.

Please turn on your computer now by pushing the button labeled "MASTER" on the right hand side of the panel underneath the screen.

[WAIT FOR SUBJECTS TO TURN ON COMPUTERS]

When the computer prompts you for your name, type your full name. Then hit the ENTER key.

[WAIT FOR SUBJECTS TO ENTER NAMES]

When you are asked to enter your color, type R if your color is RED, and B if your color is BLUE. Then hit ENTER.

[WAIT FOR SUBJECTS TO ENTER COLORS]

You now see the experiment screen. Throughout the experiment, the bottom of the screen will tell you what is currently happening, and the top will tell you the history of what happened in the previous games. Since the experiment has not begun yet, the top part of the screen is currently empty. The bottom part of the screen tells you your subject number and your color. It also tells you the subject number of the player you are matched against in the first game. Is there anyone whose color is not correct?

[WAIT FOR RESPONSE]

Please record your color and subject number on the top left hand corner of your record sheet. Also record the number of the subject you are matched against in the first game.

Each game is represented by a row in the upper screen, and the player you will be matched with in each of the ten games appears in the column labeled "OPP" (which stands for "opponent") on the right side of the screen. It is important to note that you will never be paired with the same player twice.

We will now start the first practice game. Remember, do not hit any keys until you are told to do so.

[MASTER HIT KEY TO START FIRST GAME]

You now see on the bottom part of the screen that the first game has begun, and you are told who you are matched against. If you are a RED player, you are told that it is your move, and are given a description of the choices available to you. If you are a BLUE player, you are told that it is your opponent's move, and are told the choices available to your opponent.

Will all the RED players now choose PASS by typing in P on your terminals now.

[WAIT FOR SUBJECTS TO CHOOSE]

Since RED chose P, this is recorded on the top part of the screen with a P in the first RED column, and the cursor has moved on to the second column, which is BLUE, indicating that it is BLUE's move.

On the bottom part of the screen, the BLUE players are now told that it is their turn to choose, and are told the choices they can make. The RED players are told that it is their opponent's turn to choose, and are told the choices that their opponent can make. Notice, that there is now a Large Pile of $80 and a Small Pile of $.20.

Will all the BLUE players now please choose TAKE by typing T at your terminal now.

[WAIT FOR SUBJECTS TO CHOOSE]

Since BLUE chose T, the first game has ended. On the bottom part of the screen, you are told that the game is over, and that the next game will begin shortly. On the top part of the screen, BLUE's move is recorded with a T in the second column. The payoffs from the first game for both yourself and your opponent are recorded on the right hand side of the screen in the columns labeled "Payoff." Your own payoff is in your color. That of your opponent is in the opponent's color.

Please record your own payoff on the record sheet that is provided.

[WAIT FOR SUBJECTS TO RECORD PAYOFFS]

You are not being paid for the practice session, but if this were the real experiment, then the payoff you have recorded would be money you have earned from the first game, and you would be paid this amount for that game at the end of the experiment. The total you earn over all ten real games is what you will be paid for your participation in the experiment.

We will now proceed to the second practice game.

[MASTER HIT KEY TO START SECOND GAME]

You now see that you have been matched with a new player of the opposite color, and that the second game has begun. Does everyone see this?

[WAIT FOR RESPONSE]

The rules for the second game are exactly like the first. The RED player gets the first move.

[DO RED-P, BLUE-P, RED-P]

Now notice that it is BLUE's move. It is the last move of the game. The Large Pile now contains $3.20, and the Small Pile contains $.80. If the BLUE player chooses TAKE, then the game ends. The BLUE player receives the Large Pile and the RED player receives the Small Pile. If the BLUE player chooses PASS, both piles double, and then the game ends. The RED player receives the Large Pile, which now contains $6.40, and the BLUE player receives the Small Pile, containing $1.60.

Will the BLUE player please choose PASS by typing P at your terminal now.

[WAIT FOR SUBJECTS TO CHOOSE]

The second practice game is now over. Please record your payoff on the second line of your record sheet.

[WAIT FOR PLAYERS TO RECORD PAYOFFS] [MASTER HIT KEY TO START THIRD GAME]

We now go to the third practice game. Notice again that you have a new opponent. Will all the RED players please choose TAKE by typing T at your terminal now.

[WAIT FOR PLAYERS TO CHOOSE]

Since the RED player chose TAKE on the first move, the game is over, and we proceed on to the next game. Since RED chose TAKE on the first move, BLUE did not get any chance to move.

Please record your payoff for the third game on the third line of your record sheet.

[WAIT FOR PLAYERS TO RECORD PAYOFFS]

This concludes the practice session. In the actual experiment there will be ten games instead of three, and, of course, it will be up to you to make your own decisions. At the end of game ten, the experiment ends and we will pay each of you privately, in cash, the TOTAL amount you have accumulated during all ten games, plus your guaranteed five dollar participation fee. No other person will be told how much cash you earned in the experiment. You need not tell any other participants how much you earned.

Are there any questions before we pass out the quiz?

[EXPERIMENTER TAKE QUESTIONS]

O.K., then we will now have you take the quiz.

[PASS OUT QUIZ] [COLLECT AND MARK QUIZZES] [HAND QUIZZES BACK AND GO THRU CORRECT ANSWERS]

We will now begin with the actual experiment. If there are any problems from this point on, raise your hand and an experimenter will come and assist you. When the computer asks for your name, please start as before by typing in your name. Wait for the computer to ask for your color, then respond with the correct color.

[START EXPERIMENT]
[CHECK THAT COLORS ARE OK BEFORE BEGINNING EXPERIMENT]

APPENDIX C
Experimental Data

The following tables give the data for our experiment. Each row represents a subject. The columns are

Col 1: Session number

Col 2: Subject number of Red Player

Col 2+j: Outcome of game j. Letting k be the entry in this column, and n be the number of moves in the game ($n = 4$ for Exp. 1 – 4, $n = 6$ for Exp. 5 – 7), then

$$k = \begin{cases} \leq n & \implies \text{ game ended with } T \text{ on move } k \\ = n+1 & \implies \text{ game ended with } P \text{ on move } n. \end{cases}$$

The matching scheme was: In game j, Red subject i is matched with Blue subject $[(i+j-1) \bmod m]$, where m is the number of subjects of each color in the session. Thus, with ten subjects of each color, in the first game, Red i is matched with Blue i. In the second game, Red i is matched with Blue $1 + i$, except Red 10, who is matched with Blue 1.

1	1	3	3	3	2	3	2	2	2	3
1	2	4	2	4	4	4	4	2	4	4	2
1	3	3	3	2	2	3	3	3	4	3	2
1	4	4	3	3	4	3	2	3	3	3	2
1	5	2	1	3	1	3	3	3	3	2	2
1	6	5	3	4	3	5	4	4	3	3	3
1	7	4	2	2	3	4	3	2	3	2	3
1	8	2	1	5	4	1	3	3	4	3	3
1	9	3	3	4	3	2	2	3	1	3	2
1	10	4	2	4	2	3	1	3	3	2	5

Session 1

(Four move, PCC)

2	1	4	4	3	3	2	4	2	2	2
2	2	2	1	4	1	3	2	2	2	1
2	3	3	3	2	2	1	1	1	1	1
2	4	3	3	3	3	3	2	3	2	3
2	5	3	4	2	3	2	3	3	2	3
2	6	3	3	3	2	3	3	2	3	2
2	7	2	4	3	4	5	2	3	2	2
2	8	3	2	3	3	2	3	2	3	2
2	9	2	4	2	3	4	2	3	2	2

Session 2
(Four move, PCC)

3	1	3	4	2	3	2	3	2	2	1	3
3	2	4	2	2	2	4	2	2	5	4	3
3	3	2	2	1	1	2	1	1	3	3	2
3	4	3	2	3	2	2	3	3	3	3	2
3	5	3	5	2	2	3	4	3	3	2	3
3	6	5	2	2	5	4	4	4	2	2	2
3	7	2	3	5	4	2	3	2	2	2	1
3	8	2	3	3	3	3	2	2	2	5	2
3	9	5	4	5	5	2	2	2	4	2	4
3	10	4	4	3	2	2	3	3	2	2	3

Session 3
(Four move, CIT)

4	1	2	4	5	4	2	4	4	2	4	4
4	2	3	3	2	2	2	1	1	1	3	2
4	3	4	2	3	2	3	2	3	3	2	3
4	4	2	3	2	3	2	3	3	2	2	2
4	5	3	3	3	2	5	4	2	2	2	1
4	6	3	3	2	5	4	2	2	2	2	2
4	7	3	3	5	4	2	1	3	2	1	1
4	8	3	5	4	2	3	3	2	2	2	3
4	9	3	3	3	3	3	2	2	3	3	2
4	10	3	2	1	1	1	1	1	1	1	1

Session 4
(Four move, High payoff, CIT)

5	1	5	5	7	4	4	2	4	2	4	3
5	2	3	3	3	3	3	4	2	3	2	2
5	3	5	4	4	3	4	3	3	3	3	5
5	4	3	3	3	3	3	3	3	3	3	3
5	5	5	4	4	3	5	4	4	5	5	1
5	6	4	4	4	3	4	3	3	3	3	3
5	7	3	3	3	3	3	3	5	4	4	2
5	8	5	5	4	4	3	3	3	3	2	1
5	9	5	5	5	5	5	4	4	2	4	4
5	10	5	4	5	5	4	5	2	4	4	6

Session 5
(Six move, CIT)

6	1	5	6	4	5	5	5	6	5	4
6	2	6	5	7	4	6	4	4	4	4
6	3	4	5	5	4	5	4	4	4	5
6	4	5	5	5	4	5	4	4	5	5
6	5	4	5	6	6	4	4	5	4	5
6	6	4	2	5	4	4	4	4	7	6
6	7	4	6	4	4	3	4	3	5	4
6	8	2	5	4	5	4	5	4	6	5
6	9	5	4	5	4	5	4	4	3	4

Session 6
(Six move, PCC)

7	1	4	4	3	3	4	3	3	3	3
7	2	2	5	4	2	5	4	3	5	3	4
7	3	5	3	2	5	5	4	5	5	4	4
7	4	2	5	4	6	6	5	4	4	4
7	5	2	5	5	4	5	6	4	4	4	4
7	6	7	6	6	6	5	4	4	4	4	6
7	7	6	4	4	6	4	4	4	4	6	6
7	8	4	5	5	4	4	5	5	4	5	4
7	9	4	3	5	5	5	4	4	5	4	4
7	10	6	4	2	4	3	2	3	3	4	3

Session 7
(Six move, PCC)

References

Aumann, R. (1988): "Preliminary Notes on Integrating Irrationality into Game Theory," Mimeo, International Conference on Economic Theories of Politics, Haifa.

―――― (1987): "Correlated Equilibrium as an Expression of Bayesian Rationality," *Econometrica*, 55, 1–18.

Binmore, K. (1987): "Modeling Rational Players," *Economics and Philosophy*, 3, 179–214.

Camerer, C., and K. Weigelt (1988): "Experimental Tests of a Sequential Equilibrium Reputation Model," *Econometrica*, 56, 1–36.

Cooper, R., D. DeJong, R. Forsythe, and T. Ross (1990): "Selection Criteria in Coordination Games," *American Economic Review*, 80, 218–233.

Fudenberg, D., and E. Maskin (1986): "The Folk Theorem in Repeated Games with Discounting and Incomplete Information," *Econometrica*, 54, 533–554.

Güth, W., P. Ockenfels, and M. Wendel (1991): "Efficiency by Trust in Fairness? — Multiperiod Ultimatum Bargaining Experiments with an Increasing Cake," Technical Report, J. W. Goethe Universitat, Frankfurt.

Harsanyi, J. C. (1967–68): "Games of Incomplete Information Played by Bayesian Players," Parts (I, II, and III). *Management Science*, 14, 159–182, 320–334, 486–502.

Jung, Y., J. Kagel, and D. Levin (1989): "On the Existence of Predatory Pricing in the Laboratory: An Experimental Study of Reputation and Entry Deterrence in the Chain-Store Game," Mimeo.

Kreps, D. M. (1990): *A Course in Microeconomic Theory*. New Jersey: Princeton University Press.

Kreps, D., P. Milgrom, J. Roberts, and R. Wilson (1982): "Rational Cooperation in the Finitely Repeated Prisoner's Dilemma," *Journal of Economic Theory*, 27, 245–252.

Kreps, D. M., and R. Wilson (1982a): "Reputation and Imperfect Information," *Journal of Economic Theory*, 27, 253–279.

―――― (1982b): "Sequential Equilibria," *Econometrica*, 50, 863–894.

McKelvey, R. D. (1990): "GAMBIT: Interactive Extensive Form Game Program," Mimeo, California Institute of Technology.

Megiddo, N. (1986): "Remarks on Bounded Rationality," Technical Report, IBM Research Report RJ 54310, Computer Science.

Neral, John, and Jack Ochs (1989): "The Sequential Equilibrium Theory of Reputation Building: A Further Test," Mimeo, University of Pittsburgh.

Palfrey, T. R., and H. Rosenthal (1988): "Private Incentives in Social Dilemmas: The Effects of Incomplete Information and Altruism," *Journal of Public Economics*, 35, 309–332.

Reny, P. (1988): "Rationality, Common Knowledge, and the Theory of Games," Technical Report, University of Western Ontario.

Rosenthal, R. (1982): "Games of Perfect Information, Predatory Pricing, and the Chain Store Paradox," *Journal of Economic Theory*, 25, 92–100.

Selten, R., and R. Stoecker (1986): "End Behavior in Sequences of Finite Prisoner's Dilemma Supergames," *Journal of Economic Behavior and Organization*, 7, 47–70.

Smith, V. (1976): "Experimental Economics: Induced Value Theory," *American Economic Review*, 66, 274–279.

CHAPTER 19

McKelvey and Quantal Response Equilibrium

THOMAS R. PALFREY

Giving a statistical facelift to traditional non-cooperative game theory was a very appealing idea to Richard McKelvey. Specific ideas about one way to do this emerged about 1990 and evolved over the span of a few years into the quantal response equilibrium (QRE) concept. This approach became a central node in McKelvey's complex network of inter-related research topics. It lies at the junction of econometrics, game theory, laboratory experiments, and numerical computation — four of McKelvey's greatest interests. The first half of this essay will attempt to explain these connections, and how Richard thought about these connections, based on our 15 year collaboration studying games of incomplete information. One interpretation of QRE also places the concept in the category of behavioral economics, as it is often referred to as a boundedly rational version of Nash equilibrium. In spite of Richard's strong negative reaction to any use of the term "bounded rationality," he also clearly saw it as a rigorous way to try to bring in behavioral factors to the language and equations of game theory. The second half of the essay will discuss the growing importance of QRE in political science, and describe some recent applications. It closes with some brief comments about promising avenues of future research on quantal response equilibrium.

1. Background

The easiest way to see how all these different research areas are all linked together with QRE is to provide some history about how the idea developed from the experimental game theory work he was engaged in during the late 1980s and early 1990s. The watershed article was the experimental study of the centipede game. The idea for conducting that experiment arose accidentally, and the development of a statistical model to explain the data came about later. Here's what happened.

Yossi Greenberg organized a conference in Haifa, Israel, in the spring of 1988. It was a very small group, mixing a handful of distinguished Israeli game theorists with a scraggly bunch of jet-lagged American voting theorists. Robert Aumann presented a paper on a variation of the Rosenthal's (1981) centipede game. Two players move alternately, each with the opportunity of terminating the game by grabbing the much larger of two piles of money. Both piles of money double after each passing move, and there is a known finite number of possible moves. Intuitively, if the number of possible moves is large, then players will pass at first in order to let the pile grow, and both players will do quite well no matter which player grabs it later. But in any Nash equilibrium the first mover should immediately stop the game by taking the larger pile. Aumann had a model to explain how the possible lack of common knowledge of rationality could lead to passing, but if there were common knowledge of rationality then the only reasonable solution would be for the first person to take, the latter idea eventually published in Aumann (1995).

McKelvey *qua* empiricist believed three things:

(1) Rationality probably isn't common knowledge (even though he invoked that assumption repeatedly in many theoretical articles).
(2) If rationality is not common knowledge, then we are left in a wilderness where essentially anything can happen. "Lack" of common knowledge of rationality is simply ill-defined and allows for too many possibilities.
(3) In order not to get lost in the wilderness, one needs some direction, and the direction has to come from data.

Accordingly, we designed and conducted an experiment, not to test any particular theory (as both of us had been accustomed to doing), but simply to find out what would happen.

However, after looking at the data, there was a problem. Everything happened! Some players passed all the time, some grabbed the big pile at their first opportunity, and others seemed to be unpredictable, almost random. But there were clear patterns in the average behavior, the main pattern being that the probability of taking increased as the piles grew.

This presented two challenges for analyzing the data, if it was to be done "right" (always a requirement for McKelvey). In this case "right" meant three things. First, it had to fit the aggregate pattern of take probabilities. Second, it had to account for the variation in behavior across subjects — i.e., the fact that we saw every kind of behavior at least once. Third, the theoretical model had to be internally consistent. To McKelvey this means it had to be publication-proof.

A theoretical model of behavior is publication-proof if it will still accurately describe behavior after the theory becomes public information. See McKelvey and Riddihough (1999) for elaboration.

The first attempt to analyze the data was a reputation building model similar to the explanation for cooperation in the prisoner's dilemma.[1] With some probability, q, one's opponent might be altruistic and always pass. This also provides an incentive for a greedy player to pass in order to dupe their opponent into passing, and then grab the large(r) pile on the next move. It turns out that this model indeed generates a pattern of increasing take probabilities, and it also generates statistical predictions and implies a likelihood function that can be used for a rigorous analysis of data, and to estimate the proportion of altruists in the subject population (and beliefs about this proportion). It's also a nice model because it introduces heterogeneity as an intuitive structural feature of the model. But unfortunately, the model suffers from a degeneracy problem. That is, for all values of q the equilibrium take probability is either equal to 0 or very small for at least some moves in the game. As a consequence, the model will fit very poorly any data set that exhibits significant variation in behavior, including the data set at hand.

2. Errors in Actions

To circumvent the degeneracy problem, errors in actions were introduced. These errors were a form of bounded rationality, much like Selten's trembles in the definition of perfect equilibrium. With some probability, and for reasons assumed to be completely orthogonal to the model, a player might choose a suboptimal action. The key, however, is that all players were aware that all players (including themselves!) trembled. That is, the assumption that rationality is common knowledge is replaced by the assumption that a specific form of *bounded* rationality is common knowledge!

This turns out to enrich the model sufficiently to obtain a remarkably good fit of the data. The model accounts for all the main qualitative features of the data, including a tendency for players to learn over time (modeled as decay in the tremble rate) and more passing in the 6-move game than the 4-move game. When the paper was nearly finished, we realized that a more reasonable model of trembles would be one where the tremble probabilities depended on the relative costs of the errors, measured in expected payoffs (McKelvey and Palfrey 1992, p. 827 (also see page 409 Chapter 18 of this book)).

---

[1] At the time, we were unaware of the similar one-sided incomplete information model that appeared in Kreps (1990).

It was at this point that we started playing around with the logit version of quantal response equilibrium, first looking at some simple 2 × 2 games, such as the battle of the sexes game. Two things immediately became apparent. First, the model was completely general. That is, we could apply it to any finite game. Second, the model was *statistical*, so we could use it as a statistical model to *analyze data* from any finite game. The logit version of QRE is especially easy to compute and has a free parameter that makes it possible to fit to data.[2]

The early versions of the first QRE paper (McKelvey and Palfrey 1995 (Chapter 20 of this book)) defined quantal response functions as a general class of functions that shared what we considered the desirable properties of the logit function.[3] These admissible quantal response functions were *interior* (i.e., all choice probabilities were strictly between 0 and 1), *continuous* (in expected payoffs), and *monotone* (in expected payoffs).

Interiority is simply an assumption that behavior has a stochastic component to it. Viewing game theory as an approach to make predictions how players will make choices, this simply says the quantal response approach makes statistical predictions rather than degenerate predictions. This creates a natural framework for structural models in the statistical analysis of game theoretic data.

In standard game theory, the analysis of equilibrium is plagued by discontinuities in the best response functions. That is, if your opponent's strategy changes slightly, your best response to it may change dramatically even though your expected payoffs to each of your strategies have been only slightly perturbed. The continuity assumption requires that every player's choice probabilities will change only slightly if the other player's strategies change only slightly.

We assumed two kinds of monotonicity. First, choice probabilities of an action are increasing in the expected payoffs of the action. That is, if the expected payoffs to all strategies of a player remain unchanged, except for strategy k, then the probability the player chooses strategy k increases. The second kind of monotonicity compares the choice probabilities of any pair of strategies for a player: for any player and any pair of that player's strategies, the strategy with the higher expected payoffs is chosen with higher probability than the action with the lower expected payoff. The combination of continuity and monotonicity imposes a version of neutrality, that no action is specially favored, for reasons not related to

---

[2] The computation and graphical representation of the logit equilibrium correspondence eventually became part of the Gambit package for computing equilibria in normal and extensive form games (McKelvey et al. 1995).

[3] This axiomatic approach to QRE in terms of reduced form quantal response functions has recently been resurrected as "regular QRE." See Goeree, Holt, and Palfrey (2005).

payoffs. In particular, actions with equal expected payoffs must be chosen with equal probability. This latter implication of the QRE axioms places significant restrictions on observable data.[4]

The most commonly used version of QRE is based on the logit choice model, hence called logit equilibrium. The stochastic choice probabilities are proportional to exponentiated expected payoffs. Thus, the log odds of choosing one strategy rather than another are equal to a proportionality factor times the difference in their expected payoffs. This proportionality factor, λ, can be interpreted as indexing "rationality," i.e., the responsiveness to expected payoffs. When $\lambda = 0$, a player is totally random and doesn't respond to expected payoffs at all; all strategies are chosen with equal probability, regardless of payoffs. At the other end of the rationality spectrum, as λ becomes very large, players are infinitely responsive to expected payoffs; that is, they are more likely to choose only best responses. Hence, in the limit as λ goes to infinity, logit equilibria converge to Nash equilibria. In this sense, QRE is a generalization of Nash equilibria that can accommodate varying levels of rationality of the players, including (in the limit) perfectly rational choice.

3. Payoff Disturbances instead of Errors in Actions

In the published version of the paper, we defined a more general version of QRE that allowed for non-monotone relationships between choice probabilities and expected payoffs, and also formalized QRE in terms of games of incomplete information. That more general version was inspired by the Harsanyi (1973) model of games with randomly disturbed payoffs. Based on the work of McFadden (1976) and others on stochastic models of individual discrete choice one could rationalize the "errors" in quantal response equilibrium by assuming that players had privately observed payoff disturbances, producing a game of incomplete information. The term "quantal response equilibrium" was adopted from the statistical literature which had used the terminology of "quantal choice" to describe stochastic models of discrete choice.

There are a variety of interpretations of the payoff disturbances. One is literal. That is, the game of complete information is simply a model or approximation of the real game being played. When we write the payoffs for a player as "8.3," the player actually may behave as if the payoff were 8.2 or 8.5 (for reasons we don't try to explain). That is, induced value (Smith 1976) cannot be perfectly achieved even in the context of real incentives that correspond to the payoffs of the specific

---

[4]The nature of such restrictions is illustrated with an example in Goeree, Holt, and Palfrey (2005).

game one is studying (as in a laboratory experiment). Another interpretation is that the players themselves are acting as statisticians, and somehow form an estimate of the expected payoff for each strategy, and the disturbances correspond to the players' own estimation errors.[5]

This general version of QRE is sufficiently flexible that it can allow arbitrary mappings from expected payoffs to choice probabilities, and places no restrictions on the data unless some assumptions (such as i.i.d.) are made about the joint distribution of payoff disturbances. This is explained in Haile et al. (2003). Obviously restrictions must be imposed on the stochastic terms in order to obtain empirical implications of the QRE model. To date virtually all applications of QRE have followed the approach of regular QRE, implicitly assuming that the disturbances are i.i.d.

It would be interesting to pursue more complex models of the error process, particularly in games where players have a chance to act repeatedly. Repeated play has two features that are not fully captured by the i.i.d. model. First and most obvious, there can be correlation because of learning, as discussed above in the players-as-statisticians interpretation of QRE.[6] A less obvious source of correlation is more closely related to the reputation building argument used to explain cooperation in the centipede game.

The possible existence of this kind of correlation could partially explain why the one-parameter logit QRE model does not fit the centipede game as well as one might hope. Also, the finding that QRE fits the 6-move game somewhat worse than the 4-move game may be due to the fact that each player has 3 opportunities to move rather than 2, so there are more possibilities for correlation. In these games, QRE captures the salient qualitative features of observed play (such as increasing take probabilities), but it does not fit the observed choice probabilities as well quantitatively.[7]

An extension of the basic QRE model that corrects for these kinds of correlations might be both more realistic and produce better fits to the data. The challenge is to come up with a structural model of these correlations that is simultaneously

---

[5]This approach suggests a way to integrate learning models into QRE. As players gain experience playing a game, they update their beliefs about the expected payoffs of each strategy, and the estimation errors decline over time. There has been some work fitting the logit QRE, allowing a trend in the logit noise parameter, as a rough measure of learning in these games.

[6]See Basov (2003) for a dynamic learning model of QRE with non-monotone choice probabilities.

[7]See McKelvey and Palfrey (1998, pp. 30–33). Zauner (1999) analyzes the data from centipede games using a QRE-like model with normally distributed payoff disturbances.

feasible to estimate and plausible. One possible approach is to assume the disturbance to a player's payoff can be represented as the sum of a transitory term (possibly i.i.d. across information sets) reflecting some form of bounded rationality or erratic behavior, and a more permanent term corresponding to a player-type.

Altruistic preferences or other forms of social preferences are examples of the sort of permanent disturbances that may lead to correlation of disturbances for the *same player* in *different information sets* of a multistage game. In some games, like the centipede game, altruism has a clear interpretation. A model along these lines is estimated in McKelvey and Palfrey (1998), where two parameters, one corresponding to an altruism term and the other corresponding to the usual agent logit error term, are simultaneously estimated, and result in a significant improvement in fit.

4. Applications to Political Science Experiments

The *American Political Science Review* has published three papers in the last five years that apply quantal response equilibrium to the analysis of data from laboratory experiments. The first, of which McKelvey was a coauthor, is a study of Condorcet juries. The second is a study of spatial equilibrium in a one dimensional policy space when one candidate has a valence advantage. The third is a theoretical analysis, based on a wide range of experiments that had mixed strategies where the logic rested on calculations about the probability of being pivotal — a central feature of the calculus of voting, participation, and other political phenomena.

4.1. Condorcet Juries

Guarnaschelli, McKelvey, and Palfrey (2000) reports an experimental study of small Condorcet juries. The Condorcet jury problem is an old one, mainly applying primitive versions of the law of large numbers to show that majority rule is an efficient mechanism for aggregating diverse information held by similarly inclined decision makers. That literature was given new life when it was observed that, quite generally, voting members of a Condorcet jury have incentives to vote strategically in such a way that their privately held information is not accurately reflected in their vote.[8] Of course, since members of a traditional Condorcet jury have identical preferences, any garbling of information creates inefficiencies.

---

[8]See Austen-Smith and Banks (1996).

A "worst case" (or nearly so) of this strategic garbling was identified in a paper by Feddersen and Pesendorfer (1998), which shows how the use of unanimous voting rules in juries not only can be ineffective, but can have perverse effects. The traditional rationale for requiring supermajorities in criminal court juries is to reduce the likelihood of convicting an innocent defendant, reflecting a jurisprudential philosophy that such an error is more costly than the reverse error, acquitting a guilty defendant. But strategic voting leads to an equilibrium where exactly the opposite happens, and the Nash equilibrium probability of convicting an innocent defendant is actually *higher* under unanimity than majority rule, with this flaw becoming even worse for larger juries. Indeed as the size of the jury increases, the probability of this kind of error can increase under unanimity rule.

The Pivot Principle. The logic rests heavily on the now standard reasoning that strategic voters condition their behavior only on the event that their vote is pivotal:[9] *the Pivot Principle*. Under unanimity rule, one's vote is pivotal if and only if *all* other voters are voting the same way. So, if other voters are all voting informatively, then a voter doesn't want to change the outcome by casting a single vote in the opposite direction. Hence, voters with information suggesting the defendant is innocent are reluctant to cast a vote for acquittal, as this could overturn the better collective judgment of the rest of the voters, all of whom voted to convict. As a result, even voters with information suggesting innocence will have an incentive to vote to convict.[10]

McKelvey's experimental work on juries asks two questions. First, what happens to the Feddersen-Pesendorfer results if voters are not perfectly rational, in the sense of quantal response equilibrium? Second, to what extent is the Pivot Principle an accurate reflection of how individuals decide how to vote? Is the calculus of voting as practiced by voters based on the relative likelihood of conditional pivotal events?

The answer to the first question indicates the fragility of the Feddersen- Pesendorfer results. First, theoretically, in *any regular quantal response function*, the probability of convicting an innocent defendant goes to zero in the size of the jury. Second, for the parameters we used in the experiment, the probability of convicting the innocent was greater for majority rule than unanimity rule in QRE. Indeed

---

[9] A voter is pivotal if that voter's vote is sufficient to change the outcome. For example, in a winner-take all-election a voter is pivotal if their vote makes or breaks a tie.

[10] A key assumption here is that the unanimity requirement is asymmetric. That is, a unanimous vote is not required for acquittal (i.e., assume hung jury trials are not retried). See Coughlan (2000).

most of the other Nash equilibrium qualitative comparisons between majority and unanimity rule and qualitative predictions about the effect of jury size on group decision accuracy are reversed under QRE.

The intuition behind most of these reversals is straightforward. With even a small probability of error, the chance that some member of the jury will vote to acquit is much higher than in the Nash equilibrium. In the Nash equilibrium, the probability of any single voter voting to acquit must converge to zero at an extremely slow rate in order to support the mixed strategy equilibrium, because mixing requires the probability of being pivotal to be bounded away from zero (and hence the probability of convicting an innocent must also be bounded away from zero). In a QRE, since only one such vote is needed for acquittal, and the probability of an error is bounded away from zero (because payoffs are bounded), the probability of being pivotal converges to zero rapidly (and, accordingly, so does the probability of convicting an innocent).

The answer to the second question is that there is clear evidence that voters are strategic, and that the Pivot Principle is the driving force behind the strategy. As far as individual behavior goes, the qualitative predictions of Nash equilibrium are surprisingly accurate (quantitative predictions less so). Voters do appear to condition on pivotal events. Indeed, this kind of logic is also important in QRE, and the main difference between QRE and Nash equilibrium predictions about individual behavior (aside from the pure random element) is in the quantitative probabilities of voting one way or the other. These differences are illustrated in most of the applications in the following sections.

4.2. Spatial Competition between Two Candidates: Valence Effects

When two candidates compete in one dimension with one candidate having a valence or quality advantage, the equilibrium quickly becomes very complicated. Except in trivial cases where the advantage is huge (or there is no uncertainty), pure strategies fail to exist because convergence leads to certain defeat of the weaker candidate.[11]

Mixed strategy equilibria exhibit strong asymmetries between the two candidates, and these asymmetries follow intuitive patterns which are consistent with some observations of empirical political scientists. The main effect is that the

---

[11]Schofield (Chapter 11 in this book) emphasizes this fact about valence effects on electoral equilibrium, and in particular its implication about party divergence, with an application to the Israeli elections of 1988, 1992, and 1996.

weaker candidate is likely to adopt more extreme positions than the stronger candidate. A secondary effect is that the main effect is strongest if the distribution of voters is unimodal (unpolarized) and weakest when the distribution of voters is bimodal (polarized). As the electorate becomes more polarized, weak candidates will moderate their platforms and strong candidates will drift away from the median.[12]

An experiment was conducted by Aragones and Palfrey (2004) to see if these effects could be measured in a laboratory setting. Both effects were found, and were nearly as strong as predicted by the theory. However, there were a number of anomalies. The main anomaly was that weak candidates consistently adopted moderate positions more often than predicted by the Nash equilibrium. The QRE analysis of the location game provides an explanation for this: in this kind of location game, the optimal location against a completely random opponent is to locate in the center of the issue space. As a consequence, QRE predicts the weak opponent will adopt moderate policies more frequently than the Nash equilibrium.

4.3. Participation Games

An example of a participation game is one where there are a fixed number of voters and two candidates, the act of voting is costly, and each voter simply decides whether to vote for his preferred candidate or to abstain (Palfrey and Rosenthal 1983, 1985). A related but simpler game is the threshold public goods game in which each of n individuals independently decides whether or not to contribute a fixed amount to produce a public good. The public good is provided if and only if at least k players contribute. In the case of $k = 1$ this is sometimes called the volunteer dilemma, and can be applied to many free rider problems, such as bystander intervention. These problems have been studied widely by political scientists, economists, social psychologists, and sociologists.

Goeree and Holt (2005) note that in experimental tests of games in this class, the aggregate outcomes (e.g., participation *rates*) vary systematically from the theoretical predictions. For example, in games where the equilibrium participation rates are low (for example, the volunteer's dilemma), observed participation rates in laboratory experiments are significantly higher. Such is also the common wisdom in many empirical applications based on field observations. For example, high turnout rates in mass elections don't seem to square well with the apparently

---

[12] These properties are derived formally in Aragones and Palfrey (2004). Groseclose (2001) obtained similar results in a related model.

low pivot probabilities, unless costs are miniscule or negative for a large fraction of voters, or unless one is willing to assume the benefits of affecting the outcome are several orders of magnitude higher than seems plausible.

Goeree and Holt's explanation is that almost all of this kind of systematic variation in turnout can be explained very parsimoniously with QRE. In particular, QRE predicts higher participation rates than Nash for games in which the equilibrium participation rates are low, and the reverse for games with high equilibrium participation rates.

Late in his career, McKelvey turned his attention to developing a rigorous general theory of probabilistic voting (and turnout) based on QRE. His joint paper with John Patty (McKelvey and Patty 2002) is the main product of the work he did in this area.

4.4. Other Laboratory Experiments Applying QRE

There are many other applications of QRE to experimental games. Many of these involve the study of abstract games to shed light on questions of strategic behavior, and as such, most of these should be of interest at least indirectly to many formal political theorists. This would include signaling games, information transmission games, winner-take-all contests, information cascades, and others. The interested reader should consult Holt (2000) for an extensive, albeit somewhat dated, list of references.

5. Applications to Field Data in Political Science

Most of the applications of QRE to field data in political science have focused on questions of international conflict. The pioneer in these applications is Curt Signorino, who has produced a series of papers addressing methodological issues as well as substantive questions about factors affecting the probability of international conflicts.[13]

Following the recent tradition in the field of international relations, game theory is used to model the forces by which international crises may or may not escalate into war. As Signorino (1999) and Signorino and Yilmaz (2003) argue convincingly, empirical attempts to identify the causes of escalation with simple linear reduced form models may fail because the equilibrium of the underlying

---

[13]The general approach to developing structural models of strategic interaction in these kinds of games, and discussion of a variety of statistical issues, can be found in Signorino (2003).

game is highly nonlinear in the parameters of the model.[14] They call this *strategic misspecification*.

A variety of bargaining games and signaling games have been used as models of international conflict and brinkmanship. Of course, depending on the specific game one uses, the qualitative features of the equilibrium can be quite different. For example, models with and without private information can generate different results.

In order to take these games to the data and to identify which models are better or worse, two things are needed. First, an error structure needs to be added in order to apply standard statistical techniques, as in Signorino (1999), and this error structure has to be built into the game that is being used as the basic model. Second, parameters of the game, such as the terminal node payoffs, are estimated, based on the specified error structure. Once this is done, other variables measured directly in the field can be included in a regression-like exercise to control for various factors and assess their possible influence on conflict escalation. Lewis and Schultz (2003) explore methodological issues related to estimation and identification of QRE models in the context of crisis bargaining games similar to those studied in Signorino (1999).

This approach has also been used to study deterrence theory. Various factors, such the balance of military force, past reputations of the actors, alliances, geopolitics, international organizations, the amount of uncertainty and private information, and so forth, have been proposed to explain when and why deterrence succeeds or fails. This is an ideal application of the quantal response equilibrium approach to estimation, and such an application appears in Signorino and Tarar (2004), who test a model based on the extended immediate deterrence concept of Huth (1988) and Huth and Russet (1984, 1988).

6. Concluding Remarks: Possible Directions for Future Political Science Research Using QRE

Three possible theoretical directions seem particularly fruitful; interestingly, all three tie in with other aspects of McKelvey's research. First is the study of repeated games. Such games have been widely used in political science to study cooperation and the long run viability of institutions.[15] Quantal response equilibrium may have something to contribute here because it provides a natural model

---

[14]Most, but not all. Carson (2003) applies a probit specification of QRE in an empirical study of strategic behavior by challengers and incumbents in U.S. House elections.

[15]The best known application in political science is to the prisoner's dilemma (for example, Axelrod 1984).

of behavior "off the equilibrium path." More precisely, there is no such thing as "off the equilibrium path" in QRE, since all actions are taken with positive probability. As such, it could provide a good approach for evaluating the plausibility of punishment strategies, as well as providing insights to refine the (infinite) set of subgame perfect equilibria in repeated games. There are some closely related bargaining games (e.g., Baron and Ferejohn 1989) that also have an infinite recursive structure (and many equilibria) which might prove useful to study from the QRE approach.

A second direction would be strategic voting in agendas. It is well known that voters may have an incentive to vote for alternatives they strongly dislike early in an agenda, in order to obtain a better outcome ultimately. But these arguments typically rely on assumptions of complete information, and the ability of each voter to perfectly predict the voting behavior of all members of the committee in all nodes of the game tree. Even in the case of sophisticated voting with incomplete information, the equilibria seem quite fragile and depend crucially on the predictability of the other voters' behavior (Ordeshook and Palfrey 1988).

A third direction is information aggregation. McKelvey has two experimental contributions in this area, one studying juries and the other studying information cascades. He contributed to the study of information aggregation in many other contexts as well. Recently, modeling voting as an information aggregation mechanism has emerged as a leading research area in formal theory. But significant challenges face the analysis, including multiple equilibria and broader issues of cognitive sophistication implied by the equilibrium analysis. An approach like QRE that combines strategic behavior with more limited rationality may lead to new and valuable insights about information aggregation.

References

Aragones, Enriqueta and Thomas R. Palfrey. 2004. "Spatial Competition between Two Candidates of Different Quality: An Experimental Study." *American Political Science Review* 98:77–90.

Aumann, Robert J. 1995. "Backward Induction and Common Knowledge of Rationality." *Games and Economic Behavior* 8:6–19.

Austen-Smith, David and Jeffrey S. Banks. 1996. "Information Aggregation, Rationality, and the Condorcet Jury Theorem." *American Political Science Review* 90:34–45.

Axelrod, Robert. 1984. *The Evolution of Cooperation.* New York: Basic Books.

Baron, David and John A. Ferejohn. 1989. "Bargaining in Legislatures." *American Political Science Review* 83:1181–1206.

Basov, Suren. 2003. "Quantal Response Equilibrium with Non-Monotone Probabilities: A Dynamic Approach." *Working Paper*. University of Melbourne.

Carson, Jamie L. 2003. "Strategic Interaction and Candidate Competition in U.S. House Elections: Empirical Applications of Probit and Strategic Probit Models." *Political Analysis* 11 (4):368–80.

Coughlan, Peter. 2000. "In Defense of Unanimous Jury Verdicts: Mistrials, Communication, and Strategic Voting." *American Political Science Review* 94:375–93.

Feddersen, Timothy and Wolfgang Pesendorfer. 1998. "Convicting the Innocent: The Inferiority of Unanimous Jury Verdicts under Strategic Voting." *American Political Science Review* 92:23–36.

Goeree, Jacob and Charles A. Holt. 2005. "Anomalous Behavior in Binary Choice Games: Entry, Voting, Public Goods, and the Volunteer's Dilemma." *American Political Science Review* 99:201–13.

Goeree, Jacob, Charles A. Holt, and Thomas R. Palfrey. 2005. "Regular Quantal Response Equilibrium," *Experimental Economics* 8:347–367.

Groseclose, Tim. 2001. "A Model of Candidate Location when One Candidate Has a Valence Advantage." *American Journal of Political Science* 45:862–86.

Guarnaschelli, Serena, Richard D. McKelvey, and Thomas R. Palfrey. 2000. "An Experimental Study of Jury Decision Rules." *American Political Science Review* 94 (2):407–23.

Haile, Phillip A., Ali Hortacsu, and Grigory Kosenok. 2003. "On the Empirical Content of Quantal Response Equilibrium." *Working Paper*. Madison: University of Wisconsin.

Harsanyi, John. 1973. "Games with Randomly Disturbed Payoffs." *International Journal of Game Theory* 2:1–23.

Holt, Charles A. 2000. *The Y2K Bibliography of Experimental Economics and Social Science*. http://www.people.virginia.edu/~cah2k/y2k.htm.

Huth, Paul. 1988. *Extended Deterrence and the Prevention of War*. New Haven: Yale University Press.

Huth, Paul K. 1990. "The Extended Deterrent Value of Nuclear Weapons." *Journal of Conflict Resolution* 34 (2):270–90.

Huth, Paul K. and Bruce Russett. 1984. "What Makes Deterrence Work? Cases from 1900 to 1980." *World Politics* 36 (4):496–526.

Huth, Paul K. and Bruce Russett. 1988. "Deterrence Failure and Crisis Escalation." *International Studies Quarterly* 32 (1):29–45.

Kreps, David M. 1990. *A Course in Microeconomic Theory*. Princeton: Princeton University Press.

Lewis, Jeffrey B. and Kenneth A. Schultz. 2003. "Revealing Preferences: Empirical Estimation of a Crisis Bargaining Game with Incomplete Information." *Political Analysis* 11 (4):345–67.

McFadden, Daniel. 1976. "Quantal Choice Analysis: A Survey." *Annals of Economic and Social Measurement* 5 (4):363–90.

McKelvey, Richard D., Andrew McLennan, and Theodore Turocy. 1995. "Gambit: Software Tools for Game Theory." Version 0.97.0.7 (2004). http://econweb.tamu.edu/gambit.

McKelvey, Richard D. and Thomas R. Palfrey. 1992. "An Experimental Study of the Centipede Game." *Econometrica* 60:803–36. (Chapter 18 in this book.)

McKelvey, Richard D. and Thomas R. Palfrey. 1995. "Quantal Response Equilibria for Normal Form Games." *Games and Economic Behavior* 10:6–38. (Chapter 20 in this book.)

McKelvey, Richard D. and Thomas R. Palfrey. 1998. "Quantal Response Equilibria for Extensive Form Games." *Experimental Economics* 1:9–41.

McKelvey, Richard D. and John W. Patty. 2002. "A Theory of Voting in Large Elections." *Working Paper*. Carnegie Mellon University.

McKelvey, Richard D. and Guy Riddihough. 1999. "The Hard Sciences." *Proceedings of the National Academy of Sciences* 96:10549.

Ordeshook, Peter C. and Thomas R. Palfrey. 1988. "Agendas, Strategic Voting, and Signaling with Incomplete Information." *American Journal of Political Science* 32:441–66.

Palfrey, Thomas R. and Howard Rosenthal. 1983. "A Strategic Calculus of Voting." *Public Choice* 41:7–53.

Palfrey, Thomas R. and Howard Rosenthal. 1985. "Voter Participation and Strategic Uncertainty." *American Political Science Review* 79:62–78.

Rosenthal, Robert. 1981. "Games of Perfect Information, Predatory Pricing, and the Chain-Store Paradox." *Journal of Economic Theory* 25:92–100.

Signorino, Curtis S. 1999. "Strategic Interaction and the Statistical Analysis of International Conflict." *American Political Science Review* 93 (2):279–97.

Signorino, Curtis S. 2003. "Structure and Uncertainty in Discrete Choice Models." *Political Analysis* 11 (4):316–44.

Signorino, Curtis S. and Ahmer Tarar. 2004. "A Unified Theory and Test of Extended Immediate Deterrence." *Working Paper*. University of Rochester.

Signorino, Curtis S. and Kuzey Yilmaz. 2003. "Strategic Misspecification in Regression Models." *American Journal of Political Science* 47 (3):551–66.

Smith, Vernon L. 1976. "Experimental Economics: Induced Value Theory." *American Economic Review* 66:274–79.

Zauner, Klaus. 1999. "A Payoff Uncertainty Explanation of Results in Experimental Centipede Games." *Games and Economic Behavior* 26 (1):157–85.

CHAPTER 20

Quantal Response Equilibria for Normal Form Games

RICHARD D. MCKELVEY AND THOMAS R. PALFREY

ABSTRACT. We investigate the use of standard statistical models for quantal choice in a game theoretic setting. Players choose strategies based on relative expected utility and assume other players do so as well. We define a quantal response equilibrium (QRE) as a fixed point of this process and establish existence.

For a logit specification of the error structure, we show that as the error goes to zero, QRE approaches a subset of Nash equilibria and also implies a unique selection from the set of Nash equilibria in generic games. We fit the model to a variety of experimental data sets by using maximum likelihood estimation.

1. Introduction

We investigate the possibility of using standard statistical models for quantal choice in a game theoretic setting. Players choose among strategies in the normal form of a game based on their relative expected utility, but make choices based on a quantal choice model, and assume other players do so as well. For a given specification of the error structure, we define a quantal response equilibrium (QRE) as a fixed point of this process.

We acknowledge the support of National Science Foundation Grant SBR-9223701 to the California Institute of Technology and the support of the JPL-Caltech supercomputer project. We thank Barry O'Neill, Richard Boebel, Jack Ochs, and Amnon Rapoport for sharing their data. We acknowledge valuable discussions with Mahmoud El-Gamal and Mark Fey, helpful comments at several conference and seminar presentations, suggestions by a referee, and the research assistance of Yan Chen and Eugene Grayver.

Under this process best response functions become probabilistic (at least from the point of view of an outside observer) rather than deterministic. Better responses are more likely to be observed than worse responses, but best responses are not played with certainty. The idea that players make infinitesimal errors underlies some of the refinement literature (Myerson, 1978; Selten, 1975). Introduction of noninfinitesimal errors has been specifically studied by Van Damme (1987, Chap. 4), Rosenthal (1989), and Beja (1992). Rosenthal assumes that the probability of adopting a particular strategy is linearly increasing in expected payoff. Beja, in contrast, assumes that players attempt to implement a "target" strategy but fail to do so perfectly. Recent work by El-Gamal et al. (1993), El-Gamal and Palfrey (1995, 1994), McKelvey and Palfrey (1992), Ma and Manove (1993), Chen (1994), and Schmidt (1992) also explores the equilibrium implications of error-prone decisionmaking in specific settings.

It is important to emphasize that this alternative approach does not abandon the notion of equilibrium, but instead replaces the perfectly rational expectations equilibrium embodied in Nash equilibrium with an imperfect, or noisy, rational expectations equilibrium. The equilibrium restriction in our model is captured by the assumption that players estimate expected payoffs in an unbiased way. That is, an estimate by player i about the expected payoff of action a_{ij} will on average equal the expected payoff of action a_{ij} calculated from the equilibrium probability distribution of other players' action choices, given that they are adopting estimated best responses. Thus players' expectations are correct, on average.

This model is a natural extension of well developed and commonly used statistical models of choice or quantal response that have a long tradition in statistical applications to biology, pharmacology, and the social sciences. Accordingly, we call an equilibrium of our model a quantal response equilibrium. The name is borrowed from the statistical literature on quantal choice/response models in which individual choices or responses are rational, but are based on latent variables (in our case a player's vector of estimated payoffs) that are not observed by the econometrician. The added complication is that the underlying latent variables assumed to govern the discrete responses are endogenous.

A valuable feature of this alternative approach to modeling equilibrium in games is that it provides a convenient statistical structure for estimation using either field data or experimental data. For a particular specification of the error structure, we compute the QRE as a function of the variance of the player estimation errors in several games that have been studied in laboratory experiments. We use these data to obtain maximum likelihood estimates of the error variance. This is possible because, in contrast to the traditional Nash equilibrium approach which makes strong deterministic predictions, this model makes statistical predictions.

We find that the statistical predictions of the QRE model depend in systematic ways on the precision of the players' estimates of the expected payoffs from different actions. Therefore, to the extent that we can find observable independent variables that *a priori* one would expect correlated with the precision of these estimates, one can make predictions about the effects of different experimental treatments that systematically vary these independent variables. An obvious candidate that we investigate here is *experience*. As a player gains experience playing a particular game and makes repeated observations about the actual payoffs received from different action choices, he/she can be expected to make more precise estimates of the expected payoffs from different strategies. This is only slightly different from the simple observation that, for an econometrician, standard errors of regression coefficients can be expected to decrease in the number of observations. We refer to this as *learning*.[1]

The rest of the paper consists of four sections. Section 2 lays out the formal structure and establishes existence of QRE in finite games. Section 3 specializes the QRE model to the case of logistic response, where the errors follow a log Weibull distribution. This is called the *Logit Equilibrium*. We establish several properties of the logit equilibrium correspondence and use these properties to define a generically unique selection of Nash equilibrium as the limit point (as the error variance goes to zero) to the unique connected equilibrium manifold defined by the graph of the equilibrium correspondence as a function of the estimation error. Section 4 compares QRE to other equilibrium concepts in traditional game theory and establishes a formal connection between our approach and traditional game theory by demonstrating an equivalence between a QRE of a game and a Bayesian equilibrium of an incomplete information version of the game. Section 5 presents the estimation of the model and the measurement of learning effects, using data from experimental games.

2. Quantal Response Equilibrium

Consider a finite n-person game in normal form: There is a set $N = \{1, ..., n\}$ of *players*, and for each player $i \in N$ a *strategy set* $S_i = \{s_{i1}, ..., s_{iJ_i}\}$ consisting

---

[1] The term "learning" means different things to different people. El-Gamal has suggested that what we call learning is close to what some economists call "learning-by-doing." However, we do not model the detailed mechanics of learning as is done in some of the literature on repeated games, where learning is modeled as either by fully Bayesian updating or as a myopic but deterministic process such as fictitious play or Cournot dynamics.

of J_i pure strategies. For each $i \in N$, there is a *payoff function*, $u_i : S \to \mathbb{R}$, where $S = \prod_{i \in N} S_i$.

Let Δ_i be the set of probability measures on S_i. Elements of Δ_i are of the form $p_i : S_i \to \mathbb{R}$ where $\sum_{s_{ij} \in S_i} p_i(s_{ij}) = 1$, and $p_i(s_{ij}) \geq 0$ for all $s_{ij} \in S_i$. We use the notation $p_{ij} = p_i(s_{ij})$. So Δ_i is isomorphic to the J_i dimensional simplex $\Delta_i = \{p_i = (p_{i1}, ..., p_{iJ_i}) : \sum_j p_{ij} = 1, p_{ij} \geq 0\}$. We write $\Delta = \prod_{i \in N} \Delta_i$, and let $J = \sum_{i \in N} J_i$. We denote points in Δ by $p = (p_1, ..., p_n)$ where $p_i = (p_{i1}, ..., p_{iJ_i}) \in \Delta_i$. We use the abusive notation s_{ij} to denote the strategy $p_i \in \Delta_i$ with $p_{ij} = 1$. We use the shorthand notation $p = (p_i, p_{-i})$. Hence, the notation (s_{ij}, p_{-i}) represents the strategy where i adopts the pure strategy s_{ij}, and all other players adopt their components of p.

The payoff function is extended to have domain Δ by the rule $u_i(p) = \sum_{s \in S} p(s) u_i(s)$, where $p(s) = \prod_{i \in N} p_i(s_i)$. A vector $p = (p_1, ..., p_n) \in \Delta$ is a *Nash Equilibrium* if for all $i \in N$ and all $p_i' \in \Delta_i$, $u_i(p_i', p_{-i}) \leq u_i(p)$.

Write $X_i = \mathbb{R}^{J_i}$, to represent the space of possible payoffs for strategies that player i might adopt, and $X = \prod_{i=1}^n X_i$. We define the function $\bar{u} : \Delta \to X$ by

$$\bar{u}(p) = (\bar{u}_1(p), ..., \bar{u}_n(p)),$$

where

$$\bar{u}_{ij}(p) = u_i(s_{ij}, p_{-i}).$$

Next, we define quantal response equilibrium as a statistical version of Nash equilibrium where each player's utility for each action is subject to random error.[2] Specifically, for each i and each $j \in \{1, ..., J_i\}$, and for any $p \in \Delta$, define

$$\hat{u}_{ij}(p) = \bar{u}_{ij}(p) + \varepsilon_{ij}.$$

Player i's error vector, $\varepsilon_i = (\varepsilon_{i1}, ..., \varepsilon_{iJ_i})$, is distributed according to a joint distribution with density function $f_i(\varepsilon_i)$. The marginal distribution of f_i exists for each ε_{ij} and $E(\varepsilon_i) = 0$. We call $f = (f_1, ..., f_n)$ *admissible* if f_i satisfies the above properties for all i. Our behavioral assumption is that each player selects an action j such that $\hat{u}_{ij} \geq \hat{u}_{ik}$ $\forall k = 1, ..., J_i$. Given this decision rule (i chooses action j if $\hat{u}_{ij}$ is maximal[3]), then for any given $\bar{u}$ and f this implies a probability distribution over the observed actions of the players, induced by the

---

[2] One interpretation of this is that player i calculates the expected payoff, but makes calculation errors according to some random process. An alternative interpretation is that players calculate expected payoffs correctly but have an additive payoff disturbance associated with each available pure strategy. This latter interpretation is discussed in Section 5.

[3] Standard arguments show that results do not depend on how ties ($\hat{u}_{ij} = \hat{u}_{ik}$) are treated (Harsanyi, 1973).

probability distribution over the vector of observation errors, ε. Formally, for any $\bar{u} = (\bar{u}_1, ..., \bar{u}_n)$ with $\bar{u} \in \Re^{J_i}$ for each i, we define the ij-*response set* $R_{ij} \subseteq \mathbb{R}^{J_i}$ by
$$R_{ij}(\bar{u}_i) = \{\varepsilon_i \in \Re^{J_i} | \bar{u}_{ij} + \varepsilon_{ij} \geq \bar{u}_{ik} + \varepsilon_{ik} \; \forall k = 1, ..., J_i\}.$$
Given p, each set $R_{ij}(\bar{u}_i(p))$ specifies the region of errors that will lead i to choose action j. Finally, let
$$\sigma_{ij}(\bar{u}_i) = \int_{R_{ij}(\bar{u}_i)} f(\varepsilon) d\varepsilon$$
equal the probability that a player i will select strategy j given $\bar{u}$. We then define for any admissible f and game $\Gamma = (N, S, u)$ a *quantal response equilibrium* as a vector $\pi \in \Delta$ such that $\pi_{ij} = \int_{R_{ij}(\bar{u}_i)} f(\varepsilon) d\varepsilon$, where $\bar{u} = \bar{u}(\pi)$. Formally,

DEFINITION 1. Let $\Gamma = (N, S, u)$ be a game in normal form, and let f be admissible. A *quantal response equilibrium* (QRE) is any $\pi \in \Delta$ such that for all $i \in N$, $1 \leq j \leq J_i$,
$$\pi_{ij} = \sigma_{ij}(\bar{u}_i(\pi)).$$

We call $\sigma_i : \Re^{J_i} \to \Delta^{J_i}$ the *statistical reaction function* (or quantal response function) of player i. Several results about statistical reaction functions can be verified easily:

(1) $\sigma \in \Delta$ is nonempty.
(2) σ_i is continuous on $\Re^{J_i}$.
(3) σ_{ij} is monotonically increasing in $\bar{u}_{ij}$.
(4) If, for all i and all $j, k = 1, ..., J_i$, ε_{ij} and ε_{ik} are i.i.d., then for all $\bar{u}$, for all i, and for all $j, k = 1, ..., J_i$,
$$\bar{u}_{ij} > \bar{u}_{ik} \implies \sigma_{ij}(\bar{u}) > \sigma_{ik}(\bar{u}).$$

The first two properties of σ imply Theorem 1.

THEOREM 1. *For any Γ and for any admissible f, there exists a QRE.*

Proof. A QRE is a fixed point of $\sigma \circ \bar{u}$. Since the distribution of ε has a density, $\sigma \circ \bar{u}$ is continuous on Δ. By Brouwer's fixed point theorem, $\sigma \circ \bar{u}$ has a fixed point.

Q.E.D.

The third and fourth properties say that "better actions are more likely to be chosen than worse actions." Property three specifically compares the statistical best response function if one of i's expected payoffs, $\bar{u}_{ij}$, has changed and every other component of $\bar{u}_i$ has stayed the same. In this case, the region R_{ij} expands and each other $\bar{u}_{ik}$ weakly decreases. Note that this is not the same as saying that π changed in such a way that $\bar{u}_{ij}$ increased since the change in π could, in principle, change the value of all components of $\bar{u}_i$. The fourth property states that σ orders the probability of different actions by their expected payoffs.

3. The Logit Equilibrium

In the rest of the paper, we study a particular parametric class of quantal response functions that has a tradition in the study of individual choice behavior (Luce, 1959). For any given $\lambda \geq 0$, the *logistic* quantal response function is defined, for $x_i \in \mathbb{R}^{J_i}$, by

$$\sigma_{ij}(x_i) = \frac{e^{\lambda x_{ij}}}{\sum_{k=1}^{J_i} e^{\lambda x_{ik}}}$$

and corresponds to optimal choice behavior[4] if f_i has an extreme value distribution, with cumulative density function $F_i(\varepsilon_{ij}) = e^{-e^{-\lambda x_{ij}-\gamma}}$ and the ε_{ij}'s are independent. Therefore, if each player uses a logistic quantal response function, the corresponding QRE or *Logit Equilibrium* requires, for each i, j,

$$\pi_{ij} = \frac{e^{\lambda x_{ij}}}{\sum_{k=1}^{J_i} e^{\lambda x_{ik}}}$$

where $x_{ij} = \bar{u}_{ij}(\pi)$.

For the logistic response function, we can parameterize the set of possible response functions σ with the parameter λ, which is inversely related to the level of error: $\lambda = 0$ means that actions consist of all error, and $\lambda = \infty$ means that there is no error. We can then consider the set of Logit Equilibria as a function of λ. It is obvious that when $\lambda = 0$, there is a unique equilibrium at the centroid of the simplex. In other words, $\pi_{ik} = 1/J_i$ for all i, k. On the other hand, when $\lambda \to \infty$, the following result shows that the Logit Equilibria approach Nash equilibria of the underlying game.

We define the *Logit Equilibrium correspondence* to be the correspondence $\pi^* : \mathbb{R}_+ \Longrightarrow 2^\Delta$ given by

$$\pi^*(\lambda) = \left\{ \pi \in \Delta : \pi_{ij} = \frac{e^{\lambda \bar{u}_{ij}(\pi)}}{\sum_{k=1}^{J_i} e^{\lambda \bar{u}_{ik}(\pi)}} \ \forall i, j \right\}.$$

---

[4]See, for example, McFadden (1976).

THEOREM 2. *Let σ be the logistic quantal response function. Let $\{\lambda_1, \lambda_2, ...\}$ be a sequence such that $\lim_{t\to\infty} \lambda_t = \infty$. Let $\{p_1, p_2, ...\}$ be a corresponding sequence with $p_t \in \pi^*(\lambda_t)$ for all t, such that $\lim_{t\to\infty} p_t = p^*$. Then p^* is a Nash equilibrium.*

Proof. Assume p^* is not a Nash equilibrium. Then there is some player i and some pair of strategies, s_{ij} and s_{ik}, with $p^*(s_{ik}) > 0$, and $u_i(s_{ij}, p^*_{-i}) > u_i(s_{ik}, p^*_{-i})$. Equivalently, $\bar{u}_{ij}(p^*) > \bar{u}_{ik}(p^*)$. Since $\bar{u}$ is a continuous function, it follows that for sufficiently small ε there is a T such that for $t \geq T$, $\bar{u}_{ij}(p^t) > \bar{u}_{ik}(p^t) + \varepsilon$. But as $t \to \infty$, $\sigma_k(\bar{u}_i(p^t))/\sigma_j(\bar{u}(p^t)) \to 0$. Therefore $p^t(s_{ik}) \to 0$. But this contradicts $p^*(s_{ik}) > 0$.

Q.E.D.

The following theorem establishes several properties of the equilibrium correspondence. The proof is in the Appendix.

THEOREM 3. *For almost all games $\Gamma = (N, S, u)$.*
1. *$\pi^*(\lambda)$ is odd for almost all λ.*
2. *π^* is upper hemicontinuous.*[5]
3. *The graph of π^* contains a unique branch which starts at the centroid, for $\lambda = 0$, and converges to a unique Nash equilibrium, as λ goes to infinity.*

The third property is particularly interesting and is similar to properties of the "tracing procedure" of Harsanyi and Selten[6] (1988). The third property implies that we can define a unique selection from the set of Nash equilibria by "tracing" the graph of the logit equilibrium correspondence beginning at the centroid of the strategy simplex (the unique solution when $\lambda = 0$) and continuing for larger and larger values of λ. We have already seen that all limit points of QREs as $\lambda \to \infty$ are Nash equilibria. Results in differential topology are used in the Appendix to show that for almost all games there is a unique selection as $\lambda \to \infty$. We call this Nash equilibrium the *Limiting Logit Equilibrium* of the game.

4. Relation to Other Equilibrium Notions

One may be tempted to conjecture Theorem 2 can be extended to prove that limit points of Logit Equilibria as λ grows will not only be Nash equilibria, but

---

[5] This is always true, not just generically.

[6] These properties of the tracing procedure are proven rigorously in the work of Schanuel *et al.* (1991).

will also be trembling-hand perfect. But that is not true. Consider the game in Table I.

TABLE I.
A Game with a Unique Perfect Equilibrium and Different Unique Limiting Logit Equilibrium $A > 0$, $B > 0$

	L	M	R
U	1,1	0,0	1,1
M	0,0	0,0	0,B
D	1,1	A,0	1,1

This game has a unique perfect equilibrium (D, R), and the Nash equilibria consist of all mixtures between U and D for Player 1 and L and R for Player 2. The limit of Logit Equilibria selects $p = (.5, 0, .5)$, $q = (.5, 0, .5)$ as the unique limit point. Along the limit, for finite λ, $p_D \gg p_M$ and $q_R > q_L \gg q_M$ but as λ becomes large p_2 and q_2 converge to 0. So M is eliminated in the limit.[7]

Note that the Limiting Logit Equilibrium does not depend on the magnitudes of A and B. However, the Logit Equilibria for intermediate values of λ are quite sensitive to A and B. Figures 1 and 2 illustrate the Logit Equilibrium graph as a function of λ for the cases of $A = B = 5$ and $A = B = 100$.

One might consider the fact that the limiting QREs are not always perfect equilibria to be a drawback of the QRE definition. Alternatively, it could be viewed as "independence of irrelevant alternative" property of the limiting QRE. For large values of λ, strategies that have sufficiently small probability in the QRE do not affect the play of the rest of the game.

A rational-choice justification of the logistic quantal response function, based on McFadden's (1973) random utility maximization model, leads to a connection with the literature on "purification" of Nash equilibria.[8] For any $x \in \mathbb{R}^m$, let the vector of expected utility payoffs to player i be $x + \varepsilon$, where $\varepsilon_i = (\varepsilon_{i1}, ..., \varepsilon_{im})$ is a vector of draws from a distribution with commonly known density f. If ε_i is known to i but to no one else and i is maximizing expected payoffs given his/her information, then the ordering assumptions imply that i's statistical best response function to any x will be given by σ. The connection to the purification literature is through the Bayesian equilibrium of the game $\langle N, S, u \rangle$ where ε_i is viewed as a random disturbance to i's payoff vector (Harsanyi, 1973). Suppose that for each

---

[7] In the game without strategy M it is obvious that the unique limit point of Logit Equilibria is $(0.5, 0.5)$.

[8] See Harsanyi, 1973 in particular. This has its roots in the work of Dvoretsky et al. (1951). See also Radner and Rosenthal (1981).

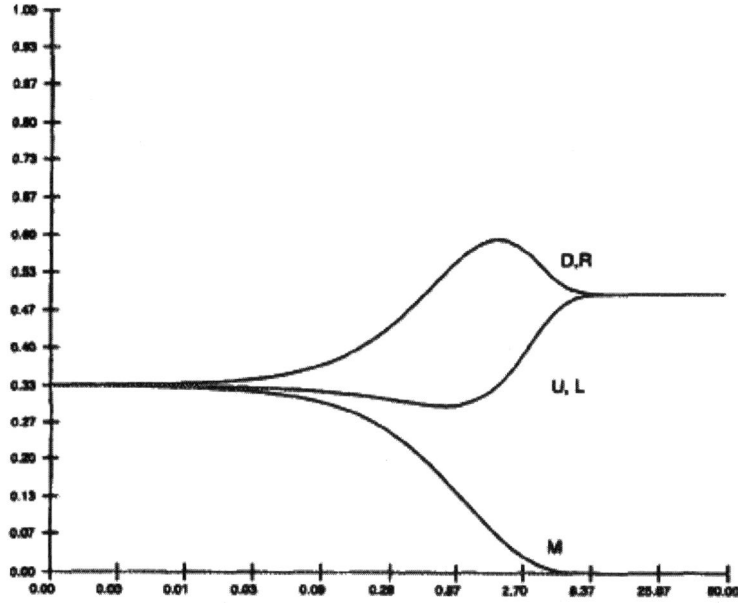

FIGURE 1. QRE for game of Table I, with $A = B = 5$

$s \in S$ each player i has a disturbance of ε_{ij} added to $u_i(s_{ij}, s_{-i})$ and that each ε_{ij} is independently and identically distributed according to f. Alternatively viewed, each player has a randomly determined "predisposition" for each of his/her different available strategies which takes the form of an extra term added to every payoff associated with that strategy. This is illustrated in Table II for a 3 × 3 game.

TABLE II.
Illustration of a Modified Harsanyi Distributed Game for a 3 × 3 Game

	s_{21}	s_{22}	s_{23}
s_{11}	$u^2_{11} + \varepsilon_{21}$ $u^1_{11} + \varepsilon_{11}$	$u^2_{12} + \varepsilon_{22}$ $u^1_{12} + \varepsilon_{11}$	$u^2_{13} + \varepsilon_{23}$ $u^1_{13} + \varepsilon_{11}$
s_{12}	$u^2_{21} + \varepsilon_{21}$ $u^1_{21} + \varepsilon_{12}$	$u^2_{22} + \varepsilon_{22}$ $u^1_{22} + \varepsilon_{12}$	$u^2_{23} + \varepsilon_{23}$ $u^1_{23} + \varepsilon_{12}$
s_{13}	$u^2_{31} + \varepsilon_{21}$ $u^1_{31} + \varepsilon_{13}$	$u^2_{32} + \varepsilon_{22}$ $u^1_{32} + \varepsilon_{13}$	$u^2_{33} + \varepsilon_{23}$ $u^1_{33} + \varepsilon_{13}$

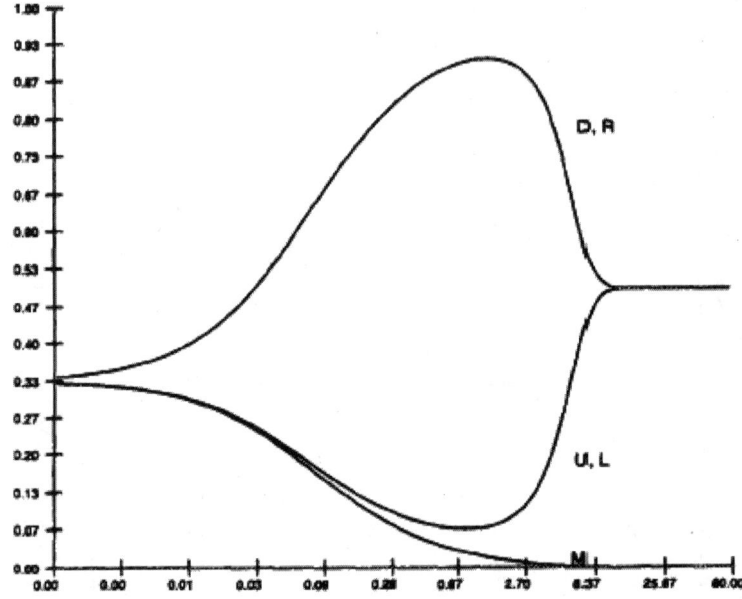

FIGURE 2. QRE for game of Table I, with $A = B = 100$

This differs only slightly from the Harsanyi (1973) setup which assumes a separate disturbance $\varepsilon_i(s)$ for i's payoff to each strategy profile, s, while we assume that this disturbance for i is the same for payoffs of all strategy profiles in which i uses the same strategy. That is, we assume $\varepsilon_i(s_i, s_{-i}) = \varepsilon_i(s_i, s'_{-i})$ for all i and for all $s_{-i}, s'_{-i} \in S_{-i}$. This violates Harsanyi's condition (1973, p. 5) that requires the existence of a density function for $\varepsilon(s)$. In spite of this, it is easy to see that the main results in Harsanyi (1973) are still true under the weaker assumption that for each i a density function exists for $\varepsilon_i = (\varepsilon_{i1}, ..., \varepsilon_{iJ_i})$. See Radner and Rosenthal (1982). This weaker assumption is met in our model.

Therefore, our model inherits the properties of Bayesian equilibrium in Harsanyi's disturbed game approach:

(1) Best replies are "essentially unique" pure strategies.
(2) Every equilibrium is "essentially strong" and in essentially pure strategies.
(3) There exists an equilibrium.

The idea of smoothing out the best response correspondence by assuming that players might adopt inferior strategies with declining, but positive, probability is the main feature of the bounded-rationality equilibrium model studied in Rosenthal (1989). Rosenthal considers a linear version of the quantal response equilibrium model and analyzes the equilibrium correspondence as a function of the slope of the (linear) response function. His analysis produces equilibrium graphs of the sort we use in later sections to estimate the response parameter of our logit specification of the response function. He points out that there is also a connection between the statistical response function approach and the "control cost" model explored by Van Damme (1987, Chap. 4). The control cost model assumes that it is costly to implement strategies that deviate from a uniform distribution over available actions. Thus, in the control cost approach good strategies will be played more often than bad strategies, but bad strategies may still be used with positive probability.

The quantal response equilibrium is also related to Beja's (1992) imperfect equilibrium. The approach taken there is that each player has a "target" (mixed) strategy that he/she attempts to play but fails to implement that strategy perfectly. The target strategy maximizes expected payoff, given the probability distribution of strategies induced by the imperfect implementation of target strategies by the other players. This idea of "equilibrium" imperfect implementation of target strategies also appears in Chen (1994), El-Gamal *et al.* (1993), El-Gamal and Palfrey (1994, 1995), Ma and Manove (1993), McKelvey and Palfrey (1992), and Schmidt (1992).[9]

The QRE concept does not use the notion of target strategies but, like Beja (1992), does assume that the probability of implementing a particular strategy is increasing in the expected payoff of the strategy. Furthermore, these expected payoffs are calculated from the equilibrium distribution of joint strategies.

5. Data

In this section we explore how well the logistic version of QRE explains some features of data from past experiments on normal form games that are anomalous

---

[9]There are a number of other papers that use explicit models of the error structure that can be interpreted as imperfect implementation. Logit and probit specifications of the errors are common (Palfrey and Rosenthal, 1991; Palfrey and Prisbrey, 1992; Harless and Camerer, 1992; Stahl and Wilson, 1993; and Anderson, 1993). However, most of these are nonequilibrium models in the sense that a player's choice strategy does not take account of other players' errors (or their own) and therefore is not an optimal response to the probability distribution of other players' actions. An exception is Zauner (1993) who uses a Harsanyi (1973) equilibrium model with independent normal errors to explain data from the centipede game (McKelvey and Palfrey, 1992).

with respect to standard game theory. We focus on experiments involving two-person games with unique Nash equilibria where there are not outcomes Pareto preferred to the Nash equilibrium. This avoids games where there are supergame equilibria which achieve more than the Nash equilibrium for both players (for example, the prisoner's dilemma game).

The experiments that we analyze were run across a span of more than 30 years. In order to have some comparability across experiments, we express payoffs in terms of the expected monetary payoff in real (1982) dollars.

For each experiment, we calculate a maximum likelihood estimate of λ in the logistic version of the QRE and see how well the model fits the data.

Lieberman (1960)

Lieberman (1960) conducted experiments on the following two person zero sum game:

	B_1	B_2	B_3
A_1	15	0	-2
A_2	0	-15	-1
A_3	1	2	0

The payoffs represent payments, in 1960 pennies, from Player 2 to Player 1. For our estimates, the payoff matrix of the above game is multiplied by 3.373 to express the 1960 payoffs in 1982 pennies.

This game can be solved by iterated elimination of strictly dominated strategies. It has a unique Nash equilibrium at (A_3, B_3). In this experiment, Lieberman reports the choice frequencies as a function of time. Each subject participated in 200 plays of the game, with a single opponent.

TABLE III.
Data and Estimates for Lieberman (1960) Experiments: $N = 300$
for Each Experience Level

Periods	Actual Data				Predicted $\hat{A}_1$ $\hat{B}_2$	$\hat{A}_3$ $\hat{B}_3$	λ	$-\mathcal{L}^*$
	A_1	A_3	B_2	B_3				
1–10	0.260	0.720	0.300	0.667	0.277	0.696	0.176	212.0
11–20	0.167	0.806	0.227	0.760	0.196	0.781	0.252	177.0
21–30	0.113	0.880	0.160	0.833	0.138	0.838	0.329	134.3
31–40	0.093	0.887	0.120	0.853	0.106	0.869	0.390	134.4
41–50	0.060	0.907	0.073	0.907	0.066	0.906	0.500	109.5
51–60	0.060	0.873	0.120	0.860	0.087	0.886	0.435	144.7
61–70	0.060	0.853	0.113	0.867	0.083	0.890	0.448	152.7
71–80	0.060	0.907	0.047	0.933	0.054	0.916	0.547	98.9
81–90	0.047	0.893	0.067	0.920	0.056	0.915	0.542	112.3
91–100	0.027	0.920	0.080	0.907	0.053	0.918	0.553	105.6
101–120	0.053	0.907	0.047	0.933	0.051	0.920	0.564	99.5
111–120	0.027	0.920	0.047	0.933	0.037	0.932	0.635	94.2
121–130	0.040	0.927	0.040	0.920	0.040	0.929	0.616	97.1
131–140	0.033	0.927	0.047	0.953	0.040	0.929	0.616	80.2
141–150	0.053	0.913	0.060	0.900	0.056	0.915	0.542	112.3
151–160	0.053	0.900	0.053	0.920	0.052	0.919	0.558	109.3
161–170	0.027	0.946	0.060	0.927	0.045	0.925	0.592	83.4
171–180	0.053	0.900	0.033	0.927	0.042	0.927	0.604	107.1
181–190	0.027	0.933	0.020	0.973	0.023	0.946	0.737	67.0
191–200	0.040	0.920	0.047	0.933	0.044	0.926	0.598	93.7

The data, broken down into 20 experience levels of 10 periods each, as well as the QRE estimates for each experience level and the negative log likelihood ($-\mathcal{L}^*$), are reported in Table III. The data and estimates from each period are also superimposed on the QRE graph in Fig. 3. The notable feature of the data is that during early rounds the row player overplays strategy A_1 and the column player overplays strategy B_2 relative to the Nash equilibrium prediction. Figure 3 shows the QRE for the Lieberman experiment as a function of λ. We see that the QRE has the feature that, for small values of λ, A_1 and B_2 are overplayed. The frequency of these strategies decreases as λ gets larger and Nash equilibrium is approached. If one hypothesizes that the amount of error individuals make decreases as they gain more experience with the game, then one would expect the time series to correspond to QRE solutions with gradually increasing λ. This is similar to what occurs in the Lieberman data and we also see that the maximum

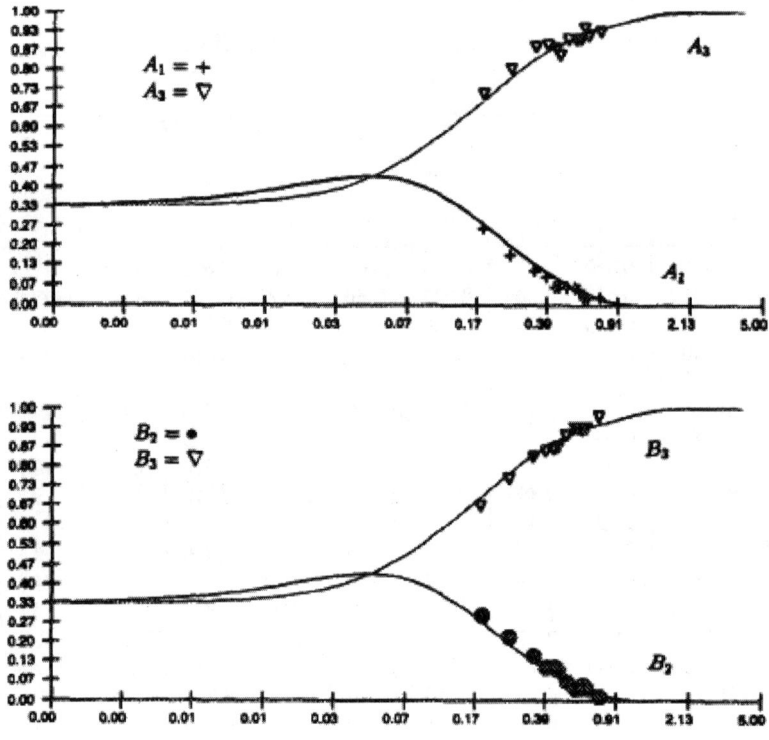

FIGURE 3. QRE as a function of λ for Lieberman experiment

likelihood estimates for λ in Table III generally increase with the period number. The Nash model is easily rejected since it predicts A_1, A_2, B_1, and B_2 will never be used. The random model (i.e., constraining $\lambda = 0$) has $-\mathcal{L}^* = 329$ and is rejected in every time period.

O'Neill (1987)

O'Neill conducted experiments on the following two person zero sum normal form game:

	B_1	B_2	B_3	B_4
A_1	5	−5	−5	−5
A_2	−5	−5	5	5
A_3	−5	5	−5	5
A_4	−5	5	5	−5

The entries represent the payoff, in pennies, from Player 2 to Player 1. Each subject participated in 105 plays of the game. Details of the procedures can be found in O'Neill (1987). In our estimates, the payoffs are multiplied by 0.913 to express them in 1982 pennies.

The game has a unique Nash equilibrium at (.4, .2, .2, .2) for both players and has the feature that the equilibrium is invariant to the choice of utility function, since the payoffs of the game take on only two values. Table IV gives the aggregate data for the O'Neill experiments.

TABLE IV. Data and Estimates for O'Neill

	Number	Frequency	Rand	NE	QRE
A_1	949	0.362	0.250	0.440	0.360
A_2	579	0.221	0.250	0.200	0.213
A_3	565	0.215	0.250	0.200	0.213
A_4	532	0.203	0.250	0.200	0.213
B_1	1119	0.426	0.250	0.400	0.426
B_2	592	0.226	0.250	0.200	0.191
B_3	470	0.179	0.250	0.200	0.191
B_4	444	0.169	0.250	0.200	0.191
λ			0	∞	1.313
$-\mathfrak{L}^*$			7278	7016	7004

O'Neill interpreted the data as providing support for the minimax hypothesis[10] and did not view as important the finding that Player 1 underplayed strategy (A_1) while Player 2 overplayed strategy (B_1). He claims that "Players' average selecting frequencies for the moves . . . were almost exactly as predicted." However, in the quantal response equilibrium we predict systematic differences ($A_1 < B_1$). The other discrepancy from the theoretical prediction involves the overplay of strategy B_2 relative to B_3 and B_4. O'Neill attributes this to a flaw

---

[10]Brown and Rosenthal (1990) reexamined these data and found a number of discrepancies with the theory.

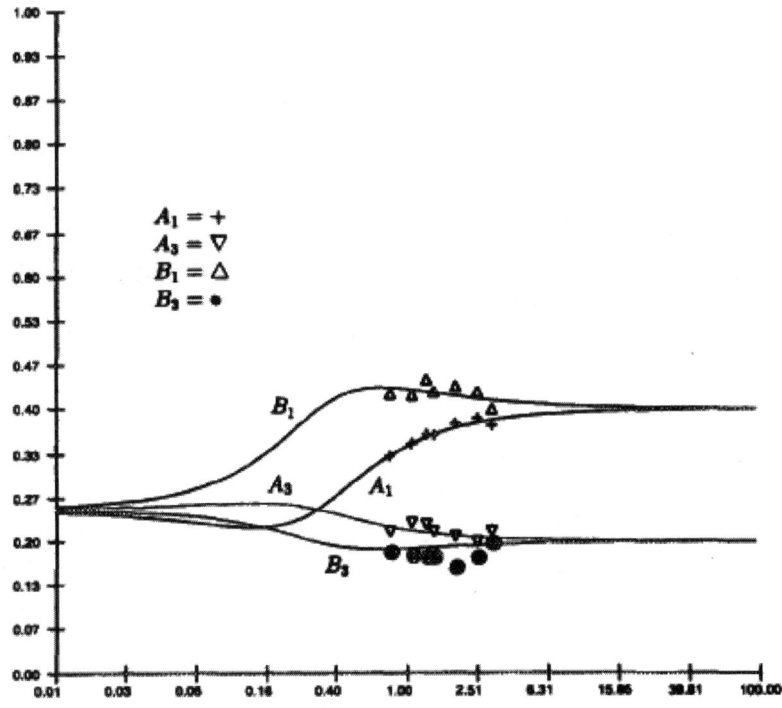

FIGURE 4. QRE as a function of λ for O'Neill experiment

in the experimental design,[11] which seems quite plausible. Given the symmetry of payoffs with respect to the last three strategies, it is hard to imagine any other explanation. Figure 4 displays a plot of the QRE predictions of the strategy frequencies of A_1, A_3, B_1, and B_3 for various values of λ. As can be seen from this figure, the QRE predicts $\{A_1$ underplayed, B_1 overplayed) for intermediate values of λ and always predicts $A_1 < B_1$. Table IV gives the maximum likelihood estimates ($\mathcal{L}^*$) of λ for the QRE. One can easily reject both the random (Rand) and Nash (NE) predictions in favor of the QRE at the 0.01 level using a likelihood ratio test.

In addition to estimating the logit QRE model using the aggregate data, we also have broken the observations down into seven different experience levels.

---

[11] Subjects chose strategies by selecting cards. Strategy 1 was a joker, and the others were Ace, Deuce, and Trey, respectively. A conjecture is that Strategy 2 was overplayed because of an Ace effect.

Each subject played 105 games, so each experience level corresponds to a 15-game sequence (games 1–15, 16–30, ...). The results are displayed in Table V, and the estimated move frequencies are superimposed on the QRE graph in Fig. 4. There is no discernible trend in the estimated values of λ, in contrast to what we found in the Lieberman experiment.

Rapoport and Boebel (1992)

Rapoport and Boebel conducted experiments on a variation of O'Neill's game. The game was also two person, zero sum, and had the following payoff matrix:

	B_1	B_2	B_3	B_4	B_5
A_1	W	L	L	L	L
A_2	L	L	W	W	W
A_3	L	W	L	L	W
A_4	L	W	L	W	L
A_5	L	W	W	L	L

Rapoport and Boebel (RB) ran two versions of the game: in one W was worth (to the row player) \$10 and L was worth $-\$6$, while in the other W was worth \$15 and L was worth $-\$1$. These versions are both equivalent from the point of view of the quantal response model. The subjects were paid for a randomly chosen 3 out of 120 rounds, leading to expected payoffs (to row) of 25 cents for a win versus -15 cents for a loss in Game 1, and 37.5 cents for a win versus -2.5 cents for a loss in Game 2. In our estimates, we multiply these payoffs by 0.713 to express them in 1982 pennies.

This payoff matrix has a unique Nash equilibrium at (.375, .250, .125, .125, .125) for each player. The aggregate data for the RB experiments are given in Tables VI and VII. They found that Player 1 underplayed the strategy A_1 and overplayed A_2, while Player 2 underplayed B_2 and overplayed B_3. Figure 5 gives the QRE as a function of λ for the RB experiments, and the maximum likelihood estimates are given in Tables VI and VII. The QRE does a fair job of predicting the behavior of Player 1, even picking up the reversal in frequency between the first two strategies for Experiment 1. It does not do as well with Player 2. The QRE does not explain Player 2's overplay of strategy B_3, although it does predict the underplay of strategy B_2. The random and Nash models are easily rejected in favor of the QRE.

TABLE V
DATA AND ESTIMATES FOR O'NEILL EXPERIMENTS, BROKEN DOWN BY PERIOD

Periods		A_1	A_2	A_3	A_4	B_1	B_2	B_3	B_4	λ	$-\mathcal{L}^*$ QRE	Nash	Rand
1–15	Actual	0.363	0.208	0.227	0.203	0.445	0.211	0.179	0.165	1.262	995	997	1040
	Predicted	0.358	0.214	0.214	0.214	0.427	0.191	0.191	0.191				
16–30	Actual	0.349	0.187	0.229	0.234	0.421	0.221	0.181	0.176	1.120	1004	1007	1040
	Predicted	0.352	0.216	0.216	0.216	0.429	0.190	0.190	0.190				
31–45	Actual	0.376	0.205	0.216	0.203	0.400	0.213	0.200	0.187	3.313	1005	1005	1040
	Predicted	0.385	0.205	0.205	0.205	0.413	0.196	0.196	0.196				
46–60	Actual	0.331	0.237	0.216	0.216	0.424	0.216	0.187	0.173	0.798	1006	1011	1040
	Predicted	0.332	0.223	0.223	0.223	0.433	0.189	0.189	0.189				
61–75	Actual	0.347	0.227	0.211	0.216	0.432	0.227	0.165	0.176	1.034	1002	1005	1040
	Predicted	0.348	0.217	0.217	0.217	0.430	0.190	0.190	0.190				
76–90	Actual	0.379	0.248	0.208	0.165	0.435	0.219	0.163	0.184	1.823	994	996	1040
	Predicted	0.372	0.209	0.209	0.209	0.420	0.193	0.193	0.193				
91–105	Actual	0.387	0.232	0.200	0.181	0.427	0.272	0.179	0.123	2.482	995	996	1040
	Predicted	0.380	0.207	0.207	0.207	0.416	0.195	0.195	0.195				

Note. The first 15 periods were practice rounds.

TABLE VI.

Data and Estimates for Rapoport-Boebel, Experiment 1

	n_{ij}	f_{ij}	Rand	NE	QRE
A_1	702	0.293	0.200	0.375	0.286
A_2	732	0.305	0.200	0.250	0.302
A_3	295	0.123	0.200	0.125	0.138
A_4	287	0.120	0.200	0.125	0.138
A_5	384	0.160	0.200	0.125	0.138
B_1	845	0.352	0.200	0.375	0.412
B_2	432	0.180	0.200	0.250	0.169
B_3	523	0.218	0.200	0.125	0.140
B_4	238	0.099	0.200	0.125	0.140
B_5	362	0.151	0.200	0.125	0.140
λ			0	∞	0.2478
$-\mathfrak{L}^*$			7725	7475	7401

TABLE VII.

Data and Estimates for Rapoport-Boebel, Experiment 2

	n_{ij}	f_{ij}	Rand	NE	QRE
A_1	736	0.307	0.200	0.375	0.309
A_2	778	0.324	0.200	0.250	0.296
A_3	239	0.100	0.200	0.125	0.132
A_4	275	0.115	0.200	0.125	0.132
A_5	372	0.155	0.200	0.125	0.132
B_1	831	0.346	0.200	0.375	0.410
B_2	463	0.193	0.200	0.250	0.184
B_3	485	0.202	0.200	0.125	0.135
B_4	279	0.166	0.200	0.125	0.135
B_5	32	0.142	0.200	0.125	0.135
λ			0	∞	0.3274
$-\mathfrak{L}^*$			7725	7400	7345

RB compare the performance of alternative models to Nash equilibrium including the totally random (equiprobable) choice model (corresponding to $\lambda = 0$, in our setup) and a win-weighted model, which says that players are more likely to choose strategies with more possible wins than those with less possible wins. This corresponds roughly to a nonequilibrium quantal response model where players believe opponents are choosing randomly. They find that the Nash model outperforms both of these alternative models. In contrast, we find that an *equilibrium* quantal response model significantly outperforms the Nash model in both of their experiments.

Table VIII breaks down the Rapoport-Boebel data to identify experience effects. Each subject participated sequentially in two sessions of one of the games, and each session consisted of 120 plays of the game. Each subject switched roles (row to column or column to row) between sessions. We break each session down into two experience levels, so that we have a total of four experience levels for each of the two games. The data and estimates are displayed on the QRE graph in Fig. 5.

In Game 2 the trend from low λ to higher λ is strong and systematic, indicating monotonic convergence to the Nash equilibrium. By the second half of the second session, the data have converged to Nash play to the point where the QRE model is not (statistically) better than the Nash model. We do not find such a trend in the first game. Specifically, the estimated value of λ is quite low throughout the game. This difference between play in the two games suggests that the statistical evidence for strategic equivalence is somewhat weaker than Rapoport and Boebel's reported finding of "no evidence to reject the hypothesis of strategic equivalence" (1992, p. 279).

Ochs (1995)

Ochs recently conducted experiments on the following three two-person non-zero-sum games:

	B_1	B_2			B_1	B_2			B_1	B_2
A_1	1,0	0,1		A_1	9,0	0,1		A_1	4,0	0,1
A_2	0,1	1,0		A_2	0,1	1,0		A_2	0,1	1,0
	Game 1				Game 2				Game 3	

These experiments are designed so that the only difference between the three tables is the payoff to Player 1 in the upper left cell. In all three tables, there is a unique Nash equilibrium. Since the Nash equilibrium for Player 1 depends only on the payoffs to Player 2, this means that the Nash equilibrium probability that Player 1 chooses A_1 or A_2 is the same (.5, .5) in all three games and that the only differences are in the predicted behavior of Player 2. The Nash equilibrium specifies that Player 1 chooses A_1 with probability .5 in all three games and Player

TABLE VIII
DATA AND ESTIMATES FOR RAPOPORT-BOEBEL EXPERIMENTS, BROKEN DOWN BY PERIOD AND SESSIONS

Game	Sess.	Periods		A_1	A_2	A_3	A_4	B_1	B_2	B_3	B_4	λ	$-\mathcal{L}^*$ QRE	$-\mathcal{L}^*$ Nash	$-\mathcal{L}^*$ Rand
1	1	1–60	Actual	0.308	0.307	0.113	0.120	0.350	0.218	0.202	0.092	0.439	1836	1843	1931
			Predicted	0.327	0.289	0.128	0.128	0.406	0.199	0.132	0.132				
1	1	61–120	Actual	0.293	0.272	0.162	0.100	0.333	0.177	0.190	0.140	0.211	1878	1896	1931
			Predicted	0.271	0.303	0.142	0.142	0.410	0.160	0.143	0.143				
1	2	1–60	Actual	0.273	0.350	0.103	0.123	0.353	0.133	0.258	0.102	0.184	1840	1881	1931
			Predicted	0.256	0.304	0.147	0.147	0.407	0.154	0.146	0.146				
1	2	61–120	Actual	0.295	0.292	0.113	0.135	0.372	0.192	0.222	0.063	0.293	1841	1855	1931
			Predicted	0.300	0.296	0.134	0.134	0.412	0.178	0.137	0.137				
2	1	1–60	Actual	0.258	0.367	0.105	0.143	0.332	0.115	0.245	0.140	0.149	1850	1906	1931
			Predicted	0.233	0.302	0.155	0.155	0.396	0.148	0.152	0.152				
2	1	61–120	Actual	0.290	0.347	0.118	0.110	0.355	0.198	0.208	0.108	0.308	1827	1844	1931
			Predicted	0.304	0.297	0.133	0.133	0.411	0.181	0.136	0.136				
2	2	1–60	Actual	0.355	0.313	0.082	0.100	0.355	0.215	0.187	0.110	0.644	1803	1808	1931
			Predicted	0.344	0.279	0.126	0.126	0.398	0.215	0.129	0.129				
2	2	61–120	Actual	0.323	0.270	0.093	0.105	0.343	0.243	0.168	0.107	1.124	1842	1843	1931
			Predicted	0.358	0.268	0.125	0.125	0.390	0.230	0.127	0.127				

Note. Data for A_5 and B_5 can be inferred from the remaining data and are omitted. The first 10 periods of each session were practice rounds and are excluded from the analysis.

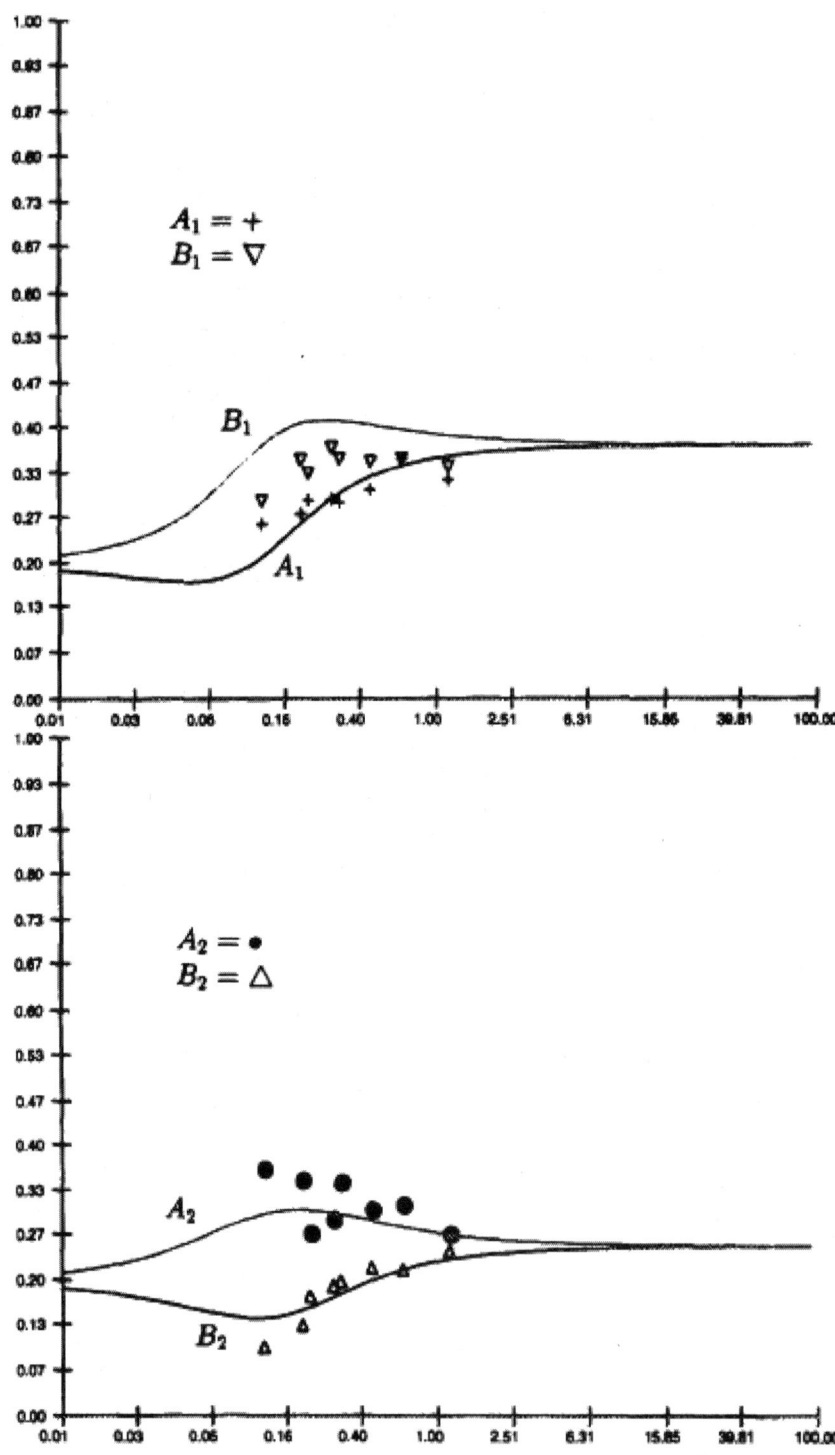

FIGURE 5. QRE as a function of λ for the Rapoport-Boebel experiment.

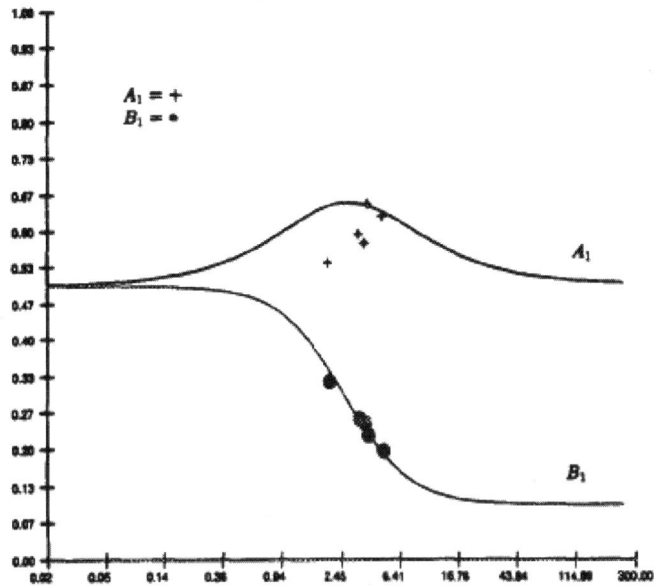

FIGURE 6. QRE as a function of λ for Game 2 of the Ochs experiment

2 chooses strategy B_1 with probability 0.5 in Game 1, 0.1 in Game 2, and 0.2 in Game 3.

In converting the above payoffs to 1982 pennies, we encounter a difficulty that did not arise in the previous, constant sum experiments. The subjects in the Ochs experiments were paid using a lottery procedure, and the probability of winning the large payoff in the lottery was determined by the total percentage of the maximum possible points that the player accumulated over the course of the experiment. Since the maximum possible number of points for each subject was different, this means that the exchange of points to expected payoff was different for each player. Most traditional theories of behavior in games are not affected by a positive scalar multiple of a player's payoffs. The quantal response equilibrium does change if one or both players' payoffs are multiplied by a positive scalar. We express each player's payoffs in terms of expected 1982 money payoff to that player. Since there was a $10 difference between the high and low payoffs in the lottery for each player, and there were a total of 640 games for each player, this means that the maximum payoff for a player is 1.5625 cents. Multiplying by 0.713

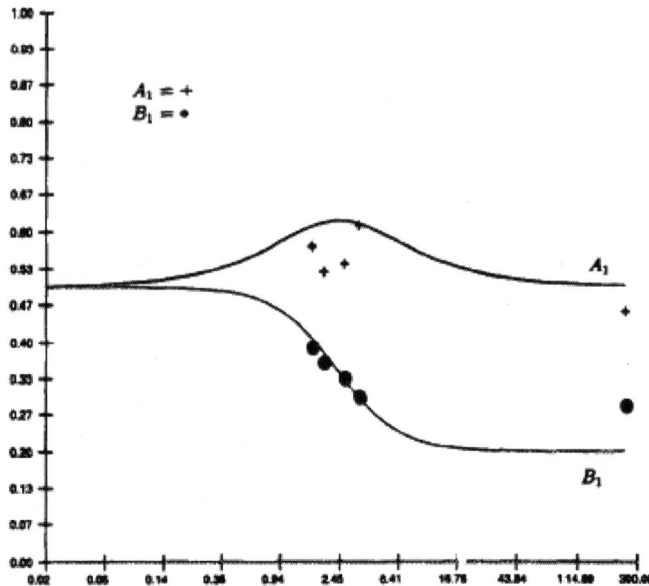

FIGURE 7. QRE as a function of λ for Game 3 of the Ochs experiment

to express the payoffs in 1982 pennies, this yields the following two games, which represent the Ochs games 2 and 3, in (expected) 1982 pennies for each player.

	B_1	B_2
A_1	1.1141, 0.0000	0.0000, 1.1141
A_2	0.0000, 1.1141	0.1238, 0.0000

Game 2

	B_1	B_2
A_1	1.1141, 0.0000	0.0000, 1.1141
A_2	0.0000, 1.1141	0.2785, 0.0000

Game 3

The aggregate data from Game 1 are close to the Nash equilibrium predictions and the Logit model makes the same prediction for all values of λ. We do not analyze that data. Data from the other games are informative. Figures 6 and 7 show the QRE as a function of λ for these two games. As QRE predicts, both A_1 and B_1 are overplayed in early rounds and this overplaying declines over time, suggesting learning is taking place. This is reflected in the overall (increasing) trend in the estimated λ for each game. The Nash model is soundly rejected in both games, using the aggregate data, consistent with Ochs' own conclusions.

Tables IX and X present the data and estimates for Games 2 and 3, respectively, broken down into four experience levels (each level corresponding to 16 plays of the game). These data and estimates are also superimposed onto Figs. 6

and 7. In both games, the QRE fitted significantly better[12] than the Nash model in early rounds and significantly better than the random model in later rounds. In Game 2, QRE fits better than both the random and Nash models in both early and later rounds. In the early rounds of Game 3, we cannot reject the random model. By the later rounds of Game 3, we cannot reject the Nash model.

6. Conclusion

This paper proposed a general statistical theory of equilibrium in normal form games based on the notion that better strategies are played more often than worse strategies, but best strategies are not always played. The quantal response equilibrium imposes a consistency requirement that the expected payoff to a strategy in equilibrium be calculated based on the equilibrium quantal response probabilities. A parametric version of this equilibrium, based on logit response functions, was analyzed and used to fit experimental data from a variety of two-person normal form games.

TABLE IX. Data and Estimates for Ochs, Game 2

Period	n	Actual		Predicted		λ	$-\mathfrak{L}^*$		
		A_1	B_1	$\hat{A}_1$	$\hat{B}_1$		QRE	Nash	Rand
1–16	128	0.541	0.326	0.645	0.347	1.951	1721	1938	1774
17–32	128	0.649	0.228	0.645	0.228	3.763	1517	1664	1774
33–48	128	0.578	0.250	0.648	0.241	3.475	1605	1725	1774
48–52	64	0.626	0.200	0.636	0.197	4.638	743	792	887
All	448	0.595	0.258	0.649	0.254	3.241	5612	6119	6210

This model predicts systematic deviations from Nash equilibrium, in spite of the fact that the error structure of the model is unbiased, in the sense that the assumed errors are not the result of a *systematic* deviation from induced preference by the players.[13] Accordingly, this model is able to account for many of the systematic deviations from Nash equilibrium in the experiments which we reanalyze. The qualitative predictions of the direction of these systematic deviations from

---

[12] Significance is at the 1% level based on a χ^2 test with one degree of freedom.

[13] This is in contrast to the model we used elsewhere (McKelvey and Palfrey, 1992 (Chapter 18 of this book)) to explain departures from equilibrium in the Centipede Game by introducing altruistic preferences.

Nash equilibrium are borne out in most of the data. In addition, the estimated error rates (i.e., inverse of the parameter λ in the logistic quantal response functions) are generally declining with subject experience, consistent with an interpretation that learning is taking place.

TABLE X. Data and Estimates for Ochs, Game 3

Period	n	Actual		Predicted		λ	$-\mathcal{L}^*$		
		A_1	B_1	$\hat{A}_1$	$\hat{B}_1$		QRE	Nash	Rand
1–16	128	0.527	0.366	0.615	0.383	1.856	1747	1822	1774
17–32	128	0.573	0.393	0.610	0.405	1.568	1735	1870	1774
33–48	128	0.610	0.302	0.614	0.301	3.306	1640	1708	1774
48–52	128	0.455	0.285	0.500	0.200	∞	1679	1679	1774
All	512	0.542	0.336	0.619	0.331	2.656	6864	7079	7098

While the QRE model picks up some of the gross departures of the aggregate behavior from the Nash equilibrium predictions, there are also aspects of the model that remain unexplained. For example, we have expressed payoffs in a common currency (1982 pennies) in an attempt to see if there is any consistency across experiments in the estimated values of λ. Despite this normalization, we find some differences across experiments in the range of λ that is estimated. Also, while we see a tendency for λ to increase with experience, this does not occur in all cases, and in many cases, despite the length of the experiments, λ remains significantly different from the Nash equilibrium even in the later periods of the experiment.

These discrepancies suggest several research directions in which to proceed from here. In light of the above observations, one direction is to attempt to endogenize the learning. The experimental evidence suggests λ may grow over time. It may be possible to infer this from optimizing (but still error prone) behavior by individuals. Also, if one tried to incorporate into the equilibrium the decision to choose λ as part of a labor–leisure tradeoff (Smith and Walker, 1993) that might explain why λ does not approach infinity and might generate testable predictions about how the "equilibrium" values of λ would be related to the magnitude of the payoffs.

A second direction is to incorporate heterogeneity across players. There is some convincing evidence emerging that models which impose homogeneity of subject behavior are inadequate.[14] Conceptually, it is not a difficult extension of the QRE to allow for different error rates across individuals (in fact the formal definition permits this), but this complicates the estimation.

A third direction is to extend this approach to extensive form games. In McKelvey and Palfrey (1994) we extend the basic model presented here to games in extensive form and apply the analysis to several experimental multistage games, including signalling games. A specific application of the extensive form quantal response model can also be found in Fey et al(1996).

Appendix

This appendix proves the properties of the quantal response correspondence stated in Theorem 3.

Let $N = \{1, ..., n\}$, and for each $i \in N$ define $m_i = J_i - 1$ and $M_i = \{1, ..., m_i\}$. Write $N_{-i} = N - \{i\}$ and $m = \sum_{i \in N} m_i$. Let $S = \prod_{i \in N} S_i$ and $u_i : S \to \mathbb{R}$ be the payoff function for player $i \in N$. As before, Δ_i is the set of mixed strategies on S_i. A mixed strategy is a function $p_i : S_i \to [0, 1]$, satisfying $p_i(s_{ik}) \geq 0$, for all $i \in N$ and $s_{ik} \in S_i$, and $\sum_{s_{ik} \in S_i} p_i(s_{ik}) = 1$ for all $i \in N$. Write $p_{ik} = p_i(s_{ik})$, for $s_{ik} \in S_i$, and $p_{i0} = p_{iJ_i}$. Define

$$D_i = \left\{ p_i \in \mathbb{R}^{m_i} : p_{ik} \geq 0 \text{ for all } k \in M_i, \text{ and } \sum_{k \in M_i} p_{ik} \leq 1 \right\},$$

and write D_i^0 for the interior of D_i. Using the identity $p_{iJ_i} = p_{i0} = 1 - \sum_{k \in M_i} p_{ik}$, a mixed strategy $p_i \in \Delta_i$ can be identified by the first m_i components, i.e., by a vector in D_i. Write $D = \prod_{i \in N} D_i$ and D^0 for the interior of D. A vector $p = (p_1, ..., p_n) \in D$ is referred to as a *mixed profile*.

Define $S_{-i} = \prod_{j \in N_{-i}} S_j$. For any $s_{-i} \in S_{-i}$, and $s_{ik}, s_{il} \in S_i$, define $u_{ikl}(s_{-i}) = u_i(s_{ik}, s_{-i}) - u_i(s_{il}, s_{-i})$. Write $u_{ik0}(s_{-i}) = u_{ikJ_i}(s_{-i})$. Define $X = D^0 \times (0, \infty)$, and $f : X \to \mathbb{R}^m$ with components given by, for any $i \in N$ and $k \in K_i$,

$$f_{ik}(p, \lambda) = \frac{1}{\lambda} \log \left\{ \frac{p_{ik}}{p_{i0}} \right\} + u_{ik0}(p),$$

where

$$u_{ikl}(p) = u_{ikl}(p_{-i}) = \sum_{s_{-i} \in S_{-i}} u_{ikl}(s_{-i}) p_{-i}(s_{-i}) \qquad p_{-i}(s_{-i}) = \prod_{j \in N_{-i}} p_j(s_j).$$

---

[14]See El-Gamal and Grether (1993), Holt (1993), Stahl and Wilson (1993), and McKelvey and Palfrey (1992).

Note that $\pi^*(\lambda) = \{p : f(p, \lambda) = 0\}$. The logistic QRE graph, $\mathcal{L} = \{(\pi^*(\lambda), \lambda) : 0 < \lambda < \infty\}$ is given by $\mathcal{L} = f^{-1}(\mathbf{0})$, where $\mathbf{0}$ is the m-dimensional vector of zeros. Since f is a continuous function, it follows that $f^{-1}(\mathbf{0})$ is a closed set. This establishes property 2 of Theorem 3, that $\mathcal{L}$ is upper hemicontinuous.

The domain X, of f, is a manifold of dimension $m + 1$. It follows from the pre-image theorem (see e.g. Guillemin and Pollack, 1974, p. 21) that if $\mathbf{0}$ is a regular value of $f : X \to \mathbb{R}^m$ that $f^{-1}(\mathbf{0})$ is a one-dimensional manifold. Writing $\varepsilon \in \mathbb{R}^m$, with components ε_{ik}, it follows by Sard's theorem that almost all values of ε are regular values of f (see Guillemin and Pollack, 1974, p. 39). Hence $f^{-1}(\varepsilon)$ is a one-dimensional manifold for almost all $\varepsilon \in \mathbb{R}^m$. But

$$f_{ik}(p, \lambda) = \varepsilon_{ik} \Leftrightarrow \frac{1}{\lambda} \log \left\{ \frac{p_{ik}}{p_{i0}} \right\} + [u_{ik0}(p) - \varepsilon_{ik}] = 0$$
$$\Leftrightarrow \frac{1}{\lambda} \log \left\{ \frac{p_{ik}}{p_{i0}} \right\} + \tilde{u}_{ik0}(p) = 0$$

where $\tilde{u}_{ik0}(p)$ is defined by $\tilde{u}_{ik0}(s_{-i}) - \varepsilon_{ik}$ for all $s_{-i} \in S_{-i}$. It follows that for all u, and almost all perturbations, $\tilde{u}$ of u the QRE graph, $\tilde{\mathcal{L}}$ of $\tilde{u}$ is a one-dimensional manifold. Hence, for almost all games, $\mathcal{L}$ is a one-dimensional manifold.

Note that the above argument can be extended to the case when the domain of f is bounded: For any $c = (\underline{c}, \bar{c})$ with $0 < \underline{c} < \bar{c}$, define $X_c \subseteq X$ by $X_c = D^0 \times [\underline{c}, \bar{c}]$. Then X_c is a $(m+1)$-dimensional manifold with boundary. It follows from the pre-image theorem for manifolds with boundary (see e.g. Guillemin and Pollack, 1974, p. 60) that if $\mathbf{0}$ is a regular value of both $f : X \to \mathbb{R}^m$ and $\partial f : \partial X_c \to \mathbb{R}^m$, then $\mathcal{L}_c = f^{-1}(\mathbf{0}) \cap X_c$ is a one-dimensional manifold with boundary. Now by Sard's theorem, it follows that for almost all values of ε that ε is a regular value of both f and ∂f (see Guillemin and Pollack, p. 62). Hence $f^{-1}(\varepsilon)$ is a one-dimensional manifold with boundary for almost all $\varepsilon \in \mathbb{R}^m$. But then by the same argument as above, it follows that for almost all games $\mathcal{L}_c$ is a one-dimensional manifold with boundary.

Now pick $M > 0$ so that for all $p \in \Delta$, $\sup_{ikl} |u_{ikl}(p)| \leq M$. Define $a_\lambda = e^{-\lambda M}$ and $b_\lambda = e^{\lambda M}$. Then it follows that for any $(p, \lambda) \in \mathcal{L}$, that

$$-\lambda \cdot M \leq \log \left(\frac{p_{ik}}{p_{i0}} \right) \leq \lambda \cdot M \Rightarrow a_\lambda p_{i0} \leq p_{ik} \leq b_\lambda p_{i0}.$$

But
$$p_{ik} \leq b\lambda p_{i0} \Rightarrow 1 - p_{i0} = \sum_{k \in M_i} p_{ik} \leq b\lambda m_i p_{i0}$$
$$\Rightarrow p_{i0} \geq 1/(b_\lambda m_i + 1)$$

and
$$p_{ik} \geq a_\lambda p_{i0} \Rightarrow p_{ik} \geq a_\lambda/(b_\lambda m_i + 1) = c_\lambda.$$

Since $a_\lambda < 1$, it follows that for all $0 < k < m_i$ (i.e., including $k = 0$) the above inequality holds. Define
$$W = \{(p, \lambda) \in X : p_{ik} \geq c_\lambda \text{ for all } i \in N, \ 0 \leq k \leq m_i\}.$$

Thus, we have shown that $\mathcal{L} \subseteq W \cap X$. Similarly, $\mathcal{L}_c \subseteq W \cap X_c$. In other words, the QRE graph can only "exit" X at the minimum and maximum values of λ.

We wish to show that in generic games, the QRE graph can be used to make a unique selection of a Nash equilibrium. To do this, we must establish two facts. First, we establish that for sufficiently small λ, there is a unique solution. Then we show that this branch of the correspondence converges to a unique Nash equilibrium as λ goes to ∞.

LEMMA 1. *For suficiently small λ, $\pi^*(\lambda)$ is a singleton.*

Proof. To see this, define the mapping $\phi : \mathbb{R}^m \to \mathbb{R}^m$ to have components

$$(*) \quad \phi_{ik}(p) = \exp[-\lambda u_i(k, p_{-i})] / \left\{ \sum_{l \in S_i} \exp[-\lambda u_i(l, p_{-i})] \right\}$$

Then, for any λ, $(p, \lambda) \in \mathcal{L}$ if and only if p is a fixed point ϕ. We will show that, for λ sufficiently small, ϕ is a contraction mapping. We use three facts to prove the result, each of which follows from easy arguments.

Fact 1. For any $p, q \in \Delta^0$ (the interior of Δ), $\max_l |p_l - q_l| \leq \max_{kl} |p_l/p_k - q_l/q_k|$.

Fact 2. Since the derivative of e^x at $x = 0$ is 1, then for all $D > 1$, there is a δ such that whenever $|x_1|, |x_2| < \delta$, $|\exp[x_1] - \exp[x_2]| \leq D \cdot |x_1 - x_2|$.

Fact 3. There is an $M > 0$ such that $\max_{ikl} |u_{ikl}(p) - u_{ikl}(q)| \leq M \cdot \max_{ik} |p_{ik} - q_{ik}|$.

Pick any $D > 1$ and let δ be defined as in Fact 2 and M be defined as in Fact 3. We pick $\underline{\lambda}$ to satisfy

(1) $\underline{\lambda} u_{ikl}(p) < \delta$ for all i, k, l, and any p.
(2) $\underline{\lambda} < 1/(D \cdot M)$

Write $\rho = \underline{\lambda} \cdot D \cdot M$. Then pick any $p, q \in \Delta$. Then, letting $\|\cdot\|$ represent the sup norm, we let

$$\begin{aligned}
\|\phi(p) - \phi(q)\| &= \max_{il} |\phi_{il}(p) - \phi_{il}(q)| \\
&\leq \max_{ikl} |\phi_{il}(p)/\phi_{ik}(p) - \phi_{il}(q)/\phi_{ik}(q)| \\
&= \max_{ikl} |\exp[\lambda u_{ikl}(p)] - \exp[\lambda u_{ikl}(q)]| \\
&\leq \lambda \cdot D \cdot \max_{ikl} |u_{ikl}(p) - u_{ikl}(q)| \\
&\leq \underline{\lambda} \cdot D \cdot M \cdot \max_{ikl} |p_{ik} - q_{ik}| = \rho \cdot |p - q|,
\end{aligned}$$

where $\rho < 1$. The steps follow, respectively, by the definition of $\|\cdot\|$, Fact 1, Equation (∗), Fact 2, Fact 3, and the definition of $\|\cdot\|$. It follows that, for $\lambda \leq \underline{\lambda}$, ϕ is a contraction mapping. Hence it has a unique fixed point.

Q.E.D.

We now have shown enough to prove Property 1 of Theorem 3, that for almost all λ there are an odd number of logistic QREs. From the above argument, seting $c = (\underline{c}, \bar{c})$, we have shown that $\mathcal{L}_c$ is a compact, one-dimensional manifold with boundary, which for small enough $\underline{c}$, has a unique intersection with $\lambda = \underline{c}$. Any such manifold has a finite number of connected, compact components, each of which must have an even number of boundary points. We have also shown that any boundary point must be at $\lambda = \underline{c}$ or $\lambda = \bar{c}$. Since there is exactly one solution at $\lambda = \underline{c}$, there must be an odd number of solutions at $\lambda = \bar{c}$.

We now show the first assertion of Property 3 of the theorem, that as $\lambda \to \infty$, the branch $\mathcal{B}$ of the manifold that passes through $\underline{\lambda}$ converges to a unique Nash equilibrium.

LEMMA 2. *Let $\underline{\lambda}$ be chosen so that $\pi^*(\underline{\lambda})$ is a singleton. Then for almost all games u, as $\lambda \to \infty$, the branch $\mathcal{B}$ of the manifold that passes through $\underline{\lambda}$ converges to a unique Nash equilibrium.*

Proof. It follows from the arguments above that for almost all games there exists an increasing sequence $\{\lambda_i\}$ with $\underline{\lambda} < \lambda_i$ for all i, such that if we define $c_i = (\underline{\lambda}, \lambda_i)$, $X_i = X_{c_i}$, and $\mathcal{L}_i = \mathcal{L}_{c_i} \subseteq \mathcal{L}$,

(1) $\mathcal{L}$ is a one-dimensional manifold with a unique point, say $(p, \underline{\lambda})$, for which $\lambda = \underline{\lambda}$ and a unique connected branch $\mathcal{B}$ that passes through $(p, \underline{\lambda})$.

(2) $\mathcal{L}_i$ is a compact one-dimensional manifold with boundary, which has a finite number of connected components.

(3) Letting $\mathcal{B}_i$ be the connected branch of $\mathcal{L}_i$ which begins at $(\underline{p}, \underline{\lambda})$, it follows that $\mathcal{B}_i$ is a compact connected one-dimensional manifold with boundary for all i, which has a unique intersection, say (p_i, λ_i), with $\lambda = \underline{\lambda}$.

Now for any i, define $\mathcal{A}_i = \{(p, \lambda) \in \mathcal{B} : \lambda > \lambda_i\}$ and A_i to be the closure of the projection of $\mathcal{A}_i$ onto D. Then $\{A_i\}$ is a decreasing sequence of sets. We show that for almost all games, $\cap_i A_i$ must be a unique point. First of all, since D is compact and each A_i is closed and nonempty, $\cap_i A_i$ cannot be empty. Suppose, by way of contradiction, that $\cap_i A_i$ contains two distinct points. Since generic games contain a finite number of Nash equilibria, we may assume that the game defined by u has a finite number of Nash equilibria. By Theorem 2, any point in $\cap_i A_i$ must be a Nash equilibrium. But if p^* and q^* are both $\cap_i A_i$, then we can construct a sequence $\{(p, \lambda)\} \subseteq \mathcal{B}$ with $p_{2i-1} \to p^*$, $p_{2i} \to p^*$, $\lambda_i \to \infty$, and a homeomorphism, $\phi : \mathbb{R} \to \mathcal{B}$, satisfying $\phi(i) = (p_i^*, \lambda_i)$, and $\phi(2i) = (q_i^*, \eta_i)$. In particular, start with any δ_i and find $(p_1^*, \lambda_1) \in \mathcal{B}$ with $\lambda_1 > 1/\delta_1$ and $||p_1 - p^*|| < \delta_1$. Since $\mathcal{B}$ is connected, it is path connected (Guillemin and Pollack, p. 38, Exercise 3), so one can construct $\phi[0, 1] \to \mathcal{B}$ with $\phi(0) = (\underline{p}, \underline{\lambda})$ and $\phi(1) = (p_1^*, \lambda_1)$. Since $\phi[0, 1]$ is compact, it is bounded. Pick δ_2 so that $1/\delta_2$ exceeds the bound and find $(p_2^*, \lambda_2) \in \mathcal{B}$ with $\lambda_2 > 1/\delta_2$ and $||p_2 - q^*|| < \delta_2$. By the same reasoning as above, one can construct $\phi[1, 2] \to \mathcal{B}$ with $\phi(1) = (p_1^*, \lambda_1)$, and $\phi(2) = (p_2^*, \lambda_2)$. Proceeding in this fashion, one can construct the sequence $\{(p_i, \lambda_i)\} \subseteq \mathcal{B}$ and a homeomorphism, $\phi : \mathbb{R} \to \mathcal{B}$ with the properties specified. Now for each i, $\phi[i, i+1]$ is a compact one-dimensional manifold with boundary. Moreover, we can pick ϕ so that $\phi(i-1, i) \cap \phi(i, i+1) = \phi(i)$.

We have constructed an infinite sequence of compact manifolds with boundary, each of whose projection on D connects a point near p^* to a point near q^*. Further, for any λ_i, at most a finite number of these manifolds intersect with X_i (since a $\mathcal{B} \cap X_i$ is a compact one-dimensional manifold with boundary, which can consist of at most a finite number of components). It follows that any separating hyperplane $H_t = \{p^* \in D : p \cdot (p^* - q^*) = t\}$ between p^* and q^* must have a nonempty intersection with $\cap_i A_i$ (by compactness of H_t). But, since there are an infinity of such separating hyperplanes, this means that $\cap_i A_i$, is infinite and hence there are an infinite number of Nash equilibria, which is a contradiction.

Q.E.D.

We have established that there is a unique branch of $\mathcal{L}$ that selects a unique Nash equilibrium as λ goes to infinity. This establishes Property 3.

References

Anderson, L. (1993). "A Logistic Error Model of Data from Information Cascade Expenments," mimeo. University of Virginia.

Bua, A. "Imperfect Equilibrium," *Games Econ. Behav.* 4 (1992), 15–36.

Brow, J., and Rosenthal, R. (1990). "Testing the Minimax Hypothesis: A Reexamination of O'Neill's Game Experiment," *Econometrics* 58, 1065–1081.

Chew, K.-Y. (1994). The Strategic Behavior of Rational Novices, Ph.D. dissertation. California Institute of Technology.

Dvoretsky, A., Wald, A., and Wolfowitz, J. (1951). "Elimination of Randomization in Certain Statistical Decision Procedures and Zero-Sum Two-Person Games," *Ann. Math. Statist.* 22, 1–21.

El-Gamal, M., and Grether, D. (1993). "Uncovering Behavioral Strategies: Likelihood-Based Experimental Data Mining," Social Science Working Paper 850. California Institute of Technology.

El-Gamal, M., McKelvey, R. D., and Palfrey, T. R. (1993). "A Bayesian Sequential Experimental Study of Learning in Games," *J. Amer. Statist. Assoc.* 88, 428–435.

El-Gamal, M., and Palfrey, T. R. (1994). "Economical Experiments: Bayesian Efficient Experimental Design," Social Science Working Paper. California Institute of Technology.

El-Gamal, M., and Palfrey, T. R. (1995). "Vertigo: Comparing Structural Models of Imperfect Behavior in Experimental Games," *Games Econ. Behav.* 8, 322–348.

Fey, M., McKelvey, R. D., and Palfrey, T. R. (1996). "Experiments on the Sum Centipede Game," *Int. J. Game Theory*, 25, 269–287.

Guillemin, V., and Pollack, A. (1974). *Differential Topology*. Englewood Cliffs, NJ: Prentice-Hall.

Harless, D., and Camerer, C. (1994). "The Predictive Utility of Generalized Expected Utility Theories," *Econometrica* 62, 1251–1289.

Harsanyi, J. (1973). "Games with Randomly Disturbed Payoffs," *Int. J. Game Theory* 2, 1–23.

Harsanyi, J., and Selten, R. (1988). *A General Theory of Equilibrium Selection in Games*. Cambridge: Massachusetts Institute of Technology Press.

Holt, D. (1993). "An Empirical Model of Strategic Choice with an Application to Coordination Games," Working Paper. Queen's University.

Lieberman, B. (1960). "Human Behavior in a Strictly Determined 3×3 Matrix Game," *Behavioral Sci.* 5, 317–222.

Luce, D. (1959). *Individual Choice Behavior*. New York: Wesley.

Ma, C. A., and Manove, M. (1993). "Bargaining with Deadlines and Imperfect Player Control," *Econometrica* 61, 1313–1339.

McFadden, D. (1976). "Quantal Choice Analysis: A Survey," *Ann. Econ. Social Measurement* 5, 363–390.

McFadden, D. (1973). "Conditional Logit Analysis of Qualitative Choice Behavior," in *Frontiers of Econometrics* (P. Zarembka, Ed.). New York: Academic Press.

McKelvey, R. D., and Palfrey, T. R. (1992). "An Experimental Study of the Centipede Game," *Econometrica* 60, 803–836. (Chapter 18 of this book.)

McKelvey, R. D., and Palfrey, T. R. (1994). "Quantal Response Equilibrium for Extensive Form Games," mimeo. California Institute of Technology.

Myerson, R. (1978). "Refinements of the Nash Equilibrium Concept," *Int. J. Game Theory* 7, 73–80.

Ochs, J. (1995). "Games with Unique Mined Strategy Equilibria: An Experimental Study," *Games Econ. Behav.* 10, 174–189.

O'Neill, B. (1987). "Nonmetric Test of the Minimax Theory of Two-Person Zerosum Games," *Proc. Natl. Acad. Sci. USA* 84, 2106–2109.

Palfrey, T. R., and Prisbrey, J. (1992). "Anomalous Behavior in Linear Public Goods Experiments: How Much and Why?" Social Science Working Paper 833. California Institute of Technology.

Palfrey, T. R., and Rosenthal, R. (1991). "Testing Game-Theoretic Models of Free Riding: New Evidence of Probability Bias and Learning," in *Laboratory Research in Political Economy* (T. Palfrey, Ed.). Ann Arbor: University of Michigan Press.

Radner, R., and Rosenthal, R. (1982). "Private Information and Pure-Strategy Equilibria," *Math. Oper. Res.* 7, 401–409.

Rapoport, A., and Boebel, R. (1992). "Mixed Strategies in Strictly Competitive Games: A Further Test of the Minimax Hypothesis," *Games Econ. Behav.* 4, 261–283.

Rosenthal, R. (1989). "A Bounded-Rationality Approach to the Study of Noncooperative Games," *Int. J. Game Theory* 18, 273–292.

Schanuel, S. H., Simon, L., and Zame, W. (1990). "The Algebraic Geometry of Games and the Tracing Procedure," in *Game Equilibrium Models*, Vol. II, *Methods, Morals and Markets* (R. Selten, Ed.). Berlin: Springer-Verlag.

Schmidt, D. (1992). "Reputation Building by Error-Prone Agents," mimeo. California Institute of Technology.

Selten, R. (1975). "Reexamination of the Perfectness Concept for Equilibrium Points in Extensive Games," *Int. J. Game Theory* 4, 25–55.

Smith, V., and Walker, J. (1993). "Monetary Rewards and Decision Cost in Experimental Economics," *Econ. Inquiry* 31, 245–261.

Stahl, D., and Wilson, P. (in press). "On Players' Models of Other Players: Theory and Experimental Evidence," *Games Econ. Behav.* 10, 218–254.

Van Damme, E. (1987). *Stability and Perfection of Nash Equilibria*. Berlin: Springer-Verlag.

Zauner, K. (1993). "Bubbles, Speculation and a Reconsideration of the Centipede Game Experiments," mimeo. U.C. San Diego.

CHAPTER 21

Computation in Finite Games: Using Gambit for Quantitative Analysis

THEODORE L. TUROCY

Richard McKelvey, in applying noncooperative game theory and quantitative analysis to problems in political science, was naturally confronted with the need for computer programs to assist in the analysis and solution of games. During the 1980s, Richard began to write computer programs to compute Nash equilibria of games, initially in the language BASIC and later in C. These programs were the ancestors of the library of routines for analyzing finite games that came to be known as Gambit.[1]

Gambit owes its current form to a redevelopment and expansion during 1994 and 1995 under a National Science Foundation grant awarded to Richard jointly with Andrew McLennan, with this author serving as principal programmer. The project currently comprises an extensive library in C++ to represent and analyze finite extensive and normal form games, as well as a graphical user interface to manipulate games and visualize results. Gambit is continuing to be developed as open source software, and is distributed freely under the terms of the GNU General Public License.

This chapter explores some of Richard's contributions to the quantitative analysis of finite games. In addition, it provides for the researcher interested in pursuing a research agenda similar in style to Richard's a quick introduction to the existing methods for computing Nash equilibria in finite games. Relative to the excellent surveys of McKelvey and McLennan (1996) and von Stengel (2002), the goal is to provide some practical guidance, based on the author's experience in the development and maintenance of Gambit, in the selection of the best methods for

---

[1] Richard chose the name "Gambit" as a play on the words "game" and "bit," the fundamental unit of information.

computing equilibria, and formation of reasonable expectations as to how large and what types of games are feasible to analyze numerically.

1. Why Compute?

Regardless of one's ultimate objectives, a handy use of computation in analyzing a formal model is the ability to build intuition about the model's behavior as its structure and parameters are changed. This process allows the modeler to play with the model, and begin formulating hypotheses about both the overall predictions and implications of the model, as well as for possible general results in the model. The intuition built from these experiments may lead to insights, which can subsequently be developed into a formal expression as a theorem. Even when a simple characterization in the form of a theorem turns out not to be available, computational experiments yield information about the quantitative predictions of the model.

The computation of Nash equilibria in finite games is a tedious process, as anyone who has manually computed equilibria in a game with more than two players or involving more than two strategies per player will attest. In fact, the number of equilibria can grow quickly in the size of the game (see, for example, McKelvey and McLennan (1997)). The precise identification of the formal computational complexity of computing Nash equilibria in finite games remains today an active area of research. What is clear, however, is that the problem is computationally difficult, meaning that automating the process is essential.

One application of formal game models involves the determination of unknown parameters based on observed data. This process requires knowledge of the equilibria of many closely-related games. For example, consider the McKelvey and Palfrey (1992 (Chapter 18 of the book)) experimental study of behavior in the centipede game. This model introduced a probability that a player has "altruistic" preferences. This rendered the centipede game an extensive form game of imperfect information, with a parameter, the probability of these preferences occurring, to be estimated from the data. What is observed in those data is the frequency with which a player chose to "pass"; from that, one backs out the underlying probability. However, the mapping from game parameters to equilibrium properties need not be straightforward, or even have a closed form; hence, iteratively computing the equilibria of the game for different probabilities is necessary to implement the estimation procedure. This idea is generalized by, for example, the recent work of Bajari, et al. (2004), who incorporate methods for computing all Nash equilibria of a game in an estimation procedure to determine underlying parameters of a game.

An alternative identification approach uses the quantal response equilibrium concept of McKelvey and Palfrey (1995 (Chapter 20 of the book), 1998). The QRE is a staple of analysis of finite games in laboratory experiments (for example, the survey of Goeree and Holt (2001) gives a set of examples where quantal response equilibrium predictions predict qualitative features of laboratory data). Quantal response equilibria can be expressed in closed form only in special cases, thereby making the problem of doing estimation using QREs inherently numerical.

2. Reasonable Expectations

As with any endeavor to numerically analyze a problem, it is best to start simple, attempting to work with "out-of-the-box" procedures available in existing packages. This chapter summarizes some of the procedures which are applicable to any finite game, and which are likely to produce results for most games of small or medium size.

It is important to keep in mind that, on average, the time required to find equilibria increases rapidly in the size of the game. Further, since the increase in running time may be exponential in the size of the game, future marginal advances in computing technology, such as processor speed or multiprocessing, may not have a significant impact on the size of game which may be adequately handled by general-purpose methods. In these cases, practical numerical analysis of a game will require techniques which avail themselves of the specific structure of the game.

Such methods are currently a topic of active development. The simplest example of reducing the effective size of a game for computational purposes is to consider symmetric games and search only for the symmetric equilibria of the game. Other classes of games have structure to their payoffs which can be exploited computationally. Echenique (2003) gives a procedure for efficiently computing all equilibria of supermodular games. Kearns, et al. (2001), among others, consider games with a particular graphical structure identifying the local interactions among players. Similarly, polymatrix games (see Govindan and Wilson (2004)), where players' payoffs are determined only by bilateral interactions, have a computationally easier structure.

3. Numerical Methods to Compute Nash Equilibria

McKelvey and McLennan (1997) observe that the definition of a Nash equilibrium may be recast in a number of different mathematical formulations. Each formulation suggests a different approach to numerically computing Nash equilibria. Since these methods are quite distinct, they are often adapted to different purposes.

A first observation is that if a game has an extensive (game tree) structure, it is generally advisable to choose methods which operate on the extensive game, rather than on its reduced normal form representation. The number of strategies in the reduced normal form of an extensive form game may grow quite (infeasibly) large for extensive forms of modest size; or, to put it another way, there is redundancy in the reduced normal form representation. The worst-case scenario for this growth is the case of an extensive form game which has many "parallel" information sets, that is, a pair of information sets for a player such that play passes through one or the other of them. The extreme examples of games like this are sequential-move games of perfect information such as tic-tac-toe.

Independent of one's ultimate objectives, the first step in analyzing a game numerically is to identify and remove from consideration dominated strategies or actions. Gilboa, et al. (1993) show that computing strictly dominated strategies is easier than computing a Nash equilibrium. Iteratively eliminating strictly dominated strategies, when possible, helps reduce the size of the game the equilibrium computation methods must confront, without removing any Nash equilibria. If one's objective will be only to compute a single equilibrium, iterative removal of weakly dominated strategies is also suggested.[2]

The second step in searching for equilibrium is to perform a search for all equilibria in pure strategies. While there is no procedure more sophisticated for doing this than a brute-force search over all possible combinations of strategies or actions, it is effective even for fairly large games. As an added benefit, equilibria in pure strategies are often considered the most compelling as a prediction of how a game would be played, so identifying them quickly is of practical interest as well.

---

[2] These comments assume the ultimate goal is identification of Nash equilibria. Some behavioral solution concepts, quantal response equilibria among them, are affected by the presence of dominated strategies.

Methods for All Finite Games

If a game has no equilibria in pure strategies, or if a fuller characterization of the equilibria of a game involving randomization is desired, more sophisticated approaches are indicated. Methods which are applicable to all games, regardless of the number of players or payoff structure, are considered next. When these methods are implemented in Gambit, their Gambit names are indicated in parentheses.

One method generalizes the idea of looking first for equilibria in pure strategies. Porter, et al. (2006) present a heuristic-based approach (PNS) for searching for equilibria which looks first for equilibria in which players give positive probability to as few strategies as possible. This method can be used to find all equilibria, but it is designed to be biased towards finding a first equilibrium as quickly as possible; this makes it ideal for searching for either one equilibrium, or two equilibria (to determine whether the game has a unique equilibrium). Since this method first searches for pure-strategy equilibria by design, doing an independent search for pure-strategy equilibria is not necessary when using this approach.

The PNS idea of searching over particular supports (i.e., sets of strategies played with positive probability) can be adapted to instead organize supports in a search tree. This method (EnumPoly) uses a top-down search that is able to prune some parts of the tree from consideration. Thus, it is better suited in general than PNS for the task of computing all equilibria.

In contrast, several methods operate by attempting to compute increasingly better approximations to a Nash equilibrium. For applications where the equilibria of interest involve randomized strategies, approximation methods may be attractive in that the sequence of strategy profiles computed by the algorithm will converge in the limit to an equilibrium. As such, the intermediate output of these methods can be viewed as giving some hint as to where an equilibrium might lie. The support-based methods outlined in the previous paragraphs give no indication whether the next support to be considered is more or less likely to contain an equilibrium.

One robust approximation method is the simplicial subdivision method for normal form games by van der Laan, et al. (1987) (Simpdiv). This procedure constructs a grid over the space of mixed strategy profiles, similar to the algorithm of Scarf (1967). This grid is then traversed to compute a fixed point on this grid. Once such a fixed point is found, the grid may be refined, and the fixed point of the coarser grid used as a starting point for a search on the refined grid. In the limit as the spacing between grid points decreases to zero, this process should compute a Nash equilibrium.

Each fixed point computed as the grid is refined can be viewed as computing a sequence of approximate equilibria, which in the limit will tend to a Nash equilibrium. In practice this is often the case, though there is no theoretical guarantee that the process will converge quickly. It is possible to appear to be converging to a particular point, only to have the computed approximate equilibrium change substantially as the grid is refined. Further, it is possible that a profile that appears to be the limit of a sequence of approximate equilibria is only revealed not to be the limit at a very fine grid size.

At every grid size, it is guaranteed that a fixed point on that grid will be found; however, on some games a very long path may be traversed to locate it. In the implementation of simplicial subdivision in Gambit, an optional "leash" parameter restricts how far afield the algorithm searches, on the principle that it is possible but unusual for an approximate fixed point to "disappear" as the grid is refined. Use of this restriction sometimes speeds convergence of the algorithm; however, it also means that the algorithm with this leash activated is not guaranteed to compute an approximate equilibrium.

The starting point for the simplicial subdivision can be any point on the initial grid. The resulting equilibrium found depends on the choice of the initial condition; therefore, it is possible to find distinct equilibria using this method by choosing different starting points. However, since the relationship between the initial point and the computed equilibrium is not easy to see, it is not possible to be sure one has found all equilibria using this approach.

Another method that computes a progressively better approximation to an equilibrium is inspired by the quantal response equilibrium concept of McKelvey and Palfrey (1995 (Chapter 20 of this book), 1998) (logit). Each branch of the logit quantal response equilibrium correspondence converges in the limit to a Nash equilibrium of the game as the randomness in payoffs is decreased to zero. A method to trace a branch of the correspondence efficiently is proposed in Turocy (2005), which is the basis for the implementation in Gambit. Asymptotically as the noise is decreased, the quantal response equilibria converge fairly rapidly to the limiting Nash equilibrium. As the quantal response equilibrium concept is now widely used for quantitative analysis of data from laboratory experiments, computation of Nash equilibria by this method has the advantage that the points necessary for such estimation are computed as a by-product.

The natural starting point for this method is the profile where all strategies (or actions, for the extensive form version) are played with equal probability, and the noise parameter is infinity; this point is always in the quantal response correspondence for all games. The equilibrium found by traversing from this point is generically unique, and is called the "logit solution" by McKelvey and Palfrey. Computing other Nash equilibria is more problematic. Other, disconnected branches may exist, each of which connects two Nash equilibria (again, generically); it is not clear how to reliably locate such branches in general. In addition, not all equilibria are limits of logit quantal response equilibria, meaning that the method is not guaranteed to compute all equilibria.

Another promising approach to computing equilibria is the global Newton method of Govindan and Wilson (2003). This method is based on facts about how the set of Nash equilibria of a game changes as payoffs are perturbed. It is observed that by making a perturbation large enough, the perturbed game will have a unique equilibrium that is easy to compute. This equilibrium is then traced back as the perturbation is made smaller to reach equilibria of the original game. Since this method may take a long time to reach the vicinity of the original game, Govindan and Wilson (2004) introduce a method to reduce this time by approximating the original game by polymatrix games, which are games where the payoffs are determined by bilateral interactions among the players. Games with this structure can be solved using an algorithm due to Lemke and Howson.[3] The global Newton (Gnm) and polymatrix (Ipa) approaches, while recent developments, currently appear to be promising as the "best" algorithms for computing equilibria for many games.[4]

Another method for approximating a Nash equilibrium is the Lyapunov function method (Liap) proposed by McKelvey (1991). This function is based on the differences between the payoff earned by each player at a given strategy profile and the payoff each player would earn by playing his best reply to the other players' choices; the function is therefore nonnegative, and zero exactly at Nash equilibria. Thus, the function is attractive since, approximately speaking, lower values of the Lyapunov function correspond to strategy profiles where players are making best-reply errors that are less costly in payoff terms.

Since the function is differentiable, standard function minimization methods can be used to compute local minima of this function, and, if the function value at the local minimum is zero, then it is a Nash equilibrium. However, local constrained minima of the Lyapunov function exist, and experience indicates that for many games, standard gradient-descent methods will tend to converge to constrained local minima that are not Nash equilibria. The properties of this function are not fully explored, and it may be possible that techniques such as simulated

---

[3] See the next section for details on this algorithm.

[4] The Gambit implementation derives from the Gametracer implementation of Blum, et al. (2004).

annealing or genetic algorithms, which are designed to operate on functions that may have many local minima, may be effective in establishing Lyapunov function methods as effective means for computing equilibria.

Methods for Games with Two Players

Games with two players enjoy some convenient properties that often make the problem of computing Nash equilibria simpler and more efficient. These derive in large part from the observation that a player's payoff for playing one of his strategies can be expressed as a linear function of the probabilities the other player assigns to her strategies.

The workhorse for computing equilibria in normal form games with two players is the method of Lemke and Howson (1964) (Lcp). The Lemke-Howson algorithm is a constructive proof of the famous existence theorem of Nash (1950). The method proceeds by following a path of mixed strategy profiles that are "almost" equilibria. Each such profile has the property that exactly one strategy that gives less than the optimal payoff for a player is used with positive probability. At the end of any such path is a profile which satisfies all the conditions of equilibrium. Because of the linearity of each player's payoff function, the Lemke-Howson algorithm can be implemented using matrix "pivoting" procedures, which are well-studied numerical methods.

The general experience is that the Lemke-Howson method finds an equilibrium quickly. However, Savani and von Stengel (2004) give an example to show that the path that the algorithm takes may be quite long in certain cases. Also, Shapley (1974) shows that there exist equilibria that cannot be located using the method; therefore, one can not use the Lemke-Howson method to compute all equilibria.

The specific operation of the Lemke-Howson method is generally opaque, and does not give an easy intuition when compared to other methods. Shapley (1974) presents a graphical interpretation of how the method operates on a simple example, though extending that visualization to a larger game may be difficult. Note that while each step of the Lemke-Howson algorithm gives an "almost" equilibrium, in that only one suboptimal strategy is used, it is not in general true that each step provides a successively better approximation to an equilibrium in the sense discussed in the previous section.

The existence of equilibria inaccessible by Lemke-Howson is addressed by an enumeration method (EnumMixed) given by Mangasarian (1964). This method essentially computes and visits all the strategy profiles that might be visited by the

Lemke-Howson method, and therefore can find even those strategy profiles that are not accessible via Lemke-Howson. Therefore, it is suitable in principle for computing all equilibria. However, because this is an enumeration method, the number of such profiles grows rapidly in the size of the game. The enumeration of these extreme points can be done using the LRS algorithm of Avis and Fukuda (1992).

When a two-player normal form game is furthermore constant-sum, it is possible to formulate the conditions for a Nash equilibrium as a linear programming problem (Lp). This observation by Dantzig (1951) serves as a constructive proof of the famous Minimax Theorem of von Neumann (1928). Linear programming problems are extensively studied numerical procedures, and many good implementations exist for solving them.

The extensive form does not lend itself as directly to solution via linear programming or linear complementarity programming. An important development in this area is an alternate representation of an extensive form, the sequence form of Koller, Megiddo, and von Stengel (1996). The sequence form allows formulation of the equilibrium problem in a way that parallels the formulation for normal form games. When the extensive form is zero-sum, characterization of equilibrium points may be done using linear programming in the sequence form. For non-constant-sum games, a variation on Lemke-Howson described by Lemke (1965) may be applied.

Compared to the reduced normal form, the sequence form grows only at the rate the extensive form grows. This occurs because the key concept in the sequence form is a sequence of choices. This representational parsimony combined with the development of efficient implementations of linear programming and linear complementarity programming solvers means that games with more than a million nodes may feasibly be solved, even when much smaller games would be infeasible using normal form methods.

Refinements of Nash Equilibrium

Since there may be many Nash equilibria of a game, many "refinement" concepts for Nash equilibria have been proposed to help eliminate Nash equilibria which are deemed to be less plausible.

Several of the algorithms described already are guaranteed to compute Nash equilibria satisfying certain refinements. The implementation of the Lemke-Howson method in Gambit, by virtue of the way degeneracies are handled, is guaranteed to compute equilibria that are trembling-hand perfect. A further refinement of perfection, a proper equilibrium, can be computed using the method of Yamamoto (1993). An equilibrium selection method due to Harsanyi and Selten (1988) can be implemented using a homotopy method of Herings and Peeters (2001). An algorithm to compute simply stable sets of equilibria was proposed by Wilson (1992).[5]

For extensive games, computation of equilibria satisfying the most basic refinement, subgame perfection, can be accomplished with any algorithm simply by solving each subgame in turn, working backwards from the end of the game. For the additional refinement of sequential equilibrium, the construction of the agent logit quantal response equilibrium and Lyapunov function method for extensive games guarantees the computation of a sequential equilibrium.[6]

4. Looking Forward

In their study of the centipede game, published in 1992, McKelvey and Palfrey acknowledged the use of donated time on a Cray XMP supercomputer to accomplish the estimation. Today, similar computations can be carried out on off-the-shelf personal computer hardware. These developments in computing power made the quantitative portion of Richard McKelvey's research program feasible. Indeed, the origins of Gambit lie in Richard's research, and Gambit represents part of Richard's legacy to future researchers seeking to pursue programs patterned on his approaches and methods.

The ubiquity of computers today continues to expand the boundaries of problems that can be tackled with computational tools. Judd (1997) makes a strong case for a significant role of computation in economics, and his comments apply with equal force to the application of rigorous and quantitative methods to political science. As exemplified by much of Richard's work, formal theorem-proving and computation are natural complements. Computational analysis can give initial insights into a model's behavior, which in turn may lead to formal statements of a model's predictions in terms of theorems. Subsequently, computation can play a significant role in the next step, that of taking the model to the data in a process of identification of a model's parameters and testing the model's quantitative predictions.

The Gambit website is http://econweb.tamu.edu/gambit.

---

[5] An implementation of Wilson's algorithm is available from the Gambit website.

[6] Note that despite the similar nomenclature, methods employing the sequence form representation do not necessarily result in finding sequential equilibria.

References

Avis, David, and Komei Fukuda. A pivoting algorithm for convex hulls and vertex enumeration of arrangements and polyhedra. *Discrete and Computational Geometry*, 8:295–313, 1992.

Bajari, Patrick, Han Hong, and Stephen Ryan. Identification and estimation of discrete games of complete information. Manuscript, Duke University, 2004.

Blum, Ben, Christian Shelton, and Daphne Koller. Gametracer. Software, version 0.2, http://dags.stanford.edu/Games/gametracer.html, 2004.

Dantzig, George. A proof of the equivalence of the programming problem and the game problem. In Tjalling C. Koopmans, editor, *Activity Analysis of Production and Allocation*, pages 330–335. Wiley, 1951.

Echenique, Federico. Finding all equilibria. Caltech Social Science working paper 1153, 2003.

Gilboa, Itzhak, Ehud Kalai, and Eitan Zemel. The complexity of eliminating dominated strategies. *Mathematics of Operations Research*, 18:553–565, 1993.

Goeree, Jacob, and Charles A. Holt. Ten little treasures of game theory, and ten intuitive contradictions. *American Economic Review*, 91:1402–1422, 2001.

Govindan, Srihari, and Robert Wilson. A global Newton method to compute Nash equilibria. *Journal of Economic Theory*, 110:65–86, 2003.

Govindan, Srihari, and Robert Wilson. Computing Nash equilibria by iterated polymatrix approximation. *Journal of Economic Dynamics and Control*, 28:1229–1241, 2004.

Harsanyi, John C., and Reinhard Selten. *A General Theory of Equilibrium Selection in Games*. MIT Press, Cambridge MA, 1988.

Herings, P. Jean-Jacques, and Ronald J. A. P. Peeters. A differentiable homotopy to compute Nash equilibria of n-person games. *Economic Theory*, 18:159–185, 2001.

Judd, Kenneth L. Computational economics and economic theory: Substitutes and complements? *Journal of Economic Dynamics and Control*, 21:907–942, 1997.

Kearns, M., M. Littman, and S. Singh. Graphical models for game theory. In *Proceedings of the Conference on Uncertainty in Artificial Intelligence*, pages 253–260, 2001.

Koller, Daphne, Nimrod Megiddo, and Bernhard von Stengel. Efficient computation of equilibria for extensive two-person games. *Games and Economic Behavior*, 14:247–259, 1996.

Lemke, C. E. Bimatrix equilibrium points and mathematical programming. *Management Science*, 11:681–689, 1965.

Lemke, C. E., and Howson, J. T. Jr. Equilibrium points of bimatrix games. *Journal of the Society of Industrial and Applied Mathematics*, 12:413–423, 1964.

Mangasarian, Oscar. Equilibrium points of bimatrix games. *Journal of the Society for Industrial and Applied Mathematics*, 12:778–780, 1964.

McKelvey, Richard D. A Liapunov function for Nash equilibria. Caltech Social Science working paper, 1991.

McKelvey, Richard D., and Andrew M. McLennan. Computation of equilibria in finite games. In Hans Amman, David A. Kendrick, and John Rust, editors, *The Handbook of Computational Economics*, volume I, pages 87–142. Elsevier, 1996.

McKelvey, Richard D., and Andrew M. McLennan. The maximal number of regular totally mixed Nash equilibria. *Journal of Economic Theory*, 72:411–425, 1997.

McKelvey, Richard D., and Thomas R. Palfrey. An experimental study of the centipede game. *Econometrica*, 60:803–836, 1992.

McKelvey, Richard D., and Thomas R. Palfrey. Quantal response equilibria for normal form games. *Games and Economic Behavior*, 10:6–38, 1995. Chapter 20 of this book.

McKelvey, Richard D., and Thomas R. Palfrey. Quantal response equilibria for extensive form games. *Experimental Economics*, 1:9–41, 1998.

Nash, John F. Equilibrium points in n-person games. *Proceedings of the National Academy of Sciences*, 36:48–49, 1950.

Porter, Ryan W., Eugene Nudelman, and Yoav Shoham. Simple search methods for finding a Nash equilibrium. *Games and Economic Behavior*, 2006. doi: 10.1016/j.geb.2006.03.015

Savani, Rahul, and Bernhard von Stengel. Exponentially many steps for finding a Nash equilibrium. CDAM Research Report LSE-CDAM-2004-03, 2004.

Scarf, Herbert. The approximation of fixed points of a continuous mapping. *SIAM Journal of Applied Mathematics*, 15:1328–1343, 1967.

Shapley, Lloyd. A note on the Lemke-Howson algorithm. *Mathematical Programming Study*, 1:175–189, 1974.

Turocy, Theodore L. A dynamic homotopy interpretation of the logistic quantal response equilibrium correspondence. *Games and Economic Behavior*, 51:243–263, 2005.

van de Laan, G., A. J. J. Talman, and L. van Der Heyden. Simplicial variable dimension algorithms for solving the nonlinear complementarity problem on a product of unit simplices using a general labeling. *Mathematics of Operations Research*, 12:377–397, 1987.

von Neumann, John. Zur Theorie der Gesellschaftsspiele. *Annals of Mathematics*, 100:295–320, 1928.

von Stengel, Bernhard. Computing equilibria for two-person games. In Robert J. Aumann and Sergiu Hart, editors, *Handbook of Game Theory, with Economic Applications*, volume 3, pages 1723–1759. North-Holland, 2002.

Wilson, Robert. Computing simply stable equilibria. *Econometrica*, 60:1039–1070, 1992.

Yamamoto, Yoshitsugo. A path-following procedure to find a proper equilibrium of finite games. *International Journal of Game Theory*, 22:249–259, 1993.

CHAPTER 22

What McKelvey Taught Us

JOHN W. PATTY AND ELIZABETH MAGGIE PENN

This volume has explored both the substance and impact of Richard McKelvey's research. Along with many of the other contributors to this volume, both of us were Richard's students. As we and many others fortunate enough to have had the experience to learn from Richard will attest, Richard was a giving and highly conscientious teacher and advisor. As this volume is meant primarily as a textbook for graduate students, we felt it important to close with a summary of what Richard taught us when we were his students. Aside from the insight it provides into Richard and his approach to science, our interactions with him during his final years will hopefully also provide the reader with an idea of how Richard thought about formal political theory and social science after finishing much of the research discussed earlier in this volume.

Before discussing some of the more specific lessons that Richard taught us, it should be noted that Richard's integrity extended beyond the traditional fiduciary duties of a scholar, such as giving credit where credit is due, being collegial with one's colleagues and students, and having one's hair cut at least once each year. Richard instilled in his students a scientific philosophy that has permeated nearly every aspect of our professional lives. He taught us to pursue our work with an honest enthusiasm; to be wary of our intuition; to recognize the proper role of assumptions; to keep in mind why one's research matters; and ultimately, that good social science research is predicated on believing in one's own work. For example, he told one of us early in our graduate training that the best way to approach a topic is to tackle the problem directly, in the way we believe is correct and true, and referring to the previous attempts and literature only after defining our own approach to the problem.[1] While achieving these goals is a tall order,

---

[1] There is an interesting similarity between Richard's advice and advice given by Herbert Simon, who instructed his students not to read any of the related literature before completing the first draft of their papers.

Richard did so consistently. What follows is a succinct list of rules of thumb — passed on to us through his comments, teaching, and work — that we have aimed to follow in our own careers, in pursuit of Richard's vision of good social science.

Be Skeptical. First and foremost, Richard was a skeptic in the classical sense.[2] However, he was not a contrarian. His skepticism was the starting point of inquiry and was predicated on maintaining an open mind: an heretofore-unproven claim is not necessarily unfounded. Richard was most easily intrigued by claims or intuitions that, at least initially, looked simultaneously plausible and refutable. He advised one of us that some of the most interesting research is begun without necessarily having an idea of where it will lead to.

Richard's skepticism extended to how he represented the importance and applicability of a theoretical model. Most famously, Richard consistently downplayed the real-world importance of his most famous theoretical results about majority preference relations, described variously as "chaos" or "instability" results. Richard felt strongly that his results and those of Norman Schofield were *not* indicative of any property of majority rule that one might observe in real-world democratic institutions. Richard realized that the theory within which the results are derived was devoid of the details of real-world political institutions and the accompanying incentives offered to the individuals within the institution. Indeed, Richard encouraged one of his students, Jeffrey Banks, to investigate the robustness of these results. Banks ultimately was able to provide a general characterization of the set of sophisticated voting outcomes, a concept that can often significantly refine the set of predicted outcomes of democratic decision making.

Be Open-Minded. Richard's curiosity and love of tinkering permeated his life and research. Richard's file cabinets and shelves contained innumerable working papers, monographs, and books that he found to be interesting, novel, or simply thought-provoking. Grabbing from this collection, Richard often handed unexpecting graduate students work from a broad spectrum of disciplines, including economics, political science, computer science, math, engineering, and evolutionary biology, and an even wider array of authors. From this collection, Richard would be as likely to pull out an early working paper by a luminary in the field as he would a term paper by an undergraduate student who had taken one of his

---

[2] As in possessing a "methodology based on an assumption of doubt with the aim of acquiring approximate or relative certainty" (*American Heritage Dictionary*, 4th Edition).

courses two decades earlier. It would be easy to claim that these recommendations were uniformly profound, on point, or even tangentially related to the student's original question. Of course this was not the case. Nevertheless (or perhaps because of this), it was the way that Richard handed these works to us — with a seeming blindness toward the author's later accomplishments, the sexiness of the paper's title or topic, or the reflected glow of making a "wise" recommendation — that often made a greater impression on us than the contents of the works themselves.

Be Wary of Intuition. Richard had a strong suspicion of his own intuitions about what predictions a model would generate. In fact, one of us began working with Richard by finding a counterexample to a claim that Richard's intuition had suggested was true.[3] Being the skeptic that he was, Richard was quite pleased with the refutation of his initial belief: the failure of intuition in this case indicated that the problem was more interesting than he had originally believed.

Perhaps this is not surprising. After all, a theorist is almost always excited to uncover a counterintuitive result. Such results can enable us to think far more deeply about a problem, and open up unexplored and/or previously unrecognized research topics. However, Richard did not view counterintuitive predictions as the sine qua non of an interesting social science model. Instead, Richard taught us that, when deriving the predictions of a theory, one's intuition can be very seductive — a blind loyalty to intuition often leads, at best, to less-than-inspired findings and, at worst, to corner-cutting and flawed logic. At the same time, we must remember that counterintuitive results can be an indicator that some aspect of the model is incorrect. This leads us to the final and most important lesson that Richard taught us.

Remember Why You're Doing What You're Doing. Perhaps most central to the lessons that Richard taught us is the admonition to motivate both the topic and methods of one's research. As firmly associated with quantitative methods and formal theory as Richard was, he was a social scientist first and foremost. Even the most technical questions were asked by Richard only with an eye toward gaining a better understanding of human behavior in some real-world situation. An example of this is his expression of exasperation with a student's insistence that Nash equilibrium is a flawed predictive tool because it does not accurately

---

[3]Richard had hypothesized that every maximal chain contains every element of the von Neumann-Morgenstern stable set, and that there was thus a unique reduced-form maximal chain. There are actually an infinite number of such chains.

predict behavior in the "dictator game."[4] Richard said to the student, "the dictator game is unrealistic; people do not drop money out their office windows."

Richard's point with expressing skepticism of the dictator game results was not that people are actually greedier than the results seem to indicate at first blush. Rather, Richard felt that the game itself was unsatisfactory as a basis for rejecting the empirical application of Nash equilibrium, as the game — while useful as an experimental tool for the measurement of subjects' preferences — did not have an obvious real-world application in the context of non-cooperative game theory. Richard taught us that, first and foremost, a successful theory matches model to situation. To be blunt, one should not expect a non-cooperative model to accurately capture a situation of pure charity. The bigger lesson to be drawn from this is that a methodological approach may be valid in certain situations and not others. A theorist should be flexible enough to realize and accommodate this.

As the works in this volume attest, one of Richard's greatest accomplishments was his ability to match model to situation. Richard's earliest work on multidimensional scaling has enabled three generations of scholars to link the spatial model of politics to the observed behavior of legislators, executives, justices, and voters. The tension between the McKelvey-Schofield "chaos" results and the realities of group decision making continues to serve as one of the starting points for the study of real-world political institutions. But it is Richard's experimental work (with Peter Ordeshook, Tom Palfrey, and others) that best exemplifies the importance Richard placed on matching model to situation. Both the competitive solution and quantal response equilibrium arose as attempts to explain experimental data with a formal theory. From our viewpoint, Richard dedicated the last years of his life to this work because he believed that matching theory to evidence was why he was doing what he did.

---

[4]The dictator game is a famous decision problem in which one player (the "dictator") is given the opportunity to keep any amount between zero and (for example) ten dollars. The amount not kept is then given to a second player (who has no role in the "game" other than to receive the leftover money). Presuming that the player faced with the decision likes money, the unique Nash equilibrium of this game is for the first player to keep the entire pot of money and leave nothing for the second player. Experimentally, many individuals do not do this, leaving nontrivial amounts of money for the second player.

Index

agenda, 12, 19, 20, 25, 26, 28–35, 49–51, 53, 56, 79, 81, 243–245, 251, 256–261, 265, 302, 315, 437
Aldrich, John, xi, 1, 2, 6, 93, 94, 98–100, 103, 104, 225
Almond, Gabriel, 296, 316
Alt, James, xi, 1
altruist, 351, 353–355, 377–422, 427, 431, 476
Arrow, Kenneth, 20, 25
Austen-Smith, David, 7, 20–24, 26–28, 222, 224, 281, 295, 300, 306, 370, 431

Banks, Jeffrey, v, 20–24, 26–28, 222, 224–227, 258, 300, 301, 303, 306, 370, 431
bargaining set, 166, 167, 173, 175, 177–179, 183, 187–189, 196–199, 202, 204, 205, 212–214, 217
Baron, David, 27, 31–34, 183, 310, 366, 369–374
beliefs, 5, 234, 235, 296–302, 305, 309, 310, 379, 380, 388–390, 393–402, 408, 427, 430
Berelson, Bernard, 296, 316
bias, 296, 300, 302, 361, 401, 442, 465, 479
  statistical, 99, 114, 115, 118, 121, 122, 124, 128, 145, 161, 164
Black, Duncan, 20, 25
Border, Kim, 269

Camerer, Colin, 183, 380, 395

centipede game, 7, 348–426, 430, 431, 476, 484
chaos, 12, 14, 21, 28, 165, 166, 184, 222, 490, 492
coalition, 19, 23, 28, 32, 51, 55, 57, 165, 166, 168, 170–172, 174–179, 182, 187–219, 223–226, 234, 243–279, 281–285, 287, 288, 290, 292, 315, 365, 366, 369–372
Condorcet winner, 20, 21, 165, 166, 183
Converse, Phillip, 296, 316
core, 8, 21–28, 54, 60, 72, 80, 165, 166, 168, 173, 183, 187–189, 195, 196, 199, 200, 202, 206, 212, 213, 217, 221, 223, 224, 243–245, 254, 261, 265, 266, 281–293
Cox, Gary, 6, 19, 27, 29, 31–34

democracy, 8–17, 35, 223
Downs, Anthony, 13, 24, 137, 194, 221, 222, 225, 243, 245, 256, 261, 265, 296, 301, 304

endorsement, 12, 13, 295–300, 302, 304–308, 310, 315–348
experiment, 1, 2, 5–9, 32, 96, 117, 118, 121, 128, 130, 167–170, 180, 181, 187, 188, 190, 197, 200, 202, 210, 212–214, 216, 217, 299, 307, 315, 318, 338–346, 349–424, 442, 443, 451–457, 460, 462–467, 476, 477, 480, 492

Feddersen, Timothy, 23, 32, 301, 302, 432
Ferejohn, John, 9, 27, 31–34
field experiment, 349, 360, 361, 368–370

493

Index

fixed point theorem, 76, 445

gambit, 7, 394, 428, 475–487
Gerber, Alan, 7, 349, 360, 368, 371, 372
Goeree, Jacob, 362, 428, 429, 434, 435, 477
Grether, David, 287, 467
Gretlein, Rodney, 53, 168–170, 177–181, 257

Holt, Charles, 362, 428, 429, 434, 435, 467, 477
Hotelling, Howard, 221, 222

information, 2, 4, 6, 7, 24, 51, 106, 107, 183, 233, 295–349, 356, 369, 377, 393–395, 427, 429, 431, 432, 435, 437, 448, 475, 476, 478
    incomplete, 2, 4, 7, 8, 104, 259, 260, 352, 357–359, 361, 377, 379, 380, 388–390, 394, 395, 408–410, 425, 427, 429, 431, 436, 437, 443, 476
intransitivity, intransitivities, 6, 21, 28, 41–92, 165

Kinder, Donald, 316
Knesset, 223, 225, 232
Kramer, Gerald, 21, 24, 25, 49, 51, 54

Ledyard, John, 296, 299–301, 303, 305, 358, 360
Lupia, Arthur, xi, 1, 7, 295, 307, 310

McKelvey, Richard D.
    biographical information, 7–8
    influence on political science, 1–3
        empirical implications of theoretical models, 3
    McKelvey-Schofield symmetry conditions, 224
Morton, Rebecca, 365

Nash equilibrium, pure strategy, 227

optima set
    critical optima set, 283, 284
    global optima set, 282–284
    local optima set, 283

Ordeshook, Peter, 165, 187, 224, 244, 302, 315, 492

Palfrey, Thomas, 2, 7, 15, 99, 226, 227, 234, 296, 302, 309, 349, 352–354, 362, 365, 366, 371, 372, 377, 379, 395, 425, 427–431, 434, 437, 441, 442, 451, 465, 467, 476, 477, 480, 481, 484, 492
Patty, John, 7, 226, 234, 435, 489
Penn, Elizabeth Maggie, 7, 489
Pesendorfer, Wolfgang, 301–303, 308, 432
Plott, Charles, 20, 21, 41, 54, 213, 221, 243, 281, 291, 292
    Plott conditions, 72, 79, 166, 196, 281, 282, 285, 287
    Plott's Theorem, 60, 78, 165, 254, 288
political science, ix, 1–7, 10, 35, 95, 96, 296, 306, 308, 310, 349, 360–362, 365, 366, 425, 431, 435, 436, 475, 484, 490
    at University of Rochester, 93, 97
poll, 295–300, 302, 304, 305, 315–318, 322, 323, 334, 337–339, 341, 343, 345, 346
Poole, Keith, 6, 93, 99, 226, 368
probit, 94, 96, 97, 144, 153–155, 157, 158, 160–162, 436, 451
    dichotomous, 143
    multinomial, 228, 232
    n-chotomous, 94–96, 157, 158, 160, 161
    NPROBIT, 151, 152, 155
    ordered, 97
    ordinal, 144
    and regression, 154, 155, 157, 158, 160, 161

quantal response equilibrium, 2, 7, 15, 225, 349, 352, 354, 356, 359, 360, 362, 372, 425, 428–437, 441–448, 451–453, 455–457, 463, 465, 467, 470, 477, 478, 480, 481, 484, 492
    graph, 453, 456, 457, 460, 464, 468, 469
    model, 14, 227
    quantal choice model, 441
    quantal response correspondence, 467, 480
    quantal response function, 428, 432, 446, 448, 466

quantal response model, 442, 443, 456, 457, 460, 466, 467

R-squared, 143, 153, 154, 158, 160
rational choice, 103, 310, 315, 372, 429, 448
rational choice theory, 9, 15
rationality, 2, 4, 15, 165, 170, 306, 311, 322, 351, 353, 362, 379, 383, 386, 388, 426, 427, 429, 437, 442
   bounded, 425, 427, 431, 451
   rational expectations, 296, 298, 299, 301, 304, 305, 317, 318, 380, 395, 399, 400, 402, 408
   rational expectations equilibrium, 297, 305, 325, 442
   voters, 296, 299–302, 304, 305, 309, 323–325, 334, 343, 432
reputation, 353, 379, 390, 430, 436
   reputation model, 379, 427
Riker, William, v, 2, 12, 16, 27, 35, 165, 188, 197, 221, 222, 225, 315, 366
   Riker-Duverger thesis, 222
   size principle, 195
Romer, Thomas, 29–33
Rosenthal, Howard, 29–33, 226, 296, 368, 378, 379, 395, 426, 434, 442, 448, 450, 451, 455

scaling, 94, 95, 98–100, 103, 104, 124, 125, 128, 130, 133, 141, 161, 492
Schofield, Norman, 6, 20, 22, 53–55, 195, 221–226, 228, 230–232, 234, 235, 243, 281, 284, 287, 290–292, 433, 490
   contribution, 22–23
   and McKelvey, 222–224, 281, 292, 492
Shepsle, Kenneth, 6, 19, 25–28, 32–34, 98, 165, 188, 243, 244, 265, 267, 315
social choice, 8, 9, 13, 22, 41, 53, 54, 81, 166, 188, 221, 224, 234, 235, 243, 244, 290, 315
   function, 53, 56, 60, 81, 245, 287, 290
   rule, 53–56, 71, 288
sophisticated voting, 12, 51, 243, 245, 256, 257, 259, 267, 437, 490
spatial instability, 19

spatial model, 6, 23–25, 27, 98, 99, 103–105, 137, 224, 227, 296, 297, 302, 303, 308, 315, 492
strong game, 248
strong simple games, 53, 54, 56, 57, 67, 68, 180, 181, 190, 202

transitivity, 20, 21, 43, 44, 54, 55, 65, 66, 72, 251, 260, 271, 273
Tullock, Gordon, 41, 50
Tullock, Theodore, 21, 24
Turocy, Theodore, 7, 475, 480

uncovered set, 24, 165, 166, 243–245, 250–253, 255, 256, 258, 260, 261, 265–267

V-set, 166–168, 170, 173, 174, 183

Weingast, Barry, 27, 28, 33, 243, 244, 265
   last-mover model, 33
Winer, Mark, 187, 213, 224, 244, 315, 366, 368

yolk, 12, 262

Zavoina, William, 2, 96, 97, 143, 151, 197